Contracting with
the Federal Government

Contracting with the Federal Government

Second Edition

Frank M. Alston
Partner, Price Waterhouse
Bethesda, Maryland

Margaret M. Worthington
Partner, Price Waterhouse
Bethesda, Maryland

Louis P. Goldsman
Partner, Price Waterhouse
Newport Beach, California

WILEY

JOHN WILEY & SONS
New York ● Chichester ● Brisbane ● Toronto ● Singapore

ISBN 0-471-63612-6

Printed in the United States of America

10 9 8 7 6 5 4 3 2 1

Preface

Since our first edition in 1984, the Federal contracting environment has undergone a rather dramatic and fundamental change. Those who are reasonably knowledgeable about this activity would recognize that government procurement is truly a dynamic process and that a certain amount of change is expected. Even so, we believe there was general surprise at the rapid and extensive change in the procurement culture; that is, change in the basic set of assumptions and ground rules that underline the rules and regulations and define the government-contractor relationship. This cultural change manifested itself in a spate of new and revised regulations as well as a noticeably different approach by the government in its enforcement practices. Unquestionably, these developments materially altered the way contractors must conduct business with the government customers. For this text to continue to fulfill its purpose of not only helping the reader to identify and understand the relevant regulations but also understand the government's attitude toward implementation, an update of the material to reflect this new environment is certainly required. With this revision, we are hopeful that the book will remain a practical guide for all who are involved in this complex activity of pricing, costing and administering federal contracts.

In its legitimate role of establishing the legal framework for the Federal acquisition process, Congress enacts legislation from time-to-time altering the basic structure in which this activity takes place. Since 1984, however, the legislators have uncharacteristically gotten involved directly in managing government contracts. Ostensibly responding to media revelation of alleged excesses in contracting, Congress enacted so-called reform legislation that prescribed detailed changes to specific provisions of the procurement regulations. This unprecedented "micromanagement" by Congress has caused difficulty for contractors and government officials; primarily because the direct involvement by Congress at a level previously reserved for implementing agencies introduced yet another variable into the government-contractor relationship, causing even greater uncertainty and complexity.

The new procurement laws are intended to remedy a broad spectrum of alleged contractor abuses such as: billing the government for labor costs mischarged to contracts, requesting reimbursement for unallowable indirect expenses, and inflating negotiated prices by failing to provide government negotiators the required cost and pricing data. Moreover, Congress concluded that these problems were widespread and, in many instances, deliberate. The legislators criticized the federal agencies for being both negligent and inept in discovering these problems and in taking appropriate actions against the guilty contractors. To ensure that agencies became more effective in ferreting out contractor fraud, waste and abuse, the new laws, among other requirements, (1) made procurement regulations more restrictive, (2) increased the penalties for violating regulations, (3) required contractors to certify under the penalty of perjury that their indirect cost submissions comply with the regulations, (4) directed the contracting agencies to impose tighter control on their suppliers, and (5) mandated an increased level of oversight of the acquisition function. Taken together, these actions had a profound impact on the procurement climate.

Stung by the harsh Congressional criticism that they were lax in their enforcement of the procurement regulations, the executive agencies, especially the Department of Defense, have become more aggressive in performing contract audits and conducting other oversight reviews. As expected, DOD has increased the number of audits and, in many instances, substantially expended the scope of these reviews. Contractors, of course, must respond to this initiative by providing more resources to support this general increase in audit activity. While the increased audit activity certainly adds to the cost of doing business with Uncle Sam, this does not represent the fundamental change in the environment. What does represent change, and is causing considerable trauma among contractors, is the lessening ability to predict how the government will characterize an audit issue or in what forum the government will seek to have the matter resolved. In other words, is the noncompliance a contractual matter or is it to be regarded as an attempt to defraud. It seems that the government is more prone to use criminal rather administrative remedies to resolve problems arising out of the contracting process.

This shift in focus has serious implications for contractors. First, what actions should contractors take to minimize the incidence of noncompliances. Secondly, when noncompliances are discovered, how can contractors improve their ability to objectively establish that the problem was inadvertent rather than a deliberate attempt to overcharge and thirdly, what must be done in the way of system design and implementation to demonstrate that adequate safeguards are present to protect the government's interests.

The Department of Defense Inspector General (DODIG) appears to emphasize using the criminal process to deal with contracting problems. Specifically, in its role as overseer of the contract audit function, the DODIG advised auditors and contracting officials *never* to make any assumption about contractor intent or good faith whenever a noncompliance is discovered. Unfortunately, this approach effectively makes every noncompliance a potential crime until a criminal investigator has determined otherwise. This is, without a doubt, a very serious change in the government's approach in resolving alleged noncompliance. Our revised edition discusses, in some detail, how contractors must manage in a business environment that involves considerably more risk as compared to pre-1984. We focus on the imperative for contractors to re-evaluate their financial management systems in light of current circumstances for the express purpose of assuring their effectiveness in avoiding, disclosing and eliminating conditions of noncompliance.

The concept of industry accountability for compliance with federal procurement regulations was given major emphasis by the President's Blue Ribbon Commission on Defense Management (The Packard Commission). Actually there is nothing new about contractors having an affirmative obligation to comply with the terms and conditions of the contracts they sign. What we believe is different and significant will be the increased emphasis the government will place on evaluating how well contractors are policing themselves for compliance with applicable regulations. The Commission in its final report recognized the limits of even the most effective enforcement and oversight activities as means for bringing about the needed improvements in the procurement process and for ensuring reasonable compliance in the future. Corporate self-governance, the Commission asserted, could redress the current weaknesses in the procurement system and could ultimately lead to a more productive relationship between the government and its suppliers. Fundamentally, self-governance requires the contractor to establish and maintain the necessary system of internal accounting and administrative controls to ensure the integrity of their own contract performance. This book describes the attributes of financial management systems that should meet these objectives.

While much has changed during the past three years; much remains the same. We have described in the preceding paragraphs what we perceive to be material changes in the government's fundamental approach to enforcing compliance with a basic procurement process that has stayed fairly constant. However, we emphasize that successfully providing the product or service only partially fulfills a company's contractual obligation to the government. What truly makes the Federal government a different customer is that, unlike a commercial contract, it regards complying with administrative requirements as important as technical performance. Our second edition is intended to reflect changes in the current procurement environment that directly impact a contractor's ability to avoid serious economic loss or legal exposure for failure to fulfill the administrative requirements (i.e., pricing and costing, and settling) of government contracts. Since so much of this process is unchanged since 1984, the Preface for the first edition is still relevant and is included with minor revisions.

Bethesda, Maryland   Frank M. Alston
Newport Beach, California   Margaret M. Worthington
January 1988   Louis P. Goldsman

EDITOR'S NOTE

While we have made every attempt to ensure that the forms included in this book are complete and current, the reader/user should investigate any changes in regulations and forms that may have been issued since the publication of the book.

Preface to the First Edition

To have any reasonable chance of success in business, the entrepreneur must understand the market in which he or she operates. An effective business strategy results not only from insight regarding how the consumer behaves, but even more important, what motivates consumer behavior.

Who are my potential customers?
How does the customer decide what to buy and when to buy?
What process is the customer likely to use in selecting the sources to fulfill his or her perceived needs?
What type of relationship will the customer seek to establish with suppliers?

These questions reflect the technical, economic, and legal characteristics of a marketplace that determine, to a large extent consumer behavior. The challenge to managers of business organizations is to be sufficiently knowledgeable about the market to anticipate, or in some cases, even influence the demand for their product. Those who succeed in this effort will be able to take the necessary actions to give their companies a competitive advantage.

While intimate knowledge of the critical factors that influence consumer behavior is important for selling in any market, it is doubly so if the consumers are Federal agencies. This is true because doing business with Uncle Sam is certainly a unique experience. For reasons that will be discussed in this book, the U.S. Government, as a customer, behaves differently than almost any other customer you will encounter. It follows then that any company planning or proceeding to do business in this market should know the rules that govern this particular customer's behavior and have some understanding of and appreciation for why the rules were written in the first place.

The many regulations that control every step of the Federal procurement process account for the major differences between government contracting and doing business in the private sector. Since these regulations determine how the Federal government behaves as a customer, it would be foolish indeed to operate in the public market without a reasonable level of knowledge about what the rules and regulations require. While the government is certainly not intent on deliberately putting anyone out of business, it, nevertheless, expects a contractor to know and understand the technical and administrative requirements of the contract that is signed. Accordingly, the procuring agency will not rescue a company from the consequences of bad business judgment made in forming or performing a government contract; neither will the government refrain from penalizing a company for violating an acquisition regulation or failing to fulfill a contractual term or condition simply because the requirements were not known or were misinterpreted. Indeed, in far too many instances, contractors have watched profits on their government work drastically shrink or totally disappear because the applicable regulations were either overlooked, misunderstood, or ignored.

This book is based on the premise that doing business with the U.S. Government can be an economically rewarding experience despite the voluminous and complex regulations. Contractors who have and continue to realize reasonable profits on their Federal contracts recognize that coping with the unique aspects of government business is much the same as coping with the idiosyncratic behavior of any distinctive market.

This book provides a practical discussion of the rules and regulations that impose special financial and accounting requirements on government contractors. It's purpose is not only to help the reader to identify and understand the relevant regulations, but equally important, to provide significant insight into how the government will go about implementing the requirements. The authors, who are all members of Price Waterhouse's Government and Other Long-Term Contractors Industry Services Group, are uniquely suited for this purpose since they include both former U.S. Government officials who were extensively involved in developing and implementing the regulations affecting procurement and individuals whose careers in public accounting have been concentrated on matters relating to government contracting. With such backgrounds, the authors are especially capable of providing the reader with practical information to assist in identifying the applicable regulations and establishing a basis for determining what constitutes reasonable compliance. Furthermore, this text represents Price Waterhouse's continuing commitment to provide full financial and accounting services to companies engaged in government business.

The ability to sucessfully deal with Federal regulations is materially enhanced if the contractor has some knowledge and appreciation of the underlying concepts and rationale followed in developing them. Therefore, the text includes a brief historical background for the major regulatory requirements discussed. Included in this coverage are the authors' views of the particular problem the government was attempting to solve. In the experience of the authors, such information has been found to be extremely helpful in identifying alternative approaches to satisfying the regulatory requirements.

This book covers that portion of the Federal procurement process involving the practices followed in making the government's needs known to the public to settling a contract at completion. Because the authors are all accountants by profession, the primary focus of this book is on the financial and accounting considerations related to this process. The book is intended to serve as a partical reference for those who are directly responsible for pricing and administering contracts with federal agencies. Those with overall management responsibilities, as well as individuals involved in marketing or providing legal advice, should also find the material useful. Knowledge of the regulations is critical in establishing short- and long-term business objectives, developing marketing plans and strategies, and avoiding or resolving disputes related to government contracts.

Anyone involved in government business must have a working knowledge of such terms as *allowability, reasonableness, allocability,* and *defective pricing.* Unfortunately, many contractors become acquainted with these concepts, as they apply to their government business, when in the midst of a crisis—too late, for often the damage is already done.

For those who are considering the government contracting market, this book should provide a fairly complete overview of the financial and accounting aspects of your decision. Responsible officials should be able to identify the changes that are necessary in management and control systems and assess the impact of those changes on the overall operation of the business. For existing contractors, the book should serve as an aid in identifying relevant regulations, and providing additional insight on what actions are in company's best interest and which satisfy the requirements of the customer—the U.S. Government.

While compliance with applicable government regulations is certainly important, contractors must be sure that their systems used for estimating, accounting, and billing costs meet management's internal needs. As indicated previously, many contract losses occur not because the contractor experienced unexpected technical difficulty in doing the work, but because its management systems failed to provide the necessary information to effectively price the contract and control the cost incurred during performance. In recognition of this need, the book also has a section on accounting systems and internal control. Additionally, throughout the text, the authors suggest what they believe are good practices to follow in estimating costs for contract negotiation purposes and monitoring and controlling costs incurred during contract performance. Particular emphasis is given to the importance of these systems as they relate to pricing the effect of changes to the contract after the date of award.

Los Angeles, California
Bethesda, Maryland
December 1983

FRANK M. ALSTON
FRANKLIN R. JOHNSON
MARGARET M. WORTHINGTON
LOUIS P. GOLDSMAN
FRANK J. DEVITO

Acknowledgments

The authors are particularly indebted to other members of the Government Consulting Services staff for their unstinting and extensive efforts in creating this text. Without their research, writing and editing, this book would not have been possible. We have drawn heavily on their individual knowledge and expertise for the various topics included in the book. We believe the wisdom of this approach is reflected in the relevancy, accuracy and practicality of the material.

The following individuals made substantial contributions to developing the material and drafting the manuscript:

Richard E. Fields
Andrew T. Habina, Jr.
Ronald M. Isaacson
James L. Ortler
Patsy Pagliarulo
Mary Edith Thomas

Special thanks are given to Frank Johnson who was a major participant in the first edition. We also recognize the contribution of Malvern J. Gross, Jr. who initially saw the need for such a book and persuaded us to make the necessary personal sacrifices to successfully complete the project.

Finally, we deeply appreciate the dedication and hard work of our administrative staff who labored tirelessly in typing and editing the very rough drafts given them by the authors. Under the inspired direction of Madge Johnston, our secretarial staff did an outstanding job in successfully completing a monumental task.

F.M.A.
M.M.W.
L.P.G.

Contents

Chapter One

Historical Perspectives and Background

EARLY STATUTES

Historians tell us that the first time the U.S. Congress exercised its constitutional authority to enact laws governing the purchase of military goods and services was in 1795. The law, the Purveyor of Public Supplies Act, enabled the Army and the Navy to meet their needs by purchasing from private business.

The next significant procurement law, passed in 1808, continues to serve as the basis for a provision that is still required to be included in Federal contracts issued today — the "officials not to benefit" clause. It expressly prohibits members of Congress from deriving personal benefits directly from procurements made by the U.S. Government.

Accusations of graft and favoritism in the award of contracts were rampant in the early nineteenth century. There was little or nothing to legally restrain members of Congress from subverting the Federal procurement process to further their own personal interests. As a result, many legislators were actively involved in securing contracts for friends or firms in which they held an interest. The ethics of some public officials in these early periods left much to be desired; the owners of businesses contracting with the government were not much better. It was clear that something had to be done.

In an attempt to bring some integrity and fairness into the process of awarding Federal contracts, Congress passed a series of statutes that virtually eliminated negotiated procurement and required, with limited exceptions, competitive bidding. By 1845, the use of sealed bids with public openings dominated the Federal procurement process.

In 1861 another major piece of procurement legislation was passed — the Civil Sundry Appropriations Act, which for the next 86 years was the primary procurement law. It continued the principle that military agencies obtain goods and services from private industry through advertised procurement. After amendments in 1874 and 1878, the act became known as Revised Statute 3709. The act was again revised in 1910 to reemphasize that the required method of procurement was formal advertising. Revised Statute 3709, as amended, was, for all practical purposes, the principal law under which all procurements were made until the Armed Services Procurement Act of 1947.

The emphasis on the use of competitive bidding practices during this period reflected a desire to free Federal contracting from favoritism, political influence, and profiteering by individuals in power. Despite the well-meaning intent of these practices, the experience of wartime procurement proved that many serious problems still needed to be resolved. As a result of shortages of available production facilities and raw materials required by World War I, an intense competition developed between the military branches that were acquiring available goods and services in the civilian marketplace. A review of the lessons learned from World War I showed that in time of war, shortages of goods and production capacity produced a seller's market. The intense competition among the buyers only served to drive prices up. In addition, formal advertising was slow and cumbersome and greatly hindered the timely receipt of the goods and services so desperately needed by the military.

Unfortunately, the time between World War I and World War II was not spent in developing alternative practices but was rather a period for recriminations. Ultimately, the manufacturers themselves became the scapegoats. It was widely believed that wars were prosecuted solely to enhance the profits of munitions and military supply manufacturers. In response to this sentiment, Congress continued to focus its attention on profit limitations, price controls and taxes. The Vinson-Trammell Act was passed in 1934 to eliminate excessive profits on military contracts. The unfortunate conflicts between the military departments and the Congress interfered with the effort to resolve procurement problems prior to the start of World War II. Indeed, the military departments were reluctant to give up the protection afforded by the strict provisions of the formal advertising procedures. They believed to do so would make them even more vulnerable to Congressional criticism.

Nevertheless, as World War II approached, it brought a slow transition to negotiation as a contract selection and award technique. By December 1941, the First War Powers Act removed most restrictions on the military services' procurement functions. It authorized agencies to make advance, progress, and other payments whenever such action would facilitate the prosecution of the war.

The complete turnabout from advertised bidding to negotiation came with Directive 2 issued in March 1942 by the War Production Board. This directive abandoned competitive bidding procurement and required that all contracts be negotiated. It also established criteria for selecting a contractor during an armed conflict. In this Federal contracting environment: (1) the primary emphasis was on delivery; (2) complex items were procured from companies that already had the required engineering and managerial capability; and (3) contracts were placed with firms that did not require a considerable amount of new equipment or facilities.

Since profits and pricing were not the most important concerns at the time, the problems of profiteering that had occurred in World War I soon reappeared during World War II. However, because of the experience of World War I, the War Department was aware of the possible consequences and provided for control of profits through proper pricing. This awareness and the associated precautions helped prevent the unfortunate experiences of World War I from recurring. As an additional safeguard, Congress gave the Federal Government certain powers to discourage contractors from making unreasonable demands in the seller's market that normally exists during a war, including the right to inspect plants and conduct audits, establish delivery priorities, allocate raw materials, unilaterally establish reasonable prices where negotiations failed, and so forth. Although the powers granted were rarely used, their existence, as intended, caused government contractors to exercise voluntary controls during World War II.

When the conflict ended, a need to rapidly change from a war to a peacetime economy was apparent. The Congress' effort to meet this challenge culminated in the enactment of the Contract Settlement Act of 1944, a law that established uniform termination procedures and related contract clauses. A new era in government procurement had begun.

CURRENT PROCUREMENT ENVIRONMENT

The experiences of World War II had shown that competitive bidding was not a viable means of producing required goods and services under emergency conditions. Nevertheless, since the statutes and regulations passed during World War II were, for the most part, temporary, procurement would revert automatically to its prewar focus on competitive bidding when the war ended. To implement the lessons of the wartime experience, the Procurement Policy Board of the War Production Board recommended that government agencies propose procurement regulations that would become effective when the emergency legislation expired. The result was the Armed Services Procurement Act (Public Law 80-413), which was later revised and codified under Title 10 of the United States Code by Public Law 84-1028.

The Armed Services Procurement Act established sealed bidding, then known as formal advertising, as the preferred procurement method. Exceptions were provided for, however, where the circumstances required or justified such action.

The Department of Defense implemented Title 10 of the United States Code through the Armed Services Procurement Regulation (ASPR). In March 1978, Department of Defense Directive 5000.35 changed the name of the regulation to the Defense Acquisition Regulation (DAR). In April 1984 the DAR was replaced by the Federal Acquisition Regulations (FAR) and the Department of Defense FAR Supplement (DFAR).

The acquisition regulations for the civilian agencies reflect many of the lessons learned in military procurement. The Federal Property and Administrative Services Act of 1949, codified under Title 41 of the United States Code, provides the contracting authority for all executive agencies except the Department of Defense, the Coast Guard, the National Aeronautics and Space Administration (NASA), and any other agency that has a separate procurement statute. Uniform policies and procedures for NASA relating to the procurement of property and services are established under the National Aeronautics and Space Act of 1958, as amended (Public Law 85-568). The statute applies to all purchases and contracts made by NASA, within or outside the United States. Prior to April 1984, the Federal Procurement Regulations (FPR), issued by the General Services Administration (GSA) in 1959, governed procurement by civilian agencies other than NASA and were very similar to the acquisition regulations that applied to defense agencies. NASA maintained its own procurement regulation.

DOD generally took the lead in developing procurement regulations, especially in the area of cost principles. NASA and GSA were usually in the posture of deciding whether the NASA Procurement Regulation and the FPR should be revised to incorporate changes made to the DAR. However, there were notable differences between the regulations. Consequently, a company had to be sure that the appropriate regulations were applied to a particular contract. In

April 1984, the NASA Procurement Regulation and the FPR were totally replaced by the Federal Acquisition Regulations (FAR) and agency FAR supplements. Unfortunately due to the somewhat uncontrolled development of the FAR supplements, acquisition regulations are far from uniform. Consequently, companies must still exercise care to assure that appropriate regulations are applied.

Predictably, war and the threat of war have had and continue to have a profound impact on the increasing complexity and sophistication of the military procurement process. The sheer magnitude of federal purchases and the uniqueness of products and services acquired have dictated the need to reassess how the risk inherent in such purchases should be apportioned between buyer and seller. It makes no sense for the government to place so high a level of risk on the contractor that performance is threatened. Unfortunately, this was one of the outcomes of the exclusive use of competitive bidding. Government officials and the contracting agencies were finding, in many instances, little resemblance between what was bid competitively and the cost of performance. To the extent the contractor could not perform for the quoted price, the government was frustrated in accomplishing its mission. Negotiated procurements were an inevitable and very necessary innovation to assure that the government would be able to meet its needs through private sector contracting. Additionally, selecting the type of procurement was, appropriately, placed with the contracting activity rather than mandated by statute.

Major changes to the procurement statutes occurred in the 1980s. The DOD budget increased significantly to strengthen military preparedness and to offset what was perceived as years of neglect. At the same time, large Federal deficits created considerable pressure to reduce budget outlays and ultimately led to the passage of the Gramm-Rudman Act. Seemingly excessive prices, most notably in the area of spare parts, and statements by senior DOD procurement officials alleging wrong doing by a number of large government contractors prompted both Congress and the Executive Branch to act.

Congress enacted the Competition in Contracting Act (CICA) as part of the Deficit Reduction Act of 1984 (Public Law 98-369). Effective April 1, 1985, CICA amended the Armed Services Procurement Act in favor of competitive procurement methods. As a result, the government is required to use competitive procedures for all procurements except under certain conditions such as where the award is to be made solely based on price. Additionally, specific circumstances exist to allow the government to restrict competition.

Contract Cost Principles

As government agencies, especially DOD and NASA, began to buy an increasingly large amount of unique, custom-made goods and services, procurement officials and private industry recognized that the forces of supply and demand could not be relied upon to establish fair and reasonable prices. This insight led to a greater use of negotiated contracts where cost of performance, either estimated or actual, became a dominant factor in setting prices. Out of this environment came the government's efforts to establish cost accounting requirements that would apply to its contracts.

After an initial attempt to provide guidance on government contract costing, nothing much happened in the way of further progress until the World War II era. In 1940 it appeared that the U.S. Government was finally serious about defining what costs should be considered in its private industry contracts. On August 7, 1940, the commissioner of the Internal Revenue Service issued Treasury Decision 5000. This document was used during the Second World War as a guide for pricing military contracts in which negotiations were based on costs. Treasury Decision 5000 is generally considered to be the precursor to the cost principles that were eventually developed and promulgated by the Department of Defense.

In April 1942, the Government Printing Office published a pamphlet that provided further elaboration of the guidance included in Treasury Decision 5000. This publication, entitled *Explanation of Principles for Determination of Costs under Government Contracts,* was known as the *Green Book* because of the color of its cover. The Green Book remained in effect until it was replaced by the contract cost principles included in the 1949 version of the Armed Services Procurement Regulation, Section XV. As previously mentioned, the civilian agencies published their cost principles (FPR 1-15) during the same year. In April 1984, cost principles in the FAR (FAR Part 31) and departmental FAR supplements replaced the cost principles previously included in the DAR, NASA Procurement Regulation, FPR, and various civilian agency regulations. The cost principles continue to change significantly as a result of efforts by the Congress as well as the Defense Acquisition Regulatory Council and Civilian Agency Acquisition Council to eliminate perceived abuses and reduce the cost of products and services purchased by the Federal Government.

Cost Accounting Requirements

Granted, the cost principles did contain some basic guidance for contractors to follow in assigning costs to contracts. However, they did not provide a complete body of cost accounting principles which the government felt was needed to assure uniformity and consistency in estimating, accumulating, and reporting costs on government contracts. This void was filled in August 1970 when the signing of Public Law 91-379 created the Cost Accounting Standards Board.

Defective Pricing

In 1962 Congress passed legislation that applies directly to estimating and negotiating the contract price. The Truth in Negotiations Act, as amended over the years, is designed to ensure that the government has the opportunity to review all significant and relevant cost or pricing data available to the contractor in arriving at the proposed price. The law requires that the contractor certify that the requirements of the act have been met. If after the negotiation it is determined that all such data were not submitted to the government, the contract price is adjusted downward for any price increase resulting from the contractor's or subcontractor's failure to comply.

Contract Audit

As the significance of cost as a factor in contract pricing increased, so did the government's need to assure itself of the validity and reasonableness of the costs proposed or charged by contractors. Consequently, government agencies began to audit contractors' books and records to determine how much the government would pay for the work performed. The military agencies (Army, Navy, and Air Force) each had their own separate audit activity until 1965. Effective July 1, 1965, contract audit activities in each of the military agencies were combined into one independent organization, the Defense Contract Audit Agency (DCAA). Although the primary purpose for the contract audit activity in DOD is to provide financial and accounting advice to DOD procurement officials, DCAA remains organizationally separate from the procurement activities it supports.

The DOD Inspector General (DODIG) also performs certain audit activity in its pursuit of fraud waste and abuse in defense procurement. The distinction between the contract audit functions assigned to DCAA and the DODIG has become increasingly blurred in recent years.

Most civilian agencies also use DCAA for their contract audit requirements. Others who have established a contract audit capability, unlike DOD, have incorporated this activity either in their financial management operations or in their offices of the inspector general.

Self-Governance

With increasing media coverage and controversy, Congress enacted legislation which increased the government's right to subpoena contractor records, shifted burden of proof for reasonableness from the government to industry, forced contractors to accept Federal travel regulations, expanded the list of unallowable costs, and amended the Truth in Negotiations Act to eliminate some contractor defenses.

The President's Blue Ribbon Commission on Defense Management, referred to as the Packard Commission, reported in June 1986 on the need for both industry and government to improve performance in the procurement process. Defense contractors were admonished to increase both internal controls and self surveillance for monitoring compliance with acquisition requirements.

As an adjunct to the Packard Commission Report, a number of defense contractors developed a document known as the Defense Industry Initiatives (DII). The DII prescribes a code of conduct and procedures to monitor compliance with Federal procurement laws and regulations.

Renegotiation

Following World War I, the Vinson-Trammell Act of 1934 was enacted to limit profits on military aircraft and naval vessels, to 12% and 10%, respectively. In 1942, profit limitation on military procurement was expanded when the first Renegotiation Act was passed. In 1951, the Renegotiation Board was legislatively established for the purpose of determining whether the overall profits earned on DOD contracts over a specified threshold were excessive. During the time the Renegotiation Act was effective, Vinson-Trammell was held in abeyance.

Profit Limitation activity under the Renegotiation Act ceased in 1979. The 1982 Defense Appropriations Act, Public Law 97-86, also suspended the application of Vinson-Trammell indefinitely. While PL 97-86 allows the president to reinstate profit limitation regulations if there is a war or national emergency, there are currently no requirements for renegotiating Federal contracts for the purpose of eliminating excess profits.

Profit

How to use the profit motive to provide an incentive to contractors to reduce costs appears to be a never-ending challenge for the government, especially DOD. Prior to the mid 1970s, profit policies followed by government agencies seemed to reward companies that incurred higher costs in performing negotiated contracts. Responding to this continuing problem, DOD conducted several studies over the years that grappled with this issue. A study, called Profit '76, was launched in August 1975 to develop policy revisions that would encourage private investment in equipment required to perform DOD contracts. As a result of Profit '76, DOD revised the profit policy, which, among other things, gave greater weight to the contractor's investment in cost-saving facilities and decreased the effect of the contractor's cost input. DOD continued to review the profit policy, making changes to achieve the elusive objective of removing the disincentive for contractors to decrease the costs of performing negotiated contracts. A notable change was implemented in 1986 pursuant to requirements in the 1987 DOD Appropriations Act continuing resolution (Public Law 99-500). This newest policy weights profit dollars even more heavily on contractor investment in productivity enhancing equipment and less on costs incurred.

Socioeconomic Laws

Further complicating the Federal procurement process is the government's use of its buying power to achieve certain social and economic goals. What has happened over the years is that social legislation is passed and then implemented by making compliance a condition for contracting with the U.S. Government. Since much of the legislation has little or no discernible relationship to the procurement process, there is continuing controversy and debate over the appropriateness of imposing compliance on government contractors. One can reasonably conclude that the debate will not end soon since the government's rationale for including many of the socioeconomic requirements in contracts was not that they were inherently related to procurement. Rather, it was simply that this is the most effective means of achieving the legislative objectives.

Some of the more notable socioeconomic legislation that has been included as contract clauses involve the following areas:

Equal employment opportunity: Implements statutes and executive orders forbidding companies that contract with the Federal government to discriminate in their employment policies and practices.

Buy American: The Buy American Act limits the extent to which a product manufactured for public use can contain components or materials from foreign suppliers. Each agency issues regulations to implement this act. DOD has substantially relaxed its Buy American barriers for NATO allies and other friendly nations to permit fair and equal competition among the industries of the participating countries.

Wage standards: Several pieces of legislation have been enacted to ensure that employees working on Federal contracts are treated fairly in payment and benefits when compared to all other workers in the country. Some of the laws affecting government contractors are the:
Service Contract Act
Contract Work Hours and Safety Standards Act
Davis-Bacon Act
Walsh-Healy Public Contract Act

Occupational Safety and Health Act: This law requires companies to maintain healthful and safe working conditions.

National Environmental Policy Act: This law, which establishes a national policy of protecting the environment, requires Federal agencies to determine the impact a particular project will have on the environment. It directly affects Federal agencies and indirectly applies to contractors that may be involved in the projects.

Clean Air Act: This legislation is directed primarily at controlling air pollution caused by industry and motor vehicle emissions. The contracting process may be delayed where there is a determination that the proposed work violates the requirement of this law.

Small business: The Small Business Act establishes as a national policy that the government should assist small businesses in obtaining their fair share of the government's business. To achieve this objective, agency officials can set aside certain procurements exclusively for small business. The four categories of set-aside contracts are:

   Partial set-aside for labor surplus areas

   Total set-aside for small business

   Partial set-aside for small business

   Set-aside for minority-disadvantaged business

TAX CONSIDERATIONS

The Research and Development Tax Credit

Since 1981, taxpayers have been entitled to a special tax break for certain expenses related to research and development ("R&D"). Until December 31, 1985 — the date that the R&D credit was scheduled to expire — a taxpayer's tax liability could be offset by as much as 25 percent of the excess of qualified expenses over a pre-defined base amount.

The Tax Reform Act of 1986 ("TRA '86"), recognizing the importance of high technology research and development, retroactively extended the R&D credit from December 31, 1985 through December 31, 1988. In doing so, however, the credit rate was reduced from 25 percent to 20 percent and the list of qualifying expenses was significantly narrowed. The new law clarifies that the credit applies only to research in the high technology areas, not for commercial production, consumer product testing, management surveys, and the like. The list of qualifying costs also excludes:

Internal-use software development unless the software is innovative, includes substantial economic risk, and is not commercially available.

Rental expenses, except for the cost of computer time.

TRA '86 also includes a look-back rule. When a contract is completed, a taxpayer using the percentage of completion method must determine how much tax would have been paid if actual costs (rather than anticipated costs) had been used to compute gross income. If this figure is greater than the tax actually paid, then interest must be paid on the difference. On the other hand, the taxpayer who paid tax earlier than if actual costs had been used will be entitled to interest on the difference.   .

Accounting for Long-Term Contracts

Prior to the enactment of TRA '86, a taxpayer could elect to use either the percentage of completion or the completed contract method of accounting for long-term contracts. A taxpayer electing the percentage of completion method would include income from the contract in proportion to the percentage of the contract completed during the year. All expenses on the contract would be deducted as incurred. A taxpayer using the completed contract method would defer all income recognition and expense deduction until the year in which the contract was completed. In the case of extended-period contracts (contracts requiring three years or more to complete), regulations specified which expenditures had to be allocated to the contract and which could be deducted currently.

TRA '86 generally repealed the completed contract method of accounting for long-term contracts. A taxpayer who does not wish to use the percentage of completion method must now use the percentage of completion-capitalized cost method, which is a hybrid of the percentage of completion method and the completed contract method. A taxpayer opting for this method must account for 40 % of the contract items on the percentage of completion method and 60 % of the contract items on the "normal method" (generally, the completed contract method). The look-back rule described above must be applied to the 40 % accounted for under the percentage of completion method.

MAJOR DIFFERENCES IN PRIVATE AND PUBLIC CONTRACTING

Given the history of the procurement process, it should be reasonably clear that many of the factors that distinguish public sector contracting from doing business with commercial organizations can be attributed to the statutory framework in which the Federal Government must operate when it enters the marketplace as a customer. When considered objectively, the unique requirements of Federal contracting should not represent an insurmountable barrier to an economically rewarding experience for those companies that elect to do business in this arena. Nonetheless, success, in a large measure, is affected by how well the contractor understands and copes with the rules that govern the Federal Government's behavior when engaged in this important activity.

The government's procedures for selecting, monitoring, and paying its contractors are somewhat more complex than those found in the commercial sector. The statutes and regulations that govern these activities are the primary cause of this additional complexity. To further compound the problem, the government is not monolithic, but in reality is a mixture of procurement people and activities using various procurement rules and regulations to obtain an incredibly diverse variety of goods and services. Whether there is a need for all of the rules and regulations is certainly the subject of considerable debate. What is important to recognize is that the government can be a good customer only when the seller has an understanding of those rules and regulations and the specific actions they require.

The need for the extensive rules and regulations stems from the government's dual role in the marketplace. Acting in its contracting capacity, the government is a vast business organization purchasing a wide variety of goods and services from every segment of the private sector. At the same time, it is a political entity—a sovereignty. In this latter role, its objectives go beyond obtaining goods and services at a stated price. The government must establish and follow practices that not only represent good business judgment but that are fair to all concerned. Therefore, the practices should reasonably ensure that (1) all known, responsible suppliers have an equal opportunity to meet the government's needs, (2) the quality of goods and services acquired is acceptable, (3) the prices paid are fair and reasonable and (4) the government buys only what the public needs. In regard to (4), if the government has entered into a formal agreement and its requirements change, it has a contractual right to cancel the contract, in whole or in part, and reimburse the contractor for costs incurred on the cancelled work.

There is a legal concept that the government, as a customer, must be treated like any other contracting party in order to protect those with whom the government deals. Another consideration is that, as a sovereign, the government deserves special treatment since it is acting in the public's interest. Trying to achieve an appropriate balance between these two concerns seems to require a more structured and controlled environment for government business than that which is required for private industry.

Some of the considerations in government contracting that appear to have no real counterparts in the commercial arena are summarized as follows:

Procedures to ensure fairness in the award of contracts from the standpoint that all interested, responsible suppliers have an equal opportunity to do all work.

Procedures for the government to unilaterally change its mind after the contract has been signed.

Procedures and techniques for technical and administrative surveillance during contract performance to ensure the reasonableness of prices and the quality of products or services.

Contractual arrangements for the government to stop performance whenever it is in the public interest.

Contractual arrangements for different payment or contract financing methods.

Miscellaneous social objectives such as:

Giving a fair share of the work to small business.

Ensuring that surplus labor areas receive appropriate amounts of work.

Fair treatment of minority groups.

Product interchangeability.

It is generally agreed that the socioeconomic requirements add a measure of complexity to the procurement process and, in most instances, require some specific action that would not apply in a purely commercial transaction. Nevertheless, they are an integral part of the contract and to ignore them can cause serious economic consequences for the contractor.

Let's now look at some differences between government and commercial contracting as they relate to specific steps in the procurement process.

Marketing

The government operates on the basic tenet that all responsible suppliers should have an equal opportunity to meet the government's needs. Consistent with this mandate, the government advertises its needs and requires strict compliance with the detailed specifications that it imposes.

As an integral part of the sealed bidding procedures, the Small Business Administration publishes the *U. S. Government Purchasing and Sales Directory*, which identifies government entities purchasing certain items or services. Further, the *Commerce Business Daily*, which is published each workday, lists procurement actions over $10,000 and contract awards over $25,000. A public posting at major Federal establishments is also used. Interested organizations use the information obtained from these sources to pursue business opportunities with the government.

Contracting agencies maintain lists of qualified companies to have ready sources to supply their needs. Being placed on a contracting agency's qualified mailing list is an important step for any company seeking to market its products or services to the U.S. Government. It is equally important for a company's marketing staff to diligently monitor the publications mentioned above. Taken together, these two actions should provide reasonable assurance that the company will be made aware, on a timely basis, of business opportunities. The requirement to make the general public aware of the government's procurement needs has no real parallel in private industry.

In addition to being aware of the published information, effective marketing to government agencies requires maintaining personal contacts with those individuals responsible for making the purchasing decisions. This aspect of government business is certainly similar to the commercial arena.

Contract Award

Government procedures leading to a contract award are detailed and precise. They are directed toward precluding partial or preferential treatment to any responsible bidder. These procedures are also intended to ensure strict compliance with detailed specifications that are set forth in the requirements data. In most instances, they require actions by the offeror that are unique to government business. We will discuss some of these actions in the paragraphs that follow.

Negotiated procurements, generally begin with a proposal that details the cost and technical aspects of the work to be done. The proposal serves as the basis for arriving at a contract price. The proposal may be subject to technical reviews, cost and price analysis, and finally, negotiation. The proposal may also have to comply with various regulations covering such things as:

Adequacy of cost or pricing data provided in support of the estimated cost.
Contract costing practices.
Allowability of specific types of costs, etc.

There are few, if any, circumstances in the private sector where a company must divulge its cost data for a customer to review as a prerequisite for negotiating a contract.

Contract Administration

For certain procurements, such as research and experimental activities, the government will closely monitor contract performance. It believes the nature of some of its purchases requires such scrutiny to ensure fair and reasonable pricing, adequate performance of the work, and remuneration to the contractor in a manner consistent with public policy.

The government, as a customer, can unilaterally direct a contract change, including ordering a delay or stopping work partially or entirely. When this occurs, the contractor is contractually entitled to compensation for the cost of making the change.

If the data provided by the contractor during the negotiations are determined to be defective, the negotiated price may be adjusted downward to eliminate any increased cost attributable to the government's reliance on the bad data in arriving at a price.

THE GOVERNMENT PROCUREMENT PROCESS

The ultimate objective of the procurement process is to acquire necessary supplies and services of the quality required, in a timely manner, and at fair and reasonable prices. An additional responsibility is to ensure that certain socioeconomic goals are met. This segment describes briefly how the Federal Government goes about determining what it is going to buy, who will be the supplier, and what price will be paid for the work performed.

Establishing the Government Need

Generally, the government has rather formal procedures for determining its procurement needs. These procedures tend to vary from agency to agency depending on the nature of the organizational mission. The process invariably starts with a legislative mandate from Congress, which may be as broad as a setting forth of the agency's overall mission or as detailed as authorizing the purchase of a specific weapon system. Describing the process of determining what each agency buys is certainly beyond the scope of this book. Nevertheless, we cannot overemphasize the importance of becoming intimately knowledgeable about this process for those agencies that represent a company's market.

Additionally, there are circumstances when a company, through its relationship with an agency, may even assist in determining the agency's needs or at least exert some influence on the process. The extent to which a company is able to anticipate agency needs can be important in making decisions regarding marketing strategies, research and development, and bid and proposal activities. Perhaps the best way to be kept informed about government needs is to have a continuing relationship with those officials who decide such matters.

Awarding the Contract

Once the government has identified its needs, the method to be used for acquiring the products or services must be determined. Federal contract awards result from either sealed bidding or negotiation. The solicitation document in a sealed bid procurement is an *invitation for bid* (IFB). The selection is made solely on the basis of the lowest price submitted by a qualified supplier.

The solicitation document in a negotiated procurement is either a *request for proposal* (RFP) or a *request for quotation* (RFQ). In this situation, the award is made on the basis of price and other technical factors. RFPs and RFQs are similar, except that the government may unilaterally accept offers made pursuant to an RFP without further negotiations. For an RFQ, a bilateral agreement must be negotiated.

In preparing for negotiations, the government contracting officer may require the assistance of engineers, accountants, and price analysts to review a proposal. The purpose of the review is to determine whether the proposal constitutes an acceptable basis for reaching an agreement. This process of bargaining between buyer and seller is, of course, a critical one. In order for it to effectively serve its stated purpose, each party must come to the negotiation table adequately prepared to vigorously and responsibly pursue its individual interest. When either party fails to do this, the procurement process is weakened. A successful negotiation is one that results in a pricing arrangement that is fair to both parties.

Contract Performance

The government enters into various contractual relationships depending on its needs. The extent to which the government remains actively involved with a contractor during contract performance is determined by the type of contract awarded. There are two basic categories— fixed price and cost reimbursable contracts. These pricing arrangements reflect the risk involved in contract performance. Under the firm fixed-price arrangement, once the price is set, there is generally no government involvement after the award. The contractor is obligated to perform at the negotiated price.

Flexibly priced (eg. cost reimbursable, incentive)contracts may provide for the final price to be determined either when the work is finished or at some interim point during contract performance. If the flexibly priced contract is cost reimbursable, the contractor can legally stop work when all contract funds are spent. If the flexibly priced contract is fixed price in nature (e.g., FPI), continued performance is required even though contract completion may cause incurrence of a loss. The major types of contracts are briefly described below:

Contract Type	Major Characteristics
Firm fixed-price (FFP)	The price is not subject to adjustment by reason of cost of performance. The contractor is obligated to perform the contract at the established price.
Fixed-price with economic price adjustment	The fixed price is adjusted upward or downward based upon the occurrence of contractually specified economic contingencies that are clearly outside the control of the contractor.
Fixed-price incentive (FPI)	The profit is adjusted and the final price is established by a formula based on the relationship of final negotiated cost to target cost previously established.
Firm fixed-price level of effort	A fixed price is established for a specified level of effort over a stated time frame. If the level varies beyond specified thresholds, the price is adjusted.
Cost	Reimbursement consists of allowable cost; there is no fee provision.
Cost-sharing	An agreed portion of allowable cost is reimbursed.
Cost plus fixed-fee (CPFF)	Reimbursement is based on allowable cost plus a fixed fee. adjsuted by a formula based on the relationship of total allowable cost to target cost.
Cost plus incentive-fee (CPIF)	Reimbursement consists of allowable cost incurred and a fee adjusted by a formula based on the relationship of total allowable cost to target cost.
Cost plus award-fee (CPAF)	Reimbursement consists of allowable cost incurred and a two-part fee (a

	fixed amount and an award amount based on an evaluation of the quality of contract performance).
Time and material (T&M)	Direct labor hours expended are reimbursed at fixed hourly rates, which usually include direct labor costs, indirect expenses, and profit. Material costs are reimbursed at actual plus a material handling charge, if applicable.
Labor hour	Direct labor hours expended are reimbursed at a fixed hourly rate, usually including all cost and profit.

During contract performance, the government can unilaterally alter the terms and conditions of the existing agreement. When it does, the contract price is equitably adjusted to reflect the impact of the change. Only the contracting officer is authorized to direct a change on behalf of the government. A contractor must be certain that directions are taken from no one other than the contracting officer and that those directions are in writing.

Contract Settlement

Ideally, all contract settlements will occur as a result of successful completion of the work. For flexibly priced contracts, a firm final price will be negotiated according to the allowable cost incurred, and adjusted for those items provided for in the contract. To settle cost reimbursement contracts, the contracting officer must obtain from the government contract auditor a report on the allowability of the total cost claimed. Based on this report, a settlement is usually reached. The contractor will be reimbursed for all acceptable costs incurred, plus an allowance for a fee as determined by contract terms and conditions.

SUMMARY

Unquestionably, the typical relationship between two commercial organizations and between the parties to a Federal procurement process are certainly different. The latter relationship is highly structured and formal. The acquisition system is designed primarily to assure that the approximately 130,000 government employees involved are reasonably uniform and effective in carrying out their responsibilities. It is also hoped that the system provides some assurance that all responsible offerors are treated fairly, that there is integrity in the process, and that actions are sufficiently documented to ensure that the necessary monitoring and surveillance can occur.

At the same time, government procurement merely represents another market. As in any separate and distinct marketplace, the entrepreneur must understand the process as well as the factors that affect the environment in which he or she operates. If you know the rules of the game, government business is probably no more or less treacherous than any other market. Without at least a basic knowledge of the rules and regulations, or if the rules and regulations are ignored, the risk of loss or expensive litigation for the supplier is real and can be considerable.

Chapter Two

Organization of the Government's Procurement Functions

A detailed description of all the procurement functions in the Federal Government is certainly beyond the scope of this book. Moreover, such an extensive exposition is unnecessary to understand and appreciate the processes the government uses to acquire goods and services. This chapter focuses on how the government has organized its procurement function and identifies key officials with whom contractors frequently come in contact.

ORGANIZATIONS

About 13 departments and 60 agencies in the executive branch award a large dollar volume of contracts. These departments and agencies, along with the specific products or services they procure, are identified in several publications which can be obtained from the U.S. superintendent of documents: *Selling to the Military, Selling to the U.S. Government, Doing Business with the Federal Government, and U.S. Government Procurement and Sales Directory.* Military contract award statistics are also available from the Pentagon DOD Office of Public Affairs. Because of the major involvement in the procurement process, several agencies and departments are mentioned briefly below.

Office of Federal Procurement Policy

The Office of Federal Procurement Policy (OFPP) is responsible for all procurement policy. The Office of Federal Procurement Policy Act, Public Law 93-400, established OFPP in 1974 as part of the Office of Management and Budget (OMB). The legislation recognized that an organization was needed to provide overall direction to departments and agencies and to enhance uniformity in procurement policies, procedures, regulations, and forms.

OFPP's greatest impact on government contractors was undoubtedly the issuance of the Federal Acquisition Regulations (FAR). Government acquisition specialists were engaged for several years in writing the FAR, which on April 1,

1984 replaced the Federal Procurement Regulations (FPR), Defense Acquisition Regulation (DAR), and other agency regulations. The stated objective of the FAR was to curb the proliferation of redundant and sometimes conflicting regulations issued by the various Federal agencies and, to the extent possible, replace them with a single, simplified set.

Public Law 96-83, the Office of Federal Procurement Policy Act Amendments of 1979, established government-wide uniformity as an objective. This legislation defined procurement as including "all stages of the acquisition process beginning with the process for determining the need for property and services through to the Federal government's disposition of such property and services."[1] In response to its legislative mandate, the administrator of OFPP submitted to Congress in 1982 a proposal for a Federal procurement system to:

Vest within the Department of Defense, General Services Administration, and National Aeronautics and Space Administration the regulatory authority to develop and promulgate a single government-wide acquisition regulation. (All federal agencies were still permitted to supplement the FAR with essential regulations unique to their missions.)

Establish an integrated procurement management framework to develop and implement policies, regulations, and standards and to identify and resolve procurement problems and issues.

Amend existing procurement statutes (Armed Services Procurement Act, Federal Property and Administrative Services Act, and Office of Federal Procurement Policy Act) to stimulate competition in procurement and streamline the procurement process.

Issuance of Presidential Executive Order 12352 on March 17, 1982 provided added impetus to implementing the Federal procurement system by calling for:

Agency heads to establish programs and procedures to make procurement more mission oriented.

The Secretary of Defense and the administrators for NASA and GSA to expedite their efforts to consolidate common procurement regulations into a single simplified FAR.

The Director of Office of Personnel Management (OPM) to ensure that Federal personnel policies and job classification standards meet the needs of executive agencies for a professional procurement work force.

OFPP to work jointly with agency heads to provide broad policy guidance and overall leadership necessary to achieve procurement reform.

OFPP is essentially a policy-making organization. It does not engage in procurement and is discouraged from monitoring or directing the day-to-day operations of departments and agencies. OFPP's regulatory authority, established by the 1974 act, was withdrawn by the 1979 amendments. Limited regulatory authority was reinstated in 1983; however, OFPP has thus far failed to exercise that authority. With the appointment of a new administrator in late 1986, OFPP announced plans in 1987 to begin exercising a more forceful role in reviewing procurement regulations for conformance with:

Established procurement policy.

Executive order 12291 requirements that Federal rules be subjected to a cost benefit test.

Paperwork reduction act requirements that information collected from the private sector meet a trifold test of necessity, practical utility, and minimization of burdensomeness.

Office of Management and Budget

In addition to overseeing OFPP, the Office of Management and Budget (OMB) plays a significant part in the procurement process through its issuance of OMB circulars, which must be followed by the departments and agencies within the Federal Government. Active OMB circulars that relate to procurement are identified in Figure 2.1 below:

A-21   Cost Principles for Educational Institutions
A-50   Audit Follow-up
A-73   Audit of Federal Operations and Programs
A-76   Performance of Commercial Activities
A-87   Cost Principles for State and Local Governments
A-88   Indirect Cost Rates, Audit, and Audit Follow-up at Educational Institutions
A-102 Uniform Administrative Requirements for Grants-in-Aid to State and Local Governments
A-110 Uniform Administrative Requirements for Grants and Other Agreements with Institutions of Higher Education, Hospitals, and Other Nonprofit Organizations
A-120 Guidelines for the Use of Consulting Services
A-122 Cost Principles for Nonprofit Organizations
A-123 Internal Control Systems
A-124 Patents—Small Business Firms and Nonprofit Organizations
A-125 Prompt Payment

Figure 2.1   Active OMB Circulars.

Department of Defense

The Department of Defense (DOD) is so large it almost defies description. Its assets have been estimated to be twice those of the 100 largest manufacturing corporations in the United States; but more important, it accounts for about 80% of all federal procurement and, next to the Department of Interior, is the nation's largest real estate operator.

The Office of the Secretary of Defense (OSD) is actually limited to purchasing relatively minor housekeeping items. The Army, Navy, Air Force, DLA, and certain other DOD agencies are responsible for the major DOD acquisitions.

As a result of the enactment of the 1986 Military Retirement Reform Act (Public Law 99-348) and the 1987 Defense Authorization Act (PL 99-661) the acquisition function within DOD was reorganized. A new position of Undersecretary of Defense for Acquisition was created to provide greater control over the acquisition process. The new Undersecretary follows directly behind the Secretary of Defense and Deputy Secretary of Defense in terms of DOD hierarchy and serves as the senior DOD procurement executive. The Undersecretary's responsibilities include:

Supervising DOD acquisition.
Setting policy for acquisition, including defense contractor oversight and contract audit.
Directing policy for maintenance of the defense industrial base.
Directing the military service secretaries and heads of DOD agencies in matters falling within the Undersecretary's responsibility.
Consulting with the Inspector General of DOD (DODIG) to prevent duplication of audit and oversight of contractor activities.

The Assistant Secretary of Defense for Acquisition and Logistics, who reports to the Deputy Undersecretary of Defense for Acquisition, has responsibility for several functions that play an important role in the acquisition process:

The Directorate for Cost Pricing and Finance is responsible for implementing DOD policy regarding cost accounting standards, independent research and development and bid and proposal costs (IR&D and B&P), progress payments, and other areas involving the costing, pricing, and financing of government contracts.

The Directorate for Defense Acquisition Regulatory System has responsibility for issuing and updating the DFARS. It has joint responsibility (with GSA) for maintaining the FAR.

The Indirect Cost Monitoring Office (ICMO) functions to assure uniform application of contracting policies and consistent treatment of cost allowability; and promote timely and equitable settlement of overhead and advance agreements for IR&D and B&P costs. ICMO guidance papers are issued to provide criteria for government field personnel to use in resolving identified problems. While the guidance papers have no contractual significance, they do reflect the official DOD position to be used as a basis for resolving the subject issues.

National Aeronautics and Space Administration

The National Aeronautics and Space Administration (NASA) conducts research in various aspects of aeronautics and space technology, including development of space transportation systems. Like OSD, NASA headquarter's procurements are relatively minor. Major NASA acquisitions are made by the various NASA field installations.

General Services Administration

The General Services Administration (GSA) was created by the Federal Property and Administrative Services Act of 1949 to consolidate dozens of agencies involved in carrying out the executive branch's many housekeeping activities, such as purchasing supplies, providing computers and communications facilities, keeping records, and acting as the Federal architect, builder, and landlord. GSA procurement is accomplished primarily by four separate groups: Property Management and Disposal Service, Public Buildings Service, Automated Data and Telecommunications Service, and the Federal Supply Service. A considerable portion of GSA procurement involves standard items that are acquired through sealed bidding. Prior to promulgation of the FAR, one of GSA's major responsibilities under the Federal Property and Administrative Services Act was issuing and maintaining the FPR. GSA currently chairs the Civilian Agency Acquisition Council which jointly maintains the FAR with the DOD Defense Acquisition Regulation Council.

Department of Energy

The Department of Energy (DOE) was established in 1977 by the Department of Energy Organization Act, Public Law 95-91. The Department's mission is to manage the energy functions in the Federal Government in meeting and solving our nation's energy problems. Most of DOE's contracts fall into one of the following caegories: atomic energy defense activities; energy conservation; energy supply research and development; fossil energy research and development; and energy production demonstration and distribution.

Department of Health and Human Services

Because of its functional responsibilities in such areas as health care, licensing of food products, and retirement security for the aged, the Department of Health and Human Services (HHS) touches the lives of most persons in the United States. Procurement in HHS is carried out by various national, regional, and field offices of the National Institutes of Health, the Public Health Service, the Food and Drug Administration, and the Social Security Administration.

Department of Interior

The Department of Interior (DOI) is responsible for about one-half billion acres of Federal lands as well as development and preservation of natural resources. Procurement activities are decentralized within the department's various bureaus, with activity concentrated in the western part of the United States.

Department of Transportation

The Department of Transportation (DOT) includes such diverse entities as the U. S. Coast Guard, Federal Aviation Administration (FAA), Federal Highway Administration (FHWA), Federal Railroad Administration (FRA), and Urban and Mass Transportation Administration (UMTA). Like DOI, procurement activities are decentralized among the various agencies.

Department of Agriculture

The Department of Agriculture (USDA) was established more than 100 years ago. The department's substantial procurement expenditures are concentrated in three services: Agricultural Stabilization and Conservation Service, Food Safety and Quality Services, and the Forest Service.

GOVERNMENT PERSONNEL

Successful government contracting largely depends upon a clear understanding of the authority, responsibility, and limitations of each government official involved. The doctrine of actual authority is well established in legal precedence. As stated by the Armed Services Board of Contract Appeals (ASBCA) in *General Electric Company*,[2] "It is appropriate that the Government cannot be bound by one acting without authority."

This point was emphasized even more emphatically by the United States Supreme Court in 1947, when it ruled:

Whatever the form in which the Government functions, anyone entering into an arrangement with the Government takes the risk of having accurately ascertained that he who purports to act for the Government stays within the bounds of his authority.[3]

Program Manager, Project Manager, and Other Technical Staff

Government officials with technical responsibilities play a major role in the procurement process.

> Program managers, found in DOD, NASA and DOE, and certain other agencies, are important officials who have overall responsibility for the procurement action. Although they have a key role in acquiring major weapon systems, they may not be widely known to smaller government contractors. In DOD, program managers are only designated for systems with anticipated costs in excess of $75 million in research, development, test, and evaluation or $300 million in production.
>
> Project managers and other government technical staff are better known to most contractors. Although generally not assigned contracting responsibilities as such, they are responsible for ensuring that goods or services meet the government's technical specifications and requirements.

While various government technical representatives may make suggestions relating to contract performance, their suggestions must be carefully evaluated. If the suggestions are expected to change the scope of the contract or result in increased costs, the contracting officer must personally authorize the necessary change orders or other contractual authorizations.

Contracting Officer (CO)

A contracting officer is the only government representative duly authorized to enter into or administer contracts. In some government agencies the term also includes the authorized representative of the contracting officer acting within designated limits of contractual authority. As firmly established in legal precedence, only a CO or the authorized representative may commit or bind the government.

In *Amis Construction and Consulting Services, Inc.*[4] the contractor asserted that work performed beyond the scope of its cost plus fixed fee contract was authorized by the contracting officer's technical representative (COTR). However, the contract explicitly stated that the COTR was a technical advisor and was not empowered to sign contractual documents or direct any actions that would change the scope, price, terms, or conditions of the contract. In denying the company's claim for reimbursement of its contract overrun, the Labor Board of Contract Appeals observed that "The doctrine of apparent authority is not binding upon the Government and accordingly, it is not stopped from denying the authority of its agents."

In another appeals proceeding, Abbott W. Thompson Associates[5] contended that additional design service performed under an architect-engineer contract was compensable because the work had been performed at the direction of the DOT regional architect. However, the changes clause in the contract required prior written approval of the CO before services could be rendered that resulted in payment by the government of an additional charge. In ruling that the contractor's claim was not compensable, the DOT Contract Appeals Board concluded that

> where such written approval [by the contracting officer] is required as a precondition for a compensable change, the failure to obtain that approval bars any recovery on account of the change. . . . Accordingly, any work performed

by the appellant under the circumstances is done as a volunteer for which no compensation is due.

In a decision involving DOT Systems Inc.,[6] the Department of Transportation Contract Appeals Board ruled that a COTR did have implied authority to direct a contractor to utilize excess warehouse space to store government property. Here the contract did not clearly specify the limitations of the COTR's authority, and the board ruled that in the particular circumstances the COTR was empowered to direct the contractor to store the government property in a particular manner. Since the requirement to use excess warehouse space constituted a constructive contract change, the government was held liable to reimburse the contractor for additional costs related to the change.

In view of the considerable financial risk in performing work at the direction of unauthorized officials, a prudent contractor should obtain the contracting officer's approval prior to proceeding with any work outside the scope, price, terms, or conditions of the contract.

Prior to implementation of the FAR, most civilian agencies designated officials who were authorized to both enter into and administer contracts. In contrast, the Army, Navy, Air Force, and the defense agencies generally designated different persons for procuring, administering, and settling terminated contracts. The FAR provides guidance aligned more closely to the DOD policy.

Procuring Contracting Officer (PCO)

In DOD, contracts are awarded by one office and administered by another. The PCO, usually located in the office responsible for the agency program, is authorized to enter into contracts. After contract award, a different office is assigned the responsibility of administering the contract. However, the PCO may retain responsibility for specific contract administration functions when such functions can best be accomplished by the purchasing office.

Administrative Contracting Officer (ACO)

This official is primarily responsible for monitoring contract performance and negotiating certain contract modifications. When authorized by the PCO, the ACO may also issue contract change orders. Within DOD the ACO is assigned to either a Defense Contract Administration Services (DCAS) office or military department contract administration office. The ACO's duties generally include inspecting the contractor's operations, monitoring contract performance, and determining whether costs are allowable and comply with cost accounting standards.

Where the government deems a significant level of oversight to be necessary, it is usually accomplished on a contractor-wide basis rather than contract by contract.In such circumstances, the contract administration office designates a Cost Monitoring Coordinator (CMC). This individual could be the administrative contracting officer or some other staff member in the contract administration office. The CMC is assisted by the Defense Contract Audit Agency (DCAA) and technical personnel as needed. The responsibilities of the CMC include the following:

Preparing and maintaining review plans. DCAA and other specialists comprising the cost monitoring team will provide assistance.
Coordinating the efforts of all team members.

Providing assistance to team members or arranging for assistance when requested.

Advising the contract administration office of deficiencies in contractors' operations and monitoring the status of recommendations made to the contractor.

Preparing for the administrative contracting officer's consideration a *notice of intent to disallow or not recognize cost* where recommendations involve a significant amount of cost or an important principle.

Termination Contract Officer (TCO)

The TCO is authorized to settle contracts which have been terminated for default or for the convenience of the government. In the latter circumstance, a TCO is appointed to examine the settlement proposal of the prime contractor and, when appropriate, subcontract settlement proposals and to effect a settlement by agreement or determination.

Tri-Service Contracting Officer (TSCO)

The TSCO is responsible for negotiating advance agreements covering the cost of independent research and development and bid and proposal (IR&D and B&P) activities. These agreements are required for companies receiving IR&D and B&P costs in excess of specified thresholds in a cost accounting period. This same official also administers Cost Accounting Standard 420, Accounting for IR&D and B&P Costs, for companies that must negotiate an advance agreement.

Defense Contract Audit Agency Auditor and Other Contract Auditors

The Defense Contract Audit Agency (DCAA) is by far the largest contract audit organization. With more than 6,000 professional auditors throughout the United States and abroad, DCAA is the agency authorized by DOD to examine the books and records of defense contractors for the purpose of establishing forward pricing, billing, and final O/H rates and contract prices. DCAA provides audit services not only for DOD and NASA but also for many civilian departments when it is considered to be in the interest of the government. This is particularly true where civilian contracts are awarded to companies already engaged in DOD work.

DCAA Organization

DCAA is a separate DOD agency that reports to the Assistant Secretary of Defense (Comptroller). However, DCAA is also subject to oversight by both the DOD Inspector General (DOGIG) and the DOD Undersecretary for Acquisition. The DODIG exercises certain oversight of DCAA operations as a result of its statutory responsibility to:

Provide policy direction for audits relating to fraud, waste, and abuse.

Monitor and evaluate the adherence of DOD auditors to contract audit principles, policies, and procedures.

Develop policy, evaluate program performance, and monitor actions taken by all components of DOD in response to contract audits.

As a result, such traditional contract audit activities as defective pricing reviews are now frequently performed by DODIG auditors, as well as by DCAA auditors. A Federal court decision to grant the DOD Inspector General access to Westinghouse's internal audit reports has considerably blurred the roles of the DODIG office and the DCAA in performing contract audits The decision has increased industry's concern over the ability of DCAA to remain independent because it clearly endorses an intermingling of the contract audit function between these two organizations.

As shown in Figure 2.2, DCAA is divided into six geographic regions: Eastern, Northeastern, Central, Southwestern, Midatlantic, and Western plus a field detachment for certain classified work. The agency operates at the field audit office level, with both resident offices and branch offices. Resident offices are established at specific contractor locations where the audit workload warrants a permanent audit staff and where either the Army, Navy, Air Force, or Defense Contract Administration Service has established an on-site contract administration activity. Branch offices are strategically located within each DCAA region to perform contract audits at other contractor locations within an assigned geographic area. The audit work is generally performed on a mobile basis with the auditors responsible for all contractors within a segment of the geographic area covered by the branch office. DCAA procurement liaison offices are established within various Army, Navy, and Air Force procurement offices to expedite communication and coordination between the procurement officials and the field audit activities.

While overall audit policy is developed by DCAA headquarters, the regional offices and the field detachment (Fig. 2.3) are the primary operating units. Regional audit managers are responsible for planning, directing, and evaluating the contract audit mission for an assigned group of field audit offices. They provide regional direction to the branch managers and resident auditors in resolving complex or controversial contract audit or cost accounting issues. They also are responsible for assuring that audits are accomplished in a timely and effective manner and in accordance with agency policy and applicable acquisition regulations.

The DCAA Mission

Department of Defense Directive 5105.36 dated June 9, 1965 (revised June 8, 1978), which established the Defense Contract Audit Agency, defined the agency's mission as:

Performing all necessary contract audits for the DOD and providing accounting and financial advisory services in connection with the negotiation, administration and settlement of contracts and subcontracts.
Providing contract audit service to other government agencies as appropriate.

As further discussed in Chapter 13, the agency's principle activities are involved in virtually every stage of the procurement process.

The FY 1986 Defense Authorization Act granted DCAA the power to subpoena books, documents, papers and records. As reflected in the Newport

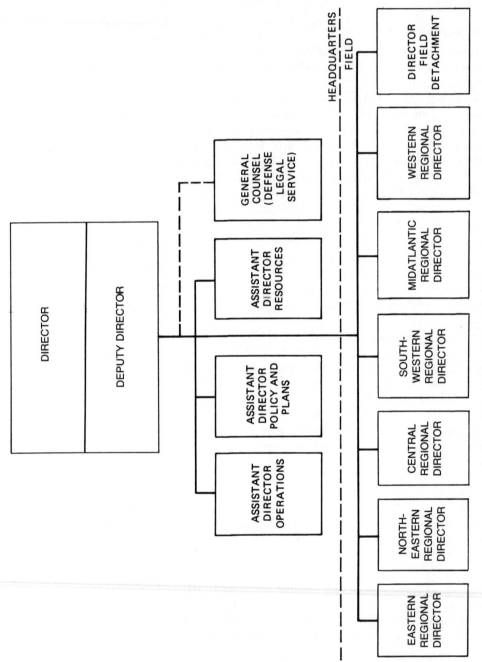

Figure 2.2 Defense Contract Audit Agency.

24

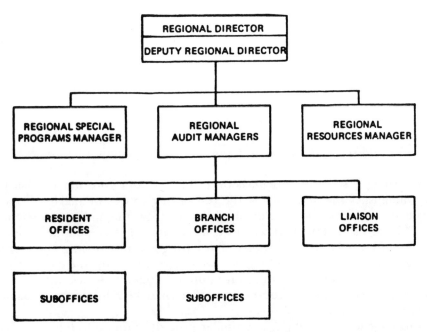

Figure 2.3 Defense Contract Audit Agency.

News and Shipbuilding[8] decision, however, DCAA's subpoena authority is more narrowly defined than that granted to the DODIG.

Audit Follow-Up

In recent years, GAO and Congress have expressed concern that the government was losing billions of dollars because executive departments were not following audit recommendations. In response to this prodding, Federal agencies have placed increased emphasis on tracking audit recommendations.

From its issuance on August 31, 1981, DOD Directive 5000.42, Policy for Follow-up on Contract Audit Recommendations, generated considerable interest and controversy. The directive basically required DOD components to track and report on the resolution of all significant contract audit recommendations where the contracting officer did not concur. To alleviate industry concerns that the directive impaired the independence of the contracting officer, the Assistant Deputy Undersecretary of Defense for Acquisition reiterated in a November 1981 memorandum that it still was the contracting officer's responsibility to make all final determinations concerning contracts. The memorandum expressed the view that the DOD Directive merely formalized review practices that previously existed rather than changed the direction of acquisition policy.

To clarify the meaning of the phrase "significant contract audit recommendations" and to reduce the number of audit reports subject to tracking, the directive was reissued on December 29, 1982, as DOD Directive 7640.2, Policy for Follow-up on Contract Audit Reports. The current version of the directive, dated July 18, 1986:

Identifies specific reports to be tracked and outlines reporting and resolution requirements.

Establishes the dollar threshold for independent review of forward pricing differences (reports with questioned cost of $500,000 or more and differences between the contracting officer and the auditor totaling 5% of questioned cost).
Clarifies responsibilities of the DOD inspector general.
Eliminates the requirement for auditors to request independent reviews of differences.
Clarifies the role of the designated independent senior acquisition official/board (advisor).
Clarifies and separates tracking, reporting, and resolution requirements.

The feeling is still widespread, both in industry and government, that the policy diminishes the authority of the contracting officer by making it more difficult to take a position materially different from the audit recommendation. This de facto shift in power to contract audit has complicated and, in some instances, delayed the process of resolving contract pricing and costing issues. In this environment, it becomes even more critical for the contractor to make every reasonable effort to resolve purely accounting issues with the contract audit activity since the contracting officer may be reluctant to go against the audit recommendation.

Civilian agencies are subject to a similar procedure for audit follow-up pursuant to revised OMB Circular A-50.

General Accounting Office (GAO)

GAO Mission

The GAO was created by the Budget and Accounting Act of 1921, and its charter has been expanded by subsequent legislation. It is a large independent agency in the legislative branch of the Federal Government and performs a wide variety of reviews that are either required by various statutes, specifically requested by Congress, or self-initiated. With its staff of about 4,500 professionals, GAO evaluates virtually every government activity. The broad range of its examinations is made possible by its almost unlimited charter and the employment of a wide variety of specialists, including accountants, auditors, attorneys, economists, social scientists, actuaries, engineers, and mathematicians.

In the late 1950s and early 1960s, GAO expended considerable effort in auditing government contractors. This activity diminished significantly in later years. The GAO now emphasizes reviews of the effectiveness of audits performed by DCAA and other contract audit organizations in Federal departments and agencies. Responding to Congressional requests and on its own initiative, GAO reviews and makes recommendations concerning virtually every activity financed by Federally appropriated funds. Acquisition policies and procedures constitute an area of considerable attention. GAO also examines profit policies, procurements of major weapon systems, logistics and communications, financial and general management, and international programs. Many of these evaluations include not only Federal departments and agencies but government contractors as well.

As stated earlier, GAO's activities have few limitations where Federal funds are involved. Their activities also include:

Review and settlement of claims against the United States.
Publication of Comptroller General (Comp. Gen.) decisions.
Audits of Federal departments and agencies, including examining financial

transactions; testing compliance with laws and regulations; and reviewing the efficiency, economy, and effectiveness of operations.

Assistance to Congress.

Bid Protests

Public Law 98-369, known as the Competition Contracting Act (CICA) significantly expanded GAO's role in the bid protest resolution. Congress believed that a strong enforcement mechanism was necessary to ensure that its mandate for competition is enforced. Accordingly, the CICA provided (for the first time) an express statutory basis for the GAO to hear bid protest cases. The parties who may protest, and the matters which may be protested, are similar to those identified in the prior bid protest regulations. Under the CICA, the Comptroller General is required to issue a final decision on a protest within 90 working days from the date the protest is submitted, with provisions for extension of that time as well as for an "express option" for accelerated resolution of "suitable" protests within 45 calendar days. Agencies are required by law to submit a report within 25 working days from the date of receipt of notice of the protest (unless a longer period is permitted by the Comp. Gen.).

Agencies are prohibited from awarding contracts after the C.O. has received notice of the protest unless the head of the procuring activity finds that urgent and compelling circumstances which significantly affect the government's interests will not permit delay. If award is made before the agency received the notice that a protest has been filed, but the protest was filed within 10 days of award, the agency must suspend performance while the protest is pending, unless the head of the procuring activity authorizes continued performance. If the head of the procuring agency finds that continued performance is merely in the "best interest" of the government,(i.e., no urgent or compelling reasons exist) the Comp. Gen.'s recommendation will be made without regard to any costs or disruption resulting from terminating, recompeting, or rewarding the contract.

If the protest is sustained, the Comp. Gen. is directed to recommend corrective action to the executive agency, and the agency must notify the Comp. Gen. if the recommendations are not implemented within 60 calendar days. The Comp. Gen. may "declare" a party entitled to the costs of filing and pursuing the protest—including attorneys' fees—and costs of bid or proposal preparation.

When signing Public Law 98-369, the President voiced objection to the CICA provisions which delegate executive agency functions to the Comp. Gen., an officer of Congress. The Department of Justice advised executive agencies that the stay of award, suspension of performance, and award of costs provisions are unconstitutional and should not be followed. However, the Comp. Gen. issued final bid protest regulations, effective January 15, 1985.[9]The CICA stay of award,and suspension of performance provisions were affirmed to be constitutional by the Court of Appeals for the Third Circuit[10] but the Department of Justice has appealed that decision to the U.S. Supreme Court.

Inspectors General (IG)

One of the major Congressional responses to rising criticisms of laxity in the government was the passage on October 12, 1978 of Public Law 95-452, the Inspector General Act of 1978. The purposes of the IG Act were to promote economy, efficiency, and effectiveness in government and to prevent and detect fraud and abuse. The act also provided a means for keeping department heads informed about deficiencies in the administration of their operations and the progress of any necessary corrective action.

The act established an Office of Inspector General in 12 Federal departments and agencies. Several IGs were already in place prior to passage of the act. The DOD Authorization Act of 1983 amended the Inspector General Act of 1978 to establish an IG for DOD, which brought the total to 18. Each IG is appointed by the President of the United States by and with the advice and consent of the Senate. The act also provides for an IG's removal from office by the President, provided the President communicates the reasons for such removal to both houses of Congress. The advice and consent of the Senate is not required for removal of an IG.

The act provides broad responsibilities and authority to the IGs for conducting audits and inspections relating to policies, practices, and operations of their respective departments. They can discharge their responsibilities in any manner they deem appropriate provided they:

Comply with the Comptroller General's Standards for Audits of Governmental Organizations, Programs, Activities, and Functions.

Report promptly to the Attorney General of the United States whenever reasonable grounds exist for belief that a Federal criminal law has been violated.

Submit to the agency/department head a semiannual comprehensive report identifying: significant problems, abuses, and deficiencies; recommendations of corrective actions; recommendations previously made for which corrective action has not been completed; matters referred to prosecutive authorities; prosecutions and convictions which have resulted; and audit reports issued during the period. (Within 30 days of submission of the semiannual report, the agency or department head must submit a copy together with any desired comments to the appropriate committee or subcommittee of Congress. No later than 60 days after transmission of the semiannual report to Congress, the agency/department head must make copies available to the public upon request and at a reasonable cost.)

Report immediately to the agency/department head any "particularly serious or flagrant problems, abuses or deficiencies." (The head of the department or agency has only 7 calendar days to forward the report to Congress with any appropriate comments.)

The act grants the IGs significant and unusual powers for accessing records, selecting audit and investigative procedures, obtaining subpoenas, and so forth. Where an IG believes requested information or assistance has been unreasonably refused, the circumstances are reported immediately to the head of the department or agency.

In recent years, DOD IG auditors have been significantly involved in the performance of contract audit activities. Major areas of IG emphasis have included defective pricing and spare parts pricing.

NOTES

1. P.L. 96–83, October 10, 1979; 93 Stat. 648; 41 U.S.C. 403, sec. 4(b).
2. General Electric Company, ASBCA no. 11990, May 25, 1967, 67–1 BCA 6,377.

3. Federal Crop Insurance Corp. v. Merrill (1947), 332 U.S. 380, 68 S. Ct. 1.

4. Amis Construction and Consulting Services, Inc., LBCA no. 81-BCA-4, March 11, 1982, 82−1 BCA 15,679.

5. Abbot W. Thompson Associates, DOT CAB no. 1098, January 21, 1981, 81−1 BCA 14,879.

6. DOT Systems, Inc., DOT CAB no. 1208, June 10, 1982, 82-2 BCA 15,817.

7. Westinghouse Electric Corporation vs. U.S., Misc. no. 11710, DC WD PA 1985, August 14, 1985, 33 CCF 73922; aff'd. CA-3 no. 85−3456, April 14, 1986, 33 CCF 74, 342.

8. Newport News Shipbuilding and Dry Dock Company vs. Reed, Misc. no. 86-182 nn, EVA, March 20, 1987. 34 CCF 75, 294.

9. 49 Federal Register 49417.

10. Amerron, Inc. vs. Army Corp of Engrs., CA-3, nos. 85−5226 and 85−5377, December 31, 1986.

Chapter Three
Obtaining Government Business

BACKGROUND

Today, the United States Government is by far the largest consumer of goods and services in the world. A government agency is likely to have a need for just about any product or service one can think of, and probably in quantities that stretch the imagination. Small wonder then that procurement by the public sector is viewed as a major market opportunity.

Understandably, there are many misconceptions about the government market, both positive and negative. Many believe that selling to the Federal Government, next to finding a pot of gold at the end of the rainbow, is perhaps the easiest way to fame and fortune. Others avoid government orders because they are certain that all the rules and regulations, as well as the unusual contractual terms and conditions, are there solely to trap the unwary, intrepid company that dares to venture into this market. Of course, both of these views are uninformed and should not be the basis for any company's decision to sell or not to sell to the government.

This chapter discusses the process of obtaining government business. It covers how the government communicates to the public what it is interested in buying, how companies interested in fulfilling government needs should respond, and finally, how the contractual relationship is ultimately established. The contracting procedures have been fairly well standardized and apply to all companies, whether foreign or domestic. We will identify the specific sources of information the government uses to publish its requirements, the procedures companies must follow in making their offers to sell, the contracting methods the government employs, and the pricing arrangements that are used to reflect the contracting environment in which the acquisition is made.

A company electing to enter this specialized market should recognize that the objective of the procurement process is to acquire necessary supplies and services of the desired quality, in a timely manner, and at fair and reasonable prices. DOD defines a fair and reasonable price as fair to both parties to the transaction, considering the quality and timeliness of contract performance. However, as in all other business dealings, the potential seller to the government must make a judgment as to whether the proposed contractual arrangement serves the best interest of the company and is consistent with the company's goals and objectives.

PRELIMINARIES FOR ENTERING THE GOVERNMENT MARKET

Before attempting to enter the government market, a company must decide exactly what it wants to sell to the government. The company must then carefully study the market to determine which of the many government agencies might be interested in the products or services that the company is capable of providing. There are hundreds of purchasing activities that may provide either a permanent or a one-time marketplace for a company's products. Only after the potential customers are identified can the company determine how best to obtain government business.

The next step is to determine the market potential. Because the military and civilian government organizations purchase literally thousands of goods and services ranging from complex space vehicles to paper clips, as well as food products, medicines, machinery, equipment, ships, airplanes, paper, ink, furniture, clothing, and so forth, a listing of all the potential government needs for any specific category would be lengthy indeed. Therefore, the company should develop a sufficient data base to identify which agencies should be the targets of its marketing strategy. This book, provides only basic guidance on how to obtain the government's business once the potential market has been identified.

No matter what the government is buying, it will be done in one of two ways: (1) using competitive procedures, which includes sealed bids, competitive negotiations, or procedures excluding a particular source, or (2) using other than competitive procedures, which can be used in only seven circumstances.

Government Marketing Defined

There is a common perception among contractors that marketing is simply the process of finding opportunities to bid or propose on government contracts. While locating opportunities to bid is an integral part of marketing, the marketing process is much more comprehensive. For example, establishing a good working relationship with a government agency through acceptable contract performance can lead to many bidding opportunities. The fact that marketing includes activities other than locating opportunities to bid requires consideration of government marketing in very broad terms. For the purposes of this discussion, government marketing is defined as all activities that contribute to winning government contracts. In the government contract environment, marketing involves two basic activities. The first is identifying and tracking potential contract opportunities. The second is conveying to the government customer the company's capability.

Strategic Marketing Planning

Marketing activity represents a significant expenditure of resources. Successful marketing is the result of careful and comprehensive planning, both at the overall business level as well as the individual contract opportunities. The purpose of strategic marketing planning is to allow a fundamental decision to be made about the government market as a source of business for the company. In making this decision, the benefits of entering or remaining in the market (return on investment, profit level, absorption of fixed operating costs, etc.)

and the costs associated with entering the market (administrative cost increases, legal liability, etc.) should be considered. The strategic plan, once developed, requires periodic updating as appropriate, in order to assess whether the government is still a viable market. Information on current contracting activity should be included in making this decision. When the strategic marketing plan is complete it should answer four questions:

Are we going to enter the government market?
What products are we going to provide, and to what customers will we provide them?
What changes to our organization or methods of doing business must we undertake in order to be successful?
What portion of the market will we enter?

Listed below are some questions to consider when preparing a strategic marketing plan.

Product

Does the government currently purchase similar product(s)?
Are the products purchased by sealed bids or negotiated procurement?
Is procurement accomplished on a centralized basis or by individual buying activities?
Is the market potential significant enough to attract us?

Agencies

Which agencies can be considered potential customers?
How are these agencies structured in terms of size and responsibility?
What type of pricing arrangements do these agencies normally award?

Profitability

Does the market offer sufficient long-term profit potential based on analysis of pricing history competition?
How effective is the competition?
What new production techniques are required?
What new or special requirements such as accounting and quality assurance are required?
What investments in technology, labor, and capital are required?

Results

Which portion of the market should we target for individual contract opportunities?

Competition in Contracting Act

Public Law 98-369 —the Competition in Contracting Act of 1984 (CICA), repealed substantial portions of the Armed Services Procurement Act of 1947 and the Federal Property and Administrative Services Act of 1949. The CICA applies to any solicitation issued after March 31, 1985.

The basic objective of the act is for each Agency to obtain full and open competition, by specifying procurement needs developing appropriate specifications and narrowing the circumstances for use of procedures other than competitive procedures.

Competitive Procurement Procedures

CICA replaces the two categories of procurement procedures recognized by the existing statutory framework, formal advertising and negotiation, with competitive procedures and procedures other than competitive procedures. Competitive procedures under CICA include sealed bidding and submission of competitive proposals. Use of either of these methods is defined as full and open competition if all responsible sources may submit bids or proposals.

Sealed Bidding

Sealed bidding is to be used when:
Time constraints permit solicitation, submission and evaluation of sealed bids,
Award can be made on the basis of price and other price-related factors,
Discussions will not be necessary, and
It is reasonably expected that more than one bid will be received.

Sealed bidding is the preferred method of procurement for all government departments. It is used when the requirements have been clearly established and are well-known by the prospective suppliers. Sealed bids are submitted in response to an *Invitation for Bid* (IFB) which must clearly, accurately, and completely describe the government's requirements. It includes bid preparation instructions; details concerning inspections, delivery and payment; technical data and specifications; and any other pertinent information concerning the purchase. The IFBs are publicized by the government through the *Commerce Business Daily* (CBD), posting in public places, distribution to known prospective bidders, and any other appropriate method to enable prospective bidders to learn about the opportunity to submit a bid. The sealed bids are submitted by prospective contractors to the contracting officer at the time and place indicated in the IFB. A public bid opening is held with the contract being awarded to the responsible bidder whose bid is most advantageous to the United States, considering only price and other price related factors included in the solicitation.

In situations where the technical specifications are not so clearly defined as to enable the government to clearly, accurately and completely describe the requirements, FAR subpart 14.5 allows contracting officers to use a two-step sealed bidding procedure. The first step requires prospective contractors to submit only technical proposals without price data. The contracting officer then determines which offerors are proposing technically acceptable supplies or services. In step two, the offerors whose technical proposals were acceptable submit sealed bids with the lowest responsible offeror receiving the award. For the two-step procedures to be effective, the contracting officer has to work very closely with technical personnel to establish reasonable and valid criteria to evaluate the technical proposals and, even more important, to judge how well they measure up.

Competitive Proposals

The competitive proposal method generally entails holding discussions with the potential contractors unless:

> it can be clearly demonstrated from the existence of full and open competition or accurate prior cost experience . . . that acceptance of an initial proposal without discussions would result in the lowest overall cost to the Government.[1]

The government must have discussions with all offerors within the competitive range. The competitive range is determined by considering only price and the other factors included in the solicitation. Discussions may be conducted for the purpose of minor clarification without requiring such discussions be held with all offerors. Award is made "to the responsible source whose proposal is most advantageous to the United States, considering only price and the other factors included in the solicitation."[2]

CICA distinguishes between sealed bids and competitive proposals. Award under sealed bidding must be made on the basis of price and price-related factors while award under competitive proposals may be made on the basis of price and other factors. Litigation will have to resolve the question of whether the "price-related factors" to be evaluated under sealed bidding must be objective or whether subjective judgment will be allowed. CICA also provides that under competitive proposals, as contrasted to sealed bids, the losing offerors are given notice of rejection of their proposals.

The Seven Exceptions to Competitive Procurement

In contrast to the 14 or 16 exceptions to the requirements for formal advertising under the predecessor statutes' specific exceptions from the use of competitive proposals,[3] the Competition in Contracting Act contains only six and a seventh broad, public interest exception determined to be necessary by the agency head.[4]

Exception 1.   The property or services needed by the executive agency are available from only one responsible source and no other type of property or service will satisfy the needs of the executive agency.

This considerably narrows the predecessor, counterpart exception. Now there is the dual test of documenting that only one source exists and that no other product or service will meet the needs of the agency. Moreover, a notice must also be published in the Commerce Business Daily that:

> Invites all responsible sources to submit bids, proposals, or quotations for consideration by the agency.
> Justifies the use of such procedures.
> Identifies the intended source.[5]

Use of the exception, without satisfying either prong of this dual test, would be subject to challenge by disappointed bidders.

This is the only exception that permits awards of either 1)follow-on contracts to firms previously awarded development or production contracts for major systems or highly specialized equipment or 2)contracts based on unsolicited proposals. However, the use of this authority for these purposes is not, according to the legislative history, "carte blanche,"[6] and is further limited by the act. When an award continuing the development or production of a major system or highly specialized equipment to a contractor other than the original source is expected to result in (i) substantial duplication of cost that is not expected to be recovered through competition, or (ii) unacceptable delays in fulfilling the agency's needs, such system or equipment may be deemed to be available only from the original source and may be procured through other than competitive procedures.

Exception 2.   The agency's need for the property or services is of such an unusual and compelling urgency that the government would be seriously injured unless the agency is permitted to limit the number of potential bidders or offerors.

This exception again is narrower than the counterpart exception contained in prior law.The restriction against use of this exception because of lack of advance planning or procurement funding concerns corrects the occasional abuse of the prior exception. The exception does not ordinarily permit sole source procurement, since agencies must request offers from as many potential sources as practicable.

Exception 3.   It is necessary to award the contract to a particular source or sources in order to (1) maintain a facility, producer, manufacturer, or other supplier available for furnishing property or services in case of a national emergency or to achieve industrial mobilization, or (2) establish or maintain an essential engineering, research or development capability to be provided by an education or other non-profit institution or a federally funded research and development center.

Exception 4.   The terms of an international agreement or treaty between the United States and a foreign government or international organization, or the written directions of a foreign government reimbursing the executive agency for the cost of the procurement of the property or services for such government, have the effect of requiring the use of procedures other than competitive procedures.

This exception relates primarily to memoranda of understanding (MOU) between the U.S. and foreign governments and to foreign military sales. The prior law contained no specific negotiation exception for these purposes.

Exception 5.   A statute expressly authorizes or requires that the procurement be made through another executive agency or from a specified source, or the agency's need is for a brand-name commercial item for authorized resale.

This exception, implemented in Part 8 of the FAR, is subject to the further statutory limitation against procuring property or services from another executive agency unless such other executive agency complies fully with the requirements of this title in its procurement of such property or services. This exception restricts the prior negotiation exception that the item be a "commercial brand-name." This exception also authorizes sole-source procurements from socially and economically disadvantaged small business firms under section 8(a) of the Small Business Act.[7]

Exception 6.   The disclosure of the executive agency's needs would compromise the national security unless the agency is permitted to limit the number of sources from which it solicits bids or proposals.

This exception parallels the prior negotiation exception, However, now when using this exception the agency must request offers from as many potential sources as practicable. The standard of "compromise the national security" may also be more restrictive than the prior negotiation exception since it requires a factual showing of harm to the national security from the disclosure incident to full and open competition. Under the prior exception the exercise of discretion by the agency head in this regard was virtually immune from GAO or court challenge.[8]

Exception 7.   The head of the agency, on a nondelegable basis, "determines that it is necessary in the public interest to use procedures other than competitive procedures in the particular procurement concerned," and notifies Congress in writing at least 30 days in advance of the award. The waiver can only be exercised "if at all, on a case by case basis, rather than for a class of procurements."[9]

Getting on the Solicitation Mailing List

An important marketing step is getting on the solicitation mailing list for each agency that represents a potential source of business. Each procuring activity maintains lists composed of those firms that have expressed interest in contracting with that agency.

To be placed on an agency solicitation mailing list, a company must submit Standard Form 129, *solicitation mailing list application* (see Fig. 3.1). Often individual departments and agencies have developed supplemental, detailed capability questionnaires that also must be used. Using the data provided in the application forms and questionnaires, the agency places the company on the mailing list only for the items listed.

To ensure complete coverage, a company should submit a solicitation mailing list application to each organization to which it is interested in selling. It should also list the items that it is offering to each organization. Firms should not send company catalogues with a request to be placed on the mailing list for all the items shown. The information should be as specific as possible since mailing lists are broken down by major commodity classification, as specified on the agency's forms.

Before placing a firm on its mailing list, an agency will often require additional information such as:

1. Production capability.
2. Description of items normally produced.
3. Number of employees.
4. Plant and transportation facilities.
5. Government contract experience.
6. Financial position.
7. Scope of the firm's operations.

Being placed on a solicitation mailing list does not necessarily mean that the company will be notified of all agency procurements specified in the application. The regulations require only that a sufficient number of bidders be solicited to ensure adequate competition. Inasmuch as a particular list may contain hundreds of firms capable of supplying the product or services desired, all will not be notified for each procurement. The agencies normally use a rotation system to ensure that each firm has a fair chance of being selected periodically.

However, any company that learns about a specific procurement, whether

SOLICITATION MAILING LIST APPLICATION	1. TYPE OF APPLICATION ☐ INITIAL ☐ REVISION	2. DATE	FORM APPROVED OMB NO. 3090-0009

NOTE—Please complete all items on this form. Insert N/A in items not applicable. See reverse for Instructions.

3. NAME AND ADDRESS OF FEDERAL AGENCY TO WHICH FORM IS SUBMITTED *(Include ZIP code)*	4. NAME AND ADDRESS OF APPLICANT *(Include county and ZIP code)*

5. TYPE OF ORGANIZATION *(Check one)*

☐ INDIVIDUAL ☐ NON-PROFIT ORGANIZATION

☐ PARTNERSHIP ☐ CORPORATION, INCORPORATED UNDER THE LAWS OF THE STATE OF:

6. ADDRESS TO WHICH SOLICITATIONS ARE TO BE MAILED *(If different than Item 4)*

7. NAMES OF OFFICERS, OWNERS, OR PARTNERS

A. PRESIDENT	B. VICE PRESIDENT	C. SECRETARY
D. TREASURER	E. OWNERS OR PARTNERS	

8. AFFILIATES OF APPLICANT *(Names, locations and nature of affiliation. See definition on reverse.)*

9. PERSONS AUTHORIZED TO SIGN OFFERS AND CONTRACTS IN YOUR NAME *(Indicate if agent)*

NAME	OFFICIAL CAPACITY	TELE. NO. *(Include area code)*

10. IDENTIFY EQUIPMENT, SUPPLIES, AND/OR SERVICES ON WHICH YOU DESIRE TO MAKE AN OFFER *(See attached Federal agency's supplemental listing and instructions, if any)*

11A. SIZE OF BUSINESS *(See definitions on reverse)*	11B. AVERAGE NUMBER OF EMPLOYEES *(Including affiliates)* FOR FOUR PRECEDING CALENDAR QUARTERS	11C. AVERAGE ANNUAL SALES OR RECEIPTS FOR PRECEDING THREE FISCAL YEARS
☐ SMALL BUSINESS *(If checked, complete items 11B and 11C)* ☐ OTHER THAN SMALL BUSINESS		$

12. TYPE OF OWNERSHIP *(See definitions on reverse) (Not applicable for other than small businesses)*	13. TYPE OF BUSINESS *(See definitions on reverse)*			
☐ DISADVANTAGED BUSINESS ☐ WOMAN-OWNED BUSINESS	☐ MANUFACTURER OR PRODUCER ☐ SERVICE ESTABLISHMENT	☐ REGULAR DEALER *(Type 1)* ☐ REGULAR DEALER *(Type 2)*	☐ CONSTRUCTION CONCERN ☐ RESEARCH AND DEVELOPMENT	☐ SURPLUS DEALER

14. DUNS NO. *(If available)*	15. HOW LONG IN PRESENT BUSINESS?

16. FLOOR SPACE *(Square feet)*		17. NET WORTH	
A. MANUFACTURING	B. WAREHOUSE	A. DATE	B. AMOUNT $

18. SECURITY CLEARANCE *(If applicable, check highest clearance authorized)*

FOR	TOP SECRET	SECRET	CONFIDENTIAL	C. NAMES OF AGENCIES WHICH GRANTED SECURITY CLEARANCES *(Include dates)*
A. KEY PERSONNEL				
B. PLANT ONLY				

CERTIFICATION — I certify that information supplied herein *(Including all pages attached)* is correct and that neither the applicant nor any person *(Or concern)* in any connection with the applicant as a principal or officer, so far as is known, is now debarred or otherwise declared ineligible by any agency of the Federal Government from making offers for furnishing materials, supplies, or services to the Government or any agency thereof.

19. NAME AND TITLE OF PERSON AUTHORIZED TO SIGN *(Type or print)*	20. SIGNATURE	21. DATE SIGNED

NSN 7540-01-152-8086
PREVIOUS EDITIONS UNUSABLE

129-106

STANDARD FORM 129 (REV. 10-83)
Prescribed by GSA
FAR (48 CFR) 53.214(c)

Figure 3.1.   Solicitation mailing list application, Standard Form 129.

38

INSTRUCTIONS

Persons or concerns wishing to be added to a particular agency's bidder's mailing list for supplies or services shall file this properly completed and certified Solicitation Mailing List Application, together with such other lists as may be attached to this application form, with each procurement office of the Federal agency with which they desire to do business. If a Federal agency has attached a Supplemental Commodity list with instructions, complete the application as instructed. Otherwise, identify in Item 10 the equipment supplies and/or services on which you desire to bid. (Provide Federal Supply Class or Standard Industrial Classification Codes if available.) The application shall be submitted and signed by the principal as distinguished from an agent, however constituted.

After placement on the bidder's mailing list of an agency, your failure to respond (submission of bid, or notice in writing, that you are unable to bid on that particular transaction but wish to remain on the active bidder's mailing list for that particular item) to solicitations will be understood by the agency to indicate lack of interest and concurrence in the removal of your name from the purchasing activity's solicitation mailing list for the items concerned.

SIZE OF BUSINESS DEFINITIONS
(See Item 11A.)

a. Small business concern—A small business concern for the purpose of Government procurement is a concern, including its affiliates, which is independently owned and operated, is not dominant in the field of operation in which it is competing for Government contracts and can further qualify under the criteria concerning number of employees, average annual receipts, or other criteria, as prescribed by the Small Business Administration. (See Code of Federal Regulations, Title 13, Part 121, as amended, which contains detailed industry definitions and related procedures.)

b. Affiliates—Business concerns are affiliates of each other when either directly or indirectly (i) one concern controls or has the power to control the other, or (ii) a third party controls or has the power to control both. In determining whether concerns are independently owned and operated and whether or not affiliation exists, consideration is given to all appropriate factors including common ownership, common management, and contractual relationship. (See Items 8 and 11A.)

c. Number of employees—(Item 11B) In connection with the determination of small business status, "number of employees" means the average employment of any concern, including the employees of its domestic and foreign affiliates, based on the number of persons employed on a full-time, part-time, temporary, or other basis during each of the pay periods of the preceding 12 months. If a concern has not been in existence for 12 months, "number of employees" means the average employment of such concern and its affiliates during the period that such concern has been in existence based on the number of persons employed during each of the pay periods of the period that such concern has been in business.

TYPE OF OWNERSHIP DEFINITIONS
(See Item 12.)

a. "Disadvantaged business concern"—means any business concern (1) which is at least 51 percent owned by one or more socially and economically disadvantaged individuals; or, in the case of any publicly owned business, at least 51 percent of the stock of which is owned by one or more socially and economically disadvantaged individuals; and (2) whose management and daily business operations are controlled by one or more of such individuals.

b. "Women-owned business"—means a business that is at least 51 percent owned by a woman or women who are U.S. citizens and who also control and operate the business.

TYPE OF BUSINESS DEFINITIONS
(See Item 13.)

a. Manufacturer or producer—means a person (or concern) owning, operating, or maintaining a store, warehouse, or other establishment that produces, on the premises, the materials, supplies, articles, or equipment of the general character of those listed in Item 10, or in the Federal Agency's Supplemental Commodity List, if attached.

b. Service establishment—means a concern (or person) which owns, operates, or maintains any type of business which is principally engaged in the furnishing of nonpersonal services such as (but not limited to) repairing, cleaning, redecorating, or rental of personal property, including the furnishing of necessary repair parts or other supplies as part of the services performed.

c. Regular dealer (Type 1)—means a person (or concern) who owns, operates, or maintains a store, warehouse, or other establishment in which the materials, supplies, articles, or equipment of the general character listed in Item 10, or in the Federal Agency's Supplemental Commodity List, if attached, are bought, kept in stock, and sold to the public in the usual course of business.

d. Regular dealer (Type 2)—In the case of supplies of particular kinds (at present, petroleum, lumber and timber products, machine tools, raw cotton, green coffee, hay, grain, feed, or straw, agricultural liming materials, tea, raw or unmanufactured cotton linters and used ADPE), Regular dealer means a person (or concern) satisfying the requirements of the regulations (Code of Federal Regulations, Title 41, 50-201.101(a)(2)) as amended from time to time, prescribed by the Secretary of Labor under the Walsh-Healey Public Contracts Act (Title 41 U.S. Code 35-45) For coal dealers see Code of Federal Regulations, Title 41, 50-201.604(a).

● COMMERCE BUSINESS DAILY—The Commerce Business Daily, published by the Department of Commerce, contains information concerning proposed procurements, sales, and contract awards. For further information concerning this publication, contact your local Commerce Field Office.

STANDARD FORM 129 BACK (REV. 10-83)

Figure 3.1. (Continued)

advertised or negotiated, can submit a bid or offer if otherwise qualified to do so. It is important to recognize that, even though a company is included on an agency's solicitation mailing list, it should nevertheless attempt to secure information about bids from other sources. This is necessary in order to maximize the opportunities to sell to the government.

Where Business Opportunities Are Publicized

Information concerning government business opportunities is contained in such publications as the *Commerce Business Daily* (CBD) and *Commerce America.* GSA *business service centers* are also excellent sources of information on what the government is buying.

Each workday the Department of Commerce publishes the *Commerce Business Daily,* which lists proposed government procurements, subcontracting leads, contract awards, sales of surplus property, and opportunities for foreign businesses to sell to U.S. Government agencies located outside the United States.

By law, virtually every proposed procurement must be published in the Commerce Daily except those under $10,000 where (1) such notice would compromise national security, (2) the procurement is made under a requirements contract or (3) the procurement is for perishable subsistence supplies. One additional exception is where an unsolicited research proposal generates a procurement and notice of such a proposal would disclose the originality or innovativeness of the proposal or would reveal proprietary information. Awards of contracts exceeding $25,000 must be snyopsized if they are likely to result in the award of subcontracts.

The CBD publication lead times have been increased. Notice must be published at least 15 days before the solicitation is issued, and at least 30 days is required between the date the solicitation is issued and the time for receipt of bids or proposals.

Commerce America is a magazine that is published biweekly by the Secretary of Commerce. The magazine provides helpful interpretations of government policies and programs that may affect daily business decisions. It gives concise, up-to-date information on worldwide trade and investment—with a special section on business leads.

GSA business service centers are responsible for (1) issuing bidder's mailing list applications, (2) furnishing invitations for bids and specifications to prospective bidders, (3) maintaining a current display of bidding opportunities, (4) safeguarding bids, (5) providing bid opening facilities, and (6) furnishing free copies of publications designed to assist business representatives in doing business with the federal government. There are 13 centers nationwide, most located in the main lobbies of federal buildings in cities having GSA regional headquarters.

Responsible Bidders/Offerors

The government is required to award contracts only to responsible bidders. The contracting officer determines whether bidders are qualified to receive contracts. The evaluation of a bidder includes considering the company's plant and testing facilities, production capabilities, quality control, financial status, credit rating, performance of previous government contracts, and overall integrity.

The Role of the Small Business Administration

Certain laws mandate that government agencies initiate procurement procedures to assist small businesses in obtaining a reasonable share of their business. Consistent with this requirement, if an offer from a small business concern is rejected solely on the grounds of insufficient capacity or inadequate credit, the contracting officer must notify the Small Business Administration (SBA). If a subsequent SBA investigation reveals that the firm is able to perform the contract, the SBA will issue a *certificate of competency.* The contracting officer normally must then award the contract to that firm.

In addition to issuing certificates of competency, the Small Business Administration acts in other ways to assist the small business concern. As provided under the Small Business Act of 1953, the SBA works closely with purchasing agencies of the Federal government to ensure that a fair proportion of the total purchases in contracts or subcontracts for property and services are given to small business concerns. The booklet *Selling to the U.S. Government,* published by the Small Business Administration, provides information on some of the programs available.

Needless to say, it is important for a company to establish whether it meets the criteria for being classified as a small business. These criteria are set forth in the SBA regulations.[10] However, in order to implement their small business programs, other executive departments have incorporated the SBA guidelines in their acquisition policies. The acquisition regulations define a small business as a concern, including its affiliates, that is independently owned and operated, is not dominant in the field of operation in which it is bidding on government contracts, and can further qualify under specified size criteria. For a company to determine whether it qualifies as a small business, the line of business must first be identified and the appropriate SBA criteria applied. For companies having more than one business line, it is possible to be a small business when proposing for a particular requirement and not be a small business when pursuing another procurement. Since being a small business offers some advantages in obtaining government contracts, companies should ensure that their classification has been appropriately determined.

A program that provides business opportunities for certain specified companies is authorized under Section 8(a) of the Small Business Act. This program is designed to assist small disadvantaged businesses to become independently viable by giving them noncompetitive government contracts. Along with the contracts, SBA provides management, technical, marketing, and financial aid. From 1969 through 1981 approximately 4600 participating firms received 8(a) contracts totaling $5.5 billion.

The original authority to help small business generally was established under Section 8(a) in 1953. However, in 1969, the eligibility criteria were revised to limit participation to firms owned or controlled by both socially and economically disadvantaged persons.

Under the 8(a) program, the Federal departments and agencies award selected contracts to the SBA. SBA then subcontracts with eligible firms for the work required by the government buying offices. The objective is to make the small disadvantaged business self-sustaining through this controlled market. When that objective is achieved, that is, when the company appears capable of competing in the general marketplace, it is then graduated from the program.

A company wishing to participate in the program must establish to the SBA's satisfaction that socially and economically disadvantaged persons operate the business and have at least 51 % ownership share. SBA regulations issued on November 23, 1981 limit the period of time a business can remain in the program. Firms are now removed from the program after five years, but can request an extension of up to two years.

Opportunities for Foreign Suppliers

The U. S. Government represents a significant market opportunity for foreign companies. The Department of Defense has entered into reciprocal purchasing *memoranda of understanding* (MOU) with members of the NATO Alliance and other friendly nations. These MOUs eliminate "buy national" barriers and other procurement obstacles that legally preclude foreign companies from competing on an equal basis for R&D and production contracts awarded by DOD. In addition to the actions taken by DOD to encourage international contracting, the U.S. Government is also a signatory to the General Agreement on Tariffs and Trade (GATT). This agreement provides a legal basis for reducing tariffs and other trade barriers and opens up about two-thirds of DOD procurement to foreign suppliers. The GATT also opens up to foreign competition procurements by civilian agencies.

It is important to note that for security reasons certain items of defense equipment have been placed on a restricted list; that is, they cannot be acquired from foreign sources. Every foreign company interested in doing business in this market should obtain a list of the restricted items from DOD to avoid wasting resources in trying to sell such products to the U.S. Government. In addition to the DOD restricted list, Congress, through the annual appropriations act, invariably prohibits government agencies from buying certain items from foreign sources. Foreign suppliers also need to know what items have been restricted by the Defense Appropriations Acts.

FAR Part 25, Foreign Acquisition, together with DOD FAR Supplement Part 25, implements DOD's international contracting policy. Among other things, it does the following:

1. Waives the "Buy American" Act and DOD balance of payment restrictions.
2. Provides for duty-free entry.
3. Waives the U.S. "Specialty Metals" restriction. This restriction requires DOD to purchase all specialty metals from U.S. sources. From time to time, Congress, in the annual Defense Appropriations Acts, will override DOD's authority to waive this restriction. As mentioned above, the content of this legislation should be of paramount importance to contracting agencies and foreign suppliers.
4. Requires DOD agencies to include on their mailing lists companies from countries with whom the U.S. has signed a MOU.
5. Requires the use of international air mail to notify sources for solicitation or allows the solicitation to be given to the foreign supplier's representative in the U.S.
6. Provides that no unusual technical or security requirements be imposed solely to exclude foreign sources.
7. States that DOD may use the results achieved by another NATO government.
8. Permits industry representatives from participating countries to attend symposia, program briefings, and prebid conferences.

9. Assures that contracting officers monitor prime contractors to make certain that no action is taken to preclude qualified foreign sources from competing for subcontracts.

The acquisition regulations only provide a framework for free and open competition among foreign and domestic suppliers for DOD work. It was never intended for the MOUs to guarantee any business to foreign sources. Non-U.S. companies, like domestic companies, must aggressively market their products and seek contracting opportunities with DOD.

Foreign sources must comply with the same procurement regulations that apply to U.S. contractors. Considerable pressure has been and continues to be exerted by participating European governments and their industrialists to exempt non-U.S. contractors from U.S. Federal Acquisition Regulations and allow them to apply their own procurement regulations. They are not likely to succeed in achieving this exemption because many of the acquisition regulations and contractual terms and conditions are based on statute, such as the Armed Services Procurement Act, Defense Production Act, Truth in Negotiations Act, and the Defense Appropriations Act. Consequently, it would require an act of Congress to remove these requirements from a contract. Another point that argues against such an exemption is that the MOU's fundamental objective is to provide foreign sources an opportunity to compete on a fair and equal basis, which could not occur if competing companies were subject to different procurement regulations. Foreign contractors are expected to comply with applicable acquisition regulations just as U.S. defense contractors are required to do so.

CONTRACTING BY NEGOTIATION

The contracting process is not complete until there is a consensus between the parties on the contractual agreement to cover the work being done. In sealed bidding that consensus is achieved when a prospective contractor accepts the terms and conditions stated by the government and submits a responsive bid. When an award is not based on sealed bidding, this final agreement is achieved through negotiation. Used in this way, the term "negotiation" has a special meaning. As defined in FAR: 15.101 and 15.102:

"Negotiation" means contracting through the use of either competitive or other-than-competitive proposals and discussions. Any contract awarded without using sealed bidding procedures is a negotiated contract.
Negotiation is a procedure that includes the receipt of proposals from offerors, permits bargaining, and usually affords an opportunity for revised offers to be submitted before award of a contract. Bargaining—in the sense of discussion, persuasion, alteration of initial assumptions and positions, and give-and-take— may apply to price, schedule, technical requirements, type of contract, or other terms of a proposed contract.

The actual bargaining which takes place is primarily dependent upon whether the negotiation is competitive or other-than-competitive. In a competitive negotiation, usually referred to as a source selection, proposals are received from more than one prospective contractor.

SOURCE SELECTION

The avowed purpose of source selection procedures is to maximize competition while ensuring impartiality and minimizing the complexity of the award decision. It is used when the supplies or services being purchased cannot be so clearly, accurately and completely described as to make price the sole determinant. The government issues either a *Request for Proposal* (RFP) or a *Request for Quotation* (RFQ). In this solicitation, the government states its minimum requirements and any other information necessary for prospective contractors to prepare and submit proposals or quotations. RFQs are used when the government does not intend to award a contract on the basis of the solicitation without further discussions but requires the data for planning purposes. RFPs are used when the award of a contract is contemplated by the government. A proposal submitted in response to an RFP is a contract offer which can be accepted by the contracting officer and become a contract. Contracting officers are instructed to provide all prospective contractors with identical information and not knowingly give any advantage to one offeror at the expense of another.

There are source selections and "formal" source selections. The formal source selection is generally used for high-dollar-value acquisitions and major system procurements and when otherwise prescribed by agency regulations. It is characterized by a specific evaluation group structure which generally includes an evaluation board, an advisory council and a source selection authority (SSA). A source selection plan is prepared which formalizes the evaluation process. In the largest system acquisitions the source selection plan is extremely detailed and specific. The key element in a formal source selection is the authority of the SSA rather than the contracting officer to make the final determination as to which competitor is awarded the contract. The source selection procedures being used will be identified.

PROPOSALS

The RFP (or RFQ) will state the time and place for the receipt of proposals. Proposals not received on time are designated as "late" and may not be considered.

Purpose of the Proposal

A proposal is an offer to supply a product, perform a service, or a combination of the two. In some cases, the products or services are simple tasks and have been done before. In other cases, they are unique R&D efforts with a number of substantial state-of-the-art problems to be solved. Nonetheless, the need for the proposal exists because the specifications for the product or a description of the services to be performed are not so definite that the use of sealed bidding can be justified.

From the government's perspective, the proposal is the primary vehicle by which a contractor will be selected to provide the goods or services needed. From the company's perspective, the function of the proposal is to sell the managerial and technical capabilities of the company to carry out the required work at a reasonable cost. The proposal is the point of sale; it should be considered the company's most important selling tool. The proposal document must convince the contracting officer that the company is offering an acceptable solution to the government's problem for a reasonable price. It also communicates that the company has an adequate organization and sufficient personnel and facilities to perform the required effort within the time specified. The offeror has considerable latitude in conveying these messages to the government. The proposal may be just a few pages or many volumes in length.

Who Takes the Initiative in Proposal Submission?

Unsolicited Proposals

When a company recognizes or anticipates a government need for a product or service, a proposal may be submitted without a solicitation. Using this marketing strategy requires a keen awareness of the government's process for determining requirements. In many cases, successful use of this strategy will be the result of existing work that the company is performing for the government or the knowledge of work being performed by others. In some cases, success may result from company knowledge about a problem an agency has. While most proposals are solicited, the unsolicited proposal does represent an effective means of selling to the government.

Solicited Proposals

There are two basic forms in which the government may request a proposal. Standard Form 33, *solicitation, offer, and award,* (See Fig. 3.2) is used in connection with requests for proposals (RFP) where written acceptance by the government would create a binding contract. The government generally accepts the proposal within the time specified unless it is withdrawn in writing prior to acceptance. This type of proposal is normally used for purchases of standard items or for procurements in which it is clearly demonstrated that accepting the most favorable initial proposal without discussion results in a fair and reasonable price. This judgment is usually based on the existence of adequate price competition or sufficient cost experience in manufacturing the product or performing the service. This procedure is similar to the manner in which an award is made in sealed bidding—that is, the contract is generally awarded to the lowest, responsible, responsive offeror. In fact, the same Standard Form 33 is used as the solicitation document for both invitations for bids and requests for proposals.

Where it is anticipated that the resulting fixed-price contract will involve extensive negotiations or that a cost type contract will be negotiated, Standard Form 18, *request for quotations* (see Fig. 3.3) will be utilized. This form is not an offer; consequently, the government cannot unilaterally accept it without further negotiation.

Types of Proposals

There are various circumstances where the government will request companies to submit proposals. The proposals are usually categorized based on circumstances. For example, where new work is involved, the proposal is considered an *initial price proposal.* Or, the government may request the contractor to submit a proposal to continue work begun under an existing contract; such proposals are normally referred to as *follow-on proposals.* Often the government will add or delete work originally included in either a sealed bid contract or a negotiated contract. When this occurs, a proposal reflecting the effect of the contract modification is required. These are considered *contract change proposals.*

SOLICITATION, OFFER AND AWARD	1. CERTIFIED FOR NATIONAL DEFENSE UNDER BDSA REG. 2 AND/OR DMS REG. 1 ▶	RATING		PAGE OF	
					PAGES

2. CONTRACT NO.	3. SOLICITATION NO.	4. TYPE OF SOLICITATION	5. DATE ISSUED	6. REQUISITION/PURCHASE NO.
		☐ ADVERTISED (IFB) ☐ NEGOTIATED (RFP)		

7. ISSUED BY	CODE	8. ADDRESS OFFER TO (If other than Item 7)

NOTE: In advertised solicitations "offer" and "offeror" mean "bid" and "bidder".

SOLICITATION

9 Sealed offers in original and _____ copies for furnishing the supplies or services in the Schedule will be received at the place specified in Item 8, or if handcarried, in the depository listed in _____ until _____ local time _____
(Hour)   (Date)

CAUTION — LATE Submissions, Modifications, and Withdrawals: See Section I, Provision No. 52.214-7 or 52.215-10. All offers are subject to all terms and conditions contained in this solicitation.

10. FOR INFORMATION CALL.	A. NAME ▶	B. TELEPHONE NO. (Include area code) (NO COLLECT CALLS)

11. TABLE OF CONTENTS

(√)	SEC.	DESCRIPTION	PAGE(S)	(√)	SEC.	DESCRIPTION	PAGE(S)
		PART I — THE SCHEDULE				PART II — CONTRACT CLAUSES	
	A	SOLICITATION/CONTRACT FORM			I	CONTRACT CLAUSES	
	B	SUPPLIES OR SERVICES AND PRICES/COSTS				PART III — LIST OF DOCUMENTS, EXHIBITS AND OTHER ATTACH.	
	C	DESCRIPTION/SPECS/WORK STATEMENT			J	LIST OF ATTACHMENTS	
	D	PACKAGING AND MARKING				PART IV — REPRESENTATIONS AND INSTRUCTIONS	
	E	INSPECTION AND ACCEPTANCE			K	REPRESENTATIONS, CERTIFICATIONS AND OTHER STATEMENTS OF OFFERORS	
	F	DELIVERIES OR PERFORMANCE					
	G	CONTRACT ADMINISTRATION DATA			L	INSTRS., CONDS., AND NOTICES TO OFFER	
	H	SPECIAL CONTRACT REQUIREMENTS			M	EVALUATION FACTORS FOR AWARD	

OFFER (Must be fully completed by offeror)

NOTE: Item 12 does not apply if the solicitation includes the provisions at 52.214-16, Minimum Bid Acceptance Period.

12 In compliance with the above, the undersigned agrees, if this offer is accepted within _____ calendar days (60 calendar days unless a different period is inserted by the offeror) from the date for receipt of offers specified above, to furnish any or all items upon which prices are offered at the price set opposite each item, delivered at the designated point(s), within the time specified in the schedule.

13. DISCOUNT FOR PROMPT PAYMENT (See Section I, Clause No. 52-232-8) ▶	10 CALENDAR DAYS	20 CALENDAR DAYS	30 CALENDAR DAYS	CALENDAR DAYS
	%	%	%	%

14 ACKNOWLEDGMENT OF AMENDMENTS (The offeror acknowledges receipt of amendments to the SOLICITATION for offerors and related documents numbered and dated:	AMENDMENT NO	DATE	AMENDMENT NO.	DATE

15A. NAME AND ADDRESS OF OFFEROR	CODE	FACILITY	16. NAME AND TITLE OF PERSON AUTHORIZED TO SIGN OFFER (Type or print)

15B. TELEPHONE NO. (Include area code)	15C. CHECK IF REMITTANCE ADDRESS IS DIFFERENT FROM ABOVE - ENTER SUCH ADDRESS IN SCHEDULE ☐	17. SIGNATURE	18. OFFER DATE

AWARD (To be completed by Government)

19. ACCEPTED AS TO ITEMS NUMBERED	20. AMOUNT	21. ACCOUNTING AND APPROPRIATION

22. SUBMIT INVOICES TO ADDRESS SHOWN IN ▶ (4 copies unless otherwise specified)	ITEM	23. NEGOTIATED PURSUANT TO ☐ 10 U.S.C. 2304(a) ( ) ☐ 41 U.S.C. 252(c) ( )

24. ADMINISTERED BY (If other than Item 7)	CODE	25. PAYMENT WILL BE MADE BY	CODE

26. NAME OF CONTRACTING OFFICER (Type or print)	27. UNITED STATES OF AMERICA (Signature of Contracting Officer)	28. AWARD DATE

IMPORTANT — Award will be made on this Form, or on Standard Form 26, or by other authorized official written notice.

NSN 7540-01-152-8064
PREVIOUS EDITION NOT USABLE

33-132

STANDARD FORM 33 (REV. 10-83)
Prescribed by GSA
FAR (48 CFR) 53.214(c)

Figure 3.2. Solicitation, offer, and award, Standard Form 33.

REQUEST FOR QUOTATIONS *(THIS IS NOT AN ORDER)*	The Notice of Small Business-Small Purchase Set-Aside on the reverse of this form ☐ is ☐ is not applicable.		PAGE OF PAGES	

1. REQUEST NO.	2. DATE ISSUED	3. REQUISITION/PURCHASE REQUEST NO.	4. CERT. FOR NAT. DEF. UNDER BDSA REG. 2 ▶ AND/OR DMS REG. 1	RATING

5A. ISSUED BY

	6. DELIVER BY *(Date)*

5B. FOR INFORMATION CALL: *(Name and telephone no.)* *(No collect calls)*

7. DELIVERY

☐ FOB DESTINATION   ☐ OTHER *(See Schedule)*

8. TO: NAME AND ADDRESS, INCLUDING ZIP CODE

9. DESTINATION *(Consignee and address, including ZIP Code)*

10. PLEASE FURNISH QUOTATIONS TO THE ISSUING OFFICE ON OR BEFORE CLOSE OF BUSINESS *(Date)*

11. BUSINESS CLASSIFICATION *(Check appropriate boxes)*

☐ SMALL   ☐ OTHER THAN SMALL   ☐ DISADVANTAGED   ☐ WOMEN-OWNED

IMPORTANT: This is a request for information, and quotations furnished are not offers. If you are unable to quote, please so indicate on this form and return it. This request does not commit the Government to pay any costs incurred in the preparation of the submission of this quotation or to contract for supplies or services. Supplies are of domestic origin unless otherwise indicated by quoter. Any representations and/or certifications attached to this Request for Quotations must be completed by the quoter.

12. SCHEDULE *(Include applicable Federal, State and local taxes)*

ITEM NO. (a)	SUPPLIES/SERVICES (b)	QUANTITY (c)	UNIT (d)	UNIT PRICE (e)	AMOUNT (f)

13. DISCOUNT FOR PROMPT PAYMENT ▶	10 CALENDAR DAYS %	20 CALENDAR DAYS %	30 CALENDAR DAYS %	CALENDAR DAYS %

NOTE: Reverse must also be completed by the quoter.

14. NAME AND ADDRESS OF QUOTER *(Street, city, county, State and ZIP Code)*	15. SIGNATURE OF PERSON AUTHORIZED TO SIGN QUOTATION	16. DATE OF QUOTATION
	17. NAME AND TITLE OF SIGNER *(Type or print)*	18. TELEPHONE NO. *(Include area code)*

NSN 7540-01-152-8084
PREVIOUS EDITION NOT USABLE

18-118

STANDARD FORM 18 (REV. 10-83)
Prescribed by GSA
FAR (48 CFR) 53.215-1(a)

Figure 3.3. Request for quotations, Standard Form 18.

REPRESENTATIONS, CERTIFICATIONS, AND PROVISIONS

The following representation applies when the contract is to be performed inside the United States, its territories or possessions, Puerto Rico, the Trust Territory of the Pacific Islands, or the District of Columbia.

52.219-1 SMALL BUSINESS CONCERN REPRESENTATION (Apr 84)

The quoter represents and certifies as part of its quotation that it ☐ is, ☐ is not a small business concern and that ☐ all, ☐ not all supplies to be furnished will be manufactured or produced by a small business concern in the United States, its possessions, or Puerto Rico. "Small business concern," as used in this provision, means a concern, including its affiliates, that is independently owned and operated, not dominant in the field of operation in which it is bidding on Government contracts, and qualified as a small business under the criteria and size standards in 13 CFR 121.

The following provision is applicable if required on the face of the form:

52.219-2 Notice of Small Business-Small Purchase Set-Aside (Apr 84)

Quotations under this acquisition are solicited from small business concerns only. Any acquisition resulting from this solicitation will be from a small business concern. Quotations received from concerns that are not small businesses shall not be considered and shall be rejected.

STANDARD FORM 18 BACK (REV. 10-83)

Figure 3.3.   (Continued)

The type of pricing arrangement contemplated by the offeror is also indicated in the proposal. Accordingly, proposals are categorized based on the type of contract that is expected to be negotiated, such as a firm fixed-price proposal, cost plus fixed-fee proposal, fixed-price incentive fee proposal, and so forth.

Notwithstanding how the proposals are classified, they must communicate to the soliciting government agency how the company intends to perform and manage the effort required by the contract. Additionally, they must state the price and provide supporting data in sufficient detail for the government to satisfy itself that the amount it will ultimately pay is fair and reasonable.

Proposal Planning

The development and submission of proposals is essential activity for most government contractors. Successful proposals require a significant commitment of both financial resources and staffing. Proposal activity, as with any expenditure of time and resources, should be adequately planned.

The Bid/No-Bid Decision

Fundamentally, the first step of proposal preparation is determining whether or not to submit a bid on a given business opportunity. Although a portion of this decision is made long before issuance of the solicitation from the government, a detailed review must be made after receipt of the solicitation to assure that all major provisions are understood. Most companies believe they approach the bid/no-bid decision scientifically. In fact, however they approach it in a highly emotional manner. What are the motivating factors in making a poor bidding decision? The reasons are indeed complex. They might include the phenomenon of the "pet interest," preservation of an empire, or a desperate grabbing at straws when business is slow.

A number of factors must be considered in making the bid/no-bid decision. These factors, while usually recognized intuitively by contractors, are nevertheless often disregarded in the quest for new business.

1. The government opportunity about to be bid should be a real, funded program or, in the case of a potential subcontractor, the prime contractor should have made the decision to buy.
2. The technical homework should be done so that a concrete solution exists.
3. There should have been significant prior customer contact pertinent to this program.
4. A marketing pursuit plan should be prepared.
5. Staffing should be available for a maximum proposal effort and for the performance of the program.
6. The company should have a positive feeling that it can win the bids.
7. The proposal should be incidental to the sale.
8. There should be compelling reasons why the company can unseat any competitors who may be in there first.
9. There should be attractive profit/risk possibilities.

Once the decision to bid has been made, the next task is to begin to prepare the proposal.

Review of the Solicitation

Once the solicitation has been received, it should be thoroughly reviewed. A single individual, who will have overall responsibility for the review (and the proposal preparation as well), should head the effort with participation by all appropriate resources within the company (technical, financial, etc.).
This review effort should have two basic results:

Identification of inconsistencies between the solicitation and the information on which the bid/no-bid decision was based. If these inconsistencies are significant, the decision to bid should be reconsidered.

Preparation of a proposal plan to establish a schedule for the proposal preparation effort and identification of the individuals who will be involved in its preparation and their responsibilities.

A listing of any unique requirements imposed by the solicitation should be developed, as well as a "wish-list" of factors which would optimize performance under a resulting contract. This information should be used during the preparation of the proposal.

Proposal Format

The proposal must adequately cover three broad areas. The first area relates to the technical solution to the problem as defined by the government in the solicitation. The second area describes how the offeror will manage contract performance, and the third area addresses how much the proposed work will cost.

Technical Section

The technical section of the proposal should demonstrate the company's understanding of the problem and the proposed method of solving it. The data should be organized and presented in a manner that is compatible with the government's request for proposal/quotation, the statement of work, and the company's organizational structure and accounting system. The technical section must be responsive to the needs of the government and be convincing that the company offers the most cost-effective approach to solving the problems.

Management Section

The purpose of the management section is to explain how the company intends to manage the effort required under the proposed contract. It should therefore reflect whether the company intends to set up a separate management organization for the specific contract contemplated or incorporate the effort into the existing structure. It should also explain how program management fits within the overall company organizational structure and point out any limits of authority or responsibility. If no specific management group is to be formed, the method of operation within the overall company management structure should be described.

Specifically, this management section should provide an explanation of organizational structure, management capability, management controls, and the assignment of key personnel with experience directly related to the work required by the contract. This section must also be tailored to the circumstances described by the government. Therefore, it should reflect the management structure the company intends to have in place to manage not only the proposed contract but the overall company operations as well.

Cost Section

The cost section of the proposal should indicate the proposed cost profit and price of the work to be performed under the anticipated contract. The proposed amount is the point from which negotiations begin. Where certified cost or pricing data are required, the offeror has little latitude in the detail and format in which the proposal is presented. The Contract Pricing Proposal Cover Sheet, Standard Form (SF) 1411 (Fig. 3.4), use of which is required for submission of certified cost or pricing data, specifies how the data should be submitted. Instructions for submission of the SF 1411 are not part of the form, itself; one must refer to FAR 15.804-6 for this guidance.

CONTRACT PRICING PROPOSAL COVER SHEET

1. SOLICITATION/CONTRACT/MODIFICATION NO.	FORM APPROVED OMB NO. 3090-0116

NOTE: This form is used in contract actions if submission of cost or pricing data is required. *(See FAR 15.804-6(b))*

2. NAME AND ADDRESS OF OFFEROR *(Include ZIP Code)*	3A. NAME AND TITLE OF OFFEROR'S POINT OF CONTACT	3B. TELEPHONE NO.

4. TYPE OF CONTRACT ACTION *(Check)*

A. NEW CONTRACT	D. LETTER CONTRACT
B. CHANGE ORDER	E. UNPRICED ORDER
C. PRICE REVISION/ REDETERMINATION	F. OTHER *(Specify)*

5. TYPE OF CONTRACT *(Check)*

☐ FFP ☐ CPFF ☐ CPIF ☐ CPAF

☐ FPI ☐ OTHER *(Specify)*

6. PROPOSED COST *(A+B=C)*

A. COST	B. PROFIT/FEE	C. TOTAL
$	$	$

7. PLACE(S) AND PERIOD(S) OF PERFORMANCE

8. List and reference the identification, quantity and total price proposed for each contract line item. A line item cost breakdown supporting this recap is required unless otherwise specified by the Contracting Officer. *(Continue on reverse, and then on plain paper, if necessary. Use same headings.)*

A. LINE ITEM NO.	B. IDENTIFICATION	C. QUANTITY	D. TOTAL PRICE	E. REF.

9. PROVIDE NAME, ADDRESS, AND TELEPHONE NUMBER FOR THE FOLLOWING *(If available)*

A. CONTRACT ADMINISTRATION OFFICE	B. AUDIT OFFICE

10. WILL YOU REQUIRE THE USE OF ANY GOVERNMENT PROPERTY IN THE PERFORMANCE OF THIS WORK? *(If "Yes," identify)*

☐ YES ☐ NO

11A. DO YOU REQUIRE GOVERNMENT CONTRACT FINANCING TO PERFORM THIS PROPOSED CONTRACT? *(If "Yes," complete Item 11B)*

☐ YES ☐ NO

11B. TYPE OF FINANCING *(√ one)*

☐ ADVANCE PAYMENTS ☐ PROGRESS PAYMENTS

☐ GUARANTEED LOANS

12. HAVE YOU BEEN AWARDED ANY CONTRACTS OR SUBCONTRACTS FOR THE SAME OR SIMILAR ITEMS WITHIN THE PAST 3 YEARS? *(If "Yes," identify item(s), customer(s) and contract number(s))*

☐ YES ☐ NO

13. IS THIS PROPOSAL CONSISTENT WITH YOUR ESTABLISHED ESTIMATING AND ACCOUNTING PRACTICES AND PROCEDURES AND FAR PART 31 COST PRINCIPLES? *(If "No," explain)*

☐ YES ☐ NO

14. COST ACCOUNTING STANDARDS BOARD (CASB) DATA *(Public Law 91-379 as amended and FAR PART 30)*

A. WILL THIS CONTRACT ACTION BE SUBJECT TO CASB REGULATIONS? *(If "No," explain in proposal)*

☐ YES ☐ NO

B. HAVE YOU SUBMITTED A CASB DISCLOSURE STATEMENT *(CASB DS-1 or 2)? (If "Yes," specify in proposal the office to which submitted and if determined to be adequate)*

☐ YES ☐ NO

C. HAVE YOU BEEN NOTIFIED THAT YOU ARE OR MAY BE IN NON-COMPLIANCE WITH YOUR DISCLOSURE STATEMENT OR COST ACCOUNTING STANDARDS? *(If "Yes," explain in proposal)*

☐ YES ☐ NO

D. IS ANY ASPECT OF THIS PROPOSAL INCONSISTENT WITH YOUR DISCLOSED PRACTICES OR APPLICABLE COST ACCOUNTING STANDARDS? *(If "Yes," explain in proposal)*

☐ YES ☐ NO

This proposal is submitted in response to the RFP contract, modification, etc. in Item 1 and reflects our best estimates and/or actual costs as of this date.

15. NAME AND TITLE *(Type)*	16. NAME OF FIRM

17. SIGNATURE	18. DATE OF SUBMISSION

NSN 7540-01-142-9845

1411-101

STANDARD FORM 1411 (10-83)
Prescribed by GSA
FAR (48 CFR) 53.215-2(c)

Figure 3.4. Contract pricing proposal cover sheet, Standard Form 1411.

As a general statement, even when certification is not required, the cost section of the proposal should be presented in a manner which is directly compatible with the company's accounting system, assuming the company will follow the existing accounting practices in pricing the contract. If the offeror intends to adopt different practices for the contract, there should be compatibility between the practices that will actually be followed and the proposal. The cost proposal should provide sufficient information and detail to support the technical and managerial aspects of the proposals. It should be an integral part of the proposal's overall use as a sales tool.

Instructions for preparing the SF 1411 outline the documentation needed to support the proposed price and require, as a minimum, submission of separate supporting schedules, detailing various cost elements, for each proposed contract line item. (The schedules should also reflect any specific requirements established by the contracting office.) Depending on the contractor's system, the breakdown of the basic cost elements would be as follows:

Materials. This should include a consolidated price summary of individual material quantities included in the various proposed tasks, orders, or contract line items, and the basis for pricing. The basis might include current written quotes, properly documented telephone quotes, historical cost, escalation factors, and rationale for quantity adjustments.

Subcontracted Items. This category includes parts, components, assemblies and services that are to be produced or performed by others in accordance with the higher tiered contractor's design, specifications, or direction, and that are applicable only to the prime contract. For each subcontract over $100,000, the support should include a listing by source, item, quantity, price, type of subcontract, degree of competition and basis for establishing source and reasonableness of price. The results of review and evaluation of subcontract proposals should also be provided when required. Cost or pricing data received from prospective subcontractors should be submitted for each subcontract cost estimate that is valued at $1,000,000 or valued at more than $100,000 and more than 10 percent of the prime contractor's proposed price; or if the information is necessary for adequately pricing the prime contract.

Standard Commercial Items. This consists of items that the contractor normally fabricates, in whole or in part, and that are generally stocked in inventory. An appropriate explanation of the basis for pricing, cost breakdowns, or justifications for exemption from submission of cost or pricing data (if applicable) should be provided. Supporting information might include price lists or other such data provided to commercial customers.

Interorganizational Transfers (at other than cost). An explanation of the pricing method used should be included. Rationale supporting this method, such as catalog price lists, should also be included.

Raw Material. This consists of materials that require further processing. Priced quantities should be provided for the items required for the proposal. Supporting documentation would be essentially the same as that detailed in the Materials paragraph, above.

Purchased Parts. Includes material items not covered above. Priced quantities of items required for the proposal should be provided, as should supporting documentation such as that detailed above.

Interorganizational Transfers (at cost). A separate breakdown of cost, by element, should be included.

Direct Labor. A time-phased breakdown of labor hours, labor rates, and costs by labor category should be provided. The basis for the estimated cost should be provided. Included items might be historical data for similar items, basis for quantity adjustments, escalation factors, union contract times, or wage projections and related rationale.

Indirect Costs. The supporting data provided should indicate the rates applied, the bases to which they are applied and the rationale used to compute the rates, including cost breakdowns, as well as any trends and budgetary factors used to provide a basis for evaluating the reasonableness of the proposed rates.

Other Costs. This consists of all other costs required to produce the product or service which are not included in the above categories. The basis and rationale used in pricing these items should be provided.

Royalties. For each royalty or license fee of more than $250, the contractor should provide a separate page detailing: name and address of licensor; date of license agreement; patent numbers, patent application or other basis on which royalty is payable; brief description of contract item or component on which royalty is payable; percentage or dollar rate of royalty per unit; unit price of contract item; number of units; and total dollar amount of royalties. If specifically requested by the contracting office, a copy of the current license agreement and identification of applicable claims of specific patents must be provided.

Facilities Capital Cost of Money. When the contractor claims facilities capital cost of money as an allowable cost, Form CASB - CMF showing the calculation of the proposed factors must be submitted. DOD contract pricing proposals also require submission of DD form 1861, as further described in chapter 4.

In addition to identifying and submitting the above detailed data, the company's cost proposal should include any information reasonably required to explain the estimating process used, including judgmental factors applied and the methods used in the estimates (including projections) and the nature and amounts of any contingencies included in the proposed price.

Relevant information which becomes available after submission of the proposal must be provided to the contracting officer prior to final contract negotiation. The contractor should maintain a record of all data provided, the date and to whom provided, and, if feasible, copies of all items provided to the contracting officer and/or the auditor.

Today's increasingly sophisticated manufacturing cost collection and reporting systems also provide substantial information for estimating the costs of future efforts. To the extent that shop-floor report systems, formal Material Requirements Planning (MRP), and other systems are utilized, the information they contain should be considered in developing cost estimates. It may be necessary to convert the format of information available to the format used for government contract estimating purposes, particularly where an SF 1411 is required.

Regardless of the certification requirements, the proposal must be compatible with the cost accounting system which the contractor anticipates will be used to measure and accumulate costs during the period of performance of the resulting contract. In order to comply with government requirements for most contracts, the cost accounting system must be able to produce information on the specific cost elements and in the same detail as proposed.

The SF 1411 also asks for information related to disclosure statement requirements as required by the Cost Accounting Standards Board under Public Law 91-379. See Chapter 8 for further discussion.

As a final point, the proposal must be compatible not only with the cost accounting system which will measure the cost of the resulting contract, but also must be compatible with the company's technical approach and management system. The cost proposal should provide sufficient information and detail to support the technical and managerial aspects of the proposal. All areas in the proposal must be directed toward one common goal, which is selling the contractor's product or services while complying with the various laws and regulations involved.

RESPONSIBLE PROSPECTIVE CONTRACTORS

General Policy

Purchases must be made from and contracts awarded to only responsible contractors. FAR 9.103 states:

> The award of a contract to a supplier based on the lowest evaluated price alone can be false economy if there is subsequent default, late deliveries, or other unsatisfactory performance resulting in additional contractual or administrative costs. While it is important that Government purchases be made at the lowest price, this does not require an award to a supplier solely because that supplier submits the lowest offer. A prospective contractor must affirmatively demonstrate its responsibility, including when necessary, the responsibility of its proposed subcontractors.

The acquisition regulations provide that the contracting officer, in connection with the award of a contract, make an affirmative determination of responsibility. The regulations state that doubt as to productive capacity or financial strength which cannot be resolved affirmatively shall require a determination of nonresponsibility. Such determination would preclude award of a contract.

To be considered a responsible prospective contractor, a contractor must:

1. Have adequate financial resources, organization, and facilities or the ability to obtain them, as required, during performance of the contract.
2. Be able to comply with the required or proposed delivery or performance schedule, taking into consideration all existing business commitments, commercial as well as governmental.
3. Have a satisfactory record of performance. Past unsatisfactory performance, due to failure to apply necessary tenacity or perserverance to do an acceptable job, shall be sufficient to justify a finding of nonresponsibility.
4. Have a satisfactory record of integrity.
5. Be otherwise qualified and eligible to receive an award under applicable laws and regulations.

Sources of Information

Information Currently Available

To the extent that the contracting officer must have sufficient information to establish that a prospective contractor currently meets the minimum standards of responsibility, maximum practical use shall be made of currently valid information already on file or within the knowledge of personnel in the agency. Additionally, information may be obtained from any of the following resources:

1. Lists of debarred, suspended, or ineligible concerns or individuals.
2. The prospective contractor. This could include representations and other information contained in or attached to bids and proposals, replies to questionnaires, financial data such as balance sheets, profit or loss statements, cash forecasts, etc.
3. Other information existing within the agency, including records on file and knowledge of personnel within the purchasing office making the procurement.
4. Publications, including credit ratings, trade and financial journals, business directories and registers.
5. Other sources including suppliers, subcontractors, customers of the prospective contractor, banks and financial insititutions.

Preaward Surveys

A preaward survey is generally required when the information available to the contracting officer for making a determination regarding the responsibility of a prospective contractor is inadequate. This is normally the case when the agency has had no previous experience with the offeror or the anticipated level of activity with the company is to be significantly increased. In a preaward survey, the procuring agency evaluates whether the prospective contractor is capable of performing the proposed contract. The survey can be utilized by the contracting officer to assist in determining if the offeror is responsible. The preaward evaluation may be accomplished by using data already in the agency files, data obtained from other government or commercial sources, on-site inspection of plants and facilities, or any combination of the above.

When a contracting officer determines that a preaward survey is desirable, his or her technical and financial advisors are directed to make the necessary reviews. The technical personnel will evaluate the prospective contractor's performance capability and productive capacity. The contract auditor will review the prospective contractor's financial capabilities, as well as the adequacy of the estimating and accounting systems.

The objective of the financial capability survey (see Fig. 3.5) is to determine whether the contractor's finances are adequate to perform the contract. In certain instances, a sound decision may be possible after a relatively simple review of a company's financial position and production commitments. In other circumstances, a more comprehensive review and analysis may be required. Where private financing is needed to supplement any government financing that may be provided, the auditor will normally verify the availability of such financing.

PREAWARD SURVEY OF PROSPECTIVE CONTRACTOR FINANCIAL CAPABILITY

	If more space is needed, continue on page 3, back. Identify continued items.	SERIAL NO. *(For surveying activity use)*	FORM APPROVED OMB NO. 3090-0110

PROSPECTIVE CONTRACTOR	LOCATION

SECTION I – BALANCE SHEET/PROFIT AND LOSS STATEMENT

PART A – LATEST BALANCE SHEET		PART B – LATEST PROFIT AND LOSS STATEMENT	
1. DATE	2. FILED WITH	1. CURRENT PERIOD	2. FILED WITH
		a. FROM b. TO	

3. FINANCIAL POSITION

a. Cash	$	
b. Other current assets		
c. Working capital		
d. Current liabilities		
e. Net worth		
f. Total liabilities		

3. NET SALES	a. CURRENT PERIOD	$
	b. First prior fiscal year	
	c. Second prior fiscal year	

4. NET PROFITS BEFORE TAXES	a. CURRENT PERIOD	$
	b. First prior fiscal year	
	c. Second prior fiscal year	

4. RATIOS

a. CURRENT ASSETS TO CURRENT LIABILITIES	b. ACID TEST *(Cash, temporary investments held in lieu of cash and current receivables to current liabilities)*	c. TOTAL LIABILITIES TO NET WORTH
:	:	:

5. OTHER PERTINENT DATA

6. FISCAL YEAR ENDS *(Date)*	7. BALANCE SHEETS AND PROFIT AND LOSS STATEMENTS HAVE BEEN CERTIFIED	a. THROUGH *(Date)*	b. BY *(Signature)*

SECTION II – PROSPECTIVE CONTRACTOR'S FINANCIAL ARRANGEMENTS

Mark "X" in appropriate column.	YES	NO	4. INDEPENDENT ANALYSIS OF FINANCIAL POSITION SUPPORTS THE STATEMENTS SHOWN IN ITEMS 1, 2, AND 3
1. USE OF OWN RESOURCES			☐ YES ☐ NO *(If "NO," explain)*
2. USE OF BANK CREDITS			
3. OTHER *(Specify)*			

SECTION III – GOVERNMENT FINANCIAL AID

1. TO BE REQUESTED IN CONNECTION WITH PERFORMANCE OF PROPOSED CONTRACT	2. EXPLAIN ANY "YES" ANSWERS TO ITEMS 1a, b, AND c

Mark "X" in appropriate column.	YES	NO
a. PROGRESS PAYMENT		
b. GUARANTEED LOAN		
c. ADVANCE PAYMENTS		

3. FINANCIAL AID CURRENTLY OBTAINED FROM THE GOVERNMENT

a. PROSPECTIVE CONTRACTOR RECEIVES GOVERNMENT FINANCING AT PRESENT	b. IS LIQUIDATION CURRENT?	c. AMOUNT OF UNLIQUIDATED PROGRESS PAYMENTS OUTSTANDING	*Complete items below only if item a., is marked "YES."*		
			DOLLAR AMOUNTS	(a) AUTHORIZED	(b) IN USE
☐ YES ☐ NO	☐ YES ☐ NO	$	a. Guaranteed loans	$	$
			b. Advance payments	$	$

4. LIST THE GOVERNMENT AGENCIES INVOLVED	5. SHOW THE APPLICABLE CONTRACT NOS.

Figure 3.5. Preaward survey of prospective contractor financial capability, Standard Form 1407.

PREAWARD SURVEY OF PROSPECTIVE CONTRACTOR FINANCIAL CAPABILITY

	If more space is needed, continue on page 3, back. Identify continued items.	SERIAL NO. (For surveying activity use)	FORM APPROVED OMB NO. 3090-0110

PROSPECTIVE CONTRACTOR	LOCATION

SECTION I – BALANCE SHEET/PROFIT AND LOSS STATEMENT

PART A – LATEST BALANCE SHEET		PART B – LATEST PROFIT AND LOSS STATEMENT		
1. DATE	2. FILED WITH	1. CURRENT PERIOD		2. FILED WITH
		a. FROM	b. TO	

3. FINANCIAL POSITION		3. NET SALES	a. CURRENT PERIOD	$
a. Cash	$		b. First prior fiscal year	
b. Other current assets			c. Second prior fiscal year	
c. Working capital		4. NET PROFITS BEFORE TAXES	a. CURRENT PERIOD	$
d. Current liabilities			b. First prior fiscal year	
e. Net worth			c. Second prior fiscal year	
f. Total liabilities				

4. RATIOS			5. OTHER PERTINENT DATA
a. CURRENT ASSETS TO CURRENT LIABILITIES	b. ACID TEST (Cash, temporary investments held in lieu of cash and current receivables to current liabilities)	c. TOTAL LIABILITIES TO NET WORTH	
:	:	:	

6. FISCAL YEAR ENDS (Date)	7. BALANCE SHEETS AND PROFIT AND LOSS STATEMENTS HAVE BEEN CERTIFIED ▶	a. THROUGH (Date)	b. BY (Signature)

SECTION II – PROSPECTIVE CONTRACTOR'S FINANCIAL ARRANGEMENTS

Mark "X" in appropriate column.	YES	NO	4. INDEPENDENT ANALYSIS OF FINANCIAL POSITION SUPPORTS THE STATEMENTS SHOWN IN ITEMS 1, 2, AND 3
1. USE OF OWN RESOURCES			☐ YES ☐ NO (If "NO," explain)
2. USE OF BANK CREDITS			
3. OTHER (Specify)			

SECTION III – GOVERNMENT FINANCIAL AID

1. TO BE REQUESTED IN CONNECTION WITH PERFORMANCE OF PROPOSED CONTRACT	2. EXPLAIN ANY "YES" ANSWERS TO ITEMS 1a, b, AND c
Mark "X" in appropriate column. YES / NO	
a. PROGRESS PAYMENT	
b. GUARANTEED LOAN	
c. ADVANCE PAYMENTS	

3. FINANCIAL AID CURRENTLY OBTAINED FROM THE GOVERNMENT

a. PROSPECTIVE CONTRACTOR RECEIVES GOVERNMENT FINANCING AT PRESENT	b. IS LIQUIDATION CURRENT?	c. AMOUNT OF UNLIQUIDATED PROGRESS PAYMENTS OUTSTANDING	Complete items below only if item a., is marked "YES."		
			DOLLAR AMOUNTS	(a) AUTHORIZED	(b) IN USE
☐ YES ☐ NO	☐ YES ☐ NO	$	a. Guaranteed loans	$	$
			b. Advance payments	$	$

4. LIST THE GOVERNMENT AGENCIES INVOLVED	5. SHOW THE APPLICABLE CONTRACT NOS.

Figure 3.5. (Continued)

6. DOES PRICE APPEAR UNREALISTICALLY LOW? ☐ YES ☐ NO

7. DESCRIBE ANY OUTSTANDING LIENS OR JUDGMENTS

	SECTION V — SALES	
CATEGORY	CURRENT DOLLAR BACKLOG OF SALES (a)	ANTICIPATED ADDITIONAL DOLLAR SALES FORECAST FOR NEXT 18 MONTHS (b)
1. Government *(Prime and subcontractor)*	$	$
2. Commercial	$	$
3. **TOTAL**	$	$

SECTION VI — RECOMMENDATION

1. RECOMMEND

☐ a. COMPLETE AWARD ☐ b. PARTIAL AWARD *(Quantity:* _____ *)* ☐ c. NO AWARD

2. REMARKS *(Cite those sections of the report which substantiate the recommendation. Give any other backup information in this space, on the back, or on additional sheet, if necessary.)*

If continuation sheets attached — mark here ☐

3. SURVEY MADE BY *(Signature and office)*	4. TELEPHONE NO. *(Include area code)*	5. DATE SUBMITTED

Figure 3.5. (Continued)

A preaward accounting system survey (see Fig. 3.6) is usually made for the purpose of determining the adequacy and suitability of the contractor's accounting practices to accumulate cost under the type of contract to be awarded. Accordingly, special emphasis may be given to the ability of the prospective contractor's cost accounting system to provide specific information the anticipated contract may require. The preaward accounting system survey should disclose the extent to which the proposed contract and the prospective contractor's cost accounting system are compatible. Additionally, if the contemplated contract is a cost-type contract, or a fixed-price contract with progress payment provisions, the auditor will normally review the accounting system to assure that it has the capability to accumulate cost by contract.

Because the preaward system survey is part of the overall determination of responsibility of the contractor, it is required prior to contract award. The time available to complete the review is normally limited. Therefore, the review may not be extensive in scope or depth. Nevertheless, a major deficiency in a cost accounting system, such as the inability to satisfy government reporting requirements, could preclude the award of a contract. Consequently, companies undergoing such a review should insist on knowing immediately any defects the government reviewers have noted. In anticipation of such a review by the government, it may be well for management to conduct its own survey and correct any deficiencies that are found.

CONTRACT NEGOTIATION

After the proposals are received, the government embarks on a procedure that has as its objective the award of the contract. This procedure starts with evaluation of the proposal and of the prospective contractor, in accordance with the evaluation criteria specified in the RFP. In a formal source selection, the more detailed procedures in the source selection plan are followed. Those performing the evaluation are prohibited from discussing the proposals with offerors until after the competitive range is determined. The result of this evaluation is the judgmental establishment by the contracting officer of the competitive range. The acquisition regulations offer some guidance by stating that the competitive range shall be determined by price or cost, and by technical and other salient factors, and shall include all proposals that have a reasonable chance of being selected for award.

Unless an award is made based on the initial evaluation, the contracting officer is required to conduct written or oral discussions with all responsible offerors who submit proposals within the competitive range. The government uses the discussions, which may be written or oral, to clarify ambiguities and to identify to the offerors any deficiencies discovered in their proposals. These discussions are not to result in what is referred to as "leveling" or "auctioning."

Leveling is defined as a condition in which the best features of each proposal are incorporated in all other competing proposals. The government is sensitive to this transfusion among proposals and has sought ways to prevent it. Auctioning occurs when the discussions take the form of a request to competing offerors to meet a certain price, or indications are given to an offeror that its proposed price is not low enough to obtain further consideration.

The discussions need not be held if it can be demonstrated that accepting an initial proposal would result in a fair and reasonable price and that the solicitation had provided for award without discussion.

PREAWARD SURVEY OF PROSPECTIVE CONTRACTOR ACCOUNTING SYSTEM

	SERIAL NO. *(For surveying activity use)*	FORM APPROVED OMB NO. 3090-0110
	PROSPECTIVE CONTRACTOR	

Mark "X" in the appropriate column	YES	NO	NOT APPLI- CABLE
1. Except as stated below, is the accounting system in accord with generally accepted accounting principles applicable in the circumstances?			
2. ACCOUNTING SYSTEM PROVIDES FOR:			
a. Proper segregation of costs applicable to proposed contract and to other work of the prospective contractor.			
b. Determination of costs at interim points to provide data required for contract repricing purposes or for negotiating revised targets.			
c. Exclusion from costs charged to proposed contract of amounts which are not allowable under terms of FAR 31, Contract Cost Principles and Procedures, or other contract provisions.			
d. Identification of costs by contract line item and by units if required by proposed contract.			
e. Segregation of preproduction costs from production costs.			
3. ACCOUNTING SYSTEM PROVIDES FINANCIAL INFORMATION:			
a. Required by contract clauses concerning limitation of cost (FAR 52.232-40 and 41) or limitation on payments (FAR 52.216-16).			
b. Required to support requests for progress payments.			
4. Is the accounting system designed, and are the records maintained in such a manner that adequate, reliable data are developed for use in pricing follow-on acquisitions?			

5. REMARKS *(Clarification of above deficiencies, and other pertinent comments. If additional space is required, continue on the back or on plain sheets of paper.)*

If continuation sheets attached — mark here ☐

6. SURVEY MADE BY *(Signature and office)*	7. TELEPHONE NO. *(Include area code)*	8. DATE SUBMITTED

NSN 7540-01-140-8529   1408-101   STANDARD FORM 1408 (10-83)
Prescribed by GSA,
FAR (48 CFR) 53.209-1(f)

Figure 3.6. Preaward survey of prospective contractor accounting system, Standard Form 1408.

When the discussions are complete, all offerors within the competitive range must be afforded the opportunity to submit a "best and final" offer, commonly referred to as the BAFO. While an offeror may submit a revised proposal at any point up to and including the time for BAFO, it is best not to wait until the close of discussions and the call for BAFOs because there is then no opportunity to clarify any misunderstandings or clear up any perceived deficiencies prior to the source selection decision. Reductions to the originally proposed price should be supported by identifiable changes in circumstances involving the work to be performed or the costs to be incurred. Arbitrary cost reductions may not be considered favorably by the government in its evaluation of the proposal. If, after reviewing the best and final offers, the government concludes that its requirements have changed, discussions must then be held with all offerors within the competitive range and a new request for a "best and final" should be issued.

A four-step source selection procedure was established by DOD as one of the ways to avoid technical leveling, which was discussed earlier. This procedure differs from the process described above since the first step of the four-step procedure involves a review and limited discussion of only the technical proposal. The government does not advise any offeror of any technical deficiencies. In step two, based on the limited discussions, all offerors submit a revised technical proposal along with their cost or pricing data. Proposals that have no chance of being selected are eliminated and a competitive range is established. For those offerors within the initial competitive range, limited discussions are held regarding their technical and cost proposals. A second elimination is made for those who fall outside the competitive range. The third step involves: establishing a common cut-off date for the receipt of clarifications and substantiations for the technical and cost proposals, receiving and evaluating the latest proposals, selecting the offeror for final contract negotiations, and advising all other offerors. The fourth step is final price negotiations with the selected source.

It is important to distinguish between the discussions held with all the offerors who submitted proposals within the competitive range and those held with the selected source. The former discussions are directed primarily at obtaining information for the purpose of source selection. The latter discussions are intended to lead to a contractually binding document. Companies should be careful about reducing their price based on the initial discussions unless it clearly results from a mutually recognized deficiency in the proposal or a change in requirements. This is important to remember since the best and final offer is usually the starting point for the final negotiations.

Before the selected source is invited to the negotiation table, the government contracting officer normally wants additional assurance that the proposed price is fair and reasonable. The acquisition regulations governing negotiated procurements require the contracting officer to utilize all appropriate organizational tools such as the advice of specialists in the fields of contracting, finance, law, contract audit, engineering, and price analysis. As a result of this requirement, the offeror is very likely to be visited by a contract auditor, a technical representative, and a cost and price analyst—all to review and evaluate the proposal.

The contract auditor will review the offeror's books and records and relevant cost data submitted in support of the proposed price for the purpose of expressing an opinion on whether the estimated costs appear reasonable. The technical evaluation will cover such things as the overall approach the company is proposing to take to solve the government's problem and the need to include in the proposal various kinds and quantities of labor hours, material, and other purchased items. Based on the specialists' reviews, they will make recommendations to the contracting officer regarding the reasonableness of the price. Of all the contracting officer's representatives that may review the proposal, the contract auditor is the one primarily authorized to examine the company's books and records.

Throughout this evaluation process, it is important to keep in mind that the contracting officer is the exclusive agent of the government with the authority to enter into and administer contracts. All of the specialists assisting the procuring contracting officer (PCO) are merely advisers; only a contracting officer is authorized to make binding agreements regarding the contract.

After all the input has been received from the specialists, final price negotiations can take place. Anyone entering the negotiation process should have some insight as to the other party's objectives. The *Armed Services Procurement Manual for Contract Pricing* (ASPM) sets forth the government's objective: to establish a fair and reasonable price and a contract type that will sustain the price. From the company's perspective, the negotiated price should provide a reasonable return on investment, and the type of contract negotiated should reflect an assumption of risk that is acceptable based on the degree of uncertainty involved in performing the contract. For example, a firm fixed-price contract would indicate that the company accepts 100 % of the risk of performing a contract within the negotiated price. A flexibly priced contract (i.e., redeterminable, incentive, or cost reimbursable) would represent a sharing of the risk between the parties.

To accomplish the government's objective, the contracting officer will formulate a negotiation plan, set objectives, assemble a team, and develop a strategy. The offeror should do no less. The offeror should enter into the negotiation process fully armed with cost and pricing data that are relevant to the proposal. Every reasonable attempt should have been made to learn about the aspects of the proposal that the government will be questioning. Often in response to the offeror's request, the government will provide a copy of the contract auditor's report. Recognizing the possibility that in some instances the contracting officer may not release the auditor's report, every effort should be made to elicit information from the auditor and the technical representative during the proposal evaluation regarding any unresolved technical or cost issues that may have arisen during their reviews. The company should insist that the auditor hold an exit conference at the completion of the audit. This conference should be used to discuss the factual data the auditor has used to arrive at the audit recommendations. While the auditor is not authorized to disclose the final recommendations, the factual bases for the judgment are appropriate matters for discussion.

Care should be exercised in forming the negotiation team. Personnel from production and support departments may be needed to respond to specific issues during the negotiation. Each team member's role in the negotiation should be clearly defined. It is important that the official spokesperson for the company be established and that the company speak with one voice.

Negotiation objectives should be established. The negotiator should be keenly aware of the price level at which it would not be reasonable for the company to accept the contract. In some instances, during the negotiation the government will change the scope of work from that which was used as the basis for the estimate. When this occurs, the company's negotiator must decide whether the effect of the change of scope can be reflected in the price without suspending the negotiation. It may be necessary to request a recess to develop a revised proposal. Depending on the extent of the change, it may be hazardous to estimate its impact while sitting around the negotiation table.

Perhaps the best way to summarize our discussion of the negotiation process is to include a slightly paraphrased version of the "Don't-But-Do" list of ideas that the government provides its negotiators:

1. Don't dictate; negotiate. Be a reasonable person.
2. Don't expose anyone to ridicule or insult.
3. Don't try to make anyone look bad.
4. Don't be predictable in your approach.
5. Do be discriminating. Accept a good offer.
6. Do fight hard on the important points; win the war, not the battles. Don't start fights you have no chance of winning or which, even if you do win, would not be worth the fight.
7. Do be courteous and considerate. Do what you say you will. Have integrity.
8. Do know when to talk and when to listen. Do stop talking when you've made your point, won your case, reached agreement.
9. Do remember that negotiation is a two-way street and that pre-negotiation preparation is the most important attribute of successful selling.

SUBCONTRACTORS

Often companies will be involved in government business as subcontractors. The contractual relationship in this case is with another company, the prime contractor or a higher tiered subcontractor, rather than a government agency. Perhaps the most important consideration in this relationship is that the terms and conditions included in the prime contractor's agreement with the government generally flow down to the subcontractor. In other words, the subcontractor is equally bound to comply with the applicable acquisition rules and regulations. Generally, all of our previous comments relating to the process of contract formation as it applies to prime contractors are equally applicable to subcontractors.

While the prime contractor is contractually obligated to administer its subcontracts, the government reserves the right to interject itself into the process on the premise of "protecting the public interest." Therefore, subcontractors may find both the prime contractor and the government reviewers looking over their shoulders.

As mentioned above, the acquisition regulations assert that basic responsibility rests with the prime contractor for selecting the subcontractors, pricing the subcontracts, and assuring satisfactory subcontractor performance. This responsibility notwithstanding, the contracting officer who negotiates the prime contract price is still required to be personally assured that all components of the price, including the subcontracts, are reasonable. Often this assurance is obtained by reviewing the prime contractor's purchasing procedures or by evaluating the actions taken by the prime contractor to establish the reasonableness of the specific subcontract price. In some instances, even with what the prime contractor has done, the government will conduct separate independent reviews, especially when the contracting officer is not satisfied.

The prime contractor may request the government to review the subcontractor's proposal in lieu of making its own. In fact, the subcontractor may object to the prime contractor having access to its books and records because of their competitive relationship. While the prime contractor is not contractually relieved of its responsibility for its subcontracts, the government, DCAA in particular, will conduct those reviews that require access to the subcontractor's formal books and records. The results of the review are provided to the prime contractor, who uses them to price or settle the subcontract.

SUMMARY

If a government agency is the potential customer, the process for making the sale is likely to be more complex, formal, and structured than selling to private industry. The Federal Government, in particular, has rather clearly defined steps to follow—from preparing and submitting the initial offer through contract execution. Companies pursuing this market must be well informed about how the government procurement process works and what is expected. It is important to know the government officials involved, their responsibilities and authority, the regulations that govern their actions, and how they go about making procurement decisions. These procedures, generally, apply also to subcontractors even though their relationship is not directly with the government.

Management should not be lulled into thinking that the elaborate procedures described in this chapter eliminate the need for aggressive, imaginative marketing. In addition to obtaining all of the published information available, successful contractors establish effective working relationships with the procurement and technical officials in the buying offices to whom they sell. These contacts are usually helpful in obtaining timely marketing information concerning anticipated procurement actions. Equally important, the relationship could afford the company the opportunity to provide input to the decision-making process since the government often looks to private industry to assist in its problem-solving activities. These activities are especially critical to potential suppliers since they usually form the basis for future procurement actions. In dealing with the Federal Government, getting the opportunity to make an offer is only the critical first step. Whether the company succeeds in receiving the contract will depend to a large measure on how well the offeror copes with the (1) rules and regulations that govern the content and format of the proposal, (2) government reviews and discussions, and (3) formal contract negotiation. Only after all of these bridges have been successfully crossed can one be assured that the government's business has been obtained.

NOTES

1. 41 USC § 235(a)(b)(2)(B); 10 USC § 2304(a)(2)(B)(ii).
2. 41 USC § 253(c)(d)(4).
3. The Armed Services Procurement Act of 1947 authorized 16 specific negotiation exceptions to procurement by formal advertising. The Federal Property and Administrative Services Act of 1949 contained 14 exceptions for the civilian agencies, omitting those for duplication of investment or delay (Exception (14) and defense mobilization requirements (Exception (16). Cf. 10 U.S.C.§ 2304(a); 41 U.S.C.§ 252(c).
4. 41 U.S.C.§ 253(c)(7); 10 U.S.C.§ 2304(c)(7).
5. 41 U.S.C.§ 416(b)(4) and (5), as amended by section 303 of the Small Business and Federal Procurement Competition Enhancement Act of 1984 (PL 98-577).
6. See House/Senate Conference Report, supra Note 5.
7. 15 U.S.C. § 631 et seq. Also supra Note 5 and 41 U.S.C. § 253(b)(3) as amended by 504(d)(1) of the Small Business and Federal Procurement Enhancement Act of 1984.

8. See prior 10 U.S.C. 2310 and 2311 providing for the finality of determinations made by the agency head with respect to determinations to negotiate under Exceptions 12-16, and the comparable provisions under prior 41 U.S.C. 257(a)(c).
9. See House/Senate report, supra Note 7.
10. Title 13, Code of Federal Regulations, Part 121.

Chapter Four

Profit

Doing business with the government requires an adequate understanding of the various rules and regulations governing the procurement process—and profit is no exception. Over the years, the government has struggled to achieve fairness, uniformity and consistency in its profit policy. Different methods have been employed by different agencies, and methods have changed over the years in an unending attempt to make them more equitable and responsive to changing needs. As an important aspect of government contracting, the methodology utilized by the contracting offices in establishing contract profit objectives warrants adequate attention by businesses involved in this market and by those planning to enter this market.

GOVERNMENT POLICY

While methods for determining specific profit objectives have varied, the general government profit policy has been relatively consistent. This policy is set forth in FAR 15.901(b) and (c), which state:

> It is in the Government's interest to offer contractors opportunities for financial rewards sufficient to (1) stimulate efficient contract performance, (2) attract the best capabilities of qualified large and small business concerns to Government contracts, and (3) maintain a viable industrial base.
> Both the Government and contractors should be concerned with profit as a motivator of efficient and effective contract performance. Negotiations aimed merely at reducing prices by reducing profit, without proper recognition of the function of profit, are not in the Government's interest.

Few would argue with this statement of policy. It does appear to promote a fair, reasonable, and equitable approach to profit determination. Nevertheless it is the application of this profit policy that affects the ultimate profits of businesses engaged in contracting with the Federal Government. While contractors have pointed with alarm to the low profit rates experienced on government contracts, Congress has viewed with suspicion the alleged high return on investment and the tremendous growth shown by many defense firms. The government's periodic studies of its profit policies frequently result in changes to the implementing regulations. These constantly changing guidelines cause confusion and hesitancy to contractors trying to respond to the government's interest while optimizing profits. The use of profit to promote the three sometimes contradictory objectives of 1) rewarding quality contract performance, 2) rewarding capital investment, and 3) rewarding support for national socio-economic policies, and the constantly shifting emphasis between the three objectives contribute to the confusion.

The purpose here is not to present the merits of each point of view, but rather to provide an overview of the approaches used by the government to reach a prenegotiation profit objective in the negotiation of contracts.

GOVERNMENT APPROACH TO DETERMINING PROFIT

Contracting Officers are charged with the responsibility to insure that the prices the government pays for the goods and services it requires are fair and reasonable. When the government purchase is a result of sealed bidding or a negotiated contact where cost or pricing data were not required, profit is not separately considered. The amount of profit is normally of no concern to the government. In such situations, fixed-price type contracts are usually awarded to the lowest responsible offeror. If the contractor earns a large profit, it is considered the normal reward of efficiency in a competitive environment.

In procurements where cost or pricing data are required, profit becomes a separate element which must be considered by contracting officers.

Statutory Limitations On Profit

Cost-type prime contracts and subcontracts are subject to statutory limitations as outlined in FAR 15.903(d). This provision states that in the case of a cost-plus-fixed-fee (CPFF) contract the fee shall not exceed 10 % of the estimated cost of the contract, exclusive of fee, as determined at the time of entering into the contract, except that:

> A fee not in excess of 15% of such estimated cost of performance is authorized in any such contract for experimental, developmental or research work.

> A fee, inclusive of the contractor's cost, not in excess of 6% of the estimated cost, exclusive of fees, of the project to which such fee is applicable is authorized in contracts for architectural or engineering services relating to any public works or utility projects.

Prenegotiation Profit Objectives

The amount of profit in the price of any negotiated contract is subject to negotiation between the contracting officer and the contractor subject to the above limits for cost-type contracts. FAR 15-807 requires the contracting officer to establish a prenegotiation objective before the negotiation of any contract action. The prenegotiation profit or fee objective is a distinct part of the required prenegotiation objective.

Until recently, contracting officers used numerous methods to establish prenegotiation profit objectives in negotiating contracts. These could generally be called structured methods. Structured methods are mechanical procedures whereby weight values are measured and assigned to such factors as contractor effort, contract cost risk, federal socioeconomic program support, capital investment, past performance, and independent development in determining a profit amount. The unstructured methods, while still considering the above performance factors, do not quantify the individual risks elements. FAR 15.902 currently requires agencies to use a structured approach for determining the profit or fee objective in those acquisitions that require cost analysis.

DOD Weighted Guidelines

Within DOD, whenever cost analysis is performed, contracting officers are required to establish a profit objective for contract negotiations that will:

Reward contractors who undertake more difficult work requiring higher skills.

Allow contractors an opportunity to earn profits commensurate with the extent of the cost risk they are willing to assume.

Reward contractors who provide their own facilities and financing and establish their competence through development work undertaken at their own risk.

Reward contractors for productivity increases.

DOD established a structured method called "weighted guidelines" for determining prenegotiation profit objectives in 1963. The weighted guidelines method for establishing prenegotiation profit objectives provided fairly precise guidance in implementing and applying these principles for tailoring profits to the circumstances of each contract in order to foster long range cost reduction objectives and spread profits commensurate with varying circumstances. While not used universally within DOD, it did go a long way toward establishing some consistency in prenegotiation profit objectives within the department.

DOD has revised its weighted guidelines several times as a result of internal studies assessing the success of the then current weights in meeting DOD's profit principles.

The first significant change to DOD's weighted guidelines profit policy was reflected in Defense Procurement Circular (DPC) 76-3, dated September 1, 1976. The changes in DPC 76-3 represented the results of a study, referred to as Profit '76, that was conducted to determine if the profits on DOD contracts were fulfilling their stated objectives. The study was based on data gathered from over 60 companies holding defense contracts totalling about $16 billion and additional information from more than 200 other companies.

The conclusion of the study was that the profit policy was not achieving DOD's objectives. While the reasons were many and varied, the major factor was the failure of defense-oriented contractors to invest in capital assets. This lack of investment was attributed to a disincentive inherent in the government technique for pricing contracts. Because profit objectives were oriented substantially to costs, investments in capital assets aimed at reducing the cost of government contracts actually resulted in less profits on future contracts to contractors making such investments.

As a result of the Profit '76 study and the concurrent implementation of CAS 414, *Cost of Money as an Element of the Cost of Facilities Capital*, DOD revised its cost allowability criteria and its profit policy to recognize, as an allowable cost, the cost of capital committed to facilities and to include the investment in facilities as a specifically identified profit factor. It was presumed, historically, that the cost of money associated with the acquisition of capital assets employed on a contract had been included in the overall negotiated profit. DOD concluded that it must provide a reasonable profit incentive to motivate contractors to invest in capital assets. Accordingly, the previously established weighted guidelines factors were revised. The relative weight attributed to contractor effort (estimated cost) was reduced by 30 % and, in part, assigned to the factor established for the amount of facilities estimated to be employed in the performance of the contract.

The objective of the changes were to increase profits to those contractors with a substantial investment in capital assets and lower profits to those contractors without such investment. Theoretically, this would result in retaining the same overall profit levels for DOD contractors collectively, and have little or no effect on the department's budget. At the same time, DOD indicated that it would study the effect of investment in more efficient equipment and consider increasing the factor in the future, if necessary.

Based on a continuing study subsequent to DPC 76-3, DOD concluded that the facilities investment profit factor was still not adequate to achieve DOD's objective of increasing contractor investment in capital assets. Therefore, Defense Acquisition Circular (DAC) 76-23, dated February 26, 1980 further increased the relative weight of the investment profit factor. At the same time DOD recognized that the performance of some types of contracts does not require the use of capital assets to the same degree as certain production contracts. It concluded that applying the same weighted guidelines profit factors to contracts not requiring significant use of capital assets produced inequitable results. The resolution of this perceived problem was to provide a separate approach in determining the profit objective for each of three different categories of contracts: Manufacturing, Services and Research and Development.

Extension of Weighted Guidelines Beyond DOD

In December 1980 the Office of Federal Procurement Policy (OFPP) issued Policy Letter 80-7. As a result of this directive, the General Services Administration (GSA) required that all agencies, unless exempt, adopt a structured approach for determining prenegotiation profit objectives by January 1, 1982. Recognizing that some agencies may have previously included cost of money as a profit factor, the OFPP stated that contractors were not to be compensated for facilities capital cost of money both as a cost and in profits or fees. OFPP stated that this could be prevented by using dollar-for-dollar offsets (i.e., reducing the government's prenegotiation profit or fee objective by the amount of allowable facilities capital cost of money) or by incorporating a common offset factor in an agency's structured approach. It further stated that an offset may not be necessary where the profit analysis factors in an agency's structured approach take into account the allowability of facilities capital cost of money.

The OFPP realized that this might be a relatively meaningless exercise if there were no further consideration of facilities employed in contract performance. For this reason, a specific profit analysis factor for facilities was prescribed in the OFPP policy letter. The intent of this factor was to result in profit and fee differentials depending on the level of capital investment required for contract performance. The OFPP went even one step further and added a profit subfactor for operating capital.

The OFPP did not specifically require, but did encourage, agencies to adopt a weighted guidelines structured approach such as that used by DOD and NASA. The OFPP stated that another structure could be used only if it "incorporates a logic and rationale similar to that of the weighted-guidelines method." While this OFPP Policy Letter has since expired, most of its provisions have been incorporated into the FAR.

CURRENT DOD PROFIT POLICY

In 1985 DOD completed another in a series of profit studies. This latest study, called Defense Financing and Investment Review (DFAIR), found that the DOD profit structure was generally sound. Two of the findings however were to have a significant impact on defense contractors. The study found that overall profit had increased about one percent since the previous profit study and that the profit policy was not effectively motivating contractors to invest in capital facilities.

As a result of this study and an analysis of the study performed by the General Accounting Office, Congress mandated that DOD revise its profit policy to incorporate certain of the recommendations immediately. To back up its demand, Congress removed about $700 million from the FY87 DOD budget which is approximately the amount that negotiated profits would be reduced by implementing the new policy. Consequently, DOD completely revised its profit approach and issued new weighted guidelines. The interim regulation was published on December 1, 1986 effective on all solicitations released after October 18, 1986. The final regulation was published on August 3, 1987, effective August 1, 1987.

The new regulation contained in DFARS 215.970, requires contractors to provide data to contracting officers which had not been previously required, namely, the distribution of capital assets into the three separate categories: land, buildings and equipment. Different weight factors are assigned to asset values in each category. Contractors must now develop this data and submit it to contracting officers so that profit objectives may be calculated.

The contracting officer has the latitude to use another structured method if it is determined to be more appropriate to the contracting situation at hand. The new regulation generally contained the same exceptions to its application as the previous weighted guidelines regulation:

Architect-engineering contracts

Construction contracts.

Contracts primarily requiring delivery of material supplied by subcontractors.

Termination settlements.

Cost-plus-award-fee contracts.

Contracts not expected to exceed $500,000.

Unusual situations where this method may not produce a reasonable overall prenegotiation profit objective.

When the weighted guidelines method is not used, a similar structured approach must be used which still considers the three primary factors of performance risk, contract type risk (with a working capital adjustment for fixed - price contracts) and facilities capital investment.

Contractors are encouraged by the new regulation to use the weighted guidelines in setting profit objectives for their negotiated subcontracts and to voluntarily submit with their proposals an analysis of their proposed profit in the weighted guidelines format.

The new weighted guidelines base prenegotiation profit objectives on three factors: performance risk, contract type risk, and facilities capital employed.

The form used to determine the prenegotiation profit objective is DD Form 1547. This form is used as both a worksheet for the contracting officer and as a transmittal sheet for statistical purposes. In addition, the contracting officer is required to prepare DD Form 1861 to report the Cost Accounting Standard (CAS) 414 Facilities Cost of Money (FCOM) negotiated.

The prenegotiation profit objective based on performance risk is the product of the contracting officer's prenegotiation cost objective (excluding FCOM, IR&D/B&P and G&A) and an assigned weight value. In assigning the weight and value, the contracting officer considers three broad categories of contract performance: Technical, Management and Cost. Each of the three categories is independently assessed. A standard range between 2 % and 6 % with a normal value of 4 % is assigned to each category. The regulation identifies a number of factors to be considered in assigning the factor to each category. The contracting officer is not limited to these considerations but must explain any other factors considered. The values for each category are weighted, based on the contracting officer's judgment, to arrive at the overall performance risk weight value.

Since Research & Development and service organizations often require minimum facilities capital in the performance of contracts, the guidelines permit the contracting officer to use an alternate range between 4 % and 8 % with a normal value of 6 % for performance risk, in lieu of the normal 4 % value described above.If the alternate factor is used, no profit is calculated for facilities capital employed.

The prenegotiation profit objective based on contract type risk is the product of the contracting officer's prenegotiation cost objective (excluding FCOM, IR&D/B&P, and G&A) and an assigned value for contract type. The normal values and ranges are as follows:

Contract Type*	Contracts With No (or Limited) Progress Provisions		Contracts With Progress Payment Provisions	
	Range	Normal Value	Range	Normal Value
Firm Fixed-Price	4% to 6%	5%	2% to 4%	3%
Fixed-Price Incentive	2% to 4%	3%	0% to 2%	1%
Cost-Plus-Incentive-Fee	0% to 2%	1%		
Cost-Plus-Fixed-Fee, Time and Material, Labor Hour, Fixed-Price-Level-of-Effort	0 to 1%	.5%		

*Cost incurred prior to contract definitization may warrent designation of a below normal risk factor.

The working capital adjustment applies only to fixed - price contracts with provisions for progress payments. The regulation provides a formula for adjusting the contract type profit objective by considering the degree of contractor funding of the effort, the length of the contract and an interest rate. In this calculation, IR&D/B&P and G&A costs are be included in the prenegotiation cost objective.

This objective is multiplied by the percent of costs financed by the contractor (1 minus the progress payment rate), and by a contract length factor taken from a table contained in DFARS 215.970-1 (b)(4)(iv). This product is then multiplied by the treasury rate which is published semiannually. There is an upward limit on the adjustment of 4% of the cost objective.

The facilities capital employed portion of the prenegotiation profit objective is based on the contractor's investment in buildings and equipment. To compute this amount, it is necessary to obtain the percentage of the net book values related to land, buildings and equipment for each business unit for each year and also the allocation base amount used to calculate the indirect rates for each pool.

The Facilities Cost of Money (FCOM) is calculated for each pool and fiscal year by multiplying the FCOM factor (from column 7 of the CASB-CMF form) by the estimated allocation base in the prenegotiation objective for the pool. The pools and fiscal years are summed into a single value and divided by the current treasury rate. The percentages of land, buildings and equipment for each pool are used to redistribute the FCOM to the three asset types. The results are the base for determining the facilities capital employed profit.

The contracting officer then assesses the usefulness of the assets to present and future DoD contracts and assigns a value within the following ranges:

Asset Type	R&D and Service Contracts Awarded to Highly Facilitized Manufacturers		Other Contracts	
	Range	Normal Value	Range	Normal Value
Land	0%	0%	0%	0%
Buildings	0% to 10%	5%	10% to 20%	15%
Equipment	15% to 25%	20%	20% to 50%	35%

The assigned value for each asset type is multiplied by the base for each asset type and the sum of the products for buildings and equipment is the profit objective for facilities capital employed.

The contracting officer's total prenegotiation profit objective is the sum of the performance risk, contract type (including the working capital adjustment, if applicable) and facilities capital employed profit objectives. The forms are straightforward and easy to prepare once the method is understood and the required data is available. Figures 4.1 through 4.5 illustrate a completed set of forms applying the DOD weighted guidelines method.

While only DOD is affected by this new regulation, NASA and the other agencies frequently follow DOD's lead in many areas. Whether they adopt the current DOD profit guidelines remains to be seen.

NASA PROFIT APPROACH

NASA uses a structured approach in determining a profit objective which is similar to the DOD policy in effect prior to October 18, 1986. Its weighted guidelines ranges, however, differ from DOD's. They are provided in Figure 4.6.

Contract length (months)   24
Contract type   FFP
Progress payments   75.0%
Cost incurred $0

	Contract Costs		
	1987	1988	Total
Subcontracts	$ 9,200	$ 8,000	$17,200
Parts and material	$ 12,424	$ 6,643	19,067
Material subtotal	21,624	14,643	36,267
Manufacturing direct labor	$316,502	$308,202	
Offsite direct labor	$ 41,024	$ 42,745	
Field engineering labor	$ 5,632	$ 7,603	
Direct labor subtotal	363,158	358,550	721,708
Manufacturing overhead	$443,103	$434,565	
Offsite eng. overhead	$ 27,076	$ 28,639	
Field eng. overhead	$ 2,534	$3,421	
Overhead subtotal	472,713	466,625	939,338
Other direct	$ 12,070	$ 22,251	34,321
Total cost input	869,565	862,069	1,731,634
G&A, R&D and B&P	$130,435	$137,931	268,366
Total cost	$1,000,000	$1,000,000	2,000,000

Figure 4.1. Weighted Guidelines Input Data Base

NASA FAR Supplement 1815.970 requires direct reduction of the profit objective by the allowable amount of the cost of money included in the contractor's proposal.

CIVILIAN

Each of the major civilian agencies now have in place a weighted guidelines type structured approach for determining prenegotiation profit objectives. For the most part, they resemble the NASA policy with much of the basis for profit based on contractor effort. Individual agency regulations should be consulted to determine the specific weights and categories used by that agency.

SUMMARY

Profit is generally considered the reward or compensation provided for (1) efforts or services performed and resources provided (both human and facilities), and (2) uncertainty or risk undertaken. The more resources provided and the higher the skills or risk involved, the higher the expected level of profit. Although government contracting differs from the commercial environment in

RECORD OF WEIGHTED GUIDELINES APPLICATION

1. REPORT NO.	2. BASIC PROCUREMENT INSTRUMENT IDENTIFICATION NO.				3. SPIIN	4. DATE OF ACTION	
	a. PURCHASING OFFICE	b. FY	c. TYPE PROC INST CODE	d. PRISN		a. YEAR	b. MONTH

5. CONTRACTING OFFICE CODE	ITEM	COST CATEGORY	OBJECTIVE

	ITEM	COST CATEGORY	OBJECTIVE
6. NAME OF CONTRACTOR	13.	MATERIAL	19,067
	14.	SUBCONTRACTS	17,200
7. DUNS NUMBER / 8. FEDERAL SUPPLY CODE	15.	DIRECT LABOR	721,708
	16.	INDIRECT EXPENSES	939,338
9. DOD CLAIMANT PROGRAM / 10. CONTRACT TYPE CODE	17.	OTHER DIRECT CHARGES	34,321
	18.	SUBTOTAL COSTS (13 thru 17)	1,731,634
11. TYPE EFFORT / 12. USE CODE	19.	GENERAL AND ADMINISTRATIVE	268,366
	20.	TOTAL COSTS (18 + 19)	2,000,000

WEIGHTED GUIDELINES PROFIT FACTORS

ITEM	CONTRACTOR RISK FACTORS	ASSIGNED WEIGHTING	ASSIGNED VALUE	BASE (ITEM 18)	PROFIT OBJECTIVE
21.	TECHNICAL	40.0 %	5.0		
22.	MANAGEMENT	30.0 %	4.0		
23.	COST CONTROL	30.0 %	4.0		
24.	PERFORMANCE RISK (COMPOSITE)		4.7	1,731,634	81,387
25.	CONTRACT TYPE RISK		3.5	1,731,634	60,607

ITEM		COSTS FINANCED	LENGTH FACTOR	INTEREST RATE	
26.	WORKING CAPITAL	500,000	.65	7.625 %	24,781

ITEM	CONTRACTOR FACILITIES CAPITAL EMPLOYED	ASSIGNED VALUE	AMOUNT EMPLOYED	
27.	LAND			
28.	BUILDINGS	16	5,629	17,770
29.	EQUIPMENT	37	370,599	137,122
30.	**TOTAL PROFIT OBJECTIVE**			321,667

NEGOTIATION SUMMARY

		PROPOSED	OBJECTIVE	NEGOTIATED
31.	TOTAL COSTS	2,000,000		
32.	FACILITIES CAPITAL COST OF MONEY (DD Form 1861)	37,156		
33.	PROFIT	321,667		
34.	TOTAL PRICE (Line 31 + 32 + 33)	2,358,823		
35.	MARKUP RATE (Line 32 + 33 divided by 31)	17.74 %	%	%

CONTRACTING OFFICER APPROVAL

36. TYPED/PRINTED NAME OF CONTRACTING OFFICER (Last, First, Middle Initial)	37. SIGNATURE OF CONTRACTING OFFICER	38. TELEPHONE NO.	39. DATE SUBMITTED (YYMMDD)

OPTIONAL USE

96.	97.	98.	99.

DD Form 1547, AUG 87   Previous editions are obsolete.   '84/259

Figure 4.2. Record of weighted guidelines application, DD Form 1547.

CONTRACT FACILITIES CAPITAL COST OF MONEY

Form Approved
OMB No. 0704-0267
Expires Oct 31, 1989

1. CONTRACTOR NAME	2. CONTRACTOR ADDRESS
3. BUSINESS UNIT	
4. RFP / CONTRACT PIIN NUMBER	5. PERFORMANCE PERIOD July 1, 1987 – June 30, 1989

6. DISTRIBUTION OF FACILITIES CAPITAL COST OF MONEY

POOL	ALLOCATION BASE	FACILITIES CAPITAL COST OF MONEY	
		FACTOR	AMOUNT
FY 1988 Manufacturing	316,502	.05019	15,884
Offsite	41,024	.00996	409
Field	5,632	.00039	2
G&A	869,565	.00361	3,139
FY 1989 Manufacturing	308,202	.04749	14,637
Offsite	42,745	.01067	456
Field	7,603	.00046	3
G&A	862,069	.00304	2,625
TOTAL			37,156
TREASURY RATE			7.625 %
FACILITIES CAPITAL EMPLOYED (TOTAL DIVIDED BY TREASURY RATE)			487,290

7. DISTRIBUTION OF FACILITIES CAPITAL EMPLOYED

	PERCENTAGE	AMOUNT
LAND	1.25 %	5,629
BUILDINGS	24.57 %	111,062
EQUIPMENT	74.18 %	370,599
FACILITIES CAPITAL EMPLOYED	100%	487,290

DD Form 1861, AUG 87   *Supersedes all previous editions of DD Forms 1861-1 and 1861-2, which are obsolete.*   79 211

Figure 4.3. Contract facilities capital cost of money, DD Form 1861.

FACILITIES CAPITAL
COST OF MONEY FACTORS COMPUTATION

CONTRACTOR:

BUSINESS UNIT:

ADDRESS:

COST ACCOUNTING PERIOD: FY 1988		1. APPLICABLE COST OF MONEY RATE 7.625%	2. ACCUMULATION & DIRECT DISTRIBUTION OF N.B.V.	3. ALLOCATION OF UNDISTRIBUTED (BASIS OF ALLOCATION)	4. TOTAL NET BOOK VALUE (COLUMNS 2+3)	5. COST OF MONEY FOR THE COST ACCOUNTING PERIOD (COLUMNS 1X4)	6. ALLOCATION BASE FOR THE PERIOD (IN UNITS OF MEASURE)	7. FACILITIES CAPITAL COST OF MONEY FACTORS (COLUMNS 5÷6)
BUSINESS UNIT FACILITIES CAPITAL	RECORDED		14,731,199					
	LEASED PROPERTY		350,750					
	CORPORATE OR GROUP		450,000					
	TOTAL		15,531,949					
	UNDISTRIBUTED			194,150				
	DISTRIBUTED		15,337,799					
	Manufacturing		12,591,249	194,150	12,785,399	974,887	19,425,000	.05019
	Offsite		320,000		320,000	24,400	2,450,000	.00996
	Field		1,800		1,800	137	350,000	.00039
OVERHEAD POOLS								
G&A EXPENSE POOLS	G&A		2,424,750		2,424,750	184,887	51,216,500	.00361
TOTAL			15,337,799	194,150	15,531,949	1,184,311	/////////	/////////

Figure 4.4 Facilities capital cost of money factors computation, Form CASB-CMF.

FACILITIES CAPITAL
COST OF MONEY FACTORS COMPUTATION

FORM CASB-CMF

CONTRACTOR:
BUSINESS UNIT:
ADDRESS:

COST ACCOUNTING PERIOD: FY 1989

		1. APPLICABLE COST OF MONEY RATE 7.625%	2. ACCUMULATION & DIRECT DISTRIBUTION OF N.B.V.	3. ALLOCATION OF UNDISTRIBUTED (BASIS OF ALLOCATION)	4. TOTAL NET BOOK VALUE (COLUMNS 2+3)	5. COST OF MONEY FOR THE COST ACCOUNTING PERIOD (COLUMNS 1X4)	6. ALLOCATION BASE FOR THE PERIOD (IN UNIT(S) OF MEASURE)	7. FACILITIES CAPITAL COST OF MONEY FACTORS (COLUMNS 5÷6)
BUSINESS UNIT FACILITIES CAPITAL	RECORDED		14,929,870					
	LEASED PROPERTY		350,750					
	CORPORATE OR GROUP		450,000					
	TOTAL		15,730,620					
	UNDISTRIBUTED		194,150					
	DISTRIBUTED		15,924,770					
OVERHEAD POOLS	Manufacturing		13,088,270	194,150	13,282,420	1,012,785	21,325,000	.04749
	Offsite		365,250		365,250	27,850	2,610,000	.01067
	Field		2,100		2,100	160	350,000	.00046
G&A EXPENSE POOLS	G&A		2,275,000		2,275,000	173,469	56,975,000	.00304
TOTAL			15,730,620	194,150	15,924,770	1,214,264	/////////	/////////

Figure 4.5. Facilities capital cost of money factors computation, Form CASB-CMF.

Profit Factors	Weight Ranges
1. Contractor effort	
Material acquisition	1 to 4%
Direct Labor	4 to 12%
Overhead	3 to 8%
Other costs	1 to 3%
General management	4 to 8%
2. Other factors	
Cost risk	0 to 7%
Investment	-2 to $+2$%
Performance	-1 to $+1$%
Socioeconomic programs	-5 to $+5$%
Special situations	

Figure 4.6. National Aeronautics and Space Administration Weighted Guidelines

ways which need to be understood, these same general principles apply. Contractors are only willing to enter the government contracting market if reasonable profit levels are provided in relation to the risks involved and the alternative opportunities for utilizing resources.

In the past, the profit policies between government agencies varied considerably, and some were not designed to capitalize on the basic profit motive. OFPP issued guidence to provide greater uniformity in the government's method of establishing a profit objective and to recognize the importance of profit in contributing to efficient contract performance. Government agencies, unless exempt, are now required to use a "structured" approach in determining profit. OFPP encouraged agencies to use a weighted guidelines approach such as used by DOD.

The DOD weighted guidelines approach was initially instituted in 1963 to be used on contracts that are subject to cost analysis. The guidelines are now intended to produce different levels of profit depending on the complexity and quality of expected contract performance and the amount of contractor investment in buildings and equipment. The current weighted guidelines include profit factors for performance risk, contract type risk (including a working capital adjustment for fixed - price contracts with progress payment provisions) and facilities investment. The objective is to encourage greater contractor investment in productivity enhancing capital facilities.

NASA and the other civilian agencies use structured approaches to establishing prenegotiation profit objectives which are different than the DOD approach. The FAR supplement for each agency specifically identifies the factors and values used.

Chapter Five

Defective Pricing and Other Pricing Issues

DEFECTIVE PRICING

Background

The requirement that cost or pricing data be submitted in negotiating government contracts is not new. The first edition of ASPR in 1948 contained a requirement for such information. However, as a result of a report to Congress by GAO[1] which "alleged" overpricing by government contractors, the ASPR was revised in 1959 to require all departments to obtain a *certificate* of current pricing.

In 1961, the ASPR was further amended to include a clause which gave the government the right to reduce a contract price in the event it was later determined that the price was overstated because of defective cost or pricing data. Nevertheless, GAO issued a number of reports to Congress indicating that cost or pricing data being obtained by government procurement officials was not current, accurate, or complete in a significant number of price negotiations. GAO asserted that the government was at a disadvantage because the contractor had all of the historical and forecast data but was not disclosing it. As a result, it was alleged that many contracts were still overpriced.

Congressional concern led to the enactment in 1962 of Public Law 87-653, known as the Truth in Negotiations Act.[2] ASPR was revised to include a new certificate and defective pricing data clause. Notwithstanding the statutory requirements of Public Law 87-653, GAO was still sharply critical, alleging DOD was not adequately implementing the law, contracting officers were not obtaining the required cost or pricing data, and overpricing was still rampant. In February 1966, GAO reported that overpricing was discovered through its postaward audits, and performing defective pricing reviews represented the best way to detect the submission of defective data. As a result, a clause was developed to obtain a right of audit, after contract award, to determine the accuracy, completeness, and currency of the cost or pricing data which formed the basis of the contractor's proposal.[3] The FPR was subsequently amended to make these requirements applicable to all government agencies. The requirements are now incorporated into the FAR.

Regulatory Implementation

Under Public Law 87-653, cost or pricing data used to support a proposal must be submitted for any negotiated contract or subcontract in excess of $100,000, except where the price is based upon adequate price competition, established catalog or market prices of commercial items, prices set by law or regulation, or when the contract is exempted by the secretary of the department. Public Law 97-86 raised the threshold for requiring cost or pricing data from $100,000 to $500,000 in 1981 but the threshold reverted back to $100,000 with the enactment of the Competition in Contracting Act effective April 1, 1985. The contractor must also sign a certificate that the data are accurate, current, and complete as of the date of agreement on price. A clause included in the negotiated contract or subcontract provides for a downward price adjustment if the negotiated price was increased because of submission of incomplete, inaccurate, or noncurrent cost or pricing data. An additional price reduction clause is included in both sealed bid contracts and negotiated contracts over $100,000 which becomes operative with respect to contract modifications in excess of $100,000.

Prime contractors who are required to submit certified cost or pricing data must also obtain cost or pricing data from prospective subcontractors in support of each subcontract estimate over $100,000. The prime contractor must submit the subcontractor's cost or pricing data to the government when the amount included in the prime contractor's submission is: (1) $1 million more, (2) both more than ten % of the prime contractor's proposed price and more than $100,000, or (3) whenever the contracting officer considers it necessary for proper pricing of the prime contract. The prime contractor is responsible for the submission of subcontractor cost or pricing data that is accurate, complete, and current as of the effective date of the certificate. The prime contractor's price will be decreased to the extent that the price was increased by reason of the defective subcontractor data.

Defective pricing also applies to modifications of negotiated and advertised contracts, contract termination actions, final pricing actions under price redeterminable contracts, final overhead rate settlement under cost type contracts, and price adjustments under Cost Accounting Standards where any of these actions exceed $100,000. Forward pricing rate agreements require the submission of current, accurate, and complete cost or pricing data. However, the negotiation of forward pricing rate agreements does not require that the contractor sign a certificate that the data is current, accurate, or complete at the time the rates are agreed upon. The certificate ultimately signed in connection with the negotiation of each contract pricing proposal will cover the data submitted in connection with the negotiation of the rates. As a result, it is important to update any data submitted in support of forward pricing rate agreements to the date of subsequent contract negotiations.

The $100,000 limitation applicable to a contract modification is not the net contract modification cost figure but is based on additive and deductive costs aggregating $100,000 or more. For example, the requirement applies to a $40,000 modification resulting from a reduction of $200,000 and an increase of $240,000. It could also apply to a modification where there is a "no cost" impact, such as when the modification results from an increase of $600,000 offset by a decrease of $600,000.

The $100,000 threshold is contained in the law. However, the procurement regulations, while indicating that it should not be requested unless necessary, do provide that certified cost or pricing data may be requested for procurements between $25,000 and $100,000.

Exemptions

Public Law 87-653 provides that the requirements of the subsection added by the Truth in Negotiations Act need not be applied where the price negotiated is based on adequate competition, established catalog or market prices of commercial items sold in substantial quantities to the general public, prices set by law or regulation, or in exceptional cases, where the head of the agency determines that the requirements of this subsection may be waived and states in writing the reasons for such determination. The statutory language "...need not be applied..." provides the contracting officer some discretion in requesting cost or pricing data. FAR 15.804-3(a) however, is more restrictive in stating "...the contracting officer shall not require submission or certification of cost or pricing data..." when one of the exemptions is determined to apply.

Adequate Price Competition

FAR 15.804-3 provides that prices based on adequate price competition exempt offerors from the requirements for submission and certification of cost or pricing data. It states that the term "adequate price competition" shall be construed in accordance with the following general guidelines.

Price competition will be assumed to exist (1) if offers are solicited; (2) at least two responsible offerors who can satisfy the purchaser's (e.g., the government's) requirements submit priced offers responsive to the express requirements of the solicitation; and (3) the offerors independently compete for a contract to be awarded to the responsive and responsible offeror submitting the lowest evaluated price.

Whether there is price competition for a given procurement is a matter for the contracting officer's judgment based on an evaluation of whether each of the above conditions are satisfied. If the above three conditions are met, price competition may be presumed to be adequate unless the contracting officer finds that:

The solicitation was made under conditions which unreasonably denied to one or more known and qualified offerors an opportunity to compete.

The low competitor has such a determinative advantage over the other competitors that it is practically immune to the stimulus of competition in proposing a price—for example, where substantial costs, such as start-up or other nonrecurring expenses, have already been absorbed in connection with previous sales, which would place a particular competitor in a preferential position.

The lowest final price is not reasonable and a contracting officer supports such a finding by an enumeration of the facts upon which it is based, provided that such finding is approved at a level above the contracting officer.

A price is assumed to be based on adequate price competition if it results directly from such competition or if price analysis (not cost analysis) shows clearly that the price is reasonable in comparison with current or recent prices of the same or substantially the same items procured in comparable quantities under contracts awarded as a result of adequate competition.

If a company concludes that the item qualifies for an exemption on the basis that it is competitively priced and refuses to furnish cost or pricing data, but the contracting officer disagrees with the conclusion, FAR 15.804-6 requires the contracting officer to make every attempt to secure such data. If the company persists in its refusal to provide necessary data, the contracting officer will withhold making the award or price adjustment and refer the procurement action to higher echelons of the department.

When requested to furnish cost or pricing data, companies should normally do so, unless the procurement clearly qualifies for an exemption under the regulation from the outset. The company does not have to certify that the data are current, accurate, and complete until after agreement is reached on the contract price, if at all. During the intervening period between the submission of the data and the agreement on final price, the company could present its arguments as to why the item is exempt from the requirements of the law.

Under the *Libby Welding Company, Inc.*[4] decision, the board concluded that if the submitted price was based upon adequate price competition, the contracting officer was prohibited from requesting cost or pricing data, let alone requiring certification of its accuracy, completeness, and currency. This situation was also addressed in *Sperry Flight Systems—Division of Sperry Rand Corporation,*[5] in which the ASBCA, while addressing a separate point, stated:

> That the ASPR authors know how unequivocally to forbid contracting officers from requesting cost or pricing data is shown by the admonition that: 'Where there is adequate price competition, cost or pricing data shall not be requested regardless of the dollar amount involved.'

If it is not established at the outset that the price is based upon adequate competition, the contracting officer may request that cost or pricing data be submitted. In the event of a subsequent determination that the award is based on adequate price competition, however, the contracting officer is precluded from requiring certification of such data.

Established Catalog or Market Price

The regulations also provide that cost or pricing data should not be requested when it has been determined that the proposed prices are, or are based on, "established catalog or market prices of commercial items sold in substantial quantities to the general public." An item developed for government end use only is not covered by this exemption. This is true even though there may be an established catalog or market price and substantial competition exists for the particular item. In these cases, the contractor must rely on the "adequate price competition" exception to preclude the application of the cost and pricing data requirements.

An "established catalog price" is a price included in a catalog, price list, schedule, or other form that (1) is regularly maintained by the manufacturer or vendor, (2) is either published or otherwise available for inspection by customers, and (3) states prices at which sales are currently made to a significant number of buyers, constituting the general public.

An "established market price" is a current price established in the usual and ordinary course of trade between buyers and sellers free to bargain, which can be substantiated from sources independent of the manufacturer or vendor.

A "commerical item" is an item which includes both supplies and services of a class or kind that (1) is regularly used for other than government purposes and (2) is sold or traded to the general public in the course of conducting normal business operations.

Commercial items are "sold in substantial quantities" when the facts or circumstances support a reasonable conclusion that the quantities regularly sold are sufficient to constitute a real commercial market for the supplies or services. Although "substantial quantity" cannot be precisely defined, sales to the general public would normally be regarded as substantial if they meet the criteria specified in FAR 15.804-3(f)(2). This provision establishes three categories of sales: category A—sales to the U.S. Government or to contractors for U.S. Government use, category B—sales to the general public at catalog prices, and category C—sales to the general public at other than catalog prices. Sales to the public will be considered to be substantial when all of the following criteria are met: categories B and C sales are not negligible in themselves and total 55% or more of the total categories A, B, and C sales, and category B sales total 75% or more of the total of categories B and C sales. If categories B and C sales total less than 35% of the total of categories A, B, and C sales, or category B sales are less than 55% of the total of categories B and C sales, the contracting officer should rarely grant an exemption. When percentages fall between those stated above, the contracting officer should make an analysis before granting an exemption.

The claim for an exemption based upon catalog or market prices does not preclude the government from requesting cost or pricing data. Even though the commerciality test has been met, the contracting officer can require cost or pricing data after determining in writing that the price is unreasonable and obtaining approval of such determination from the CO's Superior. In the *Sperry Flight Systems*[6] decision, the ASBCA said of the government's right to request cost or pricing data: "the determination as to whether to accept the catalog price or to undertake negotiations enlightened by cost data from appellant was within the discretion of the ACO, pursuant with his fundamental duty to secure a fair and reasonable price for the supplies. . . . The statute clearly states only that the contracting officer 'need not' secure certified cost or pricing data where the price is based on established catalog prices, et, not that he cannot or should not." The decision addressed the regulatory application of the statute's provisions by stating: "The regulatory guidelines also fall short of unequivocally forbidding a contracting officer from demanding cost data for catalog-priced items. Rather, they stress the necessity for the contracting officer's 'judgment and analysis on a case-by-case basis' (ASPR 3-807.1(b)(2) . . ."[7] (Note: the general concepts of the section cited by the ASBCA above are now located within FAR 15.804-3(c)(8)).

Exemptions from the requirement to submit certified cost or pricing data are claimed on Standard Form 1412 (Fig. 5.1).

Cost or Pricing Data

Definition

If one of the exemptions is not met, the critical question becomes: what is the definition of "cost or pricing data"? FAR 15.801 defines it as follows:

> "Cost or pricing data" means all facts as of the time of price agreement that prudent buyers and sellers would reasonably expect to affect price negotiations significantly. Cost or pricing data are factual, not judgmental, and are therefore verifiable. While they do not indicate the accuracy of the prospective contractor's judgment about estimated future costs or projections, they do include the data forming the basis for that judgment. Cost or pricing data are more than historical accounting data; they are all the facts that can be reasonably expected to contribute to the soundness of estimates of future costs and to the validity of determinations of costs already incurred. They also include such factors as (a) vendor quotations; (b) nonrecurring costs; (c) information on changes in production methods and in production or purchasing volume; (d) data supporting projections of business prospects and objectives

CLAIM FOR EXEMPTION FROM SUBMISSION OF CERTIFIED COST OR PRICING DATA

FORM APPROVED OMB NO.
3090-0116

1. OFFEROR (Name, address, ZIP Code)	3. SOLICITATION NO.
	4. ITEM OF SUPPLIES AND/OR SERVICES TO BE FURNISHED

2. DIVISION(S) AND LOCATION(S) WHERE WORK IS TO BE PERFORMED	5. QUANTITY	6. TOTAL AMOUNT PROPOSED FOR ITEM $

By submission of this form the offeror claims exemption from requirements for submitting certified cost or pricing data on the basis that the price offered is based on an established catalog or market price of a commercial item sold in substantial quantities to the general public or is a price set by law or regulation (see FAR 15.804-3). Complete Section I, II, or III below as applicable.

SECTION I – CATALOG PRICE (See Instructions for items 7 thru 11 on reverse.)

7. CATALOG IDENTIFICATION AND DATE	8. SALES PERIOD COVERED	
	FROM	TO

9. CATEGORIES OF SALES	TOTAL UNITS SOLD *	10. REMARKS
a. U.S. Government sales		
b. Sales at catalog price to general public		
c. Other sales to general public		

*If your accounting system does not provide precise information, insert your best estimate and explain the basis for it in Item 10, REMARKS. Continue on a separate sheet, if necessary.

11. LIST THREE SALES OF THE ITEM OFFERED

SALES CATEGORY	DATE	NO. OF UNITS SOLD	PRICE/UNIT
a. ☐ B ☐ C			$
b. ☐ B ☐ C			$
c. ☐ B ☐ C			$

SECTION II – MARKET PRICE (See Instructions for item 12 on reverse.)

12. SET FORTH THE SOURCE AND DATE OR PERIOD OF THE MARKET QUOTATION OR OTHER BASE FOR MARKET PRICE, THE BASE AMOUNT, AND APPLICABLE DISCOUNTS.

SECTION III – LAW OR REGULATION (See Instructions for item 13 on reverse.)

13. IDENTIFY THE LAW OR REGULATION ESTABLISHING THE PRICE OFFERED

REPRESENTATION (See Instructions for item 14 on reverse.)

The offeror represents that all statements made above and on attachments submitted are accurate and are submitted for the purpose of claiming exemption from requirements for submitting certified cost or pricing data. The offeror also represents that, except as stated in an attachment, a like claim for exemption involving the same or a substantially similar item has not been denied by a Government Contracting Officer within the last 2 years. Pending consideration of the proposal supported by this submission and, if this proposal or a modification of it is accepted by the Government, until the expiration of 3 years from the date of final payment under a contract resulting from this proposal, the Contracting Officer or any other authorized employee of the United States Government is granted access to books, records, documents, and other supporting data that will permit verification of the claim.

14. TYPED NAME, TITLE, AND FIRM	15. SIGNATURE	16. DATE OF SUBMISSION

NSN 7540-01-142-9846
1412-101

STANDARD FORM 1412 (10-83)
Prescribed by GSA
FAR (48 CFR) 53.215-2(b)

Figure 5.1. Claim for exemption from submission of certified cost or pricing data, Standard Form 1412.

Item 7. Attach a copy of the catalog, or the appropriate pages covering price and published discounts, or a statement that the catalog is on file in the buying office to which this proposal is being made. Catalog price, is a price that is included in a catalog, price list, schedule, or other form that is regularly maintained by the manufacturer or vendor, is either published or otherwise available for inspection by customers, and states prices at which sales are currently, or were last, made to a significant number of buyers constituting the general public. To justify a catalog price exemption for the Government item, the catalog item must be identical or must be so similar in material and design that any price difference or its absence can be evaluated solely by price analysis (see FAR 15.805-2). In the latter case, a statement must be attached identifying the specific differences and explaining, by price analysis of the differences, how the proposed price is derived from the catalog price.

Item 8. This period should include the most recent regular monthly, quarterly, or other period for which sales data are reasonably available and should extend back only far enough to provide a total period representative of average sales. You may also attach sales data for a prior representative period if for any reason recent sales are abnormal and the prior period is sufficiently recent (not more than 2 years preceding) to support the proposed price for the Government item. In the latter case, you must explain, by price analysis only, how the proposed price is derived from the catalog sales for the prior period.

Item 9. (a) Include in Category A all sales of the catalog item (a) directly to the U.S. Government and its instrumentalities and (b) for U.S. Government use (sales directly to U.S. Government prime contractors, or their subcontractors or suppliers at any tier, for use as an end item, or as part of an end item, by the U.S. Government).

(b) Include in Category B all sales of the catalog item made strictly at the catalog price, less only published discounts, to the general public (i.e., catalog price sales other than those (i) to affiliates of the offeror or (ii) included in Category A (Instruction 9(a)).

(c) Include in Category C all sales to the general public that were not made strictly at the catalog price or that were made at special discounts or discount rates not published in the catalog.

Item 11. On line a. insert information on the lowest price at which Category B or C sales of the offered item was made during the period, regardless of quantity.

On lines b. and c. insert sales information in the following manner.

a. Give the lowest price Category C sales of comparable quantities. If there were no sales of comparable quantities, then give

b. The lowest price Category C sales of quantities most nearly the quantity being offered. If there were no sales of Category C, then give

c. The lowest price Category B sales of comparable quantities. If there were no sales of comparable quantities, then give

d. The lowest price Category B sales of quantities most nearly the quantity being offered.

Attach a complete explanation (i) if you, during the period covered, offered special discounts not included in the catalog, or (ii) if the price proposed is not the lowest price at which a sale was made to any customer during that period for like items and comparable quantities.

Item 12. Market price is a current price, established in the usual and ordinary course of trade between buyers and sellers free to bargain, that can be substantiated from sources independent of the manufacturer or vendor. There must be a sufficient number of commercial buyers so that their purchases establish an ascertainable current market price for the item or service. The nature of this market should be described. To justify a market-price exemption, the item or service being purchased must be identical to the commercial item or service or must be so similar in material and design (for supplies) or in work and facilities (for services) that any price difference or its absence can be evaluated solely by price analysis (see FAR 15.805-2). In the latter case, a statement must be attached identifying the specific differences and explaining, by price analysis of the differences, how the proposed price is derived from the market price.

Item 13. Identify the law or regulation establishing the price offered. If the price is controlled under law by periodic rulings, reviews or similar actions of a governmental body, attach a copy of the controlling document, unless it was previously submitted to the contracting office.

Item 14. Insert the name, title, and firm of the person authorized by the offeror to sign this form.

Figure 5.1. (Continued)

and related operations costs; (e) unit-cost trends such as those associated with labor efficiency; (f) make-or-buy decisions; (g) estimated resources to attain business goals; and (h) information on management decisions that could have a significant bearing on costs.

In *FMC Corporation*[8] the ASBCA adopted the then substantially similar version of ASPR "as a reasonable definition of 'cost or pricing data' in the context of the clauses relating to price reduction for defective pricing in the subject contract."

The regulations make an important distinction between fact and judgment. FAR 15.804-4(b) provides:

> The certificate does not constitute a representation as to the accuracy of the contractor's judgment on the estimate of future costs or projections. It does apply to the data upon which the judgment or estimate was based. This distinction between fact and judgment should be clearly understood.

Attempts by the regulations and the courts to clarify the meaning of data and distinguish fact from judgment have not been wholly successful. Disputes have continued to arise over these terms. In an attempt to alleviate some of the vagueness concerning the definition of cost or pricing data, the 1987 DOD Authorization Act Conference Report included the following:

> The conferees were very concerned with clarifying the definition of cost or pricing data that a contractor is not required to provide and certify to data relating to judgments, business strategies, plans for the future on estimates. A contractor is required, on the other hand to disclose any information relating to execution or implementation of any such strategies or plans. For example, a corporate decision to attempt to negotiate a new labor wage rate structure with its employee union, although verifiable, is not cost or pricing data for purposes of this section. If the company has made an offer to the union, the fact that an offer has been made, and the details and status of the offer, on the other hand, is information that should be conveyed to the government.[9]

Subsequent legislative proposals have attempted to delete this language from the legislative history.

Essentially, most information relating to past or current experience is considered cost or pricing data. With respect to forecasts and projections, the situation is less clear. The factual data on which projections are made are cost or pricing data, but the projections themselves are generally not. Based on the 1987 DOD Authorization Act Conference Report language, information that is under consideration does not presently qualify as data until it is put into some kind of action plan.

In *Lockheed Aircraft Corporation, Lockheed Georgia Company Division*,[10] the ASBCA pointed out that pricing data may encompass information far beyond historical information and may include many other future factors which have a bearing on cost. This was illustrated soon after the *Lockheed* decision was rendered. In *Cutler-Hammer, Inc.*[11] the contractor had issued a request for quote to five vendors and received only one bid, this from the only company which had produced the particular item in the past. The proposed price compared favorably with Cutler-Hammer's own independent study and was included in the price proposal submitted to the government. Between that date and the date the prime contractor signed the certificate of current cost or pricing data, it received an unsolicited proposal from another company for a much lower price. It thereupon requested technical data which was finally received just two days before Cutler-Hammer signed the certificate. Although it appears that the prime's technical people were examining this technical data, the Cutler-Hammer official signing the certificate had no knowledge of the developments and the bid was not disclosed to the government.

After the prime contract was awarded, Cutler-Hammer continued negotiations and discussions with the new vendor, issued a purchase order for a limited quantity and, as the product proved satisfactory, issued additional purchase orders. The government asserted Cutler-Hammer should have disclosed the information and its failure to do so constituted a basis for price reduction because of defective data. Although the ASBCA conceded that the lower vendor bid was far from representing data on which a firm price reduction could have been made by the government, it nevertheless found that the information constituted cost or pricing data and should have been disclosed to the government. As to what the government might have done had this information been disclosed, the board conjectured that it might have excluded the item from the contract price, reserving it for further negotiation.

The ASBCA later tempered this decision in *Sparton Corporation (Sparton Electronics Division)*,[12] wherein it stated:

> In the definition of cost and pricing data which was set out in FMC Corporation, supra, it is stated that vendor's quotations are considered to be cost and pricing data which should be disclosed, but this is qualified by the caveat that such data should "reasonably be expected to have a significant bearing on costs under the proposed contract." In our opinion, unless specifically asked to do so under the contract clause in this case, a prospective contractor is not required to list each and every quote received from prospective vendors whose responsibility had not previously been evaluated and where the quote concerns a part deemed to be critical. . . . In our opinion, under the facts stated, the Government does not prove its case unless it shows that the contractor, at the time the data is submitted, did not intend to deal with the vendor listed, but did intend to do business with the lower cost vendor.

Since that time the ASBCA has issued decisions that reflected a characterization of pricing data between the above positions. As an example, in *Aerojet-General Corporation*,[13] the ASBCA ruled the contractor was liable for defective pricing because it did not submit or disclose a non-responsive vendor quotation. The ASBCA reasoned that:

> a non-responsive quotation may not always be so meaningless or unreliable that no prudent buyers and sellers would reasonably expect the quotation to have a significant effect on the price negotiations. Under certain conditions the quotation can have a significant impact on the negotiation and thus would become cost or pricing data which must be disclosed to the government.

In Grumman Aerospace Corporation,[14] the board ruled that a contractor's subcontract cost analysis report constituted cost or pricing data that was required to be disclosed. In its decision the Board concluded:

> Appellant contends that the narrative analysis contained in the report does not constitute "facts" required to be disclosed and that the bottom line itself is meaningless if the government is provided with the numbers required to perform the arithmetic to reach that bottom line. Appellant errs . . . given the nature of a Cost Analysis Report as established by the record, the narrative analysis adds meaning to the raw figures and can not be said to lack factual content simply because it contains elements of judgment. We therefore conclude that the nature of a Cost Analysis Report, including both its narrative analysis and statistical data, is such as to constitute "facts" to be disclosed as cost and pricing data.

The question has arisen as to the meaning of the term "significant" in the phrase "which prudent buyers and sellers would reasonably expect to have a significant effect on the price negotiations." The Court of Claims upheld a previous ASBCA decision, involving *Sylvania Electric Products, Inc.*[15] The AS-BCA ruled that the contractor submitted defective cost or pricing data and that the government was entitled to a price reduction. The company argued that the "significance" of each item must be viewed individually. If this were to be adopted, the court stated, the Truth in Negotiations Act would be easily circumvented. The term "significant" relates to effect on negotiation and not to amount.

In *American Bosch Arma Corporation,*[16] the Board stated that in the context of the regulation:

> Pricing data is significant if it would have any significant effect for its intended purpose, which was as an aid in negotiating a fair and reasonable price. How much it takes to be significant cannot be determined as a percentage of the total price.

Submission

Another area to be addressed in defective pricing is what data must be submitted. The contractor is expected to disclose existing verifiable data, judgmental factors used to project from known data to the estimate, and contingencies included in the proposed price. In short, the contractor's estimating process itself needs to be disclosed. The company would not be held liable if the judgment is erroneous. Nevertheless, the fact that judgment is used is a "fact" which must be disclosed to the contracting officer. Any doubt as to whether data should be submitted should be resolved in favor of submitting it. Merely making data available is not sufficient.

In *M-R-S Manufacturing Company v. United States*[17] the Court of Claims ruled that a company must either physically deliver all accurate, complete, and current pricing information relevant to negotiations, or make its significance known to the government. If a contractor does neither, it has not fulfilled its duty under the Truth in Negotiations Act. The contractor's primary argument before the Court of Claims in the case above was that it actually met its duty to submit accurate, complete, and current cost or pricing data. The facts upon which the contractor relied were that the auditor who performed the initial price evaluation: (1) received a bill of materials including all parts and parts numbers, (2) knew previous production runs had been completed, and (3) knew how to obtain all the information in the contractor's files. Since the files included all the data available to the contractor, the obligation to submit current, accurate, and complete data was fulfilled, according to the contractor. The court concluded, however, that if the contractor possesses information that is relevant to negotiations with the government, and neither physically delivers the data to the government nor makes the government aware of the information's significance to the negotiation process, "then he has not fulfilled his duty under the Act to furnish such information to the government."

The contractor in this case did not physically deliver to the government many of the production cards which showed production runs that were more current and less expensive, at least for direct labor, than the runs for which production runs were delivered. The contractor also failed to make any government agent aware of files containing production cards evidencing runs that were more current and less expensive than those runs for which the government was given information. For these reasons, and because the information was relevant to the negotiations, the Court ruled that the contractor did not fulfill its duty to submit required information to the government. The Court opined that the fact that the government chose to utilize an auditor who knew other production runs had been completed and knew how to use the contractor's files did not alter the nature of the contractor's duty. If the presence of an auditor lessened the extent of a contractor's duty to submit accurate, complete and current information, then a danger would exist, according to the Court, that a contractor could submit excessively high proposals, making voluminous incorrect data available to the auditor, and then hope that the auditor would be unable to extract the significant and correct information. The possibility of such a practice "should be eliminated as it would be contrary to the purpose of the Truth in Negotiations Act," the Court concluded.

Numerous decisions along this line of reasoning established the precedent that ultimately was incorporated in the DAR and later the FAR:[17]

> There is a clear distinction between submitting cost or pricing data and merely making available books, records and other documents without identification. The requirement for submission of cost or pricing data is met when all accurate cost or pricing data reasonably available to the offeror have been submitted either actually or by specific identification, to the contracting officer or an authorized representative.

The extent to which the Board has gone in this direction is illustrated in *The Singer Company, Librascope Division,*[18] where the contractor was declared to have failed to "submit", even though it did submit the data in question for a purpose other than the pricing proposal involved. The Board said that even physically handing over data to the government may not suffice by concluding:

> It is also necessary to advise the Government representatives involved in the proposed procurement of the kind and content of the cost or pricing data and their bearing on the prospective contractor's proposal which examination of the files would disclose.

While these rulings would appear to place a substantial obligation on the contractor to specifically identify each significant item affecting price negotiations, the ASBCA has ruled that there are reasonable limits. Hardie-Tynes Manufacturing Company[19] had submitted a proposal which reflected a quotation from vendor B although the lowest quote was from vendor C. The latter was not used because of the contractor's substantial doubts as to C's ability to make the parts. The government alleged that the lack of disclosure of C's quote represented defective pricing. The DCAA auditor who had initially reviewed the pricing proposal testified that he couldn't recall whether he had seen C's quotation but said he would have noted it if he had. The contractor testified C's quote was in a separate folder which was furnished to the preaward auditor. The Board ruled that C's quote was in the folder furnished to the auditor and that the contractor "adequately submitted that quotation to the auditor." The ASBCA further noted:

> The (C) quote was not "hidden in a mass of information" but was in a folder containing only two other quotes and three replies indicating "no quote."
> The absence of a notation on the pre-award auditor's work sheets as to why the (C) quote was not being used could indicate a failure of the auditor to realize that the quote was low or a failure in this instance to follow the prescribed policy of making such notations. In any event, the absence of a notation is not conclusive evidence of a nondisclosure.
> Under these particular circumstances, we do not believe appellant was obligated to "lead the auditor by the hand" by pointing out to him that (C) quote was low but was not being used for the reasons indicated.

Timing

The next question to be addressed is that of the currency of data. As previously discussed, cost or pricing data are defined as "all facts as of the time of price agreement. . . ." FAR 15.804-4(c) defines the time when cost or pricing data are reasonably available to the contractor, as follows:

> Closing or cutoff dates should be included as part of the data submitted with the proposal. Certain data may not be reasonably available before normal periodic closing dates (e.g., actual indirect costs). Before agreement on price, the contractor shall update all data as of the latest dates for which information is reasonably available.

However, this applies only to relatively insignificant items. The same provision (FAR 15.804-4(c)) further states that significant matters are specifically exempted from the cut-off agreement. It provides:

> Data within the contractor's or a subcontractor's organization on matters significant to contractor management and to the Government will be treated as reasonably available. What is significant depends upon the circumstances of each acquisition.

The importance of the phrase "contractor's organization" cannot be overemphasized. FAR 15.804-4(b) emphasizes that the responsibility of the contractor is not limited by the personal knowledge of the contractor's negotiator if the contractor had information reasonably available at the time of agreement, showing that the negotiated price is not based on accurate, complete, and current data. The government's interpretation of this footnote is that the signer of the certificate represents the belief and knowledge of the company as a whole as to the accuracy and completeness of the data which is being certified. This requirement for absolute knowledge on the part of the contractor's representative signing the certificate is lessened somewhat by the provisions concerning the time when cost or pricing data are reasonably available to the contractor with reference to such items as overhead expenses. However, significant matters are considered to be known to the contractor up to the time of agreement on price and are considered to be "reasonably available as of that date."

In *American Bosch Arma*[20] it was established that the cut-off date as to the point in time where cost or pricing data is reasonably available is related to the contractor's system of recordkeeping. In this instance, the ASBCA concluded that it took the contractor two weeks to a month to properly process information into its records. This amount of time and the amount of time it would have taken the contractor to extract the information from the records for negotiation purposes was used by the ASBCA to determine when the data was "reasonably available."

However, in a later decision (subsequently affirmed by the Court of Claims)[21], the ASBCA ruled that the contractor's obligations are not reduced by a lack of administrative effort or the subjective lack of knowledge on the part of the negotiating team. In its decision, the ASBCA stated:

> here the entire evidence shows that the gathering of current pricing data by the negotiation team at Mountain View was left to the initiative of its members, essentially its cost estimator, without any procedures within Sylvania other than the useless commitment run to help them assemble this information. Their duty to take the initiative and collect current pricing data on their own was clearly not fulfilled by deciding that none of the items here involved were important enough to require checking. As this Board said in Aerojet General Corporation., ASBCA No. 12264, 69-1 BCA Paragraph 7664, at p. 35,583:

'Appellant's obligation to furnish accurate, complete and current cost and pricing data to the extent that the data are significant and reasonably available cannot be reduced either by the lack of administrative effort to see that all significant data are gathered and furnished the Government, or by the subjective lack of knowledge of such data on the part of appellant's negotiators or the person who signed the certificate.'

Certification

The effect of a contractor's failure to certify that the data submitted is current, accurate, and complete has changed through case law. In *American Bosch Arma*,[22] the ASBCA ruled "the applicability of the Price Reduction Clause does not depend on the existence of a valid and meaningful Certificate of Current Cost or Pricing Data." The ASBCA reiterated this position in *Lockheed Aircraft Corporation*[27] when it *stated:* "The Certificate and the clause [price reduction] are not interdependent but are independent and each stands on its own" (parenthetical note added). The ASBCA later apparently reversed its position. It ruled in *Libby Welding Company, Inc.,*[24] by concluding that in the absence of a certificate of current cost or pricing data, the contractor is not liable under the "price reduction for defective cost or pricing data" clause in its contract. The Board again reversed its position in *S.T. Research Corporation*[25] by ruling that failure to certify cost data did not preclude the government from asserting a defective pricing claim. The Board's conclusion was based on the fact that the defective pricing clause required certification or cost or pricing data and the statute itself prohibited the submission of defective data.

The ambiguities raised by these conflicting decisions have been resolved once and for all by amendments to the statute included in the 1987 DOD Authorization Act[26] which states: "It is not a defense to an adjustment of the price of a contract . . . that . . . the prime contractor or subcontractor did not submit a certification of cost or pricing data relating to the contract . . ."

When a certificate of current cost or pricing data is required, the contracting officer must obtain an executed certificate in the specified form and include it in the contract file. Figure 5.2 is the certificate required by FAR 15.804-4. In the certificate of current cost or pricing data, the contractor certifies that the cost data are accurate, complete, and current as of the date when the price negotiation was completed and the contract price was agreed to. However, the certificate makes provision for a delay in the date of execution of the certificate as distinguished from the date of agreement. The intervening period should be utilized to verify that the data submitted were in fact current, accurate, and complete. A delay of a week or two is normally considered reasonable for this purpose.

When a contract, for which cost or pricing data was required, is executed it will contain a "price reduction for defective cost or pricing data" clause. This clause gives the government a contractual right to a price adjustment for inaccurate, incomplete, or noncurrent cost or pricing data from either the prime or a prospective or actual subcontractor. The text of the clause from FAR 52.215-22 follows:

Price Reduction for Defective Cost or Pricing Data (Apr. 1984)

(a) If any price, including profit or fee, negotiated in connection with this contract or any cost reimbursable under this contract was increased by any significant amount because:

(1) The contractor or a subcontractor furnished cost or pricing data that were not complete, accurate, and current as certified in its certificate of current cost or pricing data,

This is to certify that, to the best of my knowledge and belief, the cost or pricing data (as defined in section 15.801 of the Federal Acquisition Regulation (FAR) and required under FAR subsection 15.804-2) submitted, either actually or by specific identification in writing to the Contracting Officer or to the contracting officer's representative in support of _____* are accurate, complete, and current as of _____**

This certification includes the cost or pricing data supporting any advance agreements and forward pricing rate agreements between the offeror and the Government that are part of the proposal.

Firm _____

Name _____

Title _____

Date of Execution _____***

(End of Certificate)

*Identify the proposal, quotation, request for price adjustment, or other submission involved, giving the appropriate identifying number (e.g., RFP No. _____).

**Insert the date, month, and year when price negotiations were concluded and price agreement was reached.

***Insert the date, month, and year of signing, which should be as close as practicable to the date when the price negotiations were concluded and the contract price was agreed to.

Figure 5.2. Certificate for current cost or pricing data.

(2) A subcontractor or prospective subcontractor furnished the contractor cost or pricing data that were not complete, accurate, and current as certified in the contractor's certificate of current cost or pricing data, or

(3) Any of these parties furnished data of any description that were not accurate, the price or cost shall be reduced accordingly and the contract shall be modified to reflect the reduction.

(b) Any reduction in the contract price under paragraph (a) above due to defective data from a prospective subcontractor that was not subsequently awarded the subcontract shall be limited to the amount, plus applicable overhead and profit markup, by which (1) the actual subcontract, or (2) actual cost to the contractor, if there were no subcontract, was less than the prospective subcontract cost estimate submitted by the contractor, *provided* the actual subcontract price was not itself affected by defective cost or pricing data.

Contract Price Adjustments

In the past, questions have arisen as to the amount of the reduction that should be effected if defective data had been submitted. Assume that a cost estimate for $100 had been submitted and the price was established at $90 by negotiated agreement. Further assume it was subsequently determined that defective data, in the amount of $10, had been submitted. The guidance previously provided to government personnel by DAR 3-807.10 stated:

> In the absence of evidence to the contrary, the natural and probable consequence of defective data is an increase in the contract price in the amount of the defect plus related burden and profit or fee; therefore, unless there is a clear indication that the defective data were not used, or were not relied upon, the contract price should be reduced in that amount. In establishing that the defective data caused an increase in the contract price, the contracting officer is not expected to reconstruct the negotiation by speculating as to what would have been the mental attitude of the negotiating parties if the correct data has been submitted at the time of agreement on price.

This provision was based upon the following approach developed and stated by the ASBCA in *American Bosch Arma:*[27]

> In the absence of any more specific evidence tending to show what effect the nondisclosure of the pricing data had on the negotiated target cost, we are of the opinion that we should adopt the natural and probable consequence of the nondisclosure as representing its effect.

However, in *Levison Steel Company,*[28] the board ruled that the government must show a cause-effect relationship between the defective data and any resulting increase in negotiated contract price before it can enforce a reduction in that price.

This was further addressed in *American Machine and Foundry Company,*[29] wherein the Board did not agree with the government's estimate of the amount to be refunded by the contractor, noting that the government is not automatically entitled to a pure reduction once an overstatement has been established:

> That it was not the intent of Congress in enacting the measure so severely to punish contractors, particularly in cases of inadvertent withholding of pricing data pertaining to a component part which had little or no effect upon the final agreed price of the end item, is manifested by (1) the fact that the statute does not so expressly provide, as it readily could have, (2) by the failure of the legislative history of the measure to so indicate, and (3) by the very wordage of the Act itself.

The Board further pointed out that the statute does not expressly provide for an automatic price reduction measured by the amount of any overstatement of the cost of a component part of the end item, plus a percentage that the government chose to use for G&A and profit. Nor can it reasonably be said, according to the Board, that the act does so by necessary implication:[30]

> Rather, the remedy clearly envisioned by the statute where an overstatement in the cost of a component part has been established is an adjustment in the contract price of the end item 'to exclude any significant sums by which it may be determined . . . that the price was increased because the contractor or any subcontractor . . . furnished cost or pricing data which . . . was inaccurate, incomplete, or noncurrent.' In other words, the statute, rather than requiring an automatic price reduction in the end item equal to the amount of the dollar and cent overstatement of a component part, plus G&A and profit, as advocated by the Government, requires that first . . . there exists a causal connection between any inaccurate, incomplete, or noncurrent data with respect to a component part, on the one hand, and any increase of the contract price of the end item, on the other hand.

Interestingly, the doctrine of natural and probable cause previously contained in DAR 3-807.10 was deleted from the FAR. It has been incorporated, however, into the DOD FAR Supplement.

Reliance

Related to this point is the question of government reliance on the defective data submitted. If the defective data were not relied upon, then the logical conclusion appears to be that they did not have an effect on the ultimate price negotiated. In *Universal Restoration, Inc.*[31] the ASBCA stated that the burden of proof is upon the contractor to establish that the defective data were not relied upon. The Board stated:

> once nondisclosure has been established, it would be the natural and probable consequence that an overstated contract price resulted. The burden of persuasion is with

the appellant to establish nonreliance on the part of the Government on the inaccurate data in order to rebut the natural and probable consequences of the nondisclosure. . . . The ultimate burden of showing the causal connection between the inaccurate data and an overstated contract price, however, remains with the Government.

The concept of nonreliance as a defense against defective pricing allegations was incorporated into Public Law 87-653 by amendments in the 1987 DOD Authorization Act. At the same time the Act included circumstances when nonreliance by the Government on the defective data could not be used as a defense by companies. Specifically, the Act states:[32]

(3) It is not a defense to an adjustment of the price of a contract under a contract provision required by paragraph (1) that—
(A) the price of the contact would not have been modified even if accurate, complete and current cost or pricing data had been submitted by the contractor or subcontractor because the contractor or subcontractor—
(i) was the sole source of the property or services procured; or
(ii) otherwise was in a superior bargaining position with respect to the property or services procured;
(B) the contracting officer should have known that the cost and pricing data in issue were defective even though the contractor or subcontractor took no affirmative action to bring the character of the data to the attention of the contracting officer,
(C) the contract was based on an agreement between the contractor and the United States about the total cost of the contract and there was no agreement about the cost of each item procured under such contract; or
(D) the prime contractor or subcontractor did not submit a certification of cost and pricing data relating to the contract as required under subsection (a)(2).

These words appear to change the previously established court precedence in such decisions as *Luzon Stevedoring Corporation*[33] and *Universal Restorations, Inc.*[34] In *Luzon Stevedoring Corporation*, the ASBCA ruled that the government was not entitled to a reduction in contract price even though defective cost or pricing data may have been submitted because the contractor's strong bargaining position effectively nullified the government's use of cost or pricing data as a negotiation tool. The Court of Appeals for the Federal Circuit came to a similar decision when it concluded that Universal Restorations, Inc. would not have accepted an overhead rate lower than 115% since it was the only qualified company available to do the work. Requiring companies to prove nonreliance by the government was the only criteria used by the courts. Now, the additional restraints against sole-source contractors (or those that are otherwise in a superior bargaining position) must be considered by the government and the courts.

FAR 15.804-7(d), which requires the contracting officer to make a record of the price negotiation, provides in part:

The contracting officer shall prepare a memorandum indicating (1) the contracting officer determination as to whether or not the submitted data were accurate, complete, and current as of the certified date and whether or not the government relied on the data, and (2) the results of any contractual action taken.

The absence of a statement in the record of price negotiation that the data were not used in establishing the price would likely be asserted by the government as constituting evidence that the data were relied upon. Any agreement to the contrary should be noted in the company's memorandum of negotiations.

Offsets

What if the defective data were such that they tended to reduce the cost to the government? Unfortunately, there is nothing that the company can do to obtain an increase in the contract price. However, these data may be used to offset other defective data which tended to increase the price to the government.

In *Cutler-Hammer, Inc. v. United States*,[35] the court held that the defective pricing clause allowed the setting off of understatements against overstatements to the extent of the overstatements. In *Lockheed Aircraft Corp., Lockheed-Georgia Company Division v. the United States*,[36] the Court elaborated on its reasoning in *Cutler-Hammer*:

> The reason we allowed offsets to the extent of overstatements in Cutler-Hammer, was that including both understatements and overstatements in a price proposal, negated any attempt on the part of the contractor at creating "artificial savings." This allows them to cancel each other out, at least to the extent of the overstatements, and means that only savings which were brought about through "demonstrated performance of the work" would be available as added profit.
> The allowance of offsets does not give the contractor a windfall, nor does it penalize the government. In both the Cutler-Hammer situation and the one which prevails here, allowing offsets according to our formula merely allows the setting of the negotiated price in an amount which reflects the true cost. If overstatements exceed understatements, the government is still allowed to reduce the contract price by the amount of the excess. No raising of the price is allowed, however.

Amendments to Public Law 87-653 contained in the 1987 DOD Authorization Act specifically addressed the question of offsets. For the first time, offsets were recognized in the statute and conditions were established for the government recognizing an offset. The two conditions are:

> (i) the contractor certifies to the contracting officer (or to a designated representative to be contracting officer) that to the best of the contractor's knowledge and belief, the contractor is entitled to the offset, and
> (ii) the contractor proves that the cost or pricing data were available before the date of agreement on the price of the contract (or price of the modification) and that the data were not submitted . . . before such date.[37]

Restrictions concerning when offsets could be used were also included in the 1987 Authorization Act as follows:

A contractor shall not be allowed to offset an amount otherwise authorized to be offset . . . if—

> (i) the certification . . . with respect to the cost or pricing data involved was known to be false when signed, or
> (ii) the United States proves that, had the cost or pricing data referred to in subparagraph (A) (ii) been submitted to the United States before the date of the agreement on the price of the contract (or price of the modification), the submission of such cost or pricing data would not have resulted in an increase in that price in the amount to be offset.[38]

These conditions would eliminate claiming an offset for intentional under-statements of cost because the data is known before agreement on price. In a previous court decision Rogerson Aircraft[39] was permitted to use an intentional understatement as an offset. The above language appears to make the *Rogerson* decision invalid in the future.

Further, insight into the wording regarding false certification can be found in the legislative history wording as follows:

> The Senate recedes to the House with an amendment that would prohibit an offset, if the contractor intentionally withheld from the government information that would indicate a higher cost for an item or service and thus certified that the cost or pricing data it submitted was accurate, complete and current when, in fact, the contractor knew it to be false.

Clearly, the intent was that companies must disclose all data related to the proposal under negotiation. This does not mean that a company cannot judgmentally reduce its bid, but rather the anticipated true cost must first be disclosed. At that point the disclosure obligation is met and pricing decisions can then be made.

Use if Cost or Pricing Data

Although the defective pricing clause and the requirements of the law are such that current, accurate, and complete data must be submitted, there is no specific requirement that they be used to determine the negotiated price. In *Dworshak Dam Constructors*,[40] the Army Corps of Engineers Appeals Board stated:

> This approach erroneously assumes that the Truth in Negotiations Act dictates that contract prices must be based on the submitted cost or pricing data. The Act does not prescribe that the government adopt a contractor's actual cost in pricing situations. Further, the Act operates in the price area only after certification provisions have not been properly observed and the price to the government inflated thereby.

MOST FAVORED CUSTOMER PROVISIONS

Most Favored Customer (MFC) provisions have been included in a variety of contracting situations for years and have caused little concern. However, due to media sensationalism over the high price of spare parts and seemingly common household items such as hammers, wrenches, and coffee makers, the government is insisting on MFC treatment in more and more negotiated contracts that are not subject to full and open competition. Today the government is not accepting the reasonableness of catalog or market prices the contractor has to offer in certain situations.

The MFC provision may be a "price certification," a "price warrant," or simply a requirement that information on prices charged to other customers is disclosed. The MFC provisions should only appear in solicitations or contracts for negotiated procurements or procurements that are not subject to full and open competition. The provisions in the various contracts are subject to interpretation and compliance issues. As a general rule the contractor must demonstrate that the government received the lowest price, for similar terms and conditions, given other customers.

Noncompliance with an MFC provision could have serious consequences. If the requirements of the contract clauses are not met and the data are not accurate, complete and current, the government may be entitled to a reduction in contract price. This is similar to but distinct from the defective pricing clause. Of greater concern are the statutory remedies for fraud or misrepresentation and civil penalties for false statements and claims. Other administrative avenues could also be pursued by the government such as debarment and suspension from contracting.

Statutory Requirements

The Defense Procurement Reform Act of 1984 amended Section 2323 of the Armed Services Procurement Act to provide, with some exceptions, that defense contracts:

> entered into using other than competitive procedures . . . for the purchase of items that are offered for sale to the public may not result in a price to the United States that exceeds the lowest price at which such items are sold by the contractor to the public.

A similar but less comprehensive provision, included in the 1984 Small Business and Federal Competition Enhancement Act, also amended Section 303F of the Federal Property and Administrative Services Act. This statute differed from its defense counterpart in that it applied to a narrower range of items—components of subassemblies of a major system or spares/replenishment items.

Considerable controversy arose as a result of the passage of these statutes. Of particular concern was the broad applicability of the defense statute to all items of supply. As a result, the 1987 Defense Authorization Act further amended Section 2323 of the Armed Services Procurement Act to clarify that the provision applies only to spare or repair parts rather than all items of supply. This Act also limits the types of sales that are considered in determining the contractor's lowest commercial price.

FAR Policy and Application of MFC Provisions

To implement the most favored customer provisions of the two 1984 statutes, FAR 15.813 was promulgated in July 1985 as an interim regulation to require submission of a commercial pricing certificate on: any contract not awarded on the basis of full and open competition, any contract modification, or any orders under a basic ordering agreement. However, because of the controversy over the regulatory implementation, the DAR Council approved a deviation to FAR 15.813 on July 30, 1986 that permits contracting officers to use other means for complying with the statute. On November 18, 1986 the DAR Council issued another DAR deviation directing contracting activities to comply with the requirements of the 1987 statute. The guidance did not contain a standard solicitation provision, contract clause, or certificate.

The FAR provisions will undoubtedly be formally revised to reflect the more liberal requirements of the 1987 Act. Once the regulations are finalized, stricter enforcement of these MFC provisions can be expected through audits of price certification data.

GSA Multiple Award Schedule MCS Provisions

The Multiple Award Schedules (MAS) program used by the General Services Administration (GSA) and at times by the Veterans Administration for certain products (such as medicine and drugs) are the best known applications of the MFC concept. They were in existence many years before recent MFC legislation was passed.

In the MAS program, the agency negotiates and enters into indefinite quantity contracts at stated prices for given periods of time. These contracts result in the compilation of a Federal Supply Schedule or Multiple Award Schedule, which is a series of "catalogs" published by contractors.

Federal agencies order directly from the schedule contractors. The government's objective is to obtain an MFC discount and to avoid repetitive negotiations for standard commercial items such as typewriters, computers, copy machines, and office supplies. GSA is entitled to receive an MFC discount if the terms and conditions of the GSA contract are similar or better than the commercial sales for the same products and services. In a 1982 statement on MAS contracting, GSA stated that it is the government's goal "to obtain a discount from a firm's established catalog or commercial price which is equal to or greater than the discount given to that firm's most favored customer."
GSA's Cost or Pricing Data Requirements include:

Providing data on discounts offered to other customers on products offered to the government.

Explaining if terms and conditions differ.

Identifying factors that make the government prices different from those for other customers.

Placing a value on those factors and identifying the valuation method used.

In addition to requiring disclosure of current, complete, and accurate discount information prior to the contract award, the contract price reduction clause also requires disclosure of discounts offered to customers during performance of the MAS contract. Any change in the contractor's most favored customer pricing arrangement which disturbs the relationship between the GSA contract and the most favored commercial customer, constitutes a basis for a price reduction on the MAS contract.

Other Contractual Arrangements with MFC Provisions

The MFC provision is found in Blanket Purchase Agreements (BPA), Interorganizational Transfers, Time and Material Contracts, and Facilities Contracts. There are also individual agency requirements (policy statements and directives) and unilateral actions by contracting officers which may result in a contract with an MFC provision. These contracts and contractual arrangements are discussed briefly to give an awareness of the potential that exists for postaward adjustments if data used to negotiate such contracts were not accurate, complete and factual.

Blanket Purchase Agreements (BPAs)

BPAs are described under FAR Subpart 13.2, concerning purchases that do not exceed $25,000. However, FAR 8.406 permits use of BPAs with schedule contractors to reduce the number of orders and billing and payment documents required for repetitive orders. FAR Part 39, Automatic Data Processing and Telecommunications Contracts, also has provisions for use of BPAs.

The MFC provision found in FAR 13.203-1(j) states:

> BPAs shall contain . . . a statement that the prices to the government shall be as low or lower than those charged the supplier's most favored customer for comparable quantities under similar terms and conditions, in addition to any discounts for prompt payment.

Time and Material (T&M) Contracts

Under the optional method of pricing material addressed in FAR 16.601 (b)(3), the contractor may charge for material on a basis other than cost if:

> (iv) The contract provides (a) that the price to be paid for such material shall be based on an established catalog . . . and (b) that in no event shall the price exceed the contractor's sales prices to its most favored customer for the same item in like quantity, or the current market price, whichever is lower.

Facilities Contracts

If facilities constituting the contractor's usual commercial products (or only minor modifications thereof) are acquired by the Government under the contract, FAR 31.106-3 provides that the government shall not pay any amount in excess of the contractor's most favored customer price or the price of other suppliers for like quantities of the same of substantially the same items, whichever is lower.

Issues of Interpretation

The contractor has the burden of showing that under the MFC provisions, the government received the lowest price charged to the most favored customer under similar terms and conditions. However, there is little guidance from the courts or agencies on the meaning of these criteria.

Trackability of prices may present a problem. Recordkeeping would entail keeping prices on every product sold to every customer. Offerings of special discounts and promotions make recordkeeping even more complex. A demonstration that terms and conditions are different is required if the government is charged a higher price than the special discount or promotional sale.

Although the government is an end user, MFC provisions may give the government the lowest price charged to distributors. Even if it is an established industry practice to give discounts to distributors, the government may still insist on the lowest price. Price differences may be attributed to services provided by distributors. The controversy in the Federal Supply Schedule Program over prices charged to distributors and original equipment manufacturers (OEMs) is indicative of problems that can arise with all MFC provisions. In January 1986 a proposed revision to the 1980 GSA MAS Policy Statement defined an MFC discount as equal to the best discount given to any entity with which the firm conducts business including distributors and OEMs. The 1987 Defense Authorization Act generally excludes distributor sales from the determination of the lowest commercial price.

Terms and conditions of sale could vary greatly from one customer to another. The MFC provisions generally contain some limitation that the price provided the government be no higher than the price charged to other customers "for like quantities" or under similar terms and conditions. Consideration should be given to volume discounts, warranty terms, transportation costs, exclusive purchase agreements, and delivery.

To avoid problems and prepare for the increased use of MFC provisions in federal procurement in the future, contractors should:

Carefully review MFC provisions placed in their contracts.

Establish systems to track sales along with terms and conditions of sales.

Establish clear policies and procedures throughout the organization.

Ensure that all personnel are trained to know the MFC provisions, company procedures for compliance, and penalties for noncompliance.

Monitor policy, procedures, and systems for compliance.

SPARES PRICING

The attention devoted to the pricing of spare parts has increased geometrically in recent years. As a result, a DOD Policy Memorandum was issued in November 1985[41] requiring contracting officers to solicit voluntary refunds for spare parts that are concluded to have been overpriced.

In 1986 the Navy went one-step further by including in the Navy Acquisition Regulations Supplement (NARSUP) a mandatory refund requirement that can be imposed up to two years after date of delivery for the difference between the item's negotiated price and the intrinsic value at the date of agreement on price. The contract clause included in the NARSUP defines intrinsic value as follows:

(1) If the item is one which is sold, or is substantially similar or functionally equivalent to one that is sold in substantial quantities to the general public, intrinsic value is the established catalog or market price, plus the value of any unique requirements, including delivery terms, inspection, packaging, or labeling.

(2) If there is no comparable item sold in substantial quantities to the general public, intrinsic value is defined as the price an individual would expect to pay for the item based upon an economic quantity as defined in FAR 52.207-4, plus the value of any unique inspection, packaging, or labeling.[42]

The key to avoiding demands for refunds under this Navy provision is prenegotiation disclosure that the proposed price exceeds the item's intrinsic value since the contract clause provides that:

(g) The contractor shall not be liable for a refund if the contractor advised the contracting officer in a timely manner that the price it would propose for a spare part or item of support equipment exceeded its intrinsic value, and with such advice, specified the estimated proposed price, the estimated intrinsic value, and known alternative sources or items, if any, that can meet the requirement.[43]

This clause has major ramifications for companies who provide spare parts to the Navy since they need to develop a systems capability to calculate the intrinsic value of spare parts for comparison to prices quoted to the Navy customer.

SUMMARY

The implications of a government allegation of defective pricing are serious. The consequences can be onerous, not only on profitability for a specific contract but for operations for a given period.

Because the Truth in Negotiations Act pertains to the adequacy of data submitted for the purpose of negotiations, profitability—or lack thereof—on a specific contract may not be relevant to the potential impact of a defective pricing situation. If a $1 million fixed-price contract resulted in a $100,000 loss because of faulty judgments, and if defective data would have resulted in a further reduction of the negotiated contract price to $900,000, the government will seek and, if correct, obtain a further price reduction of $100,000. The net result for the company would be a $200,000 loss on that contract.

Additionally, the law does not make any provision for inadvertent failure to submit current, accurate, or complete data. Therefore, any company that does not have a formally designed and implemented system of estimating and proposal preparation greatly increases the risk of financial harm resulting from failure to comply with Public Law 87-653. Because of the nature of defective pricing and contract price adjustments demanded, and the continued sensitivity of the GAO, the Department of Justice and Inspector Generals, government contract auditors are continually reviewing contract proposals and performance cost data to determine that the proposals were in fact based on current, complete, and accurate data.

Exposure to downward price adjustments can also result from other pricing requirements such as disclosure of most favored customer price and intrinsic value of spare parts. Compliance with these provisions requires maintenance of pricing data to assure that required information is readily available for submission to the government customer.

NOTES

1. GAO Report B-132942, May 29, 1959.
2. P.L. 87-673, Truth in Negotiations Act, September 10, 1962. Amendment to 10 U.S.C. 2306 by adding subsection (f).
3. P.L. 90-512, September 25, 1968, amended 10 U.S.C. 2306(f) by adding paragraph (3), which states: "For the purpose of evaluating the accuracy, completeness, and currency of cost or pricing data required to be submitted by this subsection, any authorized representative of the head of the agency who is an employee of the United States Government shall have the right, until the expiration of three years after final payment under the contract or subcontract, to examine all books, records, documents, and other data of the contractor or subcontractor related to the negotiation, pricing, or performance of the contract or subcontract."
4. Libby Welding Company, Inc., ASBCA no. 15084, December 21, 1972, 73-1 BCA 9,859. (See also Lockheed Shipbuilding and Construction Company, ASBCA no. 16494, June 29, 1973, 73-2 BCA 10, 157.)
5. Sperry Flight Systems — Division of Sperry Rand Corporation, ASBCA no. 17375, May 13, 1974, 74-1 BCA 10,648.
6. Ibid.
7. Ibid.
8. FMC Corporation, ASBCA nos. 10095 and 11113, March 31, 1966, 66-1 BCA 5,483.
9. 1987 Defense Authorization Act Requirements Relating to Defense Contractors Legislative Provisions adopted, Truth in Negotiations Act Amendments (sec 952).
10. Lockheed Aircraft Corporation, Lockheed Georgia Company Division, ASBCA no. 10453, May 18, 1967, 67-1 BCA 6,356.
11. Cutler-Hammer, Inc., ASBCA no. 10900, June 28, 1967, 67-2 BCA 6,432.

12. Sparton Corporation (Sparton Electronics Division), ASBCA no. 11363, August 25, 1967, 67-2 BCA 6,539.
13. Aerojet-General Corporation, ASBCA no. 12873, March 20, 1969, 69-1 BCA 7,585.
14. Grumman Aerospace Corporation, ASBCA no. 27476, May 29, 1986, 86-3 BCA 19091.
15. Sylvania Electric Products, Inc., ASBCA no. 13622, July 14, 1970, 70-2 BCA 8,387; 202 Ct. Cl. 16, June 20, 1973, 18 CCF 82,334.
16. American Bosch Arma, ASBCA no. 10305, December 17, 1965, 65-2 BCA 5,280.
17. M-R-S Manufacturing Company v. United States, ASBCA no. 14825, March 31, 1971, 7-1 BCA 8,821; 203 Ct. Cl. 551, February 20, 1974, 19 CCF 82,862.
20. FAR 15.804-6(b), Note 3 to Table 15-3.
18. The Singer Company Librascope Division, ASBCA no. 17604, July 8, 1975, 75-2 BCA 11401.
19. Hardie-Tynes Manufacturing Company, ASBCA no. 20717, September 23, 1976, 76-2 BCA 12,121.
20. American Bosch Arma, supra note 16.
21. Sylvania Electric Products, Inc., supra note 15.
22. American Bosch Arma Corporation, supra note 16.
23. Lockheed Aircraft Corporation, Lockheed Georgia Company Division, supra note 10.
24. Libby Welding Company, supra note 4.
25. ST Research Corporation, ASBCA no. 29070, August 1, 1984, 84-3 BCA 17568.
26. 1987 Defense Authorization Act, sec. 952 Truth-in-Negotiations Act Amendments, paragraph (d)(3).
27. American Bosch Arma, supra note 16.
28. Levison Steel Company, ASBCA no. 16520, May 1, 1973, 73-2 BCA 10,116.
29. American Machine and Foundry Company, ASBCA no. 15037, December 13, 1973, 74-1 BCA 10,409.
30. Ibid.
31. Universal Restoration, Inc. ASBCA no. 22833, April 9, 1982, 82-1 BCA 15,762. Overturned on reconsideration, 83-1 BCA 16,265; Ct. Cl. no. 77-84C, July 19, 1985.
32. 1987 Defense Authorization Act, supra note 26.
33. Luzon Stevedoring Corporation, ASBCA no. 14851, February 24, 1971, 71-1 BCA 8,745.
34. Universal Restorations, Inc., v. United States, CAFC no. 85-2662, August 22, 1986.
35. Cutler-Hammer, Inc. v. United States, 189 Ct. Cl. 76, October 17, 1969, 14 CCF 83,124.
36. Lockheed Aircraft Corporation, Lockheed Georgia Company Division, 202 Ct. Cl. 787, October 16, 1970, 15 CCF 84,105 (See also October 17, 1973, 19 CCF 82, 856).
37. 1987 Defense Authorizations Act, supra note 26, paragraph (d) (4) (A).
38. Ibid., paragraph (d)(4)(B).
39. Rogerson Aircraft Controls, ASBCA No. 27954, October 15, 1984, 85-1 BCA 17, 725; CA-FC 85-2058, March 6, 1986, 33 CCF 74,262.
40. Dworshak Dam Constructors, ENG BCA no. 3198, December 16, 1971, 72-1 BCA 9,187.
41. Memorandum for Secretaries of the Military Departments, Director, Defense Logistics Afency, Subject: Refund Guidance for Spare Parts and Support Equipment, November 1, 1985.
42. Navy Acquisition Requlations Supplement, 5252.242-9000 (b) (2).
43. Ibid.

Chapter Six
Control Systems

BACKGROUND

In today's complex Federal acquisition environment, companies must be able to do more than provide accurate accounting information in order to meet the expectations of Congress and the government acquisition community. Increasing scrutiny by Congress has resulted in several "horror" stories which showed that a good accounting system, while very important, does not, in itself, prevent potential problems.

As part of the response to the Congressional inquiries, a Blue Ribbon Commission on Defense Management (also known as the Packard Commission) was established to study how companies and the Department of Defense could improve the acquisition process. One of the key recommendations in the Commission's June 1986 report was that companies should establish adequate control systems to provide reasonable assurance of compliance with government regulations. In part the Commission concluded:

> Today, defense contractors should be aware that a concerned and responsible government will aggressively enforce compliance. Contractors will be required to do much more than they have done in the past to comply with contractual, regulatory, and statutory standards and to provide adequate supervision and instruction for employees. To do so will necessitate their putting in place broad and effective systems of internal control. The effectiveness of such systems depends on a host of factors, including:
> good organizational structure, providing for proper delegation of authority and differentiation of responsibilities;
> clear policies and procedures, well adapted to business objectives and to specific tasks and functions;
> training of and communication with employees at all performance levels; and
> ongoing arrangements to monitor compliance with, and to evaluate the continuing efficacy of, internal control.[1]

Each of the above concepts is essential to an effective program of self governance and will be addressed later in the context of an overall control system.

However, as a prelude to that discussion the requirements of an accounting system as it relates to government contracting will first be addressed.

BASIC GOVERNMENT REQUIREMENTS

A contractor performing under a cost reimbursement contract has a clear need to maintain a cost system that is responsive to government cost accounting regulations in that the recording of actual transactions as reflected by the accounting system directly affects the amount paid. A company performing under a negotiated fixed-price contract has a similar need, although usually subject to less auditor oversight.

Most negotiated government contracts contain a clause similar to the one contained in FAR 52.215-2 which provides that:

> The contractor shall maintain . . . books, records, documents, and other evidence and accounting procedures and practices, sufficient to reflect properly all costs claimed to have been incurred or anticipated to be incurred in performing this contract.

The regulations do not specify that the contractor maintain any specific type of accounting system. Rather, FAR 31.201-1 states "any generally accepted method of determining or estimating costs that is equitable and is consistently applied may be used. . . ."

The obvious necessity is to capture and accumulate costs by contract so as to segregate costs that should be apportioned to government contracts from those that properly accrue to commercial business and other customers. To do this, certain costs that can be identified specifically with a given contract are treated as direct costs and charged in that manner. Most typically, direct costs are for material, subcontracts, and labor, but are by no means limited to these. Indirect costs, or costs that benefit more than one contract, must be pooled and allocated to contracts on some equitable basis.

FAR 31.201-4 requires that for a cost to be charged to a contract, it must be assigned "on a basis of the relative benefits received or other equitable relationship." In addition, to be assigned to a government contract, a cost must meet one of the following three conditions:

1. It must be incurred specifically for the contract.
2. It must benefit both the contract and other work and be distributed in reasonable proportion to the benefits received.
3. It is necessary to the overall operation of the business, although a direct relationship to any particular contract cannot be shown.

FAR 31.203 (b) is less restrictive than cost accounting standards (CAS) in its requirements for establishing indirect cost pools:

> Indirect costs shall be accumulated by logical cost groupings with due consideration of the reasons for incurring such costs. Each grouping should be determined so as to permit the distribution of the grouping on the basis of the benefits accruing to the several cost objectives. Commonly, manufacturing overhead, selling expenses, and general and administrative (G&A) expenses are separately grouped. Similarly, the particular case may require subdivision of these groupings, e.g., building occupancy

costs might be separable from those of personnel administration within the manufacturing overhead group . . . .When substantially the same results can be achieved through less precise methods, the number and composition of cost groupings should be governed by practical considerations and should not unduly complicate the allocation.

FAR 31.203 (b) and (c) similarly provide a good degree of flexibility in determining what allocation base to use to distribute costs from the indirect cost pools to contracts:

This necessitates selecting a distribution base common to all cost objectives to which the grouping is to be allocated. The base should be selected so as to permit allocation of the grouping on the basis of the benefits accruing to the several cost objectives . . . .Once an appropriate base for the distribution of indirect costs has been accepted, it shall not be fragmented by the removal of individual elements. All items properly includable in an indirect cost base should bear a pro-rata share of indirect costs irrespective of their acceptance as Government contract costs. For example, when a cost input base is used for the distribution of general and administrative (G&A) costs, all items that would properly be part of the cost input base, whether allowable or unallowable, shall be included in the base and bear their pro-rata share of G&A costs.

Indirect costs present the greatest challenge to those uninitiated in government contracting in that the government, through the acquisition regulations and particularly through CAS, has promulgated specific rules dealing with the allocability of indirect costs. In spite of these rules, there is still considerable flexibility in the number and types of pools that can be selected and the methods of allocation. An example of an allocation system for indirect costs is illustrated in Figure 6.1 for the following indirect pools and allocation bases:

Pool	Allocation Base
Use and occupancy expense	Square footage
Computer service center	Predetermed rate per CPU hour
Manufacturing overhead	Direct labor dollars for manufacturing personnel
Engineering overhead	Direct labor dollars for engineering personnel
Independent research and development/bid and proposal expense	Total cost input (direct cost plus manufacturing and engineering overhead)
General and administrative expense	Total cost input

Whatever method has been selected for classifying costs as direct and pooling and allocating indirect costs, a key requirement for satisfying government auditors is the existence of adequate audit trails. An accounting system provides satisfactory audit trails if: (1) every transaction is traceable from its origin to its final posting in the books of account, including the ledger summarizing costs by contract; (2) every posting to accounts, including the ledger summarizing contract costs, is susceptible to breakdown into identifiable transactions; and (3) adequate documentation (e.g., time cards, vendors' invoices) is available and accessible to support the accuracy and validity of individual transactions.

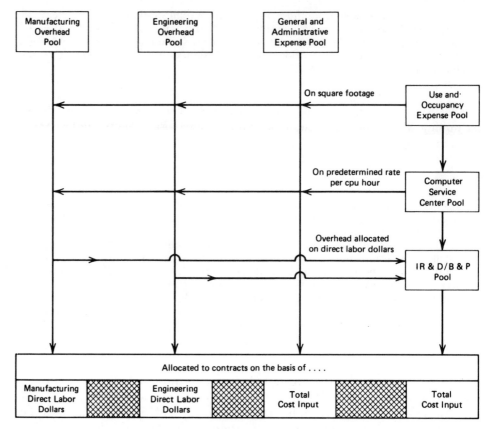

Figure 6.1. Indirect cost allocation system.

Allocation of indirect costs in a highly automated environment presents an even greater challenge since typical overhead allocation bases, such as direct labor, may represent only a minor component of total factory costs. In the factory-of-the-future environment, the need for multiple cost pools, allocated over nonlabor bases, such as machine usage, may be required.

IMPACT OF CAS ON COST ACCOUNTING SYSTEMS

Cost accounting standards have had considerable impact on the accounting systems of government contractors. Many of the standards have been incorporated into the acquisition regulations to make them apply even to the contractors not subject to CAS. Accordingly, CAS has generally affected all who contract with the government. The principal thrust of the Cost Accounting Standards Board (CASB) was to achieve greater consistency and uniformity in accounting practices.

Greater consistency has been achieved in several ways. The contract clause incorporated in government contracts concerning CAS requires those meeting the threshold (basically, $10 million in negotiated defense prime and subcontracts) to set forth in a disclosure statement their cost accounting practices. Moreover, the clause further requires the contractor to follow consistently these disclosed practices. If a contractor wants to change an accounting practice, the government requires an analysis of the change's impact on the contract costs and, in most cases, negotiates a downward adjustment of the contract price if the change would result in increased cost to the government. The process of preparing an impact statement and negotiating with the government on these accounting practice changes has proved to be tortuous for most contractors. The effect of the "cost accounting standards" clause and the disclosure statement have thus been to inhibit changes in accounting practices. Accordingly, those designing systems must realize that cost accounting practices must be selected quite carefully.

The CASB has also obtained greater consistency in accounting practice by promulgation of the first two standards, CAS 401, Consistency in Estimating, Accumulating and Reporting Costs, and CAS 402, Consistency in Allocating Costs Incurred for the Same Purpose.

Another objective of the CASB was to narrow the cost accounting alternatives available and achieve greater uniformity in the practices followed by government contractors. Options have been eliminated in some instances and narrowed in others to achieve this goal. The attempt at achieving greater uniformity has had a definite impact on accounting systems.

The CASB, while it existed, aggregated and published some of the data contained in the disclosure statements filed with it. This aggregated data provides excellent insight into the accounting practices of a wide variety of companies. This information is particularly helpful to the designer of an accounting system. Because the last year for which the CASB published this data was 1979, the impact of CAS 418 and 420 is not reflected. Nevertheless, the information highlights the decisions of the major U.S. corporations to charge direct versus indirect and the selection of allocation bases for overhead, G&A, or service centers. Consequently, the tables representing these aggregated disclosure statement responses have been included as Figures 6.2 to 6.6 as indicated below:

Table 10.   Methods of Treating Specified Functions, Elements of Cost, and Transactions
Table 11.   Allocation Bases for Overhead Pools
Table 12.   Allocation Bases for G&A Pools
Table 13.   Allocation Bases for Service Centers
Table 14.   Methods of Allocating Service Center Costs to Government Contracts and Use of Pre-determined Billing Rates

MANAGEMENT INFORMATION SYSTEMS

Basic information supplied by a government contractor's accounting system is the data necessary to bill customers. Contractors need job cost ledgers that collect costs for each contract. These ledgers can be designed in a variety of ways to permit efficient accumulation of costs for billing purposes. In practice, these records vary considerably based upon the company's need for information and the complexity of the contract terms it encounters. But there is much more to a well designed management information system than a ledger summarizing contract costs.

To successfully engage in long term contracting, it is essential that management receive the information necessary to plan and control its business. The planning phase begins when a contract proposal is made. In that process, contracts are broken down into meaningful work packages with performance responsibility assigned. Budgets of costs are prepared along with a schedule containing milestones when key phases of the contract are expected to be

10. METHODS OF TREATING SPECIFIED FUNCTIONS, ELEMENTS OF COST AND TRANSACTIONS
As of September 30, 1979

Function, Element of Cost, or Transaction		Method of Treatment for Applicable Units					Not Applicable*
		Total	Always Direct	Always Indirect	Sometimes Direct Sometimes Indirect	Others	
A. Function Applicable to Direct Materials:							
Cash Discounts	—Number	1,003	401	472	51	79	74
	—Percent	100.0%	40.0	47.1	5.0	7.9	6.9
Freight In	—Number	1,020	522	299	181	18	57
	—Percent	100.0%	51.2	29.3	17.8	1.7	5.3
Sale of Scrap	—Number	861	157	483	134	87	216
	—Percent	100.0%	18.2	56.1	15.6	10.1	20.1
Sale of Salvage	—Number	770	153	390	142	85	307
	—Percent	100.0%	19.9	50.7	18.4	11.0	28.5
Incoming Material Inspection	—Number	926	325	427	147	27	151
	—Percent	100.0%	35.1	46.1	15.9	2.9	14.0
Inventory Adjustments	—Number	738	253	285	61	139	339
	—Percent	100.0%	34.3	38.6	8.3	18.8	31.5
Purchasing	—Number	1,001	75	814	79	33	76
	—Percent	100.0%	7.5	81.3	7.9	3.3	7.1
Trade Discounts, Refunds, and Allowances on Purchases	—Number	951	711	80	110	50	126
	—Percent	100.0%	74.8	8.4	11.6	5.2	11.7
B. Function Applicable to Direct Labor:							
Health Insurance	—Number	1,050	121	849	35	45	27
	—Percent	100.0%	11.5	80.9	3.3	4.3	2.5
Holiday Differential	—Number	1,005	382	527	64	32	72
	—Percent	100.0%	38.0	52.4	6.4	3.2	6.7
Overtime Premium Pay	—Number	1,048	445	452	120	31	29
	—Percent	100.0%	42.5	43.1	11.4	3.0	2.7
Pension Costs	—Number	977	111	789	36	41	100
	—Percent	100.0%	11.4	80.8	3.6	4.2	9.3
Shift Premium Pay	—Number	959	530	348	65	16	118
	—Percent	100.0%	55.3	36.3	6.8	1.6	11.0
Training	—Number	985	180	543	238	24	92
	—Percent	100.0%	18.3	55.1	24.2	2.4	8.5
Travel	—Number	1,031	423	213	370	25	46
	—Percent	100.0%	41.0	20.7	35.9	2.4	4.3
Vacation Pay	—Number	1,051	144	800	50	57	26
	—Percent	100.0%	13.7	76.1	4.8	5.4	2.4

*Each percentage in this column is based on the total of 1,077 units in the universe.

(Continued on next page)

Figure 6.2. Direct vs. indirect costs, D/S items 3.2.1-3.2.3, methods of treating specified functions, elements of cost, and transactions as of September 30, 1979.

10. Continued

Function, Element of Cost, or Transaction		Method of Treatment for Applicable Units					
		Total	Always Direct	Always Indirect	Sometimes Direct Sometimes Indirect	Others	Not Applicable*
C. Miscellaneous							
Design Engineering	—Number	934	555	125	241	13	143
	—Percent	100.0%	59.4	13.4	25.8	1.4	13.3
Drafting	—Number	943	535	127	269	12	134
	—Percent	100.0%	56.7	13.5	28.5	1.3	12.4
Computer Operations	—Number	832	81	366	338	47	245
	—Percent	100.0%	9.7	44.0	40.6	5.7	22.8
Contract Administration	—Number	965	89	752	109	15	112
	—Percent	100.0%	9.2	77.9	11.3	1.6	10.4
Freight Out	—Number	827	445	204	98	80	250
	—Percent	100.0%	53.8	24.7	11.9	9.6	23.2
Line Inspection	—Number	849	633	125	80	11	228
	—Percent	100.0%	74.6	14.7	9.4	1.3	21.2
Packaging and Preservation	—Number	870	401	161	270	38	207
	—Percent	100.0%	46.1	18.5	31.0	4.4	19.2
Preproduction and Start Up Costs	—Number	788	529	111	93	55	289
	—Percent	100.0%	67.1	14.1	11.8	7.0	26.8
Production Shop Supervision	—Number	825	162	544	109	10	252
	—Percent	100.0%	19.6	66.0	13.2	1.2	23.4
Consultant Services	—Number	1,019	145	224	629	21	58
	—Percent	100.0%	14.2	22.0	61.7	2.1	5.4
Purchased Direct Labor (On Site)	—Number	888	766	10	62	50	189
	—Percent	100.0%	86.3	1.1	7.0	5.6	17.6
Purchased Direct Labor (Off Site)	—Number	905	823	10	45	27	172
	—Percent	100.0%	90.9	1.1	5.0	3.0	16.0
Rearrangement Costs	—Number	939	68	621	235	15	138
	—Percent	100.0%	7.2	66.2	25.0	1.6	12.8
Rework Costs	—Number	877	670	108	64	35	200
	—Percent	100.0%	76.4	12.3	7.3	4.0	18.6
Royalties	—Number	586	258	163	108	57	491
	—Percent	100.0%	44.1	27.8	18.4	9.7	45.6
Scrap Work	—Number	745	489	177	51	28	332
	—Percent	100.0%	65.6	23.8	6.8	3.8	30.8
Special Test Equipment	—Number	859	676	32	81	70	218
	—Percent	100.0%	78.7	3.7	9.4	8.2	20.2
Special Tooling	—Number	844	672	20	82	70	233
	—Percent	100.0%	79.6	2.4	9.7	8.3	21.6
Subcontracting Costs	—Number	985	818	9	125	33	92
	—Percent	100.0%	83.1	0.9	12.7	3.3	8.5
Warranty Costs	—Number	683	377	176	37	93	394
	—Percent	100.0%	55.2	25.8	5.4	13.6	36.6

*Each percentage in this column is based on the total of 1,077 units in the universe.

Figure 6.2. (Continued)

11. ALLOCATION BASES FOR OVERHEAD POOLS
1976–1979

Type of Pool and Allocation Base	Number of Units				Percentage Distribution			
	Mar 1976	Sep 1977	Sep 1978	Sep 1979	Mar 1976	Sep 1977	Sep 1978	Sep 1979
Single Plant-wide Pool Only — Total	192	222	231	215	100.0%	100.0%	100.0%	100.0%
Direct labor dollars	138	161	166	159	71.9	72.5	71.9	74.0
Direct labor hours	22	23	30	23	11.4	10.4	13.0	10.7
Other	32	38	35	33	16.7	17.1	15.1	15.3
Manufacturing — Total	346	359	377	405	100.0%	100.0%	100.0%	100.0%
Direct labor dollars	254	263	272	289	73.4	73.3	72.1	71.4
Direct labor hours	50	53	58	63	14.5	14.8	15.4	15.6
Other	42	43	47	53	12.1	11.9	12.5	13.0
Engineering — Total	394	416	439	463	100.0%	100.0%	100.0%	100.0%
Direct labor dollars	284	302	306	329	72.0	72.6	69.7	71.1
Direct labor hours	55	59	66	70	14.0	14.2	15.0	15.1
Other	55	55	67	64	14.0	13.2	15.3	13.8
Manufacturing and Engineering — Total	78	80	86	90	100.0%	100.0%	100.0%	100.0%
Direct labor dollars	65	69	74	71	83.3	86.3	86.1	78.9
Direct labor hours	8	5	7	10	10.3	6.2	8.1	11.1
Other	5	6	5	9	6.4	7.5	5.8	10.0
Off-Site — Total	99	117	128	142	100.0%	100.0%	100.0%	100.0%
Direct labor dollars	74	88	93	99	74.7	75.2	72.7	69.7
Direct labor hours	7	8	9	12	7.1	6.8	7.0	8.5
Other	18	21	26	31	18.2	18.0	20.3	21.8
Field Service — Total	140	148	157	159	100.0%	100.0%	100.0%	100.0%
Direct labor dollars	108	118	124	123	77.2	79.7	79.0	77.4
Direct labor hours	9	8	9	9	6.4	5.4	5.7	5.6
Other	23	22	24	27	16.4	14.9	15.3	17.0
Material Handling — Total	186	198	196	204	100.0%	100.0%	100.0%	100.0%
Direct material cost	137	146	148	156	73.7	73.7	75.5	76.5
Other	49	52	48	48	26.3	26.3	24.5	23.5
Departmental/Shop — Total	77	77	80	90	100.0%	100.0%	100.0%	100.0%
Direct labor dollars	41	39	41	49	53.2	50.6	51.3	54.5
Direct labor hours	16	17	17	20	20.8	22.1	21.2	22.2
Other	20	21	22	21	26.0	27.3	27.5	23.3
Use and Occupancy — Total	73	76	76	77	100.0%	100.0%	100.0%	100.0%
Square feet	57	57	56	54	78.1	75.0	73.7	70.1
Direct labor dollars	4	8	8	8	5.5	10.5	10.5	10.4
Other	12	11	12	15	16.4	14.5	15.8	19.5
Quality Control — Total	77	77	75	77	100.0%	100.0%	100.0%	100.0%
Direct labor dollars	43	43	44	45	55.8	55.8	58.7	58.4
Direct labor hours	11	10	10	10	14.3	13.0	13.3	13.0
Other	23	24	21	22	29.9	31.2	28.0	28.6
Fringe Benefits — Total	146	160	180	181	100.0%	100.0%	100.0%	100.0%
Direct labor dollars	37	44	48	41	25.3	27.5	26.7	22.7
Direct labor hours	10	10	13	10	6.9	6.2	7.2	5.5
Payroll dollars	74	79	82	82	50.7	49.4	45.6	45.3
Other	25	27	37	48	17.1	16.9	20.5	26.5

Figure 6.3. Indirect costs, D/S item 4.1.0, allocation bases for overall pools, 1976–1979.

12. ALLOCATION BASES FOR G & A POOLS
1976–1979

Type of Pool and Allocation Base	Number of Units				Percentage Distribution			
	Mar 1976	Sep 1977	Sep 1978	Sep 1979	Mar 1976	Sep 1977	Sep 1978	Sep 1979
Single G & A Pool Only — Total	430	481	524	564	100.0%	100.0%	100.0%	100.0%
Cost input	233	266	304	349	54.2	55.3	58.0	61.9
Cost of sales	108	113	96	87	25.1	23.5	18.3	15.4
Sales	16	17	14	5	3.7	3.5	2.6	0.9
Direct labor	17	25	27	22	4.0	5.2	5.2	3.9
Processing cost (value added)	6	8	24	22	1.4	1.7	4.6	3.9
Other	50	52	59	79	11.6	10.8	11.3	14.0
G & A Pool (plus other pool(s)) — Total	237	256	271	285	100.0%	100.0%	100.0%	100.0%
Cost input	68	72	106	134	28.7	28.1	39.1	47.0
Cost of sales	70	70	62	38	29.5	27.3	22.9	13.3
Processing costs (value added)	10	13	14	13	4.2	5.1	5.2	4.6
Other	89	101	89	100	37.6	39.5	32.8	35.1
Selling and Marketing Expense — Total	92	93	90	101	100.0%	100.0%	100.0%	100.0%
Cost input	25	19	27	34	27.2	20.4	30.0	33.7
Cost of sales	28	27	23	21	30.4	29.0	25.6	20.8
Other	39	47	40	46	42.4	50.6	44.4	45.5
Corporate Home Office Expense — Total	171	173	170	170	100.0%	100.0%	100.0%	100.0%
Cost input	25	28	41	52	14.6	16.2	24.1	30.6
Cost of sales	42	41	29	24	24.0	23.7	17.1	14.1
Sales	15	14	11	14	8.8	8.1	6.4	8.2
Total cost incurred	18	16	19	14	10.5	9.2	11.2	8.2
Other	72	74	70	66	42.1	42.8	41.2	38.9
I R&D Costs — Total	133	139	131	102	100.0%	100.0%	100.0%	100.0%
Cost input	37	32	41	38	27.8	23.0	31.3	37.2
Cost of sales	39	40	35	16	29.3	28.8	26.7	15.7
Sales	9	9	6	5	6.8	6.5	4.6	4.9
Direct labor	6	4	4	*	4.5	2.9	3.0	*
Other	42	54	45	43	31.6	38.8	34.4	42.2
B & P Costs — Total	107	119	111	84	100.0%	100.0%	100.0%	100.0%
Cost input	30	32	40	40	28.0	26.9	36.0	47.6
Cost of sales	20	20	16	7	18.7	16.8	14.4	8.3
Direct labor	10	7	4	*	9.4	5.9	3.6	*
Other	47	60	51	37	43.9	50.4	46.0	44.1
No Separate G & A Pool— Combined with Overhead	48	58	66	68				

* Included in Other

Figure 6.4. Indirect costs, D/S item 4.2.0, allocation bases for G&A pools, 1976–1979.

113

13. ALLOCATION BASES FOR SERVICE CENTERS
1976–1979

Type of Service Center and Allocation Base	Number of Units				Percentage Distribution			
	Mar 1976	Sep 1977	Sep 1978	Sep 1979	Mar 1976	Sep 1977	Sep 1978	Sep 1979
Scientific Computer Operations — Total	239	263	268	257	100.0%	100.0%	100.0%	100.0%
Usage	179	196	193	181	74.9	74.5	72.0	70.4
Direct labor	15	20	22	21	6.3	7.6	8.2	8.2
Cost type	11	10	11	8	4.6	3.8	4.1	3.1
Other	34	37	42	47	14.2	14.1	15.7	18.3
Business Data Processing — Total	325	354	362	367	100.0%	100.0%	100.0%	100.0%
Usage	192	217	217	220	59.1	61.3	60.0	60.0
Direct labor	22	24	24	21	6.8	6.8	6.6	5.7
Cost type	45	46	50	43	13.8	13.0	13.8	11.7
Other	66	67	71	83	20.3	18.9	19.6	22.6
Photographic Services — Total	166	177	192	186	100.0%	100.0%	100.0%	100.0%
Usage	85	90	93	89	51.2	50.9	48.4	47.9
Direct labor	40	39	39	37	24.1	22.0	20.3	19.9
Cost type	10	15	19	18	6.0	8.5	9.9	9.6
Other	31	32	41	42	18.7	18.6	21.4	22.6
Reproduction Services — Total	286	309	327	326	100.0%	100.0%	100.0%	100.0%
Usage	143	161	168	170	50.0	52.1	51.4	52.2
Direct labor	51	46	48	46	17.8	14.9	14.6	14.1
Cost type	26	32	34	30	9.1	10.4	10.4	9.2
Head count	10	11	13	13	3.5	3.5	4.0	4.0
Other	56	59	64	67	19.6	19.1	19.6	20.5
Art Services — Total	149	162	173	163	100.0%	100.0%	100.0%	100.0%
Usage	65	65	66	62	43.6	40.2	38.2	38.0
Direct labor	38	42	44	41	25.5	25.9	25.4	25.2
Cost type	12	16	20	18	8.1	9.9	11.5	11.0
Other	34	39	43	42	22.8	24.0	24.9	25.8
Technical typing services — Total	127	140	151	145	100.0%	100.0%	100.0%	100.0%
Usage	48	49	52	50	37.8	35.0	34.4	34.5
Direct labor	40	46	49	49	31.5	32.9	32.5	33.8
Cost type	11	13	14	11	8.7	9.3	9.3	7.6
Other	28	32	36	35	22.0	22.8	23.8	24.1
Communications Services — Total	244	258	269	264	100.0%	100.0%	100.0%	100.0%
Usage	108	115	119	124	44.3	44.6	44.2	47.0
Direct labor	23	23	22	20	9.4	8.9	8.2	7.6
Cost type	25	28	28	24	10.2	10.9	10.4	9.1
Headcount	11	13	15	13	4.5	5.0	5.6	4.9
Square feet	10	10	8	4	4.1	3.9	3.0	1.5
Other	67	69	77	79	27.5	26.7	28.6	29.9

(Continued on next page)

Figure 6.5. Indirect costs, D/S item 4.3.0, allocation bases for service centers, 1976–1979.

13. ALLOCATION BASES FOR SERVICE CENTERS
1976–1979

Continued

Type of Service Center and Allocation Base	Number of Units				Percentage Distribution			
	Mar 1976	Sep 1977	Sep 1978	Sep 1979	Mar 1976	Sep 1977	Sep 1978	Sep 1979
Facilities Services — Total	354	383	400	398	100.0%	100.0%	100.0%	100.0%
Usage	63	70	76	76	17.8	18.3	19.0	19.1
Direct labor	47	47	52	49	13.3	12.3	13.0	12.3
Cost type	12	15	16	13	3.4	3.9	4.0	3.3
Square feet	148	161	156	145	41.8	42.0	39.0	36.4
Other	84	90	100	115	23.7	23.5	25.0	28.9
Auto Pool Services — Total	111	119	125	121	100.0%	100.0%	100.0%	100.0%
Usage	40	46	46	44	36.1	38.7	36.8	36.4
Direct labor	17	17	17	14	15.3	14.3	13.6	11.6
Cost type	14	16	15	11	12.6	13.4	12.0	9.0
Other	40	40	47	52	36.0	33.6	37.6	43.0
Company Aircraft Services — Total	53	55	61	54	100.0%	100.0%	100.0%	100.0%
Usage	32	32	33	31	60.4	58.2	54.1	57.4
Cost type	10	11	10	6	18.9	20.0	16.4	11.1
Other	11	12	18	17	20.7	21.8	29.5	31.5
Personnel and/or Industrial Relations — Total	128	126	115	68	100.0%	100.0%	100.0%	100.0%
Direct labor	11	9	8	6	8.6	7.1	6.9	8.8
Headcount	87	85	80	51	68.0	67.5	69.6	75.0
Other	30	32	27	11	23.4	25.4	23.5	16.2
Material Handling and/or Procurement — Total	97	95	90	61	100.0%	100.0%	100.0%	100.0%
Usage	21	21	18	13	21.7	22.4	20.0	21.3
Direct labor	19	17	15	10	19.6	17.9	16.7	16.4
Headcount	8	8	9	6	8.2	8.4	10.0	9.8
Direct material cost	9	9	8	6	9.3	9.5	8.9	9.8
Other	40	40	40	26	41.2	42.1	44.4	42.7
Accounting and/or Payroll Services — Total	81	81	73	49	100.0%	100.0%	100.0%	100.0%
Usage	13	13	9	8	16.0	16.0	12.3	16.3
Direct labor	11	11	11	7	13.6	13.6	15.1	14.3
Headcount	27	27	27	18	33.3	33.3	37.0	36.7
Other	30	30	26	16	37.1	37.1	35.6	32.7
Security Services — Total	61	63	54	31	100.0%	100.0%	100.0%	100.0%
Headcount	22	23	21	11	36.0	36.5	38.9	35.5
Square feet	14	14	14	8	23.0	22.2	25.9	25.8
Other	25	26	19	12	41.0	41.3	35.2	38.7

Figure 6.5. (Continued)

115

14. METHODS OF ALLOCATING SERVICE CENTER COSTS TO GOVERNMENT CONTRACTS AND USE OF PREDETERMINED BILLING RATES
As of September 30, 1979

Type of Service Center	All Units Reporting	Allocated to Government Contracts			Predetermined Billing Rates Used*	
		Direct or Through Other Indirect Pool		Through Indirect Pool Only		
		Number of Units	Percent of All Units		Number of Units	Percent of All Units
Scientific Computer Operations	257	223	86.8	34	171	66.5
Business Data Processing	367	189	51.5	178	164	44.7
Photographic Services	186	144	77.4	42	80	43.0
Reproduction Services	326	210	64.4	116	137	42.0
Art Services	163	122	74.9	41	50	30.7
Technical Typing Services	145	123	84.8	32	38	26.2
Communications Services	264	66	25.0	198	59	22.4
Facility Services	398	132	33.2	266	98	24.6
Auto Pool Services	121	41	33.9	80	47	38.8
Company Aircraft Services	54	30	55.6	24	28	51.9
Wind Tunnels	13	9	69.2	4	2	15.4
Personnel and/or Industrial Relations	68	5	7.4	63	11	16.2
Material Handling and/or Procurement	62	8	12.9	54	13	21.0
Accounting and/or Payroll Services	49	7	14.3	42	10	20.4
Security Services	31	4	12.9	27	4	12.9
Fringe Benefits	21	5	23.8	16	5	23.8
Quality Control	30	7	23.3	23	6	20.0

*There were 414 units that reported the use of predetermined billing rates. Variances from actual costs were disposed of as follows: 89 prorated costs to users; 212 units allocated or credited variances to an indirect cost pool; 21 units used both of these methods; and 92 units used "other" methods.

Figure 6.6. Indirect costs, D/S items 4.3.0 and 4.4.0, methods of allocating service center costs to government contracts and use of predetermined billing rates, as of September 30, 1979.

completed. This plan developed for the proposal is adjusted once a contract is received and provides the basis for monitoring actual performance. Then, when comparison of actual results with the plan begins to show unfavorable variances, corrective action can be taken promptly.

The quality of a contractor's estimating system is of critical importance. Mistakes in estimating can result in losses or can result in instances of defective pricing. To prepare reliable estimates, the estimator must possess a great deal of information. He or she should possess a wealth of data on the cost of previous contracts with similar tasks. The estimator must also understand cost behavior or the impact of volume on costs. Often an understanding of the rate of improvement in performing tasks as volume increases (i.e., learning curves) is important. Well designed accounting systems can help estimators since they permit them to refer to past contracts and to draw on valuable experience. If the accounting system accounts for production by lot, it is helpful in determining the amount of learning that occurs. It is also useful if a system segregates nonrecurring costs from recurring costs. Standard cost data can also be invaluable to the estimating process. In any event, the estimating or planning process for contract costs is obviously of great importance, and design of the accounting system is all-important in providing valuable input.

Once contracts have been obtained and are being performed, a key means of assessing progress and determining if problems exist is the preparation of a comprehensive estimate of contract costs at completion. To ensure the reliability of interim financial statements and to avoid surprises that come too late for effective corrective action, such comprehensive estimates should be prepared at least quarterly.

It is important that management be informed periodically, usually once a month, of the key facts concerning contract performance. Sometimes high-level summary reports, similar to the example in Figure 6.7, are useful to provide an overview of financial, scheduling, and technical status, and the necessity for management action.

There are many facts and numbers inherent in monitoring the performance of a contract. Accordingly, it is difficult to design management reports that concisely present the key information needed, which includes:

Actual cost to date.
Budgeted cost for work scheduled.
Budgeted cost for work performed.
Estimated cost to complete.
Estimated cost at completion.
Contract amount (including changes).
Projected overrun or underrun.
Contract scheduled completion date.
Expected completion date.
Projected slippage.

Graphical presentations as shown in Figure 6.8 are often useful in portraying this important information.

In the case of major procurements, the government takes a keen interest in the management information systems of contractors. To ensure that it can monitor the contractor's progress, the government inserts a clause into contracts requiring a *cost/schedule control systems* (C/SCS). The criteria necessary to comply with this clause are quite involved and specific. The contractor's management information system must pass inspection within 90 days after contract award if this clause is contained in the contract. The military services have

Summary of Contracts
($ in 000's)

Contract Number	Financial					Schedule		Technical Status		Management Action Required
	Contract Amount	Cost Status to Date			Estimated Costs at Completion	Current	Estimated at Completion	Current	Predicted at Completion	
		Budget	Actual	Variance						
82,330	9,000	6,200	6,600	400	9,800	60 days behind	30 days behind	Quality Control Problem	OK	Meeting with Customer 6/20
82,470	6,000	4,000	4,000	—0—	5,400	On time	On time	OK	OK	OK

Figure 6.7. Summary of Contracts.

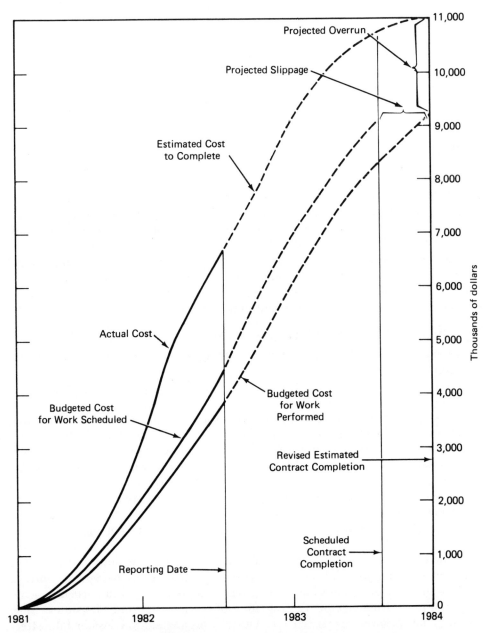

Figure 6.8. Monitoring Contract Status.

published a pamphlet entitled Cost/Schedule Control Systems Criteria Joint Implementation Guide,[2] which sets forth all the requirements. Basically, C/SCS requires breaking down the contract into work packages, identifying organizations and managers who are responsible, developing a schedule, and budgeting the costs by the work packages. Well designed systems should be able to meet the C/SCS rules without major changes. Systems without the discipline of C/SCS will require a major effort to conform.

INTERNAL CONTROLS

Proper delegation of authority and differentiation of responsibilities form the underlying concept of a system of good internal controls. The responsibility for ensuring that an adequate system of controls exists in an organization is, and has been, that of management. Boards of directors, as general overseers of all management functions, are interested in assuring themselves that management's responsibilities with respect to the control system have been thoughtfully considered and met.

The way in which a company is controlled will vary depending on such factors as size, dispersion of operating locations, complexity of the organization, and management philosophy. Smaller companies are more heavily dependent on the day-to-day involvement of management to ensure that controls are effective. Larger companies require more formal documentation and communication of policies, procedures, and control systems to ensure that control objectives are reached. What constitutes an effective internal accounting control system is a difficult question. Management, however, should establish an environment that creates the appropriate control awareness, attitude, and discipline. Management should ascertain that each control system:

Fits the company and its management philosophy.

Focuses on areas of risk, particularly those that are inherent in government contracting.

Achieves a thoughtful balance between costs of control and benefits.

Management is accustomed to dealing with traditional internal accounting controls. Executives regularly make judgments about the quality of their employees and the accuracy and reliability of their internal management reports. They have an intuitive sense based on their familiarity with what is happening as to whether the system of internal accounting control is operating effectively. The all-important feeling that "things are right" can be a real comfort to executive management.

Some companies will choose in their evaluation of internal controls to limit their consideration of aspects of business management to those that are deemed to be significant to financial and accounting functions and activities. The wiser company will evaluate the broad spectrum of management controls, which includes, but is not limited to, accounting controls for a particular activity as a part of management's evaluation of the internal control systems. In so doing, the reviewer's perspective is naturally broadened to consider how effectively and efficiently an activity is organized and how all the checks and balances ensure that employees are effectively discharging their responsibilities.

Variability in Control Systems

As indicated previously, many factors should be considered in determining the way in which a company is controlled, including the degree of centralization of the organization and the overall size of the company.

Senior executives of larger companies do not usually have the luxury of personal observation or inquiry to provide assurance that controls are operating as expected. Instead, they rely on administrative controls or internal auditors or other monitoring groups to alert them on a timely basis to failures in the internal accounting control systems. Consequently, in larger companies, management and directors should be more sensitive to the actions they take to create the appropriate control environment. The people in the organization must "feel" senior management's interest in controls and its expectation that each member within the organization will adhere to prescribed control procedures.

In smaller companies, management may not have enough people to segregate duties as fully as might be desired. Control objectives may be achieved through the supervision of day-to-day activities by top management, who also have the responsibility for authorizing most business transactions. Members of management may assure themselves of adherence to their policies by personal observation and inquiry. Under these circumstances, documentation of policies and procedures may not be critical since management is otherwise assured that the people in the organization understand what is expected of them. Accordingly, there may not be a need for an extensive internal audit function.

Executives of these companies will most likely approach the evaluation of their control systems with the confidence that they know their weaknesses and are comfortable with the risks inherent in them. These executives nevertheless should undertake an evaluation of their internal accounting control system for the reasons suggested above. Perhaps such an evaluation would emphasize those functions where there is greater reliance on the control system than upon management involvement; from management's perspective, these are the risk areas. Accordingly, it would be prudent to review any known weaknesses in the control system.

Directors of smaller companies must, of necessity, place greater reliance on top management for ensuring that internal accounting control objectives are achieved than directors in larger companies who can take comfort from sophisticated internal accounting control systems. Directors of smaller companies may therefore be particularly interested in reevaluating the delegation of authority among the top management group and the controls that restrain this group from exceeding that authority and overriding the control system. The directors may wish to consider requesting management to report to them on the evaluation of the control system—specifically, on:

Policies, including business ethics and practices, for areas of high business risk.

Weaknesses in the internal accounting control system.

Conflicts of interest, if any, of the top management group.

CONTROLS UNIQUE TO GOVERNMENT CONTRACTORS

Government contractors are not unlike any other business when it comes to the concerns of internal controls. Although the objectives are similar, the statutory, regulatory, and contractual requirements imposed on those dealing with the government are different than the requirements for those dealing with the private sector. These differences result in different assessments of risk.

Functions inherent in government contracting where risks are dissimilar to commercial enterprises not engaged in government contracting and the control objectives necessary for such functions are listed below:

Function	Control Objective
Contract administration	To establish centralized responsibility for fulfilling contractual requirements and for ensuring that adequate safeguards for the commitment of company resources are established.

Proposal preparation, estimating, and bidding	To ensure that contracts are bid or negotiated in accordance with applicable regulatory requirements and management criteria on the basis of data carefully compiled in a manner that takes into account all factors which can be compared to subsequent performance.
Project administration and contract evaluation	To establish responsibility for monitoring performance (technical, cost, and schedule) to enable periodic evaluation of the contract status, progress, and profitability of each project.
Billing	To ensure that billings are adequately supported and reflect the requirements of contractual terms and acquisition regulations. To ensure that unbilled items are identified and periodically evaluated.
Project costing: labor, overhead and material	To properly record all costs incurred to the correct project and properly accumulate, classify and summarize them in the accounts.
General accounting/ contract revenues	To ensure that contract revenue and costs are recognized in accordance with management criteria and that all factors affecting profitability have been reflected in the amounts recorded.
Job site accounting	To provide adequate control over assets located, or under the responsibility of employers, at remote locations.
Quality assurance	To assure that delivered products meet all product quality requirements included in applicable contracts.
Government furnished property	To assure that the government furnished property is properly obtained, used, and managed during the performance of contracts.
Record retention	To assure that records are retained pursuant to the government's retention requirements.
Export requirements	To assure that no defense or non-defense articles are exported unless appropriate licenses have been obtained prior to the export.
Gratuities to government employees	To assure that no gratuities are offered or given to government officials who are involved in the procurement or administration of contracts awarded to the company.
Hiring current or former government employees	To assure adherence to special restrictions and reporting requirements applicable to hiring or retaining certain government employees.
Socioeconomic requirements	To assure: Maximization of subcontracting with small and small disadvantaged businesses and labor surplus area businesses. Nondiscrimination in employment.

Compliance with Buy American Act requirements regarding domestic content of end products.

Compensation of employees consistent with applicable minimum wage, maximum hour and overtime standards.

Specific internal controls that are necessary to achieve the control objective are listed in the form of a question for each function. These questions are related specifically to government contracts and do not include all generalized controls necessary for a proper system of internal control. Further, these questions are meant to apply to a broad spectrum of operations and may not apply to every size and type of government contractor. The questions are designed so that a "no" answer to a question may indicate a control weakness.

Contract Administration

1. Does the company have a contracts organization that is responsible to the president of the operating unit and, accordingly, separate and distinct from marketing? When a contract administrator is assigned to a contract, does he or she have only dotted line responsibility to the manager responsible for contract performance?

2. Are the individuals assigned to the contracts organization experienced and mature; do they possess sound business judgment; and, most important, are they familiar with government procurement regulations and contract clauses?

3. Has the company established a training program for contract administrators and/or required their participation in outside seminars and training programs? Is it suggested that the administrators join applicable professional associations?

4. Is a senior contract administrator(s) assigned to all significant and complex contracts?

5. Are all operational entities (manufacturing, engineering, etc.) clearly informed through a policy manual or other formal means as to the restrictions placed on them in their dealings with the customer, particularly with respect to changes in the scope of work requirements set forth in the contract?

6. Is all contract-related correspondence between the company and the customer coordinated by the contract administrator responsible for the contract?

7. Are contract administrators required to attend all meetings between the company and the customer and are minutes maintained of such meetings?

8. Are executed contracts required prior to the incurrence of costs? If not, is it the responsibility of the contract administrator to obtain an advance agreement with the customer that such costs will be allowable?

9. Are contract files maintained in an orderly manner and do they include documentation of the significant factors included in negotiations and other preliminary proceedings prior to contract award, the basic contract and amendments, all internal correspondence, all correspondence to and from the customer, billing invoices, and delivery documents?

10. Does the company have a policy that outlines the circumstances under which the tasks associated with a contract's performance are required to be identified, budgeted, and scheduled?

11. Does the internal audit staff conduct examinations of contracts and summarize their findings in a report to the audit committee or president?

12. Are changes and other contract modifications coordinated with appropriate management and accounting personnel to ensure that adequate equitable adjustment claims can be submitted?

13. Are contract completion reviews performed prior to closing a contract?

Proposal Preparation, Estimating, and Bidding

Proposal Presentation and Pricing Strategy

1. Are all solicited and unsolicited contract proposals (technical and cost) reviewed by a contract administrator (and in-house legal counsel where appropriate) prior to their submission to the customer? Is a formal memorandum prepared on these reviews and forwarded to appropriate contract and company management personnel?

2. Are all firm fixed-price and high-risk contract proposals reviewed by a committee, the majority of whose members are not responsible for performance, to ensure independence of thought prior to their submission to the customer? Does the composition of the committee include representatives of finance, in-house legal counsel, and contracts? Is the committee involved in the assessment of each material revision in the proposal until source selection?

3. Are all significant firm fixed-price contracts properly approved prior to their execution? Do the formal minutes of a board or committee indicate such an approval?

4. Does the company have a formal policy as to who may commit the company to the performance of a contract, and does such a policy differentiate by type of contract and its amount?

5. Does the company generally refrain from or have a policy against "buying-in" on a contract?

6. Is every effort made by the company to assign the contract administrator associated with the bid or proposal to the contract, if awarded?

7. Is the proposed contract, prior to its execution by a designated officer of the company, reviewed by the contract administrator to determine that it is in total agreement with the proposal as amended in negotiations?

8. Are proposal efforts planned and is the proposal manager selected generally on the understanding that he or she will also be the contract performance manager?

9. Is a record maintained of all contacts with the customer from the date of submission of the proposal to the completion of final negotiations?

10. Is the contracts organization responsible for assuring that the company is maintained on the government's solicitation mailing list and not inadvertently removed?

11. Has the company established formal procedures for determining bid/no-bid decisions which incorporate pricing, financing, tooling, manufacturing and delivery schedule considerations? Is a committee established for this purpose?

12. Do prices offered for noncompetitive procurements of commercial spare or repair parts represent the lowest prices offered to other customers unless written justification for higher prices is provided to the government?

13. Are proposed prices for spare parts fair and reasonable and representative of the intrinsic value of the parts?

14. Are budgets established and approved for proposal efforts and monitored for variances and reviewed for the reasonableness of incurred costs?

15. Is the contracts organization responsible for the control and monitoring of the submission of all bids or proposals? Are records maintained on a current basis that indicate the date and other data relating to proposals submitted, anticipated dates of award, and awards received?

16. Does the contracts organization prepare a timely analysis with regard to bids or proposals that were not awarded so that company senior management may be informed and will have the opportunity to adjust its policies or procedures, if appropriate?

Cost Estimating

1. Is the estimating process formalized with written policies and procedures and preprinted forms and specific instructions?

2. Is the proposal based on detailed cost estimates prepared using formalized procedures?

3. Are estimating and costing practices consistent?

4. Where factors are used to estimate cost for such efforts as quality assurance, inspection, and test, are they documented, current, and applied in a formal and consistent manner?

5. Is actual data on similar work utilized where appropriate to validate the quality of estimates?

6. Do cost estimates based on prior cost experience reflect differences in complexity, quantity, state of development of production methods, plant capacity, and make-buy factors between items previously produced and those for which estimates are being prepared?

7. Is the learning curve used when appropriate in estimating labor costs?

8. Are material estimates based on bills of material or other material listings that are current and adequately detailed?

9. Are projected cost levels and activity volumes considered in preparing cost estimates?

10. Are cost proposals reviewed and approved by management at interim points and upon completion to assure that the proposal process is adequately documented?

11. Are procedures, such as those identifying disclosure requirements, and requiring proposal updates, and documentation of data provided to the government, established to ensure compliance with the Truth in Negotiations Act?

12. When applicable, is the certificate of current cost or pricing data signed by an individual involved in the negotiations?

Budgeting

1. Are material budgets established at the appropriate level based on defined quantities and estimated prices?

2. Are budgets established for all contract work with separate identification of cost elements (labor, material, etc.)?
3. Does the initial contract budget, including profit and management reserves, equal the negotiated value as stated in the contract?
4. Are management reserves for contingencies provided only at the overall contract level? Are the reserves adequately controlled?
5. Is a time-phased budget established and maintained at an appropriate level against which contract performance can be measured?
6. Is the budget revised in a timely manner when the contract is amended and additional work agreed to that will result in added cost?
7. Is it the contractor's practice to evaluate the effectiveness of the budgeting procedures through continuing comparisons of estimated costs with actual, particularly in relation to the original estimates if these are utilized for accounting purposes for any significant period during performance of the contract?

Project Administration and Contract Evaluation

General

1. Is all contract work defined and structured prior to performance based on the final negotiated contract statement of work at a level sufficient to monitor contract performance and prior to the assignment of organizational responsibilities?
2. Are work orders opened only with the formal written approval of officially designated officials?
3. Are work orders closed only upon evidence that established milestones have been completed?
4. Do work authorization policies and procedure clearly define and distinguish between:
   a. independent research and development (IR&D) and sponsored research.
   b. IR&D and production engineering.
   c. IR&D, bid and proposal (B&P), and selling effort.
   d. similar statements of work on multiple contracts.
5. Are separate work orders required for the following types of projects:
   a. Contracts.
   b. IR&D projects.
   c. Bids and proposals.
   d. Maintenance and repair projects.
   e. Self-constructed assets.
   f. Plant betterments and rearrangements.
6. Are the individuals responsible for the development of cost estimates also responsible for doing the work? If a central group is responsible, does it include representatives of the performing organizations?
7. Does the organizational structure clearly identify the performance (functional) organizations and subcontractors responsible for accomplishing the contract work? Are all tasks assigned to a performing organization?
8. For all significant contracts, are detailed work tasks defined for the planning and control of cost and schedule?
9. Are contract tasks adequately described and clearly defined as to start and completion dates, planned by element of cost, and assigned to a single organization?

10. Are subcontracted tasks clearly defined and identified to the appropriate prime contract task?

11. Does the company have procedures in effect to initially review and continually monitor the financial stability of major subcontractors so that the company will be aware on a timely basis of adverse financial situations and their impact on the contract? Also, does the company monitor the cost, technical progress, and delivery schedule of significant subcontractors?

12. Does the company have adequate methods for incorporating performance data from subcontractors into the reporting system being used? (This is particularly important when the subcontract is a cost reimbursement and/or intercompany type.)

13. Does the company analyze on a monthly basis the accounting for under- or over-absorbed indirect costs? Is it evident where such differences are material that consideration was given to the use of the actual rates for ₁urposes of preparing estimates of costs at completion (see estimate to complete, below) and for the recording of income or loss?

14. Does the company have procedures in effect that bring to its attention when contracts are within 75 % of the contract ceiling so that proper notice can be given in accordance with the "limitation of cost or funds" clause?

Scheduling

1. Is contract work scheduled in a manner that describes the sequence of work and that identifies the significant task interdependencies?

2. Are techniques such as PERT or CPM used where appropriate?

3. Are milestone events, technical performance goals, etc., identified at the appropriate contract task level?

4. Is a master milestone event schedule prepared and maintained?

5. Are intermediate milestone event schedules prepared and maintained that provide a logical sequence from the master milestone schedule to the detailed contract task level?

6. Do the company's procedures provide for the comparison of work accomplishment against the schedule plan? Are changes to the schedule adequately controlled?

Variance Analysis

1. Are cost and schedule performance measurement carried out monthly by contract analysts in a consistent and systematic manner?

2. Does the company have variance analysis procedures and a demonstrated capability of identifying cost and schedule variances that:
   a. Identify and isolate problems causing unfavorable cost or schedule variances?
   b. Evaluate the impact of schedule changes, etc.?
   c. Evaluate the performance of operating organizations?
   d. Identify potential or actual overruns and underruns?

3. Are actual costs used for variance analysis reconcilable with data from the accounting system?

4. Are earned value estimates made, and are they determined on a systematic basis based on technical accomplishment versus cost?

5. Are significant variances between the contract budget, earned values and actuals (cost and schedule) traced to the lowest level necessary to establish the cause of each variance?

6. Are significant differences between planned and actual schedule accomplishments identified and reasons provided for the differences?

7. Are the data disseminated to contract management timely, accurate, and usable? Are the data presented so that problems may be readily identified?

Estimates to Complete

1. Does the company prepare on a systematic basis (preferably at least quarterly) comprehensive estimates of contract profit or loss at completion of the contracts, and are such estimates reviewed by senior management for reasonableness?

2. Are written policies and procedures adequate to assure reasonably accurate estimates of costs at completion of the contract?

3. Do estimates of costs at completion consider the impact of exisiting variances?

4. Does the company, in preparing comprehensive estimates of profit or loss at completion, observe a physical inventory for the purpose of determining the stage of work in process and, when appropriate, the pricing of quantities on hand?

5. Are estimates to complete developed in conjunction with the individuals responsible for the performance of the tasks?

6. Are learning curve assumptions used for the estimate at completion based on historial company experience and modified to reflect current results on a timely basis?

7. Do the company's forecasted direct labor hourly rates used in the estimate at completion give effect to general increases and cost-of-living adjustments as required under negotiated union contracts? In this regard, is an appropriate measure of inflation used by the company as the basis for the cost-of-living adjustment? Where union contracts will be renegotiated during a contract, does the company use realistic measures such as other recent union settlements to forecast rates? Does the company give effect to salary rate increases?

8. Does the company have procedures for estimating indirect rates for future years? Are accurate budgets prepared of indirect costs based on proper assumptions?

9. Does the company have procedures for the timely settlement of subcontractor proposals for design changes and are reasonable estimates of the final negotiated amount incorporated in contract costs?

Billing

1. Are expressly unallowable costs excluded from claimed direct and indirect costs?

2. Are fee retentions billed upon completion ("close-out") of the contract (to the maximum extent permitted by contract provisions) and not held back until audited or negotiated overhead rates are available?

3. Are contract costs incurred under cost reimbursement or progress payment provisions billed at least monthly and, where possible, semi-

monthly? Are costs claimed in accordance with applicable contract provisions, e.g., quarterly funding of pension costs, prior payment to vendors (if large business), etc?

4. Are billed and unbilled receivables periodically segregated by agency and analyzed to determine if any adverse financing arrangement exists?

5. Is responsibility for delinquent accounts formalized, and are contract administrators and contract performance management notified when billed receivables are outstanding more than 30 days?

6. Is an aging analysis of unbilled accounts receivable periodically performed in order that billing may be expedited and the causes for the lack of billing identified and eliminated?

7. Is the accounting for unbilled receivables automated and integrated with the general ledger?

8. Are copies of invoices and supporting documents forwarded to the correspondence file maintained by the contract administrator?

9. Does the company periodically review cash remittance procedures to determine if deposits to its accounts can be expedited? Has the company considered whether it would be appropriate to establish several depositories throughout the United States and provide for several government payment offices?

10. Are prenumbered government receiving-inspection reports forwarded direct to the billing office from the shipping department in order to ensure that all goods delivered are billed?

Project Costing: Labor, Overhead, and Material

Payroll

1. Does the contractor have written policies and procedures in which it communicates to all employees the importance of charging the appropriate work order when completing time records? Is appropriate guidance given to employees to insure against errors in labor charging?

2. Does the company have a policy for recording uncompensated labor (mainly overtime of salaried employees) where it is considered to be material? This may affect the amount of indirect expense allocated to contracts.

3. Are time records required to be completed by the employee and approved by his or her supervisor?

4. Are floor checks performed and the charging of labor costs monitored?

5. Is compensated overtime properly authorized, including approval by the contracting officer where required?

6. With respect to labor transfer documents:
   a. Are they numerically controlled?
   b. Do they require the signature of the employee and the employee's supervisor approving the transfer prior to being processed?
   c. Do they require an explanation of the transfer and appropriate supporting data?
   d. Is it required that the documents be processed in a timely manner?

7. Have procedures been established for the coding and recording of idle time?

8. Is there a written work authorization for all labor charged?
9. Is the classification and identification of employees (i.e., direct versus indirect) appropriate to the way in which they actually charge their time?
10. Is it possible to verify the integrity of labor charging through physical progress or documented evidence of work performed?

Indirect Costs

1. Does the company evaluate on an ongoing basis the process of identifying and segregating unallowable costs?
2. Has the company complied with the provisions of the allowable cost and payment clauses, and submitted its proposed final indirect rates based on actual cost experience together with supporting data within 90 days after its year-end?
3. Is the annual indirect cost submission subject to appropriate review prior to execution of the indirect cost certificate?
4. Are annual budgets of indirect costs prepared and monitored monthly for significant fluctuations?
5. Has the company considered whether it is advantageous to obtain an advance agreement for independent research and development (IR&D) and bid and proposal (B&P) costs, although it may be incurring less than the specified threshold for obtaining such agreements? This change would be particularly important to a contractor who is under a formula ceiling and believes that costs incurred will exceed the formula limitation.
6. Has the company considered the applicability of the value-added (total cost input less materials and subcontracts) method of allocating general and administrative expense versus the total cost input method? This method prescribed under CAS 410 is particularly appropriate to service companies where certain contracts include major materials or subcontracts (e.g., computers) that under the total cost input allocation method would absorb a disproportionate amount of general and administrative expense.
7. Does the company use off-site indirect rates which generally are lower than rates used for contracts performed by the company in-house (for example, a manufacturing company performing field service contracts)?
8. Does the company evaluate for interim financial statement purposes the effect of the difference in provisional and actual rates on the financial position of contracts in process? Does the company determine the financial position of contracts in process at actual rates at year-end?
9. Does the company have a written policy for distinguishing between direct and indirect costs (CAS 418)? Is the policy consistently followed?
10. Does the company use its fiscal year as a basis for determining its indirect rates (CAS 406)?
11. Has the company considered the applicability of the cost of money on facilities capital and on assets under construction (CAS 414 and 417)?
12. Are adequate records maintained to support indirect costs claimed, and are procedures established to ensure that costs are charged to the correct cost pool?

Procurement

1. Does the company have a purchasing department organization and a formal policy and procedures manual that governs the department's activities? Are policies disseminated to an appropriate level?

2. Is company senior management (e.g., vice president finance, contract manager, president, et.) familiar with the policies and procedures of the purchasing organization and its major subcontractors, and responsive to its operating policies?

3. Does the organizational structure and level of the purchasing department allow it to operate at maximum effectiveness?

4. Has the purchasing department established standards governing the qualifications, training, and continuous evaluation of purchasing personnel? In particular, are personnel required to take part in company-sponsored training programs or participate in outside seminars on a regular basis?

5. Has the company established the use of standardized purchasing forms that adequately support the procurement function?

6. Is a summary maintained of all purchase orders let during the year by vendor, including the dollar amount?

7. Does the internal audit department periodically review the purchasing department procedures for adequacy and compliance with company policy?

8. Does the company have written policies prohibiting the acceptance of gifts, gratuities, or kickbacks from subcontractors and vendors?

9. Are conflict of interest statements required annually of all purchasing department employees? Is a statement required of employees who terminate prior to the annual circularization date?

10. Are vendors formally advised on a periodic basis that company policy prohibits the acceptance of gratuities by a purchasing representative?

11. Is there a requirement that purchasing files be maintained that represent a complete and accurate history of purchasing transactions? Is each purchase file required to indicate why the award was made?

12. Are reports of the purchasing function required on a systematic basis in order that company management may monitor its performance?

13. Does the company have policies for letting purchase orders to small and small disadvantaged businesses and firms located in labor surplus areas in accordance with the acquisition regulations?

14. Are bills of materials reviewed by the company to determine which materials or items will be purchased and which will be made in-house?

15. Does the purchasing department have available a current copy of a priced bill of materials to assure that:
    a. Material specifications recorded in the purchase order and requisition match the specifications on the bill of materials?
    b. All possible economies for ordering required materials, recognizing the total needs as reflected in the bill of materials and stock level requirements, are considered; that the price agreed to at the time of purchase is comparable to the price projected in the bill of materials; or that price increases are fully explained?

16. Are the company's make-or-buy policy and procedures documented in conformance with the acquisition regulations? Are make-or-buy decisions required to be adequately documented?

17. Are delivery dates of material required by the user organization generally sufficient to allow for adequate lead time to prevent excessive costs for expediting delivery?

18. Are follow-up procedures instituted to ensure delivery prior to the date production needs the item?

19. Is every effort made by the company (either by the contract administrator and/or purchasing department) to incorporate in purchase orders the standard and applicable clauses of the prime contract, where appropriate?

20. Are periodic reviews by company senior management undertaken of all material single or sole source procurements to determine that the procurements were justifiable?

21. Does the company have a continuing program of review and classification of single and sole source items to determine whether they can be competitively bid?

22. Are sole source procurements required to be (1) conclusively and logically substantiated by the management of the department responsible for establishing the requirements in the requisition, (2) completely documented as to the facts and approved by the appropriate procurement management, and (3) reported where material at least quarterly to company senior management?

23. Are vendors evaluated and rated on performance and financial criteria, and are such ratings kept current and used in supporting selections?

24. Is price or cost analysis performed on all quotations received?

25. Are certificates of current cost or pricing data obtained from subcontractors when appropriate?

26. Does the company support, lend direction to, and monitor the performance of subcontractors? Do representatives of the company visit subcontractors on a periodic basis or, where the subcontract is material, maintain a liaison office at the subcontractor site, and require subcontractor progress reports that incorporate cost and schedule information when appropriate?

Physical Inventories

1. Does the contractor have written instructions and procedures providing for recording transfers of materials charged to a contract but that are utilized on another contract?

2. Are detailed records maintained in the accounting department as to customer-furnished materials and equipment received, on hand, returned, or otherwise disposed of?

3. Are transfers of customer-furnished materials and equipment to and from various company locations properly documented?

4. Are detailed inventories of customer-furnished materials and equipment taken by persons independent of those charged with the physical custody thereof?

5. Has the contractor provided separate insurance coverage for customer-furnished materials or equipment when such requirement exists under the terms of the contract?

6. Has the contractor evaluated the need for any separate insurance cover-

age of government property for losses that might be sustained (excluding fire or stated casualty risks) for which it might become responsible, when no such insurance requirement exists under the terms of the special clause in the contract entitled "government property"?

General Accounting/Contract Revenues

1. Is the accounting department furnished with copies, or suitable summaries, of all pertinent contract terms, change orders, addendums, etc. of:
   a. Prime contracts?
   b. Subcontracts received?
   c. Subcontracts let?
2. Are direct costs accumulated by detailed task in a manner consistent with the budgets—using the cost accounting practices set forth in the disclosure statement—and controlled by the general ledger?
3. Does the accounting system provide for determining unit or lot costs when appropriate?
4. Are material charges recorded at the point of usage or by another acceptable method?
5. Does the accounting system provide for material price and usage variances that are essential to the effective control of cost?
6. Is the material control system adequately explained and documented, including planning, requisitioning, and issuance to performance organizations?
7. Does inventory planning support the manufacturing schedule?
8. Does the company segregate or can it otherwise identify within its accounting system costs associated with change orders and claims that have not been negotiated?
9. Are company accounting policies with respect to income recognition clearly outlined in an accounting manual or in some other formal manner?
10. Do company procedures provide for segregation (in the accounts or in worksheet analyses) of costs that are stated in the acquisition regulations to be unallowable? Are appropriate provisions made for costs subject to a disallowance as a result of government audit?
11. Does the company utilize provisional overhead rates in billings to the government or in the accumulation of unbilled costs? If so, are adequate procedures provided for adjusting the provisional rate or rates to actual at interim or year-end?
12. Can costs be determined at interim points to provide data for repricing; for negotiating revised targets; for determining progress payments?

Job Site Accounting

Note: The size and location of some projects (particularly construction projects) may require a contractor to establish an accounting office at the job site, and all or part of the accounting function relating to that project—including payrolls, purchasing, disbursements, equipment control, and billings—may be performed at the job site. Establishing a system of internal controls at job site accounting offices may be difficult because direct supervision of home office personnel may be limited and the offices may be staffed with a limited number of trained accounting personnel. When off-site locations exist, the controls documented above should be implemented as far as possible at the field site; in addition, the following controls specifically related to a field site office should be implemented:

Cash

1. Is the practice of drawing checks to "cash" prohibited? If not, do the officials satisfy themselves that such checks have been cashed in reimbursement of petty cash or used for other proper purposes?
2. Are checks restrictively endorsed immediately upon receipt and deposited on a timely basis?

Security

1. Is access and egress to the construction area gained only through check points?
2. Is a system utilized to account for the arrival and departure of employees?
3. Do procedures provide for the release of materials only upon receipt of a properly approved requisition?
4. Are there adequate controls to prevent theft or diversion of material?
5. Is material received delivered directly to the warehouse, storeroom, or production area via an inspection area?

Payroll

1. Personnel
    a. Are requisitions for craft labor initiated by craft foremen?
    b. Are these requisitions approved by supervisory personnel?
    c. Are office staff positions approved by the resident construction manager?
    d. Are referral slips from the local union halls required for all craft applicants?
    e. Are notations on the referral slip relating to rates, subsistence and mileage allowance etc., reviewed to ascertain that they are based on the appropriate labor agreements?
    f. Are tests made of distances traveled by the employee that entitle him or her to mileage and/or subsistence allowances?
    g. Are employees required to complete a personal history card and complete *two* copies of Form W-4?
    h. Is one copy of Form W-4 forwarded to the home office?
    i. Are badge numbers assigned to new employees consecutively by craft, and is a log maintained for badge assignments?
    j. Are craft termination slips completed by the craft foremen?
    k. Are these termination slips approved by supervisory personnel?
    l. Is a copy of the termination slip routed directly to the payroll department?
    m. Are the following documents maintained on file:
        Union referral slip?
        Employee personal history form?
        Field office copy of Form W-4?
        Termination slip?

Rate change authorization?

2. Timekeeping
    a. Before badges are issued, is a check made to determine that all badges are accounted for?
    b. Is the employee prevented from obtaining or returning more than one badge?
    c. Is an absentee report prepared by the timekeepers for all craft employees who have not reported to work when the badge shack is closed?
    d. Is a log maintained of craft employees who arrive or depart at irregular times?
    e. Is the log forwarded directly to the timekeeping department?
    f. Is a foremen's daily time record submitted by each craft foreman, indicating the hours worked by task for each crew member?
    g. Are these foremen's daily time records approved by supervisory personnel?
    h. Are the cost distribution accounts entered on the foremen's daily time records by the cost engineer?
    i. Are the hours on the foremen's daily time record balanced in detail or in total by craft to the hours derived from the absentee and irregular hours reports?
    j. Do the timekeepers or other appropriate personnel make daily headcounts of the craft employees while they are at work on the job site?

3. Preparation of payroll
    a. Are the hours posted from the daily time records to the payroll register?
    b. Are rates entered in the payroll register determined by reference to the appropriate labor agreements and to the daily time records for the tasks performed?
    c. Are vacation payments made to union vacation funds included in the individual employee's gross earnings for the purpose of determining payroll taxes and withholding? (This is required by Internal Revenue Service regulations.)
    d. Are the payroll calculations checked by employees who take no part in its preparation?
    e. Is the completed payroll checked against the input data?
    f. Before checks are signed, is the completed payroll reviewed and approved in writing by the:
        Field office manager?
        Resident construction manager?

4. Payment
    a. Are checks distributed so as to minimize fraud?
    b. Is presentation of a badge or other identification required?
    c. Is a report on undelivered payroll checks prepared in duplicate by the paymaster?
    d. Does the paymaster return the undelivered checks along with one copy of the above list to the field office manager?
    e. Is the other copy of the list initialed by the field office manager and retained by the paymaster?
    f. Is identification required from employees subsequently claiming their checks from the field office manager?
    g. Are such employees required to sign the list of undelivered checks upon receipt of their checks?

Quality Assurance and Testing

1. Have work instructions been prepared which identify current quality assurance requirements at the operating department level?
2. Are quality assurance procedures distributed in a timely manner to all applicable organizations?
3. Do recordkeeping requirements detail inspection steps performed at various levels of operations?
4. Is the process for correcting defects adequately documented?
5. Is vendor/subcontractor quality adequately controlled?

Government Furnished Property

1. Is government furnished property (GFP) properly segregated, secured and maintained?
2. Is use of GFP limited to the purpose intended and properly authorized prior to use?
3. Do government property accounting records conform to the requirements of FAR 45.505?
4. Are physical inventories of GFP periodically taken?
5. Is disposal of excess/unused government property properly authorized and reported?

Record Retention

1. Do written procedures require retention of books, records, documents and other supporting evidence to satisfy contract negotiation, administration and audit requirements?
2. Do written procedures specify the specific retention period required for such source documents as purchase requisitions, purchase orders, paid checks and labor distribution cards?

Export Requirements

1. Do written procedures require licenses to be obtained from the Office of Export Administration, Department of Commerce prior to export of nondefense articles and services?
2. Do written procedures require registration with the Office of Munitions Control, Department of State, prior to engaging in the business of exporting defense articles or providing defense services?
3. Do written procedures require a license to be obtained from the Office of Munitions Control prior to the permanent export of any item on the United States Munitions list?

Gratuities to Government Employees

1. Do company procedures prohibit extending offers or furnishing gratuities to government officials?
2. Are employees who regularly interface with federal procurement personnel periodically provided with guidelines which preclude offering gratuities?

Hiring Current or Former Government Employees

1. Do personnel procedures require identification of a potential employee or consultant's most recent functional responsibilities as a federal official if applicable?
2. Are potential employees or consultants requested to assert that no potential conflicts of interest resulting from federal employment exist?

Socioeconomic Requirements

1. Do written policies address subcontracting to small and small disadvantaged business concerns and labor surplus area concerns?
2. Have required small and small disadvantaged business subcontracting plans been filed?
3. Are subcontract awards to small and small disadvantaged business concerns and labor surplus area concerns monitored and required reports submitted?
4. Are programs in effect to identify potential small and small disadvantaged and labor surplus area vendors?
5. Has a written affirmative action plan been prepared?
6. Are notices required to be posted concerning equal opportunity in employment?
7. Are required Form EEO-1 (Standard Form 100) and other reports submitted as required?
8. Are records maintained that track the country of origin for parts, components and raw materials that are incorporated into deliverable end items?
9. Do written procedures require review of contracts for applicable labor standards requirements?

ELEMENTS OF EFFECTIVE CONTROL SYSTEMS

Standards of Conduct

Key to the concept of self-governance is a requirement for a strong code of conduct and business ethics. This code should address the special requirements of government contracting and establish a reporting mechanism directly to senior managment by employees who are protected against retribution.

Codes will vary from company to company but should address employee work relationships with others in the company, suppliers, customers and government employees. Codes should be in writing and clearly articulated to all employees. Many firms annually update the code as a mechanism to reinforce the standards to all employees. Having employees sign an acknowledgment that they have read and understand the code serves as documentation that management is taking an active role to ensure compliance.

The code should address major regulatory requirements that apply to the company's contracting environment. The code should also address how an employee reports a suspected violation. The reporting procedures should ensure that employees are protected and that senior management is aware of any allegation. Some firms have established an "ombudsman" to act as a reporting mechanism independent of the traditional management structure.

Policies and Procedures

A well documented policy and procedural framework is vital in achieving an effective management control system. Employees need written documentation to enable them to perform their duties in a manner consistent with management's intention. The lack of effective policies and procedures exposes companies to risks of inconsistencies in complying with various procurement rules.

Key government contracting policies and procedures include:

Labor charging.
Unallowable costs.
Cost estimating and pricing.
Quality assurance and test requirements.
Hiring practices regarding current and former government employees.
Government furnished material and equipment.

Of course, the above would be in addition to the normal policies and procedures a company should have as part of its internal control system. Individual policies and procedures should be sufficiently detailed so that employees understand the specific requirements of their roles.

To illustrate this process, an effective policy and procedural framework for the preparation of a year-end indirect cost rate proposal is outlined below:
The written policy should provide the mechanism for:

Documenting how the indirect costs proposal is prepared.
Identifying the roles and responsibilities of personnel involved in the process.
Providing management with the tools necessary to prudently evaluate proposals prior to certification.

The written procedure should address:

Accounts and/or departments for which costs are to be voluntarily conceded as unallowable.

Costs requiring special analyses (e.g., cost issues raised by DCAA in prior indirect cost proposal audit reports, etc.) to ascertain amounts to be voluntarily conceded, if any.

Disclosure of costs whose allowability is the subject of a formal dispute.

Methods used to develop indirect expense rates.

Documentation required to provide clear audit trails between the proposal and the general books of account, and to permit a prudent management review of the proposal's adherence to Federal regulations and company policies.

Independent management review and approval of indirect expense proposals, including:

Responsibility for management review by an individual knowledgeable of federal acquisition regulations and independent of the proposal preparation process.

Evaluation criteria to assure that the review process is sufficiently detailed to document the proper exclusion of unallowable costs, the disposition of costs requiring special analysis, and the disposition of cost issues previously raised by DCAA.

Designation of the individual responsible for executing the Certificate of Indirect Cost.

Compliance Monitoring

Perhaps the most important aspect of an effective control system is compliance monitoring. This process compares the actual practices employees are using to the policies and procedures and to regulatory requirements. The best policies and procedures ever written are meaningless if employees do not follow them.

Compliance monitoring serves as a kind of backbone for a good control program because it examines the whole process. A review should ensure that policies and procedures are in compliance with the various procurement regulations. Part of the determination requires a review of the accounting system to assure proper cost accumulation and good internal controls. If employees are not following the policies and procedures, the cause or solution may be training.

A riskier alternative to compliance monitoring is to establish good accounting and internal control systems and then assume compliance has been achieved. This approach has inherent risk since significant errors can occur even in the presence of effective internal controls. The government is holding company management accountable for compliance with procurement rules. The longer a noncompliant practice goes undetected, the greater the potential financial risk to the company. The best way to demonstrate that management is committed to being a responsible government contractor is to be sure employees are following the rules.

Companies who have established compliance review programs generally have done so as part of the internal audit function or as a separate compliance review group function. The Packard Commission recommendations focus on internal auditing but the same recommendations could be applied to any compliance review group. These recommendations are:

Defense contractors must individually develop and implement better systems of internal controls to ensure compliance with contractual commitments and procurement standards. To assist in this effort and to monitor its success, we recommend contractors take the following steps:
1. Establish internal auditing of compliance with government contracting procedures, corporate standards of conduct, and other requirements. Such auditing should review actual compliance as well as the effectiveness of internal control systems.
2. Design systems of internal control to ensure that they cover, among other things, compliance with the contractor's standards of ethical business conduct.
3. Establish internal audit staffs sufficient in numbers, professional background, and training to the volume, nature, and complexity of the company's government contracts business.
4. Establish sufficient direct reporting channels from internal auditors to the independent audit committee of the contractor's board of directors to assure the independence and objectivity of the audit function. Auditors should not report to any management official with direct responsibility for the systems, practices, or transactions that are the subject of an audit. Such structure assures frank reporting of and prompt action on internal audit results. To encourage and preserve the vitality of such an internal auditing and reporting process, DOD should develop appropriate guidelines heavily circumscribing the use of investigative subpoenas to compel disclosure of contractor internal auditing materials.[3]

An important question has arisen as a result of companies performing compliance reviews: What does a company do when it finds that a violation of the procurement regulation has occurred? The government expects companies to voluntarily disclose the violation. Regulations do not presently address how this voluntary disclosure will be treated by all agencies of the government. Speeches by DOD personnel have provided indications that voluntary disclosure would be looked upon favorably by the government, but there are no guarantees.

Companies need to work closely with their counsel in deciding what course of action is appropriate for the particular circumstances. Government agencies will hopefully coordinate and provide guidelines on voluntary disclosure so companies will be able to know beforehand the consequence of disclosure. Ultimately, company management will have to decide whether to disclose a violation. It may weigh the legal ramifications and potential actions the government may take, particularly considering government action if it uncovers the violation on its own.

Where a company discloses violations it finds, the concept of self-governance will work most effectively in the context of a responsible government contractor who has an isolated violation of a regulation. To establish credibility, management needs to be able to show it does monitor actual practices and that reported violations are the result of employees not following specific management direction,rather than the lack of proper procedure The consequence of the violation in this situation, can be dealt with by the government in a less onerous environment.

Training

A comprehensive longterm training plan should encompass both formal seminars in federal contract cost and pricing requirements, as well as informal on-the-job training in company policy and procedures. The training plan should provide for systematic updates of the training materials to assure that employees involved in costing, pricing, or performing federal contracts are abreast of changes in the regulatory environment. Training plans should also identify the level of training appropriate for various job classifications and records should be maintained to assure that training is provided to appropriate personnel on a timely and systematic basis.

NOTES

1. Conduct and Accountability, A Report to the President by the President's Blue Ribbon Commission on Defense management, June 1986, pgs. 7–8.
2. Departments of the Air Force, Army, Navy, and the Defense Supply Agency, *Cost/Schedle Control Systems Criteria Joint Implementation Guide* (Italics) (Washington, D.C.: October 1, 1976), AFSCP/AFLCP 173-5.
3. Conduct and Accountability . . . , supra note 1, pgs. 14-15.

Chapter Seven
Government Contract Cost Principles

DEFINITIONS AND HISTORICAL PERSPECTIVES

While this chapter is not intended to provide a comprehensive discourse on the intricacies of cost accounting, a brief look at the subject may be helpful in understanding the concepts of allocability that are expressed in the acquisition regulations. Cost accounting can be defined as the process of classifying, recording, allocating, and reporting costs of individual cost objectives, such as contracts.

The origins of cost accounting can be traced back five thousand years to the time of the Egyptian pharoahs. However, modern double entry bookkeeping and cost accounting are believed to have emerged from a more recent period— the Renaissance. Luca Paciolo, an Italian monk and mathematician, has been credited with inventing double entry bookkeeping, and the development of rudimentary techniques of modern cost accounting is ascribed to the Medici family of Florence, who were engaged in the manufacture of woolen cloth. An Englishman named James Dodson is credited with developing a job order cost system for shoe manufacturing. Although significant advances have been made in the United States and England since the eighteenth century, progress in the development of cost accounting systems can also be found in almost every industrial country since that time.

In recent years, companies have discovered that a real benefit of cost accounting is control by management. In today's complex business environment, it is not sufficient to merely accumulate costs. Costs must be controlled if a business organization is to be successful. Cost control is substantially enhanced by the establishment of budgets and systematic comparisons of actual and budgeted costs.

Elementary efforts to develop cost accounting principles for government contracts date back to the Revolutionary War. However, little in the way of formal cost criteria existed before World War I. During that war, Congress enacted the Revenue Act of 1916, known as the Munitions Manufacturers' Tax, primarily as a result of public criticism concerning alleged excess profiteering by defense contractors. However, the cost provisions of the Revenue Act of 1916 contained merely brief comments on the types of costs that would be considered allowable and no provisions concerning allocability criteria. The government appeared to lose interest in the subject of contract costing after the conclusion of World War I. In the early 1930s renewed interest in building up the nation's defenses, particularly aircraft and ships, led to the passage of the Vinson-Trammell Act and the Merchant Marine Act. However, these laws, enacted in 1934 and 1936, respectively, dealt only with the issue of profit limitation, not the broader issue of developing criteria for determining the costs against which profits are measured.

A major development occurred in August 1940, when Treasury Decision 5000 was issued to provide criteria for determining costs under the Vinson-Trammell Act. This document, a joint effort of the Treasury, Navy, and War Departments, addressed not only cost allowability but cost allocability as well. In April 1942 an unofficial booklet titled *Explanation of Principles for Determination of Cost under Government Contracts* was issued. This booklet (which became known as the Green Book because of its green cover) contained cost principles that were followed by the War and Navy Departments in determining costs under defense contracts.

The first edition of the Armed Services Procurement Regulation (ASPR) was issued in May 1948 under the authority of the Armed Services Procurement Act of 1947. The first ASPR Section XV, issued March 1, 1949, consisted of a tersely written 12 page promulgation establishing cost principles for cost type contracts.

In 1955 the Hoover Commission recommended the development of:

Cost principles for cost reimbursement type contracts that reflected generally accepted accounting principles for commercial organizations.

Audit guidelines for the determination of costs on fixed-price type contracts.

Following release of the Hoover Commission report, the Department of Defense undertook an ambitious project to completely revise the cost principles. The revised cost principles were published in September and October 1957 and discussed extensively with industry associations prior to their final promulgation in November 1959. The revised cost principles were similar in a number of respects to the current cost principles except that the November 1959 edition limited the application of the cost principles to cost reimbursement type contracts. It was not until 1970 that ASPR Section XV was made applicable to all defense contracts where cost is a factor in arriving at the price. The ASPR was redesignated as DAR in 1978.

The Federal Procurement Regulations (FPR) were established in 1959 by the administrator of the General Services Administration (GSA) under the authority of the Federal Property and Administrative Services Act of 1949.

PRESENT STATUS OF COST PRINCIPLES

General

Since the Postal Service is subject to a separate procurement statute, it has its own separate cost principles which are contained in the Postal Contracting Manual (PCM). The PCM has remained essentially unchanged over the past 10 years. Consequently, its cost principles are presently very similar to those that applied to DOD in the mid 1970's. Prior to issuance of the Federal Acquisition Regulations (FAR), DOD and NASA had their own complete cost principles while the cost principles contained in the FPR applied to civilian agencies.

Since NASA derived its procurement authority from the Armed Services Procurement Act, its cost principles prior to 1984 closely paralleled the DAR even though its procurement regulations were included in the FPR system. The FPR also tended to follow and largely adopt the cost principles in DAR Section XV with some exceptions, such as depreciation and rental costs.

The FAR and departmental FAR supplements, applicable to contracts awarded on or after April 1, 1984, replaced the cost principles previously in effect. To some extent, the FAR enhanced uniformity in the determination of acceptable costs under government contracts but agency differences still exist as indicated below

UNIQUE COST ALLOWABILITY CRITERIA CONTAINED IN AGENCY FAR SUPPLEMENTS

Cost	DOD	AID	DOE	EPA	ICA
Compensation		X			
Cost of Money	X				
IR & D/B & P	X		X	X	
Precontract Cost			X		
Selling Costs	X				
Travel					X

The various departments and agencies that have issued procurement cost principles are listed in Figure 7.1.

The FAR, FAR Supplements and Postal Contracting Manual (PCM) contain separate cost principles for contracts and/or grants awarded to the following types of organizations that have substantially differing characteristics:

Type of Organization	FAR	PCM
Commercial organizations	X	X
Educational institutions	X	X
Construction and architect-engineer firms	X*	X
State, local, and federally recognized Indian tribal governments	X	X
Nonprofit organizations	X	

*Although construction and architect-engineer contracts are subject to the cost principles for commercial organizations, separate cost principles are provided for owning, operating, and renting construction equipment.

The Veterans Administration (VA) and Department of Energy (DOE) also have separate cost principles for reimbursement for vocational rehabilitation and education contracts, and management and operating contracts respectively.

Advance Agreements on Particular Cost Items (FAR 31.109; PCM 15-107)

It is difficult to apply allowability and allocability concepts to the many different kinds of industries and accounting systems. Because of differences by industry, by contract, and by other circumstances, and in an effort to avoid unnecessary disputes on allowability of cost, the cost principles apply broadly to many accounting systems in varying contract situations. Thus, the reasonableness and allocability of certain items of cost to a given contract may be difficult to determine, particularly where firms or organizational divisions within firms

Code of Federal Regulations (CFR) Title	Organization	Procurement Acquisition Regulations	FPR/FAR System Chapter No.	Cost Principles Section/Part
Prior to issuance of FAR				
32	DOD	DAR	—	Section XV
39	Postal Service	Postal Contracting Manual (PCM)	—	Section XV
41	Civilian Agencies	FPR	1	Part 1-15
41	AID	AID PR	7	Part 7-15
41	VA	VA PR	8	Part 8-15
41	DOE	DOE PR	9	Part 9-15
41	EPA	EPA PR	15	Part 15-15
41	NASA	NASA PR	18	Part 15
41	ICA	ICA PR	19	Part 19-15
Subsequent to issuance of FAR				
39	Postal Service	PCM	—	Section XV
48	Federal Agencies	FAR	1	Part 31
48	DOD	DFARS	2	Part 31
48	GSA	GSAR	5	Part 31
48	AID	AID FAR Supplement	7	Part 31
48	VA	VA FAR Supplement	8	Part 31
48	DOE	DEAR	9	Part 31
48	EPA	EPA FAR Supplement	15	Part 31
48	NASA	NASA FAR Supplement	18	Part 31
48	ICA	ICA FAR Supplement	19	Part 31

Figure 7.1 Cost principles contrained in the acquisition regulations.

may not be subject to effective competitive restraints. To avoid possible subsequent disallowance or dispute based on unreasonableness or nonallocability, contractors are encouraged to seek advance agreement with the government as to the treatment to be accorded special or unusual costs. Such agreements may also be initiated by the government. Advance agreements may be negotiated either before or during performance of a contract but ideally should be negotiated before the cost covered by the agreement is incurred. Agreements must be in writing, executed by both contracting parties, and incorporated in the applicable contracts. Contracting officers are not authorized to enter into advance agreements for the treatment of cost inconsistent with the other provisions of the cost principles. For example, an advance agreement may not allow interest or entertainment cost since these costs are expressly stated to be unallowable in the "selected costs" section of the cost principles.

Examples of costs for which advance agreements may be particularly important include:

Compensation for personal services.

Use charges for fully depreciated assets.

Deferred maintenance costs.

Precontract costs.

Independent research and development costs.

Bid and proposal costs.

Royalties.

Selling and distribution costs.

Travel and relocation costs, as related to special or mass personnel movements and maximum per diem rates.

Travel via contractor owned, leased, or chartered aircraft.

Costs of idle facilities and idle capacity.

Costs of automatic data processing equipment.

Severance pay to employees on support service contracts.

Plant reconversion.

Professional services.

Home office and general and administrative expenses applicable to construction, job site, architect engineer, facilities, and government-owned contractor operated (GOCO) plants.

Cost of construction plant and equipment.

Costs of public relations and advertising.

Given the potentially controversial nature of many of these costs, it is readily understandable why they are suggested as items on which advance agreements may be appropriate.

COMPOSITION OF TOTAL ALLOWABLE COSTS

The cost principles for commercial organizations define the total cost of a contract as the sum of the allowable direct and indirect costs allocable to the contract, less allocable credits plus any allocable cost of money.

Direct Versus Indirect

The distinction between direct and indirect costs is a significant concept in the cost principles. A direct cost is identifiable with a specific final cost objective (e.g., the contract), whereas indirect costs are incurred for more than one cost objective. However, direct costs of insignificant amounts may be treated as indirect costs for administrative convenience. Consistent application of criteria for identifying costs as either direct or indirect is emphasized. Once a cost is identified as a direct cost to a particular contract, the same type of cost, incurred in similar circumstances, may not be included in any indirect expense pool allocated to that contract or any other contract.

The cost principles do not prescribe which costs should be charged direct as opposed to those which should be charged indirect. The criteria for charging direct versus indirect should be based on an analysis of the nature of the particular contractor's business and contracts. The criteria should be codified into a written statement of accounting principles and practices for classifying costs direct and indirect and allocating indirect costs to contracts. Indirect expenses should be accumulated into logical cost groupings to permit distribution of expenses in relation to benefits received by the cost objectives. The techniques or methods used to measure the amount of pooled costs to be allocated to cost objectives should be based on the extent of benefit derived from activities included in each pool.

In a 1981 case involving Abeles, Schwartz, Haeckel and Silverblatt, Inc.,[1] a small contractor not covered by Cost Accounting Standards (CAS), the government's assertion that G&A expenses must be allocated on a total cost input base was overturned in the appeals process. In its decision, the Board reaffirmed that the indirect expense allocation criteria contained in the acquisition regulations:

> . . . do not suggest or require the use of any particular cost distribution base. Rather they allow for the use of alternative distribution bases which will bring about a substantial matching of the indirect costs with the appropriate cost objectives . . .

Factors Affecting Allowability

Costs are not allowable merely because they were determined by application of the company's established accounting system. Factors considered in determining the allowability of individual items of cost include (1) reasonableness, (2) allocability, (3) cost accounting standards, if applicable; otherwise, generally accepted accounting principles and practices appropriate in the particular circumstances, (4) terms of the contract, and (5) limitations specified in the cost principles. A company should succeed in obtaining reimbursement for incurred costs where the contracting officer believes that all these criteria have been met.

REASONABLENESS (FAR 31.201-3; PCM 15-201.3)

Reasonableness has been one of the more difficult concepts in the regulations, and understandably so in view of the substantially subjective nature of the concept. The cost principles consider a cost to be reasonable if, in its nature and amount, it does not exceed that which would be incurred by a prudent person in the conduct of competitive business.

The cost principles recognize that reasonableness must often be determined on a case-by-case basis, with consideration given to the specific circumstances, the nature, and the amount of the cost in question.

Is the cost generally recognized as ordinary and necessary for conducting business or performing the contract?

Does the cost reflect sound business practices, arm's-length bargaining and the requirements of federal and state laws and regulations?

Would a prudent business person take similar action, considering his or her responsibilities to the business owners, employees, customers, the government, and the public?

Are significant deviations from established contractor practices inordinately increasing contract costs?

Prior to a 1987 change in the FAR, costs actually incurred by the contractor were presumed to be reasonable. The government had the burden of establishing, by a preponderance of evidence, that an incurred cost is unreasonable. As stated in *Bruce Construction Corp., et al. v. United States*[2], the Court of Claims noted that:

> Where there is an alleged disparity between "historical" and "reasonable" costs, the historical costs are presumed reasonable. Since the presumption is that a contractor's claimed cost is reasonable, the Government must carry the very heavy burden of showing that the claimed cost was of such a nature that it should not have been expended, or that the contractor's costs were more than were justified in the particular circumstance. . . .

This position was reasserted in *Western Electric Company, Inc.*,[3] where the ASBCA concluded that "if a cost is of a type that is generally recognized as ordinary and necessary for the conduct of a particular business or the performance of particular contracts, it bears the primary indication of reasonableness and allowability. . . ." While the board recognized that ". . . reasonableness, of course, relates to dollar amount as well as to the contractor's action in incurring a cost . . .", it concluded that the government ". . . failed to overcome appellant's prima facie showing of reasonableness as to the amount of its 1960 expenditures, or that appellant abused its discretion by incurring costs far in excess of what was necessary under the circumstances."

In 1983, the ASBCA overruled the government's disallowance of Data-Design Laboratories[4] reimbursements to employees for overtime hours spent in business travel outside the normal workday. In concluding that the government failed to support its assertion of unreasonableness, the Board observed:

> The Government cannot merely superimpose its opinion in contradiction to that of the contractor. It must show why the contractor's actions were not those which a prudent business person would have taken. A presumption of reasonableness attaches to costs which were actually incurred by a contractor and is measured by the situation which existed at the time of performance.

In Stanley Aviation Corporation,[5] the government, without objecting to any specific overhead item, disallowed a portion of the allocable overhead on the premise that the overhead rates were unreasonably high. The ASBCA rejected the government's argument, concluding that ". . . the appellant is entitled to be reimbursed at the actually-experienced overhead rates . . . " and ". . . there is no provision of the contract or of the Section XV cost principles . . . requiring that costs or rates be competitive in order to be reasonable. . . ."

In another case, *General Dynamics Corporation (Convair Division)*,[6] the ASBCA rejected the government's disallowance of direct material costs that were asserted to have been unreasonably incurred. The board concluded that ". . .a preponderance of evidence shows that these subcontracts incurred by the prime contractor were reasonable costs under the prime contracts and are allowable thereunder."

As can be seen from these cases which were decided prior to issuance of the 1987 cost principle revision, the government had little success in disallowing cost based on unreasonableness except where it established that the contractor abused its discretion by incurring the cost in questions. In one such case, *General Dynamics Corporation vs. United States*,[7] the Court of Claims denied the contractor's request for reimbursement of losses incurred in the construction of employee housing. The court ruled that the contractor acted unreasonably in undertaking a housing construction project when in fact, the government had declined to approve the project and had warned that the cost would not be allowed in the contract.

As the result of the 1987 change to the FAR, the burden of proof on the issue of reasonableness of contract costs has shifted from the government to the contractor. This change abolishes the presumption of reasonableness which attaches to incurred costs. The new provision is likely to result in increased audit challenges related to reasonableness of costs and the need for significant increased efforts on the part of contractors to justify the reasonableness of the costs being challenged. It will be interesting to follow such challenges as they are adjudicated by the ASBCA.

Contractor Weighted Average Share in Cost Risk (CWAS)

CWAS was a technique developed by DOD in 1966 to determine and express numerically the degree of cost risk a contractor assumed based on the mix of types of contracts that it agreed to perform for its customers. The technique was developed to offer additional inducement to contractors to accept higher-risk type contracts through reducing government controls and related costs with respect to such contracts.

The CWAS rating was determined by dividing the total costs incurred for commercial work and competitive firm fixed-price government contracts by the total costs incurred for all business. CWAS qualification (a CWAS rating of 75% or more) freed a contractor from a government review for reasonableness of costs that carried a CWAS indicator in the DOD cost principles. For CWAS-qualified contractors, selected costs designated "CWAS" were presumed reasonable as to nature and amount, even where the amounts exceeded stated ceilings. Of course, a CWAS-qualified contractor was still subject to audit for allocability, allowability, and compliance with cost accounting standards if appropriate.

In July 1983 CWAS coverage was deleted from the DAR at the direction of the Deputy Secretary of Defense and was never reinstated when the FAR became effective in 1984.

The decision to eliminate CWAS reflected an emerging government philosophy that a substantial volume of commercial and/or competitively awarded government firm fixed price contracts does not, in itself, sufficiently motivate a contractor to conserve resources. DCAA strongly supported the elimination of CWAS on the basis that contract audit, considering the degree of cost risk implicit in the contract business mix, should establish the appropriate level of review for each contract.

This policy change significantly affected defense contractors whose corporate offices were CWAS-qualified. CWAS-designated costs, which were incurred either at the corporate office or pursuant to corporate policy, had been shielded from government challenges of reasonableness. With the elimination of CWAS, these costs became subject to review to determine if they meet the government's reasonableness test.

Industry concerns about DCAA being the sole judge of whether competitive forces are sufficient to warrant a reduction in the scope of audit have not been eliminated. However, no change in the cost principles to alter the current status appears on the horizon.

ALLOCABILITY (FAR 31.201-4; PCM 15-201.4)

The second factor affecting allowability of cost is allocability. Although the concept is not complicated, specific application can become extremely difficult and frequently controversial. The cost principles consider a cost to be allocable if it is assignable or chargeable to one or more cost objectives in accordance with the relative benefits received or other equitable relationship. Subject to the foregoing, a cost is allocable to a government contract if it:

(i) is incurred specifically for the contract;

(ii) benefits both the contract and other work, or both government work and other work, and can be distributed to them in reasonable proportion to the benefits received; or

(iii) is necessary to the overall operation of the business, although a direct relationship to any particular cost objective cannot be shown.

Disputes in this area are usually not whether an expenditure is allocable, but rather how it is allocable. If it is direct (paragraph [i]), the entire cost is recoverable against a specific contract; if indirect (paragraph [ii] and [iii]), only an appropriate portion of the expense can be recovered on a given contract. As discussed further under Selected Costs, a number of disputes related to professional and consultant service fees have centered on the issue of allocability to government contracts. Frequently, litigation in this area has focused on the extent of "benefit" to the government. In such cases, there is no requirement that benefit to the government be capable of precise measurement.

In *General Dynamics/Astronautics*,[8] the ASBCA ruled that the contractor's payment to California to partially underwrite the cost of constructing a highway overpass near its plant directly benefited the government program from the standpoint of efficiency in conserving employee working time. The board concluded its decision by observing: "And this view is not altered by the circumstances that the accrued benefit is perhaps not susceptible of precise mathematical measurement."

The benefit cannot be so nebulous, however, that the assertion of benefit lacks credibility. In *Dynalectron v. United States*,[9] the contractor contended that legal expenses incurred in defense of a suit arising from a commercial venture were necessary to protect its assets and thus benefited government contracts by allowing the company to complete its contracts instead of going out of business. In sustaining the disallowance of the expenses charged to the G&A pool, the court concluded:

> The alleged benefit to the Government is far too remote and speculative to be relevant. . . . The costs in dispute . . . are not allocable to the Government contracts . . . under subparagraph (iii) because they were not necessary to the overall operation of the business, but had a direct relationship to a particular cost objective, namely, the commercial guarantee venture.

CASB STANDARDS AND THEIR PRIMACY OVER GENERALLY ACCEPTED ACCOUNTING PRINCIPLES

While cost accounting standards (CAS) are discussed in depth in the next chapter, a few comments on the relationship of CAS to the allowability of costs are appropriate at this point. Cost accounting standards relate to allocability, not allowability, of costs. In its *Restatement of Objectives, Policies, and Concepts* issued in May 1977, the CAS Board noted that:

The CASB does not determine categories or individual items of cost that are allowable. Allowability is a procurement concept affecting contract price and in most cases is expressly provided in regulatory or contractual provisions. An agency's policies on allowability of cost may be derived from law and are generally embodied in its procurement regulations. A contracting agency may include in contract terms or in its procurement regulations a provision that it will refuse to allow certain costs incurred by contractors that are unreasonable in amount or contrary to public policy. In accounting terms, those same costs may be allocable to the contract in question.[10]

The cost principles are essentially compatible with the criteria contained in the cost accounting standards for measuring, assigning, and allocating costs to government contracts. Where standards have been specifically incorporated into the cost principles (Figure 7.2), a practice inconsistent with the requirements of these standards is subject to disallowance under the cost principles as well as a finding of noncompliance with the standard. Where a contractor has submitted a disclosure statement, excess costs resulting from practices not consistent with the statement will also be disallowed. Where conflicting allocability criteria exist between CAS and the cost principles, the CAS prevails, as affirmed by the ASBCA in *The Boeing Company* [11]

If cost accounting standards are not applicable, *generally accepted accounting principles* (GAAP) may be an authoritative reference for determining appropriate accounting treatment.

In its *Codification of Statements on Auditing Standards,* the American Institute of Certified Public Accountants (AICPA) notes:

> The phrase "generally accepted accounting principles" is a technical accounting term which encompasses the conventions, rules and procedures necessary to define accepted accounting practice at a particular time. It includes not only broad guidelines of general application but also detailed practices and procedures. . . .[12]

While no single source of reference exists for all established accounting principles, the AICPA's *Codification of Statements on Auditing Standards* contains a fairly complete summary of the body of knowledge that might be classified as GAAP. Rule 203 of the AICPA Code of Professional Ethics identifies statements and interpretations issued by the Financial Accounting Standards Board, Accounting Principles Board opinions, and AICPA accounting research bulletins as authoritative pronouncements that require compliance. In the absence of these authoritative sources, the AICPA notes that

> the auditor should consider other possible sources of established accounting principles, such as AICPA accounting interpretations, AICPA industry audit guides and accounting guides and industry accounting practices. Depending on their relevance in the circumstances, the auditor may also wish to refer to APB statements, AICPA statements of position, pronouncements of other professional associations and regulatory agencies, such as the Securities and Exchange Commission, and accounting textbooks and articles. . . .[13]

Although GAAP have been defined for a variety of financial reporting practices, few of those accounting principles address the allocability of costs to specific final cost objectives (e.g., contracts). Consequently, the courts and boards of contract appeals have generally given considerable weight to GAAP only where more definitive accounting treatment is not prescribed in the acquisition regulations or the contract itself. In *Blue Cross Association and Blue Cross of Virginia,*[14] the ASBCA observed that

Cost Accounting Standard	Extent of Incorporation Into Acquisition Regulations
402- Consistency in Allocating Cost Incurred for the Same Purpose	FAR 31.202(a) and 31.203(a) require compliance with the standard on all contracts.
403- Allocation of Home Office Expenses to Segments	FAR 31.203(d) requires allocation methods to comply with CAS on CAS-covered contracts.* Otherwise, the method shall be in accordance with GAAP.
404- Capitalization of Tangible Assets	FAR 31.205-11(m) provides that items acquired by means of a capital lease, as defined by FAS 13, are subject to the standard
405- Accounting for Unallowable Costs	FAR 31.201-6 requires compliance with the standard on all costs.
406- Cost Accounting Period	FAR 31.203(e) requires compliance with the standard on all CAS-covered contracts.* For contracts not subject to CAS, a period shorter than a fiscal year may be appropriate in certain circumstances.
409- Depreciation of Tangible Capital Assets	FAR 31.205-11(b) requires compliance with the standard for all CAS-covered contracts* and permits contractors to elect adoption of the standard for all non-CAS-covered contracts.
410- Allocation of Business Unit General and Administrative Expenses to Final Cost Objectives	Same coverage as for CAS 403.
412- Composition and Measurement of Pension Cost	FAR 31.205-6(j)(2) requires compliance with the standard on all contracts.
413- Adjustment and Allocation of Pension Cost	Same coverage as for CAS 412.
414- Cost of Money as an Element of the Cost of Facilities Capital	FAR 31.205-10 provides that cost of money computed in accordance with the standard is an allowable cost on all contracts.
415- Accounting for the Cost of Deferred Compensation	FAR 31.205-6(k)(2) requires compliance with the standard on all contracts.
416- Accounting for Insurance Costs	FAR 31.205-19(a) requires compliance with the self-insurance provisions of the standard for all CAS-covered contracts* and for all non-CAS-covered contracts where the contractor wishes to establish a program of self-insurance.
417- Cost of Money as an Element of the Cost of Capital Assets under Construction	FAR 31.205-10 provides that cost of money, computed in accordance with the standard, is includible in the capitalized acquisition cost of the asset, except that actual interest in lieu of the calculated imputed cost of money is unallowable.
418- Allocation of Direct and Indirect Costs	Same coverage as for CAS 403.
420- Accounting for Independent Research and Development Cost and Bid and Proposal Cost	FAR 31.205-18(b) requires contracts subject to full CAS coverage to account for IR&D and B&P costs in accordance

Figure 7.2 Cost accounting standards incorporated into acquisition regulations.

Cost Accounting Standard	Extent of Incorporation Into Acquisition Regulations
	with the provisions of CAS 420. Contracts that are exempt from CAS or subject to only modified CAS coverage, but awarded while contracts subject to full CAS coverage are being performed, must also account for IR&D and B&P costs in accordance with the provisions of CAS 420. Other contracts must comply with all CAS 420 provisions except those pertaining to allocability. When IR&D and B&P costs cannot be allocated equitably to these contracts through the G&A base, the contracting officer may approve another base.

*Contracts subject to full CAS coverage

Figure 7.2   (Continued)

normally the contractor's established allocation practices that are in accord with generally accepted accounting principles should be accepted unless required to be changed by a new contractual provision or reexamination of the practices is warranted as a result of unusual circumstances.

On numerous occasions, the boards and courts have cautioned against using GAAP to determine the allocability of costs to government contracts by noting that" . . . such principles have been developed for asset valuation and income measurement and "are not cost accounting principles" as such. . . ."[15]

When the cost accounting treatment permitted by GAAP is contrary to the criteria provided in either the cost principles or the contract, these latter criteria generally prevail. In *Grumman Aerospace Corp. v. United States*,[16] the Court rejected the contractor's argument that, under GAAP, its 1968 state franchise tax refund resulting from the carryback of its 1971 net operating loss should be credited to 1971 costs, not 1968 costs. In its decision, the Court concluded that" . . . with regard to how GAAP and sound accounting logic might treat the refund for income tax accounting purposes, the contract language prevails here."

The ASBCA reached a similar conclusion in *Physics International Company*[17] when it decided that

even if appellant's intercompany allocations are consistent with the generally accepted accounting principles, they cannot dictate reimbursability by the Government when the cost item in question does not meet the ASPR specific allowability criteria, . . .

SELECTED COSTS

The acquisition regulations address specific limitations or exclusions for numer-ous items of cost. Although some differences still exist, the Federal Acquisition Regulations (FAR) eliminated a number of differences between the cost principles previously issued by the various departments and agencies. As a result, more companies doing business with multiple contracting offices are now able to calculate uniform indirect expense rates applicable to federal contracts awarded after April 1, 1984. Contracts awarded prior to that date remain subject to the prior regulations (e.g., DAR). Since the FAR citations differ from those in the prior regulations, a cross-reference listing is provided in Figure 7.3.

The cost principles have changed over the years with disturbing regularity in response to unique aspects of government contracting, such as public policy considerations, administrative convenience, and congressional interest. The cost principles essentially establish three categories of cost:

Expressly allowable.
Partially unallowable or require special consideration.
Expressly unallowable.

The acquisition regulations specifically require that expressly unallowable costs plus all directly associated costs be identified and excluded from proposals, billings, and claims submitted to the government. Directly associated costs are defined as those that would not have been incurred if the other cost, e.g., the unallowable cost, had not been incurred. Thus salary costs of employees who engage in activities that result in unallowable costs, such as acquisitions and mergers, could be subject to question if the employees expend a substantial portion of their time on the unallowable activity.

It is critical that a company's cost accounting system differentiate unallowable costs from otherwise allowable costs. If its cost accounting system does not have that capability, a company may be vulnerable to a determinations of noncompliance with CAS 405 or execution of a false overhead certificate for failure to delete expressly unallowable costs from claims and proposals submitted to the government.

The cost principles do not address each cost that may be incurred. The absence of a cost principle for a particular cost item does not imply that it is either allowable or unallowable. The cost principles note that determinations of allowability in these instances shall be based on the principles and standards included in the subpart and, where appropriate, the treatment of similar or related selected items.

However, the GAO[18] reported in 1985 that costs which may be unallowable by one subsection of FAR 31.205 are often allowed in the negotiation process by another section. As a result, a revision to FAR 31.204[19] has been proposed that:

> costs shall not be allowed under a cost principle when there is another more relevant cost principle which would make the costs unallowable. When more than one cost principle has reasonable applicability to a cost in question, the rules and standards in each cost principle shall be considered in determining the respective amount of allowable and unallowable costs.

Cost items described in the cost principles as either expressly allowable (assuming reasonableness and allocability tests are met) or expressly unallowable are summarized in Figure 7.4.

Certain costs that warrant special consideration or that may be either allowable or unallowable depending on the particular circumstances are discussed below.

	FAR	Regulations in Effect Prior to FAR		
	31.205	DAR 15-205	NASA PR 15.205	FPR 1-15.205
Public Relations & Advertising costs.	−1	.1	−1	−1
Automatic data processing equipment leasing costs.	−2	.48	−48	−50
Bad debts.	−3	.2	−2	−2
Bonding costs.	−4	.4	−4	−4
Civil defense costs.	−5	.5	−5	−5
Compensation for personal services.	−6	.6	−6	−6
Contingencies.	−7	.7	−7	−7
Contributions and donations.	−8	.8	−8	−8
Cost of money.	−10	.50	−50	−51
Depreciation.	−11	.9	−9	−9
Economic planning costs.	−12	.47	−47	−47
Employee morale, health, welfare, food service, and dormitory costs and credits.	−13	.10	−10	−10
Entertainment costs.	−14	.11	−11	−11
Fines and penalties.	−15	.13	−13	−13
Gains and losses on disposition of depreciable property or other capital assets.	−16	.32	−32	−32
Idle facilities and idle capacity costs.	−17	.12	−12	−12
Independent research and development and bid and proposal costs.	−18	.3 and .35	−3 and −35	−3 and −35
Insurance and indemnification	−19	.16	−16	−16
Interest and other financial costs.	−20	.17	−17	−17
Labor relations costs.	−21	.18	−18	−18
Legislative lobbying costs.	−22	.51	−51	−52
Losses on other contracts	−23	.19	−19	−19
Maintenance and repair costs.	−24	.20	−20	−20
Manufacturing and production engineering costs.	−25	.21	−21	−21
Material costs.	−26	.22	−22	−22
Organization costs.	−27	.23	−23	−23
Other business expenses.	−28	.24	−24	−24
Plant protection costs.	−29	.28	−28	−28
Patent costs.	−30	.26	−26	−26
Plant reconversion costs.	−31	.29	−29	−29
Precontract costs.	−32	.30	−30	−30
Professional and consultant service costs.	−33	.31	−31	−31
Recruitment costs.	−34	.33	−33	−33
Relocation costs.	−35	.25	−25	−25
Rental costs.	−36	.34	−34	−34
Royalties and other costs for use of patents.	−37	.36	−36	−36
Selling costs.	−38	.37	−37	−37
Service and warranty costs.	−39	.38	−38	−38
Special tooling and special test equipment costs.	−40	.40	−40	−40
Taxes.	−41	.41	−41	−41
Termination costs.	−42	.42	−42	−42
Trade, business, technical, and professional activity costs.	−43	.43	−43	−43
Training and educational costs.	−44	.44	−44	−44
Transportation costs.	−45	.45	−45	−45
Travel costs.	−46	.46	−46	−46
Defense of fraud proceedings.	−47	.52	−52	−53
Deferred research and development costs.	−48	.49		
Dividends.				−14
Goodwill.	−49			
Executive Lobbying Costs.	−50			
Cost of alcoholic beverages	−51			

Figure 7.3 Selected costs—reference citations.

Expressly Allowable Costs	Expressly Unallowable Costs
Bonding costs FAR 31.205-4, PCM 15-205.18	Bad debts FAR 31.205.3, PCM 15-205.2
Economic planning costs FAR 31.205-12, PCM 15-205.47	Contingencies FAR 31.205-7, PCM 15-205.7(b)
Labor relations costs FAR 31.205-21, PCM 15-205.18	Contributions and donations FAR 31.205-8, PCM 15-205.8
Maintenance and repair costs FAR 31.205-24, PCM 15-205.20	Entertainment FAR 31.205-14, PCM 15-205.11
Manufacturing and production engineering costs FAR 31.205-25, PCM 15-205.21	Fines and penalties FAR 31.205-15, PCM 15-205.13
Other business expenses (e.g., recurring costs for stock registry and transfer, shareholder meetings and reports, reports for taxing and regulatory bodies, etc.) FAR 31.205-28, PCM 15-205.24	Interest and other financial costs FAR 31.205-23, PCM 15-205.19 Losses on other contracts FAR 31.205-23, PCM 15-205.19 Organization costs FAR 31.205-27, PCM 15-205.23
Plant protection costs FAR 31.205-29, PCM 15-205.28	Gains or losses on disposition of capital assets other than depreciable property* FAR 31.205-16, PCM 15-205.32
Precontract costs (but an advance agreement is recommended) FAR 31.205-32, PCM 15-205.30	Lobbying costs FAR 31.205-22, 31.225-50
Service and warranty costs FAR 31.205-39, PCM 15-205.38 FAR 31.205-16, PCM 15-205.32	Goodwill FAR 31.205-49 Alcoholic beverages FAR 31.205-50

*Gains or losses on disposition of depreciable property are also unallowable under PCM 15-205.32.

Figure 7.4. Cost principles—selected costs.

Public Relations and Advertising Costs (FAR 31.205-1; PCM 15-205.1)

Effective April 7, 1986 this cost principle was retitled and revised to add coverage on public relations to the existing coverage on advertising. While the revision did not substantively change the advertising provisions, the new coverage on public relations limited allowable public relations costs to a narrower range of activities. The cost principle also added a new and significant concept that costs which are unallowable under this principle can not be allowable under other cost principles and vice versa. This concept was intended to reduce differences and disagreements among contractors, government auditors and contracting officers and reduce inconsistent treatment of costs.

The cost principle discusses advertising in the context of media advertising (such as magazines, newspapers, radio and television, direct mail, trade papers, outdoor advertising, dealer cards and window displays, conventions, exhibits, free goods and samples) and directly associated costs.

The cost principle defines public relations as all functions and activities related to maintaining, protecting, and enhancing the image of a concern or its products and maintaining or promoting reciprocal understanding and favorable relations with the public at large or any segment of the public. The term public relations includes activities associated with such areas as advertising, and customer relations.

Allowable advertising cost are limited to those that are solely for:

Recruitment of personnel for performing government contracts, when considered in conjunction with all other recruitment costs.

Procurement of scarce items for performing government contracts.

Disposal of scrap or surplus materials acquired under government contracts.

Cost of this nature, if incurred for more than one contract or for both contract work and other work of the contractor, are allowable to the extent that they are reasonably apportioned among the various benefiting objectives.

Other advertising costs, such as those related to sales promotion, are not allowable. As characterized by the ASBCA in *Aerojet General Corp.*,[20] such advertising involves direct payment for the

use of time or space to promote the sale of products either directly by stimulating interest in a product or product line, or indirectly by disseminating messages calling favorable attention to the advertiser for the purpose of enhancing its overall image to sell its products. In both instances the advertiser controls form and content of the message and selects the medium of presentation and its timing.

The government's disallowance of advertising related to sales promotions stems from two considerations:

Because of the limited number of major procurement activities, companies do not have to sell to the government in the same manner that they sell to the general public. Sales to the government are accomplished through direct contacts and submission of solicited and unsolicited proposals, and these costs are allowable as selling or bidding costs.

The annual Defense Appropriation Acts forbid the use of appropriated funds for any advertising other than that specified above.

Allowable public relations costs are limited to:

Items specifically required by contract.

Responses to inquiries on company policy and activities and communications with the public, press, stockholders, creditors and customers.

General liaison with news media and government public relations officers, limited to activities that are necessary to keep the public informed on matters of public concern such as contract awards, plant closing or openings, employee layoffs or rehires, financial information, etc.

Participation in community service activities, plant tours and open houses, keel laying, ship launching and roll out ceremonies, to the extent specifically provided for by contract.

Other public relations costs are considered to be unallowable and include costs of:

Air shows.
Conventions.
Trade shows.
Displays.
Demonstrations.
Exhibits.
Ceremonies.
Promotional material.

Motion pictures.
Videotapes.
Brochures.
Handouts.
Magazines.
Souvenirs.
Membership in civic and community organizations.
Activities designed to promote the sales of products and services by stimulating interest in a product enhancing the company's image.

Companies should properly distinguish between costs for advertising, image enhancement public relations, bidding and proposal preparation, information dissemination, and selling activities in their indirect expense accounts. Costs associated with information disseminating activities are allowable. In the 1973 *Aerojet-General Corp.* decision refered to above, the Board concluded that the following items that had been challenged as unallowable advertising costs did not fall into the definition of advertising and were thus allowable:

A monthly magazine, circulated outside the company, which contained semi-technical summaries of the company's developments in technologies, progress on government programs, and changes in personnel.

Salaried costs for the company's public communications department, which provided liaison with news media and government public information offices.

A company profile brochure that was prepared in response to business inquiries and replied to factual questions about the company. (Copies were provided to interested parties.)

A brochure describing the company's effort to increase employees' knowledge and participation in the political process. (Copies were sent to interested companies and political parties.)

A reprint of a speech made by the company president. (Copies were sent to interested parties and the news media.)

Photographs and fact sheets for news releases. (The fact sheets were distributed to the news media.)

Even before the promulgation of the current cost principle, in a decision involving Blue Cross/Blue Shield,[21] the ASBCA observed: " . . . where the major purpose of the message was image enhancement or sales, we concluded no share of the cost be allocated [to the government contact]." The Board went on to decide, however, that mass media messages relating to health education, health care cost containment, and subscriber services did not fall into the category of image enhancement or sales; therefore, the costs should not be considered unallowable.

Automatic Data Processing Equipment (ADPE) Leasing Costs (FAR 31.205-2; PCM 15-205.48)

Under FAR, as well as the predecessor DAR and NASA PR, allowable operating lease costs, as defined in FAS 13, are limited to constructive ownership costs unless the contractor can demonstrate that lease costs result in less costs to the government over the useful life of the equipment, based on the facts at the time of the decision to lease or to continue the lease. In determining the least cost to the government, the cumulative costs that would be allowed if the contractor owned the equipment (including the cost of money) should be compared with the cumulative lease costs. Section 7-206.2.b. of the DCAA *Contract Audit Manual*[22] notes the following:

Ownership vs. Rental Comparison

The contractor's submission to support the allowability of its ADPE leasing costs will generally be in the form of a comparison of constructive ownership costs with leasing costs over the anticipated useful life of the property. The major factors involved in this comparison are: constructive acquisition costs, estimated useful life, depreciation methods, residual value, and leasing costs. . . . The auditor should carefully review all pertinent factual data and estimates included in the comparison for propriety and reasonableness. Technical assistance should be obtained as necessary. The determination of whether leasing costs are more costly than ownership costs will be based upon a comparison of the respective amounts for the total estimated useful life of the property. Where this comparison shows leasing costs to be more costly, the amount of leasing costs to be disallowed in any individual year will be the excess of the cumulative leasing costs incurred through that particular year as compared with the cumulative constructive ownership costs which would have been incurred during that same total period.

Also required is an annual demonstration that:

ADPE leasing costs are reasonable and necessary for the conduct of the business.

ADPE leasing costs do not give rise to a material equity in the equipment, other than that normally given to the industry at large.

The contracting officer has approved the leasing arrangement if either total ADPE costs are allocated to flexibly priced contracts or ADPE costs for the plant, division, or cost center exceed $500,000 per year and at least 50% of the cost is allocated to flexibly priced contracts.

With regard to this annual justification, Section 7-206.2.c. of the DCAA *Contract Audit Manual* notes:

(b) ADPE—Annual Submissions. DAR 15-205.48(b)(2)/FAR 31.205-2(b)(2) provides that costs of leasing ADPE are allowable only to the extent that the contractor can demonstrate annually that leasing is in the best interests of the Government. The key word here is "annually" and this requirement applies particularly in those situations where the contractor has previously demonstrated that leasing is less costly than ownership. Annual reviews do not, however, apply where it has previously been demonstrated that the ADPE equipment is cheaper to purchase. The annual justification should recognize all new conditions such as changes in leasing arrangements, anticipated equipment acquisitions, adjustments to useful lives, and changes in residual lives. Also, it should be submitted irrespective of whether the term of the lease was renewed or otherwise extended by the contractor. For equipment already in service, the purchase price to be used in the comparison is the purchase option price under the terms of the existing lease contract, or if an option is not available, then the price in the open market.

Allowable ADPE rental costs under sale and leaseback arrangements or rental agreements between entities under common control are generally limited to constructive ownership costs.

The FPR, which preceded the FAR, and the PCM cost principles are similar to the FAR, except that they apply to all ADPE leases, not just those classified as operating leases under FAS 13.

Civil Defense Cost (FAR 31.205-5; PCM 31-205.5)

Reasonable costs of civil defense measures undertaken on the company's premises, pursuant to suggestions or requirements of civil defense authorites, are allowable. Contributions to local civil defense funds and projects are unallowable.

Compensation for Personal Services (FAR 31.205-6; PCM 31-205.6)

Compensation for personal services is essentially defined in the cost principles as including all remuneration paid currently or accrued for services rendered by employees during the period of contract performance. Allowable total compensation of individual employees must be reasonable for the services rendered. Certain types of compensation, such as bonuses, incentive compensation and severance pay, must also be paid pursuant to an employer/employee agreement or an established plan which has been consistently followed.

Allowable compensation must reflect the terms and conditions of established compensation plans or practices. No presumption of allowability exists if the government did not receive an advance notice of major changes in compensation plans.

The cost principles identify the following circumstances that the government will closely scrutinize in determining whether compensation paid is reasonable:

Compensation to owners of closely held corporations, partners, sole proprietors, or persons who have a significant financial interest in the business entity.

Increases in the company's compensation policy that coincide with an increase in government business.

Absence of a competitive environment that would operate to place controls on the reasonableness of all costs, including employee compensation.

Provisions of labor-management agreements that appear unwarranted or discriminatory against the government.

The cost principle was revised in 1986 to provide more detailed guidelines for determining the reasonableness of compensation practices. The current language makes clear that compensation is reasonable if each element of the compensation package is reasonable, and that the contractor has the burden of proof in demonstrating the reasonableness of each element that may be challenged by the government. The contractor can however, within certain specified limits, introduce other offsetting compensation elements when the reasonableness of some part of the program is challenged. Such offsets are considered only between the following allowable elements of an employee's (or a class of employees) compensation costs:

Wages and salaries.
Incentive bonuses.
Deferred compensation.

Pension and savings plan benefits.
Health insurance benefits.
Life insurance benefits.
Compensated personal absences.

The change related to burden of proof is a clear departure from previous board of contract appeals and court rulings which squarely placed the burden of proof on the government where costs were being challenged as unreasonable.

Over the years government auditors have questioned the level of compensation paid to chief executive officers (CEOs) particularly of smaller companies. Several ASBCA cases have been decided which may assist companies in establishing the reasonableness of their executive compensation when challenged by government auditors.

In *Lulejean and Associates, Inc.,*[23] the ASBCA totally reinstated the government's disallowances of executive salaries that exceeded the midpoint of salaries for comparable positions within the industry. The Board noted that, for the year in which the study was performed, the salaries of the Lulejean executives were within the range recommended by the government analyst. In the Board's view:

> There is no explanation in the record why the ACO selected the midpoint of each range as "acceptable" salary or why a salary which was above the midpoint, but still with the recommended range, was unreasonable. Since levels of reasonable compensation can be more meaningfully represented by ranges below and above a certain figure than by a precise figure, we perceive no reason why the actual salaries of these five persons were unreasonable.

In *Space Services of Georgia, Inc.,*[24] the Board considered *claimed* annual CEO salary of $100,000 to be reasonable compensation in April 1980 for a company providing mess attendant services with sales between $5 and $10 million.

In *Burt Associates, Inc.,*[25] the Board considered claimed annual CEO compensation of $63,000 ($53,000 salary and $10,000 bonus) to be reasonable compensation in 1977 for a research and consulting corporation with annual revenue of $409,000. Significantly, the Board acknowledged that CEOs who own their own companies tend to be compensated at higher levels than those who do not. In its decision, the board concluded:

> When measured against average compensation of the highest paid executives . . . Dr. Burt's compensation appears to be on the high side. However, when measured against the total compensation of executives who are majority owners of their companies, Dr. Burt's compensation falls within the range of compensation received by such executives. . . . [O]n the record before us we cannot discount Dr. Burt's overwhelming responsibility for the success of his company and the long hours devoted to achieving that success. We conclude that Dr. Burt's compensation in fiscal year 1977 was reasonable under the circumstances.

In these cases, the Board concluded that the reasonableness of compensation should be evaluated in light of the size and nature of the business.

Stock Options and Stock Appreciation Rights

A 1987 revision to the cost principle limits the allowable costs of stock appreciation rights (SAR) to the difference between the SAR base price (i.e., the price from which stock appreciation will be measured) and the market price on the first date on which both the number of shares and the SAR base price are known. Accordingly, when the SAR base price is equal to or greater than the market price on that date (as is usually the case), no costs are allowed for contract costing purposes.

Prior to the 1987 proposed revision allowable costs of stock options and SARs were to be limited to the difference between the option or SAR price and the market price of the stock on the measurement date (i.e., the first date on which the number of shares and the option or SAR price are known).

This provision had validity for a stock option plan because the measurement date is almost always the award date—the first date on which both the number of shares and the option price are known. However, the measurement date for SARs is the exercise date; by definition, appreciation can only be ascertained at a specific future date. The previous FAR provisions relating to the allowability of SARs were ambiguous. The FAR implied that SARs were allowable under certain circumstances. Yet linking the allowability of SAR costs with the cost of stock option plans could lead to the conclusion that the award date should be the date for cost measurement for both SARs and stock option plans. (In fact, in guidance to its field auditors, the Defense Contract Audit Agency took that position.) If that assumption were made, there would rarely be any allowable SAR costs because at the award date the SAR price almost always equals the market price.

The language in the 1987 revision, at least, clarified that the government intends to virtually disallow all SAR costs. The 1987 revision also make moot the ASBCA decision in the Boeing Company[26] where the Board totally overruled the government disallowance of the SAR costs by concluding that:

the costs were allowable under existing cost principles.

SARs "are far more readily described not as 'options' but as 'bonuses including stock bonuses'. . . ."

The "requirement that the agreement be entered into 'before the services are rendered' is satisfied . . ." inasmuch as SAR participants were required to remain in the firm's employ for at least six months prior to exercising a SAR.

Employee Stock Ownership Plans/Employee Stock Purchase Plans

Contributions to employee stock ownership plans (ESOPs) are generally allowable subject to certain limitations (e.g., contributions normally cannot exceed 15% of salary). However, ESOP contributions arising under tax reduction act ownership plans (TRASOPs) are not allowable costs. Neither are contributions made under payroll-based tax credit stock ownership plans (PAYSOPs). The disallowance of these costs generated considerable criticism. Some of the reasons for disagreeing with the government's position area:

TRASOP/PAYSOP contributions are a necessary cost of doing business.

Tax credits have nothing to do with government contract costing. Under GAAP, the amount contributed to the ESOP, including the portion resulting from the additional tax credit, is charged to expense so that the additional tax credit is accounted for as a reduction of federal income tax. Since the government does not recognize Federal income taxes as a cost of performance, transactions affecting the tax liability should be disregarded in determining cost recovery.

The cost principle is inconsistent with the government's position on the investment tax credit, which is considered a reduction in taxes, not a reduction in the depreciable base of the asset acquired.

The case involving *Singer Co.*[27] dealt with a stock purchase plan in which company stock was available to virtually all employees at a 20% discount from the market price. The company treated the discount as compensation costs on the books of its division, but in the consolidated financial statements the discounts were charged directly to an equity account. The government disallowed the discounted portion of the sales price of the stock issued to employees under the plan citing the following reasons:

The plan was a stock option plan for which the costs were expressly unallowable under the then existing Defense Acquisition Regulation.

The company's financial reporting of the plan as noncompensatory was contrary to GAAP.

The costs represented unallowable financing costs.

The protracted adjudication process included the following actions:

An initial ASBCA decision that sustained the disallowance on the basis that the plan was a stock option plan.

A subsequent ASBCA decision that allowed the cost solely on the basis that the plan was not a stock option plan.

Remand by the Court of Claims back to the ASBCA to consider the other issues raised by the government.

An ASBCA decision that ruled against the government on all three issues.

In its final decision, the Board concluded on the first issue that the plan was not a stock option plan within the meaning of the cost principle. Accordingly, the cost would be considered allowable as compensation unless precluded by some other provision of DAR Section XV. As to the argument that the company's accounting practice violated GAAP and thus precluded reimbursement of the costs, the Board concluded that the alleged inconsistency had no effect on the disposition of the appeal. The Board did not consider disallowing amounts that otherwise would be recoverable to be the appropriate redress for failure to follow GAAP in the financial statements. The Board also concluded that the plan was, in fact, compensatory since employees were required to treat the discount as taxable compensation in the year the stock restrictions were removed and the company was entitled to an income tax deduction in that year. The Board also disagreed with the argument that the discount should be disallowed as a financing charge. Since the plan was voluntary, the Board concluded that the employee stock purchase plan was primarily an inducement and incentive for retaining employees, rather than a vehicle for raising capital.

In *Honeywell, Inc.*[28] the ASBCA again overruled the government's challenge to the allowability of employee stock discount costs. The costs were similar to those incurred by Singer. The Honeywell Employee Stock Ownership Plan permitted employees to purchase company stock at 85% of the market price. The discount was taxable to the employee. Like Singer, Honeywell recorded the discount as an adjustment to equity rather than as a charge against earnings on its financial statements. However, it did allocate the discount costs to the appropriate division for inclusion in its indirect cost submissions. The government disallowed the cost on the basis that:

> The contractor's treatment of these costs for third party financial reporting and government costing purposes was inconsistent, and
>
> The plan was noncompensatory under Accounting Principles Board Opinion (APB) No. 25.

On the first point, the Board merely recited its earlier opinion in *Singer*—since the company treated the discount as a deductible compensation cost for tax purposes, it should be treated as a compensation cost for government contract costing purposes. On the second point, the Board found that the Honeywell Plan did not meet one of the four characteristics essential for noncompensable plans—qualification under Section 423 of the Internal Revenue Code. Therefore, the criteria in APB 25 did not support the government position.

Pensions and Deferred Compensation

Cost accounting standards have had a significant effect on the compensation cost principle since CAS 412, Composition and Measurement of Pension Cost, CAS 413, Adjustment and Allocation of Pension Cost, and CAS 415, Accounting for the Cost of Deferred Compensation, have been incorporated in toto. Thus, even contractors not otherwise subject to CAS must calculate pension and deferred compensation costs in accordance with these standards in order for the cost to be considered allowable.

In recent years, significant events have occurred which greatly affect the manner in which pension costs are calculated and allocated to government contracts.

The first major change relates to the issuance of Standard 87 by the Financial Accounting Standards Board (FAS-87). This Standard changed in several respects the way pension costs are calculated for financial accounting purposes. First, it mandates the use of the projected unit credit actuarial cost method, which is one of several methods known as an immediate-gain actuarial cost method. However, CAS 412.50(b)(2)(i) permits the use of a spread-gain actuarial cost method only if such a method is used for financial accounting purposes. Thus, because FAS-87 requires the use of an immediate-gain method for financial accounting purposes, companies that were using a spread-gain method have had to change to an immediate-gain method for government cost accounting purposes. Such a change is a cost accounting change within the definition set forth in the CAS regulations contained in 4 CFR 331.20(1). Moreover, because FAS-87's requirements for amortizing actuarial gains and losses, and valuing pension fund assets differ from CAS-412's requirements, contractors will have to prepare separate actuarial valuations for financial accounting and cost accounting purposes.

Another significant development has been the bullish stock market in recent years which resulted in pension fund assets growing more quickly than was anticipated. As a result, many pension plans have become overfunded (i.e., a fund's assets exceed its actuarial liability). There have been two significant consequences relating to overfunded plans.

Many companies have terminated their pension plans and purchased annuities for the participants' accrued benefits. The difference between the value of the assets and the cost of the annuities represents a profit to the company, generally referred to as a reversion. A major question arises as to whether the government is entitled to a portion of the reversion and, if so, how the government's share should be calculated.

Because pension plans are overfunded, companies may not be making current contributions to pension funds. One issue that has arisen is whether a contractor has a cost if nothing is funded, even though there is a CAS-calculated cost. Another issue relates to the government's right, if any, to recoup pension costs that have been included in fixed-price contracts but are not funded because of the overfunded status of the plan.

Several proposals to amend CAS 412, amend the FAR cost principle on compensation, and/or require advance agreements addressing the government's right to cost recoupment in these situations have been proposed. It will be some time before these issues are settled.

The ASBCA allowed the costs of The Boeing Company's[29] Supplemental Executive Retirement Plan which was funded only when the costs ultimately became deductible for IRS purposes. The requirements of CAS 412, "Compensation and Measurement of Pension Costs," and the cost principle on compensation in FAR 31.205-6, conflict. CAS 412 requires the actuarially computed pension costs to be assigned to a cost accounting period and allocated to cost objectives (e.g., contracts) of that period if the pension cost is funded or if payment of the benefits can be compelled. FAR more restrictively limits cost allowability to the lesser of the actuarially computed pension costs, or the amount deductible for federal income tax purposes for the year. In its decision the Board observed that

> whether based on its own official standing or on the basis of its incorporation in the Defense Acquisition Regulation, CAS 412 has the force and effect of law . . . We hold that CAS 412 is controlling with respect to the determination, measurement, assignment and allocation of SERP costs.

The government disallowed the SERP costs since they were not funded in the year the costs were claimed. In arriving at its decision the Board noted that when the DAR Council faced a similar conflict between the compensation cost principle and CAS 415 regarding the accrual of deferred compensation, the DAR Council concluded that it had no choice but to revise DAR 15-205.6 to make it compatible with the requirements of CAS 415.

This decision has far-reaching ramifications in light of government plans to issue regulations addressing such issues as overfunded pension plans. Since the standards in their present form have the force and effect of law they would likely prevail in any conflict with amended standards issued as regulations by DOD.

A revision has been proposed to the compensation cost principles[30] relating to business acquisitions. The revisions would specifically disallow the costs of "golden parachutes"—special compensation in excess of severance pay in the event of termination, and "golden handcuffs"—special compensation, in addition to normal pay, to induce employees to remain with the company.

Cost of Money (FAR 31.205-10)

Facilities capital cost of money (COM) as defined and computed in CAS 414 is allowable, except on Postal Service contracts, provided the cost is specifically identified or proposed in cost proposals. The calculation of COM is illustrated in Figures 8.7 through 8.10 in Chapter 8. The cost principle was modified in October 1984 to make unallowable the cost of money associated with goodwill.

COM as defined and computed in CAS 417 is an allowable element of the cost of a capital asset under construction, and is thus included in the depreciable base of the constructed asset. Unlike CAS 417, however, the cost principle does not allow any alternative methods for calculating COM, such as the method prescribed for financial reporting in Financial Accounting Standards Board Statement 34. Under FAS 34, interest expense on certain capital assets is capitalized at a rate based on the company's outstanding borrowings.

Bid and Proposal (B&P) and Independent Research and Development (IR&D) Costs (FAR 31.205-18; PCM 15-205.3 and 15-205.35)

B&P costs are the costs incurred in preparing, submitting, and supporting bids and proposals on potential government or nongovernment contracts. IR&D costs are the costs of technical effort that is not sponsored by a contact, grant or other arrangement and that falls in the areas of basic and applied research, development, and/or systems and other concept formulation studies.

For the purpose of allocating indirect expenses other than G&A expense, B&P and IR&D projects are accounted for as if they were contracts. Thus, B&P and IR&D costs consist of all direct labor, material, other direct costs, and all allocable indirect costs except G&A expense. IR&D and B&P costs are generally allocated to contracts on the same basis used to allocate G&A expenses.

Companies Required to Negotiate an Advance Agreement

The FAR requires any company receiving payments from the government in excess of $4.4 million for both IR&D and B&P in its prior fiscal year, to negotiate an advance agreement for the current year to establish a ceiling for allowable IR&D and B&P expenses. If the payments from DOD exceed the specified advance agreement threshold in the prior year, a DOD tri-service contracting officer is designated to negotiate the agreement. The specified threshold includes only those recoverable IR&D and B&P costs allocated during the company's previous fiscal year to government prime contracts and subcontracts for which submission and certification of cost or pricing data were required. (Prior to issuance of the FAR, the DAR and the DOE PR each required negotiation of an advance agreement for any company that in its prior fiscal year, received payments in excess of $4 million from DOD or DOE respectively. The NASA PR and FPR did not provide a dollar threshold for requiring an advance agreement.)

The penalty for not obtaining a required advance agreement is severe. No IR&D or B&P costs will be allowed if a company fails to initiate the negotiation of a required advance agreement prior to the start of the next fiscal year. If negotiations are held but agreement is not reached by the end of the fiscal year, payment for IR&D and B&P costs must be reduced by at least 25% of the amount, which, in the opinion of the contracting officer, the company or profit center would otherwise have been entitled to receive under an advance agreement.

Required advance agreements may be negotiated at the corporate level and/or with those profit centers that contract directly with the government and that in the preceding year allocated more than $550,000 in recoverable IR&D and B&P costs to DOD contracts and subcontracts for which certified cost or pricing data were required.

The advance agreement establishes separate dollar ceilings for IR&D and B&P costs. Although costs that exceed the ceilings are generally unallowable, increases in one area may be offset by decreases in the other area as long as the total expenditures do not exceed the combined ceilings for both types of cost.

The total B&P and IR&D costs allocated to DOD contracts cannot exceed the total expenditures for B&P and IR&D projects with a potential military relationship. DOE also limits recovery of IR&D costs to the lesser of the amount calculated in accordance with the FAR provision or the amount having a potential benefit to DOE programs. (These requirements apply both to companies that are negotiating an advance agreement and those that are not.)

Companies Not Required to Negotiate an Advance Agreement

The FAR, like the prior DAR and DOE Procurement Regulation, establishes cost ceilings for companies not required to negotiate an advance agreement, by using a formula based on historical IR&D and B&P costs and sales data for the preceding 3 years. The formula can be applied on either a company-wide basis or by profit center. The mechanics of the formula are illustrated in Figure 7.5. The FPR and NASA PR contained no ceiling.

	Sales ($000)	IR&D ($000)	%	B&P ($000)	%
Period for application of ceiling					
19×4	$4500	$150		$175	
Prior three periods					
19×1	$5000	$150	3.0%	$150	3.0%
19×2	$7000	$200	2.9%	$150	2.1%
19×3	$4000	$120	3.0%	$200	5.0%
Calculation of ceiling					
Historical ratio (1)			3.0%		4.0%
Average annual cost (1)		$175		$175	
Limits					
120% of average (upper limit)		$210		$210	
80% of average (lower limit)		$140		$140	
Product					
Current year sales × historical ratio					
$4500 × 3%		$135			
$4500 × 4%				$180	
19×4					
Ceiling (2)		$140		$180	
Permitted interchange (3)		5		(5)	
Total allowed		$145		$175	
Cost disallowed		$ 5			

(1) Average of the two highest of the prior three years.

(2) The ceiling equals the product of the current year sales and the historical ratio, provided that amount is not less than 80% or greater than 120% of the average.

(3) Overceiling IR&D costs are allowable to the extent that they are offset by underceiling B&P costs and vice versa.

Figure 7.5 Formula for determining IR&D/B&P ceilings for companies not required to negotiate an advance agreement.

Where the formula gives an inequitable result, the contracting officer is authorized to negotiate an advance agreement establishing the IR&D/B&P ceiling. In *Dynatrend, Inc.*[31] the company was entitled to higher recovery of B&P costs than resulted from application of the formula. The contracting officer's refusal to negotiate an advance agreement with the contractor was considered an abuse of discretion. Of particular significance is the fact that the contractor's request for advance agreement, which covered both its prior and current fiscal year, was sustained by the Board.

The PCM cost principles on B&P and IR&D costs are less prescriptive. They discuss allowability in general terms of reasonableness while concluding that it may be desirable for the Postal Service to bear less than an allocable share of the total costs. The Postal Service bases the allowability of independent development costs on the extent to which the development is related to a product line for which the Postal Service has contracts.

Depreciation (FAR 31.205-11; PCM 15.205-16)

Contractors with contracts subject to CAS 409, Depreciation of Tangible Capital Assets, must follow the provisions of the standard on these contracts and may elect to follow the standard on the remainder of their non-CAS covered contracts. For contracts not subject to CAS, the acquisition regulations rely primarily on tests of reasonableness and the Internal Revenue Code. Depreciation will ordinarily be considered reasonable if depreciation policies and procedures used for contract costing are:

Consistent with the policies and procedures followed by the company in its commercial business.

Reflected in the company's books of account and financial statements.

Used and accepted for Federal income tax purposes.

Where different depreciation costs are computed for financial statement and tax purposes, allowable depreciation is limited to the amounts used for book and statement purposes, determined in a manner consistent with the depreciation policies used on other than government business.

The FAR, like the predecessor DAR and NASA PR, incorporated the Statement of Financial Accounting Standards 13 (FAS 13), Accounting for Leases, promulgated by FASB, except where sale and leaseback transactions are involved. FAS 13 requires that a lease be classified as a capital lease for financial reporting purposes if it meets any one of four criteria; otherwise, it is classified as an operating lease. The four criteria are:

Automatic transfer of title.

Bargain purchase option.

Lease term equals or exceeds 75% of the estimated economic life of the leased property.

Present value of the minimum lease payments equals or exceeds 90% of the excess of the fair value of the leased property over any related investment tax credit retained by the lessor.

Items acquired by means of a capital lease as defined by FAS 13 are subject to the depreciation cost principle and Cost Accounting Standard 404, Capitalization of Tangible Assets. In a sale and leaseback situation, the allowable lease cost is limited to the amount the company would be allowed if it had retained title.

The FPR in effect prior to issuance of the FAR, and the PCM do not refer to FAS 13; consequently, costs of capital leases allocated to federal contracts subject to those regulations are governed by the rental cost principle, not the cost principle for depreciation.

The allowability of depreciation resulting from the "step-up" in asset values arising from business combinations has been addressed by the ASBCA in recent years. The writeup of assets under transactions that qualify for the "purchase method" of accounting in accordance with Accounting Principles Board (APB) No. 16 is permitted. The resulting depreciation can be claimed on the books of the acquiring corporation for financial reporting purposes. In the *Marquardt Company*,[32] however, the board disallowed depreciation costs resulting from the writeup of the value of Marquardt's assets following its acquisition by ISC Electronics, Inc. (ISCE). Marquardt, formerly a wholly-owned subsidiary of CCI Corporation (CCI), was acquired by and became a wholly-owned subsidiary of ISCE in 1983.

In accordance with APB No. 16, ISCE recorded the acquisition under the "purchase method" of accounting for business combination. Under the purchase method, the acquiring company allocates the cost of the acquisition to the identifiable individual assets acquired and liabilities assumed on the basis of their fair values.

On the basis of language in CAS 404.50(d), Marquardt claimed the depreciation expense attributable to the stepped-up basis of its capital assets as an allowable cost, and included this cost in its provisional and forward-pricing indirect cost rates. The contracting officer disallowed the increased depreciation expense on the basis that the sale of Marquardt merely represented a transfer of stock from CCI to ISCE. After the acquisition, Marquardt still maintained the same name, management, assets, and corporate status.

The Board concurred with the contracting officer's final decision by concluding:

> Marquardt's arguments lose sight of the fact that Marquardt and not its new parent, ISCE, is the contracting party here. Paragraph 1 of APB 16 states that a business combination occurs when one or more businesses are brought together in one accounting entity, and "The single entity carries on the activities of the previously separate, independent enterprises." Appellant's reliance on APB 16 is misplaced, since Marquardt remained an independent entity . . . APB 16, under these circumstances, has nothing to do with how the acquired corporation is to value its assets when it is acquired by another company. APB 16 deals solely with how an acquiring corporation (ISCE) is to value the assets it has acquired . . . As a result of the transaction, ISCE incurred the cost, not Marquardt, and if ISCE is to recover the purchase cost of acquiring Marquardt it can only do so under its own Government and commercial contracts. Marquardt remains a separate legal entity, obligated to perform its contracts and these contracts cannot be burdened with costs incurred by a third party.

The decision is distinguishable from an earlier case, *Gould Defense Systems, Inc.*,[33] in which the additional depreciation resulting from the stepped-up asset base was allowed. In that situation Clevite, a previously independent company, was acquired by and merged into Gould Defense Systems, Inc. Clevite ceased to exist as a result of the merger, and Clevite's contracts were novated to recognize Gould as the new contracting entity. Marquardt's situation was perceived by the Board as being clearly different. No novation agreement was required as a result of the ISC Electronics, Inc. acquisition because Marquardt's separate corporate status was not changed.

Employee Morale, Health, Welfare, and Food Service, Dormitory Costs and Credits (FAR 31.205-13; PCM 15-205.10)

Costs incurred to enhance working conditions, labor relations, employee morale, and employee productivity are generally allowable, except that special limitations apply to food and dormitory service losses. The FAR originally provided that when the company does not attempt to break even on its food and dormitory services, the loss is unallowable except in unusual circumstances (such as where commercial facilities are not reasonably available or where it is necessary to operate the facility at less than an economically practicable volume).

The cost principle was amended in 1986 to broaden the considerations available when administering the prohibition against allowability of losses on contractor operated cafeteria and lodging operations. The revision is intended to permit a more business-like evaluation of these operations than would have been permitted by a literal reading of the prior coverage. This revision draws attention to the negative impacts of reduction of cafeteria volume or cessation of operations. When workers eat away from the contractor's property the result may be longer lunch periods and when cafeteria operations are closed, many of the fixed occupancy costs do not diminish but are absorbed into other indirect cost pools of the contractor operations.

Entertainment (FAR 31.205-14; PCM 15-205.9)

Prior to April 1986 both the FAR and PCM cost principles defined unallowable entertainment as the costs of amusement, diversion, social activities and directly associated costs such as transportation and/or gratuities. In 1986 the FAR cost principle was revised to expand unallowable costs to include memberships in social, dining and country clubs, regardless of whether the costs are considered taxable income to the recipient.

Idle Facilities and Idle Capacity Costs (FAR 31.205.17; PCM 15-205.12)

Ownership costs attributable to completely unused and excess facilities are generally unallowable except if they must be maintained to accommodate workload fluctuations. However, if facilities become idle because of unforeseen events, such as a termination, the cost will be allowed for a period of up to one year.

Legislative Lobbying Costs (FAR 31.205-22) and Executive Lobbying Costs (FAR 31.205-50)

Significant changes were introduced into the cost principle in 1984. The previous language defined unallowable lobbying effort as communication or activity intended to influence Congress and state and local legislatures to favor or oppose legislation, appropriations, or other official actions.

Under the revised principle the following activities are unallowable:

Attempts to influence legislation.

Participation in election activities.

Attempts to influence government decisions through communications with legislative or government officials or employees.

Contributions to organizations that engage substantially in political advocacy.

Legislative liaison activity when such activity are in support of or in knowing preparation for an effort to engage in unallowable activities.

Certain legislative activities, when adequately documented, are allowable under FAR.

Local lobbying.

State lobbying that directly impacts a state grant or contract.

Participation in legislative public hearings or meetings in response to a specific invitation from the legislative source.

The cost principle provides for the use of estimates of time spent on such activity by indirect employees provided; less than 25% of the employee's time is spent on such activities and the company had not materially misstated any allowable or unallowable costs within the prior five years.

A new cost principle on executive lobbying costs (FAR 31.205-50) was promulgated in 1986 which disallows costs incurred to improperly influence executive branch officials of the Federal Government to give consideration to or act on a regulatory or contract matter. The prior cost principle was retitled "legislative lobbying costs."

Manufacturing and Production Engineering (FAR 31.205-25; PCM 15-205.17)

Effort related to development and deployment of new or improved materials, systems, processes, methods, equipment, tools and techniques should be considered manufacturing and production engineering if the developed items are intended for use:

1. in improving current production functions,
2. in producing the current or anticipated products or services,
3. on production lines, or
4. in production suitability analysis and manufacturing optimization.

These costs are allowable but must be carefully distinguished from effort expended in developing or deploying items that are intended for sale. Such costs should be considered IR&D which is subject to a cost reimbursability ceiling, as discussed previously in this chapter.

Material Costs (FAR 31.205-26; PCM 15-205.22)

Material costs are generally allowable, provided the costing method reasonably measures their actual costs. However, the purchase of items from affiliates is particularly sensitive. An item may be transferred at a price which includes profit rather than at cost only when:

1. it is based on an "established catalog or market price of commercial items sold in substantial quantities to the general public," or
2. it is the result of "adequate price competition."

However, in either case, the price must be reasonable and no higher than the transferor's current sales price to its most favored customer.

The terms "catalog or market price" and "adequate price competition" are discussed in Chapter 5.

Patents and Royalties (FAR 31.205-30 and 31.205-37; PCM 15-205.26 and 15-205.36)

The cost principles limit the allowability of patent costs to those applicable to:

Specific patents that are either required by contract or for which the government has royalty-free use.

General counseling services relating to patent matters.

Contractors should ensure that their cost accounting systems are capable of separately identifying allowable and unallowable patent and royalty costs.

In *Rocket Research Company*,[34] the ASBCA held that costs incurred in performing patent searches and preparing and prosecuting patent applications, which were claimed as indirect expenses on a cost type contract, were unallowable under DAR. The Board reasoned that the costs were not required for performance of the contract. The contractor contended that the disputed provision did not apply to patent costs that were charged indirectly. The board disagreed and ruled that the sole purpose of the 1971 revision to DAR 15-205.26(b) "was to disallow all patent costs not necessary to a particular contract's performance."

Plant Reconversion Costs (FAR 31.205-31; PCM 15-205.29)

Costs related to restoring or rehabilitating a contractor's facility to the same condition existing prior to undertaking contract work are unallowable except for costs of removing government property and repairing damage resulting from such removal.

Professional and Consultant Services (FAR 31.205-33 and 31.205.47; PCM 15-205.31) and Defense of Fraud Proceedings (FAR 31.205-47)

The cost principle originally incorporated in FAR stated that reasonable costs of professional and consultant services are allowable provided that:

Fees are not contingent upon recovery of costs from the government.

Retainer fees are for necessary and customary services.

The costs do not pertain to company organizations and reorganizations, defense of antitrust suits, patent infringement litigation, or prosecution of claims against the government.

The nature and scope of services performed (on other than a retainer basis) are documented.

In an appeal by Data Design Laboratories,[35] the Board clarified what constitutes the prosecution of a claim against the government. FAR 31.205-33 (formerly DAR 15-205.31) provided that costs of legal, accounting, and consulting services and directly associated costs incurred in connection with the prosecution of claims against the government are unallowable. Government auditors generally tended to view any kind of Board of Contract Appeals proceeding as the prosecution of a claim against the government and have thus disallowed professional fees associated with the litigation. In this decision the Board carefully distinguished between the prosecution of a claim against the government (which is expressly unallowable under FAR) and the defense of a government claim against the contractor (which was not then expressly unallowable under FAR). The first situation (prosecution of a claim) occurs, for instance, when: a contractor submits an equitable price adjustment proposal pursuant to the changes clause of a contract; the contracting officer refuses to pay the amount requested by the contractor; and the contractor appeals the contracting officer's final decision. The second situation (defense of a government claim) exists where the contractor appeals a government claim for a reduction in the contract amount, such as a price reduction due to asserted defective pricing or a cost disallowance due to asserted inclusion of unallowable costs in the amount submitted for reimbursement.

In the *Data Design Laboratories* decision, the contractor was appealing the government's disallowance of the differential between first class and less than first class air accommodations. While the Board agreed that the disallowance of the air fare differential was properly based on the provision of FAR 31.205-46 (formerly DAR 15-205.46), it concluded that the contractor was entitled to recover, as an indirect cost, the legal fees related to its defense of the government disallowance.

The precedence established by this decision was short lived, however, due to a 1986 revision to FAR 31.205-33 which also disallowed costs incurred in the:

Defense against government claims or appeals.

Defense or prosecution of lawsuits or appeals between contractors arising from either an agreement or contract concerning a teaming arrangement, a joint venture or similar arrangement, or dual sourcing, co-production or similar programs, unless incurred in compliance with the specific terms and conditions of the contract or written instructions from the contracting officer.

A number of disputes relating to professional and consulting services fees have centered on the allocability of such costs to government contracts. In *Walter Motor Truck Co.*,[36] legal fees were not considered allocable as an indirect expense to government contracts because they were incurred specifically for a particular cost objective, a commercial joint venture. In a similar decision, *Dynalectron Corporation*,[37] the ASBCA held that legal fees related to the defense of a suit arising out of the guarantee of a commercial sales contract were direct costs, chargeable either to the contract or to commercial business generally. The Board was not persuaded by the contractor's argument that the legal fees should not be treated as direct costs since the contractor had no way of including in the original contract price the costs of litigation that would occur in a subsequent period. The Board observed that the definition of direct costs simply does not address the "condition of ready assimilability into an accounting system."

In *Celesco Industries*,[38] a contractor was not permitted to charge a consultant fee as an indirect cost because the consulting service was applicable to a specific government contract. The Board ruled that the amount should have been charged directly to the particular contract.

In a far reaching decision, *John Doe Co., Inc.*,[39] the ASBCA considered the allowability of legal costs included in provisional billing rates and incurred in connection with a criminal investigation. The government contended that the costs should be disallowed " . . . because of their possible linkage with prior costs that might have been fraudulently charged. . . ." The contractor asserted that, regardless of the outcome of the fraud investigation, legal defense costs are ordinary and necessary expenses, reasonable in nature, and properly includable in a G&A expense pool.

In concluding that both positions were flawed, the Board ruled that

> pending completion of an investigation and possible prosecution, the Board has no assurance whether the retention of legal services and the expenditure of all costs related to alleged fraud are, in all respects, reasonable in nature.
>
> Accordingly, we may not conclude that the reasonableness in nature and allocability of such costs may not be made to depend in some cases on the ultimate outcome of an investigation and prosecution. But we may and do rule negatively; that such costs may not properly be disallowed simply because they are incurred in defense of such an investigation; nor may they be disallowed as not allocable, without regard to the circumstances, because some act of fraud might be established. . . .
>
> Unless the Government has evidence of other grounds for disallowance, e.g., that the costs are otherwise unreasonable, they should be reimbursed provisionally.

Subsequent to the ASBCA decision in *John Doe Co., Inc.* a new cost principle titled *defense of fraud proceedings* was incorporated into the regulations. This cost principle disallows costs incurred in defense of criminal or civil actions or suspension or debarment proceedings when the charges involve fraud and either result in conviction, a judgment against the contractor, debarment/suspension of the contractor, or are resolved by consent or compromise. The costs disallowed include administrative and clerical costs, costs of in-house and outside legal counsel, other professional fees, and wages of employees, officers, and directors.

A 1986 FAR revision made unallowable any costs incurred in connection with the defense of filing a false certification as well as any other directly associated costs.

This "defense of fraud" cost principle has been severely criticized by industry representatives who contend that it represents a violation of due process. The cost principle was not incorporated into the PCM.

Recruiting Costs and Relocation Costs (FAR 31.205-34 and 31.205-35; PCM 15-205.33 and 15-205.25)

Costs incident to recruitment of employees and permanent relocation of new or existing employees are generally allowable subject to certain ceilings based on time, percentages, and absolute dollar amounts (Fig. 7.6).

The cost principles also restrict the content of help-wanted advertising (e.g., use of color is prohibited) and the use of recruitment incentives intended to pirate personnel from other companies.

Rental Costs (other than ADPE) (FAR 31.205-36; PCM 15-205.34)

Under FAR, as well as the predecessor DAR and NASA PR, rental costs of operating leases (as defined by FAS 13) are generally allowable to the extent that the rates are reasonable at the time of the decision to lease the property, except that:

Rental costs under a sale and leaseback arrangement are limited to amounts that would have been allowed if title had been retained.

Rental costs of rentals between entities under common control are generally limited to normal ownership costs.

Time limitation for incurrence of transition costs (house-hunting, temporary residence, etc.)	60 days
Closing costs and continuing costs of ownership of residence being sold [as percentage of sales price]	
New employees	14%[1]
Existing employees	14%[1]
Costs incidental to acquiring a new home [as percentage of purchase price]	
New employees	5%[2]
Existing employees	5%[2]
Time limitation for incurrence of mortgage interest and rental differential payments	3 years
Loss on sale of home	Not allowable
Cancellation of unexpired lease	No ceiling
Employee income taxes incident to reimbursed relocation costs	Not allowable

[1]Continuing mortgage principal payments are unallowable.

[2]Commissions, litigation, insurance, property taxes, and operating/maintenance costs are unallowable.

Figure 7.6 Ceilings on Allowable Relocation Costs.

"Build-lease" transactions are not sale and leaseback arrangements subject to the rental cost limitation. In *HRB-Singer, Inc.*,[40] the contractor sold land to an independent party who constructed buildings that were then leased back to the contractor. The government disallowed rent paid for the facilities to the extent that it exceeded the cost of ownership on the basis that the transction was a sale and leaseback. In disagreeing with the government's position, the ASBCA concluded:

> The most that can be said is that it sold the land upon which the buildings were built and leased it back with the buildings. This land did not constitute a plant facility, specified in paragraph (c) [of ASPR 15-205.34], until the buildings were built. Even if it did, the relative value of the unimproved land . . . was so small in comparison to the value of the buildings that it cannot be considered a material factor in this question. We accordingly find that there was no sale and leaseback in this situation.

In *A. S. Thomas, Inc.*,[41] the ASBCA decision is enlightening as to the Board's views on common control. In that case the lessee was able to demonstrate that, even though he was treasurer and owned 43 % of his brother's company (lessor), there was no common control because neither brother took an active role in the management of the other brother's company. Common officers coupled with substantial ownership would potentially give a contractor the ability to exercise significant influence over the operations and financial policies of another business entity. Therefore, the management role assumed by a contractor's owners or officers in another business venture owning assets that are leased to the contractor is a critical factor in determining whether common control exists.

In a more recent decision involving Data Design Laboratories,[42] the ASBCA concluded that common control did not exist with respect to a building leased to the company by a partnership consisting of several company officers and employees. The board noted in its decision that this management group never owned more than 10% of the company's stock and that the company's Board of Directors consisted of different individuals, primarily representatives of the company's original financial backers.

When constructive ownership costs are allowed in lieu of actual rental payments, the cost of money on the capitalized value used in calculating the constructive ownership cost may be recovered. The calculation of the cost of money is covered in Chapter 8 in the discussion of CAS 414, Cost of Money as an Element of the Cost of Facilities Capital.

Under FPR in effect prior to issuance of FAR, and under PCM, allowability criteria are discussed in the context of short-term leases and longterm leases. Allowable longterm lease costs are generally limited to constructive ownership costs. Short-term lease costs (two years or less for personal property and five years or less for real property) are generally allowable where:

The rates are reasonable at the time of the decision to lease.

No material equity in the property accrues to the lessee other than that available to the public at large.

The allowability criteria for sale and leaseback transactions and rentals between entities under common control is the same as previously discussed.

Selling Costs (FAR 31.205-38; PCM 15-205.37)

Selling and marketing costs, as defined in the cost principle are acceptable to the extent that they are reasonable and allocable to government business. However, allocability to the government is defined in narrower terms than the overall allocability criteria discussed earlier. In the context of selling expense, the cost principles define allocability in terms of technical, consulting, and demonstration activities, and in terms of other services that are for such purposes as applying or adapting the contractor's products to government use. Given this strict interpretation of allocability, government personnel have generally held that selling activities relating solely to commercial products are considered unallowable on government contracts, even though the base used to allocate such costs consists of both government and commercial effort. This view by the government is longstanding. In *Cubic Corporation*[43] the ASBCA concluded:

In order to implement ASPR 15-205.37, it is obvious that the sales expenses would have to be accumulated into at least two pools. One pool would be charged with all selling costs which meet the criteria of ASPR 15-205.37 and the other pool would be charged with all selling costs which do not meet such criteria. Good accounting practice, as well as ASPR 15-201.3, 15-201.4, and 15-203(b) requires that accumulated indirect costs shall be distributed in a reasonable and equitable manner over the appropriate cost objectives. It follows that the sales costs accumulated in each pool should be distributed against the class of sales to which each applies. More specifically, we hold that ASPR 15-205.37 contemplates that the cost of acquiring Government business (as defined) shall be distributed over government business and that the cost of acquiring business which does no meet the requirements of ASPR 15-205.37 shall be distributed over such nonqualifying business.

Having reached that conclusion, however, the Board then acknowledged that the company did not keep its records in a manner which facilitated a literal application of the selling cost principle. In view of other provisions of the cost principles addressing advance agreements, allowability factors, and logical cost groupings for indirect expenses, the board concluded that a pro rata allocation of total selling expenses to all contracts was acceptable in the circumstances. Since certain Cubic selling expenses (e.g., salaries of in-house sales personnel) supported government sale while other selling expenses (e.g., outside sales commissions) supported commercial sales, the board decided that the total selling expense pool could be equitably allocated to all contracts, both government and commercial.

The cost principle on selling costs was revised in 1986 to clarify that elements of selling which are covered in other cost principles such as advertising, bid and proposal costs, and corporate image enhancement are governed by other more specific principles when determining allowability of such activities. Costs of activities correctly classified and disallowed under such cost principles cannot be reconsidered under the selling cost principles. The revised language identifies which selling and marketing costs are allowable and requires separate identification of unallowable costs. Allowable residual selling cost is limited to the costs of efforts to market particular products to particular customers.

FAR, and DAR in effect prior to issuance of FAR, specifically stated that selling costs related to foreign military sales, as defined by the Arms Export Control Act, and selling costs related to foreign sales of military products were not allocable to U.S. Government contracts for U.S. Government requirements.

In late 1986, the Armed Services Board of Contract Appeals denied Emerson Electric Company's[44] motion for summary judgment, against the government's disallowance of foreign selling expenses incurred from 1979 to 1984. The dispute focused on the provision of the prior selling cost principle (DAR 15-205.37 prior to April 1, 1984 and FAR 31.205-38 prior to April 7, 1986) which stated that selling costs related to foreign military sales or foreign sales of military products were not *allocable* to U.S. Government contracts for U.S. requirements. During the years at issue, Emerson included all selling expenses, both domestic and foreign in the G&A expense pool. After notification of the government's position that the practice of including foreign selling costs in the G&A allocation constituted noncompliance with DAR 15-205.37 and CAS 405, Emerson proposed to restructure its cost pools to separately allocate foreign and domestic selling expenses. That proposal was rejected by the ACO who concluded that the proposed method was not the only one that Emerson could use to correct the noncompliance and that it resulted in an increased cost allocation to domestic contracts. The ACO selected another method for achieving compliance—totally removing the selling expense from the G&A expense pool. Obviously, this method resulted in the highest cost disallowance. Interestingly, Emerson and the government ultimately came to terms on an acceptable method of cost allocation which effectively resulted in separate domestic and foreign selling rates for 1984 and forward.

Emerson's motion for summary judgment was based on two grounds:

Foreign selling costs were not expressly unallowable.

The allocability criteria in DAR 15-205.37 conflicted with CAS 410 Allocation of Business Unit G&A Expenses to Final Cost Objectives.

In dismissing Emerson's motion for summary judgment, the Board disagreed with Emerson's premise that foreign selling costs were not unallowable and therefore not subject to CAS 405. In coming to its conclusion, the Board focused on two key provisions of the cost principle:

Selling costs "are allowable to the extent they are allocable" to government contracts.

Foreign military products selling costs "shall not be allocable to" domestic government contracts.

In the Board's view:

It should be unmistakable to any person possessing a rudimentary familiarity with the English language and principles of deductive reasoning that the foregoing two phrases represent the first two legs of a syllogism. The third and final leg of the syllogism clearly is: *Therefore, foreign military products selling costs are not allowable under domestic Government contracts.*

The Board's apparent conclusion that foreign selling costs were automatically allocated to domestic contracts by virtue of their inclusion in the G&A expense pool did not adequately recognize that foreign contracts were also in the allocation base. Where domestic contracts require the same level of sales support as foreign contracts, no foreign selling expense included in a G&A expense pool are being allocated to domestic contracts. Where the level of selling activity required to support foreign contracts is higher than that required to support domestic contracts, the only foreign selling costs being allocated to domestic contracts through the G&A rate are those that are disproportionately higher. A logical alternative to remedy this allocation problem that complies with both the prior cost principle and CAS 405 would have been to exclude from the G&A pool the foreign selling expenses which represent the amount by which foreign selling costs are disproportionately higher than domestic selling costs. The government position, as presently sustained by the Board, was far more punitive because it allocated to foreign contracts not only 100% of foreign selling expense but a portion of the domestic selling expenses as well. Conversely, it allocated to domestic contracts none of the foreign selling expense and only some of the domestic expense. This is clearly inequitable because it results in subsidizing some selling costs incurred purely for the benefit of domestic contracts by foreign contracts.

Inasmuch as this decision was only the denial of Emerson's motion for summary judgment, we have not heard the last of this issue. Regardless of the ultimate disposition of this case, however, the FAR cost principle was revised in 1986 to provide that foreign selling expense are *unallowable*, not *unallocable*. This change may cause contractors who have foreign sales of military products to consider establishing two separate selling expense pools (domestic and foreign) since the clear implication is that foreign selling costs will be disallowed in total if they are included in a single selling, general and administrative (SG&A) pool that is allocated to all contracts.

Needless to say, this cost principle has generated considerable criticism from industry representatives who contend that selling costs are:

Necessary to the overall operation of a business.

Only one of many indirect costs incurred by a company and should not be subject to a separate analysis of benefit to the government.

Industry representatives also point with criticism to the government's inconsistent accounting treatment of B&P costs and selling costs. B&P costs that relate primarily to government work are required to be allocated to all work, including commercial contracts. In contrast, commercial selling expenses are considered allocable only to commercial effort.

Taxes (FAR 31.205-41; PCM 15-205.41)

Taxes that are accounted for in accordance with GAAP are generally allowable, except for:

Federal income and excess profits taxes.

Taxes for which an exemption is available.

Taxes related to financing, refinancing, and reorganization.

Special assessments on land.

Taxes on property used solely for nongovernment work.

Taxes on funding deficiencies or prohibited transactions relating to employee deferred compensation plans.

Deferred income taxes (tax effects of differences between taxable income and pretax income reported on the financial statements).

The unallowability of deferred taxes has generated considerable controversy. Many believe that a tax should become a cost when the conditions giving rise to the tax (such as profitable performance of contracts) occur, rather than when the liability is identified on the tax return. Generally accepted accounting principles require that taxes be recorded based on pretax accounting income and not when paid (APB no.11, Accounting for Income Taxes). The acquisition regulations are, therefore, contrary to GAAP. In recent years, the government has revised its position on some cost accruals, such as recognizing the propriety of accounting for deferred compensation on an accrual basis. Income taxes should be looked at from a similar perspective.

Major disputes have arisen over the years with regard to the allocation of state and local taxes to segments. Several of these cases are discussed in Chapter 8 in the section on CAS 403, Allocation of Home Office Expenses to Segments.

As stated above, taxes on real or personal property or on the value, use, possession, or sale of property used solely in connection with nongovernment work are unallowable. The rationale for the government's position is that real or personal property that is charged direct to flexibly priced contracts (or to fixed-price contracts for which the contractor has received progress payments) is exempt from such taxes since title vests with the government.

In *United States of America v. State of New Mexico*,[45] the U.S. Court of Appeals concluded that the following items were subject to the New Mexico gross receipts tax:

Sales of tangible personal property to the Energy Research and Development Administration (ERDA, now DOE) through its management contractors.

Advanced funds used for government operations under ERDA management contracts.

The court held that the contractors were not agents of the government; consequently, they were not immune from assessment of state tax.

Trade, Business, Technical, and Professional Activity Costs (FAR 31.205-43; PCM 15-205.43)

Cost of memberships and subscriptions related to trade, business, technical, and professional organizations are allowable.

Costs of meetings and conferences are allowable where the primary purpose of the meeting is to disseminate information or enhance production. Documentation is critical. Claimed costs must be documented as to conference participants and the purpose of the meeting. Sections 7-1102.2 and 7-1102.3 of the DCAA *Contract Audit Manual*[46] provides the following guidance to DCAA auditors as to the expected level of documentation for business conference expenses:

Documentation. Determination of allowability requires knowledge concerning the purpose and nature of activity at the meeting or conference. The contractor should maintain adequate records supplying the following information on properly prepared travel vouchers or expense records supported by copies of paid invoices, receipts, charge slips, etc.

(1) Date and location of meeting including the name of the establishment.
(2) Names of employees and guests in attendance.
(3) Purpose of meeting.
(4) Cost of the meeting, by item.

The above guidelines closely parallel the current recordkeeping requirements contained in Section 274 of the Internal Revenue Code for entertainment costs as a tax deductible expense. Where satisfactory support assuring the claimed costs are allowable conference expenses is not furnished, the claimed conference/meal costs or directly associated costs (see 8-405.1d. for description) should be questioned.

Meal Expense. Expenses for meals of contractor personnel, not in travel status, who act as hosts at contractor-sponsored business luncheons or dinners are allowable if it is determined that the activity constitutes a business meeting or conference associated with the active conduct of the contractor's business and not a social function.

Guest expenses for meals or other incidentals applicable to Federal employees should normally be questioned as unnecessary, and hence unreasonable costs, except under limited circumstances, since they are prohibited from accepting gratuities by Executive Order 11222 of 1965, 5 CFR 735(c), and various departmental implementing directives (e.g., DOD 5500.7, *Standards of Conduct*).

Training and Educational Costs (FAR 31.205-44; PCM 15-205.44)

Costs of training at the noncollege level which is designed to increase the vocational effectiveness of employees are allowable. Costs of education at the college level are allowable to the extent that the course or degree pursued relates to the field in which the employee is working or may be reasonably expected to work, except that:

Allowable, straight-time compensation of employees attending classes part-time during working hours is generally limited to 156 hours per year.
Allowable costs of full-time education at the postgraduate level are generally

limited to two school years per employee trained except for the PCM. Full-time education costs are not addressed in the PCM.

Costs of attendance of up to 16 weeks per employee per year for specialized programs for existing or potential executives or managers are allowable (not applicable to PCM). Grants to educational or training institutions are considered unallowable contributions.

Travel Costs (FAR 31.205-46; PCM 15-205.46)

FAR coverage on travel costs went through some major changes in 1986 that are having an impact on firms doing business with the government. Prior to those revisions, travel costs incurred by employees in travel status while on company business were generally allowable with certain exceptions. The excess of first-class airfare over less than first-class accommodations was allowable only where less than first-class accommodations were not reasonably available. The cost of contractor-owned aircraft was allowable if: reasonable; the use of such aircraft was necessary for the conduct of business; and any increase in cost, as compared with alternative means of transportation, was commensurate with the advantages gained.

The first of the 1986 changes in the FAR cost principle dealt with corporate aircraft costs, company furnished automobiles and unallowable commercial airfare costs. Revised criteria limit allowable cost of contrator-owned, -leased, or -chartered aircraft to the lowest customary coach airfare unless travel by such aircraft is specifically required by the contract or a higher amount is approved by the contracting officer. A higher amount may be agreed to when circumstances for justifying higher than standard airfare exist as described in the cost principle. The change also requires that manifest/ logs for all flights on company aircraft be maintained and made available as a condition of allowability.

Costs of contractor-owned or -leased automobiles are allowed to the extent that they are used for company business. Costs associated with the personal use of the automobiles (including travel to and from work) are now specifically cited as unallowable. The previous FAR stated that the difference in cost between first-class air accommodations and less than first-class air accommodations was unallowable. The revised principle clarifies that airfare costs in excess of the lowest customary standard, coach or equivalent airfare offered during normal business hours are unallowable.

The most significant change to allowable travel costs, applicable to all contracts resulting from solicitations issued on or after July 31, 1986 concerned allowable reimbursement for lodgings, meals and incidental expenses. The amendment limits reimbursement for such expenses to the maximum per diem rates applicable to government employees. If a contractor reimburses its employees per diem in lieu of actual costs, detailed receipts or other documentation are not required. However, where employee reimbursement is based on actual costs incurred documentation is required, including receipts for each expenditure in excess of $25.00.

The change not only impacts the amount of travel costs that will be reimbursable but also requires considerable administrative effort on the part of contractors to identify and eliminate the excess costs. In this regard, DCAA has concluded that a statistical sampling approach to identifying the excess costs would not, in their opinion, satisfy the requirements of CAS 405, Accounting for Unallowable Costs, and that contractors are required to specifically identify the unallowable travel costs except under circumstances addressed in CAS 405.50(c).[47] In lieu of specific identification of unallowable costs, the cost accounting standard permits the contracting parties to reach an agreement on an alternate method based on materiality considerations.

Two cases pertaining to travel are worth discussion. In *Data-Design Laboratories*,[48] the company's policy allowed first-class air accommodations but provided that travel be scheduled to the fullest extent possible outside of normal working hours. In the company's view, the government benefited from the policy since company employees traveled on their own time in exchange for the opportunity to travel first class. The ASBCA disagreed and concluded that the company's interpretation of the acquisition regulation was erroneous. Significantly, however, the Board did not permit the disallowance on a retroactive basis. There is further discussion of this decision is later under "Retroactive Disallowances."

Big Three Industries, Inc.[49] dealt with the allowability of the cost of company-owned aircraft. The ASBCA made a presumptive determination of reasonableness of the costs of an owned aircraft because the business firm obtained fixed-price contracts under competitive conditions and thus had a strong economic incentive to keep down its costs. The board further relied on IRS acceptance of the company's aircraft expenses for tax purposes as prima facie evidence that use of the aircraft was necessary to the conduct of its business. Finally, the board concluded that the government had the burden to prove that the contractor's aircraft expense was more costly than alternative means of transportation. Since the government in this case had made no attempt to demonstrate the use of the aircraft was more costly, the disputed cost was allowed in full. The applicability of this decision to future challenges to the allocability of corporate aircraft costs was effectively limited with the promulgation of the 1986 cost principle revision.

DOD's Indirect Cost Monitoring Office (ICMO) issued guidance which states:

ACO's should maintain a keen awareness that their exercise of judgment may often not be based entirely upon considerations that are susceptible to quantification. Audit reports will often contain a comparison of the operational costs of private aircraft with commercial aircraft. While this data is necessary, the ACO's decisions must embrace all of the considerations contained in DAR 15-205.46(g) to the extent that they are relevant to the situation at hand. Every sound decision by the ACO may not be arithmetically defensible and it is not reasonable to expect it to be so.

The difficulties involved in the administration and settlement of company aircraft costs are sufficient to create many situations in which both the contractor and the government will find advance agreements administratively useful in order to obviate disagreements on substantive and procedural matters that would otherwise perpetuate themselves. The Working Group recommends the use of advance agreements with respect to company aircraft wherever it is practicable to do so. In the opinion of the ICMO, as a minimum, advance agreements should be negotiated where it is anticipated that cost of $500,000 or more will be allocated to DOD flexibly-priced contracts. Additionally, the ACO should periodically review the criteria or demonstrated requirements (15-205.46(g) for contractor owned or leased aircraft.

Another problem addressed by the Working Group was that related to the documentation of aircraft usage. Many contractors contend that they are not required either to furnish documentation for the costs of trips which are not claimed, or to disclose the number of passengers for whom reimbursement is not sought. However, that information is still necessary for government auditors and ACO's to determine the acceptability of costs, determine the denominators for usage rate calculation, and to be certain of compliance with the directly associated cost provisions of CAS 405. Although specific documentation requirements are not included in the DAR, it is the

Working Group's opinion that contractors have the responsibility to support the cost of aircraft usage. Costs that are unresolved as a result of a contractor's inability or unwillingness to furnish flight manifest/log documentation should be disallowed to the extent unsupported. It would generally be appropriate to convey the documentation requirements to the contractor at the earliest possible time through the use of a "Notice of Intent to Disallow or Not Recognize Costs" (see DAR 15-206). . . .[50]

As previously noted, the present FAR language requires both an advance agreement and documentation of aircraft usage.

Goodwill (FAR 31.205-49)

In September 1983 the Defense Acquisition Regulatory Council issued for comment a new cost principle disallowing any cost for expensing, writing-off or writing-down goodwill. Goodwill is defined in FAR 31.205-49 as an unidentifiable intangible asset which

> . . . originates under the purchase method of accounting for a business combination when the price paid by the acquiring company exceeds the sum of the identifiable individual assets acquired less liabilities assumed, based on their fair value.

Unfortunately, the DAR Council action was not entirely unexpected in light of the ASBCA decision in *Gould Defense Systems*.[51] As further discussed in Chapter 8, the central issue in this appeal was whether goodwill was properly includable as an element of facilities capital under CAS 414. The Board concluded that:

> [Goodwill] amoritization expense generally is an allowable cost under the Defense Acquisition Regulations.
> There are no specific references in the Defense Acquisition Regulation cost principles to the recoverability of goodwill amortization costs nor does the Defense Acquisition Regulations preclude recovery of such costs. Amortization of goodwill not only is recognized as a cost under generally accepted accounting principles, it currently is required for financial reporting purposes. Thus, when properly incurred, goodwill amortization cost meets the general requirements of DAR 15.201.1 . . . that costs be determined in accordance with a "generally accepted" method.

When the cost principle was ultimately promulgated in the Federal Acquisition Regulation, the dispute over goodwill was, from a contractor's perspective, unfortunately just another case of winning the battle and losing the war.

Cost of Alcoholic Beverages (FAR 31.205-50)

This cost principle was added April 7, 1986 and the cost of alcoholic beverages was specifically disallowed.

RETROACTIVE DISALLOWANCES

Boards of contract appeals and the courts have consistently applied the doctrine of estoppel in preventing the government from retroactively disallowing a cost or allocation method that had previously been accepted. Cases where this doctrine figured in the decision include *Litton Systems*,[52] *H&M Moving, Inc.*,[53] *Falcon Research and Development Co.*,[54] *Data-Design Laboratories*,[55] and *Gould Defense Systems, Inc.*[56]

Elements that must be present to establish the defense of estoppel are:

The party to be estopped must know the facts.

The party to be estopped must intend that his or her conduct shall be acted upon or must so act that the party asserting estoppel has a right to believe it is so intended.

The party asserting estoppel must be ignorant of the true facts.

The party asserting estoppel must rely on the other party's conduct to his or her injury.

As previously noted in the discussion of travel costs, the ASBCA did not permit the disallowance of Data-Design Laboratories, Inc.'s[57] travel costs on a retroactive basis. The government auditors, aware of the company's policy since 1966, allowed recovery of the costs through fiscal year 1972, then disallowed 1973 costs in July 1975. In barring the disallowance of costs incurred prior to July 1975, the board cited previous ASBCA and Court of Claims decisions as a basis for its conclusion. Because of the significance of the issue of retroactive disallowances, a portion of the ASBCA decision is quoted below:

We have found that appellant, based upon its interpretation of ASPR 15-205.46, incurred first class air travel costs since as early as 1966; that Government auditors, aware of appellant's policy and the basis for it, allowed recovery of those costs through fiscal year 1972; that during fiscal year 1973, 1974, and 1975 appellant met with a series of officials in the offices of the ACO and DCAA and discussed its ongoing policy of first class air travel, even proposed changes in that policy, and recieved responses ranging from ambivalence to tacit approval. The DCAA Form 1, which disallowed 1973 costs, was not issued until 1975. Appellant contends that the cost disallowed was retractive in nature and was therefore improper. We agree.
The case of Litton Systems, Inc. v. United States [16 CCF pp 80,785] 196 Ct. Cl. 133; 449 F.2d 392 (1971), cited by appellant in support of its position, contained facts similar to those in the instant case. The issue there was the proper method of allocating G&A expense. The contractor had used the cost of sales method as a basis for allocation since at least as early as 1954. The first adverse Government comment upon the method was made during an audit meeting in June 1960, but there were no proposals at that time to change the contractor's practice. The subject next surfaced in September 1961 at a conference, during which a Government auditor "suggested" changing the allocation base. In November 1961 the resident auditor sent the contractor a memorandum advising that he considered the contractor's method to be inequitable and recommending, for that reason, that the proposed bidding rate not be approved. The contractor defended its position in a December 1961 memorandum. Further discussion followed, and in a May 1962 meeting the government proposed that the change be prospective only. The contractor later demurred to the suggestion, further correspondence ensued, and the contractor requested formal action by the Government. The Government complied and issued a DD Form 396 (Notice of Costs Suspended and/or Disapproved), apparently a forerunner of the present DCAA Form 1, on 3 December 1962, disallowing claimed reimbursements for the contractor's fiscal year 1959.
On the issue of the retroactive nature of the disallowance the Court of Claims reversed this Board and concluded that, although the Government's method of allocation was preferable, it could not impose that method upon the contractor on a retroactive basis. As the Court stated:
It was not until December 3, 1962, when the DD Form 396 was issued, that plaintiff was authoritatively informed of the Government's previously ambivalent position. This document, we think, put the plaintiff on notice that its cost of sales method would no longer be accepted as a method of computing its reimbursement billings under its CPFF contracts.
In view of plaintiff's long and consistent use of the cost of sales method with the Government's knowledge, approval and acquiescence, plaintiff was entitled to rea-

sonably adequate notice that the Government would no longer approve the use of that method with respect to the CPFF contracts. [Supra at 148]

The Court in Litton, supra., did not elaborate upon the legal theory supporting its conclusion that the retroactive disallowance was improper. Appellant also cites Falcon Research & Development Company, ASBCA No. 19784, 77-1 BCA pp 12,312 aff'd on reconsid. 77-2 BCA pp 12,795, in which this Board concluded that the Government had improperly disapproved, on a retroactive basis, one of the cost elements in the contractor's previously approved overhead pool. The cost disapproval was found to be improper based upon a line of cases which do not permit a disallowance of this nature where the cost or accounting method in question had been accepted, the contractor reasonably believed that it would continue to be approved, and relied upon such reasonable belief to its detriment.

. . . [I]n the case at hand, the record reflects, and the parties have stipulated, that during the years in question the Government was aware of appellant's practice of traveling first class and of its basis for regarding the costs of such travel to be reimbursable. . . .

Although appellant never received from the Government a formal pronouncement blessing its first class air travel policy as meeting the ASPR requirements, prior to its fiscal year 1973 appellant did discuss its travel policy with Government representatives and was certainly aware that the Government understood the nature of the costs and appellant's interpretation of ASPR 15-205.46. Appellant did not therefore react unreasonably when it construed the absence of a first class air travel cost disallowance in the 1972 audit to constitute tacit approval of its policy.

We conclude, further, that appellant relied upon the apparent Government approval to its detriment. The record demonstrates that, during discussions of the issue with Government representatives, appellant expressed that if the Government were to disallow the first class air fare costs appellant would have to modify its travel policy. We have found that if the Government had disapproved of the costs at an earlier date appellant would have made those modifications and, in fact, we see that when the costs were ultimately disallowed appellant instructed its employees to travel in less than first class accommodations, albeit during working hours.

Based upon the foregoing, we conclude that it was not until appellant received the 31 July 1975 DCAA Form 1 that it was authoritatively informed of the Government's position regarding appellant's first class air accommodation policy, that the disapproval of appellant's 1973 first class air travel costs was an improper retroactive disallowance, and that appellant is entitled to recover the 1973 costs agreed upon by stipulation.

In an interesting sequel to this case,[58] the Board later barred the government from retroactively disallowing the costs prior to issuance of the contracting officer's final decision. The Board concluded:

The DCAA Form 1 was a recommendation to the contracting officer on treatment of costs but was not, itself, a final decision disallowing such costs. Therefore, issuance of the DCAA Form 1 was not in and of itself conclusive that these costs would be disallowed. In this case, especially, the record indicates that some modification of this position by the contracting officer might have been achieved. Therefore, we conclude that under the facts here present the issuance of the DCAA Form 1 did not, in and of itself, constitute a disallowance or such likelihood of disallowance that continuing to make the expenditure became the risk of the contractor. . . .

Here, the contractor did appeal to the administrative contracting officer and was successful in negotiating approval of three of four costs for which the auditor had recommended disallowance. . . .

We, therefore, conclude that it was reasonable under the facts here present for appellant to believe it would again be successful in establishing the reasonableness of the first class air fare costs with the contracting officer and to continue to incur such costs prior to the receipt of the contracting officer's final decision so that disallowance of such costs would be a retroactive disallowance. . . .

CREDITS

Credits are defined as the applicable portion of income, rebates, allowances, and other credits that relate to allowable costs. Credits can be given to the government as either cost reductions or cash refunds.

The issue of the government's entitlement to credits has been litigated on numerous occasions.

In *Celesco Industries Inc.,* the government was precluded from sharing in a gain on a sale of land acquired through the exercise of an option under a rental agreement. In its decision, the Armed Services Board of Contract Appeals concluded that the regulatory provision was only intended to

> apply to situations where the Government has reimbursed the contractor for costs incurred and the contractor has simultaneously recovered a portion of the *same costs from another source.* . . . The Government did not participate with the contractor in the payment of any additional rental costs attributable to the option price or other factors. The gain realized was not income, rebate, allowance, or other credits related to an allowable cost within the meaning of ASPR 15-201.5. [Emphasis added.]

In a somewhat similar case, *RMK-BRJ, A Joint Venture,*[60] the government was precluded from sharing in the portion of an insurance refund that corresponded to the percentage of premiums contributed by the company's employees. In sustaining the contractor's appeal, the Board observed:

> It is not every refund which a contractor may receive to which the Government is entitled. Before any entitlement arises, the Government must have paid the costs to which the refund is applicable. . . . The Government's rights in the refund are tied to and dependent upon the amount of costs which it has reimbursed to appellant. Not one dime of the portion of the premiums paid by the employees ever became a cost of this contract or was ever reimbursed by the Government. . . .
>
> All the refund which related to the costs which respondent had paid was credited to the Government. The ASPR cost principles do not require any more than that.

In a court of claims decision, *Northrop Aircraft v. U.S.,*[61] the contractor was required to offset interest income against contract costs because the interest income was derived from a tax refund and the government had been allocated its share of the original tax payment. The Court construed the interest on the refund as a reduction in the taxes previously charged to government contracts.

In a fourth decision, *Colorado Dental Service (Delta Dental Plan of Colorado),*[62] the Board ruled that the government was entitled to interest income on monies placed in an interest-bearing account which the contractor received in advance for the purpose of paying dental claims under government contracts. Consistent with the *Northop* decision, the Board concluded that the interest income related to allowable contract costs since it was solely attributable to the government's advance reimbursement to the contractor of insurance payments that had not yet been received by claimants and deducted from the contractor's bank account.

SUMMARY

Costs are not allowable simply because they are incurred and properly recorded in the accounting records. Rather, cost allowability is determined based on such factors as reasonableness, allocability, CAS, GAAP, contractual terms, and limitations specified in the cost principles.

The regulatory environment affecting cost allowability is indeed a dynamic one. A company must keep abreast of the changes in allowability criteria to assure optimal cost recovery and to assure that appropriate measures are taken to exclude expressly unallowable costs from proposals, billings and claim's submitted to the government.

NOTES

1. Abeles, Schwartz, Haeckel and Silverblatt, Inc., HUD BCA no. 81-625-C31, September 4, 1984, 84-3 BCA 17605.
2. Bruce Construction Corporation, et al. v. United States, 163 Ct. Cl. 197, November 15, 1983, 9 CCF 721,325.
3. Western Electric Company, Inc., ASBCA no. 11056, April 18, 1969, 69-1 BCA 7,660.
4. Data-Design Laboratories, ASBCA no. 24534, June 16, 1983, 83-2 BCA 16,665.
5. Stanley Aviation Corporation, ASBCA no. 12292, June 12, 1968, 68-2 BCA 7,081.
6. General Dynamics Corporation (Convair Division), ASBCA nos. 8759, 9264, 9265, and 9266, January 31, 1965, 66-1 BCA 5,368.
7. General Dynamics Corporation v. United States, 187 Ct. Cl. 597, May 16, 1969, 13 CCF 82,732.
8. General Dynamics/Astronautics, ASBCA no. 6899, May 17, 1962, 1962 BCA 3,391.
9. Dynalectron Corporation v. United States, 212 Ct. Cl. 118, December 15, 1976, 23 CCF 80,877.
10. Elmer B. Staats, Restatement of Objectives, Policies, and Concepts (Washington, D.C.: Superintendent of Documents, May 1977), p. 2.
11. The Boeing Company, ASBCA no. 28342, September 17, 1985, 85-3 BCA 18,435.
12. American Institute of Certified Public Accountants, Codification of Statements on Auditing Standards, no. 1-39, 1982, AU sec. 411, para. 02.
13. Ibid., para. .06.
14. Blue Cross Association and Blue Cross of Virginia, ASBCA no. 25776, September 17, 1981, 81-2 BCA 15,359.
15. Lockheed Aircraft Corp. v. United States, 179 Ct. Cl. 545, April 14, 1967, 12 CCF 81,093; United States Steel Corp. v. United States, 177 Ct. Cl. 15, October 14, 1966, 11 CCF 80,706; Celesco Industries, ASBCA no. 22401, January 31, 1980, 80-1 BCA 14,271.
16. Grumman Aerospace Corp. v. United States, (Ct. Cl. 1978), November 15, 1978, 25 CCF 82,892.
17. Physics International Company, ASBCA no. 17700, June 16, 1977, 77-2 BCA 12,612.
18. Charles Bowscher, Improvements Needed in Department of Defense Procedures to Prevent Reimbursement of Unallowable Costs on Government Contracts, May 7, 1985.
19. 52 Federal Register 15884, April 30, 1987.
20. Aerojet-General Corp. ASBCA no. 13372, June 25, 1973, 73-2 BCA 10, 164; aff'd October 10, 1973, 73-2 BCA 10,307.
21. Blue Cross Association and Blue Shield Association (in the matter of Group Hospitalization, Inc., and Medical Services of the District of Columbia), ASBCA no. 25944, April 28, 1983, 83-1 BCA 16,524.
22. Superintendent of Documents U.S. Government Printing Office, *Defense Contract Audit Manual*, Washington, D.C. 20402, Catalog No. D-1.46/2.7640.1/1283.
23. Lulejean and Associates, ASBCA, no. 20094, April 27, 1976, 76-1 BCA 11880.
24. Space Services of Georgia, Inc., ASBCA no. 26021, July 19, 1982, 82-2 BCA 15,952.
25. Burt Associates, Inc., ASBCA no. 25884, April 20, 1982, 82-1 BCA 15,764.
26. The Boeing Company, ASBCA no. 24089, December 15, 1980, 81-1 BCA 14864; aff'd April 30, 1981, 81-1 BCA 15,121.
27. The Singer Company, Kearfott Division, ASBCA no. 18857, March 17, 1975, 75-1 BCA 11,185; reversed and remanded Ct. Cl. no. 381-79C, October 3, 1980, 28 CCF 80,741; May 4, 1981, 81-2 BCA 15,167; Ct. Cl. Order, November 13, 1981; March 4, 1982, 82-1 BCA 15,684.
28. Honeywell Corporation ASBCA nos. 28814, 29140, September 28, 1984, 84-3 BCA no. 17690.
29. The Boeing Company, supra, no. 11.
30. 52 Federal Register 18158, May 13, 1987.
31. Dynatrend, Inc. ASBCA no. 23463, July 25, 1980, 80-2 BCA 14,617.
32. The Marquardt Company, ASBCA no. 29888, July 19, 1985, 85-3 BCA 18,245.
33. Gould Defense Systems, Inc., ASBCA no. 24881, June 10, 1983, 83-2 BCA 16,676.

34. Rocket Research Company, ASBCA no. 24972, August 10, 1981, 81-2 BCA 15,306.
35. Data-Design Laboratories, ASBCA no. 27535.
36. Walter Motor Truck Co., ASBCA no. 8054, February 10, 1966, 66-1 BCA 5,365.
37. Dynalectron Corporation, ASBCA no. 16895, February 7, 1973, 73-1 BCA 9,909.
38. Celesco Industries, Inc., ASBCA no. 20569, March 11, 1977, 77-1 BCA 12,445.
39. The John Doe Co., Inc., ASBCA no. 24576, July 28, 1980, 80-2 BCA 14,620.
40. HRB Singer, Inc., ASBCA no. 10799, October 17, 1966, 66-2 BCA 5,903.
41. A.S. Thomas, Inc., ASBCA no. 10745, March 7, 1966, 66-1 BCA 5,438.
42. Data Design Laboratories, ASBCA no. 26753, December 27, 1984, 85-1 BCA 17,825.
43. Cubic Corporation, ASBCA no. 8125, June 17, 1963, 1963 BCA 3,775.
44. Emerson Electric Corporation, ASBCA no. 30090, November 19, 1986, 87-1 BCA.
45. United States v. State of New Mexico; Bureau of Revenue of the State of New Mexico; and Fred L. O'Cheskey, as Commissioner of Revenue of the State of New Mexico, and his successors in office, (BCA-10 1980) no. 78-1755, June 2, 1980, 38 CCF 81,365; aff'd. March 24, 1982. (S. Ct. 1982), 29 CCF 82,371.
46. Superintendent of Documents, supra note 21.
47. DCAA Memorandum for Regional Directors dated August 18, 1986, Subject: Audit Guidance on Implementing the Cost Principle on Per Diem Costs (DAR Case 85-230), reference PAD 701.40, 86 PAD-134.
48. Data-Design Laboratories, ASBCA no. 21029, May 29, 1981, 81-2 BCA 15,190, aff'd. July 8, 1982, 82-2 BCA 15,932.
49. Big Three Industries, Inc., ASBCA nos. 16949 and 17331, January 31, 1974, 734-1 BCA 10,483.
50. Memorandum for Tri-Service Contracting Officers, Company-Owned and Operated Aircraft, Indirect Cost Monitoring Office Working Group Guidance Paper.
51. Gould Defense Systems, Inc., supra note 32.
52. Litton Systems, Inc., 196 Ct. Cl. 133, October 15, 1971, 16 CFF 80785.
53. H & M Moving, Inc., Ct. Cl. 37-73, June 19, 1974, 20 CCF 83, 142.
54. Falcon Research & Development Co., ASBCA no. 19784, January 6, 1977, 77-1 BCA 12312, aff'd. October 4, 1977, 77-2 BCA 12795.
55. Data-Design Laboratories, Inc., supra note 49.
56. Gould Defense Systems, Inc., supra note 32.
57. Data-Design Laboratories, Inc., supra note 47.
58. Data-Design Laboratories, Inc., supra note 3.
59. Celesco Industries, supra note 37.
60. RMK-BRJ, A Joint Venture, ASBCA no. 10631, March 18, 1974, 74-1 BCA 10,535.
61. Northrop Aircraft, Inc. v. United States (1955), 130 t. 1.626.
62. Colorado Dental Service (Delta Dental Plan of Colorado), ASBCA no. 24,666, May 28, 1982, 82-2 BCA 15,836.

Chapter Eight
Cost Accounting Standards

HISTORICAL PERSPECTIVE

When the Defense Production Act came up for renewal in 1968, Admiral Hyman G. Rickover testified before the House Banking and Currency Committee and vigorously complained that the government could not identify costs properly to specific government negotiated contracts. He alleged that, because GAAP allowed contractors to use such a wide variety of accounting practices, it was nearly impossible to analyze contract costs and compare prices proposed by competing contractors. Rickover expressed little confidence that action to establish greater uniformity in cost accounting practices would be taken either by industry, the accounting profession, or the executive branch of the government. He challenged Congress to develop the needed accounting standards and to require contractors to comply with them. He predicted that $2 billion in savings could be achieved as a result of this action.

Based on this testimony, the House added a provision to the bill extending the Defense Production Act that required the Comptroller General of the United States to recommend legislation for the promulgation of accounting standards. The Senate also added an amendment to the bill extending the act that directed the Comptroller General to study the feasibility of applying uniform cost accounting standards to negotiated defense contracts and subcontracts. The Senate bill was ultimately accepted by the House and sent to the White House, where on July 1, 1968, it was signed into law as the Defense Production Act Amendment of 1968, Public Law 90-370.

Results of the Feasibility Study

The Comptroller General's study was completed and submitted to Congress in January 1970.[1] The principal conclusions and recommendations of the study were:

> It was feasible to establish and apply cost accounting standards to provide a greater degree of uniformity and consistency in cost accounting as a basis for negotiating and administering contracts.

Cost accounting standards should not require the application of precisely prescribed methods of computing each different type of cost.

Cost accounting standards should not be limited to defense cost reimbursement type contracts but should apply to all types of negotiated government contracts and subcontracts.

Cumulative benefits from the establishment of cost accounting standards should outweigh the cost of implementation.

Cost accounting standards for contract costing purposes should evolve from sound commercial cost accounting practices and should not be incompatible with generally accepted accounting principles.

New machinery should be established to develop cost accounting standards and to perform the continuing research and updating that will be required for effective administration.

Contractors should be required to maintain records of contract performance in conformity with the cost accounting standards and in the approved practices set forth in disclosure agreements.

Following submission of the Comptroller General's study to the House Committee on Banking and Currency, a provision to create a Cost Accounting Standards Board (CASB) to develop and promulgate cost accounting standards was included in proposed legislation to extend the Defense Production Act for two years to June 30, 1972. Public hearings were conducted by both the House and the Senate in the spring and summer of 1970 to consider the various provisions of the bill. Representatives of government, industry and the accounting profession were among the groups that testified. The principal proponents of uniform cost accounting standards were representatives of government. For the most part, industry opposed the legislation, contending among other things, that:

Uniform cost accounting standards had not been adequately defined.

The need for cost accounting standards had not been adequately demonstrated.

The probable cost of promulgating such standards could not be justified in view of the uncertainty of the benefits to be derived.

The desired objectives could be achieved within the framework of existing laws and regulations.

CAS Legislation

After vigorous debate in both houses of Congress, the legislators passed the Defense Production Act Amendments of 1970, Public Law 91-379, which was signed into law on August 15, 1970. Although resistance was strong, adoption of a law establishing the CASB was not surprising. Two unrelated factors were particularly significant in providing the framework and momentum for such legislation:

Congress was becoming increasingly disenchanted with the accounting profession's ability to express independent and objective opinions on financial matters involving private industry.

Congressional interest in defense programs had heightened.

In 1967 and 1968, the Joint Economic Subcommittee on the Economy in Government identified 23 defense contractors who were holding $15 billion in government property and allegedly using the property without approval or paying rent. In 1970, the Subcommittee cited 38 weapon systems that were overrun by $21 billion, compared to original estimates. This was viewed by many legislators and their constituencies as evidence that contract overruns were the rule rather than the exception. These findings led to questions and serious public skepticism regarding the setting of national priorities and the ability of the military to carry out its programs at reasonable costs. The mood of the times was expressed by Senator Proxmire who concluded that one of several necessities for bringing the military budget under control was better information, which would result from a uniform system of accounting for defense contractors.

The law established a five member CASB as an agent of Congress and independent of the executive departments of the government. The Board consisted of the Comptroller General as Chairman and four members appointed by him for four-year terms. Two of the appointees were from the accounting profession (one knowledgeable in the cost accounting problems of small business), one a representative of industry, and one from the Federal Government.

The Board was directed by statute to promulgate standards designed to achieve uniformity and consistency in the cost accounting principles followed by defense prime contractors and subcontractors in estimating, accumulating, and reporting costs in connection with the pricing, administration, and settlement of all negotiated national defense procurements in excess of $100,000 except where the price negotiated is based on:

Established catalog or market prices of commercial items sold in substantial quantities to the general public.

Prices set by law or regulation.

The Board was also authorized to amend its regulations and to exempt from its standards certain classes or categories of contractors as it deemed appropriate.

The enabling legislation directed the board to promulgate regulations that, as a condition of contracting, required defense contractors to:

Disclose in writing their cost accounting principles including methods of distinguishing direct costs from indirect costs and the basis used for allocating indirect costs.

Agree to contract price adjustments in favor of the government, with interest, for any net increased cost resulting from either failure to comply with duly promulgated cost accounting standards or to consistently follow their cost accounting practices in pricing contract proposals and in accumulating and reporting contract performance costs.

Ten years after the enactment of the law and the creation of the CASB, the Board ceased to exist. After a turbulent life, which included the promulgation of rules requiring the disclosure of accounting practices and the promulgation of 19 standards, Congress declined to provide funding for the Board for fiscal year 1981. There was a last-minute attempt near the close of the 96th Congress to transfer the functions of the Board to the Office of Management and Budget (OMB) but the bill failed to clear the Senate Committee on Banking, Housing, and Urban Affairs.

Even though there is no longer a CASB, the standards are still in effect. Because the standards were promulgated under the Defense Production Act, they have the full force and effect of law. The executive departments continue to enforce and monitor the provisions as they currently exist. GAO also maintains a program for reviewing executive agency implementation of CAS.

In 1984 DOD established a CAS Policy Group to administer CAS. This action was taken based on a Department of Justice opinion stating that DOD was legally free to adopt, reject, or grant exemptions to the CAS. The CAS policy group consists of representatives from the military services, Defense Logistics Agency and NASA. Nonvoting members include representatives from the Comptroller Generals Office, Office of the Assistant Secretary for acquisition and logistics, General Services Administration and the Defense Contract Audit Agency.

DOD has incorporated CAS into Part 30 of the Federal Acquisition Regulations to enable it to revise the standards on a regulatory basis. In addition DOD has proposed minor revisions to CAS 404 and 416. The CAS 404 proposal would raise the minimum capitalization threshold from $1,000 to $1,500. The CAS 416 proposed change would substitute the Treasury rate in place of state rates in discounting certain self-insured losses to present value. The policy group is also considering more substantive changes, such as revisions to CAS 404, CAS 409, CAS 412 and CAS 413. Notwithstanding the proposed changes, contractors should be cautious of implementing the proposed changes since some legal questions have been raised regarding the ability of an executive agency to amend or disregard contract requirements imposed by statute.

Legislation has been introduced in the 100th Congress (in both the House of Representatives and the Senate) to assign the responsibility previously assigned to the CASB to the Office of Federal Procurement Policy (OFPP). If enacted, this would resolve questions regarding the legal stature of the DOD CAS Policy Group. The passage of time, legislation, and the courts will determine the future impact of cost accounting standards.

Relationship to Federal Acquisition Regulations

Defense contractors subject to CAS are required by law to comply with the regulations. CAS addresses the accounting practices and allocation procedures for charging costs to contracts. Implementing and administrative requirements are contained in FAR Part 30. FAR Part 31 contains criteria governing on the allowability of specific costs on government contracts. In Boeing Company[2] the ASBCA held that CAS is controlling with respect to the determination, measurement, assignment and allocation of costs when contradictory cost accounting requirements are imposed by the DAR (FAR) cost principles and CAS.

CAS Implementation

In 1976, the Department of Defense (DOD) established a Cost Accounting Standards Steering Committee to develop policy guidelines to integrate the CASB regulations into DOD's procurement practices and to provide liaison with the CASB. Twenty-five CAS Steering Committee interim guidance papers (Fig. 8.1) were published on a variety of matters relating to the standards, contract coverage, disclosure statements, and determination of price adjustments. Since the papers have never been incorporated into the DAR or FAR, their

W.G. No.	Subject	Date
76- 1	Implementing CAS 412	Feb. 24, 1976
76- 2	Application of CAS to Contract Modifications and to Orders Placed Under Basic Agreements	Feb. 24, 1976
76- 3	Application of CAS to Subcontracts	Mar. 18, 1976
76- 4	Determining Increased Costs to the Government for CAS Covered FFP Contracts	Oct. 1, 1976
76- 5	Treatment of Implementation Costs Related to Changes in Cost Accounting Practices	Oct. 1, 1976
76- 6	Application of CAS Clauses to Changes in Contractor's Established Practices When a Disclosure Statement Has Been Submitted	Oct. 1, 1976
76- 7	Significance of "Effective" and "Applicability" Dates Included in Cost Accounting Standards	Oct. 1, 1976
76- 8	Use of the Offset Principle in Contract Price Adjustments Resulting from Accounting Changes	Dec. 17, 1976
76- 9	Measurement of Cost Impact on FFP Contracts	Dec. 17, 1976
77-10	Retroactive Implementation of Cost Accounting Standards When Timely Compliance is Not Feasible	Feb. 2, 1977
77-11	Implementation of CAS 410	Feb. 2, 1977
77-12	Deliberate Noncompliance and Inadvertent Noncompliance	Mar. 29, 1977
77-13	Applicability of CAS 405 to Costs Determined Unallowable on the Basis of Allocability	Mar. 29, 1977
77-14	Early Implementation of New Cost Accounting Standards Issued by the CAS Board	Mar. 29, 1977
77-15	Influence of CAS Regulations on Contract Terminations	Mar. 29, 1977
77-16	Applicability of CAS to Letter Contracts	Jun. 14, 1977
77-17	Identification of CAS Contract Universe at a Contractor's Plant	Jun. 14, 1977
77-18	Implementation of CAS 414 and DPC 76-3	Jun. 14, 1977
77-19	Administration of Leased Facilities Under CAS 414	Aug. 18, 1977
77-20	Policy for Withdrawing Determination of Adequacy of Disclosure Statement	Jun. 14, 1977
78-21	Implementation of CAS 410	Jan. 16, 1978
Amend. 1 to 78-21	Implementation of CAS 410	Apr. 10, 1981
78-22	CAS 409 and the Development of Asset Service Lives	Feb. 6, 1978
79-23	Administration of Equitable Adjustments for Accounting Changes Not Required by New Cost Accounting Standards	Jan. 2, 1979
79-24	Allocation of Business Unit General and Administrative (G&A) Expense to Facilities Contracts	Jan. 26, 1979
81-25	Change in Cost Accounting Practice for State Income and Franchise Taxes as a Result of Change in Method of Reporting Income From Long-Term Contracts	Feb. 10, 1981

Figure 8.1. Index of DOD CAS Steering Committee interim guidance papers.

provisions do not constitute either regulatory or contractual requirements. However, they do reflect how DOD has officially interpreted what the standards require. NASA is also bound by the CAS Steering Committee guidance pronouncements. Additionally, the General Services Administration, uses the CAS Steering Committee papers for guidance.

POLICIES, RULES, AND REGULATIONS OF THE BOARD

Objectives, Policies, and Concepts

In May 1977, the CASB published its Restatement of Objectives, Policies and Concepts for the purpose of presenting the framework within which the Board formulated the standards and related rules and regulations. The document includes statements setting forth: the Board's general objectives, among which uniformity, consistency, allowability, allocability, fairness, and verifiability assume primary importance; its cost allocation concepts; and a statement of operating policies. The document also explains how the Board developed and promulgated its rules, regulations, and standards.

Promulgation Process

The Board's procedures for developing a standard started with identifying a significant problem area in contract cost accounting. After the problem was identified, the staff began its research into the subject area. In performing the research, the staff examined existing relevant authoritative pronouncements, analyzed data available from disclosure statements, and visited various contractors, both to obtain empirical data as well as to survey actual practices.

In the early stages of developing a standard, CASB prepared questionnaires and/or statements of issues that were circulated to selected contractors, government agencies, and business and professional groups for the dual purpose of obtaining information on current practices as well as views and comments. With the information gained from these efforts, a preliminary draft standard was prepared which was distributed for comment.

After considering the comments received and the responses to the draft standard, the CAS legislation required the Board to publish the proposed standard in the *Federal Register*. Interested parties were afforded at least 30 days in which to submit views and comments. The Board reviewed and analyzed the public comments in order to determine whether revisions were appropriate or even whether the standard was necessary. The final version of a standard was then published in the *Federal Register* and submitted simultaneously to Congress.

The promulgated standard that appeared in the *Federal Register* was accompanied by prefatory comments that summarized the comments received on the proposed standard and provided the rationale for the requirements included in its provisions. The prefatory comments constitute a useful reference in explaining the technically worded regulation and are authoritative statements of the Board.

Both houses of Congress had a period of 60 days of continuous session in which to pass a concurrent resolution on any proposed final standard that they did not favor. Absent such a resolution, the standard, carrying the force of law, became effective at the beginning of the second fiscal quarter following 30 days after final publication unless a later effective date was provided by the Board.

Contract Coverage

Although the statute creating the CASB applied to negotiated defense contracts only, nondefense agencies also implemented the CASB's standards, rules, and regulations. The statutory level of coverage through December 31, 1974 was $100,000. In January 1975, the Board amended its regulations to provide that CAS coverage at a business unit* must be triggered by the award of a national defense CAS covered prime contract or subcontract in excess of

---

*Two terms, *segment* and *business unit*, are used throughout the CAS regulations and standards. A segment is defined as a subdivision of an organization, such as a division, product, department, or plant, which usually has profit responsibility and/or produces a product or service. A business unit can be either an individual segment or an entire business organization that is not divided into segments.

$500,000. After receiving such an award, a business unit is required to comply with all applicable standards for all subsequently awarded prime contracts and subcontracts in excess of $100,000 unless otherwise exempt. Proposed legislation has been introduced in the 100th Senate to raise the contract threshold for CAS coverage from $100,000 to $500,000. While enactment of legislation is uncertain, the revision would have the positive impact of reducing the administrative burden associated with CAS coverage.

Basic agreements and basic ordering agreements are, by definition, not contracts but written understandings as to future procurements. The individual orders issued under these agreements are contracts and they establish the basis for determining whether CAS applies. Modifications to covered contracts are subject to CAS. If the original contract is exempt, modifications are generally awarded on the same basis. The CASB concluded in the prefatory comments to its original publication on February 29, 1972, that its regulations

> should not cover negotiated modifications to contracts exempt at their inception. . . . however, the Board intends that the annual extension of existing negotiated contracts and similar contract modifications would not be exempt from the Board's rules, regulations and Cost Accounting Standards.[3]

In its Interim Guidance Paper W.G. 76-2, the DOD CAS Steering Committee noted that an option increment that was not contemplated under the terms of the original contract must be treated as if it were a new negotiated contract.

Effective March 10, 1978, the CAS regulations were amended to provide two levels of coverage: "full" and "modified." Under "modified" coverage a business unit must comply with only Standards 401 and 402. Full coverage requires a business unit to comply with all the Board's standards.

Conditions that determine the extent that companies must comply with CAS regulations are outlined below:

> Business units that have not received a negotiated national defense prime contract or subcontract in excess of $500,000 are exempt from complying with CAS.

> Once a business unit receives a negotiated CAS covered national defense federal contract/subcontract in excess of $500,000, that contract and all future negotiated contracts/subcontracts in excess of $100,000, must include one of the CAS clauses providing for either full or modified coverages until all CAS covered awards have been completed.

> Assuming that the requirements for initial coverages as described above have been met, national defense and nondefense contracts/subcontracts over $100,000 are eligible for modified coverage if the business unit's total CAS covered national defense awards in the preceding cost accounting period were less than $10 million and less than 10% of the business unit's total sales. A contractor who is eligible to use modified coverage must elect to do so; otherwise, full coverage will apply.

> Assuming that the requirement for initial coverage as described above has been met, negotiated national defense and nondefense contracts/subcontracts over $100,000 are subject to full coverage if total national defense awards in the preceding cost accounting period were more than 10% of the business unit's total sales or more than $10 million.

> Business units with a single national defense award of $10 million are immediately subject to full coverage.

The criteria for determining CAS applicability is illustrated in Figure 8.2.

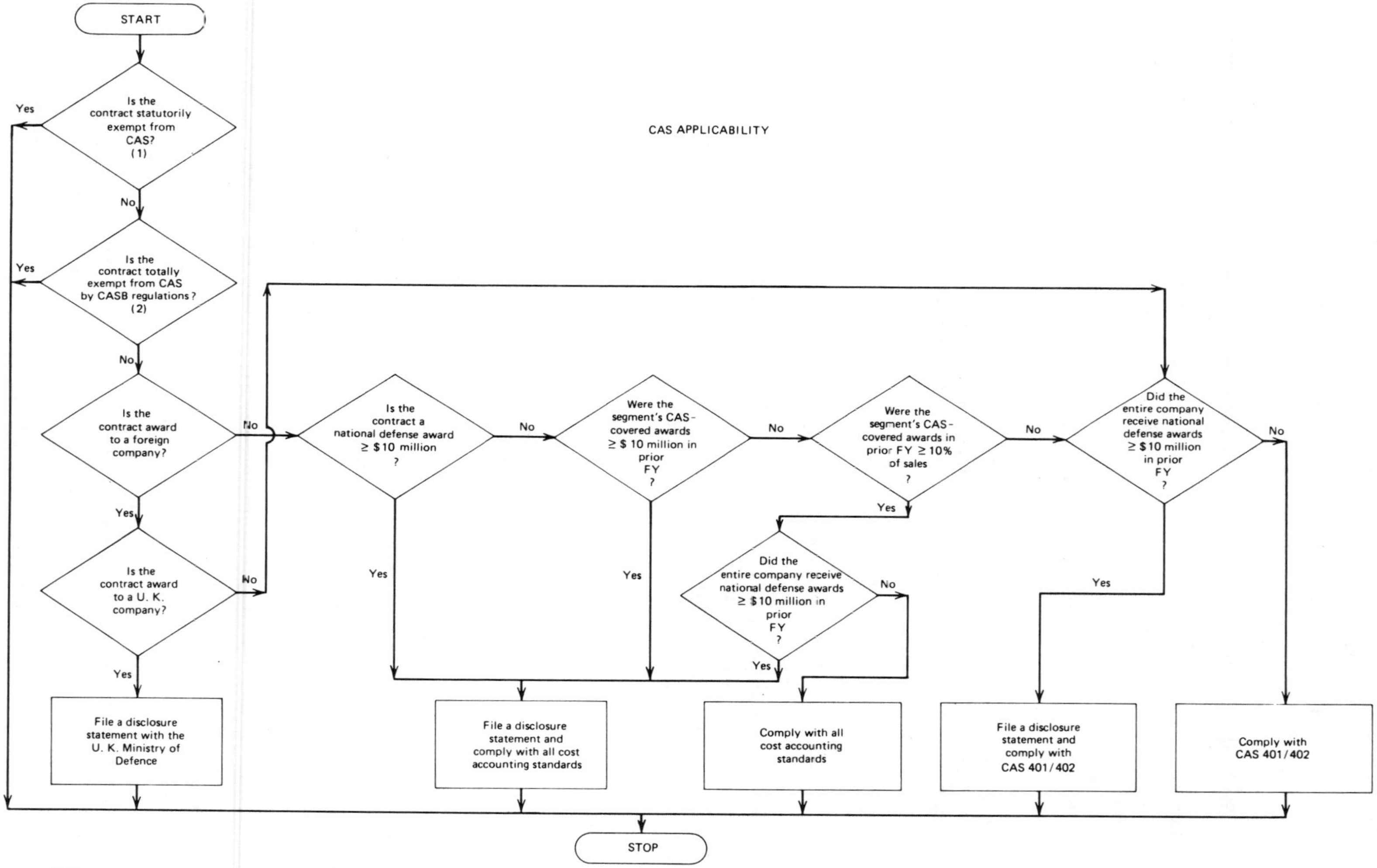

CAS APPLICABILITY

Figure 8.2. CAS applicability.

Notes:

(1) Negotiated contracts: under $100,000, based on catalog/market prices of items sold in substantial quantities to the general public, based on prices set by law or regulation; formally advertised contracts.

(2) Awards to small business concern; awards to labor surplus area concern pursuant to labor surplus area partial set asides; awards to educational institutions other than federally funded research and development centers; awards to foreign governments; fixed — price contracts awarded with cost data neither required nor submitted; awards under $500,000 where no CAS covered contracts are active.

Exemptions

In establishing the CASB, Congress recognized that in some situations it would not be in the public interest to require compliance with these regulations. Accordingly, certain exemptions were written into the statute and the Board was authorized to exempt others based on its determination.

Contracts in which the price negotiated is based upon established catalog or market prices of commercial items sold in substantial quantities to the general public or prices set by law or regulation are exempt by statute from CAS coverage. In 1976 the Comptroller General ruled that the statutory exemptions are mandatory and ". . .do not allow for agency discretion as to whether to grant the exemption. ."[4] Adequate price competition is not a criterion for exempting national defense fixed-price contracts; however, adequate price competition is a basis for exempting firm fixed-price subcontracts where:

All competing firms receive identical solicitations.
At least two offers are received from unaffiliated companies.
The successful contractor is selected solely on the basis of price.
The lowest responsive offer is accepted.

In addition to the exemptions described above, the Board further exercised its authority to exempt from its rules, regulations, and standards the following:

Any contract or subcontract awarded to a small business concern as defined by Small Business Administration regulations.

Any contract with a labor surplus area concern awarded pursuant to procedures providing for a labor surplus area partial set-aside.

Any contract with an educational institution whose cost principles are subject to OMB Circular A-21 (formerly issued as Federal Management Circular 73-8), except specifically for any parts of contracts performed at a federally funded research and development center (FFRDC).

Any contract or subcontract awarded to a foreign government or its agencies or instrumentalities.

Any contract or subcontract awarded to a foreign concern, except for Standards 401 and 402.

Any contract or subcontract with a United Kingdom (UK) contractor for performance substantially in the UK, provided that the contractor has filed with the UK Ministry of Defence a completed CASB disclosure statement. Where the contractor is already required to follow UK Government Accounting Conventions, the disclosed practices must reflect the requirements of those conventions.

Any firm fixed-price contract or subcontract awarded without submission of cost data, provided the failure to submit cost data is not due to a waiver of the requirement for certified cost or pricing data.

In addition to the exemptions contained in regulations, the acquisition regulations exempt the following categories of contracts:

	FAR	Regulations in effect prior to the FAR	
		DAR & NASA PR	FPR
Contracts executed and performed in their entirety outside the United States or its territories and possessions.	X	X	X
Nondefense contracts awarded by civilian agencies to hospitals or state, local, and tribal Indian governments.			X
Nondefense contracts awarded on the basis of adequate price competition.	X		
Nondefense contracts awarded to business units that are not currently performing any CAS covered national defense contracts.	X		

Aside from the Board's broad power to grant exemptions, it was also authorized to waive, at the request of designated DOD officials, all or part of its standards or rules for particular contracts or subcontracts. Such waivers were granted based on whether the procurement agency established to the Board's satisfaction that the contract involved was essentially a sole source procurement with such urgency that it was not feasible to find an alternative supplier. When the Board ceased operations on September 30, 1980, no Federal organization was specifically authorized to grant waivers from the CAS rules, regulations, or standards. However, in 1982, NASA granted a CAS waiver to one of its subcontractors under the provisions of Public Law 85-804, which permits Federal agencies or departments to award, modify, or amend contracts (without regard to other requirements of the law for making, performing, modifying, or amending contracts) where such action facilitates the national defense. The acquisition regulations implementing the act (FAR Part 50) provide that extraordinary contractual adjustment under the act is appropriate in circumstances where, for instance:

A loss on a government contract impairs the productive ability of a contractor whose operation is essential to the national defense.

An ambiguity in the contract fails to express clearly the agreement as understood by the contracting parties.

An obvious mistake by the contractor should have been apparent to the contracting officer.

The contracting parties make a mutual mistake as to a material fact.

NASA's rationale for the CAS waiver was based on somewhat different circumstances than those listed above:

The subcontractor was essential to the Space Shuttle program.

The subcontractor's government sales (all FFP) constituted less than 1% of total corporate sales.

Extended negotiations between the government, prime contractor, and the subcontractor failed to change the subcontractor's refusal to accept the CAS clause in its subcontracts.

Delays in the space shuttle launch schedules because of this situation would have an unacceptable effect on space and defense efforts and would have prevented NASA from accomplishing its mission.

The authority to waive Cost Accounting Standards Act requirements was vested by statute in the Cost Accounting Standards Board; however, when the Board discontinued operations at the close of the 1980 fiscal year, there was no designated alternate waiver authority. To assure maintenance of the Space Shuttle launch schedule, authority to waive cost accounting standards requirements had to be issued immediately.

The rationale provided by NASA seems very similar to criteria used by the CASB to justify waivers. Although Public Law 85-804 may be a legal basis for executive agencies to grant waivers, it is a very cumbersome process. The DOD CAS Policy Group referred to earlier has been given regulatory authority to grant waivers and exemptions.

Contract Clauses

The initial step that an agency must take to implement the Board's standards, rules, and regulations is to include a notice in the solicitation to offerors for contract award. The second step involves inserting a "CAS clause" in the negotiated contract that is subsequently awarded. All contracts subject to CASB regulations must include a clause that sets forth the obligations imposed on the contractor. The clauses distinguish between full coverage and modified coverage, which determines the number of standards that apply, as below:

Contracts	Full Coverage	Modified Coverage
Prior to FAR Implementation		
Defense	DAR 7-104.83(a)(1)	DAR 7-104.83(a)(2)
	NASA PR 7-104.55(a)(1)	NASA PR 7-104.55(a)(2)
	FPR 1-3.1204-1(a)(1)	FPR 1-3.1204-1(a)(2)
Nondefense	FPR 1-3.1204-2(a)	FPR 1-3.1204-2(b)
After FAR Implementation		
All	FAR 52.230-3	FAR 52.230-5
	Figure 8.3.	Figure 8.4.

(a) Unless the Cost Accounting Standards Board (CASB) has prescribed rules or regulations exempting the Contractor or this contract from standards, rules, and regulations promulgated pursuant to 50 U.S.C. App. 2168 (Pub. L. 91-379, August 15, 1970), the Contractor, in connection with this contract, shall:

(1) (National Defense Contracts Only) By submission of a Disclosure Statement, disclose in writing the Contractor's cost accounting practices as required by regulations of the CASB. The practices disclosed for this contract shall be the same as the practices currently disclosed and applied on all other contracts and subcontracts being performed by the Contractor and which contain a Cost Accounting Standards (CAS) clause. If the Contractor has notified the Contracting Officer that the Disclosure Statement contains trade secrets and commercial or financial information which is privileged and confidential, the Disclosure Statement shall be protected and shall not be released outside of the Government.

(2) Follow consistently the Contractor's cost accounting practices in accumulating and reporting contract performance cost data concerning this contract. If any change in cost accounting practices is made for the purposes of any contract or subcontract subject to CASB requirements, the change must be applied prospectively to this contract, and the Disclosure Statement must be amended accordingly. If the contract price or cost allowance of this contract is affected by such changes, adjustment shall be made in accordance with subparagraph (a)(4) or (a)(5) below, as appropriate.

Figure 8.3. Cost accounting standards clause, FAR 52.230-3.

(3)   Comply with all CAS in effect on the date of award of this contract or, if the Contractor has submitted cost or pricing data, on the date of final agreement on price as shown on the Contractor's signed certificate of current cost or pricing data. The Contractor shall also comply with any CAS which hereafter becomes applicable to a contract or subcontract of the Contractor. Such compliance shall be required prospectively from the date of applicability to such contract or subcontract.

(4)(i)   Agree to an equitable adjustment as provided in the Changes clause of this contract if the contract cost is affected by a change which pursuant to (3) above, the Contractor is required to make to the Contractor's established cost accounting practices.

(ii)   Negotiate with the Contracting Officer to determine the terms and conditions under which a change may be made to a cost accounting practice, other than a change made under other provisions of this paragraph 4; *provided,* that no agreement may be made under this provision that will increase costs paid by the United States.

(iii)   When the parties agree to a change to a cost accounting practice, other than a change under (4)(i) above, negotiate an equitable adjustment as provided in the Changes clause of this contract.

(5)   Agree to an adjustment of the contract price or cost allowance, as appropriate, if the Contractor or a subcontractor fails to comply with an applicable Cost Accounting Standard or to follow any cost accounting practice consistently and such failure results in any increased costs paid by the United States. Such adjustment shall provide for recovery of the increased costs to the United States together with interest thereon computed at the rate determined by the Secretary of the Treasury pursuant to Pub. L. 92-41, 85 Stat. 97, whichever is less, from the time the payment by the United States was made to the time the adjusted is effected.

(b)   If the parties fail to agree whether the Contractor or a subcontractor has complied with an applicable CAS, rule, or regulation of the CASB and as to any cost adjustment demanded by the United States, such failure to agree shall be a dispute concerning a question of fact within the meaning of the Disputes clause of this contract.

(c)   The Contractor shall permit any authorized representatives of the agency head, of the CASB, or of the Comptroller General of the United States to examine and make copies of any documents, papers, or records relating to compliance with the requirements of this clause.

(d)   The Contractor shall include in all negotiated subcontracts which the Contractor enters into, the substance of this clause, except paragraph (b), and shall require such inclusion in all other subcontracts, of any tier, including the obligation to comply with all CAS in effect on the subcontract's award date or if the subcontractor has submitted cost or pricing data, on the date of final agreement on price as shown on the subcontractor's signed Certificate of Current Cost or Pricing Data. This requirement shall apply only to negotiated subcontracts in excess of $100,000 where the price negotiated is not based on—

(1)   Established catalog or market prices of commercial items sold in substantial quantities to the general public; or

(2)   Prices set by law or regulation, and except that the requirement shall not apply to negotiated subcontracts otherwise exempt from the requirement to include a CAS clause by reason of 331.30(b) of Title 4, Code of Federal Regulations (4 CFR 331.30(b)).

Note (1):   New CAS shall be applicable to both national defense and nondefense CAS-covered contracts upon award of a new national defense CAS-covered contract containing the new Standard. The award of a new nondefense CAS-covered contract shall not trigger application of new CAS.

Note (2):   Subcontractors shall be required to submit their Disclosure Statements to the Contractor. However, if a subcontractor has previously submitted its Disclosure Statement to a Government Administrative Contracting Officer (ACO), it may satisfy that requirement by certifying to the Contractor the date of the Statement and the address of the ACO.

Note (3):   In any case where a subcontractor determines that the Disclosure Statement information is privileged and confidential and declines to provide it to the Contractor or higher tier subcontractor, the Contractor may authorize direct submission of that subcontractor's Disclosure Statement to the same Government offices to which the Contractor was required to make submission of its Disclosure Statement. Such authorization shall in no way relieve the Contractor of liability as provided in paragraph (a)(5) of this clause. In view of the foregoing and since the contract may be subject to adjustment under this clause by reason of any failure to comply with rules, regulations, and Standards of the CASB in connection with covered subcontracts, it is expected that the Contractor may wish to include a clause in each such subcontract requiring the subcontractor to appropriately indemnify the Contractor. However, the inclusion of such a clause and the terms thereof are matters for negotiation and agreement between the Contractor and the subcontractor, provided that they do not conflict with the duties of the Contractor under its contract with the Government. It is also expected that any subcontractor subject to such indemnification will generally require substantially similar indemnification to be submitted by its subcontractors.

Figure 8.3.   (Continued)

Note (4):   If the subcontractor is a business unit which, pursuant to 4 CFR 332 is entitled to elect modified contract coverage and to follow Standards 401 and 402, the clause at 52.230-5, "Disclosure Consistency of Cost Accounting Practices," of the Federal Acquisition Regulation shall be inserted in lieu of this clause.

Note (5):   The terms defined in 4 CFR 331.20 shall have the same meanings herein. As there defined, "negotiated subcontract" means any subcontract except a firm-fixed-price subcontract made by a Contractor or subcontractor after receiving offers from at least two persons not associated with each other or with such Contractor or subcontractor, providing (1) the solicitation to all competitors is identical, (2) price is the only consideration in selecting the subcontractor from among the competitors solicited, and (3) the lowest offer received in compliance with the solicitation from among those solicited is accepted.

(End of clause)

Figure 8.3. (Continued)

(a)   The Contractor, in connection with this contract, shall:

(1)   Comply with the requirements of 4 CFR Parts 401, Consistency in Estimating, Accumulating, and Reporting Costs, and 402, Consistency in Allocating Costs Incurred for the Same Purpose, in effect on the date of award of this contract.

(2)   (National Defense Contracts Only) If it is a business unit of a company required to submit a Disclosure Statement, disclose in writing its cost accounting practices as required by regulations of the Cost Accounting Standards Board (CASB). If the Contractor has notified the Contracting Officer that the Disclosure Statement contains trade secrets and commercial or financial information which is privileged and confidential, the Disclosure Statement shall be protected and shall not be released outside of the Government.

Note (1):   Subcontractors shall be required to submit their Disclosure Statements to the Contractor. However, if a subcontractor has previously submitted its Disclosure Statement to a Government Administrative Contracting Officer (ACO), it may satify that requirement by certifying to the Contractor the date of the Statement and the address of the Contracting Officer.

Note (2):   In any case where a subcontractor determines that the Disclosure Statement information is privileged and confidential and declines to provide it to the Contractor or higher tier subcontractor, the Contractor may authorize direct submission of the subcontractor's Disclosure Statement to the same Government offices to which the Contractor was required to make submission of its Disclosure Statement. Such authorization shall in no way relieve the Contractor of liability if it or a subcontractor fails to comply with an applicable Cost Accounting Standard (CAS) or to follow any practice disclosed pursuant to this paragraph and such failure results in any increased costs paid by the United States. In view of the foregoing and since the contract may be subject to adjustment under this clause by reason of any failure to comply with rules, regulations, and Standards of the CASB in connection with covered subcontracts, it is expected that the Contractor may wish to include a clause in each such subcontract requiring the subcontractor to appropriately indemnify the Contractor. However, the inclusion of such a clause and the terms thereof are matters for negotiation and agreement between the Contractor and subcontractor, provided that they do not conflict with the duties of the Contractor under its contract with the Government. It is also expected that any subcontractor subject to such indemnification will generally require substantially similar indemnification to be submitted by its subcontractors.

Note (3):   The terms defined in 4 CFR 331.20 shall have the same meanings in this clause. As there defined, "negotiated subcontract" means any subcontract except a firm-fixed-price subcontract made by a Contractor or subcontractor after receiving offers from at least two persons not associated with each other or such Contractor or subcontractor, providing (1) the solicitation to all competitors is identical, (2) price is the only consideration in selecting the subcontractor from among the competitors solicited, and (3) the lowest offer received in compliance with the solicitation from among those solicited is accepted.

(3)(i)   Follow consistently the Contractor's cost accounting practices. A change to such practices may be proposed, however, by either the Government or the Contractor, and the Contractor agrees to negotiate with the Contracting Officer the terms and conditions under which a change may be made. After the terms and conditions under which the change is to be made have been agreed to, the change must be applied prospectively to this contract, and the Disclosure Statement, if affected, must be amended accordingly.

(ii)   The Contractor shall, when the parties agree to a change to a cost accounting practice and the Contracting Officer has made the finding required in 332.51 of the CASB's regulations, negotiate an equitable adjustment as provided in the Changes clause of this contract. In the ab-

Figure 8.4.   Disclosure and consistency of cost accounting practices clause, FAR 52.230-5.

sence of the required finding, no agreement may be made under this contract clause that will increase costs paid by the United States.

(4) Agree to an adjustment of the contract price or cost allowance, as appropriate, if the Contractor of a subcontractor fails to comply with the applicable CAS or to follow any cost accounting practice, and such failure results in any increased costs paid by the United States. Such adjustment shall provide for recovery of the increased costs to the United States together with interest thereon computed at the rate determined by the Secretary of the Treasury pursuant to Pub. L. 92-41, 85 Stat. 97, from the time the payment by the United States was made to the time the adjustment is effected.

(b) If the parties fail to agree whether the Contractor has complied with an applicable CAS, rule, or regulation of the CASB and as to any cost adjustment demanded by the. United States, such failure to agree shall be a dispute within the meaning of the Disputes clause of this contract.

(c) The Contractor shall permit any authorized representatives of the agency head, of the CASB, or of the Comptroller General of the United States to examine and make copies of any documents, papers, and records relating to compliance with the requirements of this clause.

(d) The Contractor shall include in all negotiated subcontracts, which the Contractor enters into, the substance of this clause, except paragraph (b), and shall require such inclusion in all other subcontracts of any tier, except that—

(1) If the subcontract is awarded to a business unit which pursuant to Part 331 is required to follow all CAS, the clause entitled "Cost Accounting Standards," set forth in 331.50 of the CASB's regulations shall be inserted in lieu of this clause; or

(2) This requirement shall apply only to negotiated subcontracts in excess of $100,000 where the price negotiated is not based on—

(i) Established catalog or market prices of commercial items sold in substantial quantities to the general public; or (ii) Price set by law or regulation.

(3) The requirement shall not apply to negotiated subcontracts otherwise exempt from the requirement to include a CAS clause by reason of 331.30(b) of the CASB's regulations.

(End of clause)

Figure 8.4. (Continued)

Full Coverage

The clauses applicable to full coverage parallel the basic provisions of the law and require a contractor, not otherwise exempt, to:

Describe in writing its cost accounting practices used on CAS-covered contracts when a business unit is part of a company that is required to submit a disclosure statement. (This provision is not applicable to nondefense contracts awarded by civilian agencies.)

Follow its cost accounting practices consistently and apply any cost accounting practice changes prospectively to the contract.

Comply with all standards in effect either on the contract award date or the date of the signed certificate of current cost or pricing data, and comply prospectively with all standards that become applicable during the contract's performance.

Agree to an adjustment of contract price or cost allowance for the:

a. Effects of cost accounting practice changes required by new standards.

b. Net increased costs resulting from voluntary changes in practices which the contracting officer has not found to be in the interest of the government.

c. Effects of cost accounting practice changes considered desirable by the contracting officer.

d. Net increased cost resulting from failure to comply with applicable standards or to follow established practices consistently.

Process disagreements on CAS issues under the contract disputes clause.

Permit authorized government representatives to examine and copy records relating to CAS compliance.

Include an appropriate CAS clause in all applicable subcontracts.

The full CAS coverage clause imposes several requirements on contractors.

Disclosure and Compliance

First, the requirement to disclose in writing the contractor's cost accounting practices by submission of a disclosure statement reflects the legislative mandate for the CASB to

> require defense contractors and subcontractors as a condition of contracting to disclose in writing their cost accounting principles, including methods of distinguishing direct costs from indirect costs and the basis used for allocating indirect costs. . . .[5]

The contract clauses require that the practices disclosed for the proposed or actual contract be the same as the practices currently disclosed and applied on all other contracts and subcontracts being performed that contain the CAS clause.

The requirement to comply with all standards in effect on the date of award seems simple and straightforward, notwithstanding the need to interpret the requirements of the standards. However, a contractor must also comply with any future cost standards which become applicable to a contract or subcontract. The contractor is agreeing by contractual provision to make future changes which at the time are unknown. Since CASB no longer exists to promulgate new standards, this particular requirement currently has no practical effect.

Contract Price Adjustments

Three types of contract price adjustments arise under CASB standards and rules, as outlined below:

> A contract is eligible for equitable adjustment when the contractor (1) is initially required to apply a standard, or (2) implements an accounting change that the contracting officer finds to be desirable and not detrimental to the interest of the government. The price adjustment is the net increase or decrease in cost resulting from the application of the new standard or desirable changes to all covered contracts. Equitable adjustments may result in the government paying increased costs to the contractor; or the effect could be a reduction in contract price.
>
> Equitable adjustments resulting from a contractor's requirement to apply a new standard were limited to the prospective effect of the new standard on costs or prices of covered prime contracts and subcontracts awarded prior to the effective date of the standard. Thus, all uncompleted contracts subject to CAS had to be recosted and repriced in accordance with the new requirements to determine the amount of the equitable adjustment.
>
> Equitable adjustments resulting from desirable changes occur when an accounting practice change is made during the performance of CAS covered contracts. These adjustments are applied prospectively from the date of the change to covered prime contracts and subcontracts awarded before the accounting change occurred. Under DOD criteria used in determining whether an accounting practice change is desirable, the term *desirable* encompasses the test of being appropriate, warranted, equitable, fair, or reason-

able. In its implementing guidance, CAS Steering Committee Interim Guidance Paper W.G. 79-23, DOD stated that a change may be desirable and not detrimental to the interest of the government even though it causes contract costs to increase.

CAS covered contracts and subcontracts are adjusted to reflect the failure of a contractor to comply with applicable standards and disclosed or established practices. CAS legislation established the corrective action for noncompliance. It requires the company to repay net increased costs resulting from the noncompliance plus interest at the semi-annual Treasury rate. Adjustments arising from noncompliance are made only in favor of the government. The CASB regulation (4 CFR 331.70(f)) allows the offsetting of cost increases and decreases on affected CAS covered contracts.

Covered contracts and subcontracts are adjusted for the effect of voluntary changes in practice which the contracting officer has not found to be in the interest of the government. The price adjustment is the net increased cost to the government resulting from the application of the revised practice to all covered contracts. Adjustments are made only in favor of the government. Cost increases may be offset against cost decreases on affected CAS covered contracts. DOD policy on offsets is contained in CAS Steering Committee Interim Guidance Paper W.G. 76-8.

The board interpreted *increased cost* as:

Cost paid by the government that, as a result of a changed practice or a CAS noncompliance, is higher than the cost that would have been paid had the change or noncompliance not occurred—Under a cost type contract the impact is relatively simple to measure. It is the amount by which the cost resulting from the change in the contractor's cost accounting practice or failure to comply with applicable standards is higher than the cost that would have been incurred had the practices not been changed or had noncompliance not occurred .

The excess of the negotiated price on a fixed-price contract over the price that would have been negotiated if the proposal had been priced in accordance with the practices actually used during contract performance—The CAS Steering Committee expanded on this point in Interim Guidance Paper W.G. 76-4 by stating that increased costs exist when costs allocated to firm fixed-price contracts as a result of a changed practice are less than would have been allocated if the change had not occurred. This interpretation of increased costs on firm fixed-price contracts has generated considerable controversy. Industry has vigorously opposed the interpretation on the grounds that there can be no increased costs on a fixed-price contract unless the negotiated price is actually increased. Industry representatives have argued further that the cost allocations made subsequent to contract award should have absolutely no impact on the negotiated price.

The CASB legislation established the contract price adjustment as the only remedy for failure to comply with the Board's rules, regulations, and standards. A dispute that developed soon after CAS was implemented established a significant principle regarding what should happen when the cost impact of a contractor's noncompliance cannot be determined. In *AiResearch Manufacturing Company,*[6] the contracting officer found the contractor in noncompliance with two cost accounting standards but was unable to develop an estimate of cost impact resulting from the noncompliance. The contractor moved to dismiss the appeal on the grounds that the CAS clause precluded resort to the disputes process if no cost impact was asserted by the government. The ASBCA denied the contractor's motion to dismiss. The Board concluded that even the possibility that no cost impact could be computed would not deny the Board jurisdiction over the question of whether the contractor's practices complied with the standards.

Cost Accounting Practices and Cost Accounting Practice Changes

The primary purpose of the contract adjustment procedures is to hold contractors accountable for the practices used to cost government contracts. To accomplish this objective the CASB, through its regulations, established a mechanism (i.e., negotiated contract price adjustments) for reflecting the effect of deviating from established practices. It soon became evident that in order to effectively implement this requirement, it was necessary to authoritatively define a cost accounting practice and a cost accounting practice change. The term *cost accounting practice* is defined as

> any accounting method or technique which is used for measurement of cost, assignment of cost to cost accounting periods, or allocation of cost to cost objectives. . . . Measurement of cost encompasses accounting methods and techniques used in defining the components of cost, determining the basis for cost measurement, and establishing criteria for use of alternative cost measurement techniques. . . . Assignment of cost to cost accounting periods refers to a method or technique used in determining the amount of cost to be assigned to individual cost accounting periods. . . . Allocation of cost to cost objectives includes both direct and indirect allocation of costs. Examples of cost accounting practices involving allocation of cost to cost objectives are the accounting methods or techniques used to accumulate cost, to determine whether a cost is to be directly or indirectly allocated, to determine the composition of cost pools, and to determine the selection and composition of the appropriate allocation base.[7]

A *change to a cost accounting practice* is defined as an alteration in a cost accounting practice except that:

> (1) The initial adoption of a cost accounting practice for the first time a cost is incurred, or a function is created, is not a change in cost accounting practice. The partial or total elimination of a cost or the cost of a function is not a change in cost accounting practice. . . .
> (2) The revision of a cost accounting practice for a cost which previously had been immaterial is not a change in cost accounting practice.[8]

The regulation also contains practical examples of changes to cost accounting practices and changes that are not cost accounting practice changes to provide clarity to the definition.

Subsequent to the issuance of this regulation, numerous contractors changed their methods of reporting income from long term contracts for state tax purposes from the percentage of completion method to the completed contract method. This generated considerable controversy regarding whether this change actually involved cost accounting. DOD outlined its policy in CAS Steering Committee Interim Guidance Paper W.G. 81-25, which stated that such a change in method of determining actual tax liability is a change in cost accounting practice for state tax costs. The DOD decision encountered widespread opposition from industry as well as the accounting profession including Price Waterhouse. Those who disagreed argued that as long as a contractor makes no change in the practices used to measure, assign, and allocate the tax liability, there is no accounting practice change, even if the taxing authority permits alternate methods for calculating the liability. In other words, the procedures for calculating the tax amount due as permitted by the taxing authority are extraneous to the cost accounting process.

Disputes

Any disagreement under the CAS clause is considered a dispute under the "disputes" clause of the contract. This clause effectively requires disputes to be taken before the appropriate board of contract appeals or Claims Court. Without this specific clause there would have been a question as to the appropriate body for appeals of CAS disputes between contractors and the government. Inasmuch as the CASB was a legislative organization, it did not want to hear such disputes. Therefore, the Board concluded that a specific clause referencing the disputes clause already incorporated in the contract was necessary.

Government Access to Records

The requirement for government access to records is based upon a specific requirement of the Defense Production Act. Section 719(j) of the act states:

> For the purpose of determining whether a defense contractor or subcontractor has complied with the duly promulgated cost accounting standards and has followed consistently his disclosed cost accounting practices, any authorized representative of the head of the agency concerned, of the Board, or of the Comptroller General of the United States shall have the right to examine and make copies of any documents, papers, or records of such contractor or subcontractor relating to compliance of such cost accounting standards and principles.

By providing for access to any records related to compliance with the standards or the following of disclosed practices, the provision effectively allows a broad access to records for the government.

Subcontract Flow Down

An appropriate CAS clause must be inserted in negotiated subcontracts in excess of $100,000 unless one of the specific exemptions provided for in CASB rules and regulations is met. The government's claim for price adjustment in that case would be made through the prime contractor. If the clause is required but not included in a subcontract, the prime contractor (or upper tier subcontractor) may be liable for increased costs to the government resulting from the subcontractor's noncompliances or accounting practice changes, with no recourse against the subcontractor.

Modified Coverage

The clauses applicable to "modified" coverage require a contractor, not otherwise exempt, to:

Comply with Standards 401 and 402.

Describe in writing its cost accounting practices when a business unit is part of a company that is required to submit a disclosure statement. (This provision is not applicable to nondefense contracts awarded by civilian agencies.)

Follow its cost accounting practices consistently and apply any cost accounting practice changes prospectively to the contract.

Agree to an adjustment of contract price or cost allowance for the:

Net increased cost resulting from failure to comply with CAS 401 and 402 or to follow established practices consistently.

Effect of a cost accounting practice change considered desirable by the contracting officer.

Net increased costs resulting from a voluntary change in practice that the contracting officer has not found to be in the interest of the government.

Process disagreements on CAS issues under the contract's "disputes" clause.

Permit authorized government representatives to examine and copy records relating to CAS compliance.

Include an appropriate CAS clause in all applicable subcontracts.

The difference between modified and full coverage is that under modified coverage the contractor is required to comply only with CAS 401, Consistency in Estimating, Accumulating, and Reporting Costs, and CAS 402, Consistency in Allocating Costs Incurred for the Same Purpose. None of the other standards apply. The clause provides for contract adjustments for changes to cost accounting practices similar to the techniques and requirements contained in the contract clauses providing full coverage. As a practical matter, if the contractor is performing under any contract containing a full coverage CAS clause, all standards will likely be followed on all contracts whether or not they contain a provision for full or modified coverage.

CAS Administration Clause

The clause indicating the type of coverage (i.e., full or modified) is accompanied by an additional clause that specifies how the CAS requirements should be administered. The "administration" clause (Figure 8.5), which is used for both types of coverage, outlines the procedures and time requirements for the contractor to notify the contracting officer in writing of anticipated changes to any cost accounting practice. The notification must include a written description of any accounting practice change to be made, together with a general dollar magnitude cost impact showing the shift of costs between CAS covered contracts by contract type and other work. For changes required to implement a new standard, the description must be provided within 60 days of the date of award of the contract requiring the change. For any other change, it is required not less than 60 days prior to the effective date of the proposed change. For noncompliances, the written description must be provided within 60 days after the date of agreement of such noncompliance. Other dates for providing the written descriptions may be mutually agreed to by the contracting parties.

The "administration" clause also requires a contractor to submit a cost impact proposal, in the form and manner specified by the contracting officer, within 60 days after the contracting officer's determination of adequacy and compliance of the descriptions submitted above. The proposal is generally required to be submitted on a contract by contract basis. The government's position has been that this is the only way in which the true cost impact can be determined. The clause permits the ACO to withhold up to 10% of subsequent payments due under the contract until a required cost impact proposal is submitted.

The "administration" clause requires a contractor to agree to appropriate contract or subcontract amendments to reflect price adjustments or cost allowances resulting from changes in cost accounting practices or noncompliances. It

For the purpose of administering the Cost Accounting Standards (CAS) requirements under this contract, the Contractor shall take the steps outlined in (a) through (f) below:

(a)   Submit to the cognizant Contracting Officer a description of any accounting change, the potential impact of the change on contracts containing a CAS clause, and if not obviously immaterial, a general dollar magnitude cost impact analysis of the change which displays the potential shift of costs between CAS-covered contracts by contract type (i.e., firm-fixed-price, incentive, cost-plus-fixed-fee, etc.) and other contractor business activity. As related to CAS-covered contracts, the analysis should display the potential impact of funds of the various Agencies/Departments (i.e., Department of Energy, National Aeronautics and Space Administration, Army, Navy, Air Force, other Department of Defense, other Government) as follows:

(1)   For any change in cost accounting practices required to comply with a new CAS in accordance with paragraphs (a)(3) and (a)(4)(i) of the CAS clause, within 60 days (or such other date as may be mutually agreed to) after award of a contract requiring this change.

(2)   For any change in cost accounting practices proposed in accordance with paragraph (a)(4)(ii) or (a)(4)(iii) of the CAS clause or with paragraph (a)(3) or (a)(5) of the Disclosure and Consistency of Cost Accounting Practices clause, not less than 60 days (or such other date as may be mutually agreed to) before the effective date of the proposed change.

(3)   For any failure to comply with an applicable CAS or to follow a disclosed practice as contemplated by paragraph (a)(5) of the CAS clause or by paragraph (a)(4) of the Disclosure and Consistency of Cost Accounting Practices clause, within 60 days (or such other date as may be mutually agreed to) after the date of agreement of noncompliance by the Contractor.

(b)   Submit a cost impact proposal in the form and manner specified by the cognizant Contracting Officer within 60 days (or such other date as may be mutually agreed to) after the date of determination of the adequacy and compliance of a change submitted pursuant to (a) above. If the above proposal is not submitted within the specified time, or any extension granted by the cognizant Contracting Officer, an amount not to exceed 10 percent of each payment made after that date may be withheld until such time as a proposal has been provided in the form and manner specified by the cognizant Contracting Officer.

(c)   Agree to appropriate contract and subcontract amendments to reflect adjustments established in accordance with paragraphs (a)(4) and (a)(5) of the CAS clause or with paragraphs (a)(3), (a)(4), or (a)(5) of the Disclosure and Consistency of Cost Accounting Practices clause.

(d)   For all subcontracts subject either to the CAS clause or to the Disclosure and Consistency of Cost Accounting Practices clause—

(1)   So state in the body of the subcontract, in the letter of award, or in both (self-deleting clauses shall not be used); and

(2)   Include the substance of this clause in all negotiated subcontracts. In addition, within 30 days after award of the subcontract, submit the following information to the Contractor's cognizant contract administration office for transmittal to the contract administration office cognizant of the subcontractor's facility:

(i)   Subcontractor's name and subcontract number.

(ii)   Dollar amount and date of award.

(iii)   Name of Contractor making the award.

(iv)   Any changes the subcontractor has made or proposes to make to accounting practices that affect prime contracts or subcontracts containing the CAS clause or Disclosure and Consistency of Cost Accounting Practices clause, unless these changes have already been reported. If award of the subcontract results in making one or more CAS effective for the first time, this fact shall also be reported.

(e)   Notify the Contracting Officer in writing of any adjustments required to subcontracts under this contract and agree to an adjustment, based on them, to this contract's price or estimated cost and fee. This notice is due within 30 days after proposed subcontract adjustments are received and shall include a proposal for adjusting the higher tier subcontract or the prime contract appropriately.

(f) For subcontracts containing the CAS clause, require the subcontractor to comply with all Standards in effect on the date of award or of final agreement on price, as shown on the subcontractor's signed Certificate of Current Cost or Pricing Data, whichever is earlier.

(End of clause)

Figure 8.5.   CAS administration clause, FAR 52.230-4.

also provides for the flow down of the same fundamental requirements to lower tier subcontractors. Further, the contractor must advise the contracting officer within 30 days, or any other mutually agreed upon date, of an award of a CAS covered subcontract.

An integral part of the administration of this clause is the system for identifying contracts and subcontracts containing the CAS clauses. DOD CAS Steering Committee Interim Guidance Paper W.G. 77-17 has placed the responsibility for maintaining such a system on the contractor. The ACO is responsible for ensuring that the system is functioning effectively.

Materiality

The CASB stated that application of its rules and regulations requires the exercise of judgment, including application to immaterial items. In making a determination of noncompliance, the materiality of the area covered should be considered. To assist in this regard, the CASB provided criteria for determining whether costs are material or immaterial. These criteria are:

The absolute dollar amount involved.

The amount of contract costs compared with the amount under consideration.

The relation between a cost item and a cost objective. Direct cost items, especially if the amounts are themselves part of a base for allocation of indirect costs, will normally have more impact than the same amount of indirect costs.

The impact on government funding.

The cumulative impact of individually immaterial items.

The cost of administrative processing of the price adjustment modification.

When a noncompliant cost accounting practice is immaterial, the ACO is still required to notify the contractor that future price adjustments may be imposed if the cost impact later becomes material.

DISCLOSURE OF ACCOUNTING PRACTICES

Purposes and Uses

The CASB first made its influence felt when it promulgated its disclosure statement regulations. As noted earlier, Public Law 91-379 directed the CASB to promulgate regulations requiring defense contractors, as a condition of contracting, to disclose in writing and follow consistently their cost accounting practices. To accomplish this, the Board developed a detailed disclosure statement (Form CASB-DS-1) to describe and document a contractor's accounting practices. Subsequent to the development of this form, a second disclosure statement (Form CASB-DS-2) was developed for use by federally funded research and development centers. Contractors are required to adhere to their own certified practices.

The cognizant ACO is designated to review the adequacy of disclosure statements and to notify the contractor in case of any deficiency. The ACO delegates this review to his or her duly authorized agent, the DCAA auditor.

The Board, by regulation, provided that disclosure statements would not be made public in any case where, as a condition of filing the statement, a contractor requests confidentiality. Contractors should designate those parts of the statement they wish to be kept confidential. An action challenging the validity of that regulation was brought under the Freedom of Information Act (FOIA) by the Corporate Accountability Research Group. The case was dismissed following an agreement by the CASB to provide aggregate data on disclosure statement responses. The Board also agreed to comply with all disclosure statement FOIA requests where the information sought had been submitted by a respondent who did not request that it be kept confidential.

Exemptions and Filing Requirement

Under the CASB statute, the Board was authorized to exempt from its disclosure statement requirements certain classes or categories of contractors. Initially, the Board exempted those companies whose negotiated national defense prime contracts at all divisions and subsidiaries totaled less than $30 million during federal fiscal year 1971. The exemption levels were revised in 1974 and 1975 to lower the threshold to $10 million, including subcontracts.

On September 12, 1977, CASB again amended its disclosure statement filing requirements as follows:

> Any company having in excess of $10 million of negotiated national defense prime contracts and subcontracts subject to CASB coverage during its preceding cost accounting period must file a disclosure statement within 90 days after the close of that period.

> Any company receiving a single national defense prime contract or subcontract of $10 million or more subject to CASB requirements must file a disclosure statement prior to award of the contract.

> Disclosure statements must only be maintained for and applied to contracts awarded during a cost accounting period in which the $10 million filing threshold was met.

The following summarizes the history of the disclosure statement filing requirements:

Fiscal Period	Government Contracts to be Included in Computation	Amount (millions)	Effective Date
FY 1971	Net negotiated prime defense contracts in Federal fiscal year	$30	Oct. 1, 1972
FY 1972, 1973	Defense prime contracts of the type subject to CAS in Federal fiscal year	$10	Jan. 1, 1974
FY 1974, 1975	Defense prime contracts subject to CAS in Federal fiscal year	$10	Jan. 1, 1976
FY 1976	Defense prime contracts and subcontracts subject to CAS in Federal fiscal year	$10	Mar. 31, 1977

Following years	Defense prime contracts and subcontracts subject to CAS in contractor's preceding cost accounting period	$10	90 days after close of contractor's cost accounting period

Two distinctions should be emphasized about disclosure statement requirements. The $10 million filing requirement is determined only on CAS covered *defense* prime contracts and subcontracts. Statement filing was never implemented for nondefense contracts. Secondly, a company that, together with its subsidiaries, exceeds the filing requirement need only submit disclosure statements for those business units within the company that receive a covered national defense contract or subcontract.

Determination of Adequacy

Submission of a required disclosure statement is a condition of contracting embodied within the Defense Production Act. Thus, any relevant federal agency would be theoretically precluded from awarding a contract when the disclosure statement is required but has not been filed. If, in fact, a contract were awarded, it conceivably would be voidable, since the actions of the contracting officer would contravene statutory requirements and therefore not be binding on the U.S. Government. At one time the CASB's rules and regulations authorized the contracting officer to grant a 90 day delay, from the date of contract award, for submitting of a disclosure statement. That provision was deleted, effective April 1, 1981. As a result, submission of a required disclosure statement is necessary before award of a negotiated national defense contract may be legally awarded.

A contractor's disclosure statement must adequately disclose the practices the contractor intends to apply to contracts containing the CAS clause. FAR 30. 202-2 (a) provides that, for a disclosure statement to be deemed adequate, it must be current, accurate, and complete. Furthermore, the ACO must specifically determine whether a disclosure statement submitted is adequate, and notify the contractor of that determination in writing. A contract cannot be awarded until a determination has been made by the cognizant ACO that a disclosure statement is adequate. However, FAR 30. 202-1 (g) does permit the contracting officer to waive the requirement for an adequacy determination before award when necessary to protect the government's interest.

Submission of a disclosure statement does not, in itself, establish that the practices disclosed are correct. The Board stated:

> The fact that the condition of contracting has been met shall serve only to establish what the contractor's cost accounting practices are or are proposed to be. In the absence of specific regulation or agreement, *a disclosed practice shall not, by virtue of such disclosure, be deemed to have been approved by the agency involved as a proper, approved or agreed to practice for pricing proposals or accumulating and reporting contract performance cost data.*[10] [Emphasis added]

It should be obvious that submission of a disclosure statement is a serious matter. Not only does it provide a written, measurable baseline from which to measure compliance and the consistent application of accounting practices, it also can have a serious effect upon the award of contracts. If the filing requirements have been met but an *adequate* disclosure statement has not been filed with the government, a contract simply cannot be awarded.

The flow-down provisions of the CAS clause require subcontractors to submit disclosure statements if they have met the filing requirements. Generally, the filing must be made with the prime contractor and the prime contractor must assure that the disclosure statement submitted is adequate. As a practical matter, FAR 30.203 permits subcontractors to submit disclosure statements to the government instead of to the prime contractor. This may be necessary because the subcontractor does not want to divulge competitive information to the prime, or perhaps because the subcontractor is already performing as a prime contractor to the government. Even if the disclosure statement is submitted to the government, this action does not relieve the prime contractor of its responsibility for ascertaining subcontractor compliance with the requirements of the Cost Accounting Standards clause. Because of this, the CASB noted in its regulations that a prime contractor might wish to include an indemnification clause in its subcontracts. This might also be appropriate in many agreements between a subcontractor and a lower tier subcontractor.

Determination of Compliance

Neither the CAS regulations nor the acquisition regulations require the designated ACO to determine prior to contract award that the disclosure statement complies with applicable standards. However, the acquisition regulations require that subsequent to the adequacy determination, the auditor review the disclosed practices for compliance with applicable standards and report the audit findings to the ACO. The ACO is required to obtain a revised disclosure statement and negotiate any required price adjustments if the disclosed practices are determined to be in noncompliance with applicable standards. Some of the items in the disclosure statement pertain to cost accounting practices addressed in specific standards. Prudent contractors should consider the requirements of applicable standards in their disclosure statement responses.

Contents and Problem Areas

The disclosure statement is divided into eight sections. A key point in avoiding a deficient filing is complete disclosure. CAS Steering Committee Interim Guidance Paper W.G. 77-20 emphasizes that materiality is a major factor in determining the level of detail required to be disclosed. In making the determination, consideration should be given to whether a change in accounting procedure would have a material effect on the flow of costs. If it would, the practice should be disclosed. The statement includes "continuation sheets" which are to be used to expand upon specific responses to convey clearly the accounting practices followed. The disclosure statement (Form CASB-DS-1) is contained in Appendix 8.1. A description of the disclosure statement sections, along with principal areas for potential deficiencies, follows, with part numbers identified in parentheses:

> *Cover Sheet and Certification.* This section identifies the company or reporting unit, its address, and the company official to be contacted regarding the statement. A certification of the completeness and accuracy of the statement must be executed by an authorized signatory of the reporting unit.
>
> *General Information (Part I).* Part I includes industry classification, sales volume, proportion of government business to total, type of cost system, and extent of integration of the cost system with the general accounts.

Direct Costs (Part II). Contractors are asked to define direct material, direct labor, and other direct costs and disclose the bases used for making direct charges. Accounting for variances under standard costs is explored in depth. The principal problem encountered in responding to this section has been the description of classes of labor. Sufficient information is required to distinguish the principal labor rate categories.

Direct vs. Indirect Costs (Part III). Contractors must designate how various functions, cost elements, and transactions are recorded and, if indirect, what aggregating pools are used. This section appears to be the most troublesome. The basic problem has involved the extent of detail required in describing the criteria used in determining whether costs are charged directly or indirectly. DCAA representatives have generally asserted that the criteria should be the equivalent of the instructions or directions that would be given to the contractor's personnel responsible for coding or classifying items as direct or indirect.

Indirect Costs (Part IV). Allocation bases must be identified and described for all overhead, service center, and general and administrative pools used by the contractor. The accounting treatment of independent research and development and bid and proposal expenses must also be described.

Depreciation and Capitalization (Part V). The criteria for capitalization, the methods of depreciation used, the basis for determining useful life, and treatment of gains and losses on dispositions are to be specified.

Other Costs and Credits (Part VI). This section covers the methods used for charging or crediting vacation, holiday, sick pay, and other compensation for personal absences.

Deferred Compensation and Insurance Costs (Part VII). Part VII requires a description of pension plans and the determination of pension costs, as well as certain types of deferred compensation and insurance costs. Some reporting units erroneously do not complete this section because such costs are controlled at the home office. The instructions state clearly that each reporting unit must complete this section even if the information must be obtained from the home office.

Corporate or Group Expenses (Part VIII). Pooling patterns and allocation bases for distributing corporate and group expenses (home office expenses) to organizational segments must be specified and described. Contractors should submit a separate Part VIII for each group or home office operation whose costs are allocated to one or more segments. This section should only be completed by such units, not by divisions to which home office expenses are allocated.

Various sections of the disclosure statement are interrelated; consequently, responses in these sections should be compatible. Figure 8.6 contains a list of interrelationships that should assist companies in verifying the accuracy of their responses.

A separate disclosure statement must be submitted for each business unit. When the cost accounting practices under contracts are identical for more than one business unit, only one statement need be submitted, but each unit must be identified.

Amendments to disclosure statements must be submitted to the same agencies to which original filings were made. Revised sales data for items 1.4.0 through 1.7.0 of Part I and items 8.1.0 and 8.2.0 of Part VIII must be submit-

If item 1.8.0 is marked A or B, item 2.2.1 or 2.2.2 should be marked A, or item 2.5.0 should be coded C in at least one column.

A response in section 2.4.0 is required only if block A of items 2.2.1 or 2.2.2 is marked.

Section 2.6.0 should be completed only if one or more labor categories in item 2.5.0 were marked C.

Item 3.2.1(f) must be marked with a code other than Z, if item 2.2.2 is marked A,B,C,D, or Y,

If 4.1.0(a) is marked with a code other than Z, no other items in 4.1.0 are to be marked.

If items 4.2.0(a), (b), (c), or (d) are marked with a code other than Z, items (e) through (n) are not to be marked.

If item 4.7.0(a) is marked A, B, C, or D, Item 3.2.3(s) must be marked other than F or Z. If Item 4.7.0(b) is marked A, B, C, or D, Item 3.2.3(k) must be marked other than F or Z. If Item 4.7.0(d) is marked A, B, C, or D, Item 2.8.0 must be marked A, B, C, D, or Y in at least one column.

Item 4.8.1 should be marked B or D, if item 4.2.0(i) is marked with a code other than Z,

At least column 1 of the items 6.1.1 and 6.1.2 must be completed, if item 2.5.0 is checked for A,B,C, and/or Y in any column

Item 7.1.1 cannot be blank. If item 3.2.2(d) is marked other than Z, item 7.1.1 must be marked A.

Item 7.1.2 cannot be blank or marked Z in all columns if item 7.1.1 is checked A. Under ERISA, item 7.1.2 may not be checked B.

If item 7.1.3 is marked B in any column, item 7.1.2 must be marked A, and item 7.1.6 must be checked Z in the same column.

Items 7.1.3, 7.1.4, 7.1.7, 7.1.8, and 7.1.9 cannot be blank in any column for which item 7.1.2 has been marked other than Z in the same column.

Item 7.1.6 must be marked on line A,B,C, or Y in the same column, if item 7.1.2, Line C, is marked in any column.

If item 7.1.7 is marked other than Z in any column, item 7.1.8 must be marked on line A or B in the same column.

Item 7.3.1 must be marked A,B, or C, if item 3.2.2(a) is marked with a code other than Z.

If item 7.3.1 is marked A or C, items 7.3.2, 7.3.3, 7.3.4, and 7.3.5 cannot be blank.

If item 7.3.1 is marked B or C, item 7.4.0 cannot be blank or marked Z.

At least one of items, 8.3.1, 8.3.2, or 8.3.3 should have an entry against it if this part is being completed by a corporate group, or home office.

Source: Defense Contract Audit Manual, Section 8-206

Figure 8.6. Interrelationship of items in CASB disclosure statement.

ted annually at the beginning of the contractor's fiscal year. Only those pages affected by a change are to be resubmitted with a new cover sheet when the disclosure statement is revised or amended.

THE COST ACCOUNTING STANDARDS

The General Concept of the Standards

As defined in the CASB's Restatement of Objectives, Policies, and Concepts, a cost accounting standard is a statement that enunciates a principle or principles to be followed, establishes practices to be followed, or specifies criteria to be employed in selecting from alternative principles and practices in estimating, accumulating, and reporting costs. It may be stated in general or specific terms. The Comptroller General's feasibility report stated:

> cost accounting standards relate to assertions which guide or which point toward accounting procedures or applicable governing rules. Cost accounting standards are not the same as standardized or uniform cost accounting which suggests prescribed procedures from which there is limited freedom to depart.[11]

Notwithstanding these statements, the 19 standards and 3 interpretations promulgated have run the gamut from generalized statements providing for little more than consistency in certain circumstances to highly detailed dissertations on the treatment of specific costs. Which category a specific standard falls into should be readily evident from a review of each standard.

Each standard has an effective date and an applicability date. In some standards these dates are the same. The effective date designates the point in time when pricing of future covered contracts must reflect the requirements of the standard. Additionally, only those contracts existing when a standard became effective are eligible for equitable adjustment. The applicability date marks the point in time in which the contractor's accounting and reporting systems must actually conform to the standard. The significance of the effective and applicability dates are more fully discussed in CAS Steering Committee Interim Guidance Paper W.G. 76-7.

The CAS Steering Committee recognized that in unusual situations a contractor might be unable to take the required actions on the effective date or the applicability date. Interim Guidance Paper W.G. 77-10 provided for delayed implementation of a standard in such cases, with provision for appropriate retroactive price adjustment of firm fixed-price contracts and target costs and fee adjustments of cost reimbursable contracts.

As stated in its Restatement of Objectives, Policies, and Concepts, the CASB's primary objective in promulgating standards was to achieve greater uniformity in accounting practices among government contractors and consistency in accounting treatment of specific costs by individual contractors. The concept of uniformity relates to a comparison of two or more contractors, and the Board's objective was to achieve comparable accounting treatment among contractors operating under similar circumstances. Consistency, on the other hand, pertains to the practices utilized by a single contractor over periods of time. When the criteria utilized to measure costs, assign costs to cost accounting periods, and allocate costs to cost objectives remain unchanged, the results of operations under similar circumstances can be compared over different periods of time.

Cost accounting standards deal with the concepts of cost measurement, assignment to cost accounting periods, and allocability to cost objectives. They do not specifically address the question of allowability of costs. The acceptability of a specific cost for reimbursement by the government is under the purview of other laws or procurement regulations issued by the various government agencies. The CASB did not address the subject but rather left these decisions to the procuring organizations. While the standards themselves do not address the allowability of costs, two factors which determine whether a cost is allowable is its allocability to government contracts and its compliance with CAS.

The Standards

Provided below are brief summaries of each of the 19 standards that the CASB promulgated. They are not intended to be an all-inclusive interpretation of each standard. An accurate understanding of a standard requires that the entire standard, including prefatory comments (preamble), be read. The summaries include:

The more important provisions.

Exemptions and effective and applicability dates.

An indication of areas that have proved troublesome in application or have resulted in disputes.

When applicable, policy guidance given by the DOD CAS Steering Committee.

The complete standards appear in Title 4 of the Code of Federal Regulations, which is republished annually in revised form as of January 1.

Consistency in Estimating, Accumulating, and Reporting Costs (Standard 401)

The purpose of this standard is to ensure consistency in the contractor's cost accounting practices used to estimate, accumulate, and report costs on government contracts. The objective is to enhance the likelihood that comparable transactions are treated alike by a contractor.

The practices used in estimating costs for a proposal must be consistent with the cost accounting practices followed by the contractor in accumulating and reporting actual contract costs. The standard permits grouping of like costs where it is not practicable to estimate contract costs by individual cost element or function. However, costs estimated for proposal purposes must be presented in such a manner and in sufficient detail so that any significant cost can be compared with the actual cost accumulated and reported.

The standard specifically requires consistency in:

The classification of elements or functions of cost as direct or indirect.
The indirect cost pools to which each element or function of cost is charged or proposed to be charged.
The methods used in allocating indirect costs to the contract.

Many contractors have encountered difficulty in applying this standard. The principal difficulty has been with the level of detail supporting particular proposed costs when compared with the actual costs accumulated and reported on contracts. Some government auditors have required that costs presented in proposals reflect exactly the same detail as the actual costs that are accumulated and reported. The standard requires only that the practices be consistent and in sufficient detail to permit a valid comparison. The important consideration is to produce reasonable "trails" from the costs included in the proposal to those accumulated in the accounting records and subsequently reported to the government. Application of this standard has required some contractors to make changes in their cost accounting and estimating systems. However, the use of worksheets can satisfy the requirements of the standard. Therefore, it may not be necessary for a contractor to change its estimating or cost accounting system since informal (memorandum) records are acceptable. When informal records are used, they must be reconcilable to the contractor's formal books of account.

In late 1976 the CASB issued Interpretation 1 to Standard 401 in response to questions concerning consistency in estimating and recording scrap or other losses of direct materials. The interpretation does not prescribe the amount of detail required to be maintained. However, it does require, regardless of the estimating practice used (e.g., a percentage of base material cost), that the practice be supported by appropriate accounting, statistical, or other relevant records that will document actual scrap or other losses.

The question has been raised as to whether the standard mandated accounting for cost by individual contract since a separate proposal is submitted for each contract. In the dispute that focused on this issue, Texas Instruments,

Inc.[12] used a production-line cost system to manufacture homogeneous units for the covered contract as well as other orders. The cost assigned to the contract was the average cost of units produced on a production run. The ASBCA ruled that CAS 401 does not require costs to be estimated, accumulated, and reported by contract where job order costing is not consistent with the nature of the contractor's operations. Equally important, the decision stated that while the cost proposal is for a specific contract, that does not necessarily reflect the contractor's cost accounting practice.

In another ASBCA case dealing with CAS 401, Dayton T. Brown, Inc.[13] estimated bid and proposal (B&P) costs based on amounts allocated from the corporate office but reported its B&P costs based on costs incurred at the divisional level in computing the cost ceiling under the formula provided in the procurement regulations. The ASBCA initially ruled that the contractor's practice was consistent since the application of the formula was a procedure for determining allowability and therefore outside the purview of CAS. On a motion for reconsideration, ASBCA reversed its earlier decision and found that the contractor's practices were in violation of CAS 401.

The standard became effective on July 1, 1972.

Consistency in Allocating Costs Incurred for the Same Purpose (Standard 402)

The purpose of this standard is to require that each type of cost is allocated only once and on only one basis to cost objectives. The intent of the standard is to preclude the "double counting" of costs. Double counting occurs when cost items are allocated directly to cost objectives without eliminating like items from indirect cost pools. An example of double counting is charging the cost of inspecting units produced directly to a contract and at the same time including similar inspection costs incurred in substantially the same circumstances in an overhead pool that is allocated to all cost objectives, including that contract. The standard prohibits a contract from being charged more than once for the same type of cost by requiring that a cost incurred for the same purpose, in like circumstances, be classified as a direct cost only or an indirect cost only.

The standard relates to the design of the system as a whole and not necessarily to the treatment on individual contracts. Thus, a CAS noncompliance would also occur where a specific contract had a cost charged to it as a direct cost and the same costs incurred in like circumstances were also included in an overhead pool, but *not* allocated to that contract.

The key element, however, is a whether the cost is incurred for the same purpose and in like circumstances. If either the purpose or the circumstances differ, then the accounting practices related to the two separate transactions need not be consistent and would not be covered by this standard. If a contractor has submitted a disclosure statement, it should provide sufficient criteria for determining whether a particular cost in a given circumstance is treated as a direct or indirect cost.

This standard has also resulted in some conflict between contractors and government auditors regarding its requirements. The disagreements usually involve identifying and classifying costs incurred for the same purpose and in like circumstances. To avoid challenge, contractors must support their classification of costs and demonstrate that the accounting treatment of all costs of a similar type and nature, incurred in like circumstances, is the same.

Interpretation 1 of Standard 402 addresses the question of whether bid and proposal costs are always incurred for the same purpose and in like circumstances. The interpretation makes it clear that they are not. Bid and proposal costs specifically required by contractual terms and conditions can be properly treated as direct costs, while at the same time other bid and proposal costs of a contractor may be recorded as indirect costs. The condition of being "specifically required" under a contract exists, for example, when a contract option is repriced, when the government exercises an unpriced option, and when proposals result from such contract provisions, as the "changes" clause. Alternatively, all bid and proposal costs may be treated as indirect. Whatever method is used, however, must be followed consistently.

This standard also became effective on July 1, 1972.

Allocation of Home Office Expenses to Segments (Standard 403)

This standard governs the allocation of the expenses of a home office to the segments (business units) under its control. Allocation from segments to final cost objectives (e.g., contracts) is covered by Standard 410, Allocation of Business Unit General and Administrative Expenses to Final Cost Objectives.

The standard resulted from what the Board perceived as problems relating to the allocation of home office expenses and the lack of procurement regulations or authoritative accounting statements dealing with the issues surrounding the subject. It was the Board's view that the standard would provide more uniform treatment in an area that was often a source of controversy and dispute.

The standard divides home office expenses into three categories:

Expenses incurred for specific segments: Such costs should be allocated directly to those segments to the maximum extent practical.

Expenses, such as centralized services, certain line and staff management, and central payments or accruals, incurred for various segments and whose relationship to those segments can be measured on some objective basis: Such expenses should be grouped in logical and homogeneous expense pools and allocated on the most objective basis available. The standard sets forth a hierarchy of allocation techniques for centralized services and suggests several types of allocation bases for these categories of home office expenses. The suggested methods or techniques support the thrust of the standard, which requires that home office expenses be allocated on the basis of the beneficial or causal relationship between supporting and receiving activities. The hierarchy of allocation techniques for centralized services can be summarized as follows:

Preferred	A measure of the activity of the organization performing the function. Supporting functions are usually labor-oriented, machine-oriented, or space-oriented.
First alternative	A measure of the output of the supporting function, measured in the terms of the units of end product produced.
Second alternative	A measure of the activity of the segments receiving the service.

Expenses incurred to manage the organization as a whole that have no identifiable relationship to any specific segment or segments: The aggregate of such residual expenses must be allocated to segments either (1) on the basis of a three factor formula (payroll dollars, operating revenue, and net book value of tangible capital assets plus inventories) or (2) on any basis representative of the total activity of the segments. The three factor formula is required when total residual expenses exceed stated proportions of the aggregate operating revenues of all segments for the previous fiscal year as follows:

3.35% of the first $100 million
0.95% of the next $200 million
0.30% of the next $2.7 billion
0.20% of all amounts over $3 billion

A special allocation of home office expense to particular segments is permitted where it can be shown that the benefits from the expense pool to the segment(s) are significantly different.

Application of this standard was originally limited to contractors whose negotiated national defense prime contracts totaled more than $30 million during federal fiscal year 1971. Presently all contractors subject to full CAS coverage must comply.

The first CAS 403 issue to progress through the formal disputes process related to The Boeing Company's allocation of state and local taxes.[14] Property, sales, use, and fuel and vehicle taxes were accumulated at the home office and allocated to segments on the basis of headcount. The ASBCA found the contractor's practice in noncompliance with CAS 403 because the taxes allocated to the segments did not properly reflect the causal/beneficial relationship. The Board agreed with the government that using the basis on which the taxes were assessed met the requirements of the standard, whereas the contractor's method of using headcount did not comply. Boeing appealed the decision to the Court of Claims, asserting that (1) the ASBCA inappropriately rejected the "broad benefit test" and (2) the CAS Board was unconstitutional and all of its standards were therefore void. The Court of Claims affirmed the prior ASBCA decision,[15] noting that: "By literal terms of . . . the standard, the assessment base is permissible and the head-count approach seems improper." On the constitutionality issue, the Court ruled that even if the contractor's assertions were correct, the fact that DOD had adopted CAS 403 in DAR would negate the contractor's entitlement to monetary relief. By basing its decision on DOD's adoption of CAS 403, the court effectively avoided ruling on the issue of whether the CAS Board was constitutional. The Boeing Company further appealed to the U.S. Supreme Court[16] but the Supreme Court declined to accept the case.

The most controversial aspect of this standard has been the interpretation of what is required regarding the allocation of state and local taxes that are calculated based on income. The standard provides an illustration pertaining specifically to the allocation of state and local income and franchise taxes. The illustration suggests that the allocation should be made using a base, or by a method that results in an amount that equals or approximates a segment's proportionate share of the tax imposed by the jurisdiction in which the segment does business. In most states, the measures for determining taxable income are combinations of the following factors: sales, payroll dollars, and tangible property.

Citing the illustrative allocation base included in the standard as support, government representatives have taken the position that only the factors determining the taxable income for a state can be utilized in allocating the expense. However, in *Lockheed Corporation and Lockheed Missiles and Space Company, Inc.*,[17] the ASBCA ruled that state and local taxes computed on the basis of income must include income as one of the factors of the allocation base under CAS 403. The CASB disagreed with the ASBCA ruling and subsequently issued Interpretation 1 of CAS 403, which permits use of segment book income as a factor in allocating income tax expense to segments only where the segment book income is expressly used by the taxing jurisdiction in computing the income tax. The ASBCA, in rejecting the government's motion for reconsideration, challenged the legal authority of that interpretation since the CASB had neither published the interpretation for comment nor submitted it to Congress for review prior to promulgation. The issue was revisited by the ASBCA in 1985 in another dispute in which the parties agreed to retain the same issues as in the previous dispute. The ASBCA again concluded that segment net income should be included as a factor in allocating state and local taxes.[18] The significance of the second dispute is that the contract was subject to the Contract Disputes Act and could be appealed by the government. The government appealed the decision to the Court of Appeals for the Federal Circuit but the court sustained the prior ASBCA decision.[19]

In another state franchise and income tax case, McDonnell Douglas Corporation[20] allocated its multistate income and franchise taxes from the home office to its segments on the basis of gross payroll. ASBCA concluded that neither the contractor's method nor the government's method (an approach similar to the government's position in the Lockheed case) complied with CAS 403. Failure to consider segment income in either method resulted in tax allocations that were not considered comparable to the various segments' proportionate shares of the taxes.

In a third state franchise and income tax case, *Grumman Corporation*,[21] the ASBCA held that it was acceptable to include net operating losses in the allocation base used to distribute state franchise taxes and thereby assign credits to loss divisions. The government contended that CAS 403 limits the components of the allocation base to those factors used to apportion a company's total taxable income among the states, namely: property, payroll, and sales. The company stressed the principle expressed in the standard that the allocation base should reflect the causal relationship between the tax cost and the receiving segment. Regression and correlation analyses showed that there was virtually no correlation between the apportionment factors and the tax. The Board, in its opinion, clearly agreed by stating that

> we conclude that income is both the primary cause of the Grumman tax and a factor which must be considered in the home office allocation of the NYFT (New York Franchise Tax) to attain compliance with the requirements in CAS 403.40(b)(4) that an allocation base 'representative of the factors' be used.

In R & D Associates[22] the Board rejected an attempt to allocate imputed state tax expenses to a subsidiary when the actual taxes paid were considerably less due to tax credits which the company allocated to a commercial subsidiary. The company relied on CAS 403, stating that the credits were the result of economic events at the commercial segment. The Board held that it was unnecessary to address the CAS allocation issues and relied on the acquisition regulation's definition of total cost. The Board disallowed the imputed costs since they represented amounts which would never be paid or incurred.

In a more recent decision, the ASBCA ruled that General Dynamics Corporation's[23] practice of allocating data processing site office costs to user segments on the basis of an average site office cost was at variance with CAS 403. Since the site offices solely responded to ADP requests of specific facilities and divisions, the Board concluded that CAS 403 required allocation of the site costs to segments on the basis of services provided.

Contractors subject to OMB Circular A-87, formerly Federal Management Circular 74-4, *Principles for Determining Costs Applicable to Grants and Contracts with State and Local Governments,* are exempt from this standard.

The standard originally became effective on July 1, 1973. It must now be followed by each subject contractor as of the beginning of the next fiscal year after receipt of a contract subject to the standard.

Capitalization of Tangible Assets (Standard 404)

The Board's purpose in promulgating this standard was to provide uniform capitalization criteria for determining the cost of capital assets applicable to government contracts. The board concluded that existing procurement regulations did not meet that need because they relied on provisions of the Internal Revenue Code that had been developed in response to various needs other than contract costing and, further, because generally accepted accounting principles allowed alternatives that were inappropriate for contract costing purposes.

Contractors must establish and adhere to a written policy with respect to tangible asset capitalization. The policy must designate the economic and physical characteristics on which the policy is based and also identify to the maximum extent practical the components of plant and equipment that are capitalized when asset units are initially acquired or replaced. Additionally, the contractor's policy must designate minimum service life and minimum acquisition cost criteria for capitalization which may not exceed two years and $1000, respectively. The $1000 minimum acquisition cost criterion was raised from $500, effective December 20, 1980. In 1986, the DOD CAS Policy Group proposed a revision to FAR 30 to raise the threshold to $1500. [24]

Tangible capital assets constructed for a contractor's own use must be capitalized at amounts that include all allocable indirect costs, including G & A expenses that can be identified with the constructed asset and are material in amount. When the constructed assets are identical with or similar to the contractor's regular product, such assets must be capitalized at amounts that include a full allocation of G & A expense..

Donated assets that meet the contractor's criteria for capitalization must be capitalized at their fair value at the time of receipt.

A group of individual low-cost items acquired for the initial outfitting of a tangible capital asset, such as furnishings for an office, which in the aggregate represent a material investment, must be capitalized consistent with the contractor's written policy. The contractor may, however, designate a minimum acquisition cost criterion higher in the aggregate than $1000 for such original complements, provided the cost criterion is reasonable in the contractor's circumstances.

Costs incurred that extend the life or increase the productivity of an asset (betterments and improvements) must be capitalized when they exceed the contractor's specified minimum acquisition cost criterion for betterments and the asset has a remaining life in excess of two years. The cost criterion may be higher than $1000, provided it is reasonable in the circumstances.

Under this standard, the basis for determining cost, the accounting for assets acquired at other than arm's length, the accounting for assets acquired through a business combination, the treatment of repair and maintenance costs, and the accounting for assets retired do not require the use of any practices that depart from generally accepted accounting principles. However, in *The Marquardt Company*[25] the Board disallowed the increased asset values resulting from a business acquisition, even though the write - up of assets was deemed to be in accordance with generally accepted accounting principles. The Board held that the assets were to be revalued at the acquiring corporation and not at the acquired corporation which was responsible for performing on government contracts.

The standard became effective on July 1, 1973 and applicable to tangible capital assets acquired during a contractor's fiscal year beginning on or after October 1, 1973.

Accounting for Unallowable Costs (Standard 405)

This standard sets forth guidelines for both the identification in the contractor's accounting records of specific costs that are unallowable and the cost accounting treatment of such costs. The standard resulted from the board's conclusion that there was a general lack of uniformity and consistency in the accounting treatment accorded unallowable costs and that there was no regulatory requirement for contractor identification of unallowable costs. The standard does not provide criteria for determining the allowability of costs. This is a function of the appropriate procurement or reviewing authority. The standard merely establishes the accounting treatment and reporting requirements once the costs are determined to be unallowable.

Contractors must identify in their accounting records and exclude from any proposal, billing, or claim costs specifically described as unallowable either by the express wording of laws or regulations or by mutual agreement of the contracting parties.

Contractors must also:

Identify costs designated as unallowable as a result of a written decision by a contracting officer pursuant to contract disputes procedures.

Identify any costs incurred for the same purpose under like circumstances as those specifically identified as unallowable.

Account for the costs of any work project not contractually authorized in a manner that permits them to be readily separated from the costs of authorized projects.

In Interim Guidance Paper W.G. 77-13, the CAS Steering Commitee concluded that a contractor must identify costs disputed on the basis of allocability as unallowable costs represents noncompliance with this standard.

Costs that are mutually agreed to be directly associated with unallowable costs must be identified and excluded from proposals, billings, or claims. Costs that are designated as directly associated with unallowable costs pursuant to contract disputes procedures must be identified in the accounting records. A *directly associated cost* is any cost that is generated solely as a result of the incurrence of another cost and would not have been incurred had the other cost not been incurred.

Costs specifically described as unallowable as well as directly associated costs must be included in any indirect allocation base or bases in which they would normally be included.

A contractor's records must be of sufficient detail and depth to provide visibility of identified unallowable costs, as well as to establish their status in terms of allocability and to identify the accounting treatment that has been accorded these costs.

Industry's principal concern with the implementation of this standard relates to the requirement that unallowable costs remain in the base for the allocation of indirect costs. The government has used this provision, in conjunction with the cost principle requiring that all items in the indirect cost base bear their pro rata share of such indirect costs, to disallow otherwise allowable costs. This position, to many, is inequitable.

The standard became effective on April 1, 1974.

Cost Accounting Period (Standard 406)

Prior to promulgating Standard 406, the procurement regulations permitted considerable flexibility in selecting the cost accounting period to be used for contract costing. Although contractors generally used their fiscal years, shorter periods were considered appropriate:

For contracts with performance in only a minor portion of the fiscal year.

Where general industry practice permitted use of a shorter period.

Except for the following specified circumstances, this standard requires a contractor to use its normal fiscal year as its cost accounting period:

Where costs of an indirect function exist for only part of a cost accounting period, they may be allocated to cost objectives of that same part of the period.

Upon mutual agreement with the government, use of a fixed annual period other than a fiscal year is permitted if it is an established practice and is consistently used.

A transitional period may be used in connection with a change in fiscal year.

Where an expense, such as pension cost, is identified with a fixed, recurring annual period that is different from the contractor's cost accounting period, and is consistently employed, its use may be continued.

The cost accounting period used for accumulating costs in an indirect cost pool must be the same as the period used for establishing related allocation bases.

Indirect expense rates used for estimating, accumulating and reporting costs, including progress payments and public vouchers, should be based on the established annual cost accounting period.

CAS Steering Committee Interim Guidance Paper W.G. 77-15 addresses the interrelationship between the procurement cost principle for termination costs and Standards 401, 402, and 406. The paper specifically precludes the application of shorter accounting periods to contracts terminated early in the accounting year.

The standard became effective on July 1, 1974 and applicable at the start of the next fiscal year following the receipt of a contract subject to the standard.

Use of Standard Costs for Direct Material and Direct Labor (Standard 407)

Standard 407 provides criteria for establishing and revising standard costs as well as disposing of variances from standard costs for those contractors who elect to use standard costs for estimating, accumulating, and reporting costs of direct material and direct labor. The standard resulted from the board's recognition that practices concerning the use of standard costs had not been well defined in government procurement regulations and promulgation of the standard would provide needed guidance in their use. The principal requirements of the standard are:

Standard costs must be entered into the books of account.

Standard cost and related variances must be accounted for at the level of the production unit. The standard defines a production unit as a group of activities that either uses homogeneous input (e.g., direct labor and material) or yields homogeneous outputs (e.g., component parts).

Practices relating to setting and revising standards, the use of standard costs, and the disposition of variances must be stated in writing and consistently followed.

Variances must be allocated to cost objectives at least annually on the basis of material or labor cost at standard, labor hours at standard, or units of output, as is most appropriate in the circumstances. Where variances are immaterial, they may be included in appropriate indirect cost pools for allocation to applicable cost objectives.

Because of the requirement to accumulate variances at the production unit level, some prior users of standard cost accounting systems found a need to revise those systems to comply with the standard. A labor-rate standard may be used for a category of direct labor only if functions performed within that category are not materially different and employees involved perform interchangeable functions. A labor-rate standard can be set for a group of direct labor workers who perform different functions only when the group works in a single production unit yielding homogeneous outputs or when the group forms an integral team. As a result, utilization of standard costs by organizational structure (e.g., departments) are, in most cases, not acceptable under the standard.

The standard became effective on October 1, 1974 and applicable at the start of the next fiscal year following the receipt of a contract subject to the standard.

Accounting for Costs of Compensated Personal Absence (Standard 408)

Standard 408 provides criteria for measuring costs of vacation, sick leave, holiday, and other compensated personal absences, such as jury duty, military training, mourning, and personal time off, for a cost accounting period. In promulgating this standard, the CASB concluded that even though the aggregate cost of reimbursed absences was a material part of labor cost, existing procurement regulations provided no assurance that such costs would be assigned to the cost accounting period in which the service was performed or the benefit earned.

The standard requires the costs of compensated personal absence to be assigned to the cost accounting period or periods in which the entitlement was earned (accrual basis) and such costs for an entire cost accounting period be allocated pro rata on an annual basis among the final cost objectives for that period.

Entitlement is determined when the employer becomes liable to compensate the employee for such absence if the employee were terminated for lack of work. Probationary periods may be included as a part of the service time creating entitlement. Each plan or custom for compensated personal absence must be considered separately in determining when entitlement is earned. In the absence of a determinable liability, compensated personal absence will be considered to be earned only in the cost accounting period in which paid. In determining the liability for compensated personal absence, current or anticipated wage rates may be used; however, the estimated liability must be reduced to allow for anticipated nonutilization when such amounts are material.

Any adjustment occasioned by the initial adoption of the standard, the adoption of a new plan, or a change of an existing plan may not be recognized as a cost at the time of adoption or change, but must be carried in a "suspense account" and recognized as a contract cost only when the amount of the suspense account at the beginning of the cost accounting period exceeds the ending liability for such compensated absence in any future fiscal year. Contractors objected to this requirement on the basis that it created a deferral of costs. They argued that the adjustment should be recognized as a cost in the year of change. However, the board did not believe such recognition appropriate as it would result in allocating more than the cost of one year to contracts.

In an inflationary period where salaries and wage costs are increasing, the ending liability will increase even if the level of compensated absences does not increase. Consequently, the suspense account may not be liquidated for a significant number of years, if ever, if the total amount of the suspense account at the beginning of the period is compared to the total ending balance for the compensated absence. However, CAS 408.50(d)(3) also permits a comparison of the accrual for individual employees included in the suspense account with subsequent ending liability for those same employees. This method of liquidating the suspense account on an individual employee basis will generally result in a faster amortization then a liquidation based on total amounts for the work force.

Contractors subject to OMB Circular A-87, *Principles for Determining Costs Applicable to Grants and Contracts with State and Local Governments*, are exempt from this standard.

The standard became effective on July 1, 1975 and applicable at the start of the next fiscal year following the receipt of a contract subject to the standard.

Depreciation of Tangible Capital Assets (Standard 409)

Standard 409 sets forth criteria for assigning costs of tangible capital assets to cost accounting periods and for allocating such costs to cost objectives within such periods. It was the Board's belief in promulgating this standard that existing procurement regulations and IRS guidelines, as well as generally accepted accounting principles, provided too many alternatives for establishing depreciable lives, and such lives were not always supported by the company's actual record of usefulness. The purpose of the standard is to match depreciation costs with the accounting peiod and cost objectives that benefit from the use of the fixed assets.

Estimated services lives for contracting purposes must be reasonable approximations of expected actual periods of usefulness supported by records of past retirements, disposals, or withdrawals from service. A two year period, measured from the beginning of the fiscal year in which a contractor must first comply with the standard, was provided for the contractor to develop and maintain such records. Lives based on past experience may be modified to reflect expected changes in physical or economic usefulness but the contractor bears the burden of justifying estimated service lives that are shorter than experienced lives.

Estimated service lives for financial accounting purposes must be used until adequate records supporting the periods of usefulness are available, if they are not unreasonable under the criteria of the standard. Assets acquired for which the contractor has no available data or prior experience must be assigned a service life based on a projection of expected usefulness; however, that service life cannot be less than the asset guideline period (mid-range) previously published by the Internal Revenue Service. Use of any such alternative lives must cease as soon as a contractor can develop service lives supported by its own experience.

The board encouragged the use of sampling techniques in developing records in support of estimated service lives and stated in its comments accompanying the standard that procurement agencies are expected to be reasonable in the enforcement of the supporting record requirements.

Some disagreements on the appropriateness of estimated service lives have occurred. Particularly troublesome has been the determination of useful service lives of assets withdrawn from active service but still maintained for future use. Contractors' records documenting standby time or incidental use, in many instances, have not been considered adequate.

CAS Steering Committee Interim Guidance Paper W.G. 78-22 relates to two aspects of this standard. As the standard permitted a grace period of two years within which to develop records to support asset lives, the CAS Working Group noted that the equitable adjustment procedures should be applied to all CAS-covered contracts existing prior to the end of the grace period (i.e., not just those contracts existing at the more usual "effective date"). This guidance paper further requires contractors to provide sufficient detailed records to support assets retained for standby or incidental use.

The method of depreciation used for financial accounting pruposes must be used for contract costing unless it:

Does not reasonably reflect the expected consumption of services as measured by the expected activity or physical output of the assets, or
Is unacceptable for Federal income tax purposes.

Where the method used for financial accounting purposes does not meet these tests, the contractor must adopt a method that best measures the expected consumption of services. When a contractor selects a method of depreciation for new assets different from the method currently in use for like assets used in similar circumstances, that new method must be supported by a projection of the expected consumption of services. The board in its prefatory comments stated:

it is not the intent of the Board to introduce uncertainty into contract negotiation and settlement by encouraging challenge of contractors' depreciation methods. If the method selected is also used for external financial reporting and is acceptable for income tax purposes, the Board's expectation is that it will be accepted.

Gain on the disposition of assets recognized for contract costing purposes must be limited to the difference between the original acquisition cost of assets and their undepreciated balance. The gain or loss, when material in amount, must be allocated in the same manner as the related depreciation cost; however, immaterial amounts may be included in any appropriate indirect cost pool.

The standard must be applied to assets acquired after the start of the next fiscal year following the receipt of a contract subject to the standard. Application to assets acquired prior to compliance with the standard is permitted upon agreement between the contracting parties. Such application must be prospective with impact only upon the then undepreciated balance of cost.

Of the standards promulgated up to the time of its issuance, this standard received the most attention and produced the greatest criticism from industry. The board, in responding to industry's reaction, departed from its usual promulgation process and republished the proposed standard in the *Federal Register* for a second round of public comment. Over 100 commentators responded to that publication. Even after the board published the standard in final form, Congressional hearings were held to provide a forum for those wishing to express their views on whether the standard should be rescinded. The supporters of the standard prevailed on the question of rescission. However, Congress instructed the board to act expeditiously on pending standards (Cost of Money and Accounting for Inflation) that would have lessened the negative impact of CAS 409.

The principal objection to the standard centered on the requirement that service lives be based on actual periods of usefulness observed in the past. It was argued by industry that such a requirement inappropriately extends the period over which the cost of the asset is recovered, ignores the economic realities of inflation, provides little incentive for companies to contract with the government because of the standard's impact on earnings and cash flow, and erodes the productivity of government contractors. The board, in spite of these arguments, concluded that there was a need to more appropriately measure depreciation costs identified with government contracts and that consideration of capital investment in the determination of the adequacy of profits was primarily an area to be dealt with by the procuring agencies.

Notwithstanding subsequent profit decisions of procuring agencies, the long-range impact of the standard has been additional administrative costs, stemming from either maintaining separate capital asset records for contracting purposes or conforming financial accounting practices to the requirements of the standard. Members of both government and industry have continued to urge amendment or even rescission of the standard.

Standard 409 does not apply where compensation for the use of tangible capital assets is based on use allowances in lieu of depreciation.

The standard became effective on July 1, 1975. Contractors must apply the standard to assets acquired after the beginning of the next fiscal year following receipt of a covered contract and are required to support asset lives used in computing depreciation within two years of becoming subject to the standard.

Allocation of Business Unit General and Administrative Expenses to Final Cost Objectives (Standard 410)

Problems encountered with the allocation of indirect costs, and general and administrative (G&A) expenses in particular, were cited in the original CAS feasibility study as matters demanding attention. The development of this standard covered the period from the time of the CASB's creation to the standard's finalization in April 1976, and the CASB's several proposals were not without controversy.

The purpose of this standard is to provide criteria for the allocation of business unit G&A expenses to final cost objectives. To accomplish its purpose, the standard provides a much narrower definition of G&A expenses than that generally thought for such expenses. By definition, G&A expenses include only the remainder of such expenses incurred for the general management and administration of the business unit as a whole. They do not include management expenses that can be more directly related to cost objectives by a base other than a cost input base representing the total activity of a business unit. G&A expenses are thus only the "residual G&A expenses" after preallocation of management and administrative expenses having a measurable beneficial or causal relationship to cost objectives. Home office expenses that meet the definition of segment G&A expense are includable in the receiving segment's G&A expense pool. Insignificant expenses that do not qualify by definition as G&A expenses may be included in G&A expense pools..

The G&A expense pool, as defined by the standard, must be allocated to final cost objectives (i.e., contracts) by one of three cost input bases: total cost input (total production costs), value-added cost input (total production costs excluding material and subcontract costs), or single-element cost input (e.g., direct labor dollars or hours). The base selected must be the one that best represents the total activity of a typical cost accounting period.

Special allocation is permitted when the benefits from G&A expenses to a particular final cost objective are significantly different from the benefits accruing to other final cost objectives. When a special allocation is employed, the expenses allocated must be excluded from the G&A pool and the cost input of the cost objective must be removed from the cost input base employed.

Contractors that have included selling costs in a cost pool separate and apart from the G&A expense pool may continue to do so, or they may change and include selling costs in their G&A pool. However, DOD guidance permits the inclusion of selling costs in the G&A pool only where it is clear that the allocation base is appropriate for both categories of expenses. CAS Steering Committee Interim Guidance Paper W.G. 78-21 provides for separate allocation of selling expenses where a significant disparity exists in marketing activity (e.g., between domestic and foreign). In such a case, total cost input would not be the best measure, in DOD's view, of benefit received from selling costs.

The cost of items produced for stock or inventory must be included in the input base in the year the item is produced. Stock items in inventory when the standard first becomes applicable to a contractor must be included in the G&A input base in the cost accounting period in which they are assigned to final cost objectives.

To reduce the impact on G&A costs that could occur upon adoption of the standard by a contractor, an elaborate transitional procedure, including a suspense account, was provided for contractors using an output base (e.g., sales or cost of sales) to allocate G&A at the time the standard became effective, October 1, 1976. The transition method was elective, not mandatory.

The CAS Steering Committee issued three guidance papers on Standard 410. Interim Guidance Paper W.G. 77-11 deals largely with problems initially encountered by contractors who elected the transition method. Interim Guidance Paper W.G. 78-21, as revised by Amendment 1 dated April 10, 1981, covers a number of issues in a question-and-answer format. The more significant of these deal with:

Types of items includable in the G&A pool and in the cost input base: For example, significant functional costs should not be included in the residual G&A pool; interdivisional transfers should be included in the total cost input base.

Criteria for use of the value-added and single-element cost input bases: Use of the value-added base is mandated when significant distortions are reflected in a total cost input base; the single-element base is acceptable where labor dollars are significant and other input costs are a less significant measure of a segment's activities. Amendment 1 to Interim Guidance Paper W.G. 78-21 reflects a more moderate interpretation by DOD as to the conditions in which value-added or single-element allocation bases may be used. The amendment specifically recognizes that the "existence of a wide range of material and subcontract content among contracts may signal the precondition for potential significant distortion. . . ."

Separate allocations of home office expenses under Standard 403: They should be identified by the receiving segment; residual home office expenses, segment line management expenses, and directly allocated expenses related to the segment's overall management and administration are includable in the G&A pool of the segment.

Interim Guidance Paper W.G. 79-24 covers circumstances in which significant facilities contracts dictate the use of a special allocation to avoid excessive allocation of G&A expenses through the use of a total cost input allocation.

Disagreements have occurred between government and contractor representatives over what circumstances justify use of a special allocation. However, more serious disagreements in implementing this standard have related to selecting the appropriate cost input base, particularly the conditions under which including materials and subcontracts in the base distort the allocation of G&A expenses to final cost objectives. Since the standard became applicable DCAA has considered the total cost input base to best represent the total activity of the business unit in most circumstances. Many contractors believe, however, that the inclusion of materials and subcontracts in the base distorts the allocation of G&A expense when there are disparate levels of materials and subcontracts among the various contracts.

Disproportionate levels of material and subcontract costs among a contractor's cost objectives was a major consideration in a significant ASBCA decision involving CAS 410. The government argued that the standard mandated the use of total cost input to allocate segment G&A unless it could be shown that by using such a base a distorted allocation resulted. The appellant,[26] contended that a value-added base (total cost input less materials and subcontracts) was required because including materials and subcontracts destroyed the ability of the base to distribute G&A expenses to final cost objectives based on benefits received. The Board ruled that:

> In Aeronutronic's circumstances, use of the value-added base was *required* because inclusion of materials and subcontracts costs significantly distorts the benefits received by appellant's contracts from its G&A expenses.

The Board dealt meaningfully with the critical issue of how one determines whether an allocation of G&A expenses is in fact distorted when it concluded:

> (1) The material and subcontract content of appellant's contracts is disproportionate and its general management expenses pertain much more substantially to its "in-house" activity than its material and subcontract activity; and, (2) Aeronutronic's general management expenses provide substantially more benefit to its labor intensive development contracts than its material intensive production contracts.

Although the existence of Amendment 1 to Interim Guidance Paper W.G. 78-21 did not dissuade the government from continuing its appeal against Ford Aerospace, the resulting ASBCA decision, together with the amended guidance paper, should facilitate the resolution of differences of opinion in this controversial issue.

Contractors subject to OMB Circular A-87, *Principles for Determining Costs Applicable to Grants and Contracts with State and Local Governments*, are exempt from this standard.

The standard became effective on October 1, 1976 and applicable after the start of a contractor's next fiscal year beginning after January 1, 1977.

Accounting for Acquisition Costs of Material (Standard 411)

Standard 411 sets forth criteria for accumulating and allocating material costs and contains provisions concerning the use of certain inventory costing methods. Consistent with the Board's goal of uniformity, this standard resulted from what the board viewed as an absence in existing procurement regulations of a requirement that the same costing method be used for similar categories of material within the same business unit.

FIFO, LIFO, weighted or moving average, and standard cost are all acceptable methods of inventory costing. The method(s) selected must be used consistently for similar categories of material within the same business unit and must be applied "in a manner which results in systematic and rational costing of issues of materials to cost objectives." Although this standard permits the use of LIFO, the provision that the method used should result in systematic and rational costing has been interpreted by the Board to require costing on a reasonably current basis.

The standard provides for the direct allocation of the cost of units of a category of material as long as the cost objective is identified at the time of purchase or production.

The cost of material that is either used exclusively for indirect functions or is not a significant element of production cost may be allocated to cost objectives (contracts) through an indirect cost pool. Where the cost of such indirect materials remaining at the end of any cost accounting period significantly exceeds the cost at the beginning of the period, the difference must be recorded as inventory and the indirect cost pool reduced accordingly. Disagreements between government and contractor representatives have occurred on occasion as to what amount constitutes a significant increase requiring treatment as inventory.

Recent reviews of contractor Material Requirements Planning (MRP) systems have resulted in assertions by DCAA auditors that such systems may not result in material costing that complies with the requirements of CAS 411. Such issues have been raised particularly where;

1. Material charged direct to contracts is initially placed in a company storeroom;

2. Contract inventory is costed on the basis of an inventory valuation method, e.g., average cost, rather than the specific cost identified on a purchase order, or;

3. Material transfers between contracts are made on the basis of an inventory valuation method, e.g., average cost.

Many of these issues are still unresolved in terms of the specific costing practices mandated by CAS 411.

Contractors are required to maintain in writing and consistently apply their accounting policies and practices for accumulating and allocating costs of materials.

The standard, effective on January 1, 1976, must be observed for materials purchased or produced after the start of the next fiscal year following the receipt of a contract subject to the standard.

Composition and Measurement of Pension Cost (Standard 412)

Standard 412 established the components of pension cost, the bases for measuring such cost and the criteria for assigning pension cost to cost accounting periods. The need for such measurement and assignment criteria for contracts was considered critical by the Board because of the significant amounts involved in annual pension cost calculations, the changes in the mix of contractors' government and commercial business, the settlement of individual contracts long before actual pension cost could be determined, and the lack of existing authoritative guidance relative to the components of pension cost that are properly includable for contract costing purposes. The requirements of the standard are compatible with the Employee Retirement Income Security Act of 1974 (ERISA). and Accounting Principles Board Opinion 8. Certain provisions of the standard, however, conflict with the requirements of Financial Accounting Board Standards Statement 87.

Two types of pension plans are recognized: a defined-contribution plan in which benefits are determined by the amount of the contributions established in advance and a defined-benefit plan in which the benefits are stated in advance and the amount to be paid is actuarially calculated to provide for the future stated benefits. Multiemployer collective bargaining plans and state university plans are considered to be defined-contribution plans.

Components of pension cost for a cost accounting period are:

For defined-contribution plans: the payments made, less dividends and other credits.

For defined-benefit plans: normal cost, a part of the unfunded liability plus interest equivalent, and adjustment for actuarial gains and losses. Normal cost is the annual cost attributable to years subsequent to a particular valuation date. The unfunded actuarial liability is the excess of pension cost attributable to prior years over the value of the assets of a pension plan. Actuarial gains and losses represent the differences between actuarial assumptions and the actual experience for those assumptions.

Pension costs must exclude prior year costs that were unallowable under government regulations, excise taxes assessed for delayed funding, and interest attributable to pension costs computed for the cost accounting period that are not funded in that period. Unfunded actuarial liabilities must be consistently amortized in equal annual installments and such liabilities must be determined by using the same actuarial assumptions as are used for the other components of pension cost. No change in amortization period for unfunded liabilities is required when the amortization began prior to this standard; however, unfunded liabilities for new plans and improvements in existing plans must be amortized within the range of 10 to 30 years.

Pension costs for a defined benefit - plan can be measured by use of either the accrued benefit actuarial cost method or a projected benefit actuarial cost method, as long as the method used separately identifies normal costs, unfunded liability, and actuarial gains and losses. An accrued benefit method is an actuarial cost method under which units of benefit are assigned to each cost accounting period. A projected benefit method is any of several actuarial cost methods that distribute the estimated total cost of the employees' prospective benefits over a period of years, usually the employees' working careers. When the projected benefit method used does not separately identify the above cost elements (e.g. spread gain method), it may continue to be used only if:

It is also employed for financial accounting purposes and costs are spread over the remaining working lives of the work force.

Supplemental information is prepared identifying the funding status of the plan and actuarial gains and losses and pension costs for the period are reduced by the amount of any overfunding. (This supplemental information, in essence, reflects a recalculation of pension costs based on a projected benefit cost method that separately identifies each of the pension cost components).

Actuarial assumptions must be separately identified, but their validity can be evaluated on an aggregate basis. Assumptions used should reflect long term rather than short term trends. Increases or decreases to the unfunded actuarial liability resulting from changes in acturial assumptions must be separately amortized.

Pension cost must be measured by either payroll percentages where the benefit is based on salaries (and may include salary projections) or by service when the benefit is not based on salaries.

Pension cost assigned to a cost accounting period is allocable to cost objectives only to the extent that the liability is liquidated, or liquidation of the liability can be compelled. Liabilities are considered to be liquidated if funding is accomplished by the time established for filing Federal income tax returns. Excess funded amounts must be assigned to future cost accounting periods.

CAS Steering Committee Interim Guidance Paper W.G. 76-1, issued shortly after the effective date of the standard, recognized that a contractor using a projected benefit method that did not separately identify pension cost components might have difficulty in providing the required supplemental information for a prior period. The paper noted that, in such instances, contract award should be based on the actuarial method used by the contractor and the contract should include a provision for subsequent price adjustment for any significant impact resulting from the supplemental information provided subsequent to contract award.

In December 1985 the Financial Accounting Standard Board promulgated Statement 87, "Employees' Accounting for Pensions," and Statement 88, "Employees' Accounting for Settlements and Curtailments of Defined Benefit Pension Plans and for Termination Benefits." This development presents serious problems for government contractors subject to CAS 412 and 413 since provisions of the statements are not compatible with the standards. Unless the standards are revised, contractors having defined - benefit pension plans cannot comply with both sets of requirements without performing separate actuarial valuations for FASB and CAS purposes. DOD's Cost Accounting Standards Policy Group is considering several changes to CAS 412 and 413 to address these differences; however, as noted earlier, there are continuing questions as to the ability of the DOD to modify CAS standards which are promulgated by statute.

The most significant differences affecting CAS 412 and CAS 413 are:

> CAS 412 allows contractors to use a spread gain actuarial cost method if it is used for financial accounting purposes. FAS 87 mandates the use of the Projected Unit Credit Method. Therefore, contractors previously using a spread gain actuarial cost method must to change their actuarial cost method.

> FAS 87 prescribes rules for amortizing prior service costs associated with a plan amendment which are at variance with requirements of 412. Affected defense contractors may have to develop separate amortization amounts for financial and government cost accounting purposes.

> FAS 87 prescribes accounting rules for amortizing gains and losses which are at variance with CAS 413 requirements.

> In certain circumstances FAS 87 mandates that a market value method be used to establish the value of assets of a pension plan. Such a method may be inconsistent with the methods required under CAS 413.

The standard became effective on January 1, 1976 and applicable at the start of the next cost accounting period following receipt of a contract subject to the standard.

Adjustment and Allocation of Pension Cost (Standard 413)

Standard 413 addresses the measurement of actuarial gains and losses and their assignment to cost accounting periods, the valuation of pension fund assets, and the allocation of pension costs to segments.

Actuarial gains and losses must be calculated annually. Pension plans based on immediate-gain actuarial cost methods (methods that separately calculate actuarial gains and losses) must amortize the gains and losses over a 15 year period. Gains and losses that are not material may be included as a component of the current or following year's pension cost. The amount included in the current year must include the amortized amount of the gain or loss for the year plus interest for the unamortized balance as of the beginning of the period. For pension plans based on spread-gain actuarial cost methods (projected benefit methods in which actuarial gains and losses are automatically included in normal cost rather than being separately calculated), the actuarial gains and losses are included as part of normal costs and are therefore spread over the remaining average working lives of the workforce. Spread gain methods can no longer be used, as a result of FAS 87.

Any recognized pension fund valuation method may be used. However, if the method results in a value that is outside a corridor of 80 to 120% of the market value of the assets, the fund value must be adjusted to the nearest boundary of the corridor.

Pension costs for segments generally may be calculated either on a composite basis or by separate computation. However, pension costs must be separately calculated for a segment when the pension costs at the segment are materially affected by any of the following conditions:

The segment experiences material termination gains or losses.

The level of benefits, eligibility for benefits, or age distribution is materially different for the segment than for the company as a whole.

The aggregate of actuarial assumptions for termination, retirement age, or salary scale is materially different for the segment than for the company as a whole.

The ratios of pension fund assets to actuarial liabilities for merged segments are different from one another after applying the benefits in effect after the merger.

Contractors who separately calculate pension cost for one or more segments have the option of establishing a separate segment for inactive participants, such as retirees. When a segment is closed, the difference between the actuarial liability for the segment and the market value of the assets allocated to the segment as of the closure date must be determined. The difference represents an adjustment of previously determined pension costs for the segment.

The standard became effective on March 10, 1978 and applicable at the start of the next cost accounting period following receipt of a contract subject to the standard.

Cost of Money as an Element of the Cost of Facilities Capital (Standard 414)

Standard 414 recognizes the cost of facilities capital (CFC) as an allocable contract cost. The standard provides criteria for the measurement and allocation of the cost of capital committed to facilities.

Cost of money is an imputed cost that is identified with the facilities capital associated with each indirect expense pool. Cost of money is allocated to contracts over the same base used to allocate the expenses in the indirect cost pool with which it is associated. For example, manufacturing cost of money is allocated to contracts using the same manufacturing direct labor base that is used to allocate manufacturing overhead. The cost of money rate is based on a commercial borrowing rate published semiannually by the Secretary of the Treasury. Form CASB-CMF is used for calculating cost of money factors.

Procedures for calculating cost of money are:

The average net book value of facilities for each indirect expense pool is identified from accounting data used for contract costing. Unless there is a major fluctuation, the beginning and ending asset balances for the year may be averaged to arrive at the average net book value. The facilities capital values should be the same values used to generate depreciation or amortization that is allowed for Federal contract costing purposes plus the value of land that is integral to the regular operation of the business unit. DOD CAS Steering Committee Interim Guidance Paper W.G. 77-18 addressed the issue of facilities to be included in the base for the cost of money calculation on the CASB-CMF form. The DOD paper concludes that since the standard provides that the facilities should be used in the regular business activity, the following should be eliminated from the cost of money computation:

Land held for speculation or expansion.

Facilities or facility capacity that have been determined to be excess or idle.

Assets that are under construction or have not yet been put into service.

The cost of money devoted to facilities capital for each indirect pool is the product of these net book values and the commercial borrowing rate published by the Secretary of the Treasury.

Facilities capital cost of money factors (indirect expense rates) are computed by dividing the cost of money for each pool by the appropriate allocation base.

The cost of capital committed to facilities is separately estimated, accumulated, and reported for each contract.

The calculation of cost of money on Form CASB-CMF is illustrated in Figure 8.7 and explained in the notes on page 237.

Once COM indirect expense rates are calculated, they must be applied to the base costs incurred or estimated for each contract. Worksheet memorandum records may be used to allocate COM to the incurred base costs of flexibly priced contracts. An example of a worksheet distributing COM to contracts is shown in Figure 8.8.

As a result of the 1986 change in the DOD Weighted Guidelines for establishing prenegotiation profit objectives, the net book value of assets and the resultant cost of money must now be segregated between land, buildings and equipment to calculate COM applicable to a particular proposal. The calculations are made on DD Form 1861 as illustrated in Figure 8.9 The amounts for facilities cost of money on DD Form 1861 are included on the cost proposal as separate cost elements. The use of this form in calculating the preaward negotiation profit objective is discussed in greater detail in Chapter 4.

Two CAS Steering Committee Interim Guidance Papers were issued in connection with the implementation of CAS 414. Interim Guidance Paper W.G. 77-18 covers a number of issues including:

Types of facilities not subject to cost of money.
Allocation of cost of money to IR&D and B&P projects.
Revisions to disclosure statements to include procedures related to CAS 414.
Application of CAS 414 to price proposals.

FACILITIES CAPITAL
COST OF MONEY FACTORS COMPUTATION

CONTRACTOR:
BUSINESS UNIT:
ADDRESS:

COST ACCOUNTING PERIOD: 03/31/8x	1. APPLICABLE COST OF MONEY RATE ___% (A) 7.625%	2. ACCUMULATION & DIRECT DISTRIBUTION OF N.B.V.	3. ALLOCATION OF UNDISTRIBUTED — BASIS OF ALLOCATION (F)	4. TOTAL NET BOOK VALUE — COLUMNS 2+3 (G)	5. COST OF MONEY FOR THE COST ACCOUNTING PERIOD — COLUMNS 1X4 (H)	6. ALLOCATION BASE FOR THE PERIOD — IN UNIT(S) OF MEASURE (I)	7. FACILITIES CAPITAL COST OF MONEY FACTORS — COLUMNS 5÷6 (J)
BUSINESS UNIT FACILITIES CAPITAL							
RECORDED (B)		8,070,000					
LEASED PROPERTY (C)		200,000					
CORPORATE OR GROUP (D)		450,000					
TOTAL		8,720,000					
UNDISTRIBUTED (F)		3,450,000					
DISTRIBUTED (E)		5,270,000					
Material		50,000	30,000	80,000	6,100	4,500,000	.0014
Engineering		270,000	726,000	996,000	75,945	2,000,000	.0380
Manufacturing		4,750,000	2,800,000	6,750,000	514,688	3,000,000	.1716
Technical Computer			444,000	444,000	33,855	2.280/hr.	14.8487
OVERHEAD POOLS							
G&A EXPENSE POOLS G&A Expense		200,000	250,000	450,000	34,313	36,700,000	.0009
TOTAL		5,270,000	3,450,000	8,720,000	666,901	/////////	/////////

Figure 8.7. Facilities capital cost of money factors computation, Form CASB-CMF.

(A) When the cost of money (COM) is being calculated on a prospective basis for forward pricing proposals, the rate used should be the rate most recently published by the Secretary of the Treasury. In calculating final fiscal year rates for application to flexibly priced contracts, the average rates incurred for the year should be used. For example, the COM rate for fiscal year ended May 31, 1987 would be calculated as follows:

$$\frac{(9.75\% \times 5 \text{ mo.}) + (8.50\% \times 6 \text{ mo.}) + (7.625 \times 1 \text{ mo.})}{12 \text{ mo.}} = 8.95\%$$

(B) Recorded capital assets are those that are owned and recorded on the books of the business unit.

(C) Leased property consists of the capitalized value of leases for which constructive ownership costs are allowed in lieu of rental costs under the procurement regulations (discussed in Chapter 7 under depreciation and rental costs). This category also includes the capitalized value of leases that are accounted for as capital leases under FAS 13 (discussed in Chapter 7 under depreciation costs).

(D) Corporate or group capital assets consist of the business unit's allocated share of corporate owned and leased (if meeting the criteria in the paragraph above) facilities.

(E) Distributed capital assets are those that are identified to specific primary indirect expense pools (e.g., manufacturing overhead and general and administrative expense).

(F) Undistributed capital assets are those that are identified to intermediate indirect expense pools (e.g., service centers) as well as any other capital assets not categorized as "distributed" e.g., land. Undistributed assets are allocated to the primary indirect expense COM pools on (1) the same bases used to allocate the costs of the service centers to which the assets are identified, or (2) any other reasonable basis that approximates the absorption of depreciation/amortization of the facilities.

(G) The average net book value of distributed capital assets and allocated undistributed capital assets are added together.

(H) The COM pools are calculated by applying the COM rate to the total average net book values of the capital assets assigned to the various COM indirect expense pools.

(I) The allocation bases are the same allocation bases used to allocate expenses in the primary indirect expense pools and any service centers that also allocate costs directly to contracts. For example, if manufacturing direct labor dollars are used to calculate a manufacturing overhead rate, those same manufacturing labor dollars would be used to calculate the manufacturing COM rate.

(J) The various cost of money rates are calculated in the same manner as indirect expense rates for the primary indirect expense pools—the COM pools are divided by the appropriate allocation bases.

Figure 8.7. (Continued)

Interim Guidance Paper W.G. 77-19 discusses the treatment of leased property under CAS 414 and concludes that cost of money should be included as an ownership cost in making a determination whether allowable cost will be based on cost of ownership or leasing costs.

One major controversy associated with the implementation of this standard stems from DOD CAS Steering Committee Interim Guidance Paper 77-18, which disallows the cost of facilities capital allocable to IR&D and B&P ceilings. Contractors have voiced strong and persistent disagreement with that position since its adoption by DOD for the following reasons:

ALLOCATION OF COST OF MONEY TO GOVERNMENT CONTRACTS

FISCAL YEAR 19xx

Cost Element	COM Factor	Contract A	Contract B	Contract C
Direct Material Costs		$1,100,000	$200,000	$1,000,000
Material COM	.14%	$ 1,540	$ 280	$ 200,000
Engineering Direct Labor $		$ 330,000	$ 50,000	$ 200,000
Engineering COM	3.80%	$ 12,540	$ 1,900	$ 7,600
Manufacturing Direct Labor $		$1,210,000	$125,000	$ 800,000
Manufacturing COM	17.16%	$ 207,636	$ 21,450	$ 137,280
Technical Computer Hours		280	100	200
Technical Computer COM	14.85%	$ 4,158	$ 85	$ 2,970
Total Cost Input Base		$5,369,000	$705,000	$3,250,000
G&A COM	.09%	$ 4,832	$ 635	$ 2,925

Figure 8.8. Allocation of cost of money to government contracts, fiscal year 198x.

The policy acts as a disincentive to contractors investing in new facilities that are considering the incurrence of IR&D costs above negotiated ceilings.

It is inequitable to disallow a portion of cost of facilities capital when, prior to CAS 414, interest was compensated in profit without any deduction for instances of over-ceiling IR&D/B&P.

The allocation base is merely a mechanism to accomplish the task of apportioning a cost that benefits multiple cost objectives. The allocation of a cost to contracts should not be thwarted merely because the allocation base contains some unallowable costs.

None of the applicable cost accounting standards (405, 414, and 420) suggest that cost of facilities capital should be disallowed.

The cost principles and CAS 420 both indicate that G&A costs are not considered allocable to IR&D and B&P. Since cost of facilities capital is somewhat similar to G&A, it should be accorded the same treatment.

Another area of disagreement over implementation of CAS 414 has been the exclusion by DOD of land held for expansion from the net book value of assets used to calculate cost of money. Industry representatives have asserted that land held for plant expansion is integral to the operation of the business unit and should be included on the cost of money form. DOD officials disagree and continue to follow the guidance contained in CAS Steering Committee Interim Guidance Paper W.G. 77-18.

An issue involving Gould Defense Systems, Inc.,[27] addressed the inclusion of goodwill as an element of facilities capital under CAS 414. In excluding goodwill from the capital asset base, the government cited Appendix A of CAS 414 that requires the facility capital values to be 1) subject to depreciation or amortization and 2) the same values used to generate allowable depreciation or

CONTRACT FACILITIES CAPITAL COST OF MONEY

Form Approved
OMB No. 0704-0267
Expires Oct 31, 1989

1. CONTRACTOR NAME	2. CONTRACTOR ADDRESS
3. BUSINESS UNIT	
4. RFP / CONTRACT PIIN NUMBER	5. PERFORMANCE PERIOD

6. DISTRIBUTION OF FACILITIES CAPITAL COST OF MONEY

POOL	ALLOCATION BASE	FACILITIES CAPITAL COST OF MONEY	
		FACTOR	AMOUNT
Material	1,000,000	.0014	1,400
Engineering	330,000	.0380	12,540
Manufacturing	210,000	.1716	207,636
Technical Computer	280	14.8487	4,158
G&A	5,369,000	.0009	4,832
TOTAL			230,566
TREASURY RATE			7.625 %
FACILITIES CAPITAL EMPLOYED (TOTAL DIVIDED BY TREASURY RATE)			3,023,816

7. DISTRIBUTION OF FACILITIES CAPITAL EMPLOYED

	PERCENTAGE	AMOUNT
LAND	1.90 %	57,561
BUILDINGS	20.92 %	632,603
EQUIPMENT	77.18 %	2,333,652
FACILITIES CAPITAL EMPLOYED	100%	3,023,816

DD Form 1861, AUG 87   *Supersedes all previous editions of DD Forms 1861-1 and 1861-2, which are obsolete.*   79-211

Figure 8.9. Contract facilities capital cost of money, DD Form 1861.

amortization. Since Gould was neither amortizing its recorded goodwill for financial reporting purposes nor claiming such amortization as an allowable indirect expense, the government contended the goodwill failed to meet the tests provided in Appendix A. However, the government had initially accepted the contractor's proposed forward pricing cost of money rates based on the inclusion of goodwill in the capital asset values. The contractor was not formally advised until October 1979, via a DCAA Form 1, that its practice was unacceptable.

The Board agreed that only net book values used to generate allowable depreciation or amortization can be used in computing the cost of facilities capital. However, the Board went on to conclude that goodwill generally would satisfy this test if it was amortized and the amortization expense was allocated properly. At the time of the ASBCA decision, there was no specific reference in the cost principles to preclude recovery of goodwill amortization costs. Therefore, since amortization of goodwill was recognized as a cost under generally accepted accounting principles, and was required for financial reporting purposes, the Board concluded that when properly incurred, goodwill amortization cost met the general cost principle requirements that costs be determined in accordance with a generally accepted method.

Because of Gould's historical failure to amortize goodwill and claim it as an allowable cost, the disallowance of cost of facilities capital attributable to goodwill was sustained from October 1979 until such time as amortization and allocation commenced. However, because of the government's prior approval of Gould's practice, the government was estopped from excluding goodwill in the CAS 414 calculations prior to October 1979.

The Gould decision was of limited value in establishing precedence since a FAR cost principle subsequently declared goodwill to be an expressly unallowable cost.

Accounting for the Cost of Deferred Compensation (Standard 415)

Standard 415 provides criteria for measuring deferred compensation costs and assigning such costs to cost accounting periods. The standard covers deferred compensation awards made in cash, stock, stock options, or other assets. Deferred compensation costs must be assigned to current cost accounting periods whenever a valid obligation has been incurred (accrual basis) and future funding is assured.

In determining if a liability has been established, the following conditions must be met:

A future payment is required.

The payment is to be made in money, other assets, or shares of stock of the contractor.

The amount due can be measured with reasonable accuracy.

The recipient is known.

There is a reasonable probability that any conditions required for the payment will occur.

There is a reasonable probability that any stock options will be exercised.

If no obligation is incurred prior to payment, the cost must be assigned to the period(s) of payment.

The cost of deferred compensation (i.e., amounts to be paid in the future) must be measured by the present value of the future benefits to be paid. The rate published semiannually by the Secretary of the Treasury is prescribed for purposes of discounting the future payments. For awards that require future service, costs are assigned to cost accounting periods as the future services are performed. The cost of deferred compensation must be reduced by forfeitures in the cost accounting period in which the forfeiture occurs. However, the voluntary failure by a recipient to exercise stock options is not considered a forfeiture.

For deferred compensation to be paid in money, various methods are described to recognize interest, if provided for in the award. The cost assignable for awards of stock is the market value of the stock on the date the shares are awarded. The cost assignable for stock options is the excess of the market value of the stock over the option price on the date the options for the specific number of shares are awarded. Consequently, there is no cost assigned to options awarded at or above market value.

The standard became effective July 10, 1977 and applicable at the start of the next cost accounting period following award of a contract subject to the standard.

Accounting for Insurance Costs (Standard 416)

The standard provides criteria for measuring, assigning, and allocating insurance costs. The principal requirement of the standard is that the insurance cost assigned to a cost accounting period is the projected average loss for that period plus insurance administration expenses.

Insurance premiums or payments to a trusteed fund, properly prorated and adjusted for applicable refunds, dividends, or additional assessments, are considered representative of the projected average loss. For exposure to risk of loss not covered by insurance premiums or payments to a trusteed fund, a program of self-insurance accounting must be developed. If insurance could be purchased against the self-insured risk, the cost of such insurance may be used to estimate the projected average loss. If purchased insurance is not available, the projected average loss must be based on the contractor's experience, relevant industry experience, and anticipated conditions using appropriate actuarial principles. Actual losses can only be charged to insurance expense when they are expected to approximate the projected average loss or are paid to retirees under a self-insurance program.

Actual loss experience must be evaluated regularly for comparison to the self-insurance cost used to estimate the projected average loss. Actual losses are measured by the actual cash value of property destroyed, amounts paid or accrued to repair damages, amounts paid or accrued to estates and beneficiaries, and amounts paid or accrued to compensate claimants. Self-insured losses that are paid more than 1 year after definitization of a loss are recognized at the present value of the future payments.

The standard generally requires insurance costs to be allocated on the basis of the factors used to determine the premium or assessment.

Necessary records must be maintained to substantiate amounts of premiums, refunds, dividends, losses, and self-insurance charges, and the measurement and allocation of insurance costs.

The standard became effective July 10, 1979 and is applicable at the start of the next fiscal year following receipt of a contract subject to the standard.

Cost of Money as an Element of the Cost of Capital Assets under Construction (Standard 417)

Standard 417 provides for an imputed cost of money to be included in the capitalized cost of assets constructed for a contractor's own use. The concept in this standard is the same as that contained in CAS 414, which provides criteria for measuring and allocating cost of money as part of the cost of facilities capital. The cost of money to be capitalized reflects the application of the rate published semiannually by the Secretary of the Treasury to a representative investment amount for the period that considers the rate at which construction costs are incurred. A calculation of cost of money for a capital asset under construction is illustrated in Figure 8.10.

Other methods for calculating cost of money, such as the method used for financial reporting in accordance with Statement of Financial Accounting Standards 34, Capitalization of Interest Cost, may be used, provided the result is not substantially different from the amount calculated as described above. Under FAS 34, interest expense on certain capital assets is capitalized at a rate based on the company's outstanding borrowings.

	Fiscal Year 1	Fiscal Year 2	Total Period of Construction in Progress
Months project under construction	10	3	
Average investment for months under construction (A)	$245,000[1]	$1,234,000[2]	
Time-weighted cost of money (COM) rate based on rates in effect during the construction period (B)	7.5%[3]	8.0%[3]	
Portion of year to which COM rate should be applied (C)	10/12	3/12	
Amount of COM to be capitalized (A) × (B) × (C)	$15,313	$24,680	$39,993
Total construction cost			$1,500,000
COM capitalized			39,993
Depreciable base for completed asset			$1,539,993

[1] If costs are incurred at a fairly uniform rate, a simple average of the beginning and ending balances may be used to find the representative amount. If costs are not incurred at a uniform rate, each of the month end balances should be totaled to compute the average investment.

[2] The average investment includes the COM capitalized in the prior fiscal year.

[3] The COM rates are weighted by the number of months each rate is in effect during the construction period.

Figure 8.10 Calculation of cost of money for an asset under construction.

If activities necessary to prepare an asset for use are discontinued, cost of money is not capitalized during the period of the discontinuance unless the discontinuance was beyond the control of and not the fault of the contractor. Disagreements in this area may occur.

The standard became effective December 15, 1980 and applicable at the start of the next cost accounting period following receipt of a contract subject to the standard.

Allocation of Direct and Indirect Cost (Standard 418)

Standard 418 requires that a contractor have a written policy for distinguishing between direct and indirect cost and that such cost be consistently classified. A *direct cost* is defined as a cost that is identified specifically with a particular final cost objective. An *indirect cost* is defined as a cost identified with two or more final cost objectives or with at least one intermediate cost objective.

Indirect costs must be accumulated in homogeneous cost pools. A cost pool is considered homogeneous if:

The major activities in the pool have similar beneficial/causal relationships to cost objectives, or

Separate allocations of costs of dissimilar activities would not result in substantially different amounts.

Materiality is a key consideration as to whether heterogeneous cost pools must be separately allocated. No changes in the existing indirect cost pool structure are required if the allocations resulting from the existing base(s) are not materially different from the allocations that would result from use of more discrete homogeneous cost pools.

A cost pool that includes a significant amount of management of direct labor or direct material activities must be allocated on a base representative of the activity being managed. A machine-hour base may be used if the costs in the pool are predominantly facility-related. A unit of production base is appropriate if there is common production of comparable units. A material cost base is appropriate if the activity being managed or supervised is a material-related activity. If none of these bases are appropriate, a direct labor hour or direct labor cost base will be used, whichever is more likely to vary in proportion to the cost included in the pool.

A cost pool that does not include a significant amount of labor or material management activities shall be allocated in accordance with the following hierarchy of preferred bases:

A resource consumption measure.
An output measure.
A surrogate representative of resources consumed.

Like CAS 410, this standard also permits a special allocation where a particular cost objective receives significantly more or less benefit from an indirect cost pool than would result from a normal allocation of such costs.

The standard became applicable to most contractors in 1982. Problems most likely to surface are those regarding the extent and frequency of analysis required to demonstrate that separate allocations of dissimilar activities would not result in materially different allocations than amounts allocated under existing cost pools. However, the DCAA implementation guidance on CAS 418 has focused on the materiality considerations in the standard. Auditors are admonished to pursue the establishment of additional pools only where the changes result in significantly different allocations of costs to cost objectives. The guidance observes that CAS 418 is not expected to require further review of indirect cost pools if there were no audit problems with the prior pool structure.

The standard became effective September 20, 1980 and is applicable at the start of the second fiscal year after receipt of a covered contract.

Accounting for Independent Research and Development Costs and Bid and Proposal Costs (Standard 420)

Standard 420 provides criteria for accumulating independent research and development (IR&D) and bid and proposal (B&P) costs and for allocating those costs to cost objectives. The standard covers such costs incurred at both the home office and business unit levels. IR&D expenses are identified as technical effort that is neither sponsored by a grant nor required for performance of a contract and that falls into the area of basic and applied research, development, or systems and other concept formulation studies. B&P costs are those incurred in preparing, submitting, or supporting any bid or proposal that is neither sponsored by a grant, nor required for contract performance.

The standard requires IR&D and B&P costs to be identified and accumulated by project except where the costs of individual projects are not material. IR&D and B&P project costs must include all allocable costs except business unit G&A expenses. In essence, IR&D and B&P projects are accounted for the same as contracts except for the allocation of G&A expenses. IR&D costs generally may not be deferred, and B&P costs can never be deferred.

IR&D and B&P projects performed by a segment for another segment are considered final cost objectives of the performing segment rather than IR&D and B&P, unless the work is part of an IR&D or B&P project of the performing segment. In that case, costs of the IR&D or B&P project are transferred to the home office for reallocation to the benefiting segments.

IR&D and B&P costs accumulated at the home office level are allocated to specific segments where projects are identified with such segments; otherwise the costs are allocated to all segments using the CAS 403 residual expense allocation base. Segment IR&D and B&P costs are allocated to contracts using the G&A base.

The use of a special allocation of IR&D and B&P costs is permitted at either the home office or segment level when a particular segment (for home office costs) or a particular final cost objective (for segment costs) receives significantly more or less benefit from IR&D and B&P costs than would result from the normal allocation of such costs. Disagreements between government and contractor representatives over what circumstances justify use of special allocations have surfaced as they did on CAS 410.

Unlike other cost accounting standards that are administered by the designated ACO, responsibility for administering CAS 420 (including compliance determinations) has been assigned to the Tri-Service Contracting Officer (TSCO) for those companies subject to IR&D/B&P advance agreements. (Companies that receive above a specified threshold from DOD for IR&D/B&P in a fiscal year must negotiate an advance agreement with the government to establish an IR&D/B&P cost ceiling for the following year.)

Splitting CAS administration between the TSCO and the ACO raises the potential for conflict if the TSCO negotiates a different allocation base for

IR&D/B&P than is established for G&A by the ACO. In guidance to be applied by TSCOs in negotiating advance agreements, DOD's Indirect Cost Monitoring Office (ICMO) concluded that a segment using a total cost input base to allocate G&A expense may, under CAS 420, use a "modified" total cost input base to allocate IR&D/B&P expense. [28] The ICMO considers use of the modified total cost input base appropriate when certain contracts receive significantly more or less benefit from IR&D/B&P than would be allocated under the normal G&A base. This situation could occur, for example, when particular contracts contain subcontracts for work that is alien to the contractor's normal product line.

The standard became effective March 15, 1980 and is applicable at the start of the second fiscal year after receipt of a covered contract subject to the standard.

IMPACT OF COST ACCOUNTING STANDARDS

Although the legislation creating CASB limited its jurisdiction to defense contracts, nondefense agencies implemented the Board's standards and related promulgations as part of their procurement regulations for application to business units performing both defense and non defense work work. Consequently, most companies doing business with the Federal government are affected by CAS.

It is clear that CASB did not hesitate to deal with issues that many thought would be tackled by the Financial Accounting Standards Board. Pronouncements on such matters as depreciation, pension costs, vacation pay, and cost of capital affect allocation of cost to periods.

CASB pronouncements have had a significant impact upon accounting systems. Some contractors complain that now, in addition to the records needed for financial reporting and tax return preparation, they must maintain a third set of records to comply with cost accounting standards. These problems are a particular concern for contractors whose government business is immaterial in relation to their total business.

The impact of CAS on accounting systems varies with the amount of government business performed by the contractor, the contractor's size, and the sophistication of the record-keeping function. The contractor whose principal business is with the government may change its cost accounting practices to conform with CAS unless management finds that such costing techniques are not responsive to its operational requirements. Medium-sized and smaller contractors may find it necessary to change their formal cost accounting practices upon becoming subject to CAS if separate memorandum recordkeeping is not economically or practically feasible.

Implementation of changes in costing practices necessitated by new standards created additional workload problems for many contractors. Extensive contract recosting and repricing was necessary on uncompleted covered contracts when a new standard became effective.

As a result of the Board's disclosure statement requirements, some contractors have found it necessary to formalize and reduce to writing their cost accounting practices for the first time. Cost accounting practices serve management in the detailed operational analysis and control of the business. Changing business conditions and management philosophy, and improvements in accounting and operational techniques often require contractors to alter their practices. Contractors find that the procedures for effecting such changes in cost accounting practices require contract-by-contract analysis of the cost impact of any change and thus feel inhibited about improving their accounting system in response to changing business conditions.

The impact of CAS goes beyond the need to develop and maintain new accounting systems. Standards affect company profits and resulting capital accumulation. If such effect is adverse, standards can discourage companies from pursuing government work and thus weaken the base of suppliers available to satisfy the government's needs for goods and services. It is principally for these reasons that contractors, individually and collectively through industry groups, have voiced concern. The more significant issues raised by industry are:

The Board's standards are too detailed and rigid, favor the government, and give little attention to alternatives.

Costs of adoption were not sufficiently weighed against the benefits to be derived when new standards were promulgated. With regard to this latter point, the Board never, succeeded in developing a quantitative cost/benefit rationale for any of its promulgations.

Nevertheless, there have been positive effects of CAS. CAS promulgations have caused contract costing to become more comparable and consistent by requiring allocation techniques that are more objective and by limiting alternative accounting procedures by use of more specific criteria. CAS regulations have also provided a more structured framework for effecting changes to cost accounting practices. Finally, the disclosure statement has proved to be a useful document for gaining a mutual understanding of the practices to be used in costing government contracts.

Compliance with CAS should not be taken lightly. Failure to comply with the Board's standards can result in adverse adjustment of costs and profits related to work performed under government contracts. Therefore, companies subject to CAS, as well as those potentially subject, must be knowledgeable in this significant area.

NOTES

1. Elmer B. Staats, *Report on Feasibility of Applying Uniform Cost Accounting Standards to Negotiated Defense Contracts* B-39995 (Washington, D.C.: Government Printing Office, 1970).
2. *The Boeing Company* , ASBCA no. 28342, September 17, 1985, 85-3 BCA 18435.
3. CFR Part 331, Preamble A, Item 6, paragraph 2.
4. Gulf Oil Trading Company, Comptroller General's Decision No. B-184333, March 11, 1976, 22 CCF. 80153.
5. Public Law 91-379, sec. 719 para. (h)(1); 50 App. U.S.C. 2168, para. (h)(1).
6. AiResearch Manufacturing Company, ASBCA no. 20998, November 29, 1976, 76-2 BCA 12,150; aff'd. May 13, 1977, 77-1 BCA 12, 546.
7. 4 CFR 331.20(k).
8. 4 CFR 331.20(l).
9. Husky Oil NPR Operations, Inc. (Ct. Cl. 1985) no. 531-83C.
10. 4 CFR 351.100.
11. Elmer B. Staats, *Report on Feasibility of Applying Uniform Cost Accounting Standards to Negotiated Defense Contracts* (Italics) - Note 1 supra.
12. Texas Instruments, Inc., ASBCA no. 18621, March 30, 1979, 79-1 BCA 13,800; aff'd. November 20, 1979, 79-2 BCA 14, 184.
13. Dayton T. Brown, Inc., ASBCA no. 22810, September 29, 1978, 78-2 BCA 13484; reversed June 11, 1980, 80-2 BCA 14,543.
14. The Boeing Company, ASBCA no. 19224, February 4, 1977, 77-1 BCA 12,371; aff'd. January 31, 1979, 79-1 BCA 13, 708.
15. The Boeing Company, (Ct. Cl. 1982) no. 268-79C, June 2, 1982 CCF 82,630.

16. The Boeing Company, Petition for a Writ of Certiorari, no. 82-1024, Denied April 18, 1983.

17. Lockheed Corporation and Lockheed Missiles and Space Company, Inc., ASBCA no. 22451, December 26, 1979, 80-1 BCA 14,222; aff'd. June 5, 1980, 80-2 BCA 14,509.

18. Lockheed Corporation and Lockheed Missiles and Space Company, ASBCA no. 27921, December 11, 1985, 86-1 BCA 18612.

19. Lockheed Corporation and Lockheed Missiles and Space Company, CAFC No. 86-1177, April 15, 1987, 34 CCF 75, 258

20. McDonnell Douglas Corporation, ASBCA no. 19842, December 26, 1979, 80-1 BCA 14,223; aff'd. June 9, 1980, 80-2 BCA 14,508.

21. Grumman Aerospace Corporation and Grumman Corporation, ASBCA no. 23219, February 16, 1982, 82-1 BCA 15,661; aff'd. July 8, 1982, 82-2 BCA, 15,933.

22. R&D Associates, ASBCA no. 30750, May 7, 1986, 86-2 BCA 19062.

23. General Dynamics Corporation, ASBCA no. 25919, April 18, 1985, 85-2 BCA 18074.

24. 51 Federal Register, 24971, July 9, 1986.

25. The Marquardt Company, ASBCA no. 29888, June 2, 1986, 86-3 BCA 19100; aff'd. June 2, 1986.

26. Ford Aerospace and Communications Corporation, ASBCA no. 23833, August 31, 1983, 83-2 BCA 16,813.

27. Gould Defense Systems, Inc., ASBCA no. 24881, June 10, 1983, 83-2 BCA 16,676.

28. Indirect Cost Monitoring Office Memorandum dated May 11, 1981, reference NAVMAT 08CD/RWL, Subject: Application of Cost Accounting Standard 420.50 (fx2), Special Allocation - IR&D/B&P.

1. This Disclosure Statement has been designed to meet the requirements of Public Law 91–379, and persons completing it are to describe their contract cost accounting practices. For timing of requirement to file a Disclosure Statement, see 4 C.F.R. 351.4. For complete regulations and instructions concerning submission of the Disclosure Statement, refer to the *Federal Register*, Title 4, Parts 331 and 351. A Statement must be submitted by all defense contractors who enter into negotiated national defense contracts with the United States in excess of $100,-000 other than contracts where the price negotiated is based on (1) established catalog or market prices of commercial items sold in substantial quantities to the general public, or (2) prices set by law or regulation. A separate Disclosure Statement must be submitted covering the practices of each of the contractor's profit centers, divisions, or similar organizational units, whose costs included in the total price of any contract exceed $100,-000, except where such costs are based on (1) established catalog or market prices of commercial items sold in substantial quantities to the general public; or (2) prices set by law or regulation. If the cost accounting practices under contracts are identical for more than one organizational unit, then only one Statement need be submitted for those units, but each such organizational unit must be identified. A Disclosure Statement will also be required for each corporate or group office when costs are allocated to one or more corporate segments performing contracts covered by Public Law 91–379, but only Part VIII of the Statement need be completed.

2. The Statement must be signed by an authorized signatory of the reporting unit.

3. The Disclosure Statement should be answered by checking the appropriate box or inserting the applicable letter code which most nearly describes the reporting unit's cost accounting practices. Pen and ink may be used to enter the check or letter code. Part I of the Statement asks for general information concerning the reporting unit. Part VIII covers Corporate and Group (Intermediate) offices whose costs are allocated to one or more segments performing contracts covered by Public Law 91–379. Part VIII should be completed by each such office, and care should be taken to insure proper identification of such offices on the cover of the Disclosure Statement. In short, while a Corporate or Group Office may have more than one reporting unit submitting Disclosure Statements, only one Statement need be submitted to cover the Corporate or Group Office operations.

4. A number of questions in this Statement may need narrative answers requir-

ing more space than is provided. In such instances, the reporting unit should use the continuation sheets provided. The number of the question involved should be indicated and the same coding required to answer the questions in the Statement should be used in presenting the answer in the continuation sheet. The reporting unit should indicate on the last continuation sheet used, the number of such sheets that were used.

5. The Disclosure Statement is printed on both sides of the paper. To submit additional copies of the Statement, as required, companies may reproduce it on one side of the paper.

6. Amendments shall be submitted to the same offices, including the Cost Accounting Standards Board, to which submission would have to be made were an original Disclosure Statement being filed. Revised data for Items 1.4.0 through 1.7.-0, 8.1.0, and 8.2.0 must be submitted annually at the beginning of the contractor's fiscal year. If fewer than five of the other items in the Disclosure Statement on file are changed, a letter notice precisely identifying the Disclosure Statement, the specific items being amended, and the nature of the changes will suffice. If five or more items are changed, the entire Disclosure Statement shall be resubmitted. Resubmitted Disclosure Statements must be accompanied by a notation specifying the items which have been changed and the nature of the change.

7. For Item 1.3.0 of the Disclosure Statement the following codes and classification descriptions have been selected from the Standard Industrial Classification Manual 1967, Executive Office of the President (Bureau of the Budget), which is used by U.S. Government agencies to classify establishments data by industry.

For the most part, only those industries which account for a major portion of defense contracting are specifically identified to a significant 4-digit level, that is, a code whose last two digits are each greater than zero. Where the specific industries are not relatively large in defense contracting terms, either a group code (ending in zero) or a major group code (ending in two zeros) is used. An exception to this rule is made when only one specific industry is assignable to a group, e.g., Metal Cases, Code 3411, is used because it is the only industry in Group 3410. One other exception applies to the group code rule: When a specific industry code is used and the group has two or more specific industries, the remaining industry codes within the group are consolidated into a group code ending in zero, e.g., Industrial Gases, is separately identified as Code 2813 and the remaining industries in the group are consolidated into a Group Code 2810 for all other industrial organic and inorganic chemicals.

To obtain the appropriate code for en-

try in Item 1.3.0 of the Disclosure Statement, each reporting organization should first examine the list of major-group descriptions below to determine which apply to the organization's products or services. Second, the specific codes and descriptions for the major group or groups should be reviewed to select the one code that most nearly identifies the product or service which accounted for most of the organization's sales or shipments in the base fiscal year used for the Disclosure Statement.

If research and development or modification and overhaul is associated with a product, use a specific manufactured product code (Codes 1911 through 3900) rather than a service code. For example, development work associated with aircraft should be coded 3721 (aircraft) rather than 7391 (commercial research and development laboratories).

Following are the major groups whose codes and descriptions are included:

I—Manufactured Products

19 Ordnance and Accessories.
20 Food and Kindred Products.
21 Tobacco Manufactures.
22 Textile Mill Products.
23 Apparel.
24 Lumber and Wood Products except Furniture.
25 Furniture and Fixtures.
26 Paper and Allied Products.
27 Printing, Publishing and Allied Industries.
28 Chemicals and Allied Products.
29 Petroleum Refining.
30 Rubber and Miscellaneous Plastic Products.
31 Leather and Leather Products.
32 Stone, Clay, Glass and Concrete Products.
33 Primary Metal Industries.
34 Fabricated Metal Products, except Ordnance Machinery and Transportation Equipment.
35 Machinery, except Electrical.
36 Electrical Machinery, Equipment and Supplies.
37 Transportation Equipment.
38 Professional, Scientific and Controlling Instruments; Photographic and Optical Goods; Watches and Clocks.
39 Miscellaneous Manufactures.

II—Construction and Services

15 Building Construction.
16 Construction, other than Building Construction.
17 Construction, Special Trade Contractors.
40 Railroad Transportation.
42 Motor Freight Transportation and Warehousing.
44 Water Transportation.

FORM CASB–DS–1   i

Appendix 8.1.   Cost Accounting Standards Board disclosure statement required by Public Law 91–379, Form CASB-DS-1

45 Transportation by Air.

47 Transportation Services.

48 Communication.

73 Miscellaneous Business Services.

80 Medical and Other Health Services.

82 Educational Services.

PRINCIPAL PRODUCT OR SERVICE CODE

SECTION I— MANUFACTURED PRODUCTS

Code   Description

19. ORDNANCE AND ACCESSORIES

1911 *Guns, Howitzers, Mortars, and Related Equipment.* Artillery having a bore over 30 mm, or over 1.18 inches, and components.

1925 *Guided Missiles and Space Vehicles.* Completely assembled guided missiles and space vehicles. Excludes guided missile and space vehicle engines and engine parts (Code 3722); ground and airborne guidance, checkout and launch electronic systems and components (Code 3662); and guided missile and space vehicle airframes, nose cones, and space capsules (Code 3729).

1929 *Ammunition, Except for Small Arms.* Ammunition over 30 mm or 1.18 inches, and also bombs, mines, torpedoes, grenades, depth charges, chemical warfare projectiles, and component parts. Excludes explosives (Code 2892).

1931 *Tanks and Tank Components.* Complete tanks and specialized components for tanks. Excludes military vehicles other than tanks (Code 3711) and tank engines (Code 3519).

1941 *Sighting and Fire Control Equipment.* Includes bomb sights, percentage correctors, wind correctors, directors, and sound locators. Excludes computers and computer systems (Code 3573).

1951 *Small Arms.* Small firearms having a bore 30 mm or 1.18 inches and below and parts for small firearms. Includes certain weapons over 30 mm which are carried and employed by the individual, such as grenade launchers and heavy field machine guns.

1961 *Small Arms Ammunition.* Ammunition for small arms as defined in Code 1951.

1999 *Ordnance and Accessories, Not Elsewhere Classified.* Examples include flame throwers, Y-guns, and smoke generators.

20. FOOD AND KINDRED PRODUCTS

2000 Foods and beverages for human consumption, and certain related products, such as manufactured ice, chewing gum, and prepared feeds for animals.

21. TOBACCO MANUFACTURES

2100 Cigarettes, cigars, smoking and chewing tobacco, and snuff.

22. TEXTILE MILL PRODUCTS

2200 Includes any of the following: (1) Yarn, thread, braids, twine, and cordage; (2) broad woven fabric, narrow woven fabric, knit fabric, and carpets and rugs from yarn; (3) dyeing and finishing fiber, yarn, fabric and knit apparel; (4) coating, waterproofing, or otherwise treating fabric; (5) the integrated manufacture of knit apparel and other finished articles from yarn; and (6) the manufacture of felt goods, lace goods, bonded-fiber fabrics, and miscellaneous textiles.

23. APPAREL

2300 Clothing and other finished products fabricated by cutting and sewing purchased or government-furnished textile fabrics and related materials, such as leather, rubberized fabrics, plastics, and furs.

24. LUMBER AND WOOD PRODUCTS, EXCEPT FURNITURE

2400 Poles, timber and pulpwood, sawmill and planing mill products, flooring, cooperage, millwork, plywood, prefabricated buildings, and wooden containers.

25. FURNITURE AND FIXTURES

2500 Household, office, public building and restaurant furniture, and office and store fixtures.

26. PAPER AND ALLIED PRODUCTS

2600 Pulps from rags and from wood and other cellulose fibers; paper and paperboard including building paper and building board, paper bags, boxes and envelopes.

27. PRINTING, PUBLISHING AND ALLIED INDUSTRIES

2700 Printing, such as by letterpress, lithography, gravure or screen; bookbinding, typesetting, engraving, and electrotyping; and newspaper, periodical, and book publishing.

28. CHEMICALS AND ALLIED PRODUCTS

2813. *Industrial Gases.* Gases in compressed liquid, and solid forms. Excludes fluorine and ammonia (Code 2810).

2810 *Industrial Organic, Inorganic Chemicals, Except Industrial Gases.*

2820 *Plastic Materials and Synthetic Resins, Synthetic Rubber, Synthetic and Other Man-Made Fibers, Except Glass Fibers.*

2830 *Drugs and Pharmaceuticals.*

2840 *Soaps, Detergents, and Cleaning Preparations.*

2850 *Paints, Varnishes, Lacquers, and Enamels.*

2860 *Agricultural Chemicals.* Fertilizers and pesticides.

2892 *Explosives.*

2900 *Chemicals, Not Elsewhere Classified.*

29. PETROLEUM REFINING

2900 Petroleum, paving and roofing materials (asphalt and tar), and lubricating oils and greases.

30. RUBBER AND MISCELLANEOUS PLASTIC PRODUCTS

3000 Products from natural, synthetic or reclaimed rubber; and miscellaneous finished plastic products.

31. LEATHER AND LEATHER PRODUCTS

3100 Includes finished leather and artificial leather products, and also the tanning, currying, and finishing of hides and skins.

32. STONE, CLAY, GLASS, AND CONCRETE PRODUCTS

3200 Flat glass and other glass products, cement, structural clay products, pottery, concrete, and gypsum products, cut stone, abrasive and asbestos products.

33. PRIMARY METAL INDUSTRIES

3310 *Products of Blast Furnaces, Steel Works, and Rolling and Finishing Mills.*

3320 *Iron and Steel Foundry Products.*

3330 *Primary Smelting and Refining of Nonferrous Metals.*

3340 *Secondary Smelting and Refining of Nonferrous Metals.*

3350 *Rolling, Drawing, and Extruding of Nonferrous Metals.*

3360 *Nonferrous Foundry Products.*

3390 *Miscellaneous Primary Metal Products.* Iron, steel, and nonferrous forgings, and primary metal products, not elsewhere classified.

34. FABRICATED METAL PRODUCTS, EXCEPT ORDNANCE, MACHINERY, AND TRANSPORTATION EQUIPMENT

3411 *Metal cans.*

3420 *Cutlery, Hand Tools and General Hardware.*

3430 *Heating Apparatus (Except Electrical) and Plumbing Fixtures.*

3440 *Fabricated Structural Metal Products.*

3450 *Screw Machine Products and Bolts, Nuts, Screws, Rivets, and Washers.*

3461 *Metal Stampings.*

3470 *Coating, Engraving, and Allied Services.*

3481 *Miscellaneous Fabricated Wire Products.*

3490 *Miscellaneous Fabricated Metal Products.* Barrels, drums, kegs. and pails; safes and vaults; steel springs; valve and pipe fittings, except brass goods and other fabricated metal products, not elsewhere classified.

35. MACHINERY, EXCEPT ELECTRICAL

3510 *Engines and Turbines.* Steam engines; steam, gas, and hydraulic

FORM CASB–DS–1

ii

Appendix 8.1. (Continued)

turbines; steam, gas and hydraulic turbine generator set units; and internal combustion engines not elsewhere classified. Excludes aircraft and rocket engines (Code 3722) and automotive engines (Code 3714).

3522 *Farm Machinery and Equipment.*

3531 *Construction Machinery and Equipment.* Includes heavy machinery and equipment, such as bulldozers, concrete mixers, cranes, dredging machinery, pavers and power shovels.

3532 *Mining Machinery and Equipment.*

3533 *Oil Field Machinery and Equipment.*

3534 *Elevators and Moving Stairways.*

3535 *Conveyors and Conveying Equipment.*

3536 *Hoists, Industrial Cranes and Monorail Systems.*

3537 *Industrial Trucks, Tractors, Trailers and Stackers.*

3540 *Metal Working Machinery and Equipment.*

3550 *Special Industry Machinery, Except Metalworking.*

3560 *General Industrial Machinery and Equipment.*

3573 *Electronic Computing Equipment.* Includes general purpose electronic analog computers as well as electronic digital computers. The electronic computers may be used for data processing or may be incorporated as components into control equipment for industrial use, and as components of equipment used in weapons and weapons systems, space and oceanographic exploration, transportation and other systems. Electronic computer systems contain high speed arithmetic and program control units, on-line information storage devices and input/output equipment. Examples of input/output equipment are converters (card and/or tape), readers and printers. Examples of storage devices are magnetic drums and disks, magnetic cores, and magnetic film memories.

3570 *Office, Computing and Accounting Machines. Except Electronic Computing Equipment (Code 3573).*

3580 *Service Industry Machines.*

3599 *Miscellaneous Machinery, Except Electrical.*

36. ELECTRICAL MACHINERY, EQUIPMENT AND SUPPLIES

3611 *Electric Measuring Instruments and Test Equipment.* Pocket, portable, panel-board, and graphic recording instruments for measuring electricity, such as voltmeters, ammeters, watt meters, watt-hour meters, demand meters, and other meters and indicating instruments. Also includes analyzers for testing the electrical characteristics of internal combustion engines and radio apparatus.

3612 *Power, Distribution, and Specialty Transformers.* Excludes radio frequency or voice frequency transformers, coils or chokes (Code 3679).

3613 *Switchgear and Switchboard Apparatus.*

3621 *Motors and Generators.* Electric motors (except starting motors) and power generators; motor generators sets; railway motors and control equipment; and motors, generators, and control equipment for gasoline, electric, and oil electric busses and trucks.

3622 *Industrial Controls.* Motor starters and controllers, control accessories, electronic controls and other industrial controls. Excludes automatic temperature controls (Code 3822).

3620 *Electrical Industrial Apparatus, Except Motors and Generators (Code 3621) and Industrial Controls (Code 3622).*

3630 *Household Appliances.*

3640 *Electric Lighting and Wiring Equipment.*

3651 *Radio and Television Receiving Sets, except communication Types.* Electronic equipment for home entertainment. Includes public address systems, and music distribution apparatus except records.

3652 *Phonograph Records.*

3661 *Telephone and Telegraph Apparatus.*

3662 *Radio and Television Transmitting, Signaling, and Detection Equipment and Apparatus.* Radio and television broadcasting equipment; electric communication equipment and parts, except telephone and telegraph; electronic field detection apparatus, light and heat emission operating apparatus, object detection apparatus and navigational electronic equipment, and aircraft and missile control systems; and high energy particle accelerator systems and equipment designed and sold as a complete package for radiation therapy, irradiation, radiographic inspection, and research (linear accelerators, betatrons, dynamotrons, Vandergraff generators, resonant transformers, insulating core transformers, etc.); high energy particle electronic equipment and accessories sold separately for the construction of linear accelerators, cyclotrons, synchrotrons, and other high energy research installations (transmitters/modulators, accelerating waveguide structures, pulsed electron guns, vacuum systems, cooling systems, etc.); other electric and electronic communication and signaling products, not elsewhere classified. Excludes transmitting tubes (Code 3673).

3671 *Radio and Television Receiving Type Electron Tubes Except Cathode Ray.*

3672 *Cathode Ray Picture Tubes.*

3673 *Transmitting, Industrial and Special Purpose Electron Tubes.*

3674 *Semiconductors and Related Devices.* Semiconductor and related solid state devices, such as semiconductor diodes and stacks, including rectifiers, integrated microcircuits (semiconductor networks), transistors, solar cells, and light sensitive semiconductor (solid state) devices.

3679 *Electronic Components and Accessories Not Elsewhere Classified.* Establishments primarily engaged in manufacturing specialty resistors for electronic end products; inductors, transformers, and capacitors and other electronic components, not elsewhere classified.

3690 *Miscellaneous Electrical Machinery, Equipment, and Supplies.* Includes storage and primary batteries, X–ray apparatus, electrical equipment for internal combustion engines and miscellaneous electrical machinery, equipment and supplies, not elsewhere classified.

37. TRANSPORTATION EQUIPMENT

3711 *Motor Vehicles.* Complete passenger automobiles, trucks, commercial cars and buses, and special purpose motor vehicles.

3714 *Motor Vehicle Parts and Accessories.*

3715 *Truck Trailers (Full).*

3721 *Aircraft.* Complete aircraft. Also includes factory type modification and overhaul of aircraft.

3722 *Aircraft Engines and Engine Parts.*

3723 *Aircraft Propellers and Propeller Parts.*

3729 *Aircraft Parts and Auxiliary Equipment, Not Elsewhere Classified.*

3731 *Ship Building and Repairing.* Ships, barges, and lighters, whether propelled by sail or motor power or towed by other craft. Also includes the conversion and alteration of ships.

3732 *Boat Building and Repairing.*

3740 *Railroad Equipment.*

3750 *Motorcycles, Bicycles and Parts.*

3790 *Miscellaneous Transportation Equipment.*

38. PROFESSIONAL, SCIENTIFIC, AND CONTROLLING INSTRUMENTS; PHOTOGRAPHIC AND OPTICAL GOODS; WATCHES AND CLOCKS

3811 *Engineering, Laboratory, and Scientific and Research Instruments*

Appendix 8.1. (Continued)

and Associated Equipment. Laboratory, scientific, and engineering instruments such as nautical, navigational, aeronautical, surveying, drafting, and instruments for laboratory work and scientific research (except optical instruments Code 3831).

3821 *Mechanical Measuring and Controlling Instruments, Except Automatic Temperature Controls.*

3822 *Automatic Temperature Controls.* Automatic temperature controls activated by pressure, temperature, level, flow, time, or humidity (including pneumatic controls) of the type principally used as components of air conditioning, refrigeration, and comfort heating, or as components of household appliances. Excludes industrial electric controls (Code 3620).

3831 *Optical Instruments and Lenses.* Optical lenses and prisms, and optical instruments such as microscopes, telescopes, field and opera glasses; and optical measuring and testing instruments such as refractometers, spectrometers, spectroscopes, colorimeters, polariscopes.

3840 *Surgical, Medical, and Dental Instruments and Supplies.*

3851 *Ophthalmic Goods.*

3861 *Photographic Equipment and Supplies.* Photographic apparatus, equipment, parts, attachments, and accessories, such as still and motion picture cameras and projection apparatus; photocopy and microfilm equipment; blueprinting and diazotype (white printing) apparatus and equipment; and other photographic equipment; and sensitized film, paper, cloth, and plates, and prepared photographic chemicals for use therewith.

3871 *Watches, Clocks, Clockwork Operated Devices, and Parts Except Watchcases.* Clocks (including electric), watches, mechanisms for clockwork operated devices, and clock and watch parts.

39. MISCELLANEOUS MANUFACTURERS

3900 Manufacture of products not classified in any other major manufacturing groups, i.e., from Code 1911 through 3871. Includes jewelry, silverware, musical instruments, toys, sporting and athletic goods and other miscellaneous manufactured products.

II.—CONSTRUCTION AND SERVICES

Code   Description

15. BUILDING CONSTRUCTION—GENERAL CONTRACTORS

1500 Construction of residential, farm, industrial, commercial, public or other buildings.

16. CONSTRUCTION OTHER THAN BUILDING CONSTRUCTION—GENERAL CONTRACTORS

1600 Heavy construction, such as highways and streets, bridges, sewers, railroads, airports, and other types of construction work, except buildings.

17. CONSTRUCTION—SPECIAL TRADE CONTRACTORS

1700 Specialized construction activities, such as plumbing, painting, plastering, carpeting, electrical, etc.

40. RAILROAD TRANSPORTATION

4000 Transportation by line-haul railroad and certain services allied to rail transportation, such as sleeping and dining car services, railway express, and switching and terminal services.

42. MOTOR FREIGHT TRANSPORTATION AND WAREHOUSING

4200 Local or long-distance trucking, transfer, and draying services, or storage of farm products, furniture and other household goods, or commercial goods of any nature. Also includes operation of terminal facilities for handling freight, with or without maintenance facilities.

44. WATER TRANSPORTATION

4463 *Marine Cargo Handling.* Services directly related to marine cargo handling from the time cargo, for or from a vessel, arrives at shipside, dock, pier, terminal, staging area, or intransit area until cargo loading or unloading operations are completed. Includes the operation and maintenance of piers, docks, and associated buildings and facilities.

4400 *Water Transportation, Except Marine Cargo Handling.* Freight and passenger transportation on the open seas or inland waters, and incidental services such as lighterage, towing, and canal operation. Also includes excursion boats, sightseeing boats and water taxis.

45. TRANSPORTATION BY AIR

4582 *Airports and Flying Fields.* Operation and maintenance of airports and flying fields and/or the servicing, repairing (except on a factory basis), and storing of aircraft at such airports. Excludes modification and factory type overhaul of aircraft (Code 3721).

4500 *Transportation by Air, Except Airports and Flying Fields.* Domestic and foreign transportation by air and also terminal services.

47. TRANSPORTATION SERVICES

4700 Services incidental to transportation, such as forwarding, packing and crating, and rental of railroad cars.

48. COMMUNICATION

4800 Point-to-point communication service whether by wire or radio, and whether intended to be received aurally or visually; and radio broadcasting and television. Services for the exchange or recording of messages are also included.

73. MISCELLANEOUS BUSINESS SERVICES

7391 *Commercial Research and Development Laboratories.* Research and development activities on a fee or contract basis. Research and development laboratories of companies which manufacture the products developed from their research activities are classified as auxiliary to the manufacturing establishments served.

7392 *Business, Management, Administrative and Consulting Services.* Business and management administrative and consulting services, such as business analyzing business research, efficiency experts, fashion designing and consulting, industrial management, market research, personnel management, public relations counselors, sales engineers, statistical services, tax consultation, and traffic consultants.

7394 *Equipment Rental and Leasing Services.* Includes electronic equipment rental.

7300 Other miscellaneous business services, such as advertising, mailing, stenographic, employment agency, commercial testing and protective services.

80. MEDICAL AND OTHER HEALTH SERVICES

8000 Medical, surgical, and other health services to persons.

82. EDUCATIONAL SERVICES

8221 *Colleges, Universities, and Professional Schools.* Tuition fees at colleges, universities, and professional schools granting academic degrees and requiring for admission at least a high school diploma or equivalent general academic training.

8200 *Other Educational Services.* Excludes services involving colleges, universities, and professional schools and also excludes research and development activities of such institutions (Code 8921).

89. MISCELLANEOUS SERVICES

8911 *Engineering and Architectural Services.* Services of a professional nature in the fields of engineering and architecture.

8921 *Nonprofit Educational and Scientific Research Agencies.* Research at non-profit establishments including educational institutions.

8900 *Other Miscellaneous Services.*

FORM CASB–DS–1

iv

Appendix 8.1. (Continued)

251

COST ACCOUNTING STANDARDS BOARD **DISCLOSURE STATEMENT** *REQUIRED BY PUBLIC LAW 91–379*	COVER SHEET AND CERTIFICATION

Item No.	

0.1 Company or Reporting Unit:

Name

Street Address

City, State and ZIP Code

Division or Subsidiary of
(if applicable)

0.2 Reporting Unit is: (*Check one.*)

A. ☐ Corporate   B. ☐ Group   C. ☐ Division or   D. ☐ Other
    (home) office   office   subsidiary

0.3 Official to Contact Concerning this Statement:

Name and title

Phone number (including area
code and extension)

0.4 Date of:

This statement

Most recent prior statement

CERTIFICATION

I certify that to the best of my knowledge and belief this Statement is the complete and accurate disclosure as of the above date by the above-named organization of its cost accounting practices, as required by the Disclosure Regulation of the Cost Accounting Standards Board under 50 U.S.C. App. 2168, Public Law 91–379 (4 CFR 351).

_____
(*Name*)

_____
(*Title*)

**THE PENALTY FOR MAKING A FALSE STATEMENT IN
THIS DISCLOSURE IS PRESCRIBED IN 18 U.S.C. 1001**

FORM CASB–DS–1

Appendix 8.1.   (Continued)

COST ACCOUNTING STANDARDS BOARD **DISCLOSURE STATEMENT** *REQUIRED BY PUBLIC LAW 91-379*	INDEX

FORM CASB-DS-1

Appendix 8.1. (Continued)

253

COST ACCOUNTING STANDARDS BOARD **DISCLOSURE STATEMENT** *REQUIRED BY PUBLIC LAW 91–379*	**PART I—GENERAL INFORMATION** Name of Reporting Unit

Item No.	Item Description

Instructions for Part I

Sales data for this part should cover the most recently completed fiscal year of the reporting unit. "Government Sales" includes sales under both prime contracts and subcontracts. "Annual Total Sales" includes intracorporate transactions. Educational institutions may skip Items 1.4.0 and 1.6.0, and consider sales as used in Items 1.5.0 and 1.7.0 to refer to research revenues. Estimates are permitted for Items 1.4.0 through 1.7.0.

1.1.0   **Type of Business Entity of Which the Reporting Unit is a Part.** (*Check one.*)

A. ☐ Corporation   B. ☐ Partnership   C. ☐ Proprietorship

D. ☐ Not-for-profit organization   E. ☐ Joint venture   F. ☐ Educational institution

1.2.0   **Predominant Type of Government Sales.** (*Check one.*)

A. ☐ Manufacturing   B. ☐ Research and Development   C. ☐ Construction

D. ☐ Services   Y. ☐ Other (*specify*) _____

1.3.0   **Principal Product or Service Sold to the Government.** (*Specify name of product or service and enter code from Instructions.*)

Name _____   Code _____

1.4.0   **Annual Total Sales (Government and Commercial).** (*Check one.*)

A. ☐ Less than $1 million   B. ☐ $1–$10 million   C. ☐ $11–$25 million   D. ☐ $26–$50 million

E. ☐ $51–$100 million   F. ☐ $101–$200 million   G. ☐ $201–$500 million   H. ☐ Over $500 million

1.5.0   **Annual Total Government Sales.** (*Check one.*)

A. ☐ Less than $1 million   B. ☐ $1–$10 million   C. ☐ $11–$25 million   D. ☐ $26–$50 million

E. ☐ $51–$100 million   F. ☐ $101–$200 million   G. ☐ $201–$500 million   H. ☐ Over $500 million

1.6.0   **Government Sales (Item 1.5.0) as Percentage of Total Sales (Item 1.4.0).** (*Check one.*)

A. ☐ Less than 10%   B. ☐ 10%–50%   C. ☐ 51%–80%   D. 81%–95%   E. ☐ Over 95%

FORM CASB–DS–1   –1–

Appendix 8.1. (Continued)

<table>
<tr><td colspan="2">COST ACCOUNTING STANDARDS BOARD
DISCLOSURE STATEMENT
REQUIRED BY PUBLIC LAW 91–379</td><td colspan="2">PART I—GENERAL INFORMATION
Name of Reporting Unit</td></tr>
</table>

Item No.	Item Description

1.7.0 Government Subcontract Sales as Percentage of Total Government Sales (Item 1.5.0). (*Check one.*)

    A. ☐ Less than 10%   B. ☐ 10%–50%   C. ☐ 51%–80%   D. ☐ 81%–95%   E. ☐ Over 95%

1.8.0 Description of Your Cost Accounting System for Government Contracts and Subcontracts. (*Check the appropriate block(s) and if more than one is checked, explain on a continuation sheet.*)

    A. ☐ Standard costs—Job order   B. ☐ Standard costs—Process   C. ☐ Actual costs—Job order

    D. ☐ Actual costs—Process   Y. ☐ Other(s) (*Describe on a continuation sheet.*)

1.9.0 Integration of Cost Accounting with Financial Accounting. The cost accounting system is: (*Check one. If B or C is checked, describe on a continuation sheet the costs which are accumulated on memorandum records.*)

    A. ☐ Integrated with financial accounting records (Subsidiary cost accounts are all reconcilable to general ledger control accounts.)   B. ☐ Not integrated with financial accounting (Cost data are accumulated on memorandum records.)   C. ☐ Combination of A and B

1.10.0 Unit or Job Costs. Is your cost accounting system capable of producing unit or job lot costs during contract performance? (*Check one.*)

    A. ☐ Yes (*If Yes, describe on a continuation sheet the method used or which could be used to arrive at such costs.*)   B. ☐ No (Interim repricing not involved.)   C. ☐ No (*Interim repricing involved. Describe on a continuation sheet the manner in which interim repricing is developed.*)

1.11.0 Year, Month, Day on Which Your Most Recent Fiscal Year Ended. (*Enter in blocks below. Use numeric terms, e.g., 710630 for June 30, 1971; 711231 for December 31, 1971.*)

    ———————————

FORM CASB–DS–1

–2–

Appendix 8.1. (Continued)

COST ACCOUNTING STANDARDS BOARD	PART II—DIRECT COSTS
DISCLOSURE STATEMENT	
REQUIRED BY PUBLIC LAW 91-379	Name of Reporting Unit

Item No.	Item Description

Instructions for Part II

This part covers three major elements of direct costs, i.e., Direct Materials, Direct Labor, and Other Direct Costs. It is not the intent here to spell out or define the three elements of direct costs.

Rather, contractors should disclose practices based on their own definitions of what costs are, or will be, charged directly to Government contracts or similar cost objectives as Direct Materials, Direct Labor, or Other Direct Costs. For example, some contractors may charge or classify purchased labor of direct nature, as "Direct Materials" for purposes of pricing proposals, requests for progress payments, claims for cost reimbursement, etc.; some other contractors may classify the same cost as "Direct Labor," and still others as "Other Direct Costs." In these circumstances, it is expected that contractors will disclose practices consistent with their own classifications of Direct Materials, Direct Labor, and Other Direct Costs.

2.1.0   **Description of Direct Materials.** Direct Materials as used here are **not** limited to those items of materials actually incorporated into the end product; they also include materials, consumable supplies, and other costs when charged to Government contracts or similar cost objectives as Direct Materials. (*Describe on a continuation sheet the principal classes of materials and service costs which are charged as direct materials; group the materials and service costs by those which are incorporated in an end product and those which are not.*)

2.2.0   **Method of Charging Direct Materials.**

2.2.1   **Direct Charge Not Through an Inventory Account at:** (*Check the appropriate block(s) and if more than one is checked, explain on a continuation sheet.*)

     A. ☐ Standard costs (*Describe the type of standards used, e.g., current standards, basic standards, etc., on a continuation sheet.*)   B. ☐ Actual costs

     Y. ☐ Other(s) (*Describe on a continuation sheet.*)   Z. ☐ Not applicable

2.2.2   **Charged from Central or Common, Company-owned Inventory Account at:** (*Check the appropriate block(s) and if more than one is checked, explain on a continuation sheet.*)

     A. ☐ Standard costs (*Describe the types of standards used on a continuation sheet.*)   B. ☐ Average costs   C. ☐ First in, first out

     D. ☐ Last in, first out   Y. ☐ Other(s) (*Describe on a continuation sheet.*)   Z. ☐ Not applicable

FORM CASB-DS-1

– 3 –

Appendix 8.1. (Continued)

Item No.	Item Description

2.3.0 Timing of Charging Direct Materials Incorporated in End Product. (*Check the appropriate block(s) to indicate the point in time at which materials incorporated in the end product are charged to Government contracts or similar cost objectives, and if more than one block is checked, explain on a continuation sheet.*)

A. ☐ When orders are placed   B. ☐ When material is received, or when fabricated, if fabricated in-house   C. ☐ When material is issued or released to jobs

D. ☐ When consumed or incorporated in end product   E. ☐ When invoices are vouchered or paid   Y. ☐ Other(s) (*Describe on a continuation sheet.*)

Z. ☐ Not applicable

2.4.0 Variances from Standard Costs for Direct Materials. (*Do not complete this item unless you use a standard cost method, i.e., you have checked Block A of Item 2.2.1 or 2.2.2. Check the appropriate block(s) in Items 2.4.1, 2.4.2, 2.4.3 and 2.4.4, and if more than one block is checked, explain on a continuation sheet.*)

2.4.1 Type of Variance.

A. ☐ Price   B. ☐ Usage   C. ☐ Combined (A and B)

Y. ☐ Other(s) (*Describe on a continuation sheet.*)

2.4.2 Method of Accumulating Variance.

A. ☐ Plant-wide basis   B. ☐ By department   C. ☐ By product or product line

D. ☐ By contract   Y. ☐ Other(s) (*Describe on a continuation sheet.*)

2.4.3 Method of Disposing of Variance. (*Describe on a continuation sheet the basis for, and the frequency of, the disposition of the variance.*)

A. ☐ Prorated between inventories and cost of goods sold   B. ☐ Charged or credited only to cost of goods sold   C. ☐ Charged or credited only to overhead

Y. ☐ Other(s) (*Describe on a continuation sheet.*)

2.4.4 Revisions. *Standard costs for direct materials are revised:*

A. ☐ Semiannually   B. ☐ Annually   C. ☐ Revised as needed, but at least once annually

Y. ☐ Other(s) (*Describe on a continuation sheet.*)

FORM CASB–DS–1   – 4 –

Appendix 8.1. (Continued)

COST ACCOUNTING STANDARDS BOARD **DISCLOSURE STATEMENT** *REQUIRED BY PUBLIC LAW 91–379*	PART II—DIRECT COSTS
	Name of Reporting Unit

Item No.	Item Description

2.5.0 **Method of Charging Direct Labor.** (*Check the appropriate block(s) for each Direct Labor Category to show how such labor is charged to Government contracts or similar cost objectives, and if more than one block is checked, explain on a continuation sheet. Also describe on a continuation sheet the principal classes of labor or costs that are, or will be, included in Manufacturing Labor, Engineering Labor, and Other Direct Labor, as applicable.*)

	Direct Labor Category		
	Manufacturing	Engineering	Other Direct
	(1)	(2)	(3)
A. Individual/actual rates	☐	☐	☐
B. Average rates (*Describe the type of average rates on a continuation sheet.*)	☐	☐	☐
C. Standard costs/rates (*Describe the type of standards used on a continuation sheet.*)	☐	☐	☐
Y. Other(s) (*Describe on a continuation sheet.*)	☐	☐	☐
Z. Labor category is not applicable	☐	☐	☐

2.6.0 **Variances from Standard Costs for Direct Labor.** (*Do not complete this item unless you use a standard cost/rate method, i.e., you have checked Block C of Item 2.5.0 for any direct labor category. Check the appropriate block(s) in each column of Items 2.6.1, 2.6.2 and 2.6.3 and in Item 2.6.4. If more than one is checked, explain on a continuation sheet.*)

2.6.1 **Type of Variance.**

	Direct Labor Category		
	Manufacturing	Engineering	Other Direct
	(1)	(2)	(3)
A. Rate	☐	☐	☐
B. Efficiency	☐	☐	☐
C. Combined (A and B)	☐	☐	☐
Y. Other(s) (*Describe on a continuation sheet.*)	☐	☐	☐
Z. Labor category is not applicable	☐	☐	☐

2.6.2 **Method of Accumulating Variance.**

A. Plant-wide basis	☐	☐	☐
B. By department	☐	☐	☐
C. By product or product line	☐	☐	☐
D. By contract	☐	☐	☐
Y. Other(s) (*Describe on a continuation sheet.*)	☐	☐	☐
Z. Labor category is not applicable	☐	☐	☐

FORM CASB–DS–1

– 5 –

Appendix 8.1. (Continued)

258

Item No.	Item Description

2.6.3 **Method of Disposing of Variance.** (*Describe on a continuation sheet the basis for, and the frequency of, the disposition of the variance.*)

Direct Labor Category

	Manufacturing (1)	Engineering (2)	Other Direct (3)
A. Prorated between inventories and cost of goods sold	☐	☐	☐
B. Charged or credited only to cost of goods sold	☐	☐	☐
C. Charged or credited only to overhead	☐	☐	☐
Y. Other(s) (*Describe on a continuation sheet.*)	☐	☐	☐
Z. Labor category is not applicable	☐	☐	☐

2.6.4 **Revisions.** Standard costs for direct labor are revised:

A. ☐ Semiannually B. ☐ Annually C. ☐ Revised as needed, but at least once annually Y. ☐ Other(s) (*Describe on a continuation sheet.*)

2.7.0 **Credits to Contract Costs.** When Government contracts or similar cost objectives are credited for the following circumstances, are the rates of direct labor, direct materials, other direct costs and applicable indirect costs always the same as those for the original charges? (*Check one block for each circumstance, and for each "No" answer, explain on a continuation sheet how the credit differs from original charge.*)

Circumstance	A. Yes	B. No	Z. Not Applicable
(a) Transfers to other jobs/contracts	☐	☐	☐
(b) Unused or excess materials remaining upon completion of contract	☐	☐	☐

2.8.0 **Interorganizational Transfers.** This item is directed only to those materials, supplies, and services which are, or will be, transferred to **you** from divisions, subsidiaries, or affiliates under common control with you. (*Check the appropriate block(s) in each column to indicate the basis used by you as transferee to charge the cost or price of interorganizational transfers of materials, supplies, and services to Government contracts or similar cost objectives. If more than one block is checked, explain on a continuation sheet. Full cost means the cost incurred as set forth in ASPR 15–205.22(e) or other pertinent procurement regulations.*)

Basis	Materials (1)	Supplies (2)	Services (3)
A. At full cost excluding transferor's general and administrative (G&A) expenses	☐	☐	☐
B. At full cost including transferor's G&A expenses	☐	☐	☐
C. At full cost (A or B above) plus a markup percentage	☐	☐	☐
D. At established catalog or market price or prices based on adequate competition	☐	☐	☐
Y. Other(s) (*Describe on a continuation sheet.*)	☐	☐	☐
Z. Interorganizational transfers are not applicable	☐	☐	☐

FORM CASB–DS–1

– 6 –

Appendix 8.1. (Continued)

Item No.	Item Description

3.1.0 **Criteria for Determining How Costs are Charged to Government Contracts or Similar Cost Objectives.** (*Describe on a continuation sheet your criteria for determining whether costs are charged directly or indirectly.*)

3.2.0 **Treatment of Costs of Specified Functions, Elements of Cost, or Transactions.** (*For each of the functions, elements of cost or transactions listed in Items 3.2.1, 3.2.2, and 3.2.3, enter one of the Codes A through F, or Y, to indicate how the item is treated. Enter Code Z in those blocks that are not applicable to you. Also, specify the name(s) of the indirect pool(s) for each function, element of cost, or transaction coded E or F. If Code E, Sometimes direct/Sometimes indirect, is used and if there is a deviation from the criteria described in response to Item 3.1.0, explain on a continuation sheet the circumstances involved which cause the deviation.*)

Treatment Code

A. Direct material
B. Direct labor
C. Direct material and labor

D. Other direct costs
E. Sometimes direct/Sometimes indirect

F. Indirect only
Y. Other(s) (*Describe on a continuation sheet.*)
Z. Not applicable

3.2.1 **Functions, Elements of Cost, or Transactions Relative to Direct Materials.**

	Treatment Code	Name of Pool(s)
(a) Cash discounts on purchases	☐	_____
(b) Freight in	☐	_____
(c) Income from sale of scrap	☐	_____
(d) Income from sale of salvage	☐	_____
(e) Incoming material inspection	☐	_____
(f) Inventory adjustments	☐	_____
(g) Purchasing	☐	_____
(h) Trade discounts, refunds, rebates, and allowances on purchases	☐	_____

3.2.2 **Functions, Elements of Cost, or Transactions Relative to Direct Labor.**

(a) Health insurance	☐	_____
(b) Holiday differential (premium pay)	☐	_____
(c) Overtime premium pay	☐	_____
(d) Pension costs	☐	_____
(e) Shift premium pay	☐	_____
(f) Training	☐	_____
(g) Travel and subsistence	☐	_____
(h) Vacation pay	☐	_____

FORM CASB–DS–1

-7-

Appendix 8.1. (Continued)

COST ACCOUNTING STANDARDS BOARD **DISCLOSURE STATEMENT** *REQUIRED BY PUBLIC LAW 91–379*	PART III—DIRECT VS. INDIRECT
	Name of Reporting Unit

Item No.	Item Description

3.2.3	**Functions, Elements of Cost, or Transactions—Miscellaneous.**	**Treatment Code**	**Name of Pool(s)**
	(a) Design engineering (in-house)	☐_____	_____
	(b) Drafting (in-house)	☐_____	_____
	(c) Computer operations (in-house)	☐_____	_____
	(d) Contract administration	☐_____	_____
	(e) Freight out (finished product)	☐_____	_____
	(f) Line (or production) inspection	☐_____	_____
	(g) Packaging and preservation	☐_____	_____
	(h) Preproduction costs and start-up costs	☐_____	_____
	(i) Production shop supervision	☐_____	_____
	(j) Professional services (consultant fees)	☐_____	_____
	(k) Purchased labor of direct nature (on premises)	☐_____	_____
	(l) Purchased labor of direct nature (off premises)	☐_____	_____
	(m) Rearrangement costs	☐_____	_____
	(n) Rework costs	☐_____	_____
	(o) Royalties	☐_____	_____
	(p) Scrap work	☐_____	_____
	(q) Special test equipment (as defined in ASPR 15–205.40 or other pertinent procurement regulations)	☐_____	_____
	(r) Special tooling (as defined in ASPR 15–205.40 or other pertinent procurement regulations)	☐_____	_____
	(s) Subcontract costs	☐_____	_____
	(t) Warranty costs	☐_____	_____
3.3.0	**Other Costs Charged Direct to Contracts.** (*Describe on a continuation sheet all other significant functions, elements of cost, or transactions charged to Government contracts or similar cost objectives as direct material, direct labor or other direct costs. Do not include functions or costs covered in Items 2.1.0, 2.5.0, and 3.2.0 which are always charged direct. Describe also whether there are any deviations from the criteria set out in Item 3.1.0 with respect to any continuation sheet items.*)		

Appendix 8.1. (Continued)

Item No.	Item Description

Instructions for Part IV

For the purpose of this part, indirect costs have been divided into three categories: (i) manufacturing, engineering, and comparable indirect costs, (ii) general and administrative (G&A) expenses, and (iii) service center costs, as defined in Item 4.3.0. The term "overhead," as used in this part, refers only to the first category of indirect costs.

The following Allocation Base Codes are provided for use in connection with Items 4.1.0, 4.2.0 and 4.3.0. Educational institutions, to which ASPR XV, Part 3 applies, may enter Code Y for Items 4.1.0(n), 4.2.0(n) and 4.3.0(l), and describe on a continuation sheet the indirect cost pools and the bases for allocating such pools of expenses to Government contracts or similar cost objectives.

A. Sales
B. Cost of sales
C. Cost input (direct material, direct labor, other direct costs and applicable overhead)
D. Total cost incurred (cost input plus G&A expenses)
E. Prime cost (direct material, direct labor and other direct cost)
F. Processing or conversion cost (direct labor and applicable overhead)
G. Direct labor dollars
H. Direct labor hours

I. Machine hours
J. Usage
K. Unit of Product
L. Direct material cost
M. Total payroll dollars (direct and indirect employees)
N. Headcount or number of employees (direct and indirect employees)
O. Square feet
Y. Other(s) or more than one basis (*Describe on a continuation sheet.*)
Z. Pool not applicable

4.1.0 **Overhead Pools and Allocation Bases.** (*Enter for each type of overhead pool one of the Allocation Base Codes A through O or Y, to indicate the basis for allocating such pool of expenses to Government contracts or similar cost objectives, i.e., allocation to these final cost objectives without any intermediate allocations. Enter Code Z in those blocks for types of pools that are not applicable to the reporting unit; however, if you use a single plant-wide pool, Lines (b) through (n) may be left blank.*)

Type of Pool	**Allocation Base Code**
(a) Single, plant-wide pool (*If an entry other than "Z" is made here, skip to Item 4.2.0*)	☐
(b) Manufacturing	☐
(c) Engineering	☐
(d) Manufacturing and Engineering	☐
(e) Tooling	☐
(f) Off-site or out-plant (geographical pool)	☐
(g) Field service	☐
(h) Material handling	☐
(i) Departmental/shop	☐
(j) Subcontract administration	☐
(k) Use and occupancy	☐

FORM CASB–DS–1

– 9 –

Appendix 8.1. (Continued)

Item No.	Item Description

4.1.0 Continued.

		Allocation Base Code
	Type of Pool	
(l)	Quality control	☐
(m)	Fringe benefits	☐
(n)	Other Pools (*Enter Code Y on this line if other pools are used and identify on a continuation sheet each such pool and its Allocation Base Code. If no other pools are used, enter Code Z.*)	☐

4.2.0 **Reporting Unit's G&A Pools and Allocation Bases.** (*Enter for each type of G&A pool one of the Allocation Base Codes A through O, or Y, listed on Page 9 to indicate the basis for allocating G&A to Government contracts or similar cost objectives, i.e., allocation to these final cost objectives without any intermediate allocations. Enter Code Z in those blocks for types of pools that are not applicable to the reporting unit; however, if an entry other than "Z" is made on Line (a), (b), (c) or (d), Lines (e) through (n) may be left blank.*)

		Allocation Base Code
	Type of Pool	
(a)	Single G&A pool only	☐

No Separate G&A Pool

(b)	Combined with single, plant-wide overhead pool	☐
(c)	Combined with manufacturing overhead	☐
(d)	Combined with engineering overhead	☐

More Than One Pool

(e)	General and administrative	☐
(f)	Commercial—general and administrative	☐
(g)	Government—general and administrative	☐
(h)	Selling or marketing expense	☐
(i)	Independent research and development (IR&D) costs	☐
(j)	Bidding and proposal (B&P) costs	☐
(k)	IR&D and B&P costs	☐
(l)	Spares administration	☐
(m)	Corporate or home office expense	☐
(n)	Other Pools (*Enter Code Y on this line if other pools are used and identify on a continuation sheet each such pool and its Allocation Base Code. If no other pools are used, enter Base Code Z.*)	☐

FORM CASB–DS–1

– 10 –

Appendix 8.1. (Continued)

263

COST ACCOUNTING STANDARDS BOARD **DISCLOSURE STATEMENT** *REQUIRED BY PUBLIC LAW 91–379*	PART IV—INDIRECT COSTS Name of Reporting Unit

Item No.	Item Description
4.3.0	**Service Centers and Allocation Bases.** Service centers are departments or other functional units which perform specific technical and/or administrative services for the benefit of other units within a reporting unit.

Category Code

Generally, costs incurred by such centers are, or can be, charged or allocated (i) partially to specific final cost objectives as direct costs and partially to other indirect costs pools (such as a manufacturing overhead pool) for subsequent reallocation to several final cost objectives, referred to herein as Category "A" and (ii) only to several other indirect cost pools (such as manufacturing overhead pool, engineering overhead pool and G&A expense pool) for subsequent reallocation to several final cost objectives, referred to herein as Category "B".

Rate Code

Some service centers may use predetermined billing or costing rates to charge or allocate the costs (Rate Code A) while others may charge or allocate on an actual basis (Rate Code B).

(Enter in Column (1) for each service center, Code A or B to indicate the category of pool. Enter in Column (2) one of the Allocation Base Codes A through O, or Y, listed on Page 9, to indicate the basis of charging or allocating service center costs. Enter in Column (3) Rate Code A or B to describe the costing method used. Enter Code Z in Column (1) only, if any service center is not applicable to the reporting unit.)

Service Center	Category Code *(1)*	Allocation Base Code *(2)*	Rate Code *(3)*
(a) Scientific computer operations	☐	☐	☐
(b) Business data processing	☐	☐	☐
(c) Photography services	☐	☐	☐
(d) Reproduction services	☐	☐	☐
(e) Art services	☐	☐	☐
(f) Technical typing services	☐	☐	☐
(g) Communication services	☐	☐	☐
(h) Facility services (maintenance, etc.)	☐	☐	☐
(i) Auto pool services	☐	☐	☐
(j) Company aircraft services	☐	☐	☐
(k) Wind tunnels	☐	☐	☐
(l) Other service centers *(Enter Code Y on this line if other service centers are used and identify on a continuation sheet each such service center, its Category Code, Allocation Base Code, and Rate Code. If no other service centers are used, enter Code Z.)*	☐	☐	☐

FORM CASB–DS–1   – 11 –

Appendix 8.1.   (Continued)

264

Item No.	Item Description

4.4.0 **Treatment of Variances from Actual Cost (Underabsorption or Overabsorption).** Where predetermined billing or costing rates are used to charge costs of service centers to Government contracts or other indirect cost pools (Rate Code A in Column (3) of Item 4.3.0), variances from actual costs are: (*Check the appropriate blocks(s) and if more than one is checked, explain on a continuation sheet.*)

    A. ☐ Prorated to users on the basis of charges made, at least once annually   B. ☐ All charged or credited to indirect cost pool(s) at least once annually

    Y. ☐ Other(s) (*Describe on a continuation sheet.*)   Z. ☐ Service center is not applicable to reporting unit

4.5.0 **Major Types of Indirect Costs.** (*For each pool coded other than Z in Items 4.1.0, 4.2.0 and 4.3.0, list on a continuation sheet the major functions, activities, and elements of cost included.*)

4.6.0 **Allocation Base.** (*For each allocation base code used in Items 4.1.0, 4.2.0 and 4.3.0, describe on a continuation sheet the makeup of the base; for example, if direct labor dollars are used, are overtime premium, fringe benefits, etc., included?*)

4.7.0 **Application of Overhead and G&A Rates to Specified Transactions or Costs.** This item is directed to ascertaining your practice in special situations where, in lieu of establishing a separate indirect cost pool, allocation is made from an established overhead or G&A pool at less than the normal full rate for that pool. The term "less than full rate" below applies to this type of indirect cost allocation practice. The term does *not* apply to situations where, as in some cases of off-site activities, etc., a separate indirect cost pool and base are used and the rate of such activities is lower than the "in-house" rate.

(*For each of the transactions or costs listed below, enter one of the following codes to indicate your indirect cost allocation practice with respect to that transaction or cost. If Code A, Less than full rate, is entered, describe on a continuation sheet the major types of expenses that are covered by such a rate. If Code B, Full rate, is entered, identify on a continuation sheet the pool(s) reported under Items 4.1.0, 4.2.0 and 4.3.0 which are applicable. If Code C, Combination of A and B, is entered, describe on a continuation sheet the applicable expense and pool data.*)

Rate Code

A. Less than full rate   B. Full rate
C. Combination of A and B   D. No overhead or G&A is applied
Z. Transaction or cost is not applicable to reporting unit

FORM CASB–DS–1

Appendix 8.1. (Continued)

COST ACCOUNTING STANDARDS BOARD **DISCLOSURE STATEMENT** *REQUIRED BY PUBLIC LAW 91–379*	PART IV—INDIRECT COSTS Name of Reporting Unit

Item No.	Item Description

4.7.0   **Continued.**

Transaction or Cost to Which Indirect Costs May be Allocated   **Rate Code**

     (a) Subcontract costs ☐
     (b) Purchased labor ☐
     (c) Government-furnished materials ☐
     (d) Interorganizational transfers in ☐
     (e) Interorganizational transfers out ☐
     (f) Self-constructed depreciable assets ☐
     (g) Labor on installation of assets ☐
     (h) Off-site work ☐
     (i) Other transactions or costs (*Enter Code A on this line if there are other transactions or costs to which less than full rate is applied. List such transactions or costs on a continuation sheet, and for each describe the major types of expenses covered by such a rate. If there are no other such transactions or costs, enter Code Z.*) ☐

4.8.0   **Independent Research and Development (IR&D) and Bidding and Proposal (B&P) Costs.**

4.8.1   **Independent Research and Development.** IR&D costs are defined in ASPR 15–205.35 or other pertinent procurement regulations, as revised. The full rate of all allocable manufacturing, engineering, and/or other overhead is applied to IR&D costs as if IR&D projects were under contract, and the "burdened" IR&D costs are: (*Check one.*)

     A. ☐ Allocated to Government contracts or similar cost objectives as part of the G&A rate

     B. ☐ Allocated as a separate IR&D rate

     C. ☐ Transferred to the corporate or home office level. The corporate or home office level IR&D costs are subsequently allocated back to the reporting unit for allocation as part of the unit's G&A rate

     D. ☐ Treated the same as C, except that the IR&D costs are allocated as a separate IR&D rate

     Y. ☐ Other (*Describe on a continuation sheet.*)   Z. ☐ Not applicable

4.8.2   **Bidding and Proposal.** B&P costs as defined in ASPR 15–205.3 or other pertinent procurement regulations, as revised, are treated as follows: (*Check one.*)

     A. ☐ Same as IR&D costs as checked above   Y. ☐ Other (*Describe on a continuation sheet.*)

Appendix 8.1. (Continued)

Item No.	Item Description
5.1.0	**Depreciating Tangible Assets for Government Contract Costing.** (*For each of the asset categories listed on Page 15, enter a code from A through G in Column (1) describing the method of depreciation (Code F for assets that are expensed); a code from A through E in Column (2) describing the basis for determining useful life; a code from A through C in Column (3) describing how depreciation methods or use charges are applied to property units; and a Code A, B or C in Column (4) indicating whether or not residual value is deducted from the total cost of depreciable assets. Enter Code Y in each column of an asset category where another or more than one method applies. Enter Code Z in Column (1) only, if an asset category is not applicable.*)

Column (1)—Depreciation Method Code

A. Straight-line
B. Declining balance
C. Sum-of-the-years digits
D. Machine hours
E. Unit of production
F. Expensed at acquisition
G. Use charge
Y. Other or more than one method (*Describe on a continuation sheet.*)
Z. Asset category is not applicable

Column (2)—Useful Life Code

A. U.S. Treasury Department "guideline lives"
B. Replacement experience
C. Term of Lease
D. Engineering estimate
E. As prescribed for use charge by the Office of Management and Budget Circular No. A–21
Y. Other or more than one method (*Describe on a continuation sheet.*)

Column (3)—Property Units Code

A. Individual units are accounted for separately
B. Applied to groups of assets with similar service lives
C. Applied to groups of assets with varying service lives
Y. Other or more than one method (*Describe on a continuation sheet.*)

Column (4)—Residual Value Code

A. Residual value is deducted
B. Residual value is covered by the depreciation method (e.g., declining balance)
C. Residual value is not deducted
Y. Other or more than one method (*Describe on a continuation sheet.*)

FORM CASB–DS–1

– 14 –

Appendix 8.1. (Continued)

COST ACCOUNTING STANDARDS BOARD **DISCLOSURE STATEMENT** *REQUIRED BY PUBLIC LAW 91–379*	PART V—DEPRECIATION AND CAPITALIZATION PRACTICES Name of Reporting Unit

Item No.	Item Description

5.1.0 Continued.

Asset Category	Depreciation Method Code *(1)*	Useful Life Code *(2)*	Property Units Code *(3)*	Residual Value Code *(4)*
(a) Land improvements	☐	☐	☐	☐
(b) Buildings	☐	☐	☐	☐
(c) Building improvements	☐	☐	☐	☐
(d) Leasehold improvements	☐	☐	☐	☐
(e) Machinery and equipment	☐	☐	☐	☐
(f) Furniture and fixtures	☐	☐	☐	☐
(g) Automobiles and trucks	☐	☐	☐	☐
(h) Data processing equipment	☐	☐	☐	☐
(i) Programming/reprogramming costs	☐	☐	☐	☐
(j) Patterns and dies	☐	☐	☐	☐
(k) Tools	☐	☐	☐	☐
(l) Other depreciable asset categories (*Enter Code Y on this line if other asset categories are used and enumerate on a continuation sheet each such asset category and the applicable codes. Otherwise enter Code Z.*)	☐	☐	☐	☐

5.2.0 Depreciation Practices for Costing, Financial Accounting, and Income Tax. Are depreciation practices the same for costing Government contracts as for financial accounting and income tax? (*Check one block on each line under Financial Accounting and Income Tax. Educational institutions and not-for-profit organizations need not complete this item.*)

Financial Accounting	A. Yes	B. No	Income Tax	A. Yes	B. No
(a) Methods	☐	☐	(e) Methods	☐	☐
(b) Useful lives	☐	☐	(f) Useful lives	☐	☐
(c) Property units	☐	☐	(g) Property units	☐	☐
(d) Residual values	☐	☐	(h) Residual values	☐	☐

5.3.0 Fully Depreciated Assets. Is a usage charge for fully depreciated assets charged to Government contracts? (*Check one. If Yes, describe the basis for the charge on a continuation sheet.*)

A. ☐ Yes   B. ☐ No   Z. ☐ Not applicable

FORM CASB–DS–1

Appendix 8.1. (Continued)

Item No.	Item Description

5.4.0 **Treatment of Gains and Losses on Disposition of Depreciable Property.** Gains and losses are: (*Check the appropriate block(s) and if more than one is checked, explain on a continuation sheet.*)

A. ☐ Credited or charged currently to the same overhead or G&A pools to which the depreciation of the assets was charged.

B. ☐ Taken into consideration in the depreciation cost basis of the new items, where trade-in is involved

C. ☐ Not accounted for separately, but reflected in the depreciation reserve account

D. ☐ Credited or charged to Other (Miscellaneous) Income and Expense accounts

Y. ☐ Other(s) (*Describe on a continuation sheet.*)

Z. ☐ Not applicable

5.5.0 **Capitalization or Expensing of Specified Costs.** (*Check one block on each line to indicate your practices regarding capitalization or expensing of specified costs incurred in connection with capital assets. If the same specified cost is sometimes expensed and sometimes capitalized, check both blocks and describe on a continuation sheet the circumstances when each method is used.*)

Cost	A. Expensed	B. Capitalized
(a) Freight-in	☐	☐
(b) Installation costs	☐	☐
(c) Sales taxes	☐	☐
(d) Excise taxes	☐	☐
(e) Architect-engineer fees	☐	☐
(f) Overhauls (extraordinary repairs)	☐	☐
(g) Major modifications or betterments	☐	☐

5.6.0 **Criteria for Capitalization.** (*Enter (a) the minimum dollar amount of expenditures for acquisition, addition, alteration and improvement of depreciable assets, capitalized, and (b) the minimum number of expected life years of capitalized assets. Use leading zeros for dollar amount, e.g., 0150 for $150. If more than one dollar amount or number applies, show the information for the majority of your depreciable assets, and enumerate on a continuation sheet the dollar amounts and/or number of years for each category or subcategory of assets involved which differ from those for the majority of assets.*)

(a) Minimum dollar amount ☐ 　　　(b) Minimum life years ☐

5.7.0 **Group or Mass Purchase.** Are group or mass purchases (initial complement) of similar items, which individually are less than the capitalization amount indicated above, capitalized? (*Check one.*)

A. ☐ Yes 　　　　　B. ☐ No

FORM CASB–DS–1 　　　　　　　　　　　　　　　　　　　　　– 16 –

Appendix 8.1. (Continued)

COST ACCOUNTING STANDARDS BOARD **DISCLOSURE STATEMENT** *REQUIRED BY PUBLIC LAW 91–379*	PART VI—OTHER COSTS AND CREDITS
	Name of Reporting Unit

Item No.	Item Description

6.1.0 Method of Charging and Crediting Vacation, Holiday and Sick Pay. (*Check the appropriate block(s) in each column of Items 6.1.1 and 6.1.2 to indicate the method used to charge, or credit any unused or unpaid, vacation, holiday, or sick pay for direct and indirect labor. If more than one method is checked, explain on a continuation sheet.*)

		Direct Labor *(1)*	Indirect Labor *(2)*
6.1.1	**Charges.**		
	A. When accrued (earned)	☐	☐
	B. When taken	☐	☐
	Y. Other(s) (*Describe on a continuation sheet.*)	☐	☐
6.1.2	**Credits for Unused or Unpaid Vacation, Holiday, or Sick Pay.**		
	A. Credited to Government contracts at least once annually	☐	☐
	B. Credited to indirect cost pools at least once annually	☐	☐
	C. Credited to Other (Miscellaneous) Income	☐	☐
	D. Not credited	☐	☐
	Y. Other(s) (*Describe on a continuation sheet.*)	☐	☐

6.2.0 Supplemental Unemployment (Extended Layoff) Benefit Plans. Costs of such plans are charged to Government contracts: (*Check the appropriate block(s) and if more than one is checked, explain on a continuation sheet.*)

A. ☐ When actual payments are made directly to employees B. ☐ When accrued (book accrual or funds set aside but no trust fund involved) C. ☐ When contributions are made to a nonforfeitable trust fund

D. ☐ Not charged Y. ☐ Other(s) (*Describe on a continuation sheet.*) Z. ☐ Not applicable

6.3.0 Severance Pay. Costs of normal turnover severance pay, as defined in ASPR 15–205.39(b)(i) or other pertinent procurement regulations, which are charged directly or indirectly to Government contracts, are based on: (*Check the appropriate block(s) and if more than one is checked, explain on a continuation sheet.*)

A. ☐ Actual payments made B. ☐ Accrued amounts on the basis of past experience C. ☐ Not charged

Y. ☐ Other(s) (*Describe on a continuation sheet.*) Z. ☐ Not applicable

FORM CASB–DS–1

Appendix 8.1. (Continued)

Item No.	Item Description

6.4.0 **Incidental Receipts.** (*Check the appropriate block(s) to indicate the method used to account for receipts from renting real and personal property or selling services when related costs have been charged to Government contracts. If more than one is checked, explain on a continuation sheet.*)

A. ☐ The entire amount of the receipt is credited to the same indirect cost pools to which related costs have been charged

B. ☐ The amount of the receipt, less an allowance for profits, is credited to the same indirect cost pools to which related costs have been charged; the profits are credited to Other (Miscellaneous) Income

C. ☐ The entire amount of the receipt is credited directly to Other (Miscellaneous) Income

Y. ☐ Other(s) (*Describe on a continuation sheet.*)

Z. ☐ Not applicable.

6.5.0 **Proceeds from Employee Welfare Activities.** Employee welfare activities include all of those activities set forth in ASPR 15–205.10(a) or other pertinent procurement regulations. (*Check the appropriate block(s) to indicate the practice followed in accounting for the proceeds from such activities. If more than one is checked, explain on a continuation sheet.*)

A. ☐ Proceeds are turned over to an employee-welfare organization or fund; such proceeds are reduced by all applicable costs such as depreciation, heat, light and power

B. ☐ Same as A., except the proceeds are not reduced by all applicable costs

C. ☐ Proceeds are credited at least once annually to the appropriate indirect cost pools to which costs have been charged

D. ☐ Proceeds are credited to Other (Miscellaneous) Income

Y. ☐ Other(s) (*Describe on a continuation sheet.*)

Z. ☐ Not applicable

Appendix 8.1. (Continued)

COST ACCOUNTING STANDARDS BOARD **DISCLOSURE STATEMENT** *REQUIRED BY PUBLIC LAW 91-379*	PART VII—DEFERRED COMPENSATION AND INSURANCE COSTS
	Name of Reporting Unit

Item No.	Item Description

Instructions for Part VII

This part covers pension costs and certain types of deferred incentive compensation and insurance costs. Some organizations may record all of these costs at the corporate or home office level, while others may record them at subordinate organization levels. Still others may record a portion of these costs at the corporate or home office level and the balance at subordinate organization levels. Reporting units, therefore, should obtain the necessary information from the organizational level at which such costs are recorded.

7.1.0   **Pension Costs.** The actuarial terms used in this item are defined in Opinion Number 8 of the Accounting Principles Board, American Institute of Certified Public Accountants.

7.1.1   **Pension Plans Charged to Government Contracts.** Does your organization have one or more pension plans whose costs are charged to Government contracts? (*Check one.*)

    A. ☐ Yes (*If Yes, list each such plan on a continuation sheet. Indicate the approximate number and type of employees covered by each plan and whether the plan is, or is not, qualified under Internal Revenue Service criteria. Complete Items 7.1.2 through 7.1.9 for the three plans covering the greatest number of employees whose pension costs are charged to Government contracts.*)

    B. ☐ No (*If No, skip to Item 7.2.0.*)

7.1.2   **Extent of Funding.** (*Check one block for each plan. In the event the amount funded for each plan is different from the amount charged on the books of account, describe the difference on a continuation sheet.*)

	Plan I	Plan II	Plan III
A. Normal costs only	☐	☐	☐
B. Normal costs plus interest on past or prior service costs	☐	☐	☐
C. Normal costs plus an amortized portion of past or prior service costs	☐	☐	☐
Y. Other (*Describe on a continuation sheet.*)	☐	☐	☐
Z. Not applicable	☐	☐	☐

7.1.3   **Actuarial Cost Method.** (*Check one block for each plan to show the method used to compute normal and past or prior service costs.*)

A. Accrued benefit cost	☐	☐	☐
B. Aggregate	☐	☐	☐
C. Attained age—initial liability frozen	☐	☐	☐
D. Attained age—initial liability not frozen	☐	☐	☐
E. Entry age—initial liability frozen	☐	☐	☐
F. Entry age—initial liability not frozen	☐	☐	☐
G. Individual level premium	☐	☐	☐
Y. Other (*Describe on a continuation sheet.*)	☐	☐	☐
Z. Not applicable	☐	☐	☐

FORM CASB–DS–1   – 19 –

Appendix 8.1. (Continued)

<table>
<tr><td colspan="2">COST ACCOUNTING STANDARDS BOARD
DISCLOSURE STATEMENT
REQUIRED BY PUBLIC LAW 91–379</td><td>PART VII—DEFERRED COMPENSATION
AND INSURANCE COSTS</td></tr>
<tr><td></td><td></td><td>Name of Reporting Unit</td></tr>
</table>

Item No.	Item Description

7.1.4 Frequency of Actuarial Reevaluations. (*Check one block for each plan.*)

	Plan I	Plan II	Plan III
A. Annually	☐	☐	☐
B. 2–3 years	☐	☐	☐
C. 4–5 years	☐	☐	☐
Y. Other (*Describe on a continuation sheet.*)	☐	☐	☐
Z. Not applicable	☐	☐	☐

7.1.5 Criteria for Changing Actuarial Computations and Assumptions. (*Describe on a continuation sheet your criteria for determining when actuarial assumptions and computations for your funded plan(s) are changed.*)

7.1.6 Amortization of Past or Prior Service Costs. (*Check one block for each plan to show the period over which past or prior service costs are amortized.*)

	Plan I	Plan II	Plan III
A. 10 years or less	☐	☐	☐
B. 11–20 years	☐	☐	☐
C. 21–40 years	☐	☐	☐
Y. More than one amortization schedule (*Describe on a continuation sheet.*)	☐	☐	☐
Z. Not applicable	☐	☐	☐

7.1.7 Adjustment for Actuarial Gains and Losses. (*Check one block for each plan to show the period for which costs are adjusted for actuarial gains and losses. If actuarial losses for a plan are treated differently from actuarial gains, describe the difference on a continuation sheet.*)

	Plan I	Plan II	Plan III
A. Adjustment of past service costs	☐	☐	☐
B. Adjustment of current year's costs	☐	☐	☐
C. Adjustment of future years' costs	☐	☐	☐
Y. Other (*Describe on a continuation sheet.*)	☐	☐	☐
Z. Not applicable	☐	☐	☐

7.1.8 Unrealized Gains and Losses. Do the actuarial gains and losses reported in Item 7.1.7 above include unrealized gains and losses? (*Check one block for each plan. If Yes is checked, describe the method of recognition of such gains and losses on a continuation sheet.*)

	Plan I	Plan II	Plan III
A. Yes	☐	☐	☐
B. No	☐	☐	☐
Z. Not applicable	☐	☐	☐

FORM CASB–DS–1

Appendix 8.1. (Continued)

COST ACCOUNTING STANDARDS BOARD **DISCLOSURE STATEMENT** *REQUIRED BY PUBLIC LAW 91–379*	PART VII—DEFERRED COMPENSATION AND INSURANCE COSTS
	Name of Reporting Unit

Item No.	Item Description

7.1.9 **Amortization of Actuarial Gains and Losses.** (*Check one block for each plan to show the period over which actuarial gains and losses are amortized. If the amortization of actuarial losses for a plan is treated differently from the amortization of actuarial gains, describe the difference on a continuation sheet.*)

	Plan I	Plan II	Plan III
A. 10 years or less	☐	☐	☐
B. 11–20 years	☐	☐	☐
C. More than 20 years	☐	☐	☐
Y. Other (*Describe on a continuation sheet.*)	☐	☐	☐
Z. Not applicable	☐	☐	☐

7.2.0 **Deferred Incentive Compensation Charged to Government Contracts.**

7.2.1 **Deferred Incentive Compensation.** Does your organization award deferred incentive compensation (i.e., profit sharing, stock bonus, etc.) which is charged to Government contracts? (*Check one.*)

    A. ☐ Yes (*If Yes is checked, list each plan by name or title on a continuation sheet and show the approximate number and type of employees covered. Complete Items 7.2.2 and 7.2.3 for the three plans covering the greatest number of employees whose deferred incentive compensation cost is charged to Government contracts.*)

    B. ☐ No (*If No is checked, skip to Item 7.3.0.*)

7.2.2 **Qualification of Plan.** (*Check one block for each plan.*)

	Plan I	Plan II	Plan III
A. Qualifies under section 401(a) of the Internal Revenue Code of 1954, as amended	☐	☐	☐
B. Does not qualify under section 401(a) of the Internal Revenue Code of 1954, as amended	☐	☐	☐

7.2.3 **Method of Charging Costs to Government Contracts** (*Check one block for each plan.*)

	Plan I	Plan II	Plan III
A. When accrued	☐	☐	☐
B. When contributions are made to a trust fund	☐	☐	☐
C. When paid directly to employees	☐	☐	☐
D. When other "nonqualified" payments are made	☐	☐	☐
Y. Other or more than one method (*Describe on a continuation sheet.*)	☐	☐	☐

7.3.0 **Employee Group Insurance Charged to Government Contracts.** (*Includes coverage for life, hospital, surgical, medical, long-term disability, accident, etc.*)

FORM CASB–DS–1   – 21 –

Appendix 8.1. (Continued)

Item No.	Item Description

7.3.1 Method of Providing Insurance. (*Check one.*)

A. ☐ All by purchase

B. ☐ All self-insured (*If checked, skip to Item 7.4.0.*)

C. ☐ Combination of A and B above (*Describe on a continuation sheet.*)

Z. ☐ Not applicable (*If checked, skip to Item 7.5.0.*)

7.3.2 Type of Purchased Insurance Plans. (*Check one.*)

A. ☐ Retrospective rating (also called experience rating plan or retention plan)

B. ☐ Manually rated

Y. ☐ Other or more than one type (*Describe on a continuation sheet.*)

7.3.3 Treatment of Earned Refunds and Dividends from Purchased Insurance Plans. Refunds are also called experience rating credits or retroactive rating credits. All earned refunds and dividends allocable to Government contracts: (*Check one.*)

A. ☐ Are credited directly or indirectly to contracts in the policy year earned, in the same manner as the premiums are charged

B. ☐ Are credited directly or indirectly to contracts in the year received in the same manner as the premiums are charged, not necessarily in the year earned

C. ☐ Which are estimated to be received in the future are accrued each year, as applicable, to currently reflect the net annual cost of the insurance

D. ☐ Or portions thereof are not credited or refunded to the contractor each year and are retained by the carriers as reserves. (*If D is checked, describe on a continuation sheet (i) the purposes of the reserves, other than "claims reserves" retained by carriers and (ii) whether such reserves are refundable on call or upon termination of the policies, clauses, or auxiliary agreements which provide for reserve retentions.*)

Y. ☐ Other or more than one method (*Describe on a continuation sheet.*)

7.3.4 Employee Contributions (Contributory Purchased Insurance Plans). (*Check one.*)

A. ☐ Plans provide that employees contribute fixed amount, employer is responsible for balance

B. ☐ Plans provide for fixed percentage participation by both employer and employee

Y. ☐ Other or more than one method (*Describe on a continuation sheet.*)

Z. ☐ Not applicable

7.3.5 Employee Sharing in Refunds and Dividends (Contributory Purchased Insurance Plans). (*Check one.*)

A. ☐ Employees do not participate in refunds and dividends unless employer's contribution is less than the refunds and dividends

B. ☐ Employees share in refunds and dividends in the same fixed amount or percentage ratio as their contributions to premium costs

C. ☐ Employees do not share in refunds and dividends

Y. ☐ Other or more than one method (*Describe on a continuation sheet.*)

Z. ☐ Not applicable

FORM CASB–DS–1

– 22 –

Appendix 8.1. (Continued)

COST ACCOUNTING STANDARDS BOARD **DISCLOSURE STATEMENT** *REQUIRED BY PUBLIC LAW 91–379*	PART VII—DEFERRED COMPENSATION AND INSURANCE COSTS
	Name of Reporting Unit

Item No.	Item Description

7.4.0 **Self-Insurance Programs (Employee Group Insurance).** Costs of the self-insurance programs are charged to Government contracts: (*Check one.*)

A. ☐ When accrued (book accrual only)　B. ☐ When contributions are made to a nonforfeitable fund　C. ☐ When contributions are made to a forfeitable fund

D. ☐ When the benefits are paid to employees　E. ☐ When amounts are paid to an employee welfare plan or union　Y. ☐ Other or more than one method (*Describe on a continuation sheet.*)

Z. ☐ Not applicable

7.5.0 **Workmen's Compensation, Liability and Casualty Insurance (Purchased Insurance Only).** All allocable earned refunds and dividends under retrospectively rated workmen's compensation and liability insurance policies, and dividends and deposit refunds under casualty insurance policies, are: (*Check one.*)

A. ☐ Credited directly or indirectly to Government contracts in the year earned　B. ☐ Credited directly or indirectly to Government contracts in the year received, not necessarily in the year earned

C. ☐ Accrued each year, as applicable, to currently reflect the net annual cost of the insurance　D. ☐ Not credited or refunded to the contractor but are retained by the carriers as reserves

Y. ☐ Other or more than one method (*Describe on a continuation sheet.*)　Z. ☐ Not applicable

7.6.0 **Self-Insurance Programs (Workmen's Compensation, Liability and Casualty Insurance).**

7.6.1 **Workmen's Compensation and Liability.** Costs of such self-insurance programs are charged to Government contracts: (*Check one.*)

A. ☐ When claims are paid or losses are incurred (no provision for reserves)　B. ☐ When provisions for reserves are recorded based on the present value of the liability

C. ☐ When provisions for reserves are recorded based on the full or undiscounted value, as contrasted with present value, of the liability　D. ☐ When funds are set aside or contributions are made to a fund

Y. ☐ Other or more than one method (*Describe on a continuation sheet.*)　Z. ☐ Not applicable

7.6.2 **Casualty Insurance.** Costs of such self-insurance programs are charged to Government contracts: (*Check one.*)

A. ☐ When losses are incurred (no provision for reserves)　B. ☐ When provisions for reserves are recorded based on replacement costs

C. ☐ When provisions for reserves are recorded based on reproduction costs new less observed depreciation (market value) excluding the value of land and other indestructibles　D. ☐ Losses are charged to retained earnings with no charge to contracts (no provision for reserves)

Y. ☐ Other or more than one method (*Describe on a continuation sheet.*)　Z. ☐ Not applicable

FORM CASB–DS–1

Appendix 8.1. (Continued)

<table>
<tr><td colspan="2">COST ACCOUNTING STANDARDS BOARD
DISCLOSURE STATEMENT
REQUIRED BY PUBLIC LAW 91–379</td><td>PART VIII—CORPORATE OR
GROUP EXPENSES

Name of Reporting Unit</td></tr>
<tr><td>Item
No.</td><td colspan="2">Item Description</td></tr>
</table>

Instructions for Part VIII

For corporate (home) office, or group (intermediate management) office, as applicable (includes home office type operations of joint ventures, partnerships, etc.).

Sales data for this part should cover the most recently completed fiscal year. For a corporate (home) office, such data should cover the entire corporation. For a group office, they should cover the subordinate organizations managed by that group office. "Government Sales" includes sales under both prime contracts and subcontracts.

8.1.0 **Annual Total Sales (Government and Commercial).** (*Check one.*)

A. ☐ Less than $50 million   B. ☐ $50–$100 million   C. ☐ $101–$200 million

D. ☐ $201–$500 million   E. ☐ $501 million–$1 billion   F. ☐ Over $1 billion

8.2.0 **Approximate Percentage of Government Sales to Annual Total Sales.** (*Check one.*)

A. ☐ Less than 5%   B. ☐ 5%–10%   C. ☐ 11%–25%

D. ☐ 26%–50%   E. ☐ 51%–80%   F. ☐ Over 80%

8.3.0 **Expenses or Pools of Expenses and Methods of Allocation.** For classification purposes, three methods of allocation are defined: (i) Directly Chargeable—those expenses that are charged to specific corporate segments for centrally performed or purchased services; (ii) Separately Allocated—those individual or groups of expenses which are allocated only to a limited group of corporate segments; and (iii) Overall Allocation—the remaining expenses which are allocated to all or most corporate segments on an overall basis. Corporate segments, as used here, refer to divisions, product departments, plants, or profit centers of a corporation with production and, usually, profit responsibility, reporting to corporate headquarters directly or through intermediate organizations. The term includes Government-owned, contractor-operated (GOCO) plants, foreign operations, subsidiary corporations and joint ventures.

Allocation Base Codes

A. Sales
B. Cost of sales
C. Cost input (direct material, direct labor, other direct costs and applicable overhead)
D. Total cost incurred (cost input plus G&A expenses)
E. Prime cost (direct material, direct labor, and other direct costs)
F. Processing or conversion cost (direct labor and applicable overhead)
G. Direct labor dollars
H. Direct labor hours

I. Machine hours
J. Usage
K. Unit of product
L. Direct material cost
M. Total payroll dollars (direct and indirect employees)
N. Headcount or number of employees (direct and indirect employees)
O. Square feet
Y. Other or more than one basis (*Describe on a continuation sheet.*)

FORM CASB–DS–1

– 24 –

Appendix 8.1. (Continued)

Item No.	Item Description

(Enter the type of expenses or the name of the expense pool(s) and one of the Allocation Base Codes A through O, or Y, to indicate the basis of allocation. Use a continuation sheet if additional space is required.)

	Type of Expenses or Name of Pool of Expenses	**Allocation Base Code**
8.3.1	**Directly Chargeable**	
	(a)	☐
	(b)	☐
	(c)	☐
	(d)	☐
	(e)	☐
8.3.2	**Separately Allocated**	
	(a)	☐
	(b)	☐
	(c)	☐
	(d)	☐
	(e)	☐
8.3.3	**Overall Allocation**	
	(a)	☐
	(b)	☐
	(c)	☐
	(d)	☐
	(e)	☐

8.4.0 **Major Types of Expense.** *(For each pool reported in Items 8.3.1, 8.3.2 and 8.3.3, list on a continuation sheet the major functions, activities, and elements of cost included.)*

8.5.0 **Allocation Base.** *(For each Allocation Base used in Items 8.3.2 and 8.3.3, describe on a continuation sheet the makeup of the base; for example, if direct labor dollars is used, are overtime premium, fringe benefits, etc., included?)*

8.6.0 **Overall Allocation.** Are expenses in this category, Item 8.3.3, allocated to all corporate segments? *(Check one. If No is checked, list on a continuation sheet the names of excluded corporate segments and the reasons for their exclusion from the allocation.)*

A. ☐ Yes   B. ☐ No

FORM CASB–DS–1

– 25 –

Appendix 8.1. (Continued)

COST ACCOUNTING STANDARDS BOARD **DISCLOSURE STATEMENT** *REQUIRED BY PUBLIC LAW 91–379*	PART VIII—CORPORATE OR GROUP EXPENSES
	Name of Reporting Unit

Item No.	Item Description
8.7.0	**Transfer of Expenses.** Are there normally transfers of expenses from corporate segments to corporate or group office? (*Check one. If Yes is checked, identify on a continuation sheet the classifications of expense, the names of the corporate segments incurring the expense, and the corporate or group office pools in which the expenses are included.*) A. ☐ Yes B. ☐ No
8.8.0	**Fixed Management Charges.** Are fixed amounts of expenses charged to any corporate segments in lieu of a prorata or allocation basis? (*Check one. If Yes is checked, list on a continuation sheet the names of such corporate segments and the basis for making fixed management charges.*) A. ☐ Yes B. ☐ No
8.9.0	**Government Owned/Contractor Operated (GOCO) Plants.** Are corporate or group office expenses allocated to GOCO plants? (*Check one. If Yes is checked, describe on a continuation sheet the types of expenses involved and the method of allocation.*) A. ☐ Yes B. ☐ No Z. ☐ Not applicable

FORM CASB–DS–1   – 26 –

Appendix 8.1. (Continued)

COST ACCOUNTING STANDARDS BOARD **DISCLOSURE STATEMENT** *REQUIRED BY PUBLIC LAW 91–379*	CONTINUATION SHEET Page of Pages
	Name of Reporting Unit

Item No.	Item Description

FORM CASB–DS–1

Appendix 8.1. (Continued)

Chapter Nine

Contract Financing

BACKGROUND

FAR Part 32 defines government *contract financing* in terms of progress payments, guaranteed loans, and advance payments for contracts other than cost reimbursement contracts. The government's periodic reimbursement of costs incurred under cost reimbursement type contracts is not considered "financing" under this definition and thus is covered by different sections of the regulations.   The government's financing policy may appear to reflect a certain degree of altruism; however, the underlying reason for the government's willingness to provide financial assistance to contractors is the benefit derived from spreading its business to the broadest possible base of potential suppliers. A broad base of suppliers enhances competition, opportunities for alternative selections, and expansion capability in times of national emergency. The government's financing policy is also an essential element in implementing its small business policy. While government financing is designed to broaden the supplier base, it is generally available to provide working capital only, and not facilities expansion. An exception would be where the government procures facilities under contract.

To be considered eligible for government financing, a contractor must meet certain minimum standards for "responsibility," which means that the contractor must:

Have or be able to obtain (1) adequate financial resources (including government financing), (2) the necessary organization, and (3) necessary facilities to perform the contract.

Be able to meet necessary performance and delivery schedules, considering existing commercial and government commitments.

Have a satisfactory performance record.

Be considered reputable.

Be qualified and eligible to receive a contract under applicable laws and regulations.

Government financing may be necessary for successful contract performance. Therefore, a competent and capable contractor who is considered responsible but requires some form of government financing will be treated no differently than a contractor who has no need for financial assistance. FAR 32. 107 (a) states:

> If the contractor or offeror meets the standards prescribed for responsible prospective contractors . . . the contracting officer shall not treat the contractor's need for contract financing as a handicap for a contract awards; e.g., as a responsibility factor or evaluation criterion.

In selecting any appropriate financing method, contractors are not expected to resort to loans or credit at excessive interest rates or exorbitant charges, or from agencies of the government outside the specific procurement activity.

A company that did not initially request government financing may subsequently need financial assistance. A determination after contract award that government financing is required will be made if financing is essential to the successful performance of the contract. To this end, FAR 32. 107 (g) provides that:

> The contractor should not be disqualified from contract financing solely because the contractor failed to indicate a need for contract financing before the contract was awarded.

A progress payment clause is usually routine and when incorporated into a new contract at the time of award does not require any separate consideration by the contractor. However, the government must receive adequate consideration before an existing contract is modified to insert a progress payment clause. Contracts may not be modified except in the interest of the government, although the consideration need not be monetary. Where the need for progress payments is not related to an action by the government, FAR 32. 501 (c) and (d) requires some consideration . by providing that:

> The contractor may provide the new consideration by monetary or nonmonetary means. A monetary consideration could be a reduction in the contract price. A nonmonetary consideration could be the incorporation of terms in the contract modification giving the Government a new and substantial benefit.
>
> The fair and reasonable consideration should approximate as nearly as practicably ascertainable the amount by which the price would have been smaller had the Progress Payments clause been contained in the initial contract.

An example of additional consideration of this nature might be an accelerated delivery schedule.

Many forms of financing are available to government contractors, ranging from those in which the government assumes no risk at all to those in which the government assumes total risk. Although the type of financing available depends on the specific situation and conditions, the nature of the contract, the contractor's needs, and regulatory or statutory restrictions, FAR 32.106 establishes the following order of preference:

1. Private financing on reasonable terms (without governmental guarantee), supplemented by government financing to the extent reasonably required.

2. Customary progress payments (progress payments that conform to certain requirements as to preproduction period, contract size, and percentage of payments) or progress payments based on a percentage or stage of completion (confined to contracts for construction, shipbuilding, and ship conversion, alteration, or repair). Guaranteed loans may be preferable to customary progress payments when indicated by a contractor and financing institution.
3. Guaranteed loans (with appropriate participation of financial insitutions).
4. Unusual progress payments (progress payments not considered to be customary progress payments).
5. Advance payments.

PRIVATE FINANCING AND ASSIGNMENT OF CLAIMS

For obvious reasons, the government prefers that contractors secure financing from the private sector. This may be accomplished in numerous ways, such as issuing stocks or bonds, using idle funds, or obtaining bank loans. The use of incentive-type contracts may enhance a company's ability to obtain financing from private sources through the potential to increase the percentage of profit.

Although Federal law generally prohibits the assignment of claims against the government, contractors can use government contracts as collateral on loans under the provisions of the Assignment of Claims Act of 1940 (31 U.S.C. 203, 41 U.S.C. 15). The standard "assignment of claims" clause, which is included in all government contracts, provides the contractual basis pursuant to the act for a government contractor to assign monies payable under the contract to a bank or other approved financial institution.

The assignee is required to file written notice of the assignment and a copy of the assignment instrument with the contracting officer, the disbursing officer, and the surety on any contract. Timely notice is important. An assignee's claim for funds paid to the contractor after execution of an assignment may be denied if the government disbursing officer has not received the required written notification from the assignee at the time of payment.[1]

The "assignment of claims" clause (Fig. 9.1) protects a bank that lends money on the basis of the assignment of payments under the government con-

(a) The Contractor, under the Assignment of Claims Act, as amended, 31 U.S.C. 203, 41 U.S.C. 15 (hereafter referred to as the "the Act"), may assign its rights to be paid amounts due or to become due as a result of the performance of this contract to a bank, trust company, or other financing institution, including any Federal lending agency. The assignee under such an assignment may thereafter further assign or reassign its right under the original assignment to any type of financing institution decribed in the preceding sentence.

(b) Any assignment or reassignment authorized under the Act and this clause shall cover all unpaid amounts payable under this contract, and shall not be made to more than one party, except that an assignment or reassignment may be made to one party as agent or trustee for two or more parties participating in the financing of this contract.

(c) The Contractor shall not furnish or disclose to any assignee under this contract any classified document (including this contract) or information related to work under this contract until the Contracting Officer authorizes such action in writing.

(End of clause)

Figure 9.1. Assignment of claims clause, FAR 52, 232-23.

tract. Under the assignment, the government pays the bank or other approved financial institution directly. Once paid, the money is not subject to later recovery by the government. In addition, the clause provides, in time of war or national emergency, that amounts payable under the contract are generally not subject to set-off for any liability arising independently of the contract or for any liability arising from renegotiation, fines, penalties or taxes, and social security contributions whether or not independent of the contract. This provision, however, does not exempt from offsets, penalties withheld or collected in accordance with the terms of the contract. Thus, withholding that is required under the contract, such as for failure to comply with the Walsh Healy Act, are not exempt from offset.[2]

Since the Assignment of Claims Act no longer requires a loan to be tied to a particular security, the use of a revolving credit financing device is considered acceptable. However, an assignment of a claim against the government should identify the particular contract(s) involved. Banks are entitled to payments due under government contracts by virtue of a blanket security agreement where the existence of a valid assignment applicable to contract payments is adequately documented and the loan note that assigns all accounts receivable to the bank contains a schedule of the contractor's accounts receivable, including the contract account.[3] However, it has been determined that a bank is not entitled to monies owed the contractor when the blanket assignment does not comply with the Assignment of Claims Act, such as where the government has not been notified of the assignment and the bank's security agreement has not been amended to make the agreement part of the blanket assignment.[4]

Private financing through assignment of claims keeps the government out of the financing business. It also benefits the contractor in that time is not consumed by government reviews prior to the approval of loans. The substantial disadvantage is that the interest expense incurred on commercial loans is not reimbursable under government contracts.

PROGRESS PAYMENTS

Contracts requiring the use of significant contractor working capital for extended periods generally provide for progress payments when the contractor is reliable, is in satisfactory financial condition, and has an *adequate accounting and control system* (see Fig.9.2). Payments are made as work progresses, as measured by cost incurred, percentage of completion, or other measure of the specific stages of physical completion. As previously stated, progress payments based on percentages or stages of physical completion are normally restricted to construction type contracts or shipbuilding, conversion, alteration, or repair contracts. Consequently, most progress payments are based on incurred costs.

Customary Progress Payments

Customary progress payments are generally considered reasonably necessary when a contract, or a grouping of contracts, exceeds $1 Million ($100,000 for small business concerns) and lead time between the initial incurrence of cost and the first delivery or completion of service extends 6 months (4 months for small business concerns). Progress payments are not permissible if the items are quick turnover types for which progress payments are not a customary commercial practice. Examples would include clothing, medical supplies, and

PROGRESS PAYMENTS (APR 1984)

Progress payments shall be made to the Contractor when requested as work progresses, but not more frequently than monthly in amounts approved by the Contracting Officer, under the following conditions:

(a) *Computation of amounts.* (1) Unless the Contractor requests a smaller amount, each progress payment shall be computed as (i) 80 percent of the Contractor's cumulative total costs under this contract, as shown by records maintained by the Contractor for the purpose of obtaining payment under Government contracts, plus (ii) progress payments to subcontractors (see paragraph (j) below), all less the sum of all previous progress payments made by the Government under this contract. Cost of money that would be allowable under 31.205-10 of the Federal Acquisition Regulation shall be deemed an incurred cost for progress payment purposes.

(2) The following conditions apply to the timing of including costs in progress payment requests:

(i) The costs of supplies and services purchased by the Contractor directly for this contract may be included only after payment by cash, check, or other form of actual payment.

(ii) Costs for the following may be included when incurred, even if before payment, when the Contractor is not delinquent in payment of the costs of contract performance in the ordinary course of business:

(A) Materials issued from the Contractor's stores inventory and placed in the production process for use on this contract.

(B) Direct labor, direct travel, and other direct in-house costs.

(C) Properly allocable and allowable indirect costs.

(iii) Accrued costs of Contractor contributions under employee pension, profit sharing, and stock ownership plans shall be excluded until actually paid unless—

(A) The Contractor's practice is to contribute to the plans quarterly or more frequently; and

(B) The contribution does not remain unpaid 30 days after the end of the applicable quarter or shorter payment period (any contributions remaining unpaid shall be excluded from the Contractor's total costs for progress payments until paid).

(iv) If the contract is subject to the special transition method authorized in Cost Accounting Standard (CAS) 410, Allocation of Business Unit General and Administrative Expense to Final Cost Objective, General and Administrative expenses (G&A) shall not be included in progress payment requests until the suspense account prescribed in CAS 410 is less than—

(A) Five million dollars; or

(B) The value of the work-in-process inventories under contracts entered into after the suspense account was established (only a pro rata share of the G&A allocable to the excess of the inventory over the suspense account value is includable in progress payment requests under this contract).

(3) The Contractor shall not include the following in total costs for progress payment purposes in subparagraph (a)(1)(i) above:

(i) Costs that are not reasonable, allocable to this contract, and consistent with sound and generally accepted accounting principles and practices.

(ii) Costs incurred by subcontractors or suppliers.

(iii) Costs ordinarily capitalized and subject to depreciation or amortization except for the properly depreciated or amortized protion of such costs.

(iv) Payments made or amounts payable to subscontractors or suppliers, except for—

(A) Completed work, including partial deliveries, to which the Contractor has acquired title: and

(B) Work under cost-reimbursement or time-and-material subcontracts to which the Contractor has acquired title.

(4) The amount of unliquidated progress payments may exceed neither (i) the progress payments made against incomplete work (including allowable unliquidated progress payments to subcontractors) nor (ii) the value for progress payment purposes, of the incomplete work. Incomplete work shall be considered to be the supplies and services required by this contract, for which delivery and invoicing by the Contractor and acceptance by the Government are incomplete.

(5) The total amount of progress payments shall not exceed 80 percent of the total contract price.

(6) If a progress payment or the unliquidated progress payments exceed the amounts permitted by subparagraphs (a)(4) or (a)(5) above, the Contractor shall repay the amount of such excess to the Government on demand.

(b) *Liquidation* Except as provided in the Termination for Convenience of the Government clause, all progress payments shall be liquidated by deducting from any payment under this contract, other than advance or progress payments, the unliquidated progress payments, or 80 percent of the amount invoiced, whichever is less. The Contractor shall repay to the Government any amounts required by a retroactive price reduction, after computing liquidations and payments on past invoices

Figure 9.2. Progress payments clause, FAR 52.232-16.

at the reduced prices and adjusting the unliquidated progress payments accordingly. The Government reserves the right to unilaterally change from the ordinary liquidation rate to an alternate rate when deemed appropriate for proper contract financing.

(c) *Reduction or suspension.* The Contracting Officer may reduce or suspend progress payments, increase the rate of liquidation, or take a combination of these actions, after finding on substantial evidence any of the following conditions:

(1) The Contractor failed to comply with any material requirement of this contract (which includes paragraphs (f) and (g) below).

(2) Performance of this contract is endangered by the Contractor's (i) failure to make progress or (ii) unsatisfactory financial condition.

(3) Inventory allocated to this contract substantially exceeds reasonable requirements.

(4) The Contractor is delinquent in payment of the costs of performing this contract in the ordinary course of business.

(5) The unliquidated progress payments exceed the fair value of the work accomplished on the undelivered portion of this contract.

(6) The Contractor is realizing less profit than that reflected in the establishment of any alternate liquidation rate in paragraph (b) above, and that rate is less than the progress payment rate stated in subparagraph (a)(1) above.

(d) *Title.* (1) Title to the property described in this paragraph (d) shall vest in the Government. Vestiture shall be immediately upon the date of this contract, for property acquired or produced before that date. Otherwise, vestiture shall occur when the property is or should have been allocable or properly chargeable to this contract.

(2) "Property," as used in this clause. includes all of the below-described items acquired or produced by the Contractor that are or should be allocable or properly chargeable to this contract under sound and generally accepted accounting principles and practices.

(i) Parts, materials, inventories, and work in process:

(ii) Special tooling and special test equipment to which the Government is to acquire title under any other clause of this contract;

(iii) Nondurable (i.e., noncapital) tools, jigs, dies, fixtures, molds, patterns, taps, gauges, test equipment, and other similar manufacturing aids, title to which would not be obtained as special tooling under subparagraph (ii) above; and

(iv) Drawings and technical data, to the extent the Contractor or subcontractors are required to deliver them to the Government by other clauses of this contract.

(3) Although title to property is in the Government under this clause, other applicable clauses of this contract, e.g., the termination or special tooling clauses, shall determine the handling and disposition of the property.

(4) The Contractor may sell any scrap resulting from production under this contract without requesting the Contracting Officer's approval, but the proceeds shall be credited against the costs of performance.

(5) To acquire for its own use or dispose of property to which title is vested in the Government under this clause, the Contractor must obtain the Contracting Officer's advance approval of the action and the terms. The Contractor shall (i) exclude the allocable costs of the property from the costs of contract performance, and (ii) repay to the Government any amount of unliquidated progress payments allocable to the property. Repayment may be by cash or credit memorandum.

(6) When the Contractor completes all of the obligations under this contract, including liquidation of all progress payments, title shall vest in the Contractor for all property (or the proceeds thereof) not—

(i) Delivered to, and accepted by, the Government under this contract; or

(ii) Incorporated in supplies delivered to and accepted by, the Government under this contract and to which title is vested in the Government under this clause.

(7) The terms of this contract concerning liability for Government-furnished property shall not apply to property to which the Government acquired title solely under this clause.

(e) *Risk of loss.* Before delievery to and acceptance by the Government, the Contractor shall bear the risk of loss for property, the title to which vests in the Government under this clause, except to the extent the Government expressly assumes the risk. The Contractor shall repay the Government an amount equal to the unliquidated progress payments that are based on costs allocable to property that is damaged, lost, stolen, or destroyed.

(f) *Control of costs and property.* The Contractor shall maintain an accounting system and controls adequate for the proper administration of this clause.

(g) *Reports and access to records.* The Contractor shall promptly furnish reports, certificates, financial statements, and other pertinent information reasonably requested by the Contracting Officer for the

Figure 9.2. (Continued)

administration of this clause. Also the Contractor shall give the Government reasonable opportunity to examine and verify the Contractor's books, records, and accounts.

(h) *Special terms regarding default.* If this contract is terminated under the Default clause, (i) the Contractor shall on demand repay to the Government the amount of unliquidated progress payments and (ii) title shall vest in the Contractor, on full liquidation of progress payments, for all property for which the Government elects not to require delivery under the Default clause. The Government shall be liable for no payment except as provided by the Default clause.

(i) *Reservations of rights.* (1) No payment or vesting of title under this clause shall (i) excuse the Contractor from performance of obligations under this contract or (ii) constitute a waiver of any of the rights or remedies of the parties under the contract.

(2) The Government's right and remedies under this clause (i) shall not be exclusive but rather shall be in addition to any other rights and remedies provided by law or this contract and (ii) shall not be affected by delayed, partial, or omitted exercise of any right, remedy, power, or privilege, nor shall such exercise or any single exercise preclude or impair any further exercise under this clause or the exercise of any other right power, or privilege of the Government.

(j) *Progress payments to subcontractors.* The amounts mentioned in (a)(1)(ii) above shall be all progress payments to subcontractors or divisions, if the following conditions are met:

(1) The amounts included are limited to (i) the unliquidated remainder of progress payments made plus (ii) for small business concerns any unpaid subcontractor requests for progress payments that the Contractor has approved for current payment in the ordinary course of business.

(2) The subcontract or interdivisional order is expected to involve a minimum of approximately 6 months between the beginning of work and the first delivery, or, if the subcontractor is a small business concern 4 months.

(3) The terms of the subcontract or interdividional order concerning progress payments—

(i) Are substantially similar to the terms of the clause at 52.232-16, Progress Payments, of the Federal Acquisition Regulation (or that clause with its Alternate I for any subcontractor that is a small business concern);

(ii) Are at least as favorable to the Government as the terms of this clause:

(iii) Are not more favorable to the subcontractor or division than the terms of this clause are to the Contractor:

(iv) Are in conformance with the requirements of paragraph 32.504(e) of the Federal Acquisition Regulation; and

(v) Subordinate all subcontractor rights concerning property to which the Government has title under the subcontract to the Government's right to require delivery of the property to the Government if (A) the Contractor defaults or (B) the subcontractor becomes bankrupt or insolvent.

(4) The progress payment rate in the subcontract is the customary rate used by the Contracting Agency, depending on whether the subcontractor is or is not a small business concern.

(5) The parties agree concerning any proceeds received by the Government for property to which title has vested in the Government under the subcontract terms, that the proceeds shall be applied to reducing any unliquidated progress payments by the Government to the Contractor under this contract.

(6) If no unliquidated progress payments to the Contractor remain, but there are unliquidated progress payments that the Contractor has made to any subcontractor, the Contractor shall be subrogated to all the rights the Government obtained through the terms required by this clause to be in any subcontract, as if all such rights has been assigned and transferred to the Contractor.

(7) The Contractor shall pay the subcontractor's progress payment request under subdivision (j)(1)(ii) above, within a reasonable time after receiving the Government progress payment covering those amounts.

(8) To facilitate small business participation in subcontracting under this contract the Contractor agrees to provide progress payments to small business concerns, in conformity withe the standards for customary progress payments stated in Subpart 32.5 of the Federal Acquisition Regulation. The Contractor further agrees that the need for such progress payments shall not be considered as a handicap or adverse factor in the award of subcontracts.

(End of clause)

Alternate I (APR 1984). If the contract is with a small business concern, change each mention of the progress payment and liquidation rates to the customary rate of 85 percent for small business concerns (see 32.501-1), delete subparagraphs (a)(1) and (a)(2) from the basic clause, and substitute the following subparagraphs (a)(1) and (a)(2):

(a) *Computation of amounts.* (1) Unless the Contractor requests a smaller amount, each progress payment shall be computed as (i) 85 percent of the Contractor's total costs incurred under this con-

Figure 9.2. (Continued)

287

tract whether or not actually paid, plus (ii) progress payments to subcontractors (see paragraph (j) below), all less the sum of all previous progress payments made by the Government under this contract. Cost of money that would be allowable under 31.205-10 of the Federal Acquisition Regulation shall be deemed an incurred cost for progress payment purposes.

(2) Accured costs of Contractor contributions under employee pension plans shall be excluded until actually paid unless—

(i) The Contractor's practice is to make contributions to the retirement fund quarterly or more frequently; and

(ii) The contribution does not remain unpaid 30 days after the end of the applicable quarter or shorter payment period (any contribution remaining unpaid shall be excluded from the Contractor's total costs for progress payments until paid).

Figure 9.2. (Continued)

standard items not requiring a substantial accumulation of predelivery expenditures by the contractor.

Payments are based on specified percentages applied to the cost incurred. FAR 32.501-1 and DFARS 232.501-1 currently provides for the following standard reimbursement rates:

	Non Defense	Defense
Pertentage of total cost		
Other than small business (%)	80	75
Small business (%)	85	80

In lieu of the standard progress payment rates, contractors may "request" flexible progress payments on negotiated DOD contract over $1 million provided that certified cost or pricing data were submitted prior to award. The current underlying DOD policy behind flexible progress payments is that contractors should maintain a minimum 25% investment in contract work-in-process inventory over the contract performance period. By considering the contractor's cash flow on the specific contract, the flexible progress payment formula (using DOD's "CASH IV" computer program) calculates the highest possible reimbursement rate that still achieves a 25 % contractor investment in the contract work-in-process inventory.

Eligible Costs

Eligible Costs include all expenses of contract performance that are allowable, (See Chapter 7) reasonable, allocable to the contract, consistent with sound and generally accepted accounting principles and practices, and not otherwise excluded by the contract. However, costs eligible for reimbursement under monthly progress payments are limited to:

Recorded allowable costs that at the time of request for reimbursement have been paid for items or services purchased directly for the contract (not applicable to small business).

Allowable costs incurred, but not necessarily paid, for materials issued from the contractor's stores inventory, direct labor, direct travel, other direct in-house costs, and properly allocable and allowable indirect costs.

Allowable pension, deferred profit sharing, and employee stock ownership plan (ESOP) contributions that are funded on a quarterly basis.

Progress payments that have been paid to subcontractors.

Thus, for items purchased directly for a contract, the cash basis of accounting must be used unless the contractor is a small business. Furthermore, where pension, deferred profit sharing, and ESOP contributions are funded less frequently than quarterly, the accrued cost must be deleted from claimed indirect expenses until actually paid.

Title

The standard progress payment clauses provide that upon signing the contract, title to all parts, materials, inventories, work-in-process, special tooling and test equipment, nondurable tools, jigs, dies, fixtures, molds, patterns, taps, gauges, other similar manufacturing aids, drawings, and technical data acquired or produced for and allocable to the contract vest immediately in the government. Title to all like property later acquired or produced and charged to the contract also vests in the government. Such property, however, is not considered government furnished property. Vesting is intended to accomplish two things:

> The government's interests are protected in that the assets are essentially used as collateral against progress payments made.
>
> The vesting of title in the U.S. Government makes it more difficult for local jurisdictions to impose property taxes on these items.

Although title transfers to the government, the risk of loss to the property remains with the contractor prior to delivery to the government. If the property is lost, stolen, damaged, or destroyed, the contractor must refund any progress payments attributable to those items. The property must also be handled and disposed of in accordance with provisions of the contract, such as the default, termination, and special tooling clauses, as well as the special default provisions included in the progress payments clause. Production scrap may be sold by the contractor without prior government approval. However for the disposal of other property, prior government approval must be obtained; the cost allocable to the disposed property must be credited to the cost of contract performance; and the company must repay any prior progress payments allocable to the disposed property. Title to the government must be free of all encumbrances. The contractor's certification that title is free and clear generally will be relied upon unless other available information indicates that the property may be subject to an encumbrance. If any encumbrances against the property arise to prevent the contractor from transferring clear title to the government, the government will act to protect its interest in such title. When the contract terms and conditions have been completely fulfilled and all progress payments have been liquidated, the title of any property remaining in the possession of the contractor which is not deliverable to the government under the terms of the contract reverts to the contractor.

In *Marine Midland Bank v. The United States*,[5] the Court of Claims took issue with the government's assertion that upon making progress payments, title for materials, work-in-progress, and so on actually passed to the government. The Court concluded that progress payments were in effect loans and that the "progress payment" clause merely granted the government a lien against the items. The Court noted that in the progress payment clause:

> "Title" is meant to carry no risks for the government and is shifted back to the contractor when it would be unneeded or undesired. In short, the government takes an interest in the contractor's inventory but does not want, and does not take, any of the responsibilities that go with ownership.

The question raised, then, is what title vesting means for the purposes of the government's financing program, when it is evident that "title" is not used literally in the title vesting clause or the regulations. Indeed it would do violence to the system that the clause and regulations set up to say that the government "owns" covered property when it is apparent that the government specifically exempts itself from most of the incidents of ownership. Reading the clause and all of the regulations together, it is plain that ownership is not taken, but rather the government takes a security interest in the contractor's inventory, to secure the funds loaned to the contractor through progress payments. Such an interest is readily identifiable in common parlance as a lien, as plaintiff argues, despite the use of the term title.

However, even in light of this court decision, the government's interest still appears to be adequately protected, for the Court concluded:

The rule of decision we choose for this case is to make the government's security interest under its title vesting procedures paramount to the liens of general creditors.

In U.S. v. American Pouch Foods, Inc.[6], a U.S. District Court disagreed with the earlier Marine Midland decision and ruled that the progress payment clause granted to the government ". . . full, absolute title in the property covered by the vesting clause." Because of these conflicting court decisions, this issue is likely to be further litigated.

The "progress payments" clause contains a specific reservation of government rights that protects the rights and remedies available to the government under other clauses.

Liquidation

As contract items are delivered, the progress payments previously made on the items delivered must be liquidated. The regulations prescribe what percentages of payments due under the contract for delivered items are to be liquidated against outstanding progress payments.

Under the ordinary method for liquidating progress payments, the same percentage used for billing progress payments is used for liquidating progress payments. The ordinary method of liquidation is used where the original cost estimates are accurate and the profit experienced under the contract is comparable to the profit estimated. Under certain conditions, contracts may be amended to reduce the progress payment liquidation rate. This alternate method of liquidation provides payment to the contractor of earned profit, as well as cost, on items delivered and accepted. The alternate liquidation rate is explained in FAR 32.503-10. If performance is unsatisfactory, costs are abnormally high, or a substantial loss is anticipated under the contract, then the government may raise the progress payment liquidation rate to ensure that all such payments are properly liquidated and the government's interest is protected. The decision to revise the liquidation rate is normally prompted by contractor-prepared reports required under the progress payments clause, or by independent government audit or other reviews. The liquidation of progress payments is explained in Section III of Standard Form 1443, *Contractor's Request for Progress Payment* (Fig. 9.3).

The government may reduce or suspend progress payments, or increase the liquidation rate if a contractor:

CONTRACTOR'S REQUEST FOR PROGRESS PAYMENT

Form Approved
OMB No. 3090—0105

IMPORTANT. This form is to be completed in accordance with Instructions on reverse.

SECTION I — IDENTIFICATION INFORMATION

1. TO: NAME AND ADDRESS OF CONTRACTING OFFICE *(Include ZIP Code)*

PAYING OFFICE

2. FROM: NAME AND ADDRESS OF CONTRACTOR *(Include ZIP Code)*

3. SMALL BUSINESS	4. CONTRACT NO.	5. CONTRACT PRICE
☐ YES ☐ NO		$

6. RATES		7. DATE OF INITIAL AWARD		8A. PROGRESS PAYMENT REQUEST NO.	8B. DATE OF THIS REQUEST
A. PROG. PYMTS.	B. LIQUIDATION	A. YEAR	B. MONTH		
%	%				

SECTION II — STATEMENT OF COSTS UNDER THIS CONTRACT THROUGH _____ *(Date)*

9. PAID COSTS ELIGIBLE UNDER PROGRESS PAYMENT CLAUSE	$
10. INCURRED COSTS ELIGIBLE UNDER PROGRESS PAYMENT CLAUSE	
11. TOTAL COSTS ELIGIBLE FOR PROGRESS PAYMENTS *(Item 9 plus 10)*	
12. a. TOTAL COSTS INCURRED TO DATE	$
b. ESTIMATED ADDITIONAL COST TO COMPLETE	
13. ITEM 11 MULTIPLIED BY ITEM 6a	
14. a. PROGRESS PAYMENTS PAID TO SUBCONTRACTORS	
b. LIQUIDATED PROGRESS PAYMENTS TO SUBCONTRACTORS	
c. UNLIQUIDATED PROGRESS PAYMENTS TO SUBCONTRACTORS *(Item 14a less 14b)*	
d. SUBCONTRACT PROGRESS BILLINGS APPROVED FOR CURRENT PAYMENT	
e. ELIGIBLE SUBCONTRACTOR PROGRESS PAYMENTS *(Item 14c plus 14d)*	
15. TOTAL DOLLAR AMOUNT *(Item 13 plus 14e)*	
16. ITEM 5 MULTIPLIED BY ITEM 6b	
17. LESSER OF ITEM 15 OR ITEM 16	
18. TOTAL AMOUNT OF PREVIOUS PROGRESS PAYMENTS REQUESTED	
19. MAXIMUM BALANCE ELIGIBLE FOR PROGRESS PAYMENTS *(Item 17 less 18)*	

SECTION III — COMPUTATION OF LIMITS FOR OUTSTANDING PROGRESS PAYMENTS
SEE SPECIAL INSTRUCTIONS ON BACK FOR USE UNDER THE FEDERAL ACQUISITION REGULATION.

20. COMPUTATION OF PROGRESS PAYMENT CLAUSE *(a(3)(i) or a(4)(i))* LIMITATION*	$
a. COSTS INCLUDED IN ITEM 11, APPLICABLE TO ITEMS DELIVERED, INVOICED, AND ACCEPTED TO THE DATE IN HEADING OF SECTION II.	
b. COSTS ELIGIBLE FOR PROGRESS PAYMENTS, APPLICABLE TO UNDELIVERED ITEMS AND TO DELIVERED ITEMS NOT INVOICED AND ACCEPTED *(Item 11 less 20a)*	
c. ITEM 20b MULTIPLIED BY ITEM 6a	$
d. ELIGIBLE SUBCONTRACTOR PROGRESS PAYMENTS *(Item 14e)*	
e. LIMITATION a(3)(i) or a(4)(i) *(Item 20c plus 20d)* *	
21. COMPUTATION OF PROGRESS PAYMENT CLAUSE *(a(3)(ii) or a(4)(ii))* LIMITATION*	
a. CONTRACT PRICE OF ITEMS DELIVERED, ACCEPTED AND INVOICED TO DATE IN HEADING OF SECTION II	
b. CONTRACT PRICE OF ITEMS NOT DELIVERED, ACCEPTED AND INVOICED *(Item 5 less 21a)*	
c. ITEM 21b MULTIPLIED BY ITEM 6b	
d. UNLIQUIDATED ADVANCE PAYMENTS PLUS ACCRUED INTEREST	
e. LIMITATION *(a(3)(ii) or a(4)(ii))* *(Item 21c less 21d)* *	
22. MAXIMUM UNLIQUIDATED PROGRESS PAYMENTS *(Lesser of Item 20e or 21e)*	
23. TOTAL AMOUNT APPLIED AND TO BE APPLIED TO REDUCE PROGRESS PAYMENT	
24. UNLIQUIDATED PROGRESS PAYMENTS *(Item 18 less 23)*	
25. MAXIMUM PERMISSIBLE PROGRESS PAYMENTS *(Item 22 less 24)*	
26. AMOUNT OF CURRENT INVOICE FOR PROGRESS PAYMENT *(Lesser of Item 25 or 19)*	
27. AMOUNT APPROVED BY CONTRACTING OFFICER	

CERTIFICATION

I certify that the above statement (with attachments) has been prepared from the books and records of the above-named contractor in accordance with the contract and the instructions hereon, and to the best of my knowledge and belief, that it is correct, that all the costs of contract performance (except as herewith reported in writing) have been paid to the extent shown herein, or where not shown as paid have been paid or will be paid currently, by the contractor, when due, in the ordinary course of business, that the work reflected above has been performed, that the quantities and amounts involved are consistent with the requirements of the contract. That there are no encumbrances (except as reported in writing herewith, or on previous progress payment request No. _____) against the property acquired or produced for, and allocated or properly chargeable to the contract which would affect or impair the Government's title, that there has been no materially adverse change in the financial condition of the contractor since the submission of the most recent written information dated _____ by the contractor to the Government in connection with the contract, that to the extent of any contract provision limiting progress payments pending first article approval, such provision has been complied with, and that after the making of the requested progress payment the unliquidated progress payments will not exceed the maximum unliquidated progress payments permitted by the contract.

NAME AND TITLE OF CONTRACTOR REPRESENTATIVE SIGNING THIS FORM	SIGNATURE

NAME AND TITLE OF CONTRACTING OFFICER	SIGNATURE

NSN 7540-01-140-5523

1443-101

STANDARD FORM 1443 (10-82)
Prescribed by GSA (FPR 1-16.808)
FAR (48 CFR 53.232)

Figure 9.3. Contractor's request for progress payment, Standard Form 1443.

GENERAL - All entries on this form must be typewritten - all dollar amounts must be shown in whole dollars, rounded up to the next whole dollar. All line item numbers not included in the instructions below are self-explanatory.

SECTION I — IDENTIFICATION INFORMATION. Complete Items 1 through 8c in accordance with the following instructions:

Item 1. TO — Enter the name and address of the cognizant Contract Administration Office. PAYING OFFICE — Enter the designation of the paying office, as indicated in the contract.

Item 2. FROM - CONTRACTOR'S NAME AND ADDRESS/ ZIP CODE — Enter the name and mailing address of the contractor. If applicable, the division of the company performing the contract should be entered immediately following the contractor's name.

Item 3. Enter an "X" in the appropriate block to indicate whether or not the contractor is a small business concern.

Item 5. Enter the total contract price, as amended. If the contract provides for escalation or price redetermination, enter the initial price until changed and not the ceiling price; if the contract is of the incentive type, enter the target or billing price, as amended until final pricing. For letter contracts, enter the maximum expenditure authorized by the contract, as amended.

Item 6A. PROGRESS PAYMENT RATES — Enter the 2-digit progress payment percentage rate shown in paragraph (a)(1) of the progress payment clause.

Item 6B. LIQUIDATION RATE — Enter the progress payment liquidation rate shown in paragraph (b) of the progress payment clause, using three digits - Example: show 80% as 800 - show 72.3% as 723.

Item 7. DATE OF INITIAL AWARD — Enter the last two digits of the calendar year. Use two digits to indicate the month. Example: show January 1982 as 82/01.

Item 8A. PROGRESS PAYMENT REQUEST NO. — Enter the number assigned to this request. All requests under a single contract must be numbered consecutively, beginning with 1. Each subsequent request under the same contract must continue in sequence, using the same series of numbers without omission.

Item 8B. Enter the date of the request.

SECTION II — GENERAL INSTRUCTIONS. DATE In the space provided in the heading enter the date through which costs have been accumulated from inception for inclusion in this request. This date is applicable to item entries in Sections II and III.

Cost Basis. For all contracts with Small Business concerns, the base for progress payments is total costs incurred. For contracts with concerns other than Small Business, the progress payment base will be the total recorded paid costs, together with the incurred costs per the Computation of Amounts paragraph of the progress payment clause in FPR 1-30.510-1(a) or FAR 52.232-16, as appropriate. Total costs include all expenses paid and incurred, including applicable manufacturing and production expense, general and administrative expense for performance of contract, which are reasonable, allocable to the contract, consistent with sound and generally accepted accounting principles and practices, and which are not otherwise excluded by the contract.

Manufacturing and Production Expense, General and Administrative Expense. In connection with the first progress payment request on a contract, attach an explanation of the method, bases and period used in determining the amount of each of these two types of expenses. If the method, bases or periods used for computing these expenses differ in subsequent requests for progress payments under this contract, attach an explanation of such changes to the progress payment request involved.

Incurred Costs Involving Subcontractors for Contracts with Small Business Concerns. If the incurred costs eligible for progress payments under the contract include costs shown in invoices of subcontractors, suppliers and others, that portion of the costs computed on such invoices can only include costs for: (1) completed work to which the prime contractor has acquired title; (2) materials delivered to which the prime contractor has acquired title; (3) services rendered; and (4) costs billed under cost reimbursement or time and material subcontracts for work to which the prime contractor has acquired title.

SECTION II — SPECIFIC INSTRUCTIONS

Item 9. PAID COSTS ELIGIBLE UNDER PROGRESS PAYMENT CLAUSE — Line 9 will not be used for Small Business Contracts.

For large business contracts, costs to be shown in Item 9 shall include only those recorded costs which have resulted at time of request in payment made by cash, check, or other form of actual payment for items or services purchased directly for the contract. This includes items delivered, accepted and paid for, resulting in liquidation of subcontractor progress payments.

Costs to be shown in Item 9 are not to include advance payments, downpayments, or deposits, all of which are not eligible for reimbursement, or progress payments made to subcontractors, suppliers or others, which are to be included in Item 14. See "Cost Basis" above.

Item 10. INCURRED COSTS ELIGIBLE UNDER PROGRESS PAYMENT CLAUSE — For all Small Business Contracts, Item 10 will show total costs incurred for the contract.

Costs to be shown in Item 10 are not to include advance payments, downpayments, deposits, or progress payments made to subcontractors, suppliers or others.

For large business contracts, costs to be shown in Item 10 shall include all costs incurred (see "Cost Basis" above) for materials which have been issued from the stores inventory and placed into production process for use on the contract; for direct labor, for other direct in-house costs, and for properly allocated and allowable indirect costs as set forth under "Cost Basis" above.

Item 12a. Enter the total contract costs incurred to date, if the actual amount is not known, enter the best possible estimate. If an estimate is used, enter (E) after the amount.

Item 12b. Enter the estimated cost to complete the contract. The estimate may be the last estimate made, adjusted for costs incurred since the last estimate; however, estimates shall be made not less frequently than every six months.

Items 14a through 14e. Include only progress payments on subcontracts which conform to progress payment provisions of the prime contract.

Item 14a. Enter only progress payments actually paid.

Item 14b. Enter total progress payments recouped from subcontractors.

Item 14d. For Small Business prime contracts, include the amount of unpaid subcontract progress payment billings which have been approved by the contractor for the current payment in the ordinary course of business. For other contracts, enter "0" amount.

SECTION III — SPECIFIC INSTRUCTIONS. This Section must be completed only if the contractor has received advance payments against this contract, or if items have been delivered, invoiced and accepted as of the date indicated in the heading of Section II above. EXCEPTION. Item 27 must be filled in by the Contracting Officer.

Item 20a. Of the costs reported in Item 11, compute and enter only costs which are properly allocable to items delivered, invoiced and accepted to the applicable date. In order of preference, these costs are to be computed on the basis of one of the following: (a) The actual unit cost of items delivered, giving proper consideration to the deferment of the starting load costs or, (b) projected unit costs (based on experienced costs plus the estimated cost to complete the contract), where the contractor maintains cost data which will clearly establish the reliability of such estimates.

Item 20d. Enter amount from 14e.

Item 21a. Enter the total billing price, as adjusted, of items delivered, accepted and invoiced to the applicable date.

Item 23. Enter total progress payments liquidated and those to be liquidated from billings submitted but not yet paid.

Item 25. Self explanatory. (NOTE: If the entry in this item is a negative amount, there has been an overpayment which requires adjustment.)

Item 26. Self-explanatory, but if a lesser amount is requested, enter the lesser amount.

SPECIAL INSTRUCTIONS FOR USE UNDER FEDERAL ACQUISITION REGULATION (FAR).

Items 20 and 20e. Delete the references to a(3)(i) of the progress payment clause.

Items 21 and 21e. Delete the references to a(3)(ii) of the progress payment clause.

STANDARD FORM 1443 BACK (10-82)

Figure 9.3. (Continued)

Fails to comply with a material provision of the contract.

Endangers contract performance because of lack of progress or insecure financial condition.

Allocates excessive inventory to the contract.

Is delinquent in the payment of cost incurred under the contract.

Fails to make progress to the extent that unliquidated progress payments exceed the value of the work done on the undelivered portions.

Realizes less profit than that estimated and used in computing the liquidation rate.

Action to reduce or suspend progress payments is not taken precipitately. It requires notice to the contractor and an examination of the contractor's financial position, including the effect of a reduction in the progress payments. Although it is generally not in the government's interest to withhold financing, government representatives are obligated to protect the government's interest.

FAR 32. 503-6(g) prescribes a formula the government is to apply to individual progress payments for contracts considered to be in a loss position.

Preparing Progress Payment Requests

Contracts that provide for progress payments require that the contractor maintain an adequate accounting system to accumulate cost for the contract. The contractor must also furnish promptly all reasonably requested reports, certificates, and financial statements. Another contract clause specifically gives the government the right to review the contractor's books and records related to contract performance. The DCAA has developed a time-share computer program known as "PROPAY" to facilitate reviews of individual progress payments.

Requests for progress payments are submitted on a monthly or longer basis on Standard Form 1443, Contractor's Request for Progress Payment. The form and instructions for preparation are presented in Figure 9-3. The instructions are generally self-explanatory; however, two points warrant special emphasis:

1. The estimate to complete line 12b is often given little attention by a contractor. However, from the government's viewpoint, it is one of the most critical items on the progress payment request since a comparison of the estimate at completion with the contract price indicates whether the contract is in a loss position or is earning a substantially higher profit rate than was negotiated. In either event, the government may find it appropriate to change the liquidation rate. The relationship of the estimate at completion to contract price should be the same as the relationship of the cost of delivered/invoiced items to the price of delivered/invoiced items. Consequently, the government is concerned about an understatement of the estimate at completion since it results in an overstatement of the costs eligible for progress payments applicable to undelivered/invoiced items. The instructions on the form required that the contractor update the estimate to complete at least every 6 months.

2. Progress payments are liquidated on line 23 by multiplying the liquidation rate on line 6b by the billing price of items delivered and invoiced.

Unusual Progress Payments

Progress payments based on cost at higher rates than those specified in the customary progress payments clause are considered unusual progress payments. The contractor must show an actual need for such additional unusual progress payments. DFARS 232.501-2 (a) prohibits DOD contracting officers from modifying contracts to authorize unusual progress payments in excess of $25 million without the prior written consent of the Office of the Deputy Under Secretary of Defense for Research and Engineering.

Certification

Whenever indirect cost billing rates are revised, DFARS 252. 242-7003 requires contractors to certify, to the best of their knowledge and belief, under the penalty of perjury, that no claim or billing, including indirect expenses, contains any unallowable costs prescribed by part 31 of FAR. (See Chap. 10 for a more detailed discussion).

MILESTONE BILLINGS

Under regulations in effect prior to FAR (DAR Appendix E) fixed-price contracts with particularly long lead times between incurrence of cost and first delivery could convert from customary progress payments to a type of partial payment known as a milestone billing after 6 months (4 months for small business concern) of contract performance. To have been eligible for milestone billings, contracts had to meet certain size and long lead time criteria.

	Small Business	Other than Small Business
Minimum contract value	N/A	$5 million
Minimum long lead time between incurrence of costs and first delivery	6 months	12 months

Milestone billings were requested at the completion of established milestone events. The amount eligible for payment was the lesser of the actual cost to accomplish the event and the value assigned to the event in the contract. Regulations governing milestone billings were never incorporated into FAR. Since no rules specifically prohibit milestone billings, this type of financing arrangement can still be requested and negotiated on a contract by contract basis. The Defense Financial and Investment Review (DFAIR) study, issued in 1985, recommended that coverage of milestone billings be re-introduced into the regulations.

GUARANTEED LOANS

Guaranteed loans are basically commercial loans by private lending institutions to a contractor that obligate the government, on demand of the lender, to purchase a stated percentage of the loan and/or share in any losses. Guaranteed loans are normally based on the undelivered portion of all defense contracts, subcontracts, or purchase orders, as opposed to contract-by-contract financing. Unless the contractor defaults in whole or in part on the primary loan, there is no cost to the government since government funds are only involved where a percentage of the loan must actually be purchased. If government funds are expended to purchase a defaulted loan, the government recovers the amount through payments made by the contractor.

Requests for guaranteed loans are initiated by the lending institution. A contractor requiring financing applies to a private financial institution for a loan or revolving fund. If the lending institution considers a government guarantee to be necessary, it applies to its Federal Reserve Bank for the guarantee. The Federal Reserve Bank investigates the application and makes a recommendation to the Federal Reserve Board. The Federal Reserve Board forwards a copy of the application to the appropriate guaranteeing agency to determine whether a contractor is eligible to receive a loan guarantee. The Departments of the Army, Navy, and Air Force, the Department of Energy, the Department of Commerce, the Department of Interior, the Department of Agriculture, and the General Services Administration are designated as "guaranteeing agencies" under the Defense Production Act of 1950, as amended, and under Executive Order 10480. Where a company has undelivered contracts with more than one agency, the guaranteeing agency will generally be the one with the largest dollar volume of uncompleted work.

The application will only be approved if the guaranteeing agency can certify that:

The supplies or services are essential to the national defense.

Other alternative sources are not available.

The contractor is technically qualified and has adequate facilities to perform the contract.

If the guaranteeing agency approves the guarantee, the guarantee agreement is issued by the appropriate Federal Reserve Bank to the financial institution.

Loans will generally not be guaranteed for more than 90% of the borrower's investment in defense production contracts. The Defense Production Act further limits the maximum obligation of a guaranteeing agency to $20 million.

The guarantee agreement will generally require that monies payable under the contracts be assigned to the bank unless the borrower's financial condition is particularly strong or the administration of contract assignments would be unduly onerous because of the large number of small contracts involved.

ADVANCE PAYMENTS

Advance payments (Figure 9.4) are essentially loans that may be authorized for either subcontracts or prime contracts and for either cost reimbursement type or fixed-price contracts, including awards under formal advertising procedures. Advance payments may be paid up to the full amount of the unpaid contract price.

In contrast to progress payments, advance payments are loans made prior to, and in anticipation of, performance under a contract. They are authorized for defense contracts under the provisions of 10 U.S.C. 2307, as amended; the National Defense Contract Authorization Act of August 28, 1958; Public Law

ADVANCE PAYMENTS (APR 1984)

(a) *Requirements for payment.* Advance payments will be made under this contract (1) upon submission of properly certified invoices or vouchers by the Contractor and approval by the administering office. _____ [*Insert the name of the office designated under agency procedures*], or (2) under a letter of credit. The amount of the invoice or voucher submitted plus all advance payments previously approved shall not exceed $ ___ If a letter of credit is used, the Contractor shall withdraw cash only when needed for disbursements acceptable under this contract and report cash disbursements and balances as required by the administering office. The Contractor shall apply terms similar to this clause to any advance payments to subcontractors.

(b) *Special bank account.* Until (1) the Contractor has liquidated all advance payments made under the contract and related interest charges and (2) the administering office has approved in writing the release of any funds due and payable to the Contractor, all advance payments and other payments under this contract shall be made by check payable to the Contractor marked for deposit only in the Contractor's special bank account with the _____ [*Insert the name of the bank*]. None of the funds in the special bank account shall be mingled with other funds of the Contractor. Withdrawals from the special bank account may be made only by check of the Contractor countersigned by the Contracting Officer or a Government countersigning agent designated in writing by the Contracting Officer.

(c) *Use of funds.* The Contractor may withdraw funds from the special bank account only to pay for properly allocable, allowable, and reasonable costs for direct materials, direct labor, and indirect costs. Other withdrawals require approval in writing by the administering office. Determinations of whether costs are properly allocable, allowable, and reasonable shall be in accordance with generally accepted accounting principles, subject to any applicable subparts of Part 31 of the Federal Acquisition Regulation.

(d) *Repayment to the Government.* At any time, the Contractor may repay all or any part of the funds advanced by the Government. Whenever requested in writing to do so by the administering office, the Contractor shall repay to the Government any part of unliquidated advance payments considered by the administering office to exceed the Contractor's current requirements or the amount specified in paragraph (a) above. If the Contractor fails to repay the amount requested by the administering office, all or any part of the unliquidated advance payments may be withdrawn from the special bank account by check signed by only the countersigning agent and applied to reduction of the unliquidated advance payments under this contract.

(e) *Maximum payment.* When the sum of all unliquidated advance payments, unpaid interest charges, and other payments exceed ___ percent of the contract price, the Government shall withhold further payments to the Contractor. On completion or termination of the contract, the Government shall deduct from the amount due to the Contractor all unliquidated advance payments and all interest charges payable. If previous payments to the Contractor exceed the amount due, the excess amount shall be paid to the Government on demand. For purposes of this paragraph, the contract price shall be considered to be the stated contract price of $___, less any subsequent price reductions under the contract, plus (1) any price increases resulting from any terms of this contract for price redetermination or escalation, and (2) any other price increases that do not, in the aggregate, exceed $___[*Insert an amount not higher than 10 percent of the stated contract amount inserted in this paragraph*]. Any payments withheld under this paragraph shall be applied to reduce the unliquidated advance payments. If full liquidation has been made, payments under the contract shall resume.

(f) *Interest.* (1) The Contractor shall pay interest to the Government on the daily unliquidated advance payments at the daily rate specified in subparagraph (f)(3) below. Interest shall be computed at the end of each calendar month for the actual number of days involved. For the purpose of computing the interest charge—

(i) Advance payments shall be considered as increasing the unliquidated balance as of the date of the advance payment check;

(ii) Repayments by Contractor check shall be considered as decreasing the unliquidated balance as of the date on which the check is received by the Goverment authority designated by the Contracting Officer; and

(iii) Liquidiations by deductions from Government payments to the Contractor shall be considered as decreasing the unliquidated balance as of the date of the check for the reduced payment.

(2) Interest charges resulting from the monthly computation shall be deducted from payments, other than advance payments, due the Contractor. If the accrued interest exceeds the payment due, any excess interest shall be carried forward and deducted from subsequent payments. Interest carried forward shall not be compounded. Interest on advance payments shall cease to accrue upon satisfactory completion or termination of the contract for the convenience of the Government. The Contractor shall charge interest on advance payments to subcontractors in the manner described above and credit the interest to the Government. Interest need not be charged on advance payments to nonprofit educational or research subcontractors for experimental, developmental, or research work.

Figure 9.4. Advance payments clause, FAR 52-232.12.

(3) If interest is required under the contract, the Contracting Officer shall determine a daily interest rate based on the higher of (i) the published prime rate of the banking institution (depository) in which the special bank account is established or (ii) the rate established by the Secretary of the Treasury under Pub. L. 92-41 (50 U.S.C. App. 1215(b)(2)). The Contracting Officer shall revise the daily interest rate during the contract period in keeping with any changes in the cited interest rates.

(4) If the full amount of interest charged under this paragraph has not been paid by deduction or otherwise upon completion or termination of this contract, the Contractor shall pay the remaining interest to the Government on demand.

(8) *Bank Agreement.* Before an advance payment is made under this contract, the Contractor shall transmit to the administering office, in the form prescribed by the administering office, an agreement in triplicate from the bank in which the special bank account is established, clearly setting forth the special character of the account and the responsibilities of the bank under the account. If possible, the Contractor shall select a bank that is a member bank of the Federal Reserve System or is an "insured" bank within the meaning the Federal Deposit Insurance Corporation Act (12 U.S.C. 1811).

(h) *Lien on Special Bank Account.* The Government shall have a lien upon any balance in the special bank account paramount to all other liens. The Government lien shall secure the repayment of any advance payments made under this contract and any related interest charges.

(i) *Lien on property under contract.* (1) All advance payments under this contract, together with interest charges, shall be secured, when made, by a lien in favor of the Government, paramount to all other liens, on the supplies or other things covered by this contract and on all material and other property acquired for or allocated to the performance of this contract, except to the extent that the Government by virtue of any other terms of this contract, or otherwise, shall have valid title to the supplies, materials, or other property as against other creditors of the Contractor.

(2) The Contractor shall identify, by marking or segregation, all property that is subject to a lien in favor of the Government by virtue of any terms of this contract in such a way as to indicate that it is subject to a lien and that it has been acquired for or allocated to performing this contract. If, for any reason, the supplies, materials, or other property are not identified by marking or segregation, the Government shall be considered to have a lien to the extent of the Government's interest under this contract on any mass of property with which the supplies, materials, or other property are commingled. The Contractor shall maintain adequate accounting control over the property on its books and records.

(3) If, at any time during the progress of the work on the contract, it becomes necessary to deliver to a third person any items or materials on which the Government has a lien, the Contractor shall notify the third person of the lien and shall obtain from the third person a receipt in duplicate acknowledging the existence of the lien. The Contractor shall provide a copy of each receipt to the Contracting Officer.

(4) If, under the termination clause, the Contracting Officer authorizes the Contractor to sell or retain termination inventory, the approval shall constitute a release of the Government's lien to the extent that—

(i) The termination inventory is sold or retained; and

(ii) The sale proceeds or retention credits are applied to reduce any outstanding advance payments.

(j) *Insurance.* The Contractor represents and warrants that it maintains with responsible insurance carriers (1) insurance on plant and equipment against fire and other hazards, to the extent that similar properties are usually insured by others operating plants and properties of similar character in the same general locality; (2) adequate insurance against liability on account of damage to persons or property; and (3) adequate insurance under all applicable workers' compensation laws. The Contractor agrees that, until work under this contract has been completed and all advance payments made under the contract have been liquidated, it will maintain this insurance; maintain adequate insurance on any materials, parts, assemblies, subassemblies, supplies equipment, and other property acquired for or allocable to this contract and subject to the Government lien under paragraph (i) of this clause; and furnish any certificates with respect to its insurance that the administering office may require.

(k) *Default.* (1) If any of the following events occurs, the Government may by written notice to the Contractor, withhold further withdrawals from the special bank account and further payments on this contract:

(i) Termination of this contract for a fault of the Contractor.

(ii) A finding by the administering office that the Contractor has failed to—

(A) Observe any of the conditions of the advance payment terms;

(B) Comply with any material term of this contract;

(C) Make progress or maintain a financial condition adequate for performance of this contract;

(D) Limit inventory allocated to this contract to reasonable requirements; or

(E) Avoid delinquency in payment of taxes or of the costs of performing this contract in the ordinary course of business.

Figure 9.4 (Continued)

(iii) The appointment of a trustee, receiver, or liquidator for all or a subtantial part of the Contractor's property, or the institution of proceedings by or against the Contractor for bankruptcy, reorganization, arrangement, or liquidation.

(iv) The service of any writ of attachment, levy of execution, or commencement of garnishment proceedings concerning the special bank account.

(v) The commission of an act of bankruptcy.

(2) If any of the events described in subparagraph (1) above continue for 30 days after the written notice to the Contractor, the Government may take any of the following additional actions:

(i) Withdraw by checks payable to the Treasurer of the United States, signed only by the countersigning agency, all or any part of the balance in the special bank account and appy the amounts to reduce outstanding advance payments and any other claims of the Government against the Contractor.

(ii) Charge interest, in the manner prescribed in paragraph (f) above, on outstanding advance payments during the period of any event described in subparagraph (1) above.

(iii) Demand immediate repayment by the Contractor of the unliquidated balance of advance payments.

(iv) Take possession of and, with or without advertisement, sell at public or private sale all or any part of the property on which the Government has a lien under this contract and, after deducting any expenses incident to the sale, apply the net proceeds of the sale to reduce the unliquidated balance of advance payments or other Government claims against the Contractor.

(3) The Government may take any of the actions described in subparagraphs (k)(1) and (2) of this clause it considers appropriate at its discretion and without limiting any other rights of the Government.

(l) *Prohibition against assignment.* Notwithstanding any other terms of this contract, the Contractor shall not assign this contract any interest therein, or any claim under the contract to any party.

(m) *Information and access to records.* The Contractor shall furnish to the administering office (1) monthly or all other intervals as required, signed or certified balance sheets and profit and loss statements together with a report on the operation of the special bank account in the form prescribed by the administering office; and (2) if requested other information concerning the operation of the Contractor's business. The Contractor shall provide the authorized Government representatives proper facilities for inspection of the contractor's books, records, and accounts.

(n) *Other security.* The terms of this contract are considered to provide adequate security to the Government for advance payments; however, if the administering office considers the security inadequate, the Contractor shall furnish additional security satisfactory to the administering office, to the extent that the security is available.

(o) *Representations and warranties.* The Contractor represents and warrants the following:

(1) The balance sheet, the profit and loss statement and any other supporting financial statements furnished to the administering office fairly reflect the financial condition of the Contractor at the date shown or the period covered, and there has been no subsequent materially adverse change in the finanical condition of the Contractor.

(2) No litigation or proceedings are presently pending or threatened against the Contractor, except as shown in the financial statements.

(3) The Contractor has disclosed all contingent liabilities, except for liability resulting from the renegotiation of defense production contracts, in the financial statements furnished to the administering office.

(4) None of the terms in this clause conflict with the authority under which the Contractor is doing business or with the provision of any existing indenture or agreement of the contractor.

(5) The contractor has the power to enter into this contract and accept advance payments, and has taken all necessary action to authorize the acceptance under the terms of this contract.

(6) The assets of the Contractor are not subject to any lien or encumbrance of any character except for current taxes not delinquent, and except as shown in the financial statements furnished by the Contractor. There is no current assignment of claims under any contract affected by these advance payment provisions.

(7) All information furnished by the Contractor to the administering office in connection with each request for advance payments is true and correct.

(8) These representations and warranties shall be continuing and shall be considered to have been repeated by the submission of each invoice for advance payments.

(p) *Covenants.* To the extent the Government considers it necessary while any advance payments made under this contract remain outstanding, the Contractor, without the prior written consent of the administering office, shall not—

(1) Mortgage, pledge, or otherwise encumber or allow to be encumbered, any of the assets of the Contractor now owned or subsequently acquired, or permit any preexisting mortgages, liens, or

Figure 9.4 (Continued)

298

other encumbrances to remain on or attach to any assets of the Contractor which are allocated to performing this contract and with respect to which the Government has a lien under this contract:

(2) Sell, assign, transfer, or otherwise dispose of accounts receivable, notes, or claims for money due or to become due:

(3) Declare or pay any dividends, except dividends payable in stock of the corporation, or make any other distribution on account of any shares of its capital stock or purchase, redeem, or otherwise acquire for value any of its stock, except as required by sinking fund or redemption arrangements reported to the administering office incident to the establishment of these advance payment provisions:

(4) Sell, convey, or lease all or a substantial part of its assets:

(5) Acquire for value the stock or other securities of any corporation, municipality, or governmental authority, except direct obligations of United States:

(6) Make any advance or loan or incur any liability as guarantor surety, or accommodation endorser for any party:

(7) Permit a writ of attachment of any similar process to be issued against its property without getting a release or bonding the property within 30 days after the entry of the writ of attachment or other process:

(8) Pay any remuneration in any form to its directors, officers, or key employees higher than rates provided in existing agreements of which notice has been given to the administering office; accrue excess remuneration without first obtaining an agreement subordinating it to all claims of the Government; or employ any person at a rate of compensation over $ ___ a year:

(9) Change substantially the management, ownership, or control of the corporation:

(10) Merge or consolidate with any other firm or corporation, change the type of business, or engage in any transaction outside the ordinary course of the Contractor's business as presently conducted:

(11) Deposit any of its funds except in a bank or trust company insured by the Federal Deposit Insurance Corporation:

(12) Create or incur indebtedness for advances, other than advances to be made under the terms of this contract or for borrowings:

(13) Make or covenant for capital expenditures exceeding $ ___ in total:

(14) Permit its net current assets, computed in accordance with generally accepted accounting principles, to become less than $ ___; or

(15) Make any payments on account of the obligations listed below, except in the manner and to the extent provided in this contract:

[*List the pertinent obligations*]

Figure 9.4   (Continued)

85-804; and Executive Order 10789. Advance payments for civilian procurements are authorized under Section 305 of the Federal Property and Administrative Services Act.

Except for certain specialized procurements, advance payments will only be authorized where:

No other means of adequate financing is available to the contractor except at excessive interest rates or charges.

The amount of the advance payment reflects use of the contractor's own working capital to the extent possible.

The contractor provides adequate security.

It is in the public interest and facilitates the national defense.

Once these conditions have been met, a contractor's request for advance payments will generally be granted when:

The payments are necessary to supplement other funds or credit.

The contractor is otherwise considered responsible.

The government will benefit from contract performance.

Contract circumstances fit those specifically enumerated in the regulations as suitable for advance payments.

Letters of Credit

Treasury Department Circular 107501 governs the use of letters of credit advance payments are prescribed in Treasury Department 1075.10 Letters of Credit enable a contractor to withdraw government funds in amounts necessary to cover its own disbursement of cash for contract performance. The Department of the Treasury favors this method of advance payment. It generates a lower cash flow impact to the government than other financing methods because the contractor is prohibited from withdrawing funds until checks have been forwarded to payees (float delay) or presented to the contractor's bank for payment. This type of advance funding arrangement may be terminated if the contractor is unwilling or unable to minimize the elapsed time between receipt of the advance and disbursement of the funds. In such cases, if reversion to normal payment methods is not feasible, a working capital method of advance payment may be used which limits advances to the estimated disbursements for a given initial period and actual cash disbursements for subsequent periods.

Interest on Advance Payments

All advance payments provide for the payment of interest, although interest may be waived in certain specialized circumstances.

Interest on advance payments is charged at the greater of the published prime rate of the bank in which the special bank account is established or the rate established by the Secretary of the Treasury pursuant to Public Law 92-41. It is a floating interest rate, subject to revision based on fluctuations in the prime rate and the semiannual determination by the Secretary to the Treasury under Public Law 92-41. Prior to implementation of FAR, interest on advance payments for nondefense contracts was charged at a fixed rate based on the rate determined by the Secretary of the Treasury under Public Law 92-41 at the time the advance payment is authorized.

Restrictions

Advance payments and all other payments to the contractor under the contract are deposited in a special bank account. None of the funds in the special account may be commingled with other funds of the contractor prior to withdrawal by the contractor. Except in certain circumstances, funds are withdrawn by the contractor only by check signed by both an authorized company official and the contracting officer or another designated government representative. Use of advance payments is restricted to payments of direct contract costs plus allocable indirect expenses. To protect the government's interest prior to repayment of the advance payments, the government has a lien, which is paramount to all other liens, on the balance in the special account, as well as on the materials, supplies, and property allocated to the contract.

Most contracts that provide for advance payments contain covenants prohibiting the contractor from doing the following, without prior government approval, during the period of time in which advance payments are outstanding:

Mortgaging or pledging any assets.
Selling, assigning, or pledging any claims due.
Paying dividends.

Selling, conveying, or leasing all or a substantial part of the assets.

Acquiring for consideration any stock or security other than direct obligations of the United States.

Making loans or becoming liable on commercial paper.

Permitting an attachment to remain without remedial action.

Paying excessive salaries, commissions, bonuses, or other remuneration in any form or manner to the directors, officers, or key employees.

Changing the management, ownership, or control of the corporation.

Merging or consolidating with any firm or any other corporation.

Depositing funds in any bank or trust company not insured by the Federal Deposit Insurance Corporation.

Creating or incurring indebtedness for borrowed money or advances other than the advance payments themselves.

Making or agreeing to make capital expenditures exceeding a sum specified in the contract.

Permitting current assets, calculated in accordance with generally accepted accounting principles, to fall below a specified amount.

Paying, on account, obligations listed in the contract except in the manner and to the extent provided by the contract.

While advance payments are usually provided for a single contract, they can be used to finance the performance of more than one contract under a single agreement. It may be advantageous to both the government and the contractor, when several contracts are to be financed by advance payments simultaneously, to agree to pool all such contracts and their advance payments. The arrangement can cover a broad area of the contractor's financial needs rather than piecemeal segments related to particular contracts. Arrangements of this type are generally used for financing nonprofit contracts with nonprofit educational or research institutions. When an advance payment pool agreement is made, one of the contracts included in the pool will be the designated pool contract. The designated pool contract is the one to which all advance payments are charged; advances are not made on the other contracts in the pool. However, the monetary requirements of all the contracts are considered in determining the maximum amount of advance payments to be authorized.

FAST PAYMENT PROCEDURES

The fast payment procedure allows payment, under limited conditions, to a contractor prior to government verification that supplies have been received and accepted. The conditions for use of the fast payment procedure are as follows:

Individual orders cannot exceed $25,000.

Deliveries of supplies are to occur at locations that are geographically separate from and lack adequate communications with government receiving and disbursing activities that will make it impractical to make timely payment based on evidence of government acceptance.

The purchasing instrument is a firm - fixed price contract, purchase order or delivery order.

A system exists to assure (1) documentation of performance, (2) timely feedback to the contracting officer in case of contractor deficiencies, and (3) identification of suppliers who have a current history of abusing the fast payment procedures.

Fast pay orders are generally issued on DOD Form 1155.

PROMPT PAYMENT ACT

The Prompt Payment Act, effective October 1, 1982, generally requires the Federal Government to pay business concerns from whom goods and services are acquired within 45 days after receipt of a proper invoice. Requests for interim financing, such as requests for progress payments, and interim billings on cost type contracts are not considered invoices for purposes of the act. If the payment is not made within the prescribed time, the government must pay interest to the contractor commencing from the 30th day after receipt of the invoice. Interest will be paid at the same rate applied to claims adjudicated under the Contract Disputes Act of 1978.

A *business concern* is defined in the act as "any person engaged in a trade or business and nonprofit entities operating as contractors." Thus the law would appear to be fully applicable to foreign business concerns as well as U.S. firms.

The act also provides that federal agencies must notify a contractor within 15 days of receipt of an invoice whenever an error or defect in the invoice would prevent the clock from running on the 30-day time period.

The Office of Management and Budget (OMB) published OMB Circular A-125, *Prompt Payment,* to prescribe policies and procedures to federal agencies in implementing the act. The OMB circular specifically exempts payments made solely for financing purposes from the assessment of interest penalties. It also discourages agencies from paying invoices earlier than the due date. Each federal agency is required to report annually to OMB the extent of interest penalties paid by the agency.

Where the Federal Government had consistently taken more than 30 days to pay its bills, implementing the Promp Payment Act generally improved a contractor's cash flow. For certain agencies that normally paid in a time period considerably less than 30 days (for example DOD), the act has had actually the effect of slowing payment because the OMB implementing regulations require agencies to take full advantage of the 30-day period before making payments.

The regulations implementing the Prompt Payment Act point up the importance of contractors having effective accounting and billing systems to ensure the timely submission of properly prepared invoices. In far too many instances, the payment delay can be attributed to the contractor's failure to submit an acceptable invoice on a timely basis. Contractors should review their accounting and billing procedures to make certain that the systems are capable of taking full advantage of this act.

SUMMARY

Many sources of financing are available to facilitate the performance of government contracts. Potential contractors should be aware that, under most circumstances, the need for financial assistance is not considered a hindrance to the receipt of government contracts.

Notes:

1. Comptroller General Decision B-159494, September 2, 1966.
2. Comptroller General Decision B-150528, February 1, 1963.
3. Comptroller General Decision B-194945, June 16, 1979.
4. Comptroller General Decision B-195629, September 7, 1979.
5. Marine Midland Bank v. U.S. (Ct. Cl. 1982), No. 308-81C, August 25, 1982, 30 CCF 70,265.
6. American Pouch Foods, Inc., Debtor, U.S. v. American Pouch Foods, Inc., Dc NIll, No's. VIII 81 C 1616, 80 B 14821, 80 A 2375; June 20, 1983.
7. Deputy Secretary of Defense Memorandum for Secretaries of the Military Departments and Director, Defense Logistics Agency, Subject, Defense Financial and Investment Review, Attachment 1, page 10.

Chapter Ten

Other Contract Clauses

BACKGROUND

The procurement regulations require numerous clauses to be included in government contracts. Many of these clauses either directly or indirectly impact the remuneration the contractor ultimately receives for performance under the contract. Other clauses impose requirements that are totally unrelated to contract remuneration. Because the clauses are often merely incorporated by reference into the contract's general provisions, a simple perusal of the contract terms provides little insight for assessing the impact of these clauses on the potential profitability of a contract. Consequently, a more detailed review of these clauses is needed to enable a contractor to make informed judgments as to the risks and requirements of government contracting.

Because of the sheer volume of contract clauses that can be incorporated into a given contract, it is not practical to discuss each of them in this chapter. Clauses discussed below pertain to price redetermination under redeterminable and incentive type contracts, cost determination and reimbursement under cost type contracts, technical data, warranties, socioeconomic and environmental goals, and labor standards. Each of these clauses imposes significant contractual requirements as to records that must be maintained or specific actions that must be taken. However, keep in mind that the clauses discussed in this and other chapters are still only a portion of the clauses that may be incorporated into federal government contracts and subcontracts.

CONTRACT CLAUSES PROVIDING FOR SPECIFIC REPRICING ACTIONS

Several types of contract repricing actions simply respond to specific contract clauses that provide for anticipated repricing at contract inception. These repricing actions may be either positive or negative and usually relate to uncertainties about the future that exist at the time the contract is awarded. The repricing action may also represent a vehicle for making an award or making adjustments for less than anticipated levels of performance. Some of the types of contract clauses involved are discussed below.

Incentive Price Revision

Under fixed-price incentive (FPI) contracts, targets are established, with adjustments to profit based on performance as it relates to the target. The target can be based on cost or specific measures of performance. Under a FPI contract, a target cost, a target profit, a total price ceiling, and a formula for establishing the final profit and price are negotiated at the outset. After the contract is completed, the final cost is negotiated and the final price determined through application of the formula. As illustrated in Figure 10.1, the formula provides greater profits when costs are less than the target cost; conversely, profits are reduced when the costs exceed the target cost. FPI contracts may provide for either firm targets (Fig. 10.2) or successive targets (Fig. 10.3). Under the latter form, new targets are established at specified points in the contract's period of performance.

Cost plus incentive fee (CPIF) contracts are similar to FPI contracts in that the amount of the ultimate fee earned depends on the level of cost incurred compared to the previously established target cost.

Final price determination under fixed-price incentive type contracts must be submitted on Standard Form 1411 when the amount exceeds $500,000.

Example	Targets per Contract Terms	Assumption: Cost Underrun- $100,000	Assumption: Cost Overrun- $100,000
Sharing Formula	75/25		
Cost	$1,000,000	$ 900,000	$1,100,000
Profit	150,000	175,000	125,000
Price	$1,150,000	$1,075,000	$1,225,000
Price Ceiling	$1,250,000	$1,250,000	$1,250,000

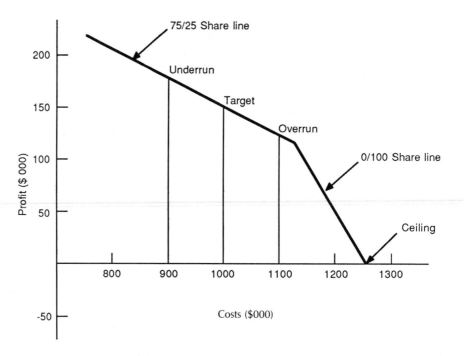

Figure 10.1. Application of fixed price incentive contract formula for final price determination.

(a) *General.* The supplies or services identified in the Schedule as Items _____ (*Contracting Officer insert Schedule line item numbers*) are subject to price revision in accordance with this clause; *provided,* that in no event shall the total final price of these items exceed the ceiling price of _____ dollars ($_____). Any supplies or services that are to be (1) ordered separately under, or otherwise added to, this contract and (2) subject to price revision in accordance with the terms of this clause shall be identified as such in a modification to this contract.

(b) *Definition.* "Costs." as usd in this clause, means allowable costs in accordance with Part 31 of the Federal Acquisition Regulation (FAR) in effect on the date of this contract.

(c) *Data submission.* (1) Within _____ (*Contracting Officer insert number of days*) days after the end of the month in which the Contractor has delivered the last unit of supplies and completed the services specified by item number in paragraph (a) above, the Contractor shall submit on Standard Form 1411 or in any other form on which the parties agree—

(i) A detailed statement of all costs incurred up to the end of that month in performing all work under the items;

(ii) An estimate of costs of further performance, if any, that may be necessary to complete performance of all work under the items;

(iii) A list of all residual inventory and an estimate of its value; and

(iv) Any other relevant data that the Contracting Officer may reasonably require.

(2) If the Contractor fails to submit the data required by subparagraph (1) above within the time specified and it is later determined that the Government has overpaid the Contractor, the Contractor shall repay the excess to the Government immediately. Unless repaid within 30 days after the end of the data submittal period, the amount of the excess shall bear interest, computed from the date the data were due to the date of repayment, at the rate established in accordance with the Interest clause.

(d) *Price revision.* Upon the Contracting Officer's receipt of the data required by paragraph (c) above, the Contracting Officer and the Contractor shall promptly establish the total final price of the items specified in (a) above by applying to final negotiated cost an adjustment for profit or loss, as follows:

(1) On the basis of the information required by paragraph (c) above, together with any other pertinent information, the parties shall negotiate the total final cost incurred or to be incurred for supplies delivered (or services performed) and accepted by the Government and which are subject to price revision under this clause.

(2) The total final price shall established by applying to the total final negotiated cost an adjustment for profit or loss, as follows:

(i) If the total final negotiated cost is equal to the total target cost, the adjustment is the total target profit.

(ii) If the total final negotiated cost is greater than the total target cost, the adjustment is the total target profit, less _____ (*Contracting Officer insert percent*) percent of the amount by which the total final negotiated cost exceeds the total target cost.

(iii) If the final negotiated cost is less than the total target cost, the adjustment is the total target profit plus _____ (*Contracting Officer insert percent*) percent of the amount by which the total final negotiated cost is less than the total target cost.

Figure 10.2. Excerpt from incentive price revision—firm target clause, FAR 523.216-16.

Economic Price Adjustment

These clauses are used to protect the contractor and the government against significant economic fluctuations in labor or material costs or to provide for contract price adjustments in the event of changes in the contract's established price. Upward or downward price adjustments are tied to the occurrence of certain contingencies that are specifically defined in the contract and beyond the control of the contractor.

(a) *General.* The supplies or services identified in the Schedule as Items _____ (*Contracting Officer insert line item numbers*) are subject to price revision in accordance with this clause; *provided,* that in no event shall the total final price of these items exceed the ceiling price of _____ dollars ($_____). The prices of these items shown in the Schedule are the initial target prices, which include an initial target profit of _____ (*Contracting Officer insert percent*) percent of the initial target cost. Any supplies or services that are to be (1) ordered separately under, or otherwise added to, this contract and (2) subject to price revision in accordance within this clause shall be identified as such in a modification to this contract.

(b) *Definition.* "Costs," as used in this clause, means allowable costs in accordance with Part 31 of the Federal Acquisition Regulation (FAR) in effect on the date of this contract.

(c) *Submitting data for establishing the firm fixed price or a final profit adjustment formula.* (1) Within _____ (*Contracting Officer insert number of days*) days after the end of the month in which the Contractor has completed. . . . [see Note 1], the Contractor shall submit the following data:

(i) A proposed firm fixed price or total firm target price for supplies delivered and to be delivered and services performed and to be performed.

(ii) A detailed statement of all costs incurred in the performance of this contract through the end of the month specified above, on Standard Form 1411 (or in any other form on which the parties may agree), with sufficient supporting data to disclose unit costs and cost trends for—

(A) Supplies delivered and services performed; and

(B) Inventories of work in process and undelivered contract supplies on hand (estimated to the extent necessary).

(iii) An estimate of costs of all supplies delivered and to be delivered and all services performed and to be performed under this contract, using the statement of costs incurred plus an estimate of costs to complete performance, on Standard Form 1411 (or in any other form on which the parties may agree), together with—

(A) Sufficient data to support the accuracy and reliability of the estimate; and

(B) An explanation of the differences between this estimate and the original estimate used to establish the initial target prices.

(2) The Contractor shall also submit, to the extent that it becomes available before negotiations establishing the total firm price are concluded—

(i) Supplemental statements of costs incurred after the end of the month specified in subparagraph (1) above for—

(A) Supplies delivered and services performed; and

(B) Inventories of work in process and undelivered contract supplies on hand (estimated to the extent necessary); and

(ii) Any other relevant data that the Contracting Officer may reasonably require.

(3) If the Contractor fails to submit the data required by subparagraphs (1) and (2) above within the time specified and it is later determined that the Government has overpaid the Contractor, the Contractor shall repay the excess to the Government immediately. Unless repaid within 30 days after the end of the data submittal period, the amount of the excess shall bear interest computed from the date the data were due to the date of repayment, at the rate established in accordance with the Interest clause.

(d) *Establishing firm fixed price or final profit adjustment formula.* Upon the Contracting Officer's receipt of the data required by paragraph (c) above the Contracting Officer and the Contractor shall promptly establish either a firm fixed price or a profit adjustment formula for determining final profit, as follows:

(1) The parties shall negotiate a total firm target cost, based upon the data submitted under paragraph (c) above.

(2) If the total firm target cost is more than the total initial target cost, the total initial target profit shall be decreased. If the total firm target cost is less than the total initial target cost, the total initial target profit shall be increased. The initial target profit shall be increased or decreased by _____ percent [see Note 2] of the difference between the total initial target cost and the total firm target cost. The resulting amount shall be the total firm target profit; *provided,* that in no event shall the total firm target profit be less than _____ percent or more than _____ percent (*Contracting Officer insert percent*) of the total initial target cost.

(3) If the total firm target cost plus the total firm target profit represent a reasonable price for performing that part of the contract subject to price revision under this clause, the parties may agree on a firm fixed price, which shall be evidenced by a contract modification signed by the Contractor and the Contracting Officer.

(4) Failure of the parties to agree to a firm fixed price shall not constitute a dispute under the Disputes clause. If agreement is not reached, or if establishment of a firm fixed price is inappropriate, the Contractor and the Contracting Officer shall establish a profit adjustment formula under

Figure 10.3. Excerpt from incentive price revision—successive targets clause, FAR 52.216-17.

which the total final price shall be established by applying to the total final negotiated cost an adjustment for profit or loss, determined as follows:

(i) If the total final negotiated cost is equal to the total firm target cost, the adjustment is the total firm target profit.

(ii) If the total final negotiated cost is greater than the total firm target cost, the adjustment is the total firm target profit, less _____ percent of the amount by which the total final negotiated cost exceeds the total firm target cost.

(iii) If the total final negotiated cost is less than the total firm target cost, the adjustment is the total firm target profit, plus _____ percent of the amount by which the total final negotiated cost is less than the total firm target cost.

(iv) The total firm target cost, total firm target profit, and the profit adjustment formula for determining final profit shall be evidenced by a modification to this contract signed by the Contractor and the Contracting Officer.

(e) *Submitting data for final price revision.* Unless a firm fixed price has been established in accordance with paragraph (d) above within _____ days after the end of the month in which the Contractor has delivered the last unit of supplies and completed the services specified by item number in paragraph (a) above, the Contractor shall sunmit on Standard Form 1411 (or in any other form on which the parties agree)—

(1) A detailed statement of all costs incurred up to the end of that month in performing all work under the items;

(2) An estimate of costs of further performance, if any, that may be necessary to complete performance of all work under the items;

(3) A list of all residual inventory and an estimate of its value; and

(4) Any other relevant data that the Contracting Officer may reasonably require.

(f) *Final price revision.* Unless a firm fixed price has been agreed to in accordance with paragraph (d) above, the Contractor and the Contracting Officer shall, promptly after submission of the data required by paragraph (e) above, establish the total final price, as follows:

(1) On the basis of the information required by paragraph (e) above, together with any other pertinent information, the parties shall negotiate the total final cost incurred or to be incurred for the supplies delivered (or services performed) and accepted by the Government and which are subject to price revision under this clause.

(2) The total final price shall be established by applying to the total final negotiated cost an adjustment for final profit or loss determined as agreed upon under subparagraph (d)(4) above.

(g) *Contract modification.* The total final price of the items specified in paragraph (a) above shall be evidenced by a modification to this contract, signed by the Contractor and the Contracting Officer. This price shall not be subject to revision, notwithstanding any changes in the cost of performing the contract, except to the extent that—

(1) The parties may agree in writing, before the determination of total final price, to exclude specific elements of cost from this price and to a procedure for subsequent disposition of these elements; and

(2) Adjustments or credits are explicitly permitted or required by this or any other clause in this contract.

Figure 10.3.   (Continued)

These are basically three types of economic price adjustment provisions:

Adjustment Based on	Method of Adjustment
Established prices (Figs 10.4 and 10.5)	Increases/decreases in published or established prices of specific items
Labor or material costs (Fig. 10.6) (actual costs method)	Increases/decreases experienced by the contractor on specified costs
Labor or material costs (cost index method)	Increases/decreases in specified cost standards or indices

The standard contract clauses limit increases to 10% of the original unit price or labor rate. However, the clauses can be modified by raising the limit on aggregate increases upon approval by the chief of the contracting office.

(a)   The Contractor warrants that the unit price stated in the Schedule for _____ (*offeror insert Schedule line item number*) is not in excess of the Contractor's applicable established price in effect on the contract date for like quantites of the same item. The term "unit price" excludes any part of the price directly resulting from requirements for preservation, packaging, or packing beyond standard commercial practice. The term "established price" means a price that (1) is an established catalog or market price for a commercial item sold in substantial quantities to the general public, (2) meets the criteria of subsection 15.804-3 of the Federal Acquisition Regulation (FAR), and (3) is the net price after applying any standard trade discounts offered by the Contractor.

(b)   The Contractor shall promptly notify the Contracting Officer of the amount and effective date of each decrease in any applicable established price. Each corresponding contract unit price shall be decreased by the same percentage that the established price is decreased. The decrease shall apply to those items delivered on and after the effective date of the decrease in the Contractor's established price, and this contract shall be modified accordingly. The Contractor shall certify (1) on each invoice that each unit price stated in it reflects all decreases required by this clause or (2) on the final invoice that all required price decreases have been applied as required by this clause.

(c)   If the Contractor's applicable established price is increased after the contract date, the corresponding contract unit price shall be increased, upon the Contractor's written request to the Contracting Officer, by the same percentage that the established price is increased, and the contract shall be modified accordingly, subject to the following limitations:

(1)   The aggregate of the increases in any contract unit price under this clause shall not exceed 10 percent of the original contract unit price.

(2)   The increased contract unit price shall be effective (i) on the effective date of the increase in the applicable established price if the Contracting Officer receives the Contractor's written request within 10 days thereafter or (ii) if the written request is received later, on the date the Contracting Officer receives the request.

(3)   The increased contract unit price shall not apply to quantities scheduled under the contract for delivery before the effective date of the increased contract unit price, unless failure to deliver before the date results from causes beyond the control and without the fault or negligence of the Contractor, within the meaning of the Default clause.

(4)   No modification increasing a contract unit price shall be executed under this paragraph (c) until the Contracting Officer verifies the increase in the applicable established price.

(5)   Within 30 days after receipt of the Contractor's written request, the Contracting Officer may cancel, without liability to either party, any undelivered portion of the contract items affected by the requested increase.

(d)   During the time allowed for the cancellation provided for in subparagraph (c)(5) above and thereafter if there is no cancellation, the Contractor shall continue deliveries according to the contract delivery schedule, and the Government shall pay for such deliveries at the contract unit price, increased to the extent provided by paragraph (c) above.

Figure 10.4.   Economic price adjustment—standard supplies clause, FAR 52.216-2.

Price Redetermination

There are two types of fixed-price redetermination clauses. The first provides for redetermination at stated intervals and is normally used where it is possible to negotiate a firm fixed-price contract for a stated period of time but not beyond (Fig. 10.7). The contract provides a fixed price for the stated period. Prior to the end of this period the contractor submits a formal pricing proposal (using a Standard Form 1411 if the amount of the contract exceeds $100,000) for the supplies to be delivered in the next succeeding period. The government and the contractor then negotiate prices for this period. The process continues for each succeeding period identified in the contract. This type of contract is only used when:

> Given the conditions surrounding the procurement, it is clear that a firm fixed-price contract does not meet the requirements of the contracting parties.

(a)   The Contractor warrants that the supplies identified as line items_____ [*offeror insert Schedule line item number*] in the Schedule are, except for modifications required by the contract specifications, supplies for which it has an established price. The term "established price" means a price that (1) is an established catalog or market price for a commercial item sold in substantial quantities to the general public, (2) meets the criteria of subsection 15.804-3 of the Federal Acquisition Regulation (FAR), and (3) is the net price after applying any standard trade discounts offered by the Contractor. The Contractor further warrants that, as of the date of this contract, any difference between the unit prices stated in the contract for these line items and the Contractor's established prices for like quantities of the nearest commercial equivalents are due to compliance with contract specifications and with any contract requirements for preservation, packaging, and packing beyond standard commercial practice.

(b)   The Contractor shall promptly notify the Contracting Officer of the amount and effective date of each decrease in any applicable established price. Each corresponding contract unit price (exclusive of any part of the unit price that reflects modifications resulting from compliance with specifications or with requirements for preservation, packaging, and packing beyond standard commercial practice) shall be decreased by the same percentage that the established price is decreased. The decrease shall apply to those items delivered on and after the effective date of the decrease in the Contractor's established price, and this contract shall be modified accordingly. The Contractor shall certify (1) on each invoice that each unit price stated in it reflects all decreases required by this clause or (2) in the final invoice that all required price decreases have been applied as required by this clause.

(c)   If the Contractor's applicable established price is increased after the contract date, the corresponding contract unit price (exclusive of any part of the unit price resulting from compliance with specifications or with requirements for preservation, packaging, and packing beyond standard commercial practice) shall be increased, upon the Contractor's written request to the Contracting Officer, by the same percentage that the established price is increased, and the contract shall be modified accordingly subject to the following limitations:

(1)   The aggregate of the increases in any contract unit price under this clause shall not exceed 10 percent of the original contract unit price.

(2)   The increased contract unit price shall be effective (i) on the effective date of the increase in the applicable established price if the Contracting Officer receives the Contractor's written request within 10 days thereafter or (ii) if the written request is received later, on the date the Contracting Officer receives the request.

(3)   The increased contract unit price shall not apply to quantities scheduled under the contract for delivery before the effective date of the increased contract unit price, unless failure to deliver before the date results from causes beyond the control and without the fault or negligence of the Contractor, within the meaning of the Default clause.

(4)   No modification increasing a contract unit price shall be executed under this paragraph (c) until the Contractin Officer verifies the increase in the applicable established price.

(5)   Within 30 days after receipt of the Contractor's written request, the Contracting Officer may cancel, without liability to either party, any undelivered portion of the contract items affected by the requested increase.

(d)   During the time allowed for the cancellation provided for in subparagraph (c)(5) above, and thereafter if there is no cancellation, the Contractor shall continue deliveries according to the contract delivery schedule, and the Government shall pay for such deliveries at the contract unit price increased to the extent provided by paragraph (c) above.

(End of clause)

Figure 10.5.   Economic price adjustment—semi standard supplies clause, FAR 52.216-3.

The contractor's accounting system is adequate for price redetermination purposes.

The prospective pricing period is compatible with the contractor's accounting system.

Timely price redetermination action is expected to be taken.

The second type of clause provides for a retroactive price redetermination after completion of the contract (Fig. 10.8). Price redeterminations after contract completion are normally limited to small contracts of short duration where it is not practical to establish a fair and reasonable firm price at the time of award.

(a)   The Contractor shall notify the Contracting Officer if, at any time during contract performance, the rates of pay for labor (including fringe benefits) or the unit prices for material shown in the Schedule either increase or decrease. The Contractor shall furnish this notice within 60 days after the increase or decrease, or within any additional period that the Contracting Officer may approve in writing, but not later than the date of final payment under this contract. The notice shall include the Contractor's proposal for an adjustment in the contract unit prices to be negotiated under paragraph (b) below, and shall include, in the form required by the Contracting Officer, supporting data explaining the cause, effective date, and amount of the increase or decrease and the amount of the Contractor's adjustment proposal.

(b)   Promptly after the Contracting Officer receives the notice and data under paragraph (a) above, the Contracting Officer and the Contractor shall negotiate a price adjustment in the contract unit prices and its effective date. However, the Contracting Officer may postpone the negotiations until an accumulation of increases and decreases in the labor rates (including fringe benefits) and unit prices of material shown in the Schedule results in an adjustment allowable under subparagraph (c)(3) below. The Contracting Officer shall modify this contract (1) to include the price adjustment and its effective date and (2) to revise the labor rates (including fringe benefits) or unit prices of material as shown in the Schedule to reflect the increases or decreases resulting from the adjustment. The Contractor shall continue performance pending agreement on, or determination of, any adjustment and its effective date.

(c)   Any price adjustment under this clause is subject to the following limitations:

(1)   Any adjustment shall be limited to the effect on unit prices of the increases or decreases in the rates of pay for labor (including fringe benefits) or unit prices for material shown in the Schedule. There shall be no adjustment for (i) supplies or services for which the production cost is not affected by such changes, (ii) changes in rates or unit prices other than those shown in the Schedule, or (iii) changes in the quantities of labor or material used from those shown in the Schedule for each item.

(2)   No upward adjustment shall apply to supplies or services that are required to be delivered or performed before the effective date of the adjustment, unless the Contractor's failure to deliver or perform according to the delivery schedule results from causes beyond the Contractor's control and without its fault or negligence, within the meaning of the Default clause.

(3)   There shall be no adjustment for any change in rates of pay for labor (including fringe benefits) or unit prices for material which would not result in a net change of at least 3 percent of the then-current total contract price. This limitation shall not apply, however, if, after final delivery of all contract line items, either party requests an adjustment under paragraph (b) above.

(4)   The aggregate of the increases in any contract unit price made under this clause shall not exceed 10 percent of the original unit price. There is no percentage limitation on the amount of decreases that may be made under this clause.

(d)   The Contractor shall include with the final invoice a certification that the Contractor either (1) has not experienced a decrease in rates of pay for labor (including fringe benefits) or unit prices for material shown in the Schedule or (2) has given notice of all such decreases in compliance with paragraph (a) above.

(e)   The Contracting Officer may examine the Contractor's books, records, and other supporting data relevant to the cost of labor (including fringe benefits) and material during all reasonable times until the end of 3 years after the date of final payment under this contract or the time periods specified in Subpart 4.7 of the Federal Acquisition Regulation (FAR), whichever is earlier.

Figure 10.6. Economic price adjustment—labor and material clause, FAR 52.216-4.

Because the entire price is redetermined retroactively, the contract itself does not provide a quantifiable incentive for effective cost control. Accordingly, the contract ceiling negotiated at the time of award is designed to provide for a reasonable assumption of risk by the contractor.

Upon completion of the contract, the contractor submits a statement of total incurred costs. The contractor and the government then negotiate a contract price. The government's objective is to negotiate a price which recognizes the degree of management effectiveness and ingenuity exhibited during contract performance. Any amounts paid during contract performance that exceed the retroactively determined contract value must be repaid to the government immediately.

(a) *General.* The unit prices and the total price stated in this contract shall be periodically rede-termined in accordance with this clause, except that (1) the prices for supplies delivered and services performed before the first effective date of price redetermination (see paragraph (c) below) shall remain fixed and (2) in no event shall the total amount paid under this contract exceed any ceiling price included in the contract.

(b) *Definition.* "Costs," as used in this clause, means allowable costs in accordance with Part 31 of the Federal Acquisition Regulation (FAR) in effect on the date of this contract.

(c) *Price redetermination periods.* For the purpose of price redetermination, performance of this contract is divided into successive periods. The first period shall extend from the date of the con-tract to _____ [see Note (1)] and the second and each succeeding period shall extend for _____ (*insert appropriate number*) months from the end of the last preceding period, except that the parties may agree to vary the length of the final period. The first day of the second and each succeeding period shall be the effective date of price redetermination for that period.

(d) *Data submission.* (1) Not more than _____ nor less than _____ [see Note (2)] days be-fore the end of each redetermination period, except the last, the Contractor shall submit—

(i) Proposed prices for supplies that may be delivered or services that may be performed in the next succeeding period, and—

(A) An estimate and breakdown of the costs of these supplies or services on Standard Form 1411, Contract Pricing Proposal Cover Sheet (or in any other form on which the parties may agree);

(B) Sufficient data to support the accuracy and reliability of this estimate; and

(C) An explanation of the differences between this estimate and the original (or last preceding) estimate for the same supplies or services; and

(ii) A statement of all costs incurred in performing this contract through the end of the _____ month [see Note (3)] before the submission of proposed prices, on Standard Form 1411, Contract Pricing Proposal Cover Sheet (or in any other form on which the parties may agree), with sufficient supporting data to disclose unit costs and cost trends for—

(A) Supplies delivered and services performed; and

(B) Inventories of work in process and undelivered contract supplies on hand (estimated to the extent necessary).

(2) The Contractor shall also submit, to the extent that it becomes available before negotiations on redetermined prices are concluded—

(i) Supplemental statements of costs incurred after the date stated in subdivision (d)(1)(ii) above for—

(A) Supplies delivered and services performed; and

(B) Inventories of work in process and undelivered contract supplies on hand (estimated to the extent necessary); and

(ii) Any other relevant data that the Contracting Officer may reasonably require.

Figure 10.7. Excerpt from price redetermination—prospective clause, FAR 52.216-5.

(a) *General.* The unit price and the total price stated in this contract shall be redetermined in ac-cordance with this clause, but in no event shall the total amount paid under this contract exceed _____ (*insert dollar amount of ceiling price*).

(b) *Definition.* "Costs," as used in this clause, means allowable costs in accordance with Part 31 of the Federal Acquisition Regulation (FAR) in effect on the date of this contract.

(c) *Data submission.* (1) Within _____ (*Contracting Officer insert number of days*) days after deliv-ery of all supplies to be delivered and completion of all services to be performed under this con-tract, the Contractor shall submit—

(i) Proposed prices;

(ii) A statement on Standard Form 1411, Contract Pricing Proposal Cover Sheet, or in any other form on which the parties agree, of all costs incurred in performing this contract; and

(iii) Any other relevant data that the Contracting Officer may reasonably require.

(2) If the Contractor fails to submit the data required by subparagraph (1) above within the time specified, the Contracting Officer may suspend payments under this contract until the data are furnished. If it is later determined that the Government has overpaid the Contractor, the excess shall be repaid to the Government immediately. Unless repaid within 30 days after the end of the data submittal period, the amount of the excess shall bear interest, computed from the date the data were due to the date of repayment, at the rate established in accordance with the Interest clause.

Figure 10.8. Excerpt from price redetermination—retroactive clause, FAR 52.216-6.

Retroactive price redetermination is used only for research and development procurements when the estimated costs are $100,000 or less and:

The contractor's accounting system is adequate for price redetermination purposes.

Timely price redetermination action is expected to be taken.

A ceiling price is established.

The head of the procuring activity has given written approval.

CONTRACT CLAUSES THAT PROVIDE THE BASIS FOR COST DETERMINATION AND REIMBURSEMENT UNDER COST TYPE CONTRACTS

Allowable Cost and Payment

The "allowable cost and payment" clause (Fig. 10.9) provides for reimbursement of costs incurred in contract performance that are deemed "allowable" by the contracting officer, in accordance with procurement regulation cost principles

---

(a) *Invoicing.* The Government shall make payments to the Contractor when requested as work progresses, but (except for small business concerns) not more often than once every 2 weeks, in amounts determined to be allowable by the Contracting Officer in accordance with Subpart 31.2 of the Federal Acquisition Regulation (FAR) in effect on the date of this contract and the terms of this contract. The Contractor may submit to an authorized representative of the Contracting Officer, in such form and reasonable detail as the representative may require, an invoice or voucher supported by a statement of the claimed allowable cost for performing this contract.

(b) *Reimbursing costs.* (1) For the purpose of reimbursing allowable costs (except as provided in subparagraph (2) below, with respect to pension, deferred profit sharing, and employee stock ownership plan contributions), the term "costs" includes only—

(i) Those recorded costs that, at the time of the request for reimbursement, the Contractor has paid by cash, check, or other form of actual payment for items or services purchased directly for the contract;

(ii) When the Contractor is not delinquent in paying costs of contract performance in the ordinary course of business, costs incurred, but not necessarily paid, for—

(A) Materials issued from the Contractor's inventory and placed in the production process for use on the contract;

(B) Direct labor;

(C) Direct travel;

(D) Other direct in-house costs; and

(E) Properly allocable and allowable indirect costs, as shown in the records maintained by the Contractor for purposes of obtaining reimbursement under Government contracts; and

(iii) The amount of progress payments that have been paid to the Contractor's subcontractors under similar cost standards.

(2) Contractor contributions to any pension, profit-sharing or employee stock ownership plan funds that are paid quarterly or more often may be included in indirect costs for payment purposes; *provided,* that the contractor pays the contribution to the fund within 30 days after the close of the period covered. Payments made 30 days or more after the close of a period shall not be included until the Contractor actually makes the payment. Accrued costs for such contributions that are paid less often than quarterly shall be excluded from indirect costs for payment purposes until the Contractor actually makes the payment.

(3) Notwithstanding the audit and adjustment of invoices or vouchers under paragraph (g) below, allowable indirect costs under this contract shall be obtained by applying indirect cost rates established in accordance with paragraph (d) below.

(4) Any statements in specifications or other documents incorporated in this contract by reference designating performance of services or furnishing of materials at the Contractor's expense or at no cost to the Government shall be disregarded for purposes of cost-reimbursement under this clause.

Figure 10.9. Allowable cost and payment clause, FAR 52.216-7.

(c) *Small business concerns.* A small business concern may be paid more often than every 2 weeks and may invoice and be paid for recorded costs for items or services purchased directly for the contract, even though the concern has not yet paid for those items or services.

(d) *Final indirect cost rates.* (1) Final annual indirect cost rates and the appropriate bases shall be established in accordance with Subpart 42.7 of the Federal Acquisition Regulation (FAR) in effect for the period covered by the indirect cost rate proposal.

(2) The Contractor shall, within 90 days after the expiration of each of its fiscal years, or by a later date approved by the Contracting Officer, submit to the cognizant Contracting Officer responsible for negotiating its final indirect cost rates and, if required by agency procedures, to the cognizant audit activity proposed final indirect cost rates for that period and supporting cost data specifying the contract and/or subcontract to which the rates apply. The proposed rates shall be based on the Contractor's actual cost experience for that period. The appropriate Government representative and Contractor shall establish the final indirect cost rates as promptly as practical after receipt of the Contractor's proposal.

(3) The Contractor and the appropriate Government representative shall execute a written understanding setting forth the final indirect cost rates. The understanding shall specify (i) the agreed-upon final annual indirect cost rates, (ii) the bases to which the rates apply, (iii) the periods for which the rates apply, (iv) any specific indirect cost items treated as direct costs in the settlement, and (v) the affected contract and/or subcontract, identifying any with advance agreements or special terms and the applicable rates. The understanding shall not change any monetary ceiling, contract obligation, or specific cost allowance or disallowance provided for in this contract. The understanding is incorporated into this contract upon execution.

(4) Failure by the parties to agree on a final annual indirect cost rate shall be a dispute within the meaning of the Disputes clause.

(e) *Billing rates.* Until final annual indirect cost rates are established for any period, the Government shall reimburse the Contractor at billing rates established by the Contracting Officer or by an authorized representative (the cognizant auditor), subject to adjustment when the final rates are established. These billing rates—

(1) Shall be the anticipated final rates; and

(2) May be prospectively or retroactively revised by mutual agreement, at either party's request, to prevent substantial overpayment or underpayment.

(f) *Quick-closeout procedures.* When the Contractor and Contracting Officer agree, the quick-closeout procedures of Subpart 42.7 of the FAR may be used.

(g) *Audit.* At any time or times before final payment, the Contracting Officer may have the Contractor's invoices or vouchers and statements of cost audited. Any payment may be (1) reduced by amounts found by the Contracting Officer not to constitute allowable costs or (2) adjusted for prior overpayments or underpayments.

(h) *Final payment.* (1) The Contractor shall submit a completion invoice or voucher, designated as such, promptly upon completion of the work, but no later than one year (or longer, as the Contracting Officer may approve in writing) from the completion date. Upon approval of that invoice or voucher, and upon the Contractor's compliance with all terms of this contract, the Government shall promptly pay any balance of allowable costs and that part of the fee (if any) not previously paid.

(2) The Contractor shall pay to the Government any refunds, rebates, credits, or other amounts (including interest, if any) accruing to or received by the Contractor or any assignee under this contract, to the extent that those amounts are properly allocable to costs for which the Contractor has been reimbursed by the Government. Reasonable expenses incurred by the Contractor for securing refunds, rebates, credits, or other amounts shall be allowable costs if approved by the Contracting Officer. Before final payment under this contract, the Contractor and each assignee whose assignment is in effect at the time of final payment shall execute and deliver—

(i) An assignment to the Government, in form and substance satisfactory to the Contracting Officer, of refunds, rebates, credits, or other amounts (including interest, if any) properly allocable to costs for which the Contractor has been reimbursed by the Government under this contract; and

(ii) A release discharging the Government, its officers, agents, and employees from all liabilities, obligations, and claims arising out of or under this contract, except—

(A) Specified claims stated in exact amounts, or in estimated amounts when the exact amounts are not known;

(B) Claims (including reasonable incidental expenses) based upon liabilities of the Contractor third parties arising out of the performance of this contract; *provided,* that the claims are not known to the Contractor on the date of the execution of the release, and that the Contractor gives notice of the claims in writing to the Contracting Officer within 6 years following the release date or notice of final payment date, whichever is earlier; and

(C) Claims for reimbursement of costs, including reasonable incidental expenses, incurred by the Contractor under the patent clauses of this contract, excluding, however, any expenses arising from the Contractor's indemnification of the Government against patent liability.

Figure 10.9. (Continued)

and contract terms. Notwithstanding the specific provisions of the cost principles (discussed in Chapter 7), the contract clause defines *cost* to include only:

> Recorded costs that at the time of request for reimbursement have been paid for items or services purchased directly for the contract (not applicable to small business).
>
> Costs incurred but not necessarily paid for materials issued from the contractor's stores inventory, direct labor, direct travel, other direct in-house costs, and properly allocable and allowable indirect costs.
>
> Pension, deferred profit sharing, and employee stock ownership plan (ESOP) contributions that are funded on a quarterly basis.
>
> Progress payments that have been paid to subcontractors.

Thus, for items purchased directly for a contract, the cash basis of accounting must be used unless the contractor is a small business. Furthermore, where pension, deferred profit sharing, and ESOP contributions are funded less frequently than quarterly, the accrued cost must be deleted from claimed indirect expenses until actually paid. The clause relies heavily on the contractor's accounting system to determine properly allocable costs. As discussed in Chapter 8, the allocation of costs to a government contract may be subject to some or all of the provisions of the Cost Accounting Standards Board's rules, regulations, and standards.

The clause also provides that for other than small businesses, payment shall not be made more frequently than biweekly.

In addition to the "audit" clause, which will be discussed later, the "allowable cost and payment" clause gives the government the right to audit the invoices or vouchers and statements of cost any time prior to final payment.

In determining the allowable costs under a contract, final indirect cost rates are applied to the appropriate contract bases. The contractor is required, within 90 days after expiration of its fiscal year, to submit to the contracting officer and cognizant audit agency a proposal for final indirect cost rates for the period, based upon actual costs. Final rates are generally computed as percentages or dollar factors that express the ratios of indirect expenses incurred in the period to direct labor, total cost input, or some other appropriate bases of the same period. Final indirect cost rates are necessary to determine the cost incurred under cost reimbursement type contracts as well as incentive and fixed-price redeterminable type contracts. They also apply to any other contracts that require settlement of indirect costs prior to establishing a final contract price. If the overhead rate proposal is covered by the Truth in Negotiations Act, FAR 42.705-2 (g) (2) (ii) requires, a signed certificate of current cost or pricing data.

Final Indirect Expense Rates

Prior to October 1985 final rates were established either by procurement determination (negotiation) or audit determination.

> The procedure for establishing final rates by negotiation was initiated by submission of the contractor's overhead proposal to the contracting officer. The auditor performed a review and issued an advisory report to the contracting officer. Negotiations ensued, and culminated in an agreement on rates. If the parties failed to agree, the contracting officer made a unilateral

final decision on behalf of the government, which could be appealed in accordance with the "disputes" clause of the contract.

The procedure for establishing rates by audit determination was also initiated by the contractor's submission of an overhead rate proposal. However, in this case the proposal was submitted to the auditor who performed the review and entered into discussions of the audit findings with the contractor. The auditor prepared a written overhead rate agreement to be jointly signed by the contractor and the auditor. In the event an agreement could not be reached, the auditor issued a formal notice of *costs suspended and/or disapproved* (DCAA FORM 1) (Fig. 10.10), detailing the exceptions, which the contractor could appeal to the contracting officer. The contracting officer's decision was appealed through the normal disputes procedure.

Overhead rates were "negotiated" where a corporate administrative contracting officer (CACO) was assigned or where an administrative contracting officer (ACO) was in residence. Audit determined rates were provided for other business concerns.

On October 17, 1985 the Deputy Secretary of Defense officially transferred the responsibility for final indirect cost rate determinations for all commercial contractor locations to the DCAA. This action extends the same procedures previously used by DCAA in determining final indirect cost rates at smaller contractors to the larger commercial contractor locations where final rates had been settled by procurement negotiation. Indirect cost settlement procedures remained unchanged for educational and similar institutions. To permit as orderly a transition as possible, ACOs retained settlement responsibility for open years in which an audit report had been issued and negotiations had begun. DCAA settlement authority would begin with the following year.

The final indirect expense rates settlement process is now initiated by the submission of the contractor's indirect cost rate proposal to both the cognizant contract auditor and the contracting officer. Upon the completion of the audit, the auditor seeks agreement with the contractor on final indirect expense rates for the fiscal year in question. The contractor has 90 days (with a potential extension to 120 days) to respond to any cost exceptions identified. The auditor has 60 days to evaluate the contractor's comments and to notify the contractor of any changes to the original audit findings. If the auditor and the contractor's representative agree on final rates, they execute a memorandum of understanding identifying the rates for incorporation into the applicable contracts. In the event an agreement cannot be reached, the auditor issues a DCAA Form 1 detailing the exceptions. The exceptions at this point can be appealed to the contracting officer, and any adverse decision by the contracting officer can be appealed through the normal disputes procedure.

Regardless of the outcome of the settlement an audit report is submitted to the ACO.

Provisional Indirect Expense Rates

Pending establishment of final indirect cost rates, the contractor and government should agree on provisional billing rates based on anticipated final annual rates. To prevent substantial over- or underpayment, billing rates should be adjusted as needed. It is incumbent on the contractor to determine the continued appropriateness of previously established billing rates given the passage of time and experience.

DEFENSE CONTRACT AUDIT AGENCY
NOTICE OF CONTRACT COSTS SUSPENDED AND/OR DISAPPROVED

PAGE _____ OF _____ PAGE(S)

TO: *(Name and Address of Contractor)*	CONTRACT NUMBER	NOTICE NUMBER
	DISBURSING OFFICE	CONTRACT ADMINISTRATION OFFICE

1.   This notice is issued pursuant to the authority of DoD Directive 5105.36, as implemented by the Defense Acquisition Regulation. It constitutes notice of costs suspended and/or disapproved incident to the audit of contractor costs incurred under referenced contract(s). Description of items and reasons for the action are stated below.

2.   SUSPENDED COSTS, as referred to herein, are costs which, for the reasons stated below, have been determined by the undersigned to be inadequately supported or otherwise questionable, and not appropriate for reimbursement under the contract terms at this time. Such costs may be determined reimbursable after the contractor provides the auditor additional documentation or explanation as specified below.

3.   DISAPPROVED COSTS, as referred to herein, are costs which, for the reasons stated below, have been determined by the undersigned to be unallowable, that is, not reimbursable under the contract terms.

4.   If the contractor disagrees with this/these determinations, the contractor may (1) request in writing the cognizant contracting officer to consider whether the unreimbursed costs should be paid and to discuss his or her findings with the contractor and/or (2) file a claim under the "Disputes" clause of the contract(s).

5.   The auditor will submit copies of the acknowledged notice to the cognizant disbursing officer for appropriate action and to the cognizant contracting officer.

DCAA AUDITOR	DATE OF NOTICE	ADDRESS	SIGNATURE

CONTRACTOR'S ACKNOWLEDGMENT OF RECEIPT - The contractor or its authorized representative shall acknowledge receipt of this notice to the DCAA auditor.

DATE OF RECEIPT	NAME AND TITLE OF AUTHORIZED OFFICIAL	SIGNATURE

ITEM NO.	DESCRIPTION OF ITEMS AND REASONS FOR ACTION	AMOUNT OF COSTS	
		SUSPENDED	DISAPPROVED

DCAA FORM 1
FEB 83

Supersedes September 1965 Edition of DCAA Form 1

☆ U.S. G.P.O. 1983-381-508/5696

Figure 10.10.   Notice of contract costs suspended and/or disapproved, DCAA Form 1.

DEFENSE CONTRACT AUDIT AGENCY NOTICE OF CONTRACT COSTS SUSPENDED AND/OR DISAPPROVED *(Continuation Sheet)*	PAGE _____ OF _____ PAGE(S)
	NOTICE NUMBER
CONTRACTOR.	

ITEM NO.	DESCRIPTION OF ITEMS AND REASONS FOR ACTION *(Continued)*

DCAA FORM 1-C
FEB 83

Supersedes September 1965 Edition of DCAA Form 1-C

Figure 10.10. (Continued)

Overhead Certificate

A new DOD certification requirement was announced March 12, 1985 amid a series of congressional hearings delving into assertions that defense contractors were improperly charging the government with unallowable costs.

The initial certificate required corporate officials to declare, under penalty of perjury, that no unallowable costs were included in the claim and that all costs that were included "benefited the Department of Defense and were demonstrably related to or necessary for the performance of the Department of Defense contracts covered by the claim."

Industry was understandably concerned about the ramifications of this new requirement since the language in the certificate could reasonably lead one to believe that DOD would seek criminal prosecution where costs, claimed and certified in good faith to be allowable, were later disallowed. In addition, the definition of "overhead" costs in that initial certificate was inconsistent with the acquisition regulations and cost accounting standards since it appeared to preclude the reimbursement of costs necessary for the overall operation of the business even though a direct relationship to a particular contract could not be shown.

A letter from the DOD General Council [1] was later issued to clarify the purpose and intent of the certificate. This letter advised:

> The form of the certificate does not require the signer to assure that the costs will be finally *allowed;* he is required to certify that in good faith he believes they are *allowable* and that he had reviewed the claim to satisfy himself that this is so. The purpose of the perjury declaration is to remind the signer of the importance of the certificate and the need to insure that it accurately states his actual knowledge and belief.
>
> Second, some commentators apparently believe that the certificate was intended to change the Federal Acquisition Regulation which defines the standards for allocating indirect costs to government contractors. This is not the case. The purpose of the certificate is to ensure that the signer, in good faith actually applies those established principles in determining which costs he claims to be chargeable to the contract.
>
> Contractors may rely on the foregoing explanation when signing the certificate.

The certificate was later revised in April 1986 to recognize that:

> The certification is a good faith assertion, not an absolute guarantee
> Costs are properly allocable to defense contracts if they are allocated in accordance with applicable acquisition regulations.

While the revised certificate has alleviated some of the ambiguities related to that intial certificate, it is clear that the certification requirement should not be taken lightly. To adequately protect itself, a defense contractor should assure that effective internal controls exist to properly screen unallowable costs from indirect expense proposals.

The Defense FAR Supplement (DFARS 242.770) requires execution of the certificate whenever provisional billing rates or final indirect cost rate proposals are submitted. The certificate must be signed by a senior management official at a level no lower than vice president or chief financial officer.

(a) The Contractor shall certify any proposal to establish or modify billing rates or to establish final indirect cost rates in the form set forth in paragraph (b) of this clause. The certificate shall be signed on behalf of the Contractor by an individual of the Contractor's organization at a level no lower than a vice president or chief financial officer of the business segment of the Contractor that submits the proposal. The Contractor understands that if the Contractor fails to submit a certificate as required herein, payments on account of indirect cost shall be at rates unilaterally established by the Government.

(b) *Certificate of Indirect Costs.* The certificate of indirect costs shall read as follows:

CERTIFICATE OF INDIRECT COSTS

This is to certify that to the best of my knowledge and belief:

1. I have reviewed the indirect cost proposal submitted herewith;

2. All costs included in this proposal (identify, date) to establish billing or final indirect cost rates for (identify, period covered by rate) are allowable in accordance with the requirements of contracts to which they apply and with the cost principles of the Department of Defense applicable to those contracts;

3. This proposal does not include any costs which are unallowable under applicable cost principles of the Department of Defense, such as (without limitation): advertising and public relations costs, contributions and donations, entertainment costs, fines and penalties, lobbying costs, defense of fraud proceedings, and good will; and

4. All costs included in this proposal are properly allocable to Defense contracts on the basis of a beneficial or causal relationship between the expense incurred and the contracts to which they are allocated in accordance with applicable acquisition regulations.

I declare under penalty of perjury that the foregoing is true and correct.

Firm: _____

Signature: _____

Name of Corporate Official: _____

Title: _____

Date of Execution: _____

(End of clause)

Figure 10.11 Certification of indirect costs clause, DFARS 252.242-7003.

A contracts clause entitled Certificate of Indirect Costs (Figure 10.11) is included in all defense contracts that provide for interim reimbursement of indirect costs, establishment of final indirect cost rates, and cost based progress payments.

Cost Reimbursement

A contractor is responsible for preparing and submitting reimbursement claims in accordance with the terms of the contract. Standard Form (SF) 1034 and 1034a, *Public Voucher for Purchases and Services Other than Personal,* are used to show the amount claimed for reimbursement. SF 1035 and 1035a, *Public Voucher for Purchases and Services other than Personal—Continuation Sheet,* are used for additional information required by the contracting officer and/or the auditor. The public voucher forms may be reproduced, obtained from an appropriate ACO, or obtained at a nominal cost from the Government Printing Office. Unless otherwise notified, public vouchers should be submitted to the auditor. The forms, together with instructions for preparation, are illustrated in Figures 10.12 and 10.13.

DCAA Publication DCAAP 7641.58 dated December 1977, *Preparation of Public Vouchers—Guidance and Instruction,* contains detailed information on preparing and processing public vouchers. The publication, which is available to

Standard Form 1034 Revised January 1980 Department of the Treasury I TFRM 4–2000 1034-118	PUBLIC VOUCHER FOR PURCHASES AND SERVICES OTHER THAN PERSONAL	VOUCHER NO. (e)

PUBLIC VOUCHER FOR PURCHASES AND SERVICES OTHER THAN PERSONAL

U.S. DEPARTMENT, BUREAU, OR ESTABLISHMENT AND LOCATION	DATE VOUCHER PREPARED (b)	SCHEDULE NO.
(a)	CONTRACT NUMBER AND DATE (c)	PAID BY (f)
	REQUISITION NUMBER AND DATE (d)	

PAYEE'S NAME AND ADDRESS	(h)	DATE INVOICE RECEIVED (f)
		DISCOUNT TERMS (f)
		PAYEE'S ACCOUNT NUMBER (g)

SHIPPED FROM (i)	TO (i)	WEIGHT (i)	GOVERNMENT B/L NUMBER (i)

NUMBER AND DATE OF ORDER	DATE OF DELIVERY OR SERVICE	ARTICLES OR SERVICES (Enter description, item number of contract of Federal supply schedule, and other information deemed necessary)	QUAN-TITY	UNIT PRICE COST	PER	AMOUNT
(j)	(k)	(l)	(m)	(n)	(n)	(n)
		(o)				

(Use continuation sheet(s) if necessary)   **(Payee must NOT use the space below)**   TOTAL

PAYMENT: ☐ PROVISIONAL ☐ COMPLETE ☐ PARTIAL ☐ FINAL ☐ PROGRESS ☐ ADVANCE	APPROVED FOR (p) (1) = $ BY ² (p) (2) TITLE (p) (3)	EXCHANGE RATE = $1.00	DIFFERENCES ____ Amount verified; correct for (Signature or initials)	

Pursuant to authority vested in me, I certify that this voucher is correct and proper for payment.

_____   _____   _____
(Date)   (Authorized Certifying Officer)³   (Title)

ACCOUNTING CLASSIFICATION

PAID BY	CHECK NUMBER	ON ACCOUNT OF U.S. TREASURY	CHECK NUMBER	ON (Name of bank)
	CASH $	DATE	PAYEE ³	

¹ When stated in foreign currency, insert name of currency.
² If the ability to certify and authority to approve are combined in one person, one signature only is necessary; otherwise the approving officer will sign in the space provided, over his official title.
³ When a voucher is receipted in the name of a company or corporation, the name of the person writing the company or corporate name, as well as the capacity in which he signs, must appear. For example: "John Doe Company, per John Smith, Secretary", or "Treasurer", as the case may be.

	PER
	TITLE

Previous edition usable   NSN 7540-00-634-4206

Figure 10.12. Public voucher for purchases and services other than personal, Standard Form 1034.

Instructions for Preparing SF1034

(a) Insert the name and address of the military department or agency that negotiated the contract.

(b) Insert the date on which the public voucher is submitted to the auditor.

(c) Insert the number and date of the contract and task order (which applicable).

(d) Insert the requisition number and date if available; otherwise leave blank.

(e) Insert the appropriate serial number of the voucher. A separate series of consecutive numbers beginning with 1 should be used for each new contract or task order (when applicable).

(f) Leave blank. The payer will complete this space.

(g) Leave blank unless such information is available.

(h) Insert the name and correct address of the contractor, except when an assignment has been made or the right to receive payment has been restricted. When the contractor has made an assignment, insert:

Name of Financial Institution
Assignee for X Company
Location (city and state) of Financial Institution

When the right to receive payment has been restricted, insert:

Name of Company
Location (city and state) of X Company
for deposit in the Y Financial Institution
Location (city and state) of Y Financial Institution
Name of Special Account

(i)-(j) Leave blank.

(k) Insert the month and year or beginning and ending dates with incurred costs claimed for reimbursement.

(l) Insert:

For detail, see SF 1035 -- Continutation Sheet, total amount claimed transferred from page ___ SF 1035.

(m) Leave blank.

(n) Insert the total amount claimed for the time indicated in (k). This should agree with the amount shown on SF 1035 -- Continuation Sheet.

(o) Insert "Cost Reimbursable -- Provisional Payment" on the interim public voucher. Insert "Cost Reimbursable -- Completion Voucher" on the final public voucher.

(p) On interim vouchers only:

(1) Insert "Provisional Payment Subject to Later Audit" after the words "Approved for"; strike out with X's, the words "Exchange Rate" and the "=" and "$" signs.

(2) Insert the name of the auditor who will sign the voucher.

(3) Insert "Auditor, Defense Contract Audit Agency"

Figure 10.12. (Continued)

Standard Form 1035 September 1973 4 Treasury FRM 2000 1035-110	**PUBLIC VOUCHER FOR PURCHASES AND SERVICES OTHER THAN PERSONAL** *CONTINUATION SHEET*	VOUCHER NO. (c) SCHEDULE NO. SHEET NO. (a)

U.S. DEPARTMENT, BUREAU, OR ESTABLISHMENT
(b)

NUMBER AND DATE OF ORDER	DATE OF DELIVERY OR SERVICE	ARTICLES OR SERVICES *(Enter description, item number of contract or Federal supply schedule, and other information deemed necessary)*	QUAN- TITY	UNIT PRICE COST	PER	AMOUNT

```
(d)  Name of Company   (e)  Contract No. _____    (f)Target/Estimated
     Address  _____                                 Costs              $xxxxxx
                                                         (f)Target/Fixed Fee    xxxxxx
                                                         (f)Total               $xxxxxx
                               (g)Analysis of Claimed Current   (f)85% of Fixed Fee $xxxxxx
                                  and Cumulative Costs and
                                  Fee Earned
                                                                              (j)
                                                         (i)Amount for        Cumulative
                                                         Current Period       Am't From In-
                                                               Billed         ception To
                                                                              Date of This
                                                                              Billing
(h)  Major Cost Elements:
     _____                                          $xxxxxx         $xxxxxx
     _____                                           xxxxxx          xxxxxx
     _____                                           xxxxxx          xxxxxx
     _____                                           xxxxxx          xxxxxx
     _____                                           xxxxxx          xxxxxx
     _____                                           xxxxxx          xxxxxx
(k)          Total Costs                                      $xxxxxx         $xxxxxx
(l)  Fixed Fee Earned                                          xxxxxx          xxxxxx
(m)          Total Amounts Claimed                           $xxxxxx         $xxxxxx

     Contract Reserves and Adjustments

(n)  Contract Reserves Withheld                              $ (xxxx)        $ (xxxx)
(o)  DCAA Form 1 -- Resubmitted (Voucher No.)                 xxxxxx          xxxxxx
(o)  DCAA Form 1 -- Outstanding Suspensions                                   (xxxx)
(p)          Net - Reserves and Adjustments                  $xxxxxx         $ (xxxx)

(q)  Adjusted Amounts Claimed:
     Current and Cumulative Costs                            $xxxxxx         $xxxxxx
     Fixed Fee                                                xxxxxx          xxxxxx
          Total                                        (r)$xxxxxx          $xxxxxx
```

Figure 10.13. Public voucher for purchases and services other than personal—continuation sheet, Standard Form 1035.

Instructions for Preparing SF 1035

(a) Insert the sheet number in numerical sequence if more than one sheet is used. Use as many sheets as necessary to show the information required by the contracting officer or the auditor.

(b) Insert the name of the military department or agency which negotiated the contract.

(c) Insert the voucher number, as shown on SF 1034.

(d) Insert payee's name and address as shown on SF 1034.

(e) Insert the contract number and the task order number (when applicable).

(f) Insert the latest: target or estimated costs, target or fixed-fee, total contract value, and amount of fee payable.

(g) Insert: analysis of claimed current and cumulative costs and fee earned.

(h) Insert the major cost elements (should be compatible with the cost elements developed in the cost accounting system). Use additional SF 1035s if necessary to show computations of overhead adjustments from provisional rates to negotiated rates or allowable actual rates, or the computation of fee claimed.

(i) Insert the amount billed by the major cost elements, contract reserves and adjustments, and adjusted amounts claimed for the current period.

(j) Insert the cumulative amounts billed by the major cost elements, contract reserves, and adjusted amounts claimed to date of this billing.

(k) Insert the total costs for current and cumulative periods.

(l) Insert the target or fixed-fee earned and due for the current and cumulative periods and the formula for the computation (percentage of costs, percentage of completion, etc.).

(m) Insert the total costs claimed and the target or fixed-fee due for the current and cumulative periods.

(n) Insert the details of the contract reserves withheld in the current period and for the cumulative period. The contractor is responsible for reducing its claims for contract reserves.

(o) Show the status of all outstanding DCAA Forrm 1's, "Notice of Contract Costs Suspended and/or Disapproved." When amounts on an outstanding DCAA Form 1 are resubmitted, they should be shown in the current period column, and the corresponding cumulative total of outstanding suspensions or disapprovals reduced to cover the resubmission so that the cumulative amounts are "net".

(p) Insert net reserves and adjustments.

(q) Show the costs and fee subject to reimbursement for the current and cumulative periods.

(r) Amount to be carried forward to SF 1034

Figure 10.13. (Continued)

the public, can be obtained from the Records Administrator, DCAA, Cameron Station, Alexandria, Va.

Within one year (or a longer period when authorized by the contracting officer) after completion of work under the contract, the contractor is required to submit to the government a *completion invoice* or *completion voucher*. The government is responsible for promptly paying to the contractor any allowable costs and fees that remain unpaid. Prior to final payment under the contract, the contractor and the assignee (if monies payable under the contract were assigned to a financial instituion pursuant to the "assignment of claims" clause which is discussed in Chapter 9) must assign to the government any refunds, rebates, credits or other amounts (including interest) properly allocable to costs for which the contractor has been reimbursed by the government under the contract. The assignment presumably extends indefinitely so that any subsequent receipt of refunds or credits associated with amounts previously paid must be forwarded to the government. In addition, the contractor and assignee, if applicable, must provide a release discharging the government, its officials, agents, and employees from all liabilities, obligations, and claims arising out of or under the contractor subject only to specified exceptions. Figures 10.14 to 10.17 contain illustrations of the Contractor's Release; Contractor's Assignment of Refunds, Rebates, Credits and Other Amounts; Assignee's Release; and Assignee's Assignment of Refunds, Rebates, Credits and other Amounts.

Cost Reimbursement to Subcontractors

Cost incurred as reimbursement to a subcontractor under a cost reimbursement type subcontract, at any tier above the first fixed-price subcontract, are allowable to the extent they are consistent with the cost principles. The subcontract may provide for the determination of allowability to be made either by the prime contractor or the government contracting officer; or the subcontract may be silent as to who is to determine the allowability of costs. If the subcontractor also performs under prime contracts of its own and has a resident government auditor and contracting officer, the subcontract may provide for the determination of allowability by those government representatives. A prime contractor has recourse to the government under the "disputes" procedures of the contract in the event of a disagreement concerning the allowability of costs. However, a subcontractor generally does not. As a result, subcontractors should avoid entering into any agreements that make the decision of government auditors or contracting officers final with regard to matters of cost without preserving some means for review of their decisions.

Limitation of Cost or Funds

The "limitation of cost" clause (Fig. 10.18) is used in fully funded cost reimbursement type contracts, whereas the "limitation of funds" clause (Fig. 10.19) is inserted in incrementally funded cost reimbursement type contracts. These clauses obligate the contractor to notify the government when the contractor has reason to believe that within the next 60 days the cumulative cost incurred to date in the performance of the contract will exceed 75% of the estimated cost of or funds allotted to the contract. The contractor must also notify the government anytime the total cost of the contract is expected to be substantially greater or less than the estimated cost or allotted funds.

CONTRACTOR'S RELEASE	CONTRACT NO.

Pursuant to the terms of Contract No. _____ and in consideration of the sum of _____
(Total of amounts paid and payable)

Dollars ($ _____), which has been or is to be paid under the said contract to _____
(Contractor's name and address)

_____
(hereinafter called the Contractor) or its assignees, if any, the Contractor upon payment of the said sum by the United States of America *(hereinafter called the Government),* does hereby remise, release, and discharge the Government, its officers, agents, and employees of and from all liabilities, obligations, claims, and demands whatsoever under or arising from the said contract, except:

   A. Specified claims in stated amounts or in estimated amounts where the amounts are not susceptible of exact statement by the Contractor, as follows *(if none, so state)*: _____

   B. Claims, together with reasonable expenses incidental thereto, based upon the liabilities of the Contractor to third parties arising out of the performance of the said contract, which are not known to the Contractor on the date of the execution of this release and of which the Contractor gives notice in writing to the Contracting Officer within the time period specified in said contract.
   C. Claims for reimbursement of costs including reasonable expenses incidental thereto, incurred by the Contractor under the provisions of the said contract relating to patents.
   D. When the contract includes an article entitled *"Optional Data Requirements,"* claims pursuant to such article when, within the one-year period after final payment under the contract, the Contracting Officer requests in writing that the Contractor furnish such data.

   The Contractor agrees, in connection with patent matters and with claims which are not released as set forth above, that it will comply with all of the provisions of the said contract, including without limitation, those provisions relating to notification to the Contracting Officer and relating to the defense or prosecution of litigation.

   The Contractor further agrees that payments on account of claims not released as set forth above shall be subject to adjustment in accordance with paragraph (i) of the clause of the contract entitled "Incentive Fee," if such clause is a provision of the contract.

   IN WITNESS WHEREOF, this release has been executed this _____ day of _____ , 19____ .

_____
(Contractor)

WITNESSES

_____   BY _____

_____   TITLE _____

   (NOTE: In the case of a corporation witnesses are not required, but the certificate below must be completed.)

CERTIFICATE

I, _____ , certify that I am the _____
(Official Title)

_____
of the corporation named as Contractor in the foregoing release; that _____
who signed said release on behalf of the Contractor was then _____ of said corporation;
(Official Title)

that said release was duly signed for and in behalf of said corporation by authority of its governing body and is within the scope of its corporate powers.

_____

(CORPORATE SEAL)

Figure 10.14 Contractor's release.

CONTRACTOR'S ASSIGNMENT OF REFUNDS, REBATES, CREDITS, AND OTHER AMOUNTS	CONTRACT NO.

Pursuant to the terms of Contract No._____ and in consideration of the reimbursement of costs and payment of fee, as provided in the said contract and any assignment thereunder, the _____

(Contractor's Name and Address)

hereinafter called the Contractor) does hereby:

1. Assign, transfer, set over and release to the UNITED STATES OF AMERICA *(hereinafter called the Government),* all right, title, and interest to all refunds, rebates, credits, and other amounts *(including any interest thereon),* arising out of the performance of the said contract, together with all the rights of action accrued or which may hereafter accrue thereunder.

2. Agree to take whatever action may be necessary to effect prompt collection of all refunds, rebates, credits, and other amounts *(including any interest thereon)* due or which may become due, and to promptly forward to the Contracting Officer checks *(made payable to the Treasurer of the United States)* for any proceeds so collected. The reasonable costs of any such action to effect collection shall constitute allowable costs when approved by the Contracting Officer as stated in the said contract and may be applied to reduce any amounts otherwise payable to the Government under the terms hereof.

3. Agree to cooperate fully with the Government as to any claim or suit in connection with refunds, rebates, credits, or other amounts due *(including any interest thereon);* to execute any protest, pleading, application, power of attorney, or other papers in connection therewith; and to permit the Government to represent him at any hearing, trial, or other proceeding; arising out of such claim or suit.

IN WITNESS WHEREOF, this assignment has been executed this_____ day of_____, 19___.

_____
(Contractor)

WITNESSES

_____ BY _____

_____ TITLE _____

(NOTE: In the case of a corporation, witnesses are not required, but the certificate below must be completed.)

CERTIFICATE

I, _____, certify that I am the _____
(Official Title)

_____
of the corporation named as Contractor in the foregoing assignment; _____
who signed said assignment on behalf of the Contractor was then _____
(Official Title)

of said corporation; that said assignment was duly signed for and in behalf of said corporation by authority of its governing body and is within the scope of its corporate powers.

_____

(CORPORATE SEAL)

Figure 10.15. Contractor's assignment of refunds, rebates, credits, and other amounts.

ASSIGNEE'S RELEASE	CONTRACT NO.

Pursuant to the terms of Contract No. _____ and in consideration of the sum _____

(Total of amounts paid and payable)

Dollars ($_____) which has been or is to be paid under the said contract by the United States of America *(herein-after called the Government)* to the Contractor or its assignees, the _____

(Assignee's name and address)

    (i) a corporation organized and existing under the laws of the State of _____ ,

    (ii) a partnership consisting of _____ ,

    (iii) an individual trading as _____ ,

(hereinafter called the Assignee), upon receipt of that part of the said sum due under its assignment does hereby remise, release, and discharge the Government, its officers, agents, and employees of and from all liabilities, obligations, claims, and demands whatsoever under or arising from the said contract and assignment, except:

    A. Specified claims in stated amounts or in estimated amounts where the amounts are not susceptible of exact statement by the Contractor, as follows: _____

(If none, so state)

    B. Claims, together with reasonable expenses incidental thereto, based upon the liabilities of the contractor to third parties arising out of the performance of the said contract, which are not known to the Contractor or Assignee on the date of the execution of this release and of which the Contractor or Assignee gives notice in writing to the Contracting Officer within the time period specified in the said contract.

    C. Claims for reimbursement of costs including reasonable expenses incidental thereto, incurred by the Contractor under the provisions of the said contract relating to patents.

    D. When the contract includes an article entitled "Data Requirements," claims pursuant to such article when, within the one-year period after final payment under the contract, the Contracting Officer requests in writing that the Contractor furnish such data.

    The Assignee agrees, in connection with claims which are not released as set forth above, that final payment under the said contract does not modify the requirements and limitations imposed on the Contractor or Assignee by the contract or the assignment, including without limitation those provisions relating to notification to the Contracting Officer and relating to the defense or prosecution of litigation.

    The Assignee further agrees that payments on amount of claims not released as set forth above shall be subject to adjustment in accordance with paragraph (i) of the clause of the contract entitled "Incentive Fee," if such clause is a provision of the contract.

    IN WITNESS WHEREOF, this release has been executed this _____ day of _____ , 19 __

WITNESSES

_____

                                          (Assignee)

_____ BY _____

_____ TITLE _____

(NOTE: In the case of a corporation witnesses are not required, but the certificate below must be completed.)

CERTIFICATE

I, _____ , certify that I am the _____

                                                            (Official Title)

of the corporation named as Assignee in the foregoing release; that _____ who signed said release on behalf of the Assignee was then _____

                                                            (Official Title)

of said corporation; that said release was duly signed for and in behalf of said corporation by authority of its governing body and is within the scope of its corporate powers.

_____

(CORPORATE SEAL)

Figure 10.16. Assignee's release.

ASSIGNEE'S ASSIGNMENT OF REFUNDS, REBATES, CREDITS, AND OTHER AMOUNTS	CONTRACT NO.

Pursuant to the terms of Contract No. _____ and in consideration of the reimbursement of costs and payment of fee, as provided in the said contract and assignment thereunder, the _____

(Assignee's name and address)

(i) a corporation organized and existing under the laws of the state of _____

(ii) a partnership consisting of _____

(iii) an individual trading as _____

(hereinafter called the Assignee), does hereby assign, transfer, set over, and release to the UNITED STATES OF AMERICA, all right, title, and interest to all refunds, rebates, credits, and other amounts *(including any interest thereon)* arising out of the performance of the said contract, together with all rights of action accrued or which may hereafter accrue thereunder.

IN WITNESS WHEREOF, this assignment has been executed this _____ day of _____ , 19___.

_____
(Assignee)

WITNESSES

_____ BY _____

_____ TITLE _____

(NOTE: In the case of a corporation, witnesses are not required, but the following certificate must be completed.)

CERTIFICATE

I, _____ , certify that I am the _____

(Official Title)

of the corporation named as Assignee in the foregoing assignment; that _____

who signed said assignment on behalf of the Assignee was then _____

(Official Title)

of said corporation; that said assignment was duly signed for and in behalf of said corporation by authority of its governing body and is within the scope of its corporate powers.

_____

(CORPORATE SEAL)

Figure 10.17. Assignee's assignment of refunds, rebates, credits, and other amounts.

(a) The parties estimate that performance of this contract, exclusive of any fee, will not cost the Government more than (1) the estimated cost specified in the Schedule or (2) if this is a cost-sharing contract, the Government's share of the estimated cost specified in the Schedule. The Contractor agrees to use its best efforts to perform the work specified in the Schedule and all obligations under this contract within the estimated cost, which, if this is a cost-sharing contract, includes both the Government's and the Contractor's share of the cost.

(b) The Contractor shall notify the Contracting Officer in writing whenever it has reason to believe that—

(1) The costs the contractor expects to incur under this contract in the next 60 days, when added to all costs previously incurred, will exceed 75 percent of the estimated cost specified in the Schedule; or

(2) The total cost for the performance of this contract, exclusive of any fee, will be either greater or substantially less than had been previously estimated.

(c) As part of the notification, the Contractor shall provide the Contracting Officer a revised estimate of the total cost of performing this contract.

(d) Except as required by other provisions of this contract, specifically citing and stated to be an exception to this clause—

(1) The Government is not obligated to reimburse the Contractor for costs incurred in excess of (i) the estimated cost specified in the Schedule or, (ii) if this is a cost-sharing contract, the estimated cost to the Government specified in the Schedule; and

(2) The Contractor is not obligated to continue performance under this contract (including actions under the Termination clause of this contract) or otherwise incur costs in excess of the estimated cost specified in the Schedule, until the Contracting Officer (i) notifies the Contractor in writing that the estimated cost has been increased and (ii) provides a revised estimated total cost of performing this contract. If this is a cost-sharing contract, the increase shall be allocated in accordance with the formula specified in the Schedule.

(e) No notice, communication, or representation in any form other than that specified in subparagraph (d)(2) above, or from any person other than the Contracting Officer, shall affect this contract's estimated cost to the Government. In the absence of the specified notice, the Government is not obligated to reimburse the Contractor for any costs in excess of the estimated cost or, if this is a cost-sharing contract, for any costs in excess of the estimated cost to the Government specified in the Schedule, whether those excess costs were incurred during the course of the contract or as a result of termination.

(f) If the estimated cost specified in the Schedule is increased, any costs the Contractor incurs before the increase that are in excess of the previously estimated cost shall be allowable to the same extent as if incurred afterward, unless the Contracting Officer issues a termination or other notice directing that the increase is solely to cover termination or other specified expenses.

(g) Change orders shall not be considered an authorization to exceed the estimated cost to the Government specified in the Schedule, unless they contain a statement increasing the estimated cost.

(h) If this contract is terminated or the estimated cost is not increased, the Government and the Contractor shall negotiate an equitable distribution of all property produced or purchased under the contract, based upon the share of costs incurred by each.

Figure 10.18. Limitation of cost clause, FAR 52.232.20.

(a) The parties estimate that performance of this contract will not cost the Government more than (1) the estimated cost specified in the Schedule or, (2) if this is a cost-sharing contract, the Government's share of the estimated cost specified in the Schedule. The Contractor agrees to use its best efforts to perform the work specified in the Schedule and all obligations under this contract within the estimated cost, which, if this is a cost-sharing contract, includes both the Government's and the Contractor's share of the cost.

(b) The Schedule specifies the amount presently available for payment by the Government and allotted to this contract, the items covered, the Government's share of the cost if this is a cost-sharing contract, and the period of performance it is estimated the allotted amount will cover. The parties contemplate that the Government will allot additional funds incrementally to the contract up to the full estimated cost to the Government specified in the Schedule, exclusive of any fee. The Contractor agrees to perform, or have performed, work on the contract up to the point at which the total amount paid and payable by the Government under the contract approximates but does not exceed the total amount actually allotted by the Government to the contract.

Figure 10.19. Limitation of funds clause, FAR 52.232.21.

(c)   The Contractor shall notify the Contracting Office in writing whenever it has reason to believe that the costs it expects to incur under this contract in the next 60 days, when added to all costs previously incurred, will exceed 75 percent of (1) the total amount so far allotted to the contract by the Government or, (2) if this is a cost-sharing contract, the amount then allottd to the contract by the Government plus the Contractor's corresponding share. The notice shall state the estimated amount of additional funds required to continue performance for the period specified in the Schedule.

(d)   Sixty days before the end of the period specified in the Schedule, the Contractor shall notify the Contracting Officer in writing of the estimated amount of additional funds, if any, required to continue timely performance under the contract or for any further period specified in the Schedule or otherwise agreed upon, and when the funds will be required.

(e)   If, after notification, additional funds are not allotted by the end of the period specified in the Schedule or another agreed-upon date, upon the contractor's written request the Contracting Officer will terminate this contract on that date in accordance with the provisions of the Termination clause of this contract. If the Contractor estimates that the funds available will allow it to continue to discharge its obligations beyond that date, it may specify a later date in its request, and the Contracting Officer may terminate this contract on that later date.

(f)   Except as required by other provisions of this contract, specifically citing and stated to be an exception to this clause—

(1)   The Government is not obligated to reimburse the contractor for costs incurred in excess of the total amount allotted by the Government to this contract; and

(2)   The Contractor is not obligated to continue performance under this contract (including actions under the Termination clause of this contract) or otherwise incur costs in excess of (i) the amount then allotted to the contract by the Government or, (ii) if this is a cost-sharing contract, the amount then allotted by the Government to the contract plus the Contractor's corresponding share, until the Contracting Officer notifies the Contractor in writing that the amount allotted by the Government has been increased and specifies an increased amount, which shall then constitute the total amount allotted by the Government to this contract.

(g)   The estimated cost shall be increased to the extent that (1) the amount allotted by the Government or, (2) if this is a cost-sharing contract, the amount then allotted by the Government to the contract plus the Contractor's corresponding share, exceeds the estimated cost specified in the Schedule. If this is a cost-sharing contract, the increase shall be allocated in accordance with the formula specified in the Schedule.

(h)   No notice, communication or representation in any form other than that specified in subparagraph (f)(2) above, or from any person other than the Contracting Officer, shall affect the amount allotted by the Government to this contract. In the absence of the specified notice, the Government is not obligated to reimburse the Contractor for any costs in excess of the total amount allotted by the Government to this contract, whether incurred during the course of the contract or as a result of termination.

(i)   When and to the extent that the amount allotted by the Government to the contract is increased, any costs the Contractor incurs before the increase that are in excess of (1) the amount previously allotted by the Government or, (2) if this is a cost-sharing contract, the amount previously allotted by the Government to the contract plus the Contractor's corresponding share, shall be allowable to the same extent as if incurred afterward, unless the Contracting Officer issues a termination or other notice and directs that the increase is solely to cover termination or other specified expenses.

(j)   Change orders shall not be considered an authorization to exceed the amount allottd by the Government specified in the Schedule, unless they contain a statement increasing the amount allotted.

(k)   Nothing in this clause shall affect the right of the Government to terminate this contract. If this contract is terminated, the Government and the Contractor shall negotiate an equitable distribution of all property produced or purchased under the contract, based upon the share of costs incurred by each.

(l)   If the Government does not allot sufficient funds to allow completion of the work, the Contractor is entitled to a percentage of the fee specified in the Schedule equalling the percentage of completion of the work contemplated by this contract.

Figure 10.19.   (Continued)

The government is not obligated to reimburse the contractor for any cost in excess of the contract estimated cost or funds allotted. Nor is the contractor obligated to continue performance or incur any costs in excess of the contract estimated costs or funds allotted. Since this limitation is equally applicable to "changes" and termination costs, cost reimbursement type contracts are sometimes spoken of as level-of-effort contracts. The "limitation of cost or funds" clauses are designed to give the government an opportunity to decide whether it can and will provide additional funds necessary to complete the work.

Because of the reporting requirements of these clauses, companies contracting with the government must have an adequate management information system to allow for timely notification of potential cost overruns. Boards of contract appeals and the Claims Court have ruled in numerous instances that an inadequate accounting or management information system is not a valid excuse for not providing the notice required by the clauses.

In *Datex, Inc.*,[1] the contractor asserted that it was unaware when contract costs exceeded 75% of total estimated costs because actual overhead rates could not be determined until after contract completion and government audit. No notice was given to the government until settlement of final overhead rates (10 months after contract completion), at which time the contractor requested a contract modification to fund the contract overrun. The contractor's request was rejected. The Board, in concluding that the contractor should have been able to foresee that its costs would exceed the contract ceiling, cited a prior ASBCA decision that a contractor is obligated to maintain an accounting and financial reporting system adequate to apprise the contractor of a possible overrun before the overrun occurs. The Board noted that the "limitation of cost" clause does not require an exact projection of the overrun but merely requires timely notice when the contractor believes total contract cost will exceed the estimated cost. The contractor was denied recovery of the overrun on the basis that it was not authorized to exceed the contractual estimated cost and that the contracting officer was authorized to deny funding of the overrun.

In an appeal heard by the DOT Contract Appeals Board, *SAI Comsystems Corp.*[2] also lost its bid for goverment funding of its CPFF contract cost overrun. SAI claimed that the goverment's failure to perform a timely audit excused the contractor's lack of notice and thus obligated the goverment to provide the requested funding. SAI also argued that since the goverment knew that its indirect expense rates were higher than projected, the goverment should also have assumed that the contract would be overrun.

The board did not agree. It noted that:

> . . . a contractor has a responsibility to maintain reasonable records and to expend reasonable effort in monitoring direct and indirect cost incurrences, in order to be able to ascertain when costs will approach the contract ceiling and to be able to cease performance in an orderly manner prior to reaching that level.

The board also rejected the notion that the goverment's knowledge concerning higher actual indirect expence rate automatically created either knowledge of the overrun or an obligation to provide funding. The Board emphasized that the limitation of cost clause limits the goverment's liability to reimburse costs incurred to the estimated cost. Consequently, unless the goverment acts to obligate additional funds, mere notice of a probable overrun will not create a funding liability.

The importance of monitoring costs incurred on cost reimbursement type contracts and of complying with the notification requirement contained in the "limitation of cost or funds" clauses is obvious—failure to comply can result in nonrecovery of cost. To assure compliance and avoid the risk of financial loss, a contractor needs a cost accounting system that monitors costs incurred and a commitment system that monitors contractor obligations to suppliers and subcontractors.

An ASBCA decision which denied an appeal by *Varigas Research Inc.*[3] for cost overrun funding, emphasizes the critical nature of these control systems.

Varigas was aware of the notification requirement in the limitation of cost clause. In fact, upon reaching 75% of the estimated cost, the contractor notified the contracting officer that it did not expect to overrun the contract. Yet shortly before contract completion, Varigas suddenly realized that an overrun would occur, due primarily to an overrun subcontract. The contracting officer denied the belated request for funding on the basis that the contractor's failure to comply with the notification requirement of the limitation of cost clause resulted from the contractor's poor management techniques and lack of control over the subcontractor. Based on a review of the evidence, the ASBCA sustained the contracting officer's decision. In concluding that Varigas had not managed its subcontract effectively, the Board noted:

> The subcontractor's failure to maintaiin adequate accounting records for its incurred costs and to notify the prime contractor of expected increases in the estimated cost does not excuse the prime contractor from the obligation to give notice to the Government pursuant to the Limitation of Cost clause.

Although the clauses explicitly relieve the government from any obligation to reimburse cost incurred in excess of the estimated cost, that does not mean that such overruns are never paid. The contracting officer may recognize and fund an overrun when the contractor failed to give timely notice in strict compliance with the clause. This discretionary authority of the contracting officer is emphasized in *ITT Defense Communications,*[4] where the ASBCA discussed the relationship between the notice requirement (paragraph [a] of the limitation of cost clause), and the government's action to fund an overrun (paragraph [b] of the clause):

> Paragraph (b) of the clause is in no way contingent upon the notice provision of paragraph (a). The notice provides a means whereby the Government receives advance notice of an anticipated shortage of funds to complete the contract, so as to give the Government an opportunity to add funds in sufficient time to prevent the interruption of the work where additional funds are unavailable or unjustified. However, the Government's exercise of its election under paragraph (b) is not conditioned on the contractor's compliance with the notice requirement of paragraph (a). Even though there has been a flagrant violation of the notice requirement, the Government may still, and frequently does, provide additional funds and continue the work under the contract. On the other hand, even though the contractor has complied fully and completely with the notice requirement, the Government may still exercise its election not to provide additional funds and continue to work under the contract.

Since the decision to fund the overrun is discretionary, under what circumstances would the government most likely grant after-the-fact funding? A company would appear to have the strongest argument for funding where it can be demonstrated that the overrun was unforeseeable and due to no fault of the contractor or where the government really needs the work. In *Metametrics, Inc.*[5] the contract overrun was caused by an unforeseeable downturn in the contractor's business in the months subsequent to contract completion. The dramatic drop-off in direct costs caused the indirect expense rates allocable to the contract to increase substantially. In sustaining the contractor's appeal, the Department of Interior Board of Contract Appeals concluded:

It is obvious that the reliability of overhead rate projections is dependent upon the timely acquisition of expected new business. An adequate accounting system is necessary to accurately project the effect that future business will have on the overhead rates. . . . The more difficult problem involved in these cases is the lack of any standards by which to measure the adequacy of the contractor's new business projections. . . . After the expected business has been lost with the resultant increase in overhead rates and a postperformance overrun, the conclusion is easily reached that the contractor should have known business would be lost many months before, when it was time to give notice of an overrun. Procurement and award procedures do not support this conclusion. These procedures often stretch over many months or years. Lengthy interfaces between the Government and contractors often precede the actual bidding or proposal effort. Evaluation and award after receipt of bids or proposals may involve extended periods. In actual practice, contractors rarely discontinue marketing efforts and expenditures until the expected business is awarded to another or a decision not to procure is announced. Under such circumstances, the placement of an unreasonable burden on the contractor to foresee the failure to secure expected business many months before the opportunity is actually lost results in reestablishing the total risk on the contractor to foresee and give notice of postperformance overhead induced overruns.

The postperformance overhead induced overrun should be funded where the contractor, through no fault or inadequacy in its accounting or business acquisition procedures, has no reason to foresee that a cost overrun will occur and the sole reason for refusal to pay the overrun is the contractor's failure to give proper notice. In the case before us, the parties agree on the adequacy of appellant's accounting system. The record discloses no basis on which appellant should have known, at the time that a notice of overrun should have been provided, that he would be markedly unsuccessful in acquiring new business.

ASBCA used similar rationale in its decision to deny reimbursement of overrun funding in *Research Applications, Inc.*[6]

The conclusion is inescapable that it was not the circumstances but appellant's own choice that produced the cost overrun as well as the lack of information on which a proper notice could have been based. Thus appellant cannot rely on the alleged unforeseeability of the overrun as an excuse.

In *American Standard, Inc.* (also known as Melpar),[7] the ASBCA concluded that the contracting officer erred in denying funding of costs that had been inadvertently omitted from an earlier request for funding. In its decision, the Board reiterated the general requirements of an adequate accounting system:

With respect to the Melpar computer costs, incurred in December, 1967, Melpar admits that the omission of these cost entries from its books of account occurred through an internal error. A contractor has the responsibility of conducting an accounting system which gives up correct and timely data, sufficient to inform the contractor what his fiscal position might be vis-a-vis a cost ceiling or a cost limitation. We do not perceive this to be an unfair or an onerous burden, and certainly not an unconscionable responsibility, as argued by appellant. Generally, where a contractor has put himself in an overrun position through his own error leading to unawareness of an overrun, contracting officers' denials of requests for funding have been sustained.

However, the Board went on further to note the mitigating circumstances of this particular appeal:

The error occurred before Melpar notified the contracting officer in March, 1968, that an overrun was imminent. While the Limitation of Cost clause requires such a notice, as well as a notice when 75% of the estimated cost will be exceeded, the clause does not require that the specific amount of the overrun be given. It does require that the contractor provide a revised estimate of the cost to complete. The notice was given, but the estimate was obviously erroneous.

With respect to the omitted computer costs, it would be appropriate for the contracting officer to consider whether the $16,800 overrun would have been funded in the larger amount had the additional $5,215 also been presented as a cost; whether the Government received the benefit of the work; whether the Government did not specifically agree that verification of the existing data should be performed. . . . Also for consideration is the fact that in the absence of an overrun, Melpar would not have been denied reimbursement for allowable costs at any time up to final payment under similar circumstances. In the Board's opinion, the contracting officer was not bound to deny the request for lack of notice. There was no bar to his exercising his discretion to allow this particular request. Accordingly, the Board will sustain the appeal with respect to the omitted computer costs only to the extent of remanding the matter to the contracting officer to permit exercise of his discretionary authority on the merits of appellant's request for additional funding for omitted computer costs.

In *Clevite Ordinance*,[8] the ASBCA sustained the contractor's appeal for funding of the overrun on the basis that the contractor was constructively authorized to proceed by the government. In its opinion, which was sharply critical of the procuring activity's actions, the Board concluded:

The limitations on money and man-hours were reduced to meaningless ciphers by the conduct of the parties; performance by Appellant was prosecuted in obedience to explicit instructions of authorized and cognizant Government personnel who were alert to the fiscal status of the contract on current and projected bases; and the Government has reaped and enjoyed the benefits of Appellant's good faith performance in reliance upon assurance of reimbursement by an official Bureau who we find to have been constituted in fact as the authorized representative of the Contracting Officer concerning the matters here in dispute. . . .

Even when the contractor has promptly reported the possibility of an overrun and has requested additional funds, the company may still be faced with delay by the government in providing written authority to continue. Whether or not to continue performance and risk not being paid is a management decision. Theoretically, perhaps the best approach is to maintain a timely record of expenditures, notify the government promptly, and then stop work when the ceiling is reached. However, while theoretically correct, this action is not together without risk. Cost may be incurred by stopping work that may be difficult or impossible to recover if and when work resumes. Also to be considered are the size of the contract in relation to the potential overrun, the funding situation of the government, the possibility of follow-on work subsequent to the current contract, and the attitude of government representatives if the company does not complete the current contract.

Another area of risk is the performance, at the request of government employees, of additional tasks or functions that are not incorporated in the contract. The only person authorized to obligate the government to reimburse a contractor for effort performed is the contracting officer. While the contracting officer may rely upon the advice of technical and financial experts, these other representatives cannot obligate the government. Therefore, it is in the company's best interest to obtain written approval from the contracting officer for all changes in work and overrun funding.

In *DBA Systems, Inc.*,[9] the contractor contended it was unable to give timely notice of its contract overrun because the overrun resulted from increased indirect expense rates recommended by DCAA after physical contract completion.

The contracting officer was advised of the overrun in a letter dated one month after contract completion. The contracting officer forwarded the letter to the contract specialist, who concluded that the contractor's position had merit; prepared a proposed contract modification to fund the overrun; and sent it to the contracting officer, with a copy to the contractor. Prior to making his decision, the contracting officer requested the opinion of the ACO as to the adequacy of the contractor's accounting methods and procedures to provide timely evidence of the potential overrun. At the ACO's request, DCAA considered the question and concluded that the accounting system had, in fact, revealed the existence of the overrun on a timely basis. The contracting officer rejected the contract modification because of the lack of timely notice of the overrun as required under the "limitation of cost" clause. The major issue in the appeal to the NASA BCA was whether the transmittal of the proposed contract modification to the contractor constituted notice, under the "limitation of cost" clause, of government approval to fund the overrun. The board concluded it did not, since it was the contracting officer, not the contract specialist, who was authorized to execute a contract on behalf of the government. In ruling against the contractor, the Board quoted from a leading Supreme Court case[10] that addressed the issue of government authority:

> Whatever the form in which the Government functions, anyone entering into an arrangement with the Government takes the risk of having accurately ascertained that he who purports to act for the Government stays within the bounds of his authority.

RIGHTS IN TECHNICAL DATA

Requirements for conveying technical data rights to the government have been particularly confusing in recent years, particularly since the passage of two FY 1984 procurement statues, the Defense Procurement Reform Act—Public Law 98-525 and the Small Business and Federal Procurement Enhancement Act—Public Law 98-577. These statutes require defense contracts to include provisions that clearly delineate the contractor's responsibility for delivering technical data. Because no government-wide regulations were promulgated soon after enactment of the 1984 statutes, military services tended to act independently in protecting the government's interest in data rights. The DAR Council's 1985 proposed revisions to the DFARS were never finalized, much to the relief of those in industry. The proposed implementation seemed unduly harsh in concluding that unlimited rights to technical data were established even where DOD sponsorship occurred only at the final stage of reducing the technology to actual practice.

The FY 1987 Defense Authorization Act amendments established a more reasoned approach for reviewing and challenging the propriety of data rights restrictions by emphasizing that, where technology has been developed partly with federal sponsorship and partly at private expense, it is appropriate for the contracting parties to negotiate the data rights issues. The amendments also provided that contractors generally cannot be forced, as a condition of responding to a solicitation's requirements, to relinquish legitimate data rights. Importantly, the conference report also contained the following language to guide the DAR Council in defining the term "developed at private expense":

> The conferees agree that, for purposes of determining whether an item or process has been developed at private expense, an item should generally be considered "developed" if the item or process exists and reasonable persons skilled in the applicable

art would conclude that a high probability exists that the item or process will work as intended. . . .

In addition, the conferees agree that as a matter of general policy "at private expense" development was accomplished without direct government payment. Payments by the government to reimburse a contractor for its indirect costs would not be considered in determining whether the government had funded the development of an item. Thus reimbursement for IR&D expenses and other indirect costs (capital funds and profits) although such payments are in indirect support of a development effort, are treated for purposes of this Act as contractor funds."

The revision to DFARS Part 227 implementing the FY 1987 Defense Authorization Act amendments establishes a third category of data rights, in addition to "limited rights" and "unlimited rights," called "government purpose license rights" to apply where the contract has contributed more than 50% of the development cost. The DFARS revision also defines "developed at private expense" along the lines suggested in the FY 1987 Authorization Act Conferences report. Provisions from the rights in technical data and computer software clause are contained in Figure 10.20.

(a) *Definitions.*

The terms used in this clause are defined in 227.471 of the Department of Defense Supplement to the Federal Acquisition Regulation (DFARS).

(b) *Rights in Technical Data.*

(1) *Limited rights.* The Government shall have limited rights in:

(i) technical data, listed or described in an agreement incorporated into the Schedule of this contract, which the parties have agreed will be furnished with limited rights in accordance with 227.472-6; and

(ii) unpublished technical data pertaining to items, components, or processes developed exclusively at private expense, and unpublished computer software documentation related to computer software that is acquired with restricted rights, other than such data included in (b)(3)(i), (iii), or (iv), below.

Limited rights shall be effective provided that only the portion or portions of each piece of data to which limited rights are to be asserted are identified (for example, by circling, underscoring, or a note), and that the piece of data is marked with the legend below:

(A.) the number of the prime contract under which the technical data is to be delivered;and

(B.) the name of the contractor and any subcontractor by whom the technical data was generated;

Limited Rights Legend

Contract No. _____.

Contractor: _____.

The restrictions governing the use of technical data marked with this legend are set forth in the definition of "Limited Rights" in DFARS 227.471. This legend, together with the indications of the portions of this data which are subject to limited rights, shall be included on any reproduction hereof which includes any part of the portions subject to such limited rights . The limited rights legend shall be honored only as long as the data continues to meet the definition of limited rights.

(2) *Government Purpose License Rights.* The Government shall have Government purpose license rights in:

(i) unpublished technical data pertaining to items, components, or processes for which the Government has funded, or will fund, a part of the development cost, unless the contracting officer has determined that the Government requires unlimited rights, and:

(A) the contractor has or will contribute more than fifty percent (50%) of the development cost of the item, component, or process; or

(B) the contractor is a small business firm or nonprofit organization that agrees to commercialize the technology; and

(ii) unpublished technical data listed or described in an agreement incorporated into the Schedule of the contract, which the parties have agreed will be furnished with Government purpose license rights in accordance with DFARS 227.472-6 or 227.472-7, 227-473-1(a) and 227.473-1 (g) (2).

Figure 10.20.   Rights in technical data and computer software clause, DFARS 252.227-7013.

Government purpose license rights shall be effective provided that only the portion or portions of each piece of data to which such rights are to be asserted are identified (for example, by circling, underscoring, or a note), and that the piece of data is marked with the legend below:

(A.) the number of the prime contract under which the technical data is to be delivered, and

(B.) the name of the contractor and /or any subcontractor Goverment Purpose License Rights.

Government Purpose License Rights Legend

Contract No. _____.

Contractor: _____.

The restrictions governing the use of technical data marked with this legend are set forth in the definition of "Government Purpose License Rights" in DFARS 227.471. This legend, together with the indications of the portions of this data which are subject to such limitations, shall be included on any reproduction hereof which includes any part of the portions subject to such limitations and shall be honored only as long as the data continues to meet the definition of Government purpose license rights.

(3) *Unlimited rights.* Unless other rights have been agreed to in writing in accordance with DFARS 227.472-7, the Government shall have unlimited rights in:

(i) technical data prepared or required to be delivered under this or any other Government contract or subcontract and constituting corrections or changes to Government-furnished data or computer software;

(ii) form, fit, or function data pertaining to items, components, or processes prepared or required to be delivered under this or any other Government contract or subcontract;

(iii) manuals or instructional materials (other than detailed manufacturing or process data) prepared or required to be delivered under this contract or any subcontract hereunder necessary for installation, operation, maintenance, or training purposes.

(iv) technical data, which is otherwise publicly available, or has been, or is normally released or disclosed by the contractor or subcontractor, without restriction on further release or disclosure;

(v) technical data pertaining to an item, component, or process for which the Government has funded, or will fund, the entire development of the item, component, or process.

(vi) technical data pertaining to an item, component, or process for which the Government has funded, or will fund, a part of the development cost of the item, component, or process, and the Contractor has not or will not contribute more than 50 percent of the development cost;

(vii) technical data pertaining to an item, component, or process for which the Government has funded, or will fund, a part of the development cost of the item, component, or process, and the contractor is a small business firm or nonprofit organization that does not agree to commercialize the technology; and

(viii) technical data pertaining to an item, component, or process for which the Government has funded, or will fund, a part of the development cost of the item, component, or process, and, notwithstanding (b)(3)(vi) and (vii) above, the Contracting Officer has determined, in accordance with DFARS 227.472-5(b), that the Government requires unlimited rights.

(ix)Technical data resulting directly from performance of experimental, developmental, or research work which was specified as an element of performance in this or any other Government contract or subcontract.

(c) *Rights in Computer Software.*

(1) *Restricted Rights.*

(i) The Government shall have restricted rights in computer software, listed or described in a license or agreement made a part of this contract, which the parties have agreed will be furnished with restricted rights, *Provided,* however, notwithstanding any contrary provision in any such license or agreement, the Government shall have the rights included in the definition of "restricted rights" in paragraph (a) above. Such restricted rights are of no effect unless the computer software is marked by the contractor with the following legend.

Restricted Rights Legend

Use, duplication, or disclosure is subject to restrictions stated in Contract No. _____ with (Name of Contractor) _____.

and the related computer software documentation includes a prominent statement of the restrictions applicable to the computer software. The contractor may not place any legend on computer software indicating restrictions on the Government's rights in such software unless the restrictions are set forth in a license or agreement made a part of this contract prior to the delivery data of the software. Failure of the contractor to apply a restricted rights legend to such computer software shall relieve the Government of liability with respect to such unmarked software.

(ii) Notwithstanding subparagraph (i)(c)(l)(i) above, commercial computer software and related

Figure 10.20. (Continued)

documentation developed at private expense and not in the public domain may, if the contractor so elects, be marked with the following legend:

Restricted Rights Legend

Use, duplication, or disclosure by the Government is subject to restrictions as set forth in subdivision (c)(1)(ii) of the Rights in Technical Data and Computer Software clause at [2]52.227-7013.

Name of contractor and Address

When acquired by the Government, commercial computer software and related documentation so legended shall be subject to the following:

(A) Title to, and ownership of, the software and documentation shall remain with the contractor.

(B) User of the software and documentation shall be limited to the facility for which it is acquired.

(C) The Government shall not provide or otherwise make available the software or documentation, or any portion thereof, in any form, to any third party without the prior written approval of the contractor. Third parties do not include prime contractors, subcontractors and agents of the Government who have the Government's permission to use the licensed software and documentation at the facility, and who have agreed to use the licensed software and documentation only in accordance with these restrictions. This provision does not limit the right of the Government to use software, documentation, or information therein, which the Government may already have or obtain without restrictions.

(D) The Government shall have the right to use the computer software and documentation with the computer for which it is acquired at any other facility to which that computer may be transferred; to use the computer software and documentation with a backup computer when the primary computer is inoperative; to copy computer programs for safekeeping (archives) or backup purposes; and to modify the software and documentation or combine it with other software, *Provided*, that the unmodified portions shall remain subject to these restrictions.

(2) *Unlimited Rights in Computer Software.* The Government shall have unlimited rights in:

(i) computer software resulting directly from performance of experimental, developmental or research work which was specified as an element of performance in this or any Government contract or subcontract;

(ii) computer software required to be originated or developed under a Government contract, or generated as a necessary part of performing a contract;

(iii) computer data bases, prepared under a Government contract, consisting of information supplied by the Government, information in which the Government has unlimited rights, or information which is in the public domain;

(iv) computer software prepared or required to be delivered under this or any other Government contract or subcontract and constituting corrections or changes to Government-furnished computer software; and

(v) computer software, which is otherwise publicly available, or has been, or is normally released, or disclosed by the contractor or subcontractor without restriction on further release or disclosure.

(d) *Technical Data and Computer Software previously Provided Without Restriction.* Contractor shall assert no restrictions on the Government's rights to use or disclose any data or computer software which the contractor has previously delivered to the Government without restriction. The limited or restricted rights provided for by this clause shall not impair the right of the Government to use similar or identical data or computer software acquired from other sources.

(e) *Copyright.*

(1) In addition to the rights granted under the provisions of paragraphs (b) and (c) above, the contractor hereby grants to the Government a nonexclusive, paid-up license throughout the world, of the scope set forth below, under any copyright owned by the contractor, in any work of authorship prepared for or acquired by the Government under this contract, to reproduce the work in copies or phonorecords, to distribute copies or phonorecords to the public, to perform or display the work publicly, and to prepare derivative works thereof, and to have others do so for Government purposes . . . With respect to technical data and computer software in which the Government has unlimited rights, the license shall be of the same scope as the rights set forth in the definition of "unlimited rights" in DFARS 227.471. With respect to technical data in which the Government has limited rights, the scope of the license is limited to the rights set forth in the definition of "limited rights". With respect to computer software which the parties have agreed will be furnished with restricted rights, the scope of the license is limited to such rights.

(2) Unless written approval of the Contracting Officer is obtained, the contractor shall not include in technical data or computer software prepared for or acquired by the Government under this contract any works of authorship in which copyright is not owned by the contractor without acquiring for the Government any rights necessary to perfect a copyright license of the scope specified herein.

Figure 10.20. (Continued)

(3) As between the contractor and the Government, the contractor shall be considered the "person for whom the work was prepared" for the purpose of determining authority under Section 201(b) of Title 17, United States Code.

(4) Technical data delivered under this contract which carries a copyright notice shall also include the following statement which shall be placed thereon by the contractor, or should the contractor fail, by the Government:

This material may be reproduced by or for the U.S. Government pursuant to the copyright license under the clause at 252.227-7013 (date).

(f) *Removal of Unjustified Technical Data Markings.*

(1) Unjustified Technical Data Markings Notwithstanding any provision of this contract concerning inspection and acceptance, the Government may, at the contractor's expense, correct, cancel, or ignore any marking not authorized by the terms of this contract on any technical data furnished hereunder in accordance with the clause of this contract entitled "Validation of Restrictive Markings on Technical Data', DFARS 252.227-7037.

(2) Nonconforming Technical Data Markings. Correction of non-conforming markings is not subject to this clause. The Goverment may at the Contractor's expense, correct any non-conforming markings if the Contracting officer notifies the Contractor and the Contractor fails to correct the non-conforming markings within 60 days.

(3) Unjustified and Non conforming Computer Software Markings notwithstanding any provision of this contract concerning inspection and acceptance, the Government may correct, cancel, or ignore any marking not authorized by the terms of this contract on any computer software furnished hereunder, if:

(i) the contractor fails to respond within sixty (60) days to a written inquiry by the Government concerning the propriety of the markings; or

(ii) the contractor's response fails to substantiate, within sixty (60) days after written notice, the propriety of restricted rights markings by identification of the restrictions set forth in the contract.

In either case, the Government shall give written notice to the contractor of the action taken.

(g) *Relation to Patents.* Nothing contained in this clause shall imply a license to the Government under any patent or be construed as affecting the scope of any license or other right otherwise granted to the Government under any patent.

(h) *Limitation on Charges for Data and Computer Software.* The contractor recognizes that it is the policy of the Government not to pay, or to allow to be paid, any charges for data or computer software which the Government has a right to use and disclose to others without restriction and contractor agrees to refund any such payments. This policy applies to contracts that involve payments by subcontractors and those entered into through the Military Assistance Program, in addition to US Government prime contracts. However, it does not apply to reasonable reproduction, handling, mailing, and similar administrative costs.

(i) *Acquisition of Data and Computer Software from Subcontractors.*

(1) Whenever any technical data or computer software is to be obtained from a subcontractor under this contract, the contractor shall use this same clause in the subcontract, without alteration, and no other clause shall be used to enlarge or diminish the Government's or the contractor's rights in the subcontractor data or computer software which is required for the Government.

(2) Technical data required to be delivered by a subcontractor shall normally be delivered to the next higher-tier contractor. However, when there is a requirement in the prime contract for data which may be submitted with other than unlimited rights by a subcontractor, then said subcontractor may fulfill its requirement by submitting such data directly to the Government, rather than through the prime contractor.

(3) The contractor and higher-tier subcontractors will not use their power to award subcontracts as economic leverage to obtain rights in technical data or computer software from their subcontractors.

(j) *Notice on limitations of Government Rights.*

(1) Unless the Schedule provides otherwise, and subject to (j) (2) below, the Contractor will promptly notify the Contracting Officer in writing of the intended use by the contractor or a subcontractor in performance of this contract of any item, component, or process for which technical data would contain any restrictions on the Government's right to use, disclose, or have others use such data.

(2) Such notification is not required with respect to:

(i) standard commercial items which are manufactured by more than one source of supply; or

(ii) items, components, or processes for which such notice was given pursuant to prenotification of rights in technical data in connection with this contract.

(3) Unless the schedule provides otherwise, Contracting Officer approval is not necessary under this clause for the contractor to use the item, component, or process in the performance of the contract.

Figure 10.20. (Continued)

CONTRACT WARRANTIES

The FY 1985 Defense Authorization Act imposed new warranty requirements on prime contractors producing weapon systems. An interim revision to DFARS Subpart 246.7 was issued in January 1985 to implement the statute's requirements. DFARS 246. 770, issued as a final rule in May 1986 requires the contracting officer to obtain cost effective warranties on large mature full scale production contracts for weapon systems. Where a warranty provision is not considered cost effective, a waiver may be obtained from a seniro defense official.

No standard warranty clause has been established due to recognition of the need for the contract clause to be tailored to the unique requirements of the contract. DFAR 246.770-3 provides the following guidance as to appropriate content for warranty clauses:

> As the objectives and circumstances vary considerably among weapon system acquisition programs, contracting officers shall appropriately tailor the required warranties on a case-by-case basis, including remedies, exclusion, limitations, and duration; *Provided,* such are consistent with the specific requirements of this section (see also FAR 46.706). The duration specified in any warranty should be clearly related to the contract requirements and allow sufficient time to demonstrate achievement of the requirements after acceptance. Contracting officers may exclude from the terms of the warranty certain defects for specified supplies (exclusions) and may limit the contractor's liability under the terms of the warranty (limitations), as appropriate, if necessary to derive a cost effective warranty in light of the technical risk, contractor financial risk, or other program uncertainties. All subsystems and components will be procured in such a manner so as not to invalidate the weapon system warranty. Contracting officers are encouraged to structure broader and more comprehensive warranties where such are advantageous and in accordance with agency policy. Likewise, the contracting officer may narrow the scope of a warranty where such is appropriate (e.g., where it would be inequitable to require a warranty of all essential performance requirements because a contractor had not designed the system). It is Department of Defense policy not to include in warranty clauses any terms that cover liability for loss, damage or injury to third parties.

CONTRACT CLAUSES RELATING TO SOCIOECONOMIC AND ENVIRONMENTAL PROTECTION GOALS

The government's various socioeconomic goals have given rise to a number of contract clauses that do not otherwise directly relate to the procurement process.

The "utilization of small business concerns and small disadvantaged business concerns" clause (FAR 52.219-8) is included in all contracts over $10,000 except contracts which are performed entirely outside the United States or for personal services. The clause underscores the government's policy to maximize procurement opportunities for small and small disadvantaged business concerns and require contractors to implement that policy in awarding subcontracts.

Pursuant to Section 8(d) of the Small Business Act (Public Law 95-507), the small business and small disadvantaged business subcontracting plan clause (FAR 52.219-9) is included in all solicitations for negotiated or formally advertised contracts or modifications that offer subcontracting possibilities; are expected to exceed $500,000 ($1 million for public facility construction); and are required to include the "utilization of small business concerns and small disadvantaged business concerns" clause. The clause is not included in solicitations that have been set aside for small business concerns or that are to be procured through the Small Business Administration Section 8(a) program. The clause requires a successful offeror/bidder to submit to the PCO a comprehensive subcontracting plan for incorporation into the contract. The plan must include:

Percentage goals for utilizing small and small disadvantaged subcontractors.

Dollars planned for subcontracting, in total, to small business concerns, and to small disadvantaged business concerns.

The name of the company representtive who administers the plan.

A description of the contractor's efforts to provide procurement opportunities to small and small disadvantaged business.

Assurance that the "utilization of small business and small disadvantaged business concerns" clause will be inserted in all subcontracts that offer further subcontracting possibilities.

Assurance that any reports required to demonstrate compliance with the plan will be furnished. SF 294, *Subcontracting Report for Individual Contracts* (Fig. 10.21), must be submitted on a semiannual basis, and SF 295, *Summary Subcontract Report* (Fig. 10.22), is required on a quarterly basis.

Identification of records that will be maintained to document subcontracting actions; contacts with small and small disadvantaged business organizations; and internal activities to guide buyers.

In lieu of separate subcontracting plans for individual contracts, a defense contractor may establish a master subcontracting plan on a division-wide or plant-wide basis. Master subcontracting plans must contain all of the elements listed above, except for the goals. Failure to submit a subcontracting plan makes the offeror ineligible for contract award. Failure to comply in good faith with the plan is considered a material breach of contract. Clearly, Public Law 95-507 has added a significant administrative requirement to the performance of defense contracts.

The "utilization of women-owned small business" clause (FAR 52.219-13) is included in contracts over $10,000 except contracts peformed entirely outside the United States or for personal services. The clause iterates the government's policy to maximize procurement opportunities for women-owned small businesses and requires contractors to use their best efforts to achieve that objective.

The "utilization of labor surplus area concerns" clause (FAR 52.220-3) is inserted in all contracts over $10,000 except contracts with foreign contractors which will be performed entirely outside the United States; for personal services; for construction; and with the petroleum and petroleum products industry. The clause restates the government's policy to award contracts to contractors located in designated high unemployment areas who agree to perform the contract effort in those areas. Contractors are required to use their best efforts to achieve that objective in their subcontracting actions. An additional clause, "labor surplus area subcontracting program" (FAR 52.220-4) is included in contracts over $10,000 with substantial subcontracting potential. This clause requires a contractor to establish a program to enhance competitive subcontracting opportunities for labor surplus area firms. The program must include:

Designation of a program administrator.

SUBCONTRACTING REPORT FOR INDIVIDUAL CONTRACTS
(Report to be submitted semi-annually. See back of form for instructions)

FORM APPROVED OMB NO.

3090-0052

1. REPORTING PERIOD		2. REPORT NO.	3. TYPE OF CONTRACT	4. DATE SUBMITTED
FROM *(Date)*	TO *(Date)*		☐ PRIME CONTRACT ☐ SUBCONTRACT	

GENERAL INFORMATION

5. AGENCY/CONTRACTOR AWARDING CONTRACT *(Name & Address)*	7. REPORTING CONTRACTOR *(Name and Address)*

6. PRIME CONTRACT NO. *(And Subcontract No., if applicable)*	8. BUSINESS CLASS. CODE	9. DUNS NO. *(If applicable)*
10. ADMINISTERING AGENCY	11. DATE OF LAST GOVERNMENT REVIEW	12. REVIEWING AGENCY

13. DOLLAR VALUE OF PRIME OR SUBCONTRACT.	14. ESTIMATED DOLLAR VALUE OF COMMITMENTS AS IN PLAN.	15. GOALS	DOLLARS	PERCENT
		a. SMALL BUSINESS CONCERNS		
		b. SMALL DISAD. BUSINESS CONCERNS		

SUBCONTRACT AND PURCHASE COMMITMENTS

COMMITMENTS		THIS REPORTING PERIOD		CUMULATIVE	
		DOLLARS	PERCENT	DOLLARS	PERCENT
16. TOTAL DIRECT SUBCONTRACT COMMITMENTS *(Sum of a & b)*			100		100
a. TOTAL SMALL BUSINESS CONCERNS					
(1) SMALL DISADVANTAGED BUSINESS CONCERNS	*(% of 16)*				
(2) OTHER SMALL BUSINESS CONCERNS	*(% of 16)*				
b. LARGE BUSINESS CONCERNS	*(% of 16)*				
17. TOTAL INDIRECT COMMITMENTS *(Sum of a & b)*					
a. TOTAL SMALL BUSINESS CONCERNS					
(1) SMALL DISADVANTAGED BUSINESS CONCERNS	*(% of 17)*				
(2) OTHER SMALL BUSINESS CONCERNS	*(% of 17)*				
b. LARGE BUSINESS CONCERNS	*(% of 17)*				

18. REMARKS:

19. TYPE THE NAME AND TITLE OF THE INDIVIDUAL ADMINISTERING CONTRACT	SIGNATURE	TELEPHONE NO. *(and Area Code)*
20. TYPE THE NAME AND TITLE OF THE APPROVING OFFICER	SIGNATURE	

NSN 7540-01-152-8078
PREVIOUS EDITION USABLE

294-102

STANDARD FORM 294 (REV. 10-83)
Prescribed by GSA
FAR (48 CFR) 53.219(a)

Figure 10.21. Subcontracting report for individual contracts, Standard Form 294.

GENERAL INSTRUCTIONS

1. This reporting form is prescribed for use in the collection of subcontract data from all Federal contractors and subcontractors which, pursuant to the Small Business Act of 1958, as amended by Public Law 95-507, are required to establish plans for subcontracting with small and small disadvantaged business concerns. Reports shall be submitted to the contracting officer semiannually as of March 31 and September 30, as well as at contract completion. This report is due by the 25th day of the month following the close of the reporting periods, in accordance with instructions contained in the contract or subcontract, or as directed by the contracting officer.

2. This report is not required to be submitted by small business concerns.

3. This report is not required for commercial products for which a company-wide annual plan has been approved. The Summary Subcontract Report is required for commercial products in accordance with the instructions on that form.

4. Only subcontract and purchase commitments involving performance within the U.S., its possessions, Puerto Rico, and the Trust Territory of the Pacific Islands will be included in this report.

SPECIFIC INSTRUCTIONS

ITEM 1 — Specify the period covered by this report (e.g., April 1, 1981 - September 30, 1981).

ITEM 2 — Specify the sequential report covering this contract. The initial report shall be identified as Report Number 1. Add "Final Report" for the last report being made.

ITEM 3 — Specify whether this report covers either a Prime Contract awarded by a Federal Department or Agency or a Subcontract awarded by a Federal prime contractor or subcontractor.

ITEM 5 — Enter the name and address of the Federal Department or Agency or Prime Contractor awarding the Prime or Subcontract.

ITEM 6 — Enter the prime contract number. If this report covers a subcontract, enter both the prime contract and subcontract numbers.

ITEM 7 — Enter the name and address of the Prime Contractor or Subcontractor submitting the report.

ITEM 8 — Enter the Business Classification Code as follows:

Code	Definition
LB	Large Business
NP	Non-Profit Organization (including Educational Institutions).

ITEM 9 — Enter Dun and Bradstreet Universal Numbering System (DUNS) number (if available).

ITEM 10 — Identify Federal agency administering the contract. For Department of Defense, identify appropriate military department; i.e., Army, Navy, Air Force, or Defense Logistics Agency. Civilian agencies should be identified as noted in the contract award document; i.e., NASA, DOE, GSA, HHS, SBA, etc.

ITEM 11 & 12 — Enter the date of the last formal surveillance review conducted by the cognizant Department or Agency Small and Disadvantaged Business Specialist or other review personnel. For DOD, also identify the military department or Defense Contract Administration Service, as appropriate, that conducted the review. In those cases where the Small Business Administration conducts its own review, show the date and "SBA".

ITEM 13 — Specify the face value of the Prime or Subcontract covered by this report. If the value changes, the face value shall be adjusted accordingly.

ITEM 14 — Enter the estimated dollar value of subcontract and purchase commitments as set forth in the Subcontract Plan.

ITEM 15 — Specify in the appropriate blocks the dollar amount and percent of the reporting contractor's total subcontract awards contractually agreed upon as goals for subcontracting with Small Business and Small Disadvantaged Business concerns. NOTE: Should the original goals agreed upon at contract awards be either increased or decreased as a result of a contract modification, the amount of the revised goals shall be indicated.

ITEM 16 — Specify in the appropriate block the total amount of all direct subcontract commitments and the dollar amount and percentage of the total placed with the subcontractor classification indicated in a and b, both for this period and cumulative. Do not include in this report purchase commitments made in support of commercial business being performed by reporting contractor.

ITEM 17 — Complete Item 17 only if indirect contract commitments were included in establishing the small and small disadvantaged business goals for the contract being reported. Specify in the appropriate block the total allocable dollar amount of indirect commitments and the dollar amount and percentage of the total placed with the subcontractor classifications indicated in a(1), a(2), and b, both for this period and cumulative.

ITEM 18 — Enter any remarks. If the goals were not met, explain why on the final report.

ITEM 19 — Enter name and title of company individual responsible for administering contract.

ITEM 20 — The approving officer shall be the senior official of the company, division, or subdivision (plant or profit center) responsible for contract performance.

DEFINITIONS

1. A Small Business Concern is a concern that meets the pertinent criteria established by the Small Business Administration.

2. (a) A Small Disadvantaged Business means any small business concern:

   (1) which is at least 51 per centum owned by one or more socially and economically disadvantaged individuals; or, in the case of any publicly-owned business, at least 51 per centum of the stock of which is owned by one or more socially and economically disadvantaged individuals; and

   (2) whose management and daily business operations are controlled by one or more of such individuals.

   (b) The contractor shall presume that socially and economically disadvantaged individuals include Black Americans, Hispanic Americans, Native Americans, Asian-Pacific Americans, and other minorities, or any other individual found to be disadvantaged by the Small Business Administration pursuant to Section 8(a) of the Small Business Act. "Native Americans" include American Indians, Eskimos, Aleuts, and native Hawaiians. "Asian-Pacific Americans" include U.S. citizens whose origins are from Japan, China, the Philippines, Vietnam, Korea, Samoa, Guam, the Trust Territory of the Pacific Islands, Northern Marianas, Laos, Cambodia, and Taiwan.

   (c) Contractors acting in good faith may rely on written representations by their subcontractors certifying their status as either a small business concern or a small business concern owned and controlled by socially and economically disadvantaged individuals.

   (d) The Office of Minority Small Business and Capital Ownership Development in the Small Business Administration will answer inquiries from prime contractors and others relative to the class of eligibles and has final authority to determine the eligibility of a concern to be designated as a small disadvantaged business.

3. Commercial Products means products sold in substantial quantities to the general public and/or industry at established catalog or market prices.

4. Commitments as used herein is defined as a contract, purchase order, amendment, or other legal obligation executed by the reporting corporation, company, or subdivision for goods and services to be received by the reporting corporation, company, or subdivision.

5. Direct Commitments are those which are identified with the performance of a specific government contract, including allocable parts of awards for material which is to be incorporated into products under more than one Government contract.

6. Indirect Commitments are those which, because of incurrence for common or joint purposes, are not identified with specific Government contracts; these awards are related to Government contract performance but remain for allocation after direct awards have been determined and identified to specific Government contracts.

STANDARD FORM 294 BACK (REV. 10-83)

Figure 10.21. (Continued)

345

SUMMARY SUBCONTRACT REPORT

(Report to be submitted quarterly. See Instructions on reverse) (Type or Print)

FORM APPROVED OMB NO.

3090-0053

1. CONTRACTING AGENCY	2. ADMINISTERING AGENCY		

3. DATE OF LAST GOVERNMENT REVIEW	4. REVIEWING AGENCY	5. DUNS NO.	6. REPORT SUBMITTED AS:

6. REPORT SUBMITTED AS: ☐ PRIME CONTRACTOR ☐ SUBCONTRACTOR ☐ BOTH

7. CORPORATION, COMPANY, OR SUBDIVISION COVERED *(Name, Address, ZIP Code)*

8. MAJOR PRODUCTS OR SERVICE LINES:

a.

b.

c.

CUMULATIVE COMMITMENTS

Subcontract and Purchase Commitments for the Period October 1, 19 _____ through _____ , 19 _____

COMMITMENTS	CURRENT FISCAL YEAR *(To date)*		SAME PERIOD LAST YEAR	
	DOLLARS	PERCENT	DOLLARS	PERCENT
9. TOTAL *(Sum of a and b)*		100		100
a. SMALL BUSINESS CONCERNS				
b. LARGE BUSINESS CONCERNS				
10. SMALL DISADVANTAGED BUSINESS CONCERNS *(\$ & % of 9)*				
11. LABOR SURPLUS AREA CONCERNS *(\$ & % of 9)*				

SUBCONTRACT GOAL ACHIEVEMENT

GOALS	NO. OF CONTRACTS	$ VALUE OF SUBCONTRACTS (000)	$ VALUE OF SUBCONTRACT GOALS	ACTUAL GOAL ACHIEVEMENT	
				DOLLARS	%
12. CONTRACTS WITH SMALL BUSINESS SUBCONTRACT GOALS					
a. ACTIVE CONTRACTS					
b. CONTRACTS COMPLETED THIS QUARTER WHICH MET GOALS					
c. CONTRACTS COMPLETED THIS QUARTER NOT MEETING GOALS					
13. CONTRACTS WITH SMALL DISADVANT. BUS. SUBCONTRACT GOALS					
a. ACTIVE CONTRACTS					
b. CONTRACTS COMPLETED THIS QUARTER WHICH MET GOALS					
c. CONTRACTS COMPLETED THIS QUARTER NOT MEETING GOALS					

14. REMARKS *(Enter a short narrative explanation if: (a) Zero is entered in Blocks 9a or 10 for current fiscal year, (b) the percent entry in Block 9a for current fiscal year is more than 5 percentage points below the percent reported for same period last year, or (c) the percent entry in Block 10 for current fiscal year is lower than the percent reported for same period last year.)*

15. NAME AND TITLE OF LIAISON OFFICER	SIGNATURE	DATE	TELEPHONE NO. *(and Area Code)*

16. NAME AND TITLE OF APPROVING OFFICIAL	SIGNATURE	DATE	

NSN 7540-01-152-8079
PREVIOUS EDITION USABLE

295-102

STANDARD FORM 295 (REV. 10-83)
Prescribed by GSA
FAR (48 CFR) 53.219(b)

Figure 10.22. Summary of subcontract report, Standard Form 295.

INSTRUCTIONS

GENERAL INSTRUCTIONS

1. This reporting form is prescribed for use in the collection of subcontract data from Federal contractors and subcontractors which hold one or more contracts over $500,000 ($1 million for construction) and are required to subcontract with small and small disadvantaged business concerns under a subcontract plan as required by the Small Business Act of 1958, as amended by Public Law 95-507. (See Items 9 and 10 of Specific Instructions.)

2. The report may be submitted on a corporate, company, or subdivision (e.g., plan or division operating as a separate profit center) basis unless otherwise directed. After submission of the first report on this form, succeeding reports shall be submitted on the same basis.

3. Reports shall be submitted by the 25th day of the month following the close of the reporting period, as follows: (a) quarterly, in accordance with instructions below, or as directed by the contracting activity, or (b) annually for subcontracts covered by an approved company-wide annual subcontracting plan for commercial products. The annual report should summarize all Federal contracts for commercial products performed during the year and should be submitted in addition to required quarterly reports, for other than commercial products, if any. Show in Item 14 or in an attachment to the report, the share of this total attributable to each agency from which contracts for such commercial products were received. Send a copy of this report to each listed agency.

4. If a contractor is performing work for more than one Federal agency, a separate report shall be submitted to each agency covering its contracts. However, for DOD contracts, see paragraph 5, below.

5. (a) For reports covering contracts awarded by the military departments or agencies of the Department of Defense (DOD) or subcontracts awarded by DOD prime contracts, each reporting corporation, company, or subdivision (except contractors involved in maintenance, repair, and construction) shall report its total DOD business on one report (i.e., it shall not segregate subcontracts arising from work for the Army, Navy, Air Force, or Defense Agencies). All contractors shall submit:

    (i) The original of each report directly to the Office of the Deputy Secretary of Defense, Attention: Director of Small and Disadvantaged Business Utilization, The Pentagon, Washington, DC 20301.

    (ii) A copy of the report to the office listed below whose military activity is responsible for contract administration of the contractor:

ARMY — Director of Small and Disadvantaged Business Utilization, Office of the Secretary of the Army, Washington, DC 20360

NAVY — Director of Small and Disadvantaged Business Utilization, Office of the Secretary of the Navy, Washington, DC 20360

AIR FORCE — Director of Small and Disadvantaged Business Utilization, Office of the Secretary of the Air Force, Washington, DC 20330

DLA — Staff Director of Small and Disadvantaged Business Utilization, HQ Defense Logistics Agency (Attention U) Cameron Station, Alexandria, VA 22314

    (iii) A copy of the report, in accordance with instructions contained in the contract or subcontract, to the Federal agency or military department or defense agency, which is administering the prime or subcontractor.

(b) Contractors involved in maintenance, repair and construction shall also submit this report, similarly on a quarterly basis, to the appropriate construction contract administration activity. If a construction contractor is involved with more than one contract administration activity, this report should be submitted to each activity reflecting the contract awards under the supervision of the particular contract administration activity.

6. For NASA contracts forward reports to NASA - Office of Procurement (HM-1) Washington, DC 20546. For Department of Energy, forward reports to DOE - Small Business Division, Washington, DC 20585. For reports covering contracts awarded by other Federal Departments or Agencies and subcontracts placed by prime contractors of such departments or agencies, the original copy shall be sent to the Department or Agency Director of Small and Disadvantaged Business Utilization or as otherwise provided for in instructions issued by the Department or Agency.

7. Only subcontract or purchase commitments involving performance within the U.S., its possessions, Puerto Rico, and the Trust Territory of the Pacific Islands will be included in this report.

8. This report is not required to be submitted by small business concerns.

SPECIFIC INSTRUCTIONS

ITEM 1. Enter the agency which awarded the prime contract (e.g., DOD, HUD, GSA, etc.)

ITEM 2. Enter the department or agency administering the contracts (if different from Item 1). For DOD contracts enter the military department or agency which has responsibility for the subcontracting program of the corporation or plant (i.e., Army, Navy, Air Force, or Defense Logistics Agency), not the "Office of the Deputy Secretary of Defense."

ITEMS 3 & 4. Enter the date of the last formal surveillance review conducted by the cognizant department or agency Small and Disadvantaged Business Specialist or other review personnel. For DOD, also identify the military department or Defense Contract Administration Service, as appropriate, that conducted the review. In those cases where the Small Business Administration conducts its own review, show "SBA" and the date.

ITEM 5. Enter Dun and Bradstreet Universal Numbering System (DUNS) number (if available).

ITEM 6. Check whether reporting business is performing as a prime or subcontractor or both.

ITEM 7. Enter the name and address of the reporting corporation, company, or subdivision thereof (e.g., division or plant) which is covered by the data submitted.

ITEM 8. Identify the major product or service lines of the reporting corporation, company, or subdivision.

ITEMS 9 & 10. Report all commitments and purchase orders, regardless of dollar value, made by the reporting organization under all Federal prime contracts and subcontracts (whether or not prime contracts are over $500,000 ($1 million for construction) and small and small disadvantaged business subcontracting plans and goals are required). Report on a quarterly cumulative basis until the end of the fiscal year on September 30 after which a new quarterly reporting cycle is to be initiated commencing with the first quarter from October 1 through December 31. Dollar amounts reported should include direct awards and the appropriate prorated portion of the prime contractor's indirect awards (see definition below) contracted with small and small disadvantaged business concerns and other than small business concerns. The indirect award portion should be based on the percentages of the Federal department or agency work being performed by the reporting contractor in relation to other work performed for other departments or agencies. Particular care should be taken not to include in quarterly reports purchase commitments made in support of commercial business being performed by the contractor.

ITEM 11. Show dollar amount of commitments valued over $10,000 placed with labor surplus area (LSA) concerns (i.e., those that will perform substantially in labor surplus areas). Prime contractors are also encouraged to include awards valued less than $10,000 if such additional reporting does not impose a burden upon the contractor. LSA's are identified in the Department of Labor (DOL) publication "Labor Surplus Area Listings" which can be obtained from the Federal Agency contracting officer or by writing to Employment and Training Administration, (Attention: TPPL), Department of Labor, 601 "D" Street, NW, Washington, DC 20213.

ITEMS 12 & 13. Enter the information as indicated regarding contracts with small and small disadvantaged business goals. For each item (as applicable), enter the number of contracts, the total value of subcontracts, the dollar value of subcontract goals (as expressed in the subcontract plans) and actual goal achievement expressed in dollars and percent of goal. This item does not apply to reports covering commercial products.

ITEM 16. The approving official shall be the chief executive officer or, in the case of a separate division or plant, the senior individual responsible for overall division or plant operations.

DEFINITIONS

1. A Small Business Concern is a concern that meets the pertinent criteria established by the Small Business Administration.

2. (a) A Small Disadvantaged Business means any small business concern—
    (i) which is at least 51 per centum owned by one or more socially and economically disadvantaged individuals; or, in the case of any publicly-owned business, at least 51 per centum of the stock of which is owned by one or more socially and economically disadvantaged individuals; and
    (ii) whose management and daily business operations are controlled by one or more of such individuals.

(b) The contractor shall presume that socially and economically disadvantaged individuals include Black Americans, Hispanic Americans, Native Americans, Asian-Pacific Americans, and other minorities, or any other individual found to be disadvantaged by the Small Business Administration pursuant to Section 8(a) of the Small Business Act. "Native Americans" include American Indians, Eskimos, Aleuts, and native Hawaiians. "Asian-Pacific Americans" include U.S. citizens whose origins are from Japan, China, the Philippines, Vietnam, Korea, Samoa, Guam, Trust Territory of the Pacific Islands, Northern Marianas, Laos, Cambodia, and Taiwan.

(c) Contractors acting in good faith may rely on written representations by their subcontractors certifying their status as either a small business concern or a small business concern owned and controlled by socially and economically disadvantaged individuals.

(d) The Office of Minority Small Business and Capital Ownership Development in the Small Business Administration will answer inquiries from prime contractors and others relative to the class of eligibles and has final authority to determine the eligibility of a concern to be designated as a small disadvantaged business.

3. Commercial Products means products sold in substantial quantities to the general public and/or industry at established catalog or market prices.

4. Commitments as used herein is defined as a contract, purchase order, amendment, or other legal obligation executed by the Reporting corporation, company, or subdivision for goods and services to be received by the reporting corporation, company, or subdivision.

5. Direct Commitments are those which are identified with the performance of a specific government contract, including allocable parts of awards for material which is to be incorporated into products under more than one Government contract.

6. Indirect Commitments are those which, because of incurrence for common or joint purposes, are not identified with specific Government contracts; these awards are related to Government contract performance but remain for allocation after direct awards have been determined and identified to specific Government contracts.

7. A contract is considered to be completed when the supplies or services which are required to be delivered under the contract have been provided to the Government.

Figure 10.22. (Continued)

347

Consideration of potential for labor surplus area subcontracting in make-buy decisions.

Arrangement of subcontracting actions to enhance opportunities for labor surplus areas to compete for subcontracts.

Maintenance of records to document subcontracting actions.

Inclusion of "utilization of labor surplus area concerns" clauses in subcontracts with lower-tier subcontracting possibilities.

The "equal opportunity" clause (FAR 52.222-26) is included in all contracts except for transactions of $10,000 or less; work outside the United States; contracts with state or local governments; work on or near Indian reservations; and contracts exempted by the Office of Federal Contractor Compliance Programs in the Department of Labor in the national interest.

This clause prohibits discrimination against qualified employees or applicants because of race, color, religion, sex, or national origin and requires submission of periodic reports of employment statistics as required by Executive Orders 11246 and 11375 and Department of Labor orders. Standard Form 100 (EEO-1) (Figure 10.23) must be filed 30 days following the award of a contract, unless the form has already been filed within the preceding 12 months. Contractors determined to be in noncompliance with the EEO clause or rules, regulations, and orders may be declared ineligible to receive further government contracts.

The "affirmative action for special disabled veterans and Vietnam era veterans" clause (FAR 52.222-35) is included in all contracts for $10,000 or more except for work performed outside the United States by employees who were not recruited within the United States. The clause prohibits discrimination against qualified employees or applicants on the basis that the employee or applicant is a disabled veteran or veteran of the Vietnam era and requires reporting of employment openings and hirings.

The "affirmative action for handicapped workers" clause (FAR 52.222-36) is included in all contracts for $2500 or more except work performed outside the United States by employees who were not recruited within the United States. The clause prohibits discrimination against qualified employees or applicants on the basis of mental or physical handicap.

The "buy American act-trade balance act-balance of payments program" clause (FAR 52.225-8) implements the Buy American Act and the Department of Defense Balance of Payments Program by providing a preference to domestic end products over certain foreign end products. The clause is inserted in all contracts not utilizing small purchase procedures for suppliers. Certain waivers from these acts are available under DOD's international contracting policy, as discussed in Chapter 3.

The "clean air and water" clause (FAR 52.222-3) is inserted in all contracts except contracts that are less than $100,000 unless the contract facility has been convicted of Clean Air Act or Federal Water Pollution Control Act violations; performed entirely outside the United States; or exempted by one of the departmental secretaries in the national interest. The clause requires compliance with sections of the Clean Air and Federal Water Pollution Control Acts relating to inspection, monitoring, entry, reports, and information and also prohibits performance of contract effort in facilities on the EPA List of Violating Facilities.

Joint Reporting
Committee

- Equal Employment
  Opportunity Com-
  mission
- Office of Federal
  Contract Compli-
  ance Programs (Labor)

EQUAL EMPLOYMENT OPPORTUNITY

EMPLOYER INFORMATION REPORT EEO–1

Standard Form 100
(Rev. 5–84)
O.M.B. No. 3046–0007
EXPIRES 3/31/85
100–211

Section A—TYPE OF REPORT
Refer to instructions for number and types of reports to be filed.

1. Indicate by marking in the appropriate box the type of reporting unit for which this copy of the form is submitted (MARK ONLY ONE BOX).

(1) ☐ Single-establishment Employer Report

Multi-establishment Employer:

(2) ☐ Consolidated Report (Required)

(3) ☐ Headquarters Unit Report (Required)

(4) ☐ Individual Establishment Report (submit one for each establishment with 50 or more employees)

(5) ☐ Special Report

2. Total number of reports being filed by this Company (Answer on Consolidated Report only) _____

Section B—COMPANY IDENTIFICATION (To be answered by all employers)	OFFICE USE ONLY

1. Parent Company

a. Name of parent company (owns or controls establishment in item 2) omit if same as label

a.

Name of receiving office	Address (Number and street)	b.

City or town	County	State	ZIP code	b. Employer Identification No.							

OFFICE USE ONLY

2. Establishment for which this report is filed. (Omit if same as label)

a. Name of establishment

c.

Address (Number and street)	City or Town	County	State	ZIP code	d.

b. Employer Identification No.								(Omit if same as label)	e.

Section C—EMPLOYERS WHO ARE REQUIRED TO FILE (To be answered by all employers)

☐ Yes ☐ No 1. Does the entire company have at least 100 employees in the payroll period for which you are reporting?

☐ Yes ☐ No 2. Is your company affiliated through common ownership and/or centralized management with other entities in an enterprise with a total employment of 100 or more?

☐ Yes ☐ No 3. Does the company or any of its establishments (a) have 50 or more employees AND (b) is not exempt as provided by 41 CFR 60–1.5, AND either (1) is a prime government contractor or first-tier subcontractor, and has a contract, subcontract, or purchase order amounting to $50,000 or more, or (2) serves as a depository of Government funds in any amount or is a financial institution which is an issuing and paying agent for U.S. Savings Bonds and Savings Notes?

If the response to question C–3 is yes, please enter your Dun and Bradstreet identification number (if you have one): ☐☐☐☐☐☐☐☐☐

☐ Yes ☐ No 4. Does the company receive financial assistance from the Small Business Administration (SBA)?

NOTE: If the answer is yes to questions 1, 2, or 3, complete the entire form, otherwise skip to Section G.

NSN 7540–00–180–6384

Figure 10.23. Equal employment opportunity employer information report, EEO-1, standard form 100.

Section D—EMPLOYMENT DATA

Employment at this establishment—Report all permanent full-time or part-time employees including apprentices and on-the-job trainees unless specifically excluded as set forth in the instructions. Enter the appropriate figures on all lines and in all columns. Blank spaces will be considered as zeros.

JOB CATEGORIES		OVERALL TOTALS (SUM OF COL. B THRU K)	MALE					FEMALE				
			WHITE (NOT OF HISPANIC ORIGIN)	BLACK (NOT OF HISPANIC ORIGIN)	HISPANIC	ASIAN OR PACIFIC ISLANDER	AMERICAN INDIAN OR ALASKAN NATIVE	WHITE (NOT OF HISPANIC ORIGIN)	BLACK (NOT OF HISPANIC ORIGIN)	HISPANIC	ASIAN OR PACIFIC ISLANDER	AMERICAN INDIAN OR ALASKAN NATIVE
		A	B	C	D	E	F	G	H	I	J	K
Officials and Managers	1											
Professionals	2											
Technicians	3											
Sales Workers	4											
Office and Clerical	5											
Craft Workers (Skilled)	6											
Operatives (Semi-Skilled)	7											
Laborers (Unskilled)	8											
Service Workers	9											
TOTAL	10											
Total employment reported in previous EEO–1 report	11											

(The trainees below should also be included in the figures for the appropriate occupational categories above)

Formal On-the-job trainees	White collar	12											
	Production	13											

NOTE: Omit questions 1 and 2 on the Consolidated Report.

1. Date(s) of payroll period used: 2. Does this establishment employ apprentices?
       1 ☐ Yes   2 ☐ No

Section E—ESTABLISHMENT INFORMATION *(Omit on the Consolidated Report)*

1. Is the location of the establishment the same as that reported last year?

1 ☐ Yes   2 ☐ No   3 ☐ No report last year

2. Is the major business activity at this establishment the same as that reported last year?

1 ☐ Yes   2 ☐ No   3 ☐ No report last year

OFFICE USE ONLY

3. What is the major activity of this establishment? (Be specific, i.e., manufacturing steel castings, retail grocer, wholesale plumbing supplies, title insurance, etc. Include the specific type of product or type of service provided, as well as the principal business or industrial activity.)

f.

Section F—REMARKS

Use this item to give any identification data appearing on last report which differs from that given above, explain major changes in composition or reporting units and other pertinent information.

Section G—CERTIFICATION *(See Instructions G)*

Check one   1 ☐ All reports are accurate and were prepared in accordance with the instructions (check on consolidated only)
       2 ☐ This report is accurate and was prepared in accordance with the instructions.

Name of Certifying Official	Title	Signature		Date
Name of person to contact regarding this report (Type or print)	Address (Number and street)			
Title	City and State	ZIP code	Telephone Area Code	Number Extension

All reports and information obtained from individual reports will be kept confidential as required by Section 709(e) of Title VII
WILLFULLY FALSE STATEMENTS ON THIS REPORT ARE PUNISHABLE BY LAW, U.S. CODE, TITLE 18, SECTION 1001.

Figure 10.23. (Continued)

CONTRACT CLAUSES RELATING TO LABOR STANDARDS

The "Walsh-Healy Public Contracts Act" clause (FAR 52.222-20), inserted in contracts over $10,000 for the manufacture or furnishing of materials, supplies, articles, or equipment, prohibits:

The payment to employees of less than the prevailing minimum wages for persons employed on similar work within the geographic area.

Work by employees in excess of 40 hours in any one week except where an employer-employee agreement pursuant to Title 29, Section 207 of the U.S. Code, provides otherwise.

The employment of children (males under 16 and females under 18) or convicts.

Contract performance under working conditions that are unsanitary, hazardous, or dangerous to the health and safety of employees.

The "Davis Bacon Act" clause, included in construction contracts, prohibits the payment to mechanics and laborers of less than the prevailing minimum wages for comparable classes of laborers and mechanics employed on similar construction projects in the same geographical area.

The "Contract Work Hours and Safety Standards Act—Overtime Compensation" clauses (FAR 52.222-4 and -5), inserted in supply, research and development, and construction contracts, prohibit work by laborers or mechanics in excess of 40 hours in any one week without payment of overtime compensation at least at time and a half the basic rate of pay.

The "Service Contract Act of 1965" clause (FAR 52.222-41) inserted in fixed-price service contracts over $25,000, prohibits the payment to employees of less than the prevailing minimum monetary wage and fringe benefits.

SUMMARY

A review of various contract clauses emphasizes the fact that doing business with the Federal Government is far different than doing business with a typical commercial customer.

Because many contract clauses are merely incorporated into the contract by reference, a contractor must become knowledgeable about their requirements. Prior to accepting any contract, a potential contractor should carefully read the complete text of each clause being incorporated into the contract to ensure that its requirements are understood and that reasonable compliance with its provisions during contract performance is achievable.

NOTES

1. Datex, Inc., ASBCA no. 24794, March 20, 1982, 81-1 BCA 15,060.
2. SAI Comsystems Corp., DOT CAB no. 1406, March 27, 1984, 84-2 BCA 17, 234.
3. Varigas Research Inc., ASBCA no. 28610, January 25, 1984, 84-1 BCA 17, 154.
4. ITT Defense Communications, ITT Federal Laboratories, ASBCA no. 14270, June 25, 1970, 70-2 BCA 8,370.
5. Metametrics, Inc., IBCA no. 1552-2-82, October 27, 1982, 82-2 BCA 16,095.
6. Research Applications, Inc., ASBCA no. 23834, October 4, 1979, 79-2 BCA 14,120.
7. American Standard, Inc., ASBCA no. 15660, September 24, 1971, 71-2 BCA 9,109.
8. Clevite Ordinance, ASBCA no. 5859, Navy Appeals Panel, March 26, 1962, 1962 BCA 3,330.
9. DBA Systems, Inc., NASA BCA no. 481-5, November 20, 1981, 82-1 BCA 15,468.
10. Federal Crop Insurance Corp. v. Merrill, 1947, 332 U.S. 380, 68 S. Ct. 1.
11. FY 1987 Defense Authorization Act Conference Report no. 52638, section 953.

Chapter Eleven
Equitable Adjustments

BACKGROUND

Throughout the negotiation and administration of a government contract there always lurks the knowledge that the government has the right to change its mind, to revise what it wants or how it wants it accomplished, to just "stop and think about it," or to forget it entirely. In Chapter 12, Terminations, we discuss the latter situation.

The government's reservation of the right to change the terms and conditions of an existing contract originates in its desire to exclude contingencies in its initial pricing. Government contracts include provisions for contract price adjustments resulting from government-directed changes, acts, or omissions. As a result the government has accepted the risk for potential future price increases or decreases. This risk is assumed in exchange for the elimination of the pricing of contingencies for these actions in the initial contract value. This assumption of risk by the government manifests itself in various contract clauses, all of which provide for an equitable adjustment to the contract price for various government actions or inactions. These changes can be related to the design of the product, government-furnished material or property, inspection, government suspension of work, differing site conditions, cost accounting changes required or agreed to by the government, and so on. Accordingly, changes to a contract, and the need for a resulting adjustment to the contract price, are a normal part of contracting with the Federal Government. It is for these reasons that a contractor need to submit a request for an equitable adjustment should not be looked upon as an undesirable event. Rather, it is the result of a recognition by both the government and the contractor that the need for an equitable adjustment is a normal part of the contracting process. In fact, the government prefers equitable adjustments to the inclusion of sums in the initial contract to provide for events that may or may not take place.

While any one of a number of reasons may result in the need for an adjustment to a contract price, the most common is simply the fact that the government changed what was contracted for. The change could be in the item or services themselves, or the manner in which each party to the contract will perform. While the reasons may be many and varied, the government's right to change the contract and the need for an equitable adjustment, are more often than not contained in a specific "changes" contract clause. While this clause may vary from agency to agency and by type of contract, all versions share some common concepts. All "changes" clauses contain words similar to those found in the *changes—fixed-price clause* (FAR 52. 243-1) which states:

> The contracting officer may at any time, by written order, and without notice to the sureties, if any, make changes within the general scope of this contract. . . . If any such change causes an increase or decrease in the cost of, or the time required for, performance of any part of the work under this contract, whether or not changed by the order, the Contracting Officer shall make an equitable adjustment in the contract price, delivery schedule, or both, and shall modify the contract.

Changes directed by the government under the provisions of these clauses are referred to as "formal" changes. However, it is not the only way a change in a contractual obligation may occur. A "constructive" change occurs where government action or inaction, other than a formally directed change, causes a contractor to perform in a manner different from that required by the contract. Constructive changes may also require that an equitable adjustment be made to the contract.

The purpose of this chapter is to discuss the circumstances under which either a formal or constructive change may take place and to address some of the key accounting concepts related to the pricing of the resultant equitable adjustment. While the distinction between the accounting issues and the legal issues involved may not always be clear, it is not our intent to address the questions and concepts more appropriately covered in a legal forum. Accordingly, we will generally not discuss the questions related to proof of entitlement or which party has the burden of proof and how that burden must be met. Rather, our purpose is to discuss the issues and questions related to the determination of the amount of the adjustment necessary in various circumstances where it has been determined that an equitable adjustment is appropriate.

The False Claims Act deserves serious consideration in any discussion of equitable adjustments. The act states that any demand upon the government for payment of money or transfer of property which is known to be false, fictitious or fraudulent is a criminal violation subject to a fine and/or imprisonment and triple damages. Furthermore, if any part of a claim is found to be fraudulent, the entire proposal is disallowed. Avoiding a false claim allegation in connection with an equitable adjustment proposal submission is a simple matter. The contractor need only be straightforward and tell the truth. The government may disagree with the interpretations of contract terms or the amount of compensation requested but the fact that the government has a different position should not in itself lead to fraud allegations.

Because changes can occur for many and varied reasons, the techniques used to determine the necessary price adjustment are many and varied as well. This chapter, will cover some of these different types of changes and related pricing techniques in connection with the more common types of changes. Changes related to cost accounting standards are separately addressed in Chapter 8. First, it is necessary to determine the objective of the equitable adjustment.

DEFINITION OF AN EQUITABLE ADJUSTMENT

Certain clauses require that an equitable adjustment be made to the contract for any change made pursuant to the particular clause. Like many things, the adjustment necessary to create equity may be highly dependent on the perspective of the parties to the action. A dictionary would probably define equity using terms such as *fairness, impartiality, and justice*. This type of definition has generally proved to be too broad for use in contract pricing actions. The Court of Claims recognized that the term has developed specific meaning in a Federal Government contracting environment. In *General Builders Supply v. United States*[1] the court stated:

> [The meaning of "equitable adjustment" has become so to speak, a "trade usage" for those engaged in contracting with the Federal Government. The knowledgeable federal contractor would understand it, and plaintiff if it were not so knowledgeable, was charged with making itself aware of that usage. . . . Since it was dealing with the government, as to which a whole body of special contract provisions has developed, plaintiff could hardly take the naive stance that it had the right to read its contract as an unsophisticated layman might, without bothering to inquire into the established meaning and coverage of phrases and provisions which appear to be unusual or special to federal procurement.

In a key case, *Bruce Construction Corp.* v. *United States*,[2] the Court of Claims defined equitable adjustment as "simply corrective measures utilized to keep a contractor whole when the government modifies a contract." While this may sound simple enough, a long history of disputes and litigation would indicate that there is not a clear-cut anwer in many situations. In addressing what is meant by "keeping a contractor whole" the Court of Claims stated in *Pacific Architects and Engineers, Incorporated* v. *United States:*[3]

> It is well established that the equitable adjustment may not properly be used as an occasion for reducing or increasing the contractor's profit or loss or for converting a loss to a profit or vice-versa, for reasons unrelated to a change. A contractor who has understated his bid or encountered unanticipated expense or inefficiencies may not properly use a change order as an excuse to reform the contract or to shift its own risk or losses to the government.

In other words, the profit or loss that would be experienced on the portion of the contract not affected by the change should not be disturbed.

In a more recent case, the calculation of the equitable adjustment was looked upon in much simpler terms. In *Celesco Industries, Inc.,*[4] the Armed Services Board of Contract Appeals stated:

> The measure of the equitable price adjustment is the difference between the reasonable cost of performing without the change or deletion and the reasonable cost of performing with the change or deletion.

In summary, it can be stated that an equitable adjustment is that which reimburses the contractor or the government, as the case may be, for the reasonable cost or savings resulting from the difference in cost of performance with and without the change, while not disturbing the profit or loss that will be experienced on the unchanged portion of the contract. Or, as put very succinctly in *Montag-Halvorson-Cascade-Austin.*[5]

> The true objective of an equitable adjustment . . . is to leave the parties in the same position costwise and profitwise as they would have occupied had there been no change, preserving to each as nearly as possible the advantages and disadvantages of their bargain. . . .

REASONABLE COSTS

"Reasonable" costs are defined in the FAR 31.201-3 as costs which do not exceed those that would be incurred by an ordinary prudent person in the conduct of competitive business.

In discussing the reasonable cost of performance, which is the basis for equitable adjustments, the Court of Claims in *Nager Electric Company, Inc. and Keystone Engineering Corporation* v. *United States*[6] stated that:

> the objective focus is on the cost that would have been incurred by a prudent businessman placed in a similar overall competitive situation. . . . However, unless it also takes into account the subjective situation of the contractor a test of 'reasonable cost' is incomplete.

The result is that while the cost of another contractor or the government to perform a task which had been added or deleted may be used to evaluate the reasonableness of the adjustment, this test alone is not sufficient. The anticipated or actual cost of performance by the contractor must be shown to be unreasonable before it may be departed from as a measure of the equitable adjustment. In *Bruce Construction Corp.,*[7] the Court of Claims, in quoting from a Law Review article, stated: "But the standard of reasonable cost must be viewed in the light of a particular contractor's cost . . . and not the universal objective determination of what the cost would have been to other contractors at large."

In Bruce Construction Corp., the Court of Claims documented the presumption that incurred (historical) costs are considered to be reasonable by stating:

> To say that "reasonable cost" rather than "historical cost" should be the measure does not depart from the test applied in the past, for the two terms are often synonymous. And where there is an alleged disparity between "historical" and "reasonable" costs, the historical costs are presumed reasonable.
> Since the presumption is that a contractor's claimed cost is reasonable, the Government must carry the very heavy burden of showing that the claimed cost was of such a nature that it should not have been expended, or that the contractor's costs were more than were justified in the particular circumstance.

While Bruce Construction established precedence for establishing the presumption of reasonableness, a 1987 change to FAR 31.201-3 shifted the burden of proving reasonableness to the contractor in certain circumstances. Under the new definition of reasonableness:

> No presumption of reasonableness shall be attached to the incurrence of costs by a contractor, and upon challenge of a specific cost by the contracting officer, the burden of proof shall be upon the contractor to establish that such a cost is reasonable.

This FAR revision represents a dramatic change in the treatment of reasonable costs, which will undoubtedly impact future court decisions in this area.

Even if the presumption of reasonableness is sustained, the incurred costs must also meet the other tests of allowability provided for in the contract and applicable procurement regulations.

DEDUCTIVE CHANGES

Savings to the government may result from changes that reduce contractual requirements. If a deletion occurs before work associated with the deleted item is performed, costs will not be incurred. In this case, it will be necessary to estimate the amount of the equitable adjustment required to reflect the reduced contract requirements. One piece of information that may be available is the original contract price for the item or items deleted. Another piece of information that may be available is the amount that was included in the original bid.

Because one objective of the equitable adjustment is to leave the profit or loss which would have been experienced unchanged on the unchanged portion of the contract, the use of the contract value or original bid price may not be appropriate. If the profit on the deleted item is anticipated to vary from that contemplated in the original contract price, the estimated costs which would have been experienced may be a better measure of the appropriate adjustment. As stated earlier, the equitable adjustment may not be used to increase profit or decrease a loss for reasons not related to the change.[8] As a result, boards of contract appeals and courts have taken the position that the proper measure of a deductive change is the reasonable cost that would have been incurred for the deleted item, plus a profit thereon. Thus, if the estimated cost of performance is less than the amount included in the contract for the item deleted, the contractor will retain the benefit of the difference.[9] Conversely, if the estimated cost of performance is greater than the contract price for the item, the contractor will suffer that loss. The estimated cost of performance for these calculations should be based upon the information available at the time the change was directed or negotiated.

In boards of contract appeals and court decisions, the burden of proof for a price reduction has been placed upon the government. In *Nager Electric Company, Inc.*[10] the Court of Claims stated:

> Another principle which is intricately involved in this case is that the government has the burden of proving how much of a downward equitable adjustment in price should be made on account of the deletion of the original [items]. Just as the contractor has that task when an upward adjustment is sought under the changes clause so the [government] has the laboring oar, and bears the risk of failure of proof, when a decrease is at issue.

Given the situation that the costs have not been incurred, the burden of proof ascribed to the government may be a difficult burden. However, in the situation where a portion of the costs were incurred before a change deleted the requirement for an item, the actual costs incurred will be utilized in determining the amount of the adjustment.

ADDITIVE CHANGES

Just as changes can delete contract items so can they add items or services. Indeed, it is more common that changes increase overall contractual obligations rather than reduce such obligations. The focus of the accounting issues related to additive changes are generally the same as those for deductive changes. The key task is the determination of the "reasonable costs" to perform the additional work. One of the critical issues concerning the determination of reasonable costs is the timing of the pricing action. The timing of the action will determine the approach to be used and what information will be utilized to calculate the specific amounts involved. The timing of the action will also influence the determination of which party will bear the cost risk.

PROSPECTIVE PRICING

As a general rule, the government prefers prospective pricing. It is not at all unusual for the government to request an estimate or proposal for a change that is under consideration. This is normally desired by the government for budgetary and funding purposes. In this case, the contractor is providing an estimate, or indeed may be making an offer, prior to the government even directing a change in a contract. It should be readily apparent in this situation that, to the extent the actual cost may be somewhat different than the estimated cost, the risk is placed primarily upon the contractor. The importance of this assignment of risk to the contractor will be dependent upon the type of contract adjustment to be negotiated (firm fixed-price or cost type) and how much confidence the contractor has in its ability to forecast the cost to be incurred.

As stated earlier, the key element here is the determination of "reasonable cost" and the addition of a profit thereon. This pricing activity may therefore not be significantly different than the pricing activity related to the award of the initial contract. However, because the relative negotiating positions of the parties is not the same as that for an initial contract (the contractor is already performing under the contract and it may not be possible to seek another contractor to perform the changed work), the government may seek to limit its liability through the inclusion of a predetermined contract price in the change order itself. It is not at all uncommon for a change order to include a phrase such as "at no increased cost" or "not to exceed." In these situations, even if the contractor is able to prove "reasonable cost" above the level specified, the payment for the additional items will be limited to the agreed-upon amount.

Although it is the policy of the government to attempt to negotiate the equitable adjustment associated with the contract changes prior to the performance of the changed activity, it will do so only if this will not adversely affect the interest of the government. FAR 43.102 notes that if a significant cost increase could result from a modification and time does not permit the negotiation of a price, at least a maximum price shall be negotiated prior to the work being performed unless to do so would be impractical.

Because the prospective pricing of contract changes is substantially similar to the pricing activity associated with the initial award of a contract, the same rules of conduct generally apply. As a statutory provision, the Truth in Negotiations Act (Defective Pricing) discussed in Chapter 5 is applicable to any change orders where the estimated cost exceeds the statutory limits. In addition, the contracting officer may request cost or pricing data for change orders which are not anticipated to exceed the statutory thresholds. Whether or not the submission of cost or pricing data is required, the determination of the "reasonable cost" to perform the changed work will be based upon the best information available at the time the contractor prepares the pricing proposal. To the extent that additional information becomes available between the time the proposal is prepared and the time the negotiation of the equitable adjustment for the change takes place, this additional information should also be presented.

RETROACTIVE PRICING

While the government prefers to negotiate the equitable adjustment prior to the performance of the changed work, there are many situations when it is not practical or desirable to do so. If the contractor can estimate the cost of anticipated performance with a high degree of confidence, it may be desirable to negotiate the equitable adjustment on a prospective basis. If a sufficient degree of confidence does not exist, it may be in the contractor's best interest to wait until after the costs have been incurred to negotiate the equitable adjustment. As discussed earlier, this tends to shift the risk of cost performance to the government.

However, the use of retroactive pricing does place some additional burdens on the contractor. These are related to the degree to which the contractor must "prove" the incurred cost. Even if incurred costs are presumed to be reasonable, they must be shown to have been incurred specifically for performance of the changed effort or allocable to that effort. If incurred costs are the preferred basis for the retroactive pricing of a contract change, then the absence of a showing of incurred costs must be overcome for the contractor to successfully negotiate the adjustment. The importance of incurred cost information relating to the change was demonstrated in *Cen-Vi-Ro.*[11] In that case, the Court of Claims stated:

> [Plaintiff should have the opportunity to justify its equitable adjustment by a showing of actual costs. If . . . plaintiff is unable to come forward with acceptable records of its actual costs for particular claims, further adjustment as to those items should be denied.

In this particular case, the Court of Claims noted that the contractor was a subsidiary of a sophisticated, multidivision organization with an elaborate system of record-keeping. It could be inferred that the detailed record-keeping requirements implied in the decision could be limited to a contractor in the same circumstances. As a result, it may be possible to overcome a lack of adequate accounting records to support the amount of an equitable adjustment being priced on a retroactive basis. However, to the extent that actual cost data are not available, the contractor's request for an equitable adjustment may be more vulnerable to a government challenge of the reasonableness of the proposed amounts.

Not only because it is desired by the courts, but because it is also in the contractor's best interest, the production of records showing the actual cost of performance for the changed effort is highly desirable. It may therefore be necessary for a contractor to evaluate the adequacy of the accounting system in terms of its ability to segregate the cost of changed work whenever possible.

The government's recognition of the importance of incurred cost data in negotiating contract changes on a retroactive basis is evidenced in FAR 43.203 which states, in part:

> Contractors' accounting systems are seldom designed to segregate the costs of performing changed work. Therefore, before prospective contractors submit offers, the contracting officer should advise them of the possible need to revise their accounting procedures to comply with the cost segregation requirements of the Change Order Accounting clause. . .

The clause cited above is one which may be inserted in contracts. Under its provisions, contractors may be directed to segregate change order costs in their accounting records. FAR 43.203 indicates that the following costs are normally segregable and accountable under the terms of the clause:

> Nonrecurring costs; e.g., engineering costs and costs of obsolete work or reperformed work.

Cost of added distinct work caused by the change order; e.g., new subcontract work, new prototypes, or new retrofit or backfit kits.

Costs of recurring work; e.g., labor and material costs.

Whether an equitable adjustment should be negotiated on a prospective or retroactive basis is dependent upon the particular circumstances of each change. Because of the complexities normally encountered in the actual implementation of contract changes, and the resulting need for contract repricing actions, many derivations of prospective and retroactive changes may be utilized. Indeed, it is entirely likely that a combination of methods will prove to be the most desirable approach for a specific change.

While we have not yet discussed specific types of changes, it can be seen from the above discussion that actual costs incurred, estimated costs to be incurred, or costs that would have been incurred are the starting point for determining the amount of an equitable adjustment resulting from a contract change. In summary, it can be said that the pricing of equitable adjustments may not be significantly different from the activities associated with the pricing of an initial contract. Changes may be based upon costs incurred or on estimates of costs expected to be incurred. A change may be related to the addition of contract requirements, the deletion of contract requirements, a substitution of one contract obligation for another, or a combination of all of these. The pricing action may take place before the change has occurred, while the change is occurring, or after the change has occurred. There may be specific accounting records measuring the precise impact, or it may be necessary to resort to subjective approximations or estimates.

We will now discuss the various types of contract changes, the various costs covered by the different types of changes, and various methods that may be used to price changes.

COSTS

Direct Costs

In determining the amount of the equitable adjustment necessary as a result of a change, the simpler elements of cost to calculate may be the direct costs. In general, direct costs are those that are incurred exclusively for the performance of the particular activity and are measurable with a reasonable degree of precision. As a result, once the changed activity is identified, it is usually a matter of applying the normal estimating and accounting processes to that activity to determine the amount of the direct cost. Therefore, adjustments related to the pricing of changes for direct labor, direct material purchases, subcontracts, and so on may be a straightforward exercise. The difficulties in this area are more likely to relate to the determination of the activity being changed and the amount of the change rather than to the estimating and accounting techniques used to measure the impact.

Overhead

The determination of the proper amount of overhead to be applied to the changed effort may not be so clear cut. That an overhead adjustment is necessary is normally not the issue. Rather, the determination of the amount is the question to be addressed. Some government agencies include as a contract provision a specific overhead percentage to be applied for changes. These clauses may also include a provision for certain other costs and profit at a prescribed amount or rate. When a contract has such a provision, the equitable adjustment will normally be made using the stated percentage applied to the appropriate base (the normal base applied through the accounting system application or the base specified in the contract).

Where the rate is not specified in the contract, the determination of the proper amount is usually dependent upon a subjective evaluation of the circumstances. This may present some difficulties. In *Kemmons-Wilson, Inc.*,[12] the ASBCA stated:

> It is always more desirable to reimburse a contracting party for its actual expended or incurred indirect costs, exactly in the same manner as direct costs if it is practicable or feasible. Such treatment of indirect cost is usually neither practicable nor feasible.

The issues to be addressed in determining the proper amount of overhead costs to be applied to the contract are substantially the same as determining any other costs of performing the change. That is, the costs must be reasonable in amount, allowable under the contract cost principles, not prohibited by the contract, and properly allocable. It is this latter point that usually is the most difficult to properly ascertain.

When the amount of the change requiring the equitable adjustment is not so significant as to have a measurable impact on the allocation base, difficulties are not normally encountered. In this case, the normal overhead rate applied to all contracts (either incurred or projected) would be applied to the component of the change that represents the normal allocation base for those indirect expenses. However, where the change is of such a magnitude as to have an impact on the overhead rates for all jobs, a determination must be made as to the proper portion of the overhead expenses that should be applied to measure the equitable adjustment. Normally, an attempt is made to isolate the components of the indirect expenses that are impacted by the change. This may be accomplished by account analysis of the indirect expenses pool or by a determination of the proportionate impact on the total pool. The determination of the proper adjustment must of necessity be handled on a case-by-case basis. The ultimate objective is to isolate the impact of the change on the indirect expense pool much in the same manner as the impact on direct costs must be isolated.

Delay-Related Costs

The concept of delay can be extremely complicated. However, it is important to distinguish between government-caused delays and other "excusable delays." Excusable delays, which are the result of causes beyond the control and without the fault or negligence of the contractor, entitle a contractor to an increased period of performance. However, only excusable delays that are caused by the government entitle the company to an equitable adjustment for increased cost due to the delay. Because the government acts in the capacity of a sovereign, any delays caused by government action or inaction are considered to be excusable delays.

There are various methods used to calculate the impact of government-caused delays. However, certain factors normally recur. The principle elements usually include (1) unabsorbed overhead, (2) cost of labor and equipment, (3) loss of efficiency, and (4) performance in a later, and higher cost, period.

Unabsorbed Overhead

When a government-caused delay requires that the contractor stop performance, certain expenses will continue to be incurred. Among these are fixed indirect (overhead) expenses. Fixed overhead expenses should be considered to also include those variable expenses which cannot, as a practical matter, be prevented through the use of good management procedures. Since the normal method of absorbing indirect expenses is to allocate these expenses over direct activity, to the extent there is no performance there is no way to recover these costs. If a single contract has a delay in performance, the indirect expenses which would have been absorbed by this contract will be absorbed by other contracts unless an adjustment is made. This is true even though the delay can specifically be identified with a reduction in the anticipated indirect expense allocation base.

To provide for this adjustment, case law has established several formulas. One of the first formulas established was in *Carteret Work Uniforms*[13] Under the assumption that all other work of the contractor is unaffected by the delay and is proceeding in a normal manner, this formula provides recovery of all overhead expenses incurred during the delay period above the amount paid through the contract price. The adjustment can be expressed by the following formula:

$$\begin{array}{l}
\text{Incurred overhead} \\
\text{rate during} \\
\text{delay period}
\end{array} - \text{Normal overhead rate} = \text{Excess rate}$$

$$\text{Excess rate} \quad \times \quad \dfrac{\text{Total base costs}}{\text{during delay period}} = \dfrac{\text{Unabsorbed}}{\text{overhead}}$$

In this case, the contractor was using the entire plant for performance of the contract that experienced the delay. As a result, any unabsorbed overhead was specifically identified with the contract.

Another formula that was subsequently developed compares the rate actually incurred during the actual period of performance and the rate during the originally projected period of performance. If the actual rate is higher than the rate during the anticipated period of performance, then the difference is applied to the contract base cost to determine the unabsorbed overhead. This was established in *Allegheny Sportswear Company*.[14] The formula can be stated as:

$$\begin{array}{l}
\text{Incurred overhead} \\
\text{rate during} \\
\text{actual period}
\end{array} - \begin{array}{l}
\text{Incurred overhead} \\
\text{rate for projected} \\
\text{period}
\end{array} = \text{Excess rate}$$

$$\text{Excess rate} \quad \times \text{Contract base costs} = \text{Unabsorbed overhead}$$

One of the characteristics of this method is that the two periods of overhead are intermixed. The period originally projected for performance is included in the actual period of performance.

The most widely used formula evolved after the Allegheny Sportswear formula. In *Eichleay Corp.*,[15] a daily overhead rate was calculated on the basis that there had been no delay. This daily rate was then applied to each day of delay. It is expressed by the following formula:

$$\frac{\text{Contract billings}}{\text{Total billings for ac-}} \times \frac{\text{Total overhead incurred}}{\text{during contract period}} = \frac{\text{Overhead allocable}}{\text{to contract}}$$
tual contract period

$$\frac{\text{Allocable overhead}}{\text{Actual days of per-}} = \frac{\text{Overhead allocable}}{\text{to contract per day}}$$
formance

Daily overhead $\times$ Number of days of delay = Unabsorbed overhead

In its pamphlet on *Audit Guidance—Delay and Disruption Claims*,[16] the Defense Contract Audit Agency indicates a preference for the Allegheny method. However, over the last 20 years, boards of contract appeals have shown a decided preference for the Eichleay formula in calculating a contractor's additional overhead costs attributable to delay and extended performance.

In *Propserv, Inc.*,[17] the government argued that the contractor was not entitled to recovery of unabsorbed general and administrative (G&A) expenses because such expenses are relatively stable costs applicable to total company operations irrespective of the nature of individual production jobs. The ASBCA disagreed and concluded:

> If the claim is for "unabsorbed" expense, it is really for a decrease in allocability to other work, which bore too great a proportion of all indirect costs because of the disruption and delay. In this aspect, general and administrative expense stands on the same footing as other overhead expense.
> Hence, the fact that no specific increase in G&A expenses has been shown herein is immaterial. We find the "Eichleay" method employed by the appellant to allocate these expenses as a function of time to be particularly appropriate in cases of suspension of work where the direct costs incurred are minimal or nonexistent.

Boards of contract appeals' support for the use of the formula developed in Eichleay is further evidenced in other cases. In *Charles W. Schroyer, Inc.*,[18] the ASBCA stated:

> The Government argues that appellant was able to utilize its direct labor elsewhere and, therefore, no overhead was unabsorbed. That begs the question since direct labor is only one of the costs involved in contract performance. The "Eichleay" formula has been developed to be used where direct costs are low or proof of actual allocation difficult or impossible. It is an effort to arrive at an approximate allocation. We conclude it is an appropriate approach to use here.

In *Dawson Construction Company, Inc.*,[19] the GSA Board of Contract Appeals expressed the following view when it discussed the government's objection to the use of the Eichleay formula:

> The thrust of the Government's objections to the use of the Eichleay formula can be summed up as a contention that its method of estimating and applying values to Appellant's own projected work schedule is more precise. As we observed, the task of separating suspended from nonsuspended work is less than precise, and we are not ready to say that the Eichleay is the only fair method of allocating home office overhead incurred by a contractor during a suspension. However, the Eichleay formula is more precise than the method proposed by the Government which fails to take into consideration the period of delay and the impact of that delay over the term of the contract. Accordingly, we conclude that in the absence of a contractually-prescribed

method for allocating overhead, the Eichleay formula is not only acceptable but preferable to the method proposed by the Government.

In a more recent board of contract appeals case, it appears that the government has accepted the use of the Eichleay formula. In *Two State Construction Company*,[20] DCAA used the Eichleay formula, only recommending that certain unallowable costs (such as bad debts, advertising, contributions, and entertainment) be deleted from the overhead pool used to calculate the daily rate. The Board adopted the DCAA recommendation.

In 1983 two cases (Capital Electric Company and Savoy Construction Company, Inc.) established a need to go beyond a showing of underabsorption of overhead expenses during the actual period of delay. In *Capital Electric Company*,[21] the GSA Board of Contract Appeals initially denied a contractor's request for underabsorbed overhead because the contractor did not consider the benefits to future jobs resulting from reduced indirect expense allocations. The Board stated: ". . . a contractor claiming recovery of underabsorbed . . . overhead must also account for the possible benefit of direct costs deferred to later cost accounting periods that might result in a balancing overabsorption."

However, the Court of Appeals for the Federal Circuit subsequently remanded the decision and ordered the GSBCA to award the contractor extended overhead costs calculated by the *Eichleay* formula[22].

The concept of offsetting an underabsorption of overhead by a later overabsorption was addressed in *Savoy Construction Co., Inc.*[23] In this decision, the court addressed the concept of identifying underabsorbed costs solely on the basis of a delay in performance, as follows:

> the concept of awarding additional home office overhead on a per diem basis simply because the performance time on a project has been extended presents logical difficulties. As noted, this overhead cost is not related to contract performance. The cost will continue regardless of when any one contract is completed. Having a contract in progress for an additional period of time does not necessarily increase or decrease home office costs. Only if an extended performance period on one contract served to preclude the receipt of new revenue would the contractor actually suffer a loss of sums otherwise available to offset its continuing home office overhead expense. In recent decisions, courts and boards have cast a critical eye on the concept of an automatic recovery of home office overhead whenever a contract completion is delayed.

Consistent with the decision in *Capital Electric Co.*, the Claims Court reversed its decision and remanded Savoy Construction Co.,[24] stating to the ASBCA:

> The Government implies, in its brief on remand, that to award appellant such additional compensation would constitute reliance upon an "ipso facto" approach which does not give proper credit for amounts already paid through the application of overhead percentage rates to direct costs. However, the Board's record, as supplemented, shows that this is not the case. After giving full credit for the $15,231 previously paid, a significant balance of $151,135.20 remains in appellant's favor. The delays due to the 14 changes started at the beginning of the project, continued sporadically throughout the period of construction, and it appears that appellant was unable to shift its forces to other projects. Under the circumstances we are persuaded that merely allowing appellant a percentage markup of the direct costs would not adequately compensate it. The Eichleay formula, in our view, presents a well settled means of providing a fair allocation in this situation.
> That these appeals involved changes providing for the performance of additional work does not militate against the use of the Eichleay formula, where, as here, proper adjustment is made for overhead already paid so as to avoid over recovery.

As can be seen from these more recent cases, the *Eichleay* method for calculating unabsorbed overhead continues to be accepted by the boards and courts as long as the contractor's records are adequate to clearly show that the damages are not offset by future effort and that overhead adjustments are made for amounts already paid.

Idle Labor and Equipment

When a contractor is faced with a government-caused delay, some direct costs may be incurred on a contract from nonproductive activities that are a result of the delay. This can happen despite the contractor's best efforts to productively divert resources. It is especially true in construction contracting where there may be no other work to transfer the resources to because of the remote work site or by the very nature of the construction work itself. It can also occur on supply or service contracts with delays of short duration. In such cases, where a contractor is not able to productively divert direct resources, the resulting costs may be recoverable in a request for equitable adjustment. The direct costs most frequently encountered are for idle labor and equipment.

Whenever disruptions in work flow occur, there is normally a question about the utilization of those employees assigned to the disrupted work. The effective utilization of employees in such situations is a management responsibility and is no different in the government contracting environment.

The basic rule applied is that only those direct costs that the contractor cannot avoid through the use of good management should be included in an equitable adjustment request. Therefore, those direct personnel that cannot be effectively utilized elsewhere should continue charging the delayed contract unless they can be transferred or discharged. This decision requires a good deal of management judgment. It may also require a contractor to try to forecast the length of the delay since it may be the critical factor affecting the decision. For example it may not be feasible to release an employee only to attempt to hire the employee back in a short time.

Delays may also result in idle equipment. Where such equipment is used exclusively on one contract and cannot be used elsewhere, depreciation may continue to be allocated directly to a delayed contract if this was the prior practice. If equipment costs are included in overhead, idle equipment costs would be recovered through unabsorbed overhead. For construction contractors, the method of recovering idle equipment costs in equitable adjustments may be quite different. For equipment that is rented from third parties, the specific rental charges, on a daily or other periodic basis, will continue to be charged at the rental rates. For company-owned equipment the method of calculating the cost of idle equipment will be dependent upon the contractor's method of identifying equipment utilization cost by job.

If the company maintains records that segregate ownership and operating costs by individual pieces of equipment, those records will form the basis for the calculation of idle equipment costs. Generally equipment ownership costs (depreciation, insurance, taxes, etc.) and certain maintenance costs are includable.

If the company does not maintain cost records by individual piece of equipment, it may be appropriate to resort to industrywide experience. Construction industry trade associations and equipment groups publish tables with equipment usage rates which some contractors use. Some tables include rates for equipment that is in a standby status (assigned to a job but not being used). FAR 31.105 (d) (2) (i) (b) provides for the evaluation of equipment usage rates based upon predetermined schedules of construction equipment use rates, such as the construction ownership and operating schedule published by the U.S. Army Corps of Engineers.

A contractor claiming idle labor or equipment should be prepared to show that it has taken appropriate action to reduce the cost of a delay similar to mitigating damages after a breach of contract. This will substantially aid in the ultimate recovery of claimed costs. The requirement to reduce the cost of delay was established by the ASBCA in *Hardeman-Morier-Hutcherson*,[25] in which it stated:

> A contractor has the duty to minimize its cost in the execution of a change order in the same manner as he must mitigate his damages after a breach. Normally he would be required to transfer or discharge idle men, and find uses for his equipment pending the time that work can commence.

Loss of Efficiency

Even in cases where labor is not totally idled by a government-caused delay, increased costs may result from the inefficient utilization of labor or equipment. Such inefficiences may be the result of confusion, interrruptions in the orderly progress of work, or increased start-ups.

To the extent any of these losses of efficiency cause increased costs, they should be included in the calculation of costs associated with a delay. While it is clear that contractors are entitled to such adjustments from government-caused delays, the determination of the amount of adjustment is extremely difficult.

Normally, the amount of adjustment is calculated based on subjective judgments rather than segregated accounting data. Accounting data alone will not normally provide the needed information without the use of judgment. Two methods used in determining the amount of loss of efficiency are: (1) application of a percentage factor and (2) "estimated cost." The first method involves application of a percentage factor, typically between 10 and 40%, to labor hours or costs incurred during the disrupted period. This represents the additional costs (hours) incurred as a result of the disruption. The "estimated cost" method measures the difference between actual labor costs incurred and an estimate of what labor costs would have been without the disruption.

Regardless of the method used, estimates will be required. The boards and courts have accepted approximations because of the difficulty of proving exact amounts. Nevertheless, there must be some underlying basis for the estimate related to the specific circumstances of the delay. For example, a contractor could develop objective evidence comparing the amount of work accomplished during the period of disruption with the amount of work accomplished during normal operations. Without such an underlying basis, the amount of the calculated loss of efficiency may be denied or at least reduced. In court or board proceedings, it is usually advisable to use an expert witness to testify on the amount of lost efficiency rather than an employee of the contractor. Such experts are looked upon as being more objective and more widely known for their expertise in such matters. However, again, the testimony of such expert witnesses should be backed up with objective evidence.

Performance in a Later Period

One of the consequences of a significant delay is usually an extension of the period of contract performance. In some cases, the period of delay may be recovered through the use of additional labor or accelerated performance. However, when a contractor is required to perform the contract in a period later than originally planned because of a government-caused delay, it is entitled to recover any resulting increased costs in an equitable adjustment.

Such increased costs may occur because of increased labor rates or higher material costs than would have been incurred had performance occurred as originally planned. In these circumstances, the contractor must be able to show that actual labor rates and material prices increased and not just total labor or material costs. Increases in total labor or material costs may be due to inefficiencies or other causes not necessarily related to performance in a later period.

The inability of a contractor to prove the exact amount of labor rate increases applicable to a specific contract may not be a basis for complete denial of a claim. Although expressing a preference for actual labor cost data, the ASBCA in *Keco Industries, Inc.*[26] allowed the contractor to use plant-wide labor rates in the calculation of the equitable adjustment.

ACCELERATION

An equitable adjustment may also be required if the government, for whatever reason, decides to "accelerate" performance under a contract. This may be the result of a unilateral government decision that it needs the items sooner than originally contemplated. However, in most cases it will result from a "constructive acceleration" related to a need to "make-up" time lost due to delays. Equitable adjustments for constructive accelerations are limited to situations where a contractor would be entitled to schedule extensions because of excusable delays.

Excusable Delays and Successful Claims

Excusable delays are generally defined in contract clauses as delays resulting from "causes beyond the control and without the fault or negligence of the contractor. . . ." Examples of such causes are acts of God, fires, floods, strikes, and unusually severe weather. The general criterion above takes precedence over the specific examples cited. For example, while "strikes" is listed as a cause for excusable delay, a contractor that was found to be engaged in an unfair labor practice would not be entitled to an excusable delay. In this case, the strike would *not* be "beyond the control and without the fault or negligence of the contractor. . . ." In the case of unusually severe weather, the basic issue is that the weather was *unusually* severe and not necessarily the *severity* of the weather. If the weather was extremely severe, even to the point of making any work impossible, the delay would not be excusable if such weather conditions were not unusual for the location. If the effect of the weather could not have been foreseen in making the original cost estimate, the resulting delay should be excusable. However, the contractor must be able to prove that the delay was a direct result of unusual weather.

The determination of the existence of a constructive acceleration is no easy task. Based on an analysis of prior court and board cases, the ASBCA in *Fermont Division, Dynamics Corporation of America*[27] established the following conditions as a prerequisite to a successful acceleration claim based on a government failure to grant a time extension for excusable delay:

1. Existence of a given period of excusable delay;
2. Contractor notice to the government of the excusable delay, and request for extension of time together with supporting information sufficient to allow the government to make a reasonable determination.
    Exceptions:
    a. Such notice, request and information are not necessary if the government's order (see (3) below) directs compliance with a given schedule expressly without regard to the existence of any excusable delay.
    b. The supporting information is unnecessary if it is already reasonably available to the government;
3. Failure or refusal to grant the requested extension within a reasonable time;
4. A government order, either express or implied from the circumstances, to (a) take steps to overcome the excusable delay, or (b) complete the work at the earliest possible date, or (c) complete the work by a given date earlier than that to which the contractor is entitled by reason of the excusable delay. Circumstances from which such an order may be implied include expressions of urgency by the government, especially if coupled with (i) a threat of default or liquidated damages for not meeting a given accelerated schedule, or (ii) actual assessment of liquidated damages for not meeting a given accelerated schedule;
5. Reasonable efforts by the contractor to accelerate the work, resulting in added costs, even if the efforts are not actually successful.

The notice to the contracting officer of excusable delay and request for schedule extension should, like other communications to the government, be in writing. Contractors meeting the above conditions and strictly following the prescribed procedures should be able to prove an acceleration and negotiate an equitable adjustment.

Nevertheless, some of the statements are generalizations that require interpretation. For example, one of the conditions is that there is a "failure or refusal to grant the requested extension within a reasonable time. . . ." How long is a reasonable time? Undue delays in granting a request for schedule extension places a contractor in a precarious position. Does it incur acceleration costs to make up lost time that may not be recoverable or does it run the risk that not meeting delivery schedules will result in assessment of liquidated damages or a termination for default? In *Ashton Co.,*[28] the Department of Interior Board of Contract Appeals commented on government witness testimony that no action was taken on requests for time extensions due to weather conditions until the contract was completed. The Board stated that "the duty is upon the Government to obtain the climatological data without unnecessary delay. . . . To wait until the contract work is completed . . . could well force a contractor into acceleration." This example demonstrates a need for effective communications between the contracting parties.

Another problem in acceleration claims occurs when a contractor has experienced both excusable and contractor-caused delays and the contracting officer issues an acceleration order. The question is whether the order is to make up the time of excusable or unexcusable delay. Unless the contract contains a special clause giving the contracting officer the right to order the contractor to make-up lost time for contractor caused delays, the order could be assumed to be for excusable delays. When in doubt, a contractor should clarify the intent with the contracting officer.

One of the most difficult questions involved in acceleration claims is what communications from the government constitute a constructive acceleration order. It has been held by the boards and courts that "requests" to accelerate can be considered an order to accelerate if the request is firm. Threats to terminate for default or pressure to complete a schedule can also be construed as an acceleration order. Again, when in doubt, the matter should be clarified with the contracting officer.

Acceleration Costs

Once a contractor is found to be entitled to an equitable adjustment for an acceleration, the next step is to determine which costs were incurred as a result of the acceleration order. Generally, a contractor is reimbursed only for costs incurred to make up for excusable delays. If a contractor can show that it was otherwise on schedule, except for the excusable delays, the only problem is identifying and proving the acceleration costs incurred. However, problems are encountered when a contractor has experienced both excusable and contractor-caused delays. In such cases, the contracting parties need to reach agreement on the costs related to the acceleration effort and a reasonable allocation of such costs to excusable and contractor-caused delays. The parties might agree to share all of the acceleration costs on a pro rata basis.

The most frequent types of cost encountered in acceleration-related equitable adjustments follow, along with comments about determining and supporting amounts claimed.

Overtime and Shift Premiums

Overtime and shift premiums are the most common costs incurred in acceleration situations. The costs represent only the premium portion of pay for overtime or extra shift work. The basic labor costs are part of the normal costs of performing the work and are not included in an acceleration claim. Such premium costs should be easily extracted from the accounting records and should be acceptable if the contractor can show that the work was performed as part of the acceleration.

Expedited Material Costs

Expedited material costs are incurred for efforts to acquire materials earlier than originally expected. For example, higher-priced transportation or higher prices paid to vendors or subcontractors for earlier deliveries may be recoverable. Also included might be the costs of extra internal expediters required to ensure prompt movement of materials through production.

Loss of Efficiency

Loss of efficiency or productivity is generally one of the most difficult costs to compute in an acceleration claim because of the inability to segregate such costs. Loss of efficiency in acceleration situations is the added cost involved because of the inability of workers to be as productive as they might be without the acceleration. For example, workers tend to be less productive when working long hours or when working in adverse weather. Also, accelerations may result in the need to hire new, untrained workers, which would be less productive than existing workers. The most effective way of calculating a loss of efficiency is to determine a factor representing the general decline in productivity as a result of the acceleration. This can be done by comparing the work accomplished per labor hour or dollar during the acceleration period with the work accomplished per labor hour or dollar in a normal period.

Other Costs

There are significant other costs that may be attributed to an acceleration. The list is almost limitless. The key is to identify all costs that can be reasonably attributed to the acceleration and that would not have been incurred but for the acceleration. Applicable overhead and profit are normally included as part of the acceleration claim.

DEFECTIVE SPECIFICATIONS

Another action that may result in the need to reprice the contract is when specifications provided in a government contract are defective. The identification and correction of these defective specifications may cause increses in the cost of performance under the contract. The calculation of the impact of the delay caused by the defective specifications should be calculated as discussed earlier. Defective specifications may not be discovered until sometime after the beginning of contract performance. As a result, there may also be the cost of wasted effort. The boards of contract appeals and the courts have held that the cost of work performed in accordance with defective specifications is clearly to be included in the equitable adjustment. In *Hol-Gar Manufacturing Corp.* v. U.S.,[29] the Court of Claims stated:

> The Armed Services Board of Contract Appeals has recognized the correctness of the allowance of costs incident to an attempt to comply with defective specifications. See, e.g., J. W. Hurst & Son Awnings, Inc., 59-1 BCA 2095 at 8965 (1959), where the Board stated:
> 'Where, as here, the change is necessitated by defective specifications and drawings, the equitable adjustment to which a contractor is entitled must, if it is to be equitable, i.e., fair and just, include the costs which it incurred in attempting to perform in accordance with the defective specifications and drawings. Under these circumstances the equitable adjustment may not be limited to costs incurred subsequent to the issuance of the change orders.'
> We hold that the [contractor] is entitled to an equitable adjustment which will compensate it for the costs which it incurred in trying to perform in accordance with the original specifications that turned out to be defective.

There may also be costs incurred in connection with effort necessary to actually correct the defective specification. Not only may the company be required to identify the defective specifications, but it also must correct those specifications so as to allow for continued contract performance. The costs directly related to the additional activity associated with correcting the defective specifications are to be included in the equitable adjustment.

Finally, the correction of the defective specifications may entail the use of production techniques or the incurrence of cost for performance different than those that were originally anticipated. In this regard, the contract would require repricing to incorporate the cost associated with different production techniques or the utilization of different labor or materials.

TOTAL COST APPROACH

The method of calculating the costs of an equitable adjustment that is most favored by contractors and least favored by the government is the total cost approach. Essentially, this method determines the total cost of performance and deducts from that the total negotiated contract cost. It ascribes the difference as being the measure of the cost portion of the equitable adjustment. As is apparent, the total responsibility for the cost impact is ascribed to the government. Under this method, a cause and effect showing of the change is not attempted. Because the connection between the government change and the cost impact is not presented, the boards and courts have traditionally not favored this approach. In *WRB Corp. of Texas,*[36] the Court of Claims stated:

> This court has tolerated the use of the total cost method only when no other procedure was available and then only when the reliability of the supporting evidence was fully substantiated. There must be proof that (1) the nature of the particular losses make it impossible or highly impracticable to determine them with a reasonable degree of accuracy; (2) the plaintiff's bid or estimate was realistic; (3) it's actual costs were reasonable; and (4) it was not responsible for the added expenses.

As a result, this approach should only be used when no other approach is appropriate and the conditions for its use, as discussed in the above case, have been properly addressed.

JURY VERDICT APPROACH

When all else fails, the board or court must determine the proper amount of the equitable adjustment. This is referred to as a jury verdict. Once the contractor has proven entitlement to an adjustment and the only issue is determining the amount, a jury verdict may be used as a last resort. The responsibility of the board or court in this situation has been stated in *E. Arthur Higgins:*[31]

> When a contractor has proven entitlement, but cannot define his costs with exact data, courts and appels boards have been reluctant either to send the dispute back to the Contracting Officer for determination of excess costs or to send the contractor away empty handed when it is at all possible to make a fair and reasonable approximation of extra costs. . . . It is not necessary that the amount be ascertainable with absolute exactness or mathematical precision. . . . It is enough if the testimony and evidence adduced is sufficient to enable the court or board (acting as a jury) to make a fair and reasonable approximation. . . .

The responsibility of the court or board to reach a jury verdict approach has been emphasized in *S.W. Electronics & Manufacturing Corp.*[32] In this case, the Court of Claims stated that where entitlement was clear, the Board is under a heavy obligation to provide some compensation and should render a jury verdict giving a fair and reasonable approximation of the damages.

Generally, in rendering a jury verdict decision, the board or court will only announce its determination of the amount. It will generally not explain or justify how the result was obtained.

PROFIT

That an application of profit to the amount of the cost portion of the equitable adjustment is appropriate is usually not at issue. The appropriateness of adding profit has been addressed by the U.S. Supreme Court. In *United States* v. *Callahan Walker Construction Co.,*[33] it stated "an equitable adjustment of the [government's] additional payment for extra work involved merely the ascertainment of the cost of [the work added] and the addition to that cost of a reasonable and customary allowance for profit." It is therefore considered appropriate that profit be added to the changed effort for the same reasons that profit must be added to the original cost estimates used to establish the original contract amount.

However, because the circumstances are different, the application of the original contract profit rate may not be appropriate. If the equitable adjustment is being calculated on a retroactive basis, the cost risk is less than the situation where the activity has not as yet taken place. The regulations generally require that the structured approach to profit determination be used for contract changes in the same manner that it is utilized to determine the government's profit objective to negotiate contracts. This method will recognize the differing circumstances existing between the initial contract pricing activity and the activity related to the pricing of changes. Methods of establishing profit objectives are discussed in Chapter 4, Profit. If the changes are not significant in amount, it may be appropriate to apply the same profit rate reflected in the original contract . However, if the changes entail significantly different activities from that originally contemplated, it may be more appropriate to determine a rate that is either higher or lower than the originally contemplated profit rate.

In the case of deleted contract effort, there has been some debate as to whether it is appropriate to reduce profit on the contract. While the issue has been handled both ways, it has been generally agreed by the boards and courts that it is appropriate to add a factor for profit to contract reductions for deductive changes. The factors to be addressed in determining the amount of the reduced profit would be the same as those for adding profit to contract increases.

INTEREST

Interest is generally not includable in an equitable adjustment computation. Since the early 1970s, a "pricing of adjustments" clause has been used in contracts. It incorporates the cost principles in contracts, both cost type and fixed-price, where the pricing action is subject to cost analysis.

Inasmuch as the cost principles provide that interest is not an allowable cost (refer to Chapter 7, Government Contract Cost Principles), interest is not includable in the contract price adjustment. If the equitable adjustment becomes subject to a dispute and any claim over $50,000 is certified pursuant to FAR 33.207, interest would be included in any subsequent contract adjustment as provided under the "disputes" clause. FAR 33.208 provides that simple interest at the rate fixed by the Secretary of the Treasury is due and payable from (i) the date of receipt of the certified claim by the Contracting Officer or (ii) the date payment would have been due, whichever is later, to the date payment is received by the contractor. A more complete discussion is contained in Chapter 14, Disputes.

ACCOUNTING SYSTEM IMPLICATIONS

As can be seen from the discussion in this chapter, the key concept related to the amount of an equitable adjustment is the determination of "reasonable costs." Whether the equitable adjustment is to be calculated before the change takes place or after, the key element is the measurement or estimation of the costs that have been or will be incurred to perform the changed activity. Accordingly, an accounting system should be designed to reasonably measure the cost of changes in all circumstances determined to be appropriate. Indeed, it may be absolutely necessary to protect the contractor's rights to a contract adjustment. The boards of contract appeals have ruled that if a contractor should have maintained accurate records but failed to do so, even a jury verdict award may be inappropriate.[34]

NOTES

1. General Builders Supply v. United States, 163 Ct. Cl. 477, April 11, 1968, 13 CCF 82,642.
2. Bruce Construction Corp. et al. v. United States, 163 Ct. Cl. 97, November 15, 1963, 9 CCF 72, 325.
3. Pacific Architects and Engineers Incorporated, a California Corporation and Advanced Maintenance Corp. v. United States, 203 Ct. Cl. 449, January 23, 1974, 19 CCF 82,415.
4. Celesco Industries, Inc., ASBCA no. 22251, November 30, 1978, 79-1 BCA 82,415.
5. Montag-Halvorson-Cascase-Ayustin; CC 1121 (1958).
6. Nager Electric Company, Inc. and Keystone Engineering Corporation v. United States, 194 Ct. Cl. 835, April 30, 1970, 14 CCF 83,571. (Note: Report of Trial Commissioner of the Court of Claims. For review by court, see note 13).
7. Bruce Construction Corp. et al v. United States, supra note 2.
8. Pacific Architects and Engineers Incorporated, supra note 3.
9. Nager Electric Company, Inc. and Keystone Engineering Corporation v. United States, 194 Ct. Cl. 835, May 14, 1971, 16 CCF 80,367.
10. Ibid.
11. Cen-Vi-Ro of Texas, Inc. v. United States, Ct. Cl. no. 334-73, June 24, 1975, 21 CCF 84,057.
12. Kemmons-Wilson, Inc. and South & Patton, Joint Venture, ASBCA no. 16167, September 8, 1972, 72-2 BCA 9,689.
13. Carteret Work Uniforms, ASBCA no. 1647, August 20, 1954, 6 CCF 61,561.
14. Allegheny Sportswear Company ASBCA no. 4163, March 25, 1958, 58-1 BCA 1,684.
15. Eichleay Corp., ASBCA no. 5183, July 29, 1960, 60-2 BCA 2,688.
16. Audit Guidance-Delay and Disruption Claims, Defense Contract Audit Agency Pamphlet 7641.45, January 1983.
17. Propserv, Inc., ASBCA no. 20768, February 28, 1978, 78-1 BCA 13,066.
18. Charles W. Schroyer, Inc., ASBCA no. 21859, October 13, 1978, 78-2 BCA 13,513.
19. Dawson Construction Company, Inc., ASBCA no. 4956, July 31, 1979, 79-2 BCA 13,989.
20. Two State Construction Company, DOT CAB nos. 78-31, 1006,1070, and 1081, May 29, 1981, 81-1 BCA 15,149.
21. Capital Electric Company, GSBCA nos. 5316 & 5317, February 17, 1983, 83-2 BCA 16,548.
22. Capital Construction Company, CAFC no. 83-965, February 7, 1984, 31 CCF 72119.
23. Savoy Construction Co., Inc. v. United States, Ct. Cl. no. 579-81C, April 29, 1983, 31 CFF 71,109.
24. Savoy Construction Co., Claims Court Order no. 579-81C, March 6, 1984, ASBCA nos. 21218, 21925, 22300, 22336, 22691, 22763, 22915, April 23, 1985, 85-2 BCA 18,073.
25. Hardeman-Monier-Hutcherson, a Joint Venture, ASBCA no. 11785, March 13, 1967, 67-1 BCA 6,210.
26. Keco Industries, Inc., ASBCA nos. 15184 and 15547, June 30, 1972, 72-2 BCA 9,576.
27. Fermont Division, Dynamics Corporation of America, ASBCA no. 15806, February 20, 1975, 75-1 BCA 11,139.
28. Ashton Co., IBCA no. 1070-6-75, June 16, 1976, 76-2 BCA 11,934.
29. Hol-Gar Manufacturing Corp. v. United States, 175 Ct. Cl. 518, May 13, 1966, 11 CCF 80,438.

30. WRB Corp., et al. a Joint Venture dba Robertson Construction Company v. United States, 183 Ct. Cl. 409, 12 CCF 81,781.
31. E. Arthur Higgins, AGBCA no. 76-128, September 20, 1979, 79-2 BCA 14,050.
32. S.W. Electronics Manufacturing Corp. v. United States, Ct. Cl. 1981, no. 207-78, July 29, 1981, 29 CCF 81,726.
33. United States v. Callahan Walker Construction Co., 317 U.S. 56 (1942).
34. Soledad Enterprises, Inc. ASBCA no. 20376, September 6, 1977, 72-2 BCA 12,757.

Chapter Twelve

Terminations

BACKGROUND

One of the major differences in contracting with the government, as compared to contracting in the commercial environment, is the government's right to unilaterally terminate a contract. While the government normally reserves the right to terminate a contract by speciic contract provision, its authority for this action is based on the application of its role as a sovereign. The original court cases cited "the public interest" of the sovereign as the basis for the right of termination.

In *United States* v. *Corliss Steam-Engine Company,* the United States Supreme Court ruled in 1876 that the government had the right to terminate a contract even though there was no contract provision to that effect. In this case, the Navy directed a contractor to discontinue work on a contract for engines and boilers. The contractor and the contracting officer reached agreement on payment as settlement for the termination. However, the Comptroller of the Treasury refused to approve the certification for Congressional appropriation of funds. The contractor filed a suit in the Court of Claims which ruled in favor of the contractor. The government appealed to the Supreme Court of the United States. In ruling for the contractor, the Supreme Court stated that, "the contracting officer, when representing the public's interest must have the right to suspend or terminate otherwise contractually agreed to work. . . ." The Court further stated that

> with the improvements constantly made . . . some parts originally contracted have to be abandoned; and other parts substituted, and it would be of serious detriment to the public service if the power of the head of the Navy Department did not extend to providing for all such possible contingences by modification or suspension of the contracts and settlement with the contractor. . . .

Even though the courts held that the government's right to terminate existed without a contract clause providing for such action, the procurement regulations generally require insertion of specific clauses reserving the government's rights. Therefore, either by specific incorporation or by the "operation of law," termination clauses exist in almost all government contracts. The principle of a contract provision incorporated by operation of law was the holding by the Court of Claims in *G. L. Christian and Associates* v. *United States.*[2] The court found that (1) the Armed Services Procurement Regulations (ASPR) governed the contract, (2) this regulation was promulgated pursuant to law (The Armed Services Procurement Act of 1947, 10 U.S.C. 2301, et. seq.), (3) the ASPR therefore had the force and effect of law, (4) the ASPR required the clause, and (5) no authorized deviation was granted. The result of this ruling is that if the procurement regulations require the inclusion of a clause, the clause exists in that contract whether physically incorporated in the contract or not.

To implement termination procedures through the incorporation of contract clauses, the government makes use of various termination clauses. These clauses cover:

> Fixed-price supply contracts.
> Cost reimbursement type contracts.
> Construction contracts.
> Fixed-price research and development contracts.
> Fixed-price service contracts.
> Fixed-price architect-engineer contracts.
> Contracts with educational and other nonprofit institutions.
> Consolidated facilities or facilities acquisition contracts.
> Personal services contracts.

Additionally, there are recommended modifications to the clauses for inclusion in subcontracts. Generally, there is a single clause for cost type contracts which covers both termination for convenience and termination for default, and separate clauses for convenience and default terminations on fixed-price contracts. See Figures 12.1 through 12.3 for examples of these clauses. Additionally, there are recommended modifications to the clauses for inclusion in subcontracts. We will be discussing the procedures under the various contract clauses later.

TYPES OF TERMINATIONS

There are basically two types of terminations. The first is a termination for convenience and is related to the government's right to terminate a contract, either in whole or in part, for any reason deemed to be in the public's best interest. The second type of termination is a termination for default. Default terminations occur when a contractor either fails or refuses to deliver the required supplies or perform the required services or otherwise perform the contract, or where there is a failure of the contractor to make progress so as to endanger performance of the contract.

While the government's right to terminate a contract for its convenience has in the past been broadly interpreted, a Court of Claims decision added some protection to contractors. In overruling *Colonial Metals Company v. U.S.,*[3] the Court of Claims in *Torncello & Soledad Enterprises, Inc. v. United States*[4] stated that the termination for convenience clause is only applicable to situations where the circumstances of the bargain or the expectations of the parties have

(a) The Government may terminate performance of work under this contract in whole or, from time to time, in part, if—

(1) The Contracting Officer determines that a termination is in the Government's interest; or

(2) The Contractor defaults in performing this contract and fails to cure the default within 10 days (unless extended by the Contracting Officer) after receiving a notice specifying the default. "Default" includes failure to make progress in the work so as to endanger performance.

(b) The Contracting Officer shall terminate by delivering to the Contractor a Notice of Termination specifying whether termination is for default of the Contractor or for convenience of the Government, the extent of termination, and the effective date. If, after termination for default, it is determined that the Contractor was not in default or that the Contractor's failure to perform or to make progress in performance is due to causes beyond the control and without the fault or negligence of the Contractor as set forth in the Excusable Delays clause, the rights and obligations of the parties will be the same as if the termination was for the convenience of the Government.

(c) After receipt of a Notice of Termination, and except as directed by the Contracting Officer, the Contractor shall immediately proceed with the following obligations, regardless of any delay in determining or adjusting any amounts due under this clause:

(1) Stop work as specified in the notice.

(2) Place no further subcontracts or orders (referred to as subcontracts in this clause), except as necessary to complete the continued portion of the contract.

(3) Terminate all subcontracts to the extent they relate to the work terminated.

(4) Assign to the Government, as directed by the Contracting Officer, all right, title, and interest of the Contractor under the subcontracts terminated, in which case the Government shall have the right to settle or to pay any termination settlement proposal arising out of those terminations.

(5) With approval or ratification to the extent required by the Contracting Officer, settle all outstanding liabilities and termination settlement proposals arising from the termination of subcontracts, the cost of which would be reimbursable in whole or in part, under this contract; approval or ratification will be final for purposes of this clause.

(6) Transfer title (if not already transferred) and, as directed by the Contracting Officer, deliver to the Government (i) the fabricated or unfabricated parts, work in process, completed work, supplies, and other material produced or acquired for the work terminated, (ii) the completed or partially completed plans, drawings, information, and other property that, if the contract had been completed, would be required to be furnished to the Government, and (iii) the jigs, dies, fixtures, and other special tools and tooling acquired or manufactured for this contract, the cost of which the Contractor has been or will be reimbursed under this contract.

(7) Complete performance of the work not terminated.

(8) Take any action that may be necessary, or that the Contracting Officer may direct, for the protection and preservation of the property related to this contract that is in the possession of the Contractor and in which the Government has or may acquire an interest.

(9) Use its best efforts to sell, as directed or authorized by the Contracting Officer, any property of the types referred to in subparagraph (6) above; *provided, however,* that the Contractor (i) is not required to extend credit to any purchaser and (ii) may acquire the property under the conditions prescribed by, and at prices approved by, the Contracting Officer. The proceeds of any transfer or disposition will be applied to reduce any payments to be made by the Government under this contract, credited to the price or cost of the work, or paid in any other manner directed by the Contracting Officer.

(d) After expiration of the plant clearance period as defined in Subpart 45.6 of the Federal Acquisition Regulation, the Contractor may submit to the Contracting Officer a list, certified as to quantity and quality, of termination inventory not previously disposed of, excluding items authorized for disposition by the Contracting Officer. The Contractor may request the Government to remove those items or enter into an agreement for their storage. Within 15 days, the Government will accept the items and remove them or enter into a storage agreement. The Contracting Officer may verify the list upon removal of the items, or if stored, within 45 days from submission of the list, and shall correct the list, as necessary, before final settlement.

(e) After termination, the Contractor shall submit a final termination settlement proposal to the Contracting Officer in the form and with the certification prescribed by the Contracting Officer. The Contractor shall submit the proposal promptly, but no later than 1 year from the effective date of termination, unless extended in writing by the Contracting Officer upon written request of the Contractor within this 1-year period. However, if the Contracting Officer determines that the facts justify it, a termination settlement proposal may be received and acted on after 1 year or any extension. If the Contractor fails to submit the proposal within the time allowed, the Contracting

Figure 12.1. Termination (cost-reimbursement) clause, FAR 52.249-6.

Officer may determine, on the basis of information available, the amount, if any, due the Contractor because of the termination and shall pay the amount determined.

(f) Subject to paragraph (e) above, the Contractor and the Contracting Officer may agree on the whole or any part of the amount to be paid (including an allowance for fee) because of the termination. The contract shall be amended, and the Contractor paid the agreed amount.

(g) If the Contractor and the Contracting Officer fail to agree to whole or in part on the amount of costs and/or fee to be paid because of the termination of work, the Contracting Office shall determine, on the basis of information available, the amount ,if any, due the Contractor, and shall pay that amount, which shall include the following:

(1) All costs reimbursable under this contract, not previously paid, for the performance of this contract before the effective date of the termination, and those costs that may continue for a reasonable time with the approval of or as directed by the Contracting Officer; however, the Contractor shall discontinue these costs as rapidly as practicable.

(2) The cost of settling and paying termination settlement proposals under terminated subcontracts that are properly chargeable to the terminated portion of the contract if not included in subparagraph (1) above.

(3) The reasonable costs of settlement of the work terminated, including—

(i) Accounting, legal, clerical, and other expenses reasonably necessary for the preparation of termination settlement proposals and supporting data;

(ii) The termination and settlement of subcontracts (excluding the amounts of such settlements); and

(iii) Storage, transportation, and other costs incurred, reasonably necessary for the preservation, protection, or disposition of the termination inventory, If the termination is for default, no amounts for the preparation of the Contractor's termination settlement proposal may be included.

(4) A portion of the fee payable under the contract, determined as follows:

(i) If the contract is terminated for the convenience of the Government, the settlement shall include a percentage of the fee equal to the percentage of completion of work contemplated under the contract, but excluding subcontract effort included in subcontractors' termination proposals, less previous payments for fee.

(ii) If the contract is terminated for default, the total fee payable shall be such proportionate part of the fee as the total number of articles (or amount of services) delivered to and accepted by the Government is to the total number of articles (or amount of services) of a like kind required by the contract.

(5) If the settlement includes only fee, it will be determined under subparagraph (g)(4) above.

(h) The cost principles and procedures in Part 31 of the Federal Acquisition Regulation, in effect on the date of this contract, shall govern all costs claimed, agreed to, or determined under this clause.

(i) The Contractor shall have the right of appeal, under the Disputes clause, from any determination made by the Contracting Officer under paragraph (e) or (g) above or paragraph (k) below, except that if the Contractor failed to submit the termination settlement proposal within the time provided in paragraph (e) and failed to request a time extension, there is no right of appeal. If the Contracting Officer has made a determination of the amount due under paragraph (e), (g) or (k), the Government shall pay the Contractor (1) the amount determined by the Contracting Officer if there is no right of appeal or if no timely appeal has been taken, or (2) the amount finally determined on an appeal.

(j) In arriving at the amount due the Contractor under this clause, there shall be deducted—

(1) All unliquidated advance or other payments to the Contractor, under the terminated portion of this contract;

(2) Any claim which the Government has against the Contractor under this contract; and

(3) The agreed price for, or the proceeds of sale of materials, supplies, or other things acquired by the Contractor or sold under this clause and not recovered by or credited to the Government.

(k) The Contractor and Contracting Officer must agree to any equitable adjustment in fee for the continued portion of the contract when there is a partial termination. The Contracting Officer shall amend the contract to reflect the agreement.

(l) (1) The Government may, under the terms and conditions it prescribes, make partial payments and payments against costs incurred by the Contractor for the terminated portion of the contract, if the Contracting Officer believes the total of these payments will not exceed the amount to which the Contractor will be entitled.

(2) If the total payments exceed the amount finally determined to be due, the Contractor shall

Figure 12.1. (Continued)

repay the excess to the Government upon demand, together with interest computed at the rate established by the Secretary of the Trasury under 50 U.S.C. App. 1215(b)(2). Interest shall be computed for the period from the date the excess payent is received by the Contractor to the date the exccss is repaid. Interest shall not be charged on any excess payment due to a reduciton in the Contractor's termination settlement proposed because of retention or other disposition of termination inventory until 10 days after the date of the retention or disposition, or a later date determined by the Contracting Officer because of the circumstances.

(iii) The provisions of this clause relating to fee are inapplicable if this contract does not include a fee.

Figure 12.1. (Continued)

(a) The Government may terminate performance of work under this contract in whole or, from time to time, in part if the Contracting Officer determines that a termination is in the Government's interest. The Contracting Officer shall terminate by delivering to the Contractor a Notice of Termination specifying the extent of termination and the effective date.

(b) After receipt of a Notice of Termination, and except as directed by the Contracting Officer, the Contractor shall immediately proceed with the following obligations, regardless of any delay in determining or adjusting any amounts due under this clause:

(1) Stop work as specified in the notice.

(2) Place no further subcontracts or orders (referred to as subcontracts in this clause) for materials, services, or facilities, except as necessary to complete the continued portion of the contract.

(3) Terminate all subcontracts to the extent they relate to the work terminated.

(4) Assign to the Government, as directed by the Contracting Officer, all right, title, and interest of the Contractor under the subcontracts terminated, in which case the Government shall have the right to settle or to pay any termination settlement proposal arising out of those terminations.

(5) With approval or ratification to the extent required by the Contracting Officer, settle all outstanding liabilities and termination settlement proposals arising from the termination of subcontracts; the approval or ratification will be final for purposes of this clause.

(6) As directed by the Contracting Officer, transfer title and deliver to the Government (i) the fabricated or unfabricated parts, work in process, completed work, supplies, and other material produced or acquired for the work terminated, and (ii) the completed or partially completed plans, drawings, information, and other property that, if the contract had been completed, would be required to be furnished to the Government.

(7) Complete performance of the work not terminated.

(8) Take any action that may be necessary, or that the Contracting Officer may direct, for the protection and preservation of the property related to this contract that is in the possession of the Contractor and in which the Government has or may acquire an interest.

(9) Use its best efforts to sell, as directed or authorized by the Contracting Officer, any property of the types referred to in subparagraph (6) above; *provided,* however, that the Contractor (i) is not required to extend credit to any purchaser and (ii) may acquire the property under the conditions prescribed by, and at prices approved by, the Contracting Officer. The proceeds of any transfer of disposition will be applied to reduce any payments to be made by the Government under this contract, credited to the price or cost of the work, or paid in any other manner directed by the Contracting Officer.

(c) After expiration of the plant clearance period as defined in Subpart 45.6 of the Federal Acquisition Regulation, the Contractor May submit to the Contracting Officer a list, certified as to quantity and quality, of termination inventory not previously disposed of, excluding items authorized for disposition by the Contracting Officer. The Contractor may request the Government to remove those items or enter into an agreement for their storage. Within 15 days, the Government will accept title to those items and remove them or enter into a storage agreement. The Contracting Officer may verify the list upon removal of the items, or if stored, within 45 days from submission of the list, and shall correct the list, as necessary, before final settlement.

(d) After termination, the Contractor shall submit a final termination settlement proposal to the Contracting Officer in the form and with the certification prescribed by the Contracting Officer. The Contractor shall submit the proposal promptly, but no later than 1 year from the effective date of termination, unless extended in writing by the Contracting Officer upon written request of the Contractor within this 1-year period. However, if the Contracting Officer determines that the facts justify it, a termination settlement proposal may be received and acted on after 1 year or any

Figure 12.2. Termination for convenience of the government (fixed-price), FAR 52.249-2.

extension. If the Contractor fails to submit the proposal within the time allowed, the Contracting Officer may determine, on the basis of information available, the amount, if any, due the Contractor because of the termination and shall pay the amount determined.

(e) Subject to paragraph (d) above, the Contractor and the Contracting Officer may agree upon the whole or any part of the amount to be paid because of the termination. The amount may include a reasonable allowance for profit on work done. However, the agreed amount, whether under this paragraph (e) or paragraph (f) below, exclusive of costs shown in subparagraph (f)(3) below, may not exceed the total contract price as reduced by (a) the amount of payments previously made and (2) the contract price of work not terminated. The contract shall be amended, and the Contractor paid the agreed amount. Paragraph (f) below shall not limit, restrict, or affect the amount that may be agreed upon to be paid under this paragraph.

(f) If the Contractor and the Contracting Officer fail to agree on the whole amount to be paid because of the termination of work, the Contracting Officer shall pay the Contractor the amounts determined by the Contracting Officer as follows, but without duplication of any amounts agreed on under paragraph (e) above:

(1) The contract price for completed supplies or services accepted by the Government (or sold or acquired under subparagraph (b)(9) above) not previously paid for, adjusted for any saving of freight and other charges.

(2) The total of—

(i) The costs incurred in the performance of the work terminated, including initial costs and preparatory expense allocable thereto, but excluding any costs attributable to supplies or services paid or to be paid under subparagraph (f)(1) above;

(ii) The cost of settling and paying termination settlement proposals under terminated subcontracts that are properly chargeable to the terminated portion of the contract if not included in subdivision (i) above; and

(iii) A sum, as profit on subdivision (i) above, determined by the Contracting Officer under 49.202 of the Federal Acquisition Regulation, in effect on the date of this contract, to be fair and reasonable; however, if it appears that the Contractor would have sustained a loss on the entire contract had it been completed, the Contracting Officer shall allow no profit under this subdivision (iii) and shall reduce the settlement to reflect the indicated rate of loss.

(3) The reasonable costs of settlement of the work terminated, including—

(i) Accounting, legal, clerical, and other expenses reasonably necessary for the preparation of termination settlement proposals and supporting data;

(ii) The termination and settlement of subcontracts (excluding the amounts of such settlements); and

(iii) Storage, transportation, and other costs incurred, reasonably necessary for the preservation, protection, or disposition of the termination inventory.

(g) Except for normal spoilage, and except to the extent that the Government expressly assumed the risk of loss, the Contracting Officer shall exclude from the amounts payable to the Contractor under paragraph (f) above, the fair value, as determined by the Contracting Officer, of property that is destroyed, lost, stolen, or damaged so as to become undeliverable to the Government or to a buyer.

(h) The cost principles and procedures of Part 31 of the Federal Acquisition Regulation, in effect on the date of this contract, shall govern all costs claimed, agreed to, or determined under this clause.

(i) The Contractor shall have the right of appeal, under the Disputes clause, from any determination made by the Contracting Officer under paragraph (d), (f), or (k), except that if the Contractor failed to submit the termination settlement proposal within the time provided in paragraph (d) or (k), and failed to request a time extension, there is no right of appeal. If the Contracting Officer has made a determination of the amount due under paragraph (d), (f), or (k), the Government shall pay the Contractor (1) the amount determined by the Contracting Officer if there is no right of appeal or if no timely appeal has been taken, or (2) the amount finally determined on an appeal.

(j) In arriving at the amount due the Contractor under this clause, there shall be deducted—

(1) All unliquidated advance or other payments to the Contractor under the terminated portion of this contract;

(2) Any claim which the Government has against the Contractor under this contract; and

(3) The agreed price for, or the proceeds of sale of, materials, supplies, or other things acquired by the Contractor or sold under the provisions of this clause and not recovered by or credited to the Government.

(k) If the termination is partial, the Contractor may file a proposal with the Contracting Officer for an equitable adjustment of the price(s) of the continued portion of the contract. The Contract-

Figure 12.2. (Continued)

ing Officer shall make any equitable adjustment agreed upon. Any proposal by the Contractor for an equitable adjustment under this clause shall be requested within 90 days from the effective date of termination unless extended in writing by the Contracting Officer.

(l) (1) The Government may, under the terms and conditions it prescribes, make partial payments and payments against costs incurred by the Contractor for the terminated portion of the contract, if the Contracting Officer believes the total of these payments will not exceed the amount to which the Contractor will be entitled.

(2) If the total payments exceed the amount finally determined to be due, the Contractor shall repay the excess to the Government upon demand, together with interest computed at the rate established by the Secretary of the Treasury under 50 U.S.C. App. 1215(b)(2). Interest shall be computed for the period from the date the excess payment is received by the Contractor to the date the excess is repaid. Interest shall not be charged on any excess payment due to a reduction in the Contractor's termination settlement proposal because of retention or other disposition of termination inventory until 10 days after the date of the retention or disposition, or a later date determined by the Contracting Officer because of the circumstances.

(m) Unless otherwise provided in this contact or by statute, the Contractor shall maintain all records and documents relating to the terminated portion of this contract for 3 years after final settlement. This includes all books and other evidence bearing on the Contractor's costs and expenses under this contract. The Contractor shall make these records and documents available to the Government, at the Contractor's office, at all reasonable times, without any direct charge. If approved by the Contracting Officer, photographs, microphotographs, or other authentic reproductions may be maintained instead of original records and documents.

Figure 12.2.   (Continued)

(a) (1) The Government may, subject to paragraphs (c) and (d) below, by written notice of default to the Contractor, terminate this contract in whole or in part if the Contractor fails to—

(i) Deliver the supplies or to perform the services within the time specified in this contract or any extension;

(ii) Make progress, so as to endanger performance of this contract (but see subparagraph (a)(2) below); or

(iii) Perform any of the other provisions of this contract (but see subparagraph (a)(2) below).

(2) The Government's right to terminate this contract under subdivisions (l)(ii) and (l)(iii) above, may be exercised if the Contractor does not cure such failure within 10 days (or more if authorized in writing by the Contracting officer) after receipt of the notice from the Contracting Officer specifying the failure.

(b) If the Government terminates this contract in whole or in part, it may acquire, under the terms and in the manner the Contracting officer considers appropriate, supplies or services similar to those terminated, and the Contractor will be liable to the Government for any excess costs for those supplies or services. However, the Contractor shall continue the work not terminated.

(c) Except for defaults of subcontractors at any tier, the Contractor shall not be liable for any excess costs if the failure to perform the contract arises from causes beyond the control and without the fault or negligence of the Contractor. Examples of such causes include (1) acts of God or of the public enemy, (2) acts of the Government in either its sovereign or contractual capacity, (3) fires, (4) floods, (5) epidemics, (6) quarantine restrictions (7) strikes, (8) freight embargoes, and (9) unusually severe weather. In each instance the failure to perform must be beyond the control and without the fault or negligence of the Contractor.

(d) If the failure to perform is caused by the default of a subcontractor at any tier, and if the cause of the default is beyond the control of both the Contractor and subcontractor, and without the fault or negligence of either, the Contractor shall not be liable for any excess costs for failure to perform, unless the subcontracted supplies to services were obtainable from other sources in sufficient time for the Contractor to meet the required delivery schedule.

(e) If this contract is terminated for default, the Government may require the Contractor to transfer title and deliver to the Government, as directed by the Contracting Officer, any (1) completed supplies, and (2) partially completed supplies and materials, parts, tools, dies, jigs, fixtures, plans, drawings, information, and contract rights (collectively referred to as "manufacturing materials" in this clause) that the Contractor has specifically produced or acquired for the terminated portion of this contract. Upon direction of the Contracting Officer, the Contractor shall also protect and preserve property in its possession in which the Government has an interest.

Figure 12.3.   Default (fixed-price supply and service), FAR 52.249-8.

(f) The Government shall pay contract price for completed supplies delivered and accepted. The Contractor and Contracting Officer shall agree on the amount of payment for manufacturing materials delivered and accepted and for the protection and preservation of the property. Failure to agree will be a dispute under the Disputes clause. The Government may withhold from these amounts any sum the Contracting Officer determines to be necessary to protect the Government against loss because of outstanding liens or claims of former lien holders.

(g) If, after termination, it is determined that the Contractor was not in default, or that the default was excusable, the rights and obligations of the parties shall be the same as if the termination had been issued for the convenience of the Government.

(h) The rights and remedies of the Government in this clause are in addition to any other rights and remedies provided by law or under this contract.

Figure 12.3.   (Continued).

changed. However, the Court of Claims and the various boards of contract appeals have been reluctant to apply the holding in *Torncello* beyond the scope of the fact situation of that case. In *Automated Services, Inc.*[5], the Department of Transportation Board of Contract Appeals concluded that validity of invoking the termination for convenience clause continues to be measured by the presence or absence of bad faith on the part of the government.

Termination for Convenience

A contract is completely terminated when a notice of termination directs complete cessation of all work remaining to be performed, while partial termination requires that a portion of the contract effort continue. That part of the work not completed at the effective date of the termination and for which the contractor must continue to perform is referred to as the" continued portion" of the contract. That portion of the contract relating to work or articles completed and accepted prior to the effective date of the contract termination is the "completed portion" of the contract.

Once the government decides to terminate a contract, notification must be given to the contractor. FAR 49.601 sets forth the approved forms of termination notices. Generally, the procedures used involve the sending of a telegraphic notification followed by a letter. It is possible, however, to give the notice by letter alone. Whatever the means used to convey the notice, it:

Must specify the extent of the termination—It should specify whether it is a partial or complete termination and, if a partial termination, what part of the contract is terminated.

Must specify the effective date of the termination—The contract may be terminated immediately upon receipt of notification, on a given future date, or upon the date of completion of a particular item or the happening of a particular event.

Must specify when the work must be stopped and when the prime contractor must notify any subcontractors to stop work.

Should establish that the termination inventory of the prime and all subcontractors is to be taken into account when the claim is submitted.

Should establish policy with regard to the acceptance and invoicing of the completed items.

Should enclose settlement forms and include a request for prompt presentation of settlement proposals.

Should include a requirement for the disclosure of patents, inventions, and discoveries, when applicable.

Should include a statement indicating the contractor's liability for settlement with subcontractors.

Should indicate the government office that is charged with the settlement of the contractor's claim, and it should request acknowledgement of the receipt of the notice of termination.

Should include recommended action to minimize the impact on the contractor's employees.

Must specify instructions, if any.

Upon receipt of the termination, and in accordance with its provisions, the contractor generally must:

Stop work immediately, or at the time specified, on the terminated portion of the contract and discontinue placing any subcontracts.

Terminate any subcontracts related to the terminated portion of the contract.

Immediately advise the contracting office of any reasons why the work cannot be immediately stopped.

If it is a partial termination, continue performance on the nonterminated portion of the contract and submit a request for equitable adjustment for any increased costs associated with the continuing portion.

Take any action necessary or directed by the contracting officer to protect government property in the possession of the contractor; this will include delivery of such property to the government as directed.

Promptly notify the contracting office in writing of any legal proceedings against the contractor growing out of any subcontract or other commitment related to the terminated portion of the contract.

Settle all outstanding liabilities and all claims arising out of the termination of subcontracts.

Promptly submit the contractor's own inventory and its settlement proposal to the contracting office.

Dispose of any termination inventory as directed or authorized by the contracting officer.

Basis for Settlement

A contractor whose cost type contract has been terminated has three alternatives: (1) voucher-out all reimbursable costs, using the Standard Form 1034 (Public Voucher) for all costs including any costs applicable to the terminated portion of the contract; (2) settle by negotiation the amount to be paid for unreimbursed costs and fixed fee; or (3) voucher-out costs for a while, then discontinue vouchering-out the costs and settle by negotiation the amount to be paid for the balance of unreimbursed cost and fixed fee.

The vouchering-out procedure is limited to that time period ending on the last day of the sixth month following the termination. The contractor should attempt to submit a voucher covering all costs prior to the expiration of the six-month limitation. At the end of the six-month period, or any earlier time at the contractor's election, the contractor may submit a settlement proposal. The form used to submit a settlement proposal under a cost type contract is Standard Form 1437 shown as Figure 12.4. Once the contractor elects to submit a settlement proposal, it is not permissible to submit any more vouchers.

Under fixed-price contracts, the contractor must negotiate a settlement with the government. There are three methods by which the settlement proposal may be prepared: (1) inventory basis, (2) total cost basis, or (3) percentage of completion basis.

The inventory basis for settlements is generally preferred by the government. Under this method, the contractor lists only its costs relating or allocable to the terminated portion of the contract. The costs are broken down between raw materials, purchased parts, finished components, and work-in-process at the purchase price or manufactured costs. To this amount are added other costs such as startup costs, preproduction costs, and allocable indirect expenses. To the total of the above items are added profit on the work completed, the cost of settlements with any subcontractors, specific settlement expenses associated with the termination, and the price of finished items that were completed but had not as yet been delivered at the time of the termination. Deducted from the foregoing are any disposal credits and any advance progress payments associated with the terminated portion of the contract. The form used for submitting a settlement proposal using the inventory basis is Standard Form 1435 and is shown as Figure 12.5.

Under the total cost method, all costs incurred for the entire contract are added to a reasonable profit on all the costs. From this amount is deducted the contract price for items completed and delivered to the government, along with unliquidated advance and progress payments, and disposal and other known credits. Where a complete termination occurs, all costs incurred prior to the date of the termination are calculated and an adjustment is made for profit or loss. These costs are added to the costs of any settlements with subcontractors and other settlement expenses. Where a partial termination occurs, all costs incurred under the contract will be summarized including those costs incurred after termination on the nonterminated portion of the contract. An adjustment is made for profit or loss. Payments made by the government for completed units will then be deducted and settlements with subcontractors and other applicable termination costs will be added. The form used to submit a settlement proposal on a total cost basis is Standard Form 1436 and is shown as Figure 12.6.

The forms used to support termination inventory items for settlement proposals under either the inventory or total cost basis are included as Figures 12.7 through 12.10. Also, for fixed price-settlement proposals of less than $10,000, there is a short form (Standard Form 1438) included as Figure 12.11., and an inventory schedule (Standard Form 1434) shown as Figure 12.12.

The total cost basis normally requires approval for its use. The use of the total cost method will generally be authorized only under a complete termination where (1) production has not commenced and accumulated costs represent planning and preproduction costs, (2) the accounting system will not lend itself to the establishment of unit cost for work-in-process, (3) the contract does not specify unit prices or (4) the termination is complete and involves a yet to be definitized letter contract.

The percentage of completion method is rarely used. Under this method, the percentage of contract completion is estimated and this percentage is applied to the total contract price. From this is deducted payments the contractor has already received either in progress or advance payments or for contract payments for items completed and delivered.

SETTLEMENT PROPOSAL FOR COST-REIMBURSEMENT TYPE CONTRACTS

FORM APPROVED OMB NO. 3090-0115

To be used by prime contractors submitting settlement proposals on cost-reimbursement type contracts under Part 49 of the Federal Acquisition Regulation. Also suitable for use in connection with terminated cost-reimbursement type subcontracts.

COMPANY	PROPOSAL NUMBER	CHECK ONE
		☐ PARTIAL ☐ FINAL
STREET ADDRESS	GOVERNMENT PRIME CONTRACT NO.	REFERENCE NO.
CITY AND STATE (Include ZIP Code)	EFFECTIVE DATE OF TERMINATION	

ITEM (a)	TOTAL PREVIOUSLY SUBMITTED (b)	INCREASE OR DECREASE BY THIS PROPOSAL (c)	TOTAL SUBMITTED TO DATE (d)
1. DIRECT MATERIAL	$	$	$
2. DIRECT LABOR			
3. INDIRECT FACTORY EXPENSE			
4. SPECIAL TOOLING AND SPECIAL TEST EQUIPMENT			
5. OTHER COSTS			
6. GENERAL AND ADMINISTRATIVE EXPENSE			
7. TOTAL COSTS (Items 1 thru 6)	$	$	$
8. FEE			
9. SETTLEMENT EXPENSES			
10. SETTLEMENTS WITH SUBCONTRACTORS			
11. GROSS PROPOSED SETTLEMENT (Items 7 thru 10)			
12. DISPOSAL AND OTHER CREDITS			
13. NET PROPOSED SETTLEMENT (Items 11 less 12)	$	$	$
14. PRIOR PAYMENTS TO CONTRACTOR	$	$	$
15. NET PAYMENT REQUESTED (Items 13 less 14)	$	$	$

CERTIFICATE

This is to certify that the undersigned, individually, and as an authorized representative of the Contractor, has examined this termination settlement proposal and that, to the best knowledge and belief of the undersigned:

(a) AS TO THE CONTRACTOR'S OWN CHARGES. The proposed settlement (exclusive of charges set forth in Item 10) and supporting schedules and explanations have been prepared from the books of account and records of the Contractor in accordance with recognized commercial accounting practices; they include only those charges allocable to the terminated portion of this contract; they have been prepared with knowledge that they will, or may, be used directly or indirectly as the basis of settlement of a termination settlement proposal or claim against an agency of the United States; and the charges as stated are fair and reasonable.

(b) AS TO THE SUBCONTRACTORS' CHARGES. (1) The Contractor has examined, or caused to be examined, to an extent it considered adequate in the circumstances, the termination settlement proposals of its immediate subcontractors (exclusive of proposals filed against these immediate subcontractors by their subcontractors); (2) The settlements on account of immediate subcontractors' own charges are fair and reasonable, the charges are allocable to the terminated portion of this contract, and the settlements were negotiated in good faith and are not more favorable to its immediate subcontractors than those that the Contractor would make if reimbursement by the Government were not involved; (3) The Contractor has received from all its immediate subcontractors appropriate certificates with respect to their termination settlement proposals, which certificates are substantially in the form of this certificate; and (4) The Contractor has no information leading it to doubt (i) the reasonableness of the settlements with more remote subcontractors or (ii) that the charges for them are allocable to this contract. Upon receipt by the Contractor of amounts covering settlements with its immediate subcontractors, the Contractor will pay or credit them promptly with the amounts so received, to the extent that it has not previously done so. The term "subcontractors," as used above, includes suppliers.

NOTE: The Contractor shall, under conditions stated in FAR 15.804-2, be required to submit a Certificate of Current Cost or Pricing Data (see FAR 15.804-2(a) and 15.804-6).

NAME OF CONTRACTOR	BY (Signature of authorized official)	
	TITLE	DATE
NAME OF SUPERVISORY ACCOUNTING OFFICIAL	TITLE	

1437-101

STANDARD FORM 1437 (10-83)
Prescribed by GSA
FAR (48 CFR) 53.249(a)(4)

Figure 12.4. Settlement proposal for cost-reimbursement type contracts, Standard Form 1437.

SETTLEMENT PROPOSAL
(INVENTORY BASIS)

FOR USE BY A FIXED-PRICE PRIME CONTRACTOR OR FIXED-PRICE SUBCONTRACTOR

THIS PROPOSAL APPLIES TO *(Check one)*
☐ A PRIME CONTRACT WITH THE GOVERNMENT
☐ SUBCONTRACT OR PURCHASE ORDER

COMPANY

SUBCONTRACT OR PURCHASE ORDER NO(S).

STREET ADDRESS

CONTRACTOR WHO SENT NOTICE OF TERMINATION

CITY AND STATE

NAME

NAME OF GOVERNMENT AGENCY

ADDRESS

GOVERNMENT PRIME CONTRACT NO. | CONTRACTOR'S REFERENCE NO.

If moneys payable under the contract have been assigned, give the following:

NAME OF ASSIGNEE

EFFECTIVE DATE OF TERMINATION

ADDRESS

PROPOSAL NO. | CHECK ONE
☐ INTERIM ☐ FINAL

SF 1439, SCHEDULE OF ACCOUNTING INFORMATION ☐ IS ☐ IS NOT ATTACHED *(If not, explain)*

SECTION I — STATUS OF CONTRACT OR ORDER AT EFFECTIVE DATE OF TERMINATION

PRODUCTS COVERED BY TERMINATED CONTRACT OR PURCHASE ORDER (a)		PREVIOUSLY SHIPPED AND INVOICED (b)	FINISHED ON HAND		UNFINISHED OR NOT COMMENCED		TOTAL COVERED BY CONTRACT OR ORDER (g)
			PAYMENT TO BE RECEIVED THROUGH INVOICING (c)	INCLUDED IN THIS PROPOSAL (d)	TO BE COMPLETED *(Partial termination only)* (e)	NOT TO BE COMPLETED (f)	
	QUANTITY						
	$						
	QUANTITY						
	$						
	QUANTITY						
	$						

SECTION II — PROPOSED SETTLEMENT

NO.	ITEM (a)	TOTAL PREVIOUSLY PROPOSED (b)	INCREASE OR DECREASE BY THIS PROPOSAL (c)	TOTAL PROPOSED TO DATE (d)	FOR USE OF CONTRACTING AGENCY ONLY (e)
		(Use Column (b) and (c) only where previous proposal has been filed)			
1	METALS				
2	RAW MATERIALS *(other than metals)*				
3	PURCHASED PARTS				
4	FINISHED COMPONENTS				
5	MISCELLANEOUS INVENTORY				
6	WORK-IN-PROCESS				
7	SPECIAL TOOLING AND SPECIAL TEST EQUIPMENT				
8	OTHER COSTS *(from Schedule B)*				
9	GENERAL AND ADMINISTRATIVE EXPENSES *(from Schedule C)*				
10	**TOTAL** *(Items 1 to 9 inclusive)*				
11	PROFIT *(explain in Schedule D)*				
12	SETTLEMENT EXPENSES *(from Schedule E)*				
13	**TOTAL** *(Items 10 to 13 inclusive)*				
14	SETTLEMENTS WITH SUBCONTRACTORS *(from Schedule F)*				
15	ACCEPTABLE FINISHED PRODUCT				
16	GROSS PROPOSED SETTLEMENT *(Items 13 thru 15)*				
17	DISPOSAL AND OTHER CREDITS *(from Schedule G)*				
18	NET PROPOSED SETTLEMENT *(Item 16 less 17)*				
19	ADVANCE, PROGRESS & PARTIAL PAYMENTS *(from Schedule H)*				
20	**NET PAYMENT REQUESTED** *(Item 18 less 19)*				

When the space provided for any information is insufficient, continue on a separate sheet.

Figure 12.5. Settlement proposal for (inventory basis), Standard Form 1435.

SCHEDULE A — ANALYSIS OF INVENTORY COST *(Items 4 and 6)*

Furnish the following information *(unless not reasonably available)* for inventories of finished components and work-in-process included in this proposal:

	TOTAL DIRECT LABOR	TOTAL DIRECT MATERIALS	TOTAL INDIRECT EXPENSES	TOTAL
FINISHED COMPONENTS				
WORK-IN-PROCESS				

NOTE.—Individual items of small amounts may be grouped into a single entry in Schedules B, C, D, E, and G.

SCHEDULE B — OTHER COSTS *(Item 8)*

ITEM	EXPLANATION	AMOUNT	FOR USE OF CONTRACTING AGENCY ONLY

SCHEDULE C — GENERAL AND ADMINISTRATIVE EXPENSES *(Item 9)*

DETAIL OF EXPENSES	AMOUNT	FOR USE OF CONTRACTING AGENCY ONLY

SCHEDULE D — PROFIT *(Item 11)*

EXPLANATION	AMOUNT	FOR USE OF CONTRACTING AGENCY ONLY

Where the space provided for any information is insufficient, continue on a separate sheet.

STANDARD FORM 1435 (10-83)
PAGE 2

Figure 12.5. (Continued)

SCHEDULE E — SETTLEMENT EXPENSES *(Item 12)*			
ITEM	EXPLANATION	AMOUNT	FOR USE OF CONTRACTING AGENCY ONLY

SCHEDULE F — SETTLEMENTS WITH IMMEDIATE SUBCONTRACTORS AND SUPPLIERS *(Item 14)*			
NAME AND ADDRESS OF SUBCONTRACTOR	BRIEF DESCRIPTION OF PRODUCT CANCELED	AMOUNT OF SETTLEMENT	FOR USE OF CONTRACTING AGENCY ONLY

SCHEDULE G — DISPOSAL AND OTHER CREDITS *(Item 16)*		
DESCRIPTION	AMOUNT	FOR USE OF CONTRACTING AGENCY ONLY

(If practicable, show separately amount of disposal credits applicable to acceptable finished product included on SF 1428.)

Where the space provided for any information is insufficient, continue on a separate sheet.

STANDARD FORM 1436 (10-83)
PAGE 3

Figure 12.5. (Continued)

DATE	TYPE OF PAYMENT	AMOUNT	FOR USE OF CONTRACTING AGENCY ONLY

Where the space provided for any information is insufficient, continue on a separate sheet.

CERTIFICATE

This is to certify that the undersigned, individually, and as an authorized representative of the Contractor, has examined this termination settlement proposal and that, to the best knowledge and belief of the undersigned:

(a) AS TO THE CONTRACTOR'S OWN CHARGES. The proposed settlement (exclusive of charges set forth in Item 14) and supporting schedules and explanations have been prepared from the books of account and records of the Contractor in accordance with recognized commercial accounting practices; they include only those charges allocable to the terminated portion of this contract; they have been prepared with knowledge that they will, or may, be used directly or indirectly as the basis of settlement of a termination settlement proposal or claim against an agency of the United States; and the charges as stated are fair and reasonable.

(b) AS TO THE SUBCONTRACTORS' CHARGES. (1) The Contractor has examined, or caused to be examined, to an extent it considered adequate in the circumstances, the termination settlement proposals of its immediate subcontractors (exclusive of proposals filed against these immediate subcontractors by their subcontractors); (2) The settlements on account of immediate subcontractors' own charges are fair and reasonable, the charges are allocable to the terminated portion of this contract, and the settlements were negotiated in good faith and are not more favorable to its immediate subcontractors than those that the Contractor would make if reimbursement by the Government were not involved; (3) The Contractor has received from all its immediate subcontractors appropriate certificates with respect to their termination settlement proposals, which certificates are substantially in the form of this certificate; and (4) the Contractor has no information leading it to doubt (i) the reasonableness of the settlements with more remote subcontractors or (ii) that the charges for them are allocable to this contract. Upon receipt by the Contractor of amounts covering settlements with its immediate subcontractors, the Contractor will pay or credit them promptly with the amounts so received, to the extent that it has not previously done so. The term "subcontractors," as used above, includes suppliers.

NOTE: The Contractor shall, under conditions stated in FAR 15.804-2, be required to submit a Certificate of Current Cost or Pricing Data (see FAR 15.804-2(a) and 15.804-6).

NAME OF CONTRACTOR	BY *(Signature of authorized official)*	
	TITLE	DATE
NAME OF SUPERVISORY ACCOUNTING OFFICIAL	TITLE	

STANDARD FORM 1436 (10-83)
PAGE 4

Figure 12.5. (Continued)

SETTLEMENT PROPOSAL
(TOTAL COST BASIS)

FORM APPROVED OMB NO.
3090-0115

FOR USE BY A FIXED-PRICE PRIME CONTRACTOR OR FIXED-PRICE SUBCONTRACTOR

THIS PROPOSAL APPLIES TO (Check one)
☐ A PRIME CONTRACT WITH THE GOVERNMENT   ☐ A SUBCONTRACT OR PURCHASE ORDER

COMPANY

SUBCONTRACT OR PURCHASE ORDER NO.(S)

STREET ADDRESS

CONTRACTOR WHO SENT NOTICE OF TERMINATION

CITY AND STATE

NAME

NAME OF GOVERNMENT AGENCY

ADDRESS

GOVERNMENT PRIME CONTRACT NO. | CONTRACTOR'S REFERENCE NO.

If moneys payable under the contract have been assigned, give the following:

NAME OF ASSIGNEE

EFFECTIVE DATE OF TERMINATION

ADDRESS

PROPOSAL NO.

CHECK ONE
☐ INTERIM   ☐ FINAL

SF 1439, SCHEDULE OF ACCOUNTING INFORMATION ☐ IS   ☐ IS NOT ATTACHED (If not, explain)

SECTION I – STATUS OF CONTRACT OR ORDER AT EFFECTIVE DATE OF TERMINATION

PRODUCTS COVERED BY TERMINATED CONTRACT OR PURCHASE ORDER (a)		PREVIOUSLY SHIPPED AND INVOICED (b)	FINISHED		UNFINISHED OR NOT COMMENCED		TOTAL COVERED BY CONTRACT OR ORDER (g)
			ON HAND				
			PAYMENT TO BE RECEIVED THROUGH INVOICING (c)	PAYMENT NOT TO BE RECEIVED THROUGH INVOICING (d)	SUBSE- QUENTLY COMPLETED AND INVOICED * (e)	NOT TO BE COMPLETED (f)	
	QUANTITY						
	$						
	QUANTITY						
	$						
	QUANTITY						
	$						

SECTION II – PROPOSED SETTLEMENT

NO	ITEM (a)	(Use Columns (b) and (c) only where previous proposal has been filed)		TOTAL PROPOSED TO DATE (d)	FOR USE OF CONTRACTING AGENCY ONLY (e)
		TOTAL PREVIOUSLY PROPOSED (b)	INCREASE OR DECREASE BY THIS PROPOSAL (c)		
1	DIRECT MATERIAL				
2	DIRECT LABOR				
3	INDIRECT FACTORY EXPENSE (from Schedule A)				
4	SPECIAL TOOLING AND SPECIAL TEST EQUIPMENT (SF 1432)				
5	OTHER COSTS (from Schedule B)				
6	GENERAL AND ADMINISTRATIVE EXPENSES (from Schedule C)				
7	TOTAL COSTS (Items 1 thru 4)				
8	PROFIT (Explain in Schedule D)				
9	TOTAL (Items 7 and 8)				
10	DEDUCT FINISHED PRODUCT INVOICED OR TO BE INVOICED *				
11	TOTAL (Item 9 less Item 10)				
12	SETTLEMENT EXPENSES (from Schedule E)				
13	TOTAL (Items 11 and 12)				
14	SETTLEMENTS WITH SUBCONTRACTORS (from Schedule F)				
15	GROSS PROPOSED SETTLEMENT (Items 13 thru 14)				
16	DISPOSAL AND OTHER CREDITS (from Schedule G)				
17	NET PROPOSED SETTLEMENT (Item 15 less 16)				
18	ADVANCE, PROGRESS & PARTIAL PAYMENTS (from Schedule H)				
19	NET PAYMENT REQUESTED (Item 18 less 19)				

*Column (e), Section I, should only be used in the event of a partial termination, in which the total cost reported in Section II should be accumulated to date of completion of the continued portion of the contract and the deduction for finished product (Item 10, Section II) should be the contract price of finished product in Column (b), (c) and (e), Section I.

NOTE.—File inventory schedules (SF 1426, 1428, 1430, and 1432) for allocable inventories on hand at date of termination (See 49.2 06 and SF 1425).

Where the space provided for any information is insufficient, continue on a separate sheet.

NSN 7540-01-140-5521   1436-101   STANDARD FORM 1436 (10-83)
Prescribed by GSA
FAR (48 CFR) 53.249(a)(3)

Figure 12.6. Settlement proposal (total cost basis), Standard Form 1436.

SCHEDULE A – INDIRECT FACTORY EXPENSE *(Item 3)*			
DETAIL OF EXPENSES	METHOD OF ALLOCATION	AMOUNT	FOR USE OF CONTRACTING AGENCY ONLY

NOTE.—Individual items of small amounts may be grouped into a single entry in Schedules B, C, D, E, and G.

SCHEDULE B – OTHER COSTS *(Item 5)*			
ITEM	EXPLANATION	AMOUNT	FOR USE OF CONTRACTING AGENCY ONLY

SCHEDULE C – GENERAL AND ADMINISTRATIVE EXPENSES *(Item 6)*			
DETAIL OF EXPENSES	METHOD OF ALLOCATION	AMOUNT	FOR USE OF CONTRACTING AGENCY ONLY

SCHEDULE D – PROFIT *(Item 8)*		
EXPLANATION	AMOUNT	FOR USE OF CONTRACTING AGENCY ONLY

Where the space provided for any information is insufficient, continue on a separate sheet

STANDARD FORM 1436 (10-83)
PAGE 2

Figure 12.6. (Continued)

SCHEDULE E — SETTLEMENT EXPENSES *(Item 12)*			
ITEM	EXPLANATION	AMOUNT	*FOR USE OF CONTRACTING AGENCY ONLY*

SCHEDULE F — SETTLEMENTS WITH IMMEDIATE SUBCONTRACTORS AND SUPPLIERS *(Item 14)*			
NAME AND ADDRESS OF SUBCONTRACTOR	BRIEF DESCRIPTION OF PRODUCT CANCELED	AMOUNT OF SETTLEMENT	*FOR USE OF CONTRACTING AGENCY ONLY*

SCHEDULE G — DISPOSAL AND OTHER CREDITS *(Item 17)*		
DESCRIPTION	AMOUNT	*FOR USE OF CONTRACTING AGENCY ONLY*

(If practicable, show separately amount of disposal credits applicable to acceptable finished product included in Item 15.)

Where the space provided for any information is insufficient, continue on a separate sheet.

STANDARD FORM 1435 (10-83)
PAGE 3

Figure 12.6. (Continued)

392

SCHEDULE H — ADVANCE, PROGRESS AND PARTIAL PAYMENTS *(Item 19)*			
DATE	TYPE OF PAYMENT	AMOUNT	FOR USE OF CONTRACTING AGENCY ONLY

Where the space provided for any information is insufficient, continue on a separate sheet.

CERTIFICATE

This is to certify that the undersigned, individually, and as an authorized representative of the Contractor, has examined this termination settlement proposal and that, to the best knowledge and belief of the undersigned:

(a) AS TO THE CONTRACTOR'S OWN CHARGES. The proposed settlement (exclusive of charges set forth in Item 14) and supporting schedules and explanations have been prepared from the books of account and records of the Contractor in accordance with recognized commercial accounting practices; they include only those charges allocable to the terminated portion of this contract; they have been prepared with knowledge that they will, or may, be used directly or indirectly as the basis of settlement of a termination settlement proposal or claim against an agency of the United States; and the charges as stated are fair and reasonable.

(b) AS TO THE SUBCONTRACTORS' CHARGES. (1) The Contractor has examined, or caused to be examined, to an extent it considered adequate in the circumstances, the termination settlement proposals of its immediate subcontractors (exclusive of proposals filed against these immediate subcontractors by their subcontractors); (2) The settlements on account of immediate subcontractors' own charges are fair and reasonable, the charges are allocable to the terminated portion of this contract, and the settlements were negotiated in good faith and are not more favorable to its immediate subcontractors than those that the Contractor would make if reimbursement by the Government were not involved; (3) The Contractor has received from all its immediate subcontractors appropriate certificates with respect to their termination settlement proposals, which certificates are substantially in the form of this certificate; and (4) the Contractor has no information leading it to doubt (i) the reasonableness of the settlements with more remote subcontractors or (ii) that the charges for them are allocable to this contract. Upon receipt by the Contractor of amounts covering settlements with its immediate subcontractors, the Contractor will pay or credit them promptly with the amounts so received, to the extent that it has not previously done so. The term "subcontractors," as used above, includes suppliers.

NOTE: The Contractor shall, under conditions stated in FAR 15.804-2, be required to submit a Certificate of Current Cost or Pricing Data (see FAR 15.804-2(a) and 15.804-6).

NAME OF CONTRACTOR	BY *(Signature of authorized official)*	
	TITLE	DATE
NAME OF SUPERVISORY ACCOUNTING OFFICIAL	TITLE	

STANDARD FORM 1435 (10-83)
PAGE 4

Figure 12.6. (Continued)

393

INVENTORY SCHEDULE A
(METALS IN MILL PRODUCT FORM)
(See SF 1425 for Instructions)

FORM APPROVED OMB NO. 3090-0120

TYPE OF CONTRACT	DATE	PAGE NO.	NO. OF PAGES

PROPERTY CLASSIFICATION

TYPE
- [ ] TERMINATION
- [ ] NONTERMINATION

THIS SCHEDULE APPLIES TO (Check one)
- [ ] PARTIAL [ ] FINAL
- [ ] A PRIME CONTRACT WITH THE GOVERNMENT
- [ ] SUBCONTRACT(S) OR PURCHASE ORDER(S)

GOVERNMENT PRIME CONTRACT NO. SUBCONTRACT OR P.O. NO. | REFERENCE NO.

COMPANY PREPARING AND SUBMITTING SCHEDULE

CONTRACTOR WHO SENT NOTICE OF TERMINATION

NAME

STREET ADDRESS

ADDRESS (Include ZIP Code)

CITY AND STATE (Include ZIP Code)

PRODUCT COVERED BY CONTRACT OR ORDER

LOCATION OF MATERIAL

FOR USE OF CON-TRACT-ING AGENCY ONLY	ITEM NO.	DESCRIPTION			DIMENSIONS				CONDITION (Use code)	QUAN-TITY	UNIT OF MEASURE	COST		CONTRACTOR'S OFFER	FOR USE OF CON-TRACT-ING AGENCY ONLY
		FORM, SHAPE, ROLLING TREATMENT (When applicable, type of edge. Example: HR coiled strip, CR flat sheets box rod, tubing in straight length, etc.)	HEAT TREAT-MENT, TEMPER, HARDNESS FINISH, ETC. (Example: Annealed and pickled ¼ hard, polished, etc.)	SPECIFICA-TIONS, AND ALLOY OR OTHER VARIA-TION IN THE SPECIFICATION (Example: 00-T-981-D B16-42 Alloy 7 Grade B)	THICK-NESS (Wall for tubing, class for pipe, type for copper watertube)	WIDTH (O.D. for tube diameter of rod. size for pipe, manufac-turer's die no. for ex-truded shapes)	LENGTH					UNIT	TOTAL		
							FEET	INCHES							
(a)		(b)	(b1)	(b2)	(b3)	(b4)	(b5)		(c)	(d)	(d1)	(e)	(f)	(g)	

INVENTORY SCHEDULE CERTIFICATE

The undersigned, personally and as representative of the Contractor, certifies that this inventory Schedule consisting of page numbers _____ to _____ inclusive, dated _____ has been examined, and that in the exercise of the signer's best judgment and to the best of the signer's knowl-edge, based upon information believed by the signer to be reliable, said Schedule has been prepared in accordance with applicable instructions; that the inventory described is allocable to the designated contract and is located at the places specified; if the property reported is termination inventory, that the quantities are not in excess of the reasonable quantitative requirements of the terminated portion of the contract; that this Schedule does not include any items reasonably usable, without loss to the

Contractor, on its other work; and that the costs shown on this Schedule are in accordance with the Contractor's records and books of account.

The Contractor agrees to inform the Contracting Officer of any substantial change in the status of the inventory shown in this Schedule between the date hereof and the final disposition of such in-ventory.

Subject to any authorized prior disposition, title to the inventory listed in this Schedule is hereby tendered to the Government and is warranted to be free and clear of all liens and encumbrances.

NAME OF CONTRACTOR

BY (Signature of Authorized Official) | TITLE

NAME OF SUPERVISORY ACCOUNTING OFFICIAL

TITLE | DATE

NSN 7540-01-140-5515
1426-101

STANDARD FORM 1426 (10-83)
Prescribed by GSA
FAR (48 CFR) 53.245(f)

Figure 12.7. Inventory schedule A (metals in mill product form), Standard Form 1426.

INVENTORY SCHEDULE A – CONTINUATION SHEET
(METALS IN MILL PRODUCT FORM)

TYPE ☐ TERMINATION ☐ NONTERMINATION

FORM APPROVED OMB NO.
3090-0120

DATE

GOVERNMENT PRIME CONTRACT NO. | SUBCONTRACT OR P.O. NO. | REFERENCE NO. | PROPERTY CLASSIFICATION

PAGE NO. | NO. OF PAGES

FOR USE OF CON-TRACT-ING AGENCY ONLY	ITEM NO.	DESCRIPTION			DIMENSIONS			CONDITION (Use code)	QUAN-TITY	UNIT OF MEASURE	COST		CONTRACTOR'S OFFER	FOR USE OF CON-TRACT-ING AGENCY ONLY
		FORM, SHAPE, ROLLING TREATMENT	HEAT TREATMENT, TEMPER, HARDNESS, FINISH, ETC.	SPECIFICA-TIONS, AND ALLOY OR OTHER VARIA-BLE DESIGNA-TION IN THE SPECIFICATION	THICK-NESS	WIDTH	LENGTH				UNIT	TOTAL		
							FEET	INCHES							
	(a)	(b)	(b1)	(b2)	(b3)	(b4)	(b5)		(c)	(d)	(d1)	(e)	(f)	(g)	

NSN 7540-0-140-5531,
1427 101

STANDARD FORM 1427 (10-83)
Prescribed by GSA
FAR (48 CFR) 53.245(f)

Figure 12.7. (Continued) Standard Form 1427.

INVENTORY SCHEDULE B
(See SF 1425 for Instructions)

FORM APPROVED OMB NO. **3090-0120**

TYPE
☐ PARTIAL ☐ FINAL ☐ TERMINATION ☐ NONTERMINATION

TYPE OF CONTRACT

DATE

PAGE NO. NO. OF PAGES

TYPE OF INVENTORY
☐ RAW MATERIALS (Other than metals)
☐ FINISHED PRODUCT
☐ PURCHASED PARTS
☐ PLANT EQUIPMENT
☐ FINISHED COMPONENTS
☐ MISCELLANEOUS

PROPERTY CLASSIFICATION

COMPANY PREPARING AND SUBMITTING SCHEDULE

THIS SCHEDULE APPLIES TO (Check one)
☐ A PRIME CONTRACT WITH THE GOVERNMENT
☐ SUBCONTRACT OR PURCHASE ORDER

GOVERNMENT PRIME CONTRACT NO. SUBCONTRACT OR P.O. NO. REFERENCE NO.

STREET ADDRESS

CONTRACTOR WHO SENT NOTICE OF TERMINATION

CITY AND STATE (Include ZIP Code)

NAME

ADDRESS (Include ZIP Code)

LOCATION OF MATERIAL

PRODUCT COVERED BY CONTRACT OR ORDER

FOR USE OF CONTRACTING AGENCY ONLY	ITEM NO.	DESCRIPTION			CONDITION (Use code)	QUAN-TITY	UNIT OF MEASURE	COST (For finished product, show contract price instead of cost)		CONTRACTORS OFFER	FOR USE OF CONTRACTING AGENCY ONLY
		ITEM DESCRIPTION	GOVERNMENT PART OR DRAWING NUMBER AND REVISION NUMBER	TYPE OF PACKING (Bulk, bbls., crates, etc.)				UNIT	TOTAL		
(a)		(b)	(b1)	(b2)	(c)	(d)	(d1)	(e)	(f)	(g)	

INVENTORY SCHEDULE CERTIFICATE

The undersigned, personally and as representative of the Contractor, certifies that this inventory _____ has been examined, and that in the exercise of the signer's best judgment and to the best of the signer's knowledge, based upon information believed by the signer to be reliable, said Schedule has been prepared in accordance with applicable instructions, that the inventory described is allocable to the designated contract and is located at the places specified, if the property reported is termination inventory, that the quantities are not in excess of the reasonable quantitative requirements of the terminated portion of the contract; that this Schedule does not include any items reasonably usable, without loss to the

Contractor, on its other work; and that the costs shown on this Schedule are in accordance with the Contractor's records and books of account.

The Contractor agrees to inform the Contracting Officer of any substantial change in the status of the inventory shown in this Schedule between the date hereof and the final disposition of such inventory.

Subject to any authorized prior disposition, title to the inventory listed in this Schedule is hereby tendered to the Government and is warranted to be free and clear of all liens and encumbrances.

NAME OF CONTRACTOR

BY (Signature of Authorized Official)   TITLE   DATE

NAME OF SUPERVISORY ACCOUNTING OFFICIAL   TITLE

NSN 7540-01-142-0135
1428-101

STANDARD FORM 1428 (10-83)
Prescribed by GSA
FAR (48 CFR) 53.245(g)

Figure 12.8. Inventory schedule B, Standard Form 1428.

Figure 12.8. (Continued) Standard Form 1429.

398

INVENTORY SCHEDULE C
(WORK-IN-PROCESS)
(See SF 1428 for Instructions)

FORM APPROVED OMB NO.
3090-0120

TYPE OF CONTRACT

PAGE NO. NO. OF PAGES

TYPE

☐ TERMINATION
☐ NONTERMINATION

DATE

THIS SCHEDULE APPLIES TO (Check one)

☐ PARTIAL   ☐ FINAL

☐ A PRIME CONTRACT WITH THE GOVERNMENT
☐ SUBCONTRACT(S) OR PURCHASE ORDER(S)

COMPANY PREPARING AND SUBMITTING SCHEDULE

GOVERNMENT PRIME CONTRACT NO. SUBCONTRACT OR P.O. NO. REFERENCE NO.

STREET ADDRESS

CONTRACTOR WHO SENT NOTICE OF TERMINATION

NAME

CITY AND STATE (Include ZIP Code)

ADDRESS (Include ZIP Code)

LOCATION OF MATERIAL

PRODUCT COVERED BY CONTRACT OR ORDER

FOR USE OF CON-TRACT-ING AGENCY ONLY	ITEM NO.	DESCRIPTION		CONDITION (See code)	QUAN-TITY	UNIT OF MEASURE	COST		CONTRACTORS OFFER	FOR USE OF CON-TRACT-ING AGENCY ONLY
		ITEM DESCRIPTION	ESTIMATED WEIGHT				UNIT	TOTAL		
(a)		(b)	(b1)	(c)	(d)	(d1)	(e)	(f)	(g)	

INVENTORY SCHEDULE CERTIFICATE

The undersigned, personally and as representative of the Contractor, certifies that this inventory Schedule consisting of page numbers ___ to ___ inclusive, dated ___ has been examined, and that in the exercise of the signer's best judgment and to the best of the signer's knowl-edge, based upon information believed by the signer to be reliable, said Schedule has been prepared in accordance with applicable Instructions; that the inventory described is allocable to the designated contract and is located at the places specified; if the property reported is termination inventory, that the quantities are not in excess of the reasonable quantitative requirements of the terminated portion of the contract; that this Schedule does not include any items reasonably usable, without loss to the

Contractor, on its other work; and that the costs shown on this Schedule are in accordance with the Contractor's records and books of account.

The Contractor agrees to inform the Contracting Officer of any substantial change in the status of the inventory shown in this Schedule between the date hereof and the final disposition of such in-ventory.

Subject to any authorized prior disposition, title to the inventory listed in this Schedule is hereby tendered to the Government and is warranted to be free and clear of all liens and encumbrances.

NAME OF CONTRACTOR

BY (Signature of Authorized Official)   TITLE

NAME OF SUPERVISORY ACCOUNTING OFFICIAL   TITLE   DATE

NSN 7540-01-140-5518
1430-101

STANDARD FORM 1430 (10-83)
Prescribed by GSA
FAR (48 CFR) 53.245(h)

Figure 12.9.   Inventory schedule C (work in process), Standard Form 1430.

INVENTORY SCHEDULE C — CONTINUATION SHEET
(WORK-IN-PROCESS)

FORM APPROVED OMB NO.
3090-0120

TYPE
☐ TERMINATION   ☐ NONTERMINATION

GOVERNMENT PRIME CONTRACT NO. | SUBCONTRACT OR P.O. NO. | REFERENCE NO. | DATE | PAGE NO. | NO. OF PAGES

FOR USE OF CONTRACTING AGENCY ONLY	ITEM NO.	DESCRIPTION		CONDITION (See code)	QUANTITY	UNIT OF MEASURE	COST		CONTRACTOR'S OFFER	FOR USE OF CONTRACTING AGENCY ONLY
		ITEM DESCRIPTION	ESTIMATED WEIGHT				UNIT	TOTAL		
(a)		(b)	(b1)	(c)	(d)	(d1)	(e)	(f)	(g)	

NSN 7540-01-140-9848
1431-101

STANDARD FORM 1431 (10-83)
Prescribed by GSA
FAR (48 CFR) 53.245(n)

Figure 12.9. (Continued) Standard Form 1431.

INVENTORY SCHEDULE D
(SPECIAL TOOLING AND SPECIAL TEST EQUIPMENT)
(See SF 1425 for Instructions)

THIS SCHEDULE APPLIES TO (Check one)

☐ PARTIAL ☐ FINAL

☐ A PRIME CONTRACT WITH THE GOVERNMENT
☐ SUBCONTRACT OR PURCHASE ORDER

GOVERNMENT PRIME CONTRACT NO. | SUBCONTRACT OR P.O. NO. | REFERENCE NO.

TYPE

☐ TERMINATION
☐ NONTERMINATION

TYPE OF CONTRACT | DATE | FORM APPROVED OMB NO. 3090-0120

PROPERTY CLASSIFICATION | PAGE NO. | NO. OF PAGES

COMPANY PREPARING AND SUBMITTING SCHEDULE

CONTRACTOR WHO SENT NOTICE OF TERMINATION

NAME

STREET ADDRESS

ADDRESS (Include ZIP Code)

CITY AND STATE (Include ZIP Code)

PRODUCT COVERED BY CONTRACT OR ORDER

LOCATION OF MATERIAL

FOR USE OF CONTRACTING AGENCY ONLY	ITEM NO.	ITEM DESCRIPTION	CONDITION (Use code)	QUANTITY	COST					CONTRACTOR'S OFFER	FOR USE OF CONTRACTING AGENCY ONLY
					UNIT	TOTAL	APPLICABLE TO THIS CONTRACT				
							TO ENTIRE CONTRACT	TO PORTION NOT TO BE COMPLETED			
(a)		(b)	(c)	(d)	(e)	(f)	(f1)	(f2)		(g)	

INVENTORY SCHEDULE CERTIFICATE

The undersigned, personally and as representative of the Contractor, certifies that this inventory Schedule consisting of page numbers _____ to _____ inclusive, dated _____ has been examined, and that in the exercise of the signer's best judgment and to the best of the signer's knowledge, based upon information believed by the signer to be reliable, said Schedule has been prepared in accordance with applicable instructions; that the inventory described is allocable to the designated contract and is located at the places specified; if the property reported is termination inventory, that the quantities are not in excess of the reasonable quantitative requirements of the terminated portion of the contract, that this Schedule does not include any items reasonably usable, without loss to the

Contractor, on its other work; and that the costs shown on this Schedule are in accordance with the Contractor's records and books of account.

The Contractor agrees to inform the Contracting Officer of any substantial change in the status of the inventory shown in this Schedule between the date hereof and the final disposition of such inventory.

Subject to any authorized prior disposition, title to the inventory listed in this Schedule is hereby tendered to the Government and is warranted to be free and clear of all liens and encumbrances.

NAME OF CONTRACTOR | BY (Signature of Authorized Official) | TITLE | DATE

NAME OF SUPERVISORY ACCOUNTING OFFICIAL | TITLE

NSN 7540-01-140-5519
1432-:01

STANDARD FORM 1432 (10-83)
Prescribed by GSA
FAR (48 CFR) 53.245(I)

Figure 12.10. Inventory schedule D (special tools and special test equipment), Standard Form 1432.

INVENTORY SCHEDULE D — CONTINUATION SHEET
(SPECIAL TOOLING AND SPECIAL TEST EQUIPMENT)

TYPE: ☐ TERMINATION ☐ NONTERMINATION

FORM APPROVED OMB NO. 3090-0120

GOVERNMENT PRIME CONTRACT NO. | SUBCONTRACT OR P.O. NO. | REFERENCE NO. | PROPERTY CLASSIFICATION | DATE | PAGE NO. | NO. OF PAGES

FOR USE OF CONTRACT- ING AGENCY ONLY	ITEM NO. (a)	ITEM DESCRIPTION (b)	CONDITION (Use code) (c)	QUAN- TITY (d)	COST					CONTRACTOR'S OFFER	FOR USE OF CON- TRACT- ING AGENCY ONLY (g)
					UNIT (e)	TOTAL (f)	APPLICABLE TO THIS CONTRACT				
							TO ENTIRE CONTRACT (f1)	TO PORTION NOT TO BE COMPLETED (f2)			

NSN 7540-01-141-3918
1433-101

STANDARD FORM 1433 (10-83)
Prescribed by GSA
FAR (48 CFR) 53.245(i)

Figure 12.10. (Continued) Standard Form 1433.

401

SETTLEMENT PROPOSAL
(SHORT FORM)

FORM APPROVED OMB NO.

3090-0115

For Use by a Prime Contractor or Subcontractor In Settlement of a Fixed Price Terminated Contract When Total Charges Claimed Are Less Than $10,000.

THIS PROPOSAL APPLIES TO *(Check one)*
☐ A PRIME CONTRACT WITH THE GOVERNMENT
☐ SUBCONTRACT OR PURCHASE ORDER

COMPANY *(Prime or Subcontractor)*

SUBCONTRACT OR PURCHASE ORDER NO.(S)

STREET ADDRESS

CONTRACTOR WHO SENT NOTICE OF TERMINATION

NAME

CITY AND STATE

ADDRESS

NAME OF GOVERNMENT AGENCY | GOVERNMENT PRIME CONTRACT NO.

If moneys payable under the contract have been assigned, give the following:

NAME OF ASSIGNEE

CONTRACTOR'S REFERENCE NO. | EFFECTIVE DATE OF TERMINATION

ADDRESS

SECTION I – STATUS OF CONTRACT OR ORDER AT EFFECTIVE DATE OF TERMINATION

PRODUCTS COVERED BY TERMINATED CONTRACT OR PURCHASE ORDER		FINISHED			UNFINISHED OR NOT COMMENCED		TOTAL COVERED BY CONTRACT OR ORDER
		PREVIOUSLY SHIPPED AND INVOICED	ON HAND		TO BE COMPLETED *(Partial termination only)*	NOT TO BE COMPLETED	
			PAYMENT TO BE RECEIVED THROUGH INVOICING	INCLUDED IN THIS PROPOSAL			
(a)		(b)	(c)	(d)	(e)	(f)	(g)
	QUANTITY						
	$						
	QUANTITY						
	$						
	QUANTITY						
	$						

SECTION II – PROPOSED SETTLEMENT

NO.	ITEM *(Include only items allocable to the terminated portion of contract)*	AMOUNT OF CHARGE
1	CHARGE FOR ACCEPTABLE FINISHED PRODUCT NOT COVERED BY INVOICING *(from SF 1434)*	$
2	CHARGE FOR WORK-IN-PROCESS, RAW MATERIAL, ETC., ON HAND *(from SF 1434)*	$
3	OTHER CHARGES INCLUDING PROFIT AND SETTLEMENT EXPENSES	$
4	CHARGES FOR SETTLEMENT(S) WITH SUBCONTRACTORS	$
5	GROSS PROPOSED SETTLEMENT *(Sum of Items 1 thru 4)*	$
6	DISPOSAL AND OTHER CREDITS *(from SF 1434, Col. 2)*	$
7	NET PROPOSED SETTLEMENT *(Item 5 less 6)*	$
8	ADVANCE, PROGRESS, AND PARTIAL PAYMENTS	$
9	NET PAYMENT REQUESTED *(Item 7 less 8)*	$

List your inventory on SF 1434 and attach a copy thereto. Retain for the applicable period specified in the prime contract all papers and records relating to this proposal for future examination.

GIVE A BRIEF EXPLANATION OF HOW YOU ARRIVED AT THE AMOUNTS SHOWN IN ITEMS 3, 4, 6, AND 7

I CERTIFY that the above proposed settlement includes only charges allocable to the terminated portion of the contract or purchase order. That the total charges (Item 5) and the disposal credits (Item 6) are fair and reasonable, and that this proposal has been prepared with knowledge that it will, or may, be used directly or indirectly as a basis for reimbursement under a settlement proposal(s) against agencies of the United States.

NAME OF YOUR COMPANY

BY *(Signature of authorized official)*

TITLE | DATE

Where the space provided for any information is insufficient, continue on a separate sheet.

NSN 7540-01-140-5522

1438-101

STANDARD FORM 1438 (10-83)
Prescribed by GSA
FAR (48 CFR) 53.249(a)(5)

Figure 12.11. Settlement proposal (short form), Standard Form 1438.

INSTRUCTIONS

1. This settlement proposal should be submitted to the contracting officer, if you are a prime contractor, or to your customer, if you are a subcontractor. The term contract as used hereinafter includes a subcontract or a purchase order.

2. Proposals that would normally be included in a single settlement proposal, such as those based on a series of separate orders for the same item under one contract should be consolidated wherever possible, and must not be divided in such a way as to bring them below $10,000.

3. You should review any aspects of your contract relating to termination and consult your customer or contracting officer for further information. Government regulations pertaining to the basis for determining a fair and reasonable termination settlement are contained in Part 49 of the Federal Acquisition Regulation. Your proposal for fair compensation should be prepared on the basis of the costs shown by your accounting records. Where your costs are not so shown, you may use any reasonable basis for estimating your costs which will provide for fair compensation for the preparations made and work done for the terminated portion of the contract, including a reasonable profit on such preparation and work.

4. Generally your settlement proposal may include under items 2, 3, and 4, the following:

a. COSTS—Costs incurred which are reasonably necessary and are properly allocable to the terminated portion of your contract under recognized commercial accounting practices, including direct and indirect manufacturing, selling and distribution, administrative, and other costs and expenses incurred.

b. SETTLEMENT WITH SUBCONTRACTORS— Reasonable settlements of proposals of subcontractors allocable to the terminated portion of the subcontract. Copies of such settlements will be attached hereto.

c. SETTLEMENT EXPENSES—Reasonable costs of protecting and preserving termination inventory in your possession and preparing your proposal.

d. PROFIT—A reasonable profit with respect to the preparations you have made and work you have actually done for the terminated portion of your contract. No profit should be included for work which has not been done, nor shall profit be included for settlement expenses, or for settlement with subcontractors.

5. If you use this form, your total charges being proposed (line 5), must be less than $10,000. The Government has the right to examine your books and records relative to this proposal, and if you are a subcontractor your customer must be satisfied with your proposal.

STANDARD FORM 1438 BACK (10-83)

Figure 12.11. (Continued)

TERMINATION INVENTORY SCHEDULE E
(SHORT FORM FOR USE WITH SF 1438 ONLY)
(See SF 1425 for Instructions)

☐ PARTIAL ☐ FINAL

DATE

PAGE NO. | NO. OF PAGES | FORM APPROVED OMB NO.

3090-0120

THIS SCHEDULE APPLIES TO *(Check one)*
☐ A PRIME CONTRACT WITH THE GOVERNMENT
☐ SUBCONTRACT(S) OR PURCHASE ORDER(S)

COMPANY PREPARING AND SUBMITTING SCHEDULE

GOVERNMENT PRIME CONTRACT NO. | SUBCONTRACT OR P.O. NO. | REFERENCE NO.

STREET ADDRESS

CONTRACTOR WHO SENT NOTICE OF TERMINATION

NAME

CITY AND STATE *(Include ZIP Code)*

ADDRESS *(Include ZIP Code)*

LOCATION OF MATERIAL

PRODUCT COVERED BY CONTRACT OR ORDER

FOR USE OF CON-TRACT-ING AGENCY ONLY	ITEM NO.	DESCRIPTION		CONDITION *(Use code)*	QUAN-TITY	UNIT OF MEASURE	COST *(For finished product, show contract price instead of cost)*		CONTRACTOR'S OFFER	FOR USE OF CON-TRACT-ING AGENCY ONLY
		ITEM DESCRIPTION	GOVERNMENT PART OR DRAWING NUMBER AND REVISION NUMBER	TYPE OF PACKING *(Bulk, bbls., crates, etc.)*				UNIT	TOTAL		
(a)		(b)	(b1)	(b2)	(c)	(d)	(d1)	(e)	(f)	(g)	

TERMINATION INVENTORY SCHEDULE CERTIFICATE

The undersigned, personally and as representative of the Contractor, certifies that this Inventory Schedule consisting of page numbers _____ to _____ inclusive, dated _____ has been examined, and that in the exercise of the signer's best judgment and to the best of the signer's knowledge, based upon information believed by the signer to be reliable, said Schedule has been prepared in accordance with applicable instructions; that the inventory described is allocable to the designated contract and is located at the places specified; if the property reported is termination inventory, that the quantities are not in excess of the reasonable quantitative requirements of the terminated portion of the contract; that this schedule does not include any items reasonably usable, without loss to the

Contractor, on its other work; and that the costs shown on this Schedule are in accordance with the Contractor's records and books of account.

The Contractor agrees to inform the Contracting Officer of any substantial change in the status of the inventory shown in this Schedule between the date hereof and the final disposition of such inventory.

Subject to any authorized prior disposition, title to the inventory listed in this Schedule is hereby tendered to the Government and is warranted to be free and clear of all liens and encumbrances.

NAME OF CONTRACTOR

BY *(Signature of Authorized Official)* | TITLE | DATE

NAME OF SUPERVISORY ACCOUNTING OFFICIAL | TITLE

NSN 7540-01-140-5520
1434-101

STANDARD FORM 1434 (10-83)
Prescribed by GSA
FAR (48 CFR) 53.245(i)

Figure 12.12. Termination inventory schedule E (short form), Standard Form 1434.

The government prefers the inventory basis because the settlement is related directly to the cost of the items actually terminated. The unterminated portion of the contract will continue, and unit prices will remain the same unless changed through an equitable adjustment. The difficulty in the use of this method is that it requires a determination of the price of work-in-process. It also requires considerable effort in the isolation of startup costs and contract preparatory costs and the proper allocation of these costs between the terminated and nonterminated portions of the contract.

One of the deficiencies of the inventory basis is its lack of recognition of the impact of a termination on the unterminated portion of the contract. As we discuss later in this chapter, many costs are incurred for the benefit of the contract as a whole and, as such, recovery is provided for in the unit price of all items. To the extent a termination results in less units or items, unless the costs which will be incurred are reduced proportionately, unit costs will increase. Unless the continuing portion of the contract is revised through an equitable adjustment, the contractor will earn a lower rate of profit, or will suffer a loss on the continuing portion, solely because of the termination.

Because the total amount of the termination settlement is limited to the contract price of the items terminated plus settlement expenses, the need for an equitable adjustment should be addressed in either partial or complete terminations. If the costs incurred on a completely or partially terminated contract have been increased because of government action or inaction, then an equitable adjustment will result in (1) increasing the level at which a possible limitation on the termination settlement amount may apply, (2) calculating a higher rate of profit earned to allow for a higher profit in the settlement, and (3) preventing a degradation of profit on the unterminated portion of the contract. Included in government actions that could cause an increase in the costs of performance would be the termination. Equitable adjustments are discussed in Chapter 11.

The total cost method allows the contractor to recover all the costs incurred to date and profit if a profit would have been earned. This could be an advantage to a company that was incurring profit at a rate lower than originally negotiated and would be to the disadvantage of a company incurring a profit at a rate higher than initially negotiated if the originally negotiated profit rate is conclude to be fair and reasonable. In *Lockley Manufacturing Co., Inc.*,[6] the AS-BCA limited the profit rate for the terminated portion of the contract to the rate actually experienced by the contractor. The ASBCA stated that it "perceives no reason why the adjustment should provide the appellant more profit than it would have realized had the contarct been completed on time." Determining the appropriate profit level does not necessarily follow this rule. The factors which will be considered by the government in negotiating or determining profit are delineated in FAR 49.202(b). Only one of these factors is the rate contemplated by the parties at the time the contract was originally negotiated.

Contractors may submit Standard Form 1440, Request for Partial Payment (Figure 12.13.), which provides the basis for the government to make partial payments against costs incurred for the terminated portion of the contract before a final settlement is reached. When and how much of a partial payment is made is at the discretion of the contracting officer.

Termination for Default

As stated earlier, the government has the right to terminate a contract when a company fails to: (1) deliver the supplies or perform the services within the

APPLICATION FOR PARTIAL PAYMENT

FORM APPROVED OMB NO.
3090-0115

For use by Prime Contractor or Subcontractor under contracts terminated for the convenience of the Government.

THIS APPLICATION APPLIES TO *(Check one)*
☐ A PRIME CONTRACT WITH THE GOVERNMENT ☐ SUBCONTRACT OR PURCHASE ORDER

SUBCONTRACT OR PURCHASE ORDER NUMBER(S)

APPLICANT

STREET ADDRESS

CONTRACTOR WHO SENT NOTICE OF TERMINATION

NAME

CITY AND STATE *(Include ZIP Code)*

ADDRESS *(Include ZIP Code)*

NAME OF GOVERNMENT AGENCY

IF CONTRACTOR HAS GUARANTEED LOANS OR HAS ASSIGNED MONEYS DUE UNDER THE CONTRACT, GIVE THE FOLLOWING:

GOVERNMENT PRIME CONTRACT NUMBER

NAME AND ADDRESS OF FINANCING INSTITUTION *(Include ZIP Code)*

CONTRACTOR'S REFERENCE NUMBER

NAME AND ADDRESS OF GUARANTOR *(Include ZIP Code)*

EFFECTIVE DATE OF TERMINATION

DATE OF THIS APPLICATION

NAME AND ADDRESS OF ASSIGNEE *(Include ZIP Code)*

AMOUNT REQUESTED
$

APPLICATION NUMBER UNDER THIS TERMINATION

SECTION I – STATUS OF CONTRACT OR ORDER AT EFFECTIVE DATE OF TERMINATION

PRODUCTS COVERED BY TERMINATED CONTRACT OR PURCHASE ORDER		FINISHED			UNFINISHED OR NOT COMMENCED		TOTAL COVERED BY CONTRACT OR ORDER
		PREVIOUSLY SHIPPED AND INVOICED	ON HAND		TO BE COMPLETED	NOT TO BE COMPLETED	
			PAYMENT TO BE RECEIVED THROUGH INVOICING	INCLUDED IN THIS APPLICATION			
(a)		(b)	(c)	(d)	(e)	(f)	(g)
	QUANTITY						
	$						
	QUANTITY						
	$						
	QUANTITY						
	$						

SECTION II – APPLICANT'S OWN TERMINATION CHARGES
(Exclusive of its Subcontractors' Charges)

SETTLEMENT PROPOSAL
☐ ATTACHED
☐ PREVIOUSLY SUBMITTED

NO.	ITEM	CHARGES AS LISTED IN SETTLEMENT PROPOSAL
1	ACCEPTABLE FURNISHED PRODUCT *(at contract price)*	$
2	WORK-IN-PROCESS	
3	RAW MATERIALS, PURCHASED PARTS, AND SUPPLIES	
4	GENERAL AND ADMINISTRATIVE EXPENSE	
5	**TOTAL** *(Sum of lines 1, 2, 3, and 4)*	$
6	SPECIAL TOOLING AND SPECIAL TEST EQUIPMENT	
7	OTHER COSTS	
8	SETTLEMENT EXPENSES	
9	**TOTAL** *(Sum of lines 5, 6, 7, and 8)*	$
10	SUBCONTRACTOR SETTLEMENTS APPROVED BY CONTRACTING OFFICER OR SETTLED UNDER A DELEGATION OF AUTHORITY AND PAID BY APPLICANT	$
	11. AMOUNTS RECEIVED	
a	UNLIQUIDATED PARTIAL, PROGRESS, AND ADVANCE PAYMENTS RECEIVED	$
b	DISPOSAL AND OTHER CREDITS	
c	**TOTAL** *(Sum of lines a and b)*	
d	AMOUNT OF PARTIAL PAYMENT REQUESTED	
e	**TOTAL** *(Sum of lines c and d)*	$

NSN 7540-01-142-0131

1440-101

STANDARD FORM 1440 (10-83)
Prescribed by GSA
FAR (48 CFR) 53.249(a)(7)

Figure 12.13. Application for partial payment, Standard Form 1440.

406

time specified in the contract, (2) perform any other provisions of the contract, or (3) make progress so as to endanger performance of the contract. Under the first circumstance, if the company fails to deliver the supplies or services within the time specified in the contract, unless there are excusable delays, the government has the right to terminate the contract immediately, regardless of how slight the delay may be. The government is not obligated to provide any prior notice. However, in the situation of failure to perform any other provision of the contract or failure to make progress, the government must provide an opportunity for the company to cure the defect. The contracting officer may notify the company that within a period of ten days after receipt of a notice, or such other longer period as the contracting officer may authorize in writing, the company must cure the defect. After this time period, if the problem is not remedied, the government may terminate the contract.

Under cost type contracts, the accounting procedures for default and convenience terminations are the same. The only real difference is that settlement expenses are not allowable costs on a termination for default and fee is only considered for acceptable work.

Under fixed-price contracts, the contractor will be paid only for items completed and accepted. The payment will be at the contract price. The government is not liable for payment of the contractor's costs incurred on any undelivered work and is entitled to the repayment of any advance or progress payments applicable to the terminated portion of the contract. As in cost type contracts terminated for default, settlement expenses are not considered allowable costs. In addition, the government may require the contractor to transfer title and deliver to the government any materials and supplies on hand related to the terminated portion of the contract. The government may then turn these items over to another contractor to reprocure the items terminated. If the cost of reprocuring the items from another supplier is greater than the cost that would have been incurred on the terminated contract, the government may recover the increased cost from the contractor whose contract was terminated.

There are several defenses against a termination for default. While the available defenses depend very much on the specific circumstances, they generally can be classified as either procedural defects or excuses. Boards of contract appeals and courts have generally held that the government must adhere strictly to the procedures established. This applies particularly to a termination for failure to perform. Under applicable procedures, the government cannot terminate a contract for failure to make timely delivery until all the time for performance has expired. If the contract is terminated even one day early, the termination may be determined to be for the convenience of the government and not for default by the contractor. (However, a contract may be terminated for a failure to make adequate progress.) This in only one example of a procedural defect that would cause a contract that was originally terminated for default to be converted to a termination for convenience.

Excuses that may result in converting a termination for default into a termination for convenience generally must relate to actions and causes beyond the control of the contractor or unreasonable acts by the government. Some excuses which may fall within these criteria include: (1) government actions caused or contributed to the nonperformance; (2) the defects used as a basis for the termination for default were minor; (3) the defects could have been cured within a reasonable time, which was not granted by the contracting officer; (4) the government's actions indicated its intent that the contractor continue performance; (5) the failure to perform was due to causes beyond the control and without the fault or negligence of the contractor; or (6) performance by any contractor was impossible. In the case of an excusable delay, an extension of the period of performance may have been in order, thus justifying the classification of a termination prior to the end of the "extended" period as one for convenience rather than default.

The specific critieria that must be met to successfully convert a termination for default to a termination for convenience are perhaps best left to a legal forum. However, while those criteria may be stringent, they have been successfully met in many circumstances and should be considered whenever a contract is terminated for default. This is important because of the substantial financial and other consequences resulting from a termination for default.

TERMINATION ACCOUNTING PROBLEMS

Accounting Procedures

One of the difficulties faced in accounting for the cost of terminated contracts is the fact that accounting systems are normally designed to reflect an ongoing, continuous situation. Most cost accounting systems have not been designed to handle terminations. As a result of a termination, certain costs will be incurred which otherwise would not have been incurred. In addition, the premise upon which allocation procedures were established may no longer be valid. Unless accounting procedures are changed to reflect the change in circumstances, costs may not be properly allocated nor proper recovery obtained. It is highly unlikely that the cost accounting system for a fixed-price contract, would identify, isolate, and report costs unique to a termination action. Indeed, this was concluded in *Algonac Manufacturing Company*,[7] where it was also concluded that the acquisition regulation does not require a fixed-price contractor to maintain elaborate cost accounting systems or follow prescribed accounting principles simply because the contract might be terminated.

This lack of a requirement to maintain specific accounting systems does not, however, shift the burden of proving the amounts of any entitlement to the government. In *Clary Corporation*,[8] the Board stated:

> Although it may have been legitimate for the appellant to have estimated its costs of performance where those costs were not shown on its accounting records, it was still necessary to demonstrate the bases and accuracy of those estimates.

This case is consistent with other cases in which the burden of proof of costs incurred and entitlement fall to the contractor. The boards have permitted estimates where accounting records were unavailable through no fault of the contractor. In such cases, however, the contractor is still required to support its claim by the best available competent evidence.

The cost principle on termination costs (FAR 31.205-42) recognizes this by stating: "Contract terminations generally give rise to the incurrence of costs or the need for special treatment of costs that would not have arisen had the contract not been terminated." This FAR provision covers cost areas that are unique to terminations. It also addresses the need for revisions to normal accounting practices to reflect the unique environment created by a termination. The areas covered are (1) common items, (2) costs continuing after termination, (3) initial costs, (4) loss of useful value of special tooling, machinery, and equipment, (5) rental costs under unexpired leases, (6) alterations of leased property, (7) settlement expenses, and (8) subcontractor claims. These cost principles are based upon the premise that the contractor will take all necessary action to minimize expenses. This includes the diversion of materials and supplies to any other work of the contarctor. It is also based upon the premise that the government is not a guarantor of the business of the company and therefore will not reimburse a company for indirect expenses that would have been allocated to the terminated portion of a completely terminated contract (i.e., unabsorbed overhead), which will be discussed in more detail later in this chapter.

In addition to the settlement forms discussed earlier, contractors will generally be required to submit Standard Form 1439, Schedule of Accounting Information (Figure 12.14) which contains general information about the accounting system and specific information about accounting methods used in preparing the settlement proposal.

Initial Costs

It typically costs a contractor a great deal more to produce the first unit contracted for than the last unit. During the initial stages of many contracts, especially production contracts, the contractor will incur abnormally high direct and indirect labor, material and administrative costs. The regulations recognize essentially two types of such "initial costs": starting-load and preparatory costs.

Starting-load costs are the costs resulting from labor inefficiencies and excessive material losses due to inexperienced labor, employee training, changing processing methods, etc. during the early stages of a program. Preparatory costs are the costs incurred in preparing to perform the contract, including costs of plant rearrangement and alterations, management and personnel organization, and production planning.

In Baifield Industries,[9] the ASBCA decided that a van container supply contractor was entitled, upon a convenience termination, to recover as preparatory costs the costs of reasonable modifications necessary to outfit an existing facility for contract performance.

The basic issue with initial costs is not one of allowability but of identifiability. The regulations generally allow initial costs if they can be adequately identified and supported. The theory is that if the contract was completed, such costs would be spread over all units and recouped in the total contract price. If a contract is terminated, however, while such costs may have been largely expended, they will be allocated only to completed units. As a result, the contractor would suffer a loss through no fault of its own. Therefore, identification and adequate support are the keys to recovering initial costs in a settlement proposal.

The regulations provide that if initial costs are claimed and have not been segregated in the contractor's books, segregation for settlement purposes is to be made from cost reports and schedules reflecting the high unit cost incurred during the early stages of the contract. Because contractors do not normally account for contract costs in anticipation of a termination and because of the difficulty of identification, contractors rarely segregate initial costs in their formal books of account. As a result, computations will normally be based on informal records, cost reports, budgetary and actual production data, and judgmental estimates.

The relative ease of identifying all allocable initial costs depends on the quality of supporting records as well as the nature of the costs. Some initial costs should be relatively easy to identify; others will be very difficult.

SCHEDULE OF ACCOUNTING INFORMATION

FORM APPROVED OMB NO.
3090-0115

To be used by prime contractors submitting termination proposals under Part 49 of the Federal Acquisition Regulation. Also suitable for use by subcontractor in effecting subcontract settlements with prime contractor or intermediate subcontractor.

THIS PROPOSAL APPLIES TO *(Check one)*	COMPANY *(Prime or Subcontractor)*		
☐ A PRIME CONTRACT WITH THE GOVERNMENT ☐ SUBCONTRACT OR PURCHASE ORDER			

SUBCONTRACT OR PURCHASE ORDER NO. (S)	STREET ADDRESS		

CONTRACTOR WHO SENT NOTICE OF TERMINATION	CITY AND STATE *(Include ZIP Code)*		
NAME AND ADDRESS *(Include ZIP Code)*			
	NAME OF GOVERNMENT AGENCY		
	GOVERNMENT PRIME CONTRACT NO.	CONTRACTOR'S REFERENCE NO.	EFFECTIVE DATE OF TERMINATION

1. INDIVIDUAL IN YOUR ORGANIZATION FROM WHOM ADDITIONAL INFORMATION MAY BE REQUESTED ON QUESTIONS RELATING TO:

ACCOUNTING MATTERS		PROPERTY DISPOSAL	
NAME		NAME	
TITLE	TELEPHONE NO.	TITLE	TELEPHONE NO.
ADDRESS *(Include ZIP Code)*		ADDRESS *(Include ZIP Code)*	

2. ARE THE ACCOUNTS OF THE CONTRACTOR SUBJECT TO REGULAR PERIODIC EXAMINATION BY INDEPENDENT PUBLIC ACCOUNTANTS?

☐ YES ☐ NO *(Name and address of accountants)*

3. INDEPENDENT ACCOUNTANTS, IF ANY, WHO HAVE REVIEWED OR ASSISTED IN THE PREPARATION OF THE ATTACHED PROPOSAL

NAME	ADDRESS *(Include ZIP Code)*

4. GOVERNMENTAL AGENCY (IES) WHICH HAVE REVIEWED YOUR ACCOUNTS IN CONNECTION WITH PRIOR SETTLEMENT PROPOSALS DURING THE CURRENT AND PRECEDING FISCAL YEAR

NAME	ADDRESS *(Include ZIP Code)*

5. HAVE THERE BEEN ANY SIGNIFICANT DEVIATIONS FROM YOUR REGULAR ACCOUNTING PROCEDURES AND POLICIES IN ARRIVING AT THE COSTS SET FORTH IN THE ATTACHED PROPOSAL? *(If "Yes," explain briefly)*

☐ YES ☐ NO

6. WERE THE DETAILED COST RECORDS USED IN PREPARING THE PROPOSAL CONTROLLED BY AND IN AGREEMENT WITH YOUR GENERAL BOOKS OF ACCOUNT? ☐ YES ☐ NO

7. STATE METHOD OF ACCOUNTING FOR TRADE AND CASH DISCOUNTS EARNED, REBATES, ALLOWANCES, AND VOLUME PRICE ADJUST-MENTS. ARE SUCH ITEMS EXCLUDED FROM COSTS PROPOSED? ☐ YES ☐ NO

Where the space provided for any information is insufficient, continue on a separate sheet.

NSN 7540-01-142-9852

1439-101

STANDARD FORM 1439 (10-83)
Prescribed by GSA
FAR (48 CFR) 53.249(a)(6)

Figure 12.14. Schedule of accounting information, Standard Form 1439.

410

8. STATE METHOD OF RECORDING AND ABSORBING (1) GENERAL ENGINEERING AND GENERAL DEVELOPMENT EXPENSE AND (2) ENGINEERING AND DEVELOPMENT EXPENSE DIRECTLY APPLICABLE TO THE TERMINATED CONTRACT.

9. STATE TYPES AND SOURCE OF MISCELLANEOUS INCOME AND CREDITS AND MANNER OF RECORDING IN THE INCOME OR THE COST ACCOUNTS SUCH AS RENTAL OF YOUR FACILITIES TO OUTSIDE PARTIES. ETC.

10. METHOD OF ALLOCATING GENERAL AND ADMINISTRATIVE EXPENSE.

11. ARE COSTS AND INCOME FROM CHANGE ORDERS SEGREGATED FROM OTHER CONTRACT COSTS AND INCOME? *(If "Yes," by what method)*
[ ] YES   [ ] NO

12. METHOD OF COMPUTING PROFIT SHOWN IN THE ATTACHED PROPOSAL AND REASON FOR SELECTING THE METHOD USED. FURNISH ESTIMATE OF AMOUNT OR RATE OF PROFIT IN DOLLARS OR PERCENT ANTICIPATED HAD THE CONTRACT BEEN COMPLETED.

13. ARE SETTLEMENT EXPENSES APPLICABLE TO PREVIOUSLY TERMINATED CONTRACTS EXCLUDED FROM THE ATTACHED PROPOSALS? *(If "No," explain)*
[ ] YES   [ ] NO

14. DOES THIS PROPOSAL INCLUDE CHARGES FOR MAJOR INVENTORY ITEMS AND PROPOSALS OF SUBCONTRACTORS COMMON TO THIS TERMINATED CONTRACT AND OTHER WORK OF THE CONTRACTOR? *(If "Yes," explain the method used in allocating amounts to the terminated portion of this contract.)*
[ ] YES   [ ] NO

15. EXPLAIN BRIEFLY YOUR METHOD OF PRICING INVENTORIES, INDICATING WHETHER MATERIAL HANDLING COST HAS BEEN INCLUDED IN CHARGES FOR MATERIALS.

16. ARE ANY PARTS, MATERIALS, OR FINISHED PRODUCT, KNOWN TO BE DEFECTIVE, INCLUDED IN THE INVENTORIES? *(If "Yes," explain.)*
[ ] YES   [ ] NO

Where the space provided for any information is insufficient, continue on a separate sheet.

STANDARD FORM 1439 (10-83)
PAGE 2

Figure 12.14.   (Continued)

17. WERE INVENTORY QUANTITIES BASED ON A PHYSICAL COUNT AS OF THE DATE OF TERMINATION? *(If "No," explain exceptions)*

☐ YES ☐ NO

18. DESCRIBE BRIEFLY THE NATURE OF INDIRECT EXPENSE ITEMS INCLUDED IN INVENTORY COSTS *(See Schedule A, SF 1435)* AND EXPLAIN YOUR METHOD OF ALLOCATION USED IN PREPARING THIS PROPOSAL, INCLUDING IF PRACTICABLE, THE RATES USED AND THE PERIOD OF TIME UPON WHICH THEY ARE BASED.

19. STATE GENERAL POLICIES RELATING TO DEPRECIATION AND AMORTIZATION OF FIXED ASSETS, BASES, UNDERLYING POLICIES.

20. DO THE COSTS SET FORTH IN THE ATTACHED PROPOSAL INCLUDE PROVISIONS FOR ANY RESERVES OTHER THAN DEPRECIATION RESERVES? *(If "Yes," list such reserves)*

☐ YES ☐ NO

21. STATE POLICY OR PROCEDURE FOR RECORDING AND WRITING OFF STARTING LOAD.

22. STATE POLICIES FOR DISTINGUISHING BETWEEN CHARGES TO CAPITAL (FIXED) ASSET ACCOUNTS AND TO REPAIR AND MAINTENANCE ACCOUNTS.

23. ARE PERISHABLE TOOLS AND MANUFACTURING SUPPLIES CHARGED DIRECTLY TO CONTRACT COSTS OR INCLUDED IN INDIRECT EXPENSES?

Where the space provided for any information is insufficient, continue on a separate sheet.

STANDARD FORM 1439 (10-83)
PAGE 3

Figure 12.14. (Continued)

24. HAVE ANY CHARGES FOR SEVERANCE, DISMISSAL, OR SEPARATION PAY BEEN INCLUDED IN THIS PROPOSAL? *(If "Yes," furnish brief explanation and estimates of amounts included.)*

☐ YES ☐ NO

25. STATE POLICIES RELATING TO RECORDING OF OVERTIME SHIFT PREMIUMS AND PRODUCTION BONUSES.

26. DOES CONTRACTOR HAVE A PENSION PLAN? *(If "Yes," state method of funding and absorption of past and current pension service costs.)*

☐ YES ☐ NO

27. IS THIS SETTLEMENT PROPOSAL BASED ON STANDARD COSTS?

☐ YES *(If "Yes," has adjustment to actual cost or adjustment for any significant variations been made?*   ☐ YES ☐ NO *(If "No," explain.)*

☐ NO

28. DOES THIS PROPOSAL INCLUDE ANY ELEMENT OF PROFIT TO THE CONTRACTOR OR A RELATED ORGANIZATION, OTHER THAN (a) PROFIT SET FORTH SEPARATELY IN THE PROPOSAL OR (b) PROFIT INCLUDED IN THE CONTRACT PRICE AT WHICH ACCEPTABLE FINISHED PRODUCT, IF ANY, IS INCLUDED IN THE PROPOSAL? *(If "Yes," explain briefly.)*

☐ YES ☐ NO

29. WHAT IS LENGTH OF TIME (PRODUCTION CYCLE) REQUIRED TO PRODUCE ONE OF THE END ITEMS FROM THE TIME THE MATERIAL ENTERS THE PRODUCTION LINE TO THE COMPLETION AS THE FINISHED PRODUCT?

30. STATE POLICY AND PROCEDURE FOR VERIFICATION AND NEGOTIATION OF SETTLEMENTS WITH SUBCONTRACTORS AND VENDORS.

CERTIFICATE

THIS CERTIFIES THAT, TO THE BEST KNOWLEDGE AND BELIEF OF THE UNDERSIGNED, THE ABOVE STATEMENTS ARE TRUE AND CORRECT.

NAME OF CONTRACTOR	BY *(Signature of supervisor accounting official)*	
	TITLE	DATE

Where the space provided for any information is insufficient, continue on a separate sheet.

STANDARD FORM 1439 (10-83)
PAGE 4

Figure 12.14. (Continued)

413

Some initial costs and the records that can be used to support them are:

Rate of Production Loss. These can be based on scrap reports, efficiency reports, spoilage tickets, etc. In proving excessive losses early in a program, the contractor could use trends and/or rely on historical experience.

Initial Plant Rearrangement and Alterations. These are usually based on a work order or service order, with costs accumulated against the order.

Management and Personnel Organization and Production Planning. These are difficult to develop. There may be a need to base these on estimates using the assistance of technical personnel.

Idle Time, Subnormal Production, Employee Training, and Unfamiliarity with the Product, Materials or Processes. As production continues, these costs should diminish due to "learning." This learning process may be expressed through the use of the "learning curve" theory. Additionally, many contractors maintain data on these factors in a collective manner in the form of efficiency reports, equivalent units produced, etc. These are often found to be acceptable support for starting-load costs.

After identifying initial costs, the problem then becomes one of allocating them to the terminated and nonterminated portions of the contract. Usually this can be done on the basis of quantities. For example, the improvement curve could be used to project total direct labor hours if the contract had been completed. Unit hours can then be determined and applied to the delivered units. The hours allocated could then be deducted from the total hours required to produce the delivered units. The difference could be costed using historical labor and overhead rates to determine the initial costs allocable to the terminated portion of the contract. Depending upon the type of contract involved and the nature of the settlement proposal, it may be necessary to use the increased per unit costs attributable to the nonterminated portion of the contract as a basis for an equitable adjustment.

Two important points should be remembered about initial costs. First, although segregation of initial costs is not necessary for cost recovery, the better the accounting for these costs, the easier it will be to identify them and establish their validity in case of termination. The other point involves proving the nonrecurring nature of these costs. Unless nonrecurrence can be adequately shown, it may lead to the conclusion that the contract would have been performed at a loss, and the government will seek a credit for the loss of the termination settlement.

Indirect to Direct Reclassifications

Closely related to the issue of initial costs and sometimes involving the same types of costs (e.g., preparatory costs) is the reclassification of costs from indirect to direct. As stated before, contractors' accounting systems are established to accurately determine costs on contracts expected to be completed. It would not normally be appropriate to maintain cost records with the expectation of a termination. Therefore, when a termination occurs, especially in the early stages of contract performance, normal costing procedures will not likely yield reasonable amounts of termination costs. As a result, it is frequently necessary to reclassify costs from an indirect to a direct charge to fairly and accurately represent the real cost allocable to the terminated contract. While such reallocations are specifically allowed for post-termination settlement expenses, it may also be appropriate for costs incurred prior to the termination notice.

Often there is no relationship in terms of time between the incurrence of overhead and other indirect costs and their recoupment when allocated to contracts. Contractors must abandon their usual accounting methods for the allocation of indirect expenses. They must directly identify all the cost elements concerned with the performance of the contract to ensure that they will recover all the expenses incurred to date at the time of termination.

This applies to all categories of costs included in indirect expenses—engineering, purchasing, top management, plant management, production control, first line supervisors, and so forth.

Conventional accounting methods may not be suitable for preparing termination claims in that an allocation based on direct labor, or a similar base, will often result in an inadequate recovery. An example illustrates the inequities that may result from using normal accounting practices for a terminated contract. A contractor received a production contract for which most of the required material was purchased and received in the early stages of performance. Assume that purchasing and receiving expenses are charged to a manufacturing overhead pool that is allocated to contracts on the basis of direct labor hours. It is apparent that in the early stages of the contract when little direct labor hours have been expended, an allocation of manufacturing overhead using direct labor hours will not produce equitable results. Therefore, direct costing of the purchasing and receiving expenses would be more appropriate in the circumstances.

Recognizing the problem, however, is considerably easier than implementing an acceptable solution. Once a contractor departs from its usual, accepted accounting practices, there is an implication of "double counting" (i.e., charging the same type of cost indirectly in one instance and directly in another). In such cases, either (1) the costs would remain in the indirect cost pool, which would not alleviate the problem of inequity, or (2) all similar costs would need to be removed from the pool and charged direct, which would likely prove very difficult. The regulations and cost accounting standards, however, provide an escape clause. Double counting can exist only for "costs incurred for the same purpose, in like circumstances. . . ." Therefore, inconsistent treatment of indirect costs in a termination claim can be justified as not "like circumstances." Refer to DOD CAS Steering Committee Interim Guidance W.G. 77-15, dated March 29, 1977.

As can be seen from this discussion, it is very important to review terminated contracts to determine the existence of any special situations requiring indirect to direct reclassifications. Such reclassifications can have a significant effect on the ultimate costs recovered in a termination settlement.

Common Items

Common items are materials that are common to both the terminated contract and the contractor's other work. The regulations state that the cost of common items that are reasonably usable on the contractor's other work are not allowable in a terminaion claim unless the contractor can show that it could not retain such items at cost without sustaining a loss. The items must be usable specifically by the contractor. It is not enough to show the items are commonly used in the industry. It seems reasonable for the government to decline to accept and pay for materials which the contractor can reasonably use in the normal course of its work without sustaining a loss. The key considerations involving common items are the phrases "reasonably usable" and "retain without sustaining a loss."

The contractor is not expected to retain common items acquired for the contract if the quantities on hand and on order exceed its reasonable requirements. To show this, a contractor must present convincing evidence that plans and orders for production are insufficient to merit retention of the material. If the contractor has no other work and despite sufficient efforts is unable to obtain any work, it need not retain the common items, for in doing so a loss would be sustained.[10] It is clear that common items are not automatically unallowable but, rather, their allowability is a factual matter.

Excess Inventory

When raw materials are common to a contractor's other work but the amount resulting from the termination would be equal to an amount largely in excess of the contractor's usual inventory, the retention of the material might adversely affect its cash or working capital position and result in a financial hardship. In such cases, common items need not be so classified.

However, the retention of a large inventory does not in itself entitle the contractor to claim an amount for excess inventory. When the inventory can be used within a reasonable period, regardless of size, the excess inventory claim would likely not be accepted.

Under FAR 45.605-2 contractors can return excess inventory to suppliers for full credit less a normal restocking charge or 25% of cost, whichever is less. It is also appropriate to seek reimbursement in the termination settlement proposal for transportation, handling and restocking charges. Returning excess inventory to suppliers may represent a reasonable resolution of this problem.

In some cases, contractors can negotiate an allowance for reworking, rewarehousing, and so forth to retain inventory items with the contracting officer's approval.

Production supplies are normally part of overhead; but if unusually large quantities are purchased or are not the kind used in unterminated business, then it is acceptable to include these as well in a request for reimbursement of excess inventory.

Nonspecification Inventory

As the name implies, nonspecification inventory is the contract inventory on hand at termination that does not comply in all respects with specification requirements. Because the regulations are not specific, cost recoverability for nonspecifiation inventory has evolved through case law. The basic issues affecting allowability of these costs have been (1) reasonableness, (2) whether due to contractor or government fault, (3) whether the items are reworkable, and (4) the government's right to assess the costs of correcting the deficiencies. Generally, the costs of nonspecification inventory are recoverable if they are reasonable, whether due to contractor or government fault, and whether or not the items are reworkable.

Reasonableness has been viewed in relation to the circumstances of the procurement. Key considerations in a determination of reasonableness are the degree of difficulty in producing a product to specification and the stage of performance in which the contract is terminated. Obviously, the more complex or difficult the production process and the earlier in a contract's planned performance period it is terminated, the more significant nonspecification material would be expected to be.

The boards of contract appeals have held that the costs of producing defective work are normally reimbursable under a cost reimbursement contract unless it is established that the defective production resulted from the contractor's careless work conduct. And although a fixed-price contractor is not entitled to be paid for items that do not comply with specification requirements, a termination for convenience deprives the contractor of the opportunity to recoup expenses associated with defective work incurred in the early stages of performance. Therefore, the general effect of a termination for convenience of a fixed-price contract is to convert the terminated portion into a cost reimbursement contract.

One other issue involves the government's ability to assess counterclaims for the cost of correcting deficiencies. This issue was decided by the ASBCA in *New York Shipbuiling Co.*[11] The contract for construction of a submarine was terminated for the convenience of the government before completion and the remaining work was awarded to another contractor. During the completion work, deficiencies were found in New York Shipbuilding's work. The cost of correcting these deficiencies was asserted by the government as a counterclaim by concluding " . . . that the termination for convenience precludes the Government from recovering amounts paid for correcting the alleged deficiencies, even if the existence of such deficiencies were proved and the Government's cost to correct them were established." The Board relied on the principle established in earlier cases that "upon terminating a contract for convenience the Government loses whatever right it might have possessed to hold the contractor responsible for correcting deficiencies in the work included in the terminated portion of the contract."

Continuing Costs

As a general rule the termination clauses in government contracts require that all work be stopped for any portion of a contract that is terminated. It is anticipated that all work will be stopped almost immediately. However, it is also recognized that not all activities nor the incurrence of all costs can be immediately halted. The incurrence of some costs will continue for a period of time after a contract is terminated. The nature of the costs and the actions taken to mitigate or prevent the incurrence of these costs will determine their acceptability as part of a termination settlement proposal. The government will resist payment for any costs that are attributed solely to a loss of business. This concept will be discussed later in this chapter under unabsorbed overhead.

In *Lowell O. West Lumber Sales*[12] the ASBCA ruled that cost can be recovered where it is impossible to discontinue those costs and expenses in spite of all reasonable efforts to stop work immediately. Included in this category, among other items allowed in this case, was depreciation expense from the date of termination until the date the contract was originally contemplated to be completed.

In Baifield *Industries, Division of A-T-O, Inc.,*[13] the contractor was entitled to recover such continuing costs as plant rent, security, depreciation maintenance and other costs pending disposal of its plant equipment (rendered completely idle by the termination), and termination inventory. The government contended that the costs did not bear a necessary relationship to the termination but rather to A-T-O's overall corporte needs. The Board responded with the following significant points:

The Government correctly states that neither the plant nor some of the equipment installed therein were acquired by A-T-O or appellant specifically for performance of the . . . contract. However, that fact does not control the disposition of appellant's claim. The cost principles applicable to continuing contract costs do not condition allowability upon the acquisition of facilities, etc., solely for performance of the terminated contract. The relationship which must be shown is a clear connection between the costs claimed and the terminated contract and, further, that those costs could not have been reasonably shut off upon the termination.

The government also contended that the company, by delaying its disposition of inventory and equipment, did not obtain the best possible price. The Board's opinion was that the company exercised reasonable business judgment with regard to its disposition of termination inventory and equipment and the government is not entitled to second guess the judgment. The amounts allowed were incurred over a 10-month period which the Board concluded was a reasonable period consistent with the additional time needed to complete the contract had it not been terminated.

Finally, the ASBCA, in *Fiesta Leasing & Sales, Inc.*[14], allowed the continuing costs of depreciation on buses used on a bus lease contract terminated by the government. The depreciation was allowed over the full 18-month lease period even though the contract was terminated very early in contract performance. After termination, the company immediately attempted the mitigate the government's damages by advertising to sell some of the buses. When the buses could not be sold, the company began placing the buses under long term leases and a daily rental program. All income from the lease and daily rental programs was credited to the government in the termination claim. In allowing the depreciation costs, the Board stated:

> Such depreciation costs are appropriately recoverable as continuing costs under DAR 15-205.42(b) where, as here, they could not be reasonably discontinued immediately upon termination. . . . There is . . . a clear connection between the costs claimed and the terminated contract and it is clear to us that these costs could not be discontinued immediately upon termination.

Unexpired Leases

An additional item of cost that is specifically addressed as a continuing cost is the cost of unexpired leases. Under the FAR termination cost principle, the costs for the unexpired portion of leases that were reasonably required for the performance of the terminated contract may be an appropriate charge in the termination settlement. The contractor must show that all reasonable efforts were made to terminate, assign, settle, or otherwise reduce the costs of the lease.

This was the case in *Baifield Industries*,[15] described above. When the contract was terminated, the company no longer had a need for its manufacturing plant where the contract was being performed; however it needed to retain the plant until disposition of the inventory and equipment was substantially accomplished. The plant was being leased under a long term lease arrangement with an unaffiliated lessor. The company diligently attempted to dispose of the plant in a timely basis. Its attempts to cancel the lease, however, were unsuccessful. Attempts to interest other companies (including other divisions of A-T-O, Inc.) in subleasing the plant were also unsuccessful, primarily because of the relatively isolated location of the plant.

The company finally located an interested sublessee, which assumed the rental obligation. The Board, in allowing the continuing rent on the unexpired lease until the sublessee took over the payments, concluded that the company's efforts to dispose of the plant after the termination were reasonable in the circumstances.

The ASBCA reached a similar conclusion in *Southland Manufacturing Corp.*[16] The Board concluded that Southland made a reasonable effort to cancel or otherwise dispose of a building lease, and allowed continuing lease costs after termination until the building was sublet to an outside party.

Idle Facilities and Idle Capacity

The costs of idle facilities and capacity are not specifically addressed in the termination cost principle. However, FAR 31.205-17 recognizes tht idle facilities and idle capacity may result from a contract termination and may be allowable. In *Celesco Industries, Inc.,*[17] the ASBCA allowed the costs of two buildings as idle facilities for a period of five weeks subsequent to the termination of the contract. The two buildings were assigned for the exclusive use of the project during performance of the contract and remained idle for four months after the termination. The Board concluded that nothing in the record supported the four-month period of idleness as necessary or reasonable. The Board decided that five weeks was a reasonable period for dismantling the production line and making the buildings available for other purposes.

Generally, both idle facilities and idle capacity-costs are reflected as allowable overhead costs and are allocated to all applicable work of the company, instead of being directly charged to the terminated contract. However, special tooling or equipment that was for specific use on the contract should be charged directly to the contract if it is not allocable to other work.

Settlement Expenses

The cost principles recognize that certain costs will be incurred, as a direct result of a termination, that would not have been incurred under normal contract performance. These specifically include the costs associated with stopping performance, terminating and settling subcontracts and costs associated with preparing and settling the termination proposal. FAR 31.205-42 (g) provides that the following are generally allowable.

(i) accounting, legal, clerical, and similar costs reasonably necessary for the preparation and presentation to contracting officers of settlement claims and supporting data with respect to the terminated portion of the contract, and for the termination and settlement of subcontracts.

(ii) reasonable costs for storage, transportation, protection, and disposition of property acquired for the contract; and

(iii) indirect costs related to salary and wages incurred as settlement expenses in (i) and (ii); normally, such indirect costs shall be limited to payroll taxes, fringe benefits, occupancy costs, and immediate supervision.

Another cost may be severance pay for employees who would have worked on the terminated contract.

During its existence the Cost Accounting Standards Board (CASB) (which is discussed in Chapter 8) studied the art of accounting for the costs of terminated contracts. While the CASB did not issue a standard on the subject, it sent a letter to the Department of Defense summarizing the results of the research of the CASB staff.[18] The CASB staff advised the DAR Council in November 1978 that its study revealed that the problems were related to allowability and reasonableness rather than allocability; accordingly, it was suspending further work and abandoning the project. The letter suggested several minor DAR revisions to: (1) require contractors to account for costs related to termination in a separate final cost objective established for such costs, (2) make more "explicit" the provisions to obtain uniform treatment in allocating indirect costs as settlement expenses, and (3) sharpen up the requirements concerning allocating indirect expenses to the cost of settlements with subcontractors.

Some two years later, the DAR Council published the following as a new subparagraph 15-205.42(f)(2): "When settlement expenses of a termination are significant, a separate cost account(s) or work order(s) shall be established to accumulate and identify these expenses separately." FPR1-15.205.42 was similarly revised in 1982, and comparable language was also incorporated into the FAR 31.205-42 (g) (2).

This separation of settlement expenses from other expenses is the responsibility of the contractor. One area that should be specifically considered is legal and accounting fees. Legal and accounting fees incurred in connection with the settlement of a terminated contract, including the preparation of the settlement proposal, are acceptable settlement expenses. Other legal fees are not. This was addressed in great detail in *A.C.E.S., Inc.*[19] where the ASBCA, in relying on prior cases, noted:

> For recovery of legal fees as settlement expenses, claimants have been required to make a showing that the legal expenses claimed were incurred in "settlement negotiations with the contracting officer" . . as distinguished from litigation or other nonsettlement activities.

Accordingly, when a notice of termination is received, a separate account or work order should be established to collect and maintain separate identification of legal and accounting fees associated with the termination. Because of the highly specialized nature of terminations these expenses are normally incurred and reimbursed if properly segregated.

The boards[20] and courts have generally allowed outside legal and accounting fees as settlement expenses when the following conditions exist:

> Both the rate per hour and the time charged are reasonable considering the complexity of the termination claim and nature of the work performed.

> The contractor has limited experience in government contracts in general or in termination claims in particular and the outside legal and accounting advisors have the necessary expertise.

> Services performed are consistent with the level of expertise.

> Time charged is supported by records indicating specific descriptions of activities performed.

Other significant issues related to the allowability of settlement expenses should be kept in mind. Anyone involved in supporting a termination settlement proposal should keep a contemporaneous record of time charged to the termination and identify the specific activity performed. Also, any costs normally charged to overhead or G&A expenses should be excluded from such indirect expenses if the costs are charged directly as a settlement expense.

The government may attempt to disallow a portion of settlement expenses on the basis that such expenses represent an unreasonable percentage of the total claim. The boards have generally concluded that the reasonableness of settlement expenses will be determined by analysis of the specific expenses claimed and not by an arbitrary percentage amount.

Cost Principles

In calculating the costs to be included in termination settlement proposals, questions often arise as to which cost principles govern. The FAR Part 49 termination provisions discuss a fairness concept in a broad sense, while the government has often used the precise tests found in the cost principles. The *General Electric Company*[21] case has established that the answer is somewhere in between. In that case the ASBCA stated: "To dispose of this appeal, we now turn to the fatal flaw in the Government's position: its reliance exclusively on strict accounting principles and the standards of ASPR Section XV." The ASBCA, in this case, relied upon *Codex Corporation v. United States*[22] which overturned a prior ASBCA decision,[23] which had ruled that the Section 15 (now Part 31 of the FAR) cost principles governed. In referring to the Codex Court of Claims decision, the ASBCA stated:

> The court held, not that section 8-301 "governs" a termination settlement, "but that the application of the cost principles in part 2 of section 15 .. must be made 'subject to the general policies set forth'" in section 8-301.

> The decision in *Codex Corporation v. United States, supra,* states in part that the "proper reconciliation of the strict standard of allowable costs" in ASPR Section XV and the "fairness concept" in section 8-301 "is a matter primarily within the discretion of the Board." This discretion is conferred upon this Board, not because we are a dispenser of discretionary equity, which we are not, but because of our responsibility to adjudicate *de novo* contract disputes involving questions of allowable costs strictly in accordance with the terms of the contract and applicable law and regulations. In this case, the applicable regulations is ASPR 8-214, which, by its express terms, mandates consideration of the fair compensation policies of section 8-301.

PROFIT

As we previously noted, part of the settlement of a contract terminated for the convenience of the government includes the negotiation of the profit on preparations made (e.g., initial costs) and the work that was actually performed (but not including settlement expenses). Anticipatory profits and consequential damages are not allowed. Any reasonable method may be used to arrive at a fair settlement. Generally, the factors to be considered in determining the profit in a termination for convenience action are not unlike those considered in other pricing actions for contract changes. While many of these relate to the contract as a whole, special consideration should be given to the relative complexity of the tasks and risk performed in the early stages of a contract. Generally, management attention and financial investments are greater in the early periods of contract performance than the later stages of performance. The proposed profit settlement should reflect any such differences.

However, FAR 49.203 provides that if a contractor would have suffered a loss on a contract if it were completed, then that anticipated rate of loss shall be reflected in the termination settlement.. This is to assure that the termination of a contract is not used as a "bail out" from a contract loss by the contractor.

In the case where a contract is terminated during the early stages of contract performance, the government may have to assume that the contract, if performed to anticipated completion, would have resulted in a profit. However, if a substantial amount of the work has been performed or substantial costs have been incurred, the government will likely attempt to estimate the total costs that would have been incurred had the contract been completed in order to determine whether or not a loss would have been experienced. While the government may request that the contractor prepare this estimate to complete the contract, there is no contractual obligation to do so. Whether it should be done or not depends on the specific circumstances of each case. If the government prepares an estimate to complete, consideration will be given to expected production efficiencies.[24] This has been interpreted to mean that, among other things, the application of learning-curve theory shall be considered.

If it has been determined that a loss would have been experienced, the loss adjustment is developed by relating the contract price to the total estimated costs that would have been incurred had the contract been completed. The resulting percentage will be applied, by the government, to those costs accepted by the government (excluding settlement expenses) to determine the total termination costs allowed outside of settlement expenses. Profit will not be allowed.

If the contract can be shown to be one that was impossible to perform, the loss adjustment would not be appropriate. In *Scope Electronics, Inc.*[25] the ASBCA stated: "The fact that the appellant performed unsuccessfully in a loss position has no effect on the termination allowance since we are convinced that performance of this contract was objectively impossible." Accordingly, all reasonable costs incurred, even if contract performance would be anticipated to produce a loss, are fully recoverable.

UNABSORBED OVERHEAD

Separate and special attention is warranted on the subject of unabsorbed overhead. Chapter 11 includes formulas computing equitable price adjustments as a result of delays, disruptions and other instances where the government acted (or failed to act) in such a manner as to cause a contractor to incur increased costs. In many instances proposed equitable price adjustments appropriately include unabsorbed overhead and, generally, it is only the computation method which is in dispute.

What is unabsorbed overhead? In the case of equitable price adjustments resulting from delays or disruptions, the courts and boards of contract appeals have defined it simply as the additional amount of overhead which ongoing contracts had to bear because the contractor could not continue working on a contract due to government action. Thus, the other contracts each had to pick up a portion of the overhead which would have otherwise been absorbed by the delayed contract. It is important to note that there is no need to demonstrate that the total overhead increased.

Why is unabsorbed overhead accepted by boards of contract appeals and courts in the case of delays and disruptions, even when the time frame exceeds a year, but not accepted by them in the case of complete terminations? This is a difficult question. Answers are not to be found in either the statutes or regulations which are silent on this issue. The answers are found only in what attorneys call "case law," decisions by judicial and quasijudicial bodies.

In *Chamberlain Manufacturing Corp.*,[26] the ASBCA concluded:

> The continuing costs to which ASPR 15-205.42 refers clearly are only those costs directly related to the terminated contract which cannot reasonably be shut off immediately upon termination. It is obvious that appellant's overhead is a cost which will

continue so long as appellant continues to exist as an ongoing organization and is thus not directly related to the terminated contract. . . . Moreover, the continuation of overhead after a termination is a common occurrence and if the drafters of the regulation had intended to allow such costs they could have done so simply and clearly as they did for rental costs.

In thus circumscribing those continuing costs which are allowable, the regulation is neither unfair nor inequitable. In practical effect, if claims such as presented by appellant were allowed the Government would be guaranteeing a contractor's overhead costs, without receiving any benefit therefrom, as a "penalty" for exercising its contractual rights.

In *Pioneer Recovery Systems, Inc.,*[27] the ASBCA expanded on the above cited decision in observing:

the board recognizes that in individual instances the impact of a termination on overhead absorption may be practially indistinguishable from the impact of a comparable suspension of work, where unabsorbed overhead may be recoverable. But, in view of the innumerable circumstances in which delays or terminations may result in under absorption, or even "over absorption" (e.g., opportunity for other more profitable business), and in view of the long standing precedent, construing ASPR 15-205.42, any change in the rule should be a matter for regulatory consideration.

Tracing the subject to the mass terminations following World War II, we find no written prohibition against unabsorbed overhead and in practice it was generally allowed. The first edition of ASPR did not specifically address this subject nor did the subsequent revisions. In 1965, after experiencing problems with contract auditors and contracting officers, industry rquested the ASPR committee to address this subject but the DOD policy group refused. It suggested that perhaps a problem really did not exist. In any case, it gave no indication as to whether it was for or against allowing unabsorbed overhead when contracts were completely terminated. In 1971 industry tried again, this time in a recommendation to the Commission on Government Procurement. The Council of Defense and Space Industry Associations requested formal recognition to be given to continuing costs under contracts terminated for the convenience of the government, including "unabsorbed ongoing fixed overhead which would have to be unfairly absorbed against other business of the contractor, if not allowed on the termination claim."

Industry's efforts remained unsuccessful, but about that time certain government officials took the initiative and proposed an ASPR revision to specifically cite unabsorbed overhead as unallowable under terminated contracts. A subcommittee was persuaded but the ASPR committee again closed the case without a definitive decision.

As discussed earlier, the subject of accounting for terminated contracts, with particular emphasis on unabsorbed overhead, was brought to the attention of the Cost Accounting Standards Board staff when that group was exploring areas suitable for promulgating standards. The assigned project manager saw this problem as just a small part of a much larger subject and, after considerable time, distributed for comment an issues paper on Accounting for Capacity-Related Costs. The project was later abandoned without promulgation of any cost accounting standards on the subject.

The cost of the disruptive effects of partial terminations can generally be adequately recovered at least to the extent of obtaining equitable price adjustments for the unterminated portion. Here again, there is not much to be found in law or regulation and one must look to case law. Without quite spelling it out, the boards of contract appeals and the courts have looked sympathetically at unabsrobed overhead in determining the cost of the unterminated items as they have in instances of delays and disruptions attributable to the government. When it comes to a complete termination, however, somehow all the ground-rules and philosophy change.

Attempts to recover unabsorbed overhead for a period of, say, six months, while new business is pursued to fill the void left by a major contract completely terminated by the government for its convenience, encounter heavy obstacles. On the other hand, chances are infinitely better for recovering unabsorbed overhead for a much longer period when the void is caused by work stoppage on a contract.

SUMMARY

For companies contracting with the Federal Government, the possibility that the contract may be terminated is a "fact of life." While the results are usually less than desired when a termination does occur, there are several actions which must be taken to mitigate any adverse impact. Paramount among these is a nccd to evaluate the contractor's financial position at the time of the termination and the reasons for that position. This may entail redefining thc appropriate accounting practices that must be used to measure the results of operations for the terminated work. After this, the process of negotiating a settlement can begin using the procedures appropriate to this unique environment.

NOTES

1. United States V. Corliss Steam-Engine Company, 91 U.S. 3211 (1876).
2. G.L. Charistian and Associates v. United States, 160 Ct. Cl. 1 January 11, 1963, 9 CCF 71,964; Cert. denied, 375 U.S. 954 (1963, 9 CCF 72,180.
3. Colonial Metals Company v. United States, 204 Ct. Cl. 320, April 17, 1974, 20 CCF 82,973.
4. Ronald A. Torncello & Soledaad Enterprises, Inc. v. United States, (Ct. Cl. 1982), June 16, 1982, 30 CCF 70,005.
5. Automated Services, Inc., DOT BCA No. 1753, November 25, 1986, 87-1 BCA 19,459.
6. Lockley Manufacturing Co., Inc., ASBCA no. 21231, January 26, 1978, 78-1 BCA 12,987.
7. Algonac Manufacturing Company, ASBCA no. 10534, August 1, 1966, 66-2 BCA 5,731.
8. Clary Corporation, ASBCA no. 19274, November 1, 1974, 74-2 BCA 10,947.
9. Baifield Industries, Division of A-T-O, Inc., ASBCA no. 20006, August 18, 1976, 76-2 BCA 12,096.
10. Southland Manufacturing Corp., ASBCA no. 16830, November 29, 1974, 75-1 BCA 10,944.
11. New York Shipbuilding Co., A Division of Merritt-Chapman & Scott Corp., ASBCA no. 15443, December 21, 1972, 73-1 BCA 9,852.
12. Lowell O. West Lumber Sales, ASBCA no. 10879, January 18, 1967. 67-1 BCA 6,101.
13. Baifield Industries, Division of A-T-O, Inc., supra note 9.
14. Fiesta Leasing and Sales, Inc., ASBCA no. 29311, January 30, 1987, 871-BCA 19,622.
15. Baifield Industries, Division of A-T-O, Inc., supra note 9.
16. Southland Manufacturing Corp., supra note 10.
17. Celesco Industries, Inc., ASBCA no. 22460, March 30, 1984, 84-2 BCA 17,295.
18. Cost Accounting Standards Board, minutes of meeting no. 67, November 3, 1978.
19. A.C.E.S., Inc., ASBCA no. 21417. March 23, 1979, 79-1 BCA 13,809.
20. Fiesta Leasing and Sales Inc. supra note 14.
21. General Electric Company, ASBCA no. 24111, March 29, 1982, 82-1 BCA 15,725.
22. Codex Corporation v. United States (Ct. Cl. 1981) February 24, 1981, 28 CCF 81,099.
23. Codex Corporation, ASBCA no. 17983, August 26, 1974, 74-2 BCA 10,827, recon. den. October 22, 1975, 75-2 BCA 11,554.
24. Codex Corporation v. United States, supra note 24.
25. Scope Electronics, Inc. ASBCA no. 20359, February 16, 1977, 77-1 BCA 12,404.

26. Chamberlain Manufacturing Corporation, ASBCA no. 16877, June 22, 1973, 73-2 BCA 10,139 (See also Nolan Brothers, Inc., v. United States, 194 Ct. Cl. 1, February 19, 1971, 16 CCF 80,119; KDI Precision Products, Inc., ASBCA no. 21522, January 15, 1979, 79-1 BCA 13,640; Celesco Industries, Inc., supra note 18; Technology, Incorporated, ASBCA no. 14083, June 28, 1971, 71-2 BCA 8,956, recon. den. January 18, 1972, 72-1 BCA 9,281.
27. Pioneer Recovery Systems, Inc., ASBCA no. 24658, February 20, 1981, 81-1 BCA 15,059.

Chapter Thirteen
Contract Audit Reviews

BACKGROUND

As previously mentioned in Chapter 2, the Defense Contract Audit Agency is the principal contract audit organization for the Federal Government. The principle activities of DCAA include virtually every stage of the procurement process such as:

Reviewing pricing proposals.

Auditing costs incurred under flexibly-priced government contracts, including reviews of the economy and efficiency of contractor operations (e.g. "operations audits").

Reviewing the adequacy of contractor's accounting and financial management systems and estimating procedures.

Reviewing contractor compliance with cost accounting standards.

Auditing contractor compliance with the Truth in Negotiations Act, Public Law 87-653.

The DCAA Contract Audit Manual[1] (CAM) (see Fig. 13.1 for the table of contents) contains audit guidance, audit techniques, audit standards, policies, and procedures to be followed by DCAA personnel in the performance of the contract audit function. The CAM, is a comprehensive document that provides valuable insight into CAA's reasons for performing various type of audits.

AUDIT AUTHORITY

Contract Audits

Audits by contract auditors are generally performed in two broad situations. The first situation involves the submission of a proposal prior to award of a contract. When a contractor submits cost or pricing data to support a proposal,

Foreword & Contents
Introduction to the DCAA Contract Audit Manual
Abbreviations
Revisions
Topical Index

Figure 13.1. DCAA Contract Audit Manual Contents

7-500 Section 5 Insurance Costs
7-600 Section 6 Pension Costs
7-700 Section 7 Patent and Royalty Costs
7-800 Section 8 Labor Settlement and Strike Period Costs
7-900 Section 9 Employee Training and Educational Costs
7-1000 Section 10 Employee Travel and Relocation costs
7-1100 Section 11 Dues, Memberships, and Conference Costs
7-1200 Section 12 Publications and Public Relations Costs
7-1300 Section 13 Selling Costs
7-1400 Section 14 Taxes
7-1500 Section 15 Independent Research and Development and Bid and Proposal Costs
7-1600 Section 16 Warranty and/or Correction of Defect Costs
7-1700 Section 17 Business Combination Costs
7-1800 Section 18 Accounting for Joint Ventures—Reserved
7-1900 Section 19 Other Areas of Cost

8-000 Chapter 8 Cost Accounting Standards
8-100 Section 1 Overview of Cost Accounting Standards Rules and Regulations
8-200 Section 2 Review of Disclosure Statements for Adequacy
8-300 Section 3 Compliance with Cost Accounting Standards Board (CASB) Rules, Regulations and Standards and with DAR Section XV
8-400 Section 4 Cost Accounting Standards
8-500 Section 5 Review of Cost Impact Proposals Submitted Pursuant to the Cost Accounting Standards Clause

9-000 Chapter 9 Review of Cost Estimates and Price Proposals
9-100 Section 1 Administrative Procedures for Field Pricing Support
9-200 Section 2 Evaluating the Adequacy of Cost or Pricing Data in the Proposal—Reserved
9-300 Section 3 General Evaluation Procedures for Estimates
9-400 Section 4 Evaluation of Direct Material Cost Estimates
9-500 Section 5 Evaluation of Direct Labor Cost Estimates
9-600 Section 6 Evaluation of Other Direct Cost Estimates
9-700 Section 7 Evaluation of Indirect Cost Estimates
9-800 Section 8 Economic Considerations in Price Proposals
9-900 Section 9 Profit in Price Proposals
9-1000 Section 10 Review of Parametric Cost Estimates
9-1100 Section 11 Joint Team Surveys of Contractor Estimating Systems
9-1200 Section 12 Forward Pricing Rate Agreements—Reserved
9-1300 Section 13 Should-Cost Team Reviews

10-000 Chapter 10 Preparation and Distribution of Audit Reports
10-100 Section 1 Principles of Effective Writing
10-200 Section 2 Common Elements of Audit Reports
10-300 Section 3 Audit Reports on Pricing Proposals
10-400 Section 4 Audit Reports on Functional/Operational Reviews
10-500 Section 5 Audit Reports on Annual Indirect Costs
10-600 Section 6 Audit Reports on Postaward Reviews of Cost or Pricing Data
10-700 Section 7 Audit Reports on Termination Settlement Proposals
10-800 Section 8 Audit Reports on Cost Accounting Standards Matters
10-900 Section 9 Final Audit Reports on Cost-Reimbursement Type Contracts and Subcontracts
10-1000 Section 10 Audit Reports on Interim and Final Price Redetermination Proposals under FPR/FPI Contracts and Subcontracts—Reserved
10-1100 Section 11 Audit Reports on Claims—Reserved
10-1200 Section 12 Audit Reports on Other Matters
10-S10 Suppl. General Purpose Address Lists for Audit Reports

11-000 Chapter 11 Review of Contractor Compliance with Contract Financial Management Requirements
11-100 Section 1 Review of Contractor Compliance with "Limitation of Cost" and "Limitation on Payments" Clauses
11-200 Section 2 Review of Contractor Compliance with Cost/Schedule Control Systems Criteria

Figure 13.1. (Continued)

11-300 Section 3 Review of Contractor Compliance with DoD Program Management Systems Reporting Requirements
12-000 Chapter 12 Audits in Connection with Terminated Contracts
12-100 Section 1 General
12-200 Section 2 Audit Guidance, Terminated Contracts—General
12-300 Section 3 Audit of Terminated Fixed-Price Contracts
12-400 Section 4 Audit of Terminated Cost-Type Contracts
13-000 Chapter 13 Contract Audits at Educational Institutions
13-100 Section 1 Federal Audit Agency Cognizance at Educational Institutions
13-200 Section 2 Contract Regulations Applicable to Educational Institutions
13-300 Section 3 General Concepts for Audit of Costs at Educational Institutions
13-400 Section 4 Audit of Direct Costs at Educational Institutions
13-500 Section 5 Audit of Indirect Costs at Educational Institutions
13-600 Section 6 Administrative Procedures for Establishing Indirect Cost Rates at Educational Institutions
13-700 Section 7 Audit Reports on Educational Institutions
13-S10 Supplement-Federal Cost Principles for Educational Institutions
14-000 Chapter 14 Other Contract Audit Assignments
14-100 Section 1 Postaward Reviews of Cost or Pricing Data Under PL 87-653
14-200 Section 2 Review of Contract Claims
14-300 Section 3 Review of Contractor Cash Flow Forecasts
14-400 Section 4 Contract Audits of Government Property
14-500 Section 5 Other Special Purpose Audits
15-000 Chapter 15 Other DCAA Functions
15-100 Section 1 Special Administrative Procedures for Non-DoD Agencies
15-200 Section 2 Contract Audit Coordinator Program
15-300 Section 3 Procurement Liaison Auditor Services
15-400 Section 4 Audit Support of Negotiation Conferences
15-500 Section 5 Special Procedures for Actual or Potential Board of Contract Appeals (BCA) Cases
15-600 Section 6 Contract Audit Followup

APPENDIXES
A-000 Appendix A Contract Cost Principles and Procedures
A-100 Cross Index—FAR, DAR, DFARS Contract Cost Principles and Procedures
A-200 Defense Acquisition Regulation—Section 15—Contract Cost Principles and Procedures
A-300 Federal Acquisition Regulation—Part 31—Contract Cost Principles and Procedures
A-400 DoD FAR Supplement—Part 31—Contract Cost Principles and Procedures
B-000 Appendix B Statistical Sampling Techniques
B-100 Section 1 Impact of Other Sources of Reliance on Amount of Sampling
B-200 Section 2 Design of the Sampling Plan
B-300 Section 3 Random Selection Procedures
B-400 Section 4 Sampling for Attributes
B-500 Section 5 Sampling for Variables
C-000 Appendix C Electronic Data Processing Systems
C-100 Section 1 Background on Automatic Data Processing Systems
C-200 Section 2 Design of Automated Systems
C-300 Section 3 Audit Trails in Automated Systems
C-400 Section 4 Surveying Automated Systems
C-500 Section 5 Auditing Automated Systems Data
D-000 Appendix D Reserved
E-000 Appendix E Graphic and Computational Analysis Techniques
E-100 Section 1 Correlation and the Use of Scatter Diagrams
E-200 Section 2 Regression and Correlation Analysis
E-300 Section 3 Time Series Charts
E-400 Section 4 Audit Applications of Graphic and Computational Techniques
F-000 Appendix F Improvement Curve Analysis Techniques
F-100 Section 1 The Improvement Curve Theory
F-200 Section 2 Types of Improvement Curves

Figure 13.1. (Continued)

Figure 13.1. (Continued)

the government generally requires that the contractor grant to the contracting officer or authorized representatives the right to examine books, records, documents, and other data submitted, along with related computations and projections. Submission of a standard government proposal form automatically grants this right to review, prior to contract award. The instructions contained in FAR 15.804-6(b) for preparing Standard Form 1411, Contract Pricing Proposal Cover Sheet, provide that:

> By submitting offeror's proposal, the offeror if selected for negotiation, grants the contracting officer or an authorized representative the right to examine those books, records, documents and other supporting data that will permit adequate evaluation of the proposed price. This right may be exercised at any time before award.

Proposals for products or services that are exempt from the cost or pricing data requirement on the basis of established catalog or market price, or price set by law or regulation, require submission of Standard Form 1412 (Figure 5.1), which includes a preaward provision for verification of submitted data pertaining to the exemption.

Once the contract is awarded, the audit-sealed bidding (Figure 13.2) and audit negotiation (Figure 13.3) clauses provide to the government the right to audit costs after contract award to determine the accuracy, completeness, and currency of cost or pricing data submitted. These "audits" may take place at any time after contract award and prior to the expiration of three years from the date of final payment of the contract.

The other general situation in which the government has the right to audit is when payments are to be based on incurred costs. The audit negotiation clause specifically addresses the government's right to audit a contractor's books and records to ensure that direct and indirect costs are properly claimed for reimbursement on flexibly priced contracts. When either interim or final payments are based on the incurrence of costs, such as progress payments on fixed-price contracts or reimbursement of cost on cost reimbursement type contracts, the government also establishes a contractual right to audit by including specific clauses to that effect, such as the progress payments clause (Figure 9.2) and the allowable cost and payment clause (Figure 10.9).

The government's right of audit access to records has been defined to some extent by both the boards of contract appeals and the courts. In *Grumman Aircraft Engineering Corporation*,[2] the government disapproved certain costs

(a) *Cost or pricing data.* If the Contractor has submitted cost or pricing data in connection with the pricing of any modification to this contract, unless the pricing was based on adequate price competition, established catalog or market prices of commercial items sold in substantial quantities to the general public, or prices set by law or regulation, the Contracting Officer or a representative who is an employee of the Government shall have the right to examine and audit all books, records, documents, and other data of the Contractor (including computations and projections) related to negotiating, pricing or performing the modification, in order to evaluate the accuracy, completeness, and currency of the cost or pricing data. In the case of pricing any modification, the Comptroller General of the United States or a representative who is an employee of the Government shall have the same rights.

(b) *Availability.* The Contractor shall make available at its office at all reasonable times the materials described in paragraph (a) above, for examination, audit, or reproduction, until 3 years after final payment under this contract, or for any other period specified in Subpart 4.7 of the Federal Acquisition Regulation (FAR). FAR Subpart 4.7, Contractor Records Retention, in effect on the date of this contract, is incorporated by reference in its entirety and made a part of this contract.

(1) If this contract is completely or partially terminated, the records relating to the work terminated shall be made available for 3 years after any resulting final termination settlement.

(2) Records pertaining to appeals under the Disputes clause or to litigation or the settlement of claims arising under or relating to the performance of this contract shall be made available until disposition of such appeals, litigation, or claims.

(c) The Contractor shall insert a clause containing all the provisions of this clause, including this paragraph (c), in all subcontracts over $10,000 under this contract, altering the clause only as necessary to identify properly the contracting parties and the contracting office under the Government prime contract.

Figure 13.2. Audit—sealed bidding clause, FAR 52.214-26.

(a) *Examination of costs.* If this is a cost-reimbursement, incentive, time-and-materials, labor-hour, or price-redeterminable contract, or any combination of these, the Contractor shall maintain—and the Contracting Officer or representatives of the Contracting Officer shall have the right to examine and audit—books, records, documents, and other evidence and accounting procedures and practices, sufficient to reflect properly all costs claimed to have been incurred or anticipated to be incurred in performing this contract. This right of examination shall include inspection at all reasonable times of the Contractor's plants, or parts of them, engaged in performing the contract.

(b) *Cost or pricing data.* If, pursuant to law, the Contractor has been required to submit cost or pricing data in connection with pricing this contract or any modification to this contract, the Contracting Officer or representatives of the Contracting Officer who are employees of the Government shall have the right to examine and audit all books, records, documents, and other data of the Contractor (including computations and projections) related to negotiating, pricing, or performing the contract or modification, in order to evaluate the accuracy, completeness, and currency of the cost or pricing data. The right of examination shall extend to all documents necessary to permit adequate evaluation of the cost or pricing data submitted, along with the computations and projections used.

(c) *Reports.* If the Contractor is required to furnish cost, funding, or performance reports, the Contracting Officer or representatives of the Contracting Officer who are employees of the Government shall have the right to examine and audit books, records, other documents, and supporting materials, for the purpose of evaluating (1) the effectiveness of the Contractor's policies and procedures to produce data compatible with the objectives of these reports and (2) the data reported.

(d) *Availability.* The Contractor shall make available at its office at all reasonable times the materials described in paragraphs (a) and (b) above, for examination, audit, or reproduction, until 3 years after final payment under this contract, or for any shorter period specified in Subpart 4.7, Contractor Records Retention, of the Federal Acquisition Regulation, or for any longer period required by statute or by other clauses of this contract. In addition—

(1) If this contract is completely or partially terminated, the records relating to the work terminated shall be made available for 3 years after any resulting final termination settlement; and

(2) Records relating to appeals under the Disputes clause or to litigation or the settlement of claims arising under or relating to this contract shall be made available until such appeals, litigation, or claims are disposed of.

(e) The Contractor shall insert a clause containing all the terms of this clause, including this paragraph (e), in all subcontracts over $10,000 under this contract, altering the clause only as necessary to identify properly the contracting parties and the Contracting Officer under the Government prime contract.

Figure 13.3. Audit—negotiation clause, FAR 52.215-2.

because of the contractor's refusal to make franchise tax returns available. The tax returns directly supported the franchise tax expenses that were included in the indirect expense rates allocated to the contractor's cost reimbursable type contracts. The ASBCA stated in its decision:

> When it entered into these cost-type contracts, appellant agreed "to maintain books, records, documents and other evidence pertaining to the costs and expenses of this contract (hereinafter collectively called the 'records') to the extent and in such detail as will properly reflect all net costs, direct and indirect, of labor, materials, equipment, supplies and services, and other costs and expenses of whatever nature for which reimbursement is claimed under the provisions of this contract." It is also agreed "to make available . . . any of the records for inspection, audit or reproduction by any authorized representative of the Department or of the Comptroller General." That language is broadly inclusive. We would find it difficult to say that the Franchise Tax Return is not a "document" or "evidence pertaining to the costs and expenses of this contract."
>
> This is not a situation in which the government is asking that the contractor create new records or establish a new recordkeeping system. It is asking to see a document which is already in existence. The appellant, in essence, is responding that it will decide how much the Government auditor needs to see and which of the documents in its files are pertinent and proper for the auditor's perusal.
>
> At the same time the Government agrees to pay a contractor's cost of contract performance, it also reserves the right to satisfy itself with reasonable certainty what those costs truly are. When a contractor's obligation is to deliver the Government something for a competitively-arrived-at fixed price, it retains the right to keep its own counsel and strict privacy as to its cost of delivering that item. When, on the other hand, a contractor enters into a contract in which the Government agrees essentially to pay him what it costs him to perform, that contractor has also invited the Government into his office to determine what those costs are. Thereafter a Government auditor looks over his shoulder. The marriage of Government auditor and contractor is not easily dissoluble. That auditor certainly has no right to roam without restriction through all the contractor's business documents which have no connection with the government contract. But he has a right to satisfy himself as to items claimed to be part of the costs of performing the government contract. When the claim is as to an overhead or indirect cost, there may be some necessity to look at entries other than those of labor, material, and equipment used directly in the performance of the Government contract. We conceive of the audit function, when it applies, as a broad rather than a narrow one.

In a later case, *SCM Corporation* v. *United States*,[3] the Court of Claims upheld the government's right to refuse to reimburse the contractor for claimed costs incurred on a cost reimbursable type contract because of undue restrictions that the contractor placed on the conduct of the audit. The contractor had refused to let the DCAA auditors:

> Notate in their working papers such information as vendor names or employee names and compensation.
>
> Make copies of any company documents.
>
> Remove their working papers from the contractor's premises without the contractor's review and consent.

The Court upheld the ASBCA's prior decision that the contractor was not entitled to reimbursement of its costs until it allowed the government to perform a proper audit of its claim. The Court concluded that the audit procedures used by the auditors were in accordance with generally accepted auditing standards and within the scope of the "audit" clause in the contract and that nothing in the contract entitled the contractor to payment for costs incurred without an unrestricted audit.

As these cases show, the government does not have the right to roam unrestricted; but the right of access to records is fairly broad where the requested information directly or indirectly supports costs claimed for reimbursement on flexibly priced contracts. However, these two cases do address very limited situations: one where a contractor declined to furnish a document directly supporting an expenditure allocated to a CPFF contract and the other where a contractor unreasonably refused to permit the auditors to copy pertinent information in their working papers or carry such working papers out of the contractor's facility.

In connection with flexibly priced contracts, the "audit" clause refers to ". . . books, records, documents and other evidence and accounting procedures and practices, sufficient to reflect properly all costs claimed to have been incurred or anticipated to be incurred in performing this contract." In connection with the review of cost or pricing data, the clause refers to "all books, records, documents and other data . . . related to negotiating, pricing or performing contract or modification. . . ." Numerous controversies have surfaced over whether a literal interpretation of these words requires unlimited access to such records as board of directors' minutes, internal audit reports and working papers, management letters submitted by CPA firms, long term business forecasts, and nonfinancial records pertinent to the performance of operations audits.

In 1985 the DOD Inspector General subpoenaed Westinghouse Electric Corporation's internal audit reports. The issue involved a number of formal actions, including the following chronological events:

DCAA's request for access to the contractor's internal audit reports.

The contractor's denial of access to such records.

DCAA's disallowance of the cost of the contractor's internal audit department.

The contractor's appeal to the ASBCA of the DCAA cost disallowance.

DCAA's request that the DOD IG issue a subpoena requiring the contractor to produce the requested records.

The DOD IG's issuance of a subpoena for "any and all documents" generated by the contractor's internal audit department to be turned over to DCAA.

The contractor's refusal to comply with the subpoena and subsequent appeal to the District Court.

The Court emphatically rejected the contractor's argument that the DODIG issued the subpoena not for his own purpose but only to force the contractor to hand over the records to DCAA. In concluding that the subpoena was issued as a tool of the DO DIG, not a tool of DCAA, the Court relied on testimony by the DODIG that he had "taken over" the DCAA audit and that one of the DOD Assistant IGs had been directed to report on the progress of the audit.

The Court clearly considered this action to be appropriate, for the decision notes that:

> . . . even if . . . the DCAA is an independent component of the DOD, it is completely available for use when called upon by the IG both as a source of information and to carry out investigative delegations and assignments. . . .
> Through the magical dexterity of Congress . . . the nineteen thousand auditors and investigators in the scattered, disjointed DOD agencies were brought under the inde-

pendent authority of the IG who could more effectively combat fraud, waste, abuse, and mismanagement. . .

While it may be that the IG should not have used the DCAA because the DCAA had reasons of its own for getting information about internal audit reports, it was nevertheless a discretionary right which Congress had given him, lacking his own personnel with which to act. . . . Under such circumstances, it is not for this court to forbid the IG from using DCAA employees. . . .[4]

Because the case involved an IG subpoena rather than a DCAA request for access to records, the question of whether internal audit reports and workpapers constituted records which must be furnished pursuant to the audit clause was never addressed.

The Court clearly distinguished the IG's broader access rights from DCAA's potentially more limited access rights by noting:"Whether or not the DCAA itself has any rights to access of such records as demanded, which the respondent has refused, is of no concern to this enforcement proceeding."

The District Court decision was sustained on appeal.

The implications of this decision, coupled with DCAA's subsequent action requesting the DOD IG to issue subpoenas for internal audits of other contractors and subsequent legislation granting DCAA its own subpoena power, are clearly ominous, raising such questions as:

Will the roles of the IG and DCAA become so blurred that it is difficult to say who is directing the contract audit function?

Will the limitations on government access to records that are contained in the audit clause cease to be considered when the records are the subject of a subpoena?

Will the use of subpoenas (issued either by the DODIG or DCAA) be confined to internal audit reports or expanded to cover corporate board of director minutes, special studies performed by outside consultants, executive correspondence files, and other documents which may not be related either directly or indirectly to costs charged to government contracts?

Some of these questions were answered (at least on an interim basis) after DCAA served a subpoena on Newport News Shipbuilding and Dry Dock Company (Newport News) on October 24, 1986, demanding that Newport News produce certain internal audit materials. These materials included schedules of performed and planned audits, audit working papers, audit reports, follow-up actions on expense reports, and time-charging records of the internal auditors. Newport News refused to provide the internal audit materials and DCAA filed a petition for summary enforcement of the subpoena in the U.S. District Court for the Eastern District of Virginia.

The Court concluded that the subpoena power granted to DCAA did not expand DCAA's access to records but merely provided DCAA with subpoena authority for enforcement of its existing access rights. The Court distinguished this situation from Westinghouse where the DOD Inspector General, using the broad statutory subpoena granted by the IG Act, subpoenaed Westinghouse's internal audit reports and chose to turn them over to DCAA for review. In the Newport News case, the Court agreed with the contractor that DCAA lacks the authority to subpoena certain internal records. It concluded that:

When the DCAA's purpose under the statute and subpoena power are viewed along side the Inspector General's statutory purpose and subpoena power, the Court must find that the DCAA is limited to what materials it can and cannot subpoena. Whereas the DCAA's access to contractor records, etc. is limited to pricing and cost data, the Inspector General's subpoena power is not so limited.[5]

Based on the legislative history and the limiting language of the law and implementing regulations, the Court determined that Newport News' internal audit reports are not cost or pricing data. The government has appealed this decision.

In a separate but somewhat related matter, the ASBCA [6] overruled the government's disallowance of the cost of Martin Marietta Corp.'s internal audit department in response to the company's refusal to grant unlimited access to all internal audit reports and working papers. The company routinely provided to DCAA, upon request, reports relating to government contracting areas. Its reservations about unlimited government access to all internal audit reports related (1) to the government's ability to protect sensitive company data from release under the Freedom of Information Act and (2) to SEC requirements concerning the release of inside information about potential acquisitions. In its decision the Board concluded that the cost disallowance was unreasonable and arbitrary. In its view:

> the internal audit documents were not necessary to determine if its costs were properly chargeable to the G&A of the contractor. Thus the suspension of the entire costs of appellant's internal audit function for three fiscal years has no reasonable relationship to the nature of the demand for access to the records or to the appellant's response. Where specific costs are questioned, the Government may suspend payment of such costs but the use of withholding payments, as a club to insure compliance with demands unrelated to the costs suspended must, at the very least, be exercised with discretion.

Just as controversial is the issue of whether the clause grants to government officials the right to question contractor personnel and require them to prepare responses to questionnaires. The DCAA places a major emphasis on the use of interviews as an audit technique. CAM[7] Section 2-307(a) states:

> It is the auditor's responsibility to accumulate sufficient evidence to provide an appropriate factual basis for his conclusions and recommendations. Evidence needed to support the auditor's findings may be (1) observation, photograph, or similar means, (2) interviewing or taking statements from involved persons, (3) documentary evidence consisting of letters, contracts, extracts from books of account, etc, and (4) analysis of information the auditor has obtained. The evidence involved should meet the basic tests of sufficiency, competency, and relevance. . . .

CAM[8] Section 3-105.7 further discusses the use of oral evidence as follows:

> Generally, oral evidence is useful in disclosing situations that may require examination or may corroborate other types of evidence already obtained by the auditor. Oral evidence can determine audit direction and, when appropriate, should be recorded and made part of the audit file. While useful, this type of evidence should not be completely relied upon to support an audit conclusion or opinion; other confirming evidence should generally be used, particularly where the matter is significant.

CAM[9] Section 6-408.3, which delineates specific procedures for performing physical observations (floor checks), instructs the auditor to:

> Determine whether the employee is performing in the proper capacity as direct or indirect labor and whether time is being charged correctly by *discussing the nature of*

the work being performed with the employee and observing the actual work performance. If an employee's time for the prior period was charged to a cost code or work project other than the one he is working on during the floor check and the nature of his work is not such that it obviously entails frequent job changes, the employee should be queried regarding his work assignment in the prior period. This procedure may disclose errors, adjustments or alterations to the prior period labor distribution records which require further analysis. [Emphasis added.]

An April 1, 1981 DCAA Headquarters Memorandum for Regional Directors on the subject of "Floor Checks" further emphasized that:

regardless of the types of audit tests performed, it would appear that interviews of employees are an essential and critical prerequisite to any conclusion on the adequacy, reasonableness, and reliability of labor records. . . .

Given the DCAA emphasis on interviews and floor checks, a carefully managed program regarding government access to records and people becomes even more critical.

Examination of Records by the Comptroller General

The General Accounting Office (GAO) is authorized to audit the books and records of government contractors by a standard clause inserted in virtually all negotiated contracts exceeding $10,000. Under this clause (Fig. 13.4), the contractor agrees, generally until the expiration of three years after final payment under the contract, that the GAO has "access to and the right to examine any of the Contractor's directly pertinent books, documents, papers, or other records involving transactions related to this contract." A clause establishing GAO's authority to perform similar audits of subcontractors is also required in most negotiated subcontracts exceeding $10,000. Although the clause appears constrained by such phrases as "directly pertinent" and "transactions related to this contract", GAO has continually expanded its activities and sought to review many aspects of a contractor's operations. Its efforts have been facilitated by special congressional requests encompassing government programs that extend beyond books and records. However, in *Elmer B. Staats, Comptroller General of the United States, et al.* v. *Bristol Laboratories Division of Bristol-Myers Company*[10] and *Charles A. Bowsher, Comptroller General of the United States, et al., v. Merck Co. Inc.,*[11] the Supreme Court affirmed earlier Court of Appeals decisions that limited GAO's access to directly pertinent contract data by concluding that the "examination of records" clause did not require GAO access to data concerning a company's research, development, marketing, promotion, distribution, and administration costs.

AUDIT APPROACH

Audit Planning

How a contract auditor approaches a specific audit depends in part on the auditor's professional judgment regarding the type of audit to be performed and the contractor being audited. However, guidelines have been established to assist the auditor with the audit planning process. The audit planning process

(a) This clause applies if this contract exceeds $10,000 and was entered into by negotiation.

(b) The Comptroller General of the United States or a duly authorized representative from the General Accounting Office shall, until 3 years after final payment under this contract or for any shorter period specified in Federal Acquisition Regulation (FAR) Subpart 4.7, Contractor Records Retention, have access to and the right to examine any of the Contractor's directly pertinent books, documents, papers, or other records involving transactions related to this contract.

(c) The Contractor agrees to include in first-tier subcontracts under this contract a clause to the effect that the Comptroller General or a duly authorized representative from the General Accounting Office shall, until 3 years after final payment under the subcontract or for any shorter period specified in FAR Subpart 4.7, have access to and the right to examine any of the subcontractor's directly pertinent books, documents, papers, or other records involving transactions related to the subcontract. "Subcontract," as used in this clause, excluded (1) purchase orders not exceeding $10,000 and (2) subcontracts or purchase orders for public utility services at rates established to apply uniformly to the public, plus any applicable reasonable connection charge.

(d) The periods of access and examination in paragraphs (b) and (c) above for records relating to (1) appeals under the Disputes clause. (2) litigation or settlement of claims arising from the performance of this contract, or (3) costs and expenses of this contract to which the Comptroller General or a duly authorized representative from the General Accounting Office has taken exception shall continue until such appeals, litigation, claims, or exceptions are disposed of.

Figure 13.4 .Examination of records by comptroller general clause, FAR 52.215-1.

includes a vulnerability assessment, application of minimum annual audit requirements, and identification of audit leads for the various types of audits to be performed.

Identification of the need for audits may result from a variety of events including:

Audit requests from procurement or administrative agencies.

Contractual requirements.

Contract proposals or modification to existing contracts.

Changes in contractor organization, operations or systems.

Audit leads, or other matters which lead the auditor to believe an audit is necessary to protect the government's interest.

While certain audits may be predictable as the result of such events as submission of a cost proposal, final indirect cost proposal, or voucher, an audit may be internally initiated without a contractor's specific knowledge of the planned audit or understanding of the audit objectives.

Once an audit assignment has been established, the audit planning process is performed to determine the scope of the audit and specific procedures to be applied.

Vulnerability Assessment

Vulnerability assessment is a method of measuring the government's exposure to contractor fraud, waste and error based on the auditor's experience in prior audits and perception of the contractor's systems and internal controls. The assessment process requires that the auditor assign risk factors to a set of questions relative to 10 different categories.

The categories included in the vulnerability assessment, Figure 13.5, generally incorporate prior audit experience, confidence in internal controls and accounting systems, government participation in total business activity, financial condition and allegations of noncompliance with procurement regulations. As risk factors increase, the scope of future audits increase.

Prior DCAA Audit Results:

Suggested criteria for rating this
factor are as follows: *Suggested Range*

Factors	Suggested Range
Contractor location reviewed in past two years and no known incidents of fraud, waste or error.	1-4
Contractor location reviewed prior to last two-year period and no known incidents of fraud, waste or error.	4-5
Contractor location reviewed within last five years and no known incidents of fraud, waste or error.	6-8
Contractor location never reviewed.	7-10
Recent serious incidents of fraud, waste or error detected.	8-10

Contractor location reviewed prior to last
two-year period and known incidents of
fraud, waste or error where corrective action
was:

Accomplished rapidly	1-4
Accomplished very slowly	5-8
Never Accomplished	7-10

Adequacy of Internal Controls:

The adequacy of existing general and accounting
internal controls affecting government business must be
ascertained to rate this factor. When assessing internal
controls the following points should be considered. Do
existing internal controls provide for:

1. Safeguarding of company assets?
2. Reliability of financial records?
3. A system of authorization and approvals?
4. Separation of duties and responsibilities?
5. An organization plan with all the necessary methods
   and procedures to promote operational efficiency and
   assure adherence to prescribed managerial policies?

Suggested criteria for rating the adequacy of internal
control factors are as follows: *Suggested Range*

No internal control weakness noted.	1-3
Minor internal control weakness noted.	4-6
Major internal control weakness noted.	7-10

Adequacy of Accounting System:

Is the contractors' accounting system suitable for properly
costing and administering government contracts including
the capability of providing reasonable data for cost
projections?

Suggested criteria for rating this factor: *Suggested Range*

No accounting system weaknesses noted which affect government business.	1-3
Accounting system weaknesses noted with minor dollar impact on government business.	4-6
Accounting system weaknesses noted with major dollar impact on government business.	7-10

Unusual Trends or Deviations in Financial Figures and Ratios:

Some examples:

The amount of incurred overhead expenses allocated to
government business are disproportionate with the percentage of government sales to the total company sales.

Figure 13.5. DCAA vulnerability assessment.

    The amount of forecasted overhead expenses are significantly out of pattern (with those experienced for a representative base period) without apparent reason(s) for the deviation.

Suggested criteria for rating this factor:	*Suggested Range*
No unusual trends or deviations noted.	1-3
Unusual trends or deviations noted with minor potential dollar impact on government business.	4-6
Unusual trends or deviations noted with major potential dollar impact on government business.	7-10

Mix of Contracts:

    Does the contractor have a mix of commercial work, fixed-price and cost type contracts thus creating conditions for potential mischarging of cost to cost type work?

Suggested criteria for rating this factor:	*Suggested Range*
100% Fixed-Price work	1-3
100% Cost Type work	1-3
75/25 (Fixed-Price/Cost Type)	4-5
50/50 (Fixed-Price/Cost Type)	6-7
25/75 (Fixed-Price/Cost Type)	8-10

Internal/CPA Audits:

    Does the contractor maintain an internal audit staff and/or retain a CPA firm? Do the activities of these groups include areas which impact government contracts? Are the results of these reviews available to DCAA? Have past findings through compliance testing indicated poor internal controls which could lead to fraud, waste and error and were they followed up by transaction testing? Were noted deficiencies corrected?

Suggested criteria for rating this factor:	*Suggested Range*
Contractor maintains an internal audit staff and retains a CPA firm. Activities of these groups cover areas which impact government business. Internal audit reports are available for DCAA use.	1-3
Contractor maintains an internal audit staff and retains a CPA firm. Activities of these groups do not include all areas which impact government business. Internal audit reports are not made available to DCAA.	4-6
Contractor does not maintain an internal audit staff and/or retain a CPA firm.	7-10

Company Management Dominated by One or Few Individuals:

    1. Are there unusual amounts of receivables/payables to employees, affecting working capital or an abuse of resources to the detriment of government work?

    2. Do management officials have interests in related firms or suppliers, creating potential for overpricing of costs by elimination of competition in purchases, diversion of competition in purchases, diversion of resources, etc.

    3. Are management officials' salaries, and salaries of related employees, commensurate with services performed:

Suggested criteria for rating this factor:	*Suggested Range*
Company management is not dominated by one or a few individuals. There are no indications of management abuse of company resources and/or conflicts of interest.	1-3
Company management is dominated by one or a few individuals. There are indications of management abuse	

Figure 13.5. (Continued)

Factors	Rating
of company resources and/or conflicts of interest which have a relatively small dollar impact on government business.	4-6
Company management is dominated by one or a few individuals. There are indications of management abuse of company resources and/or conflicts of interest which have a relatively significant dollar impact on government business.	7-10

Defective Pricing

Have there been instances of defective pricing in postaward reviews which evidence poor control over pricing of subcontracting procedures and vulnerability to improper transactions in this area?

Suggested criteria for rating this factor:	*Suggested Range*
No instances of defective pricing have been noted during postaward reviews.	1-3
Instances of defective pricing with a small dollar impact on government business have been noted during postaward reviews.	4-6
Instances of defective pricing with a significant dollar impact on government business have been noted during postaward reviews.	7-10

Budgetary Controls:

Does the contractor maintain an effective and realistic budgetary system to preclude improper charging of costs by operating personnel in order to achieve management goals otherwise unattainable?

Suggested criteria for rating this factor:	*Suggested Range*
Reviews of budgetary system have disclosed no discrepancies.	1-3
Review of budgetary system has disclosed minor discrepancies with small dollar impact on government business. Access to budgetary data has been denied or restricted.	4-6
Review of budgetary system has disclosed major discrepancies with significant dollar impact on government business.	7-10

Financial Condition:

A poor profit history and lack of working capital either for the company or a particular organization within a company. These circumstances can lead to over-statements of claims for reimbursement and/or deliberate mischarging of costs to the more profitable segments of the business.

Suggested criteria for rating this factor:	*Suggesting Range*
Contractor has a good profit history, adequate working capital and a favorable financial outlook.	1-5
Contractor has a poor profit history, has marginal working capital and a questionable financial future.	6-10

TOTAL

NOTE:

Factors can be quantified by assigning values (such as 0-10) to indicate contribution to risk. Since the highest risk environment for a particular contractor location would be 10 × the number of factors, there is now a useful point for beginning to make decisions.

Date of initial or last update _____

Date of current assessment _____

Figure 13.5. (Continued)

Vulnerability assessments such as these are required at least annually and are usually performed in conjunction with some aspect of internal control reviews.

Mandatory Annual Audit Requirements

DCAA has established minimum annual audit requirements (MAARs) which must be performed at each contractor location either as separate reviews or as integral components of routine audits. The minimum requirements have been established in a MAARs planning control sheet (Figure 13.6.) A more detailed discussion of the MAARs objectives and purposes is contained in Figure 13.7. The auditor must consider incorporating these requirements when planning assigned audits. Therefore, the scope of assigned audits may be expanded to incorporate one or more of these requirements.

The MAARs normally necessitates audits sufficient in scope to evaluate some aspect of the contractor's internal controls and business systems.

Audit Leads

Audit leads are reviewed and considered in the audit planning process to ensure that any matters of concern identified in prior audits are adequately considered in the scope of the assigned audit. Audit lead sheets (Figure 13.8) are

MAAR	*Assignment Nos.*	*Check when Complete*	*Notes*
1. Update internal control survey			
2. Contract cost analysis and reconciliation to books			
3. Permanent files			
4. Tax returns and financial statements			
5. General ledger and income/credit adjustments			
6. Labor floor checks, etc.			
7. Changes in direct/indirect charging			
8. Comparative analysis-sensitive labor accounts			
9. Payroll/labor distribution reconciliation and tracing.			
10. Labor adjusting entries/exception reports			
11. Purchases adjusting entries/exception reports			
12. Auditable subcontracts/assist audits			
13. Purchases existence/consumption			
14. Pools/bases reconciliation to books			
15. Indirect cost comparison w/prior year budgets			
16. Indirect account analysis			
17. IR&D/B&P compliance			
18. Indirect allocation bases			
19. Indirect rate computations			
20. Indirect adjusting entries			

Figure 13.6. Mandatory annual audit requirements planning control sheet.

Objectives to be Satisfied	*Purpose*
1. *Update Internal Control Survey* Prepare/update internal control survey and evaluate changes in the contractor's internal controls.	To determine the extent of reliance that can be placed on the internal controls for contract costs and the need for and extent of substantive testing that may be required based on the observed strengths or weaknesses of contractor systems.
2. *Contract Cost Analysis and Reconciliations to Books* Review summaries of the contractor's total annual contract costs by major cost element (material, subcontractors, intracompany charges, other purchases, labor, indirect, other charges and credits, etc.) and verify that the auditable contract costs reconcile to contractor accounting records by cost element (typically using work in process or other contract control accounts in the general ledger).	To provide an overview and order-of-magnitude frame of reference for direction of audit effort and other audit planning/performance considerations, and to verify that the auditable costs claimed or to be claimed on government contracts tie into the amounts produced by the accounting system in the contractor's official books and records.
3. *Permanent Files* Maintain/update permanent files (CAM 4-404.1) for new or changed contractor organizations, operations, policies, procedures, internal controls, and accounting methods that influence the nature, level, and accounting treatment of costs being charged or to be charged to government contracts.	To provide an efficient and effective repository of current audit information. Permanent file maintenance should help identify the need for further audit reviews and analyses and help in determining the extent of further testing required in specific cost accounts, functions, operations, departments, etc.
4. *Tax Returns and Financial Statements* Review applicable tax returns and financial statements of the contractor.	To highlight possible areas requiring further attention and/or to reduce the extent of DCAA audit effort that might otherwise be required.
5. *General Ledger and Income/Credit Adjustments* Review the contractor's general ledger and other income/accounting adjustments (for example, unusual and/or sensitive journal entries).	To help identify any income and credits which the government may be entitled to obtain or share, and to evaluate the exclusion of any adjustments not reflected by the contractor in government contract costs.
6. *Labor Floor Checks, Etc.* Perform floor checks, interviews, and/or other physical observations and related analyses.	To test the reliability of employee time records, that employees are actually at work, that they are performing in assigned job classifications, and that time is charged to the proper cost objective.
7. *Changes in Direct/Indirect Charging* Review changes in procedures and practices for direct/indirect time charging of contractor employees for consistency with generally accepted accounting principles, the applicable cost principles per contracts, and any applicable cost accounting standards requirements.	To verify that changes in direct/indirect charging practices do not have the effect of improperly circumventing cost targets or ceilings of certain contracts or other significant cost categories.
8. *Comparative Analysis-Sensitive Labor Accounts* Perform comparative analysis of sensitive labor accounts.	To identify for further review any sensitive labor charges (for example, indirect charging by direct labor employees) that vary significantly from the prior period and/or budgetary estimates.
9. *Payroll/Labor Distribution Reconciliation and Tracing* Review the contractor's labor cost distributions.	To test the overall integrity of labor cost records at the general ledger levels and to reconcile payroll accruals and disbursements making sure that distribution entries trace to and from the cost accumulations records.
10. *Labor Adjusting Entries/Exception Reports* Review adjusting journal entries and exception reports for labor costs.	To identify adjustments and/or exceptions that require further audit analysis and/or explanation.
11. *Purchases Adjusting Entries/Exception Reports* Review adjusting journal entries and exception reports for costs of purchases services and material (including subcontract costs and intracompany charges).	To identify adjustments and/or exceptions that require further audit analysis and/or explanation.
12. *Auditable Subcontracts/Assist Audits* Review auditable type subcontracts and intracompany orders issued by the contractor under auditable type government con-	To protect the government's interests concerning the ensuing costs.

Figure 13.7. Schedule of mandatory annual audit requirements.

Objectives to be Satisfied	*Purpose*

tracts and subcontracts, and arrange for any independent assist audits required.

13. *Purchase Existence/Consumption*
Review (make physical observations and/or inquiries in addition to documentation verification) contract charges for purchases, etc.

To test that materials were in fact received (exist or were consumed) and that services were in fact performed.

14. *Pools/Bases Reconciliation to Books*
Review proposed pools and bases to accounting records.

To determine that the claimed indirect cost pools and allocation bases under government contracts reconcile to amounts in the contractor's official books and records.

15. *Indirect Cost Comparison with Prior Year and Budgets*
Review the current year's indirect cost accounts and prior years' costs and budgetary estimates.

To identify changes in cost accounting practices, reclassifications of costs, and areas with substantial increases or decreases in cost incurrence that require further audit analysis and/or explanation.

16. *Indirect Account Analysis*
Review selected indirect cost accounts or transactions such as sensitive accounts, new accounts, accounts with large variances,

To obtain sufficient evidence to support an opinion on the allowability, allocability, and reasonableness of the costs.

17. *IR&D/B&P Compliance*
Review the contractor's independent research and development and bid and proposal costs.

To verify for proper classification and compliance with the terms of government contracts and any related agreements.

18. *Indirect Allocation Bases*
Review the contractor's indirect cost allocation bases for consistency with generally accepted accounting principles, the applicable cost accounting standards requirements.

To assure that allocation bases are equitable for allocation of indirect costs to interim and final cost objectives.

19. *Indirect Rate Computations*
Review the accuracy of the contractor's rate computations for distributing interim and final indirect costs to intermediate and final cost objectives.

To confirm that contractor's rate computations are accurate for distributing indirect costs in government contracts.

20. *Indirect Adjusting Entries*
Review adjusting journal entires for indirect costs.

To identify adjustments that require further audit analysis and/or explanation.

Figure 13.7.   (Continued)

generated by each auditor upon completion of an audit assignment. These leads identify specific system deficiencies, internal control weaknesses, and other matters which the auditor considers pertinent. They are maintained in a permanent file for audit planning purposes. Contractors can frequently anticipate these areas of concern and rectify any deficiencies or weaknesses based on auditor comments during conferences. However, specific matters relating to questioned costs on proposals cannot usually be anticipated.

Scope of Audit

The final step in the audit approach is establishing the scope of the audit. The audit may represent a "desk review", a review of specified elements, or a comprehensive review of a contractor's supporting documentation and books and records.

A desk review is generally limited tó the analysis of the documents submitted by the contractor without additional audit procedures at the contractor's facility. Desk reviews are typically limited to proposals of $5 million or less for cost type contracts; $750,000 or less for incentive type contracts; and $100,000 or less for fixed-price contracts. In addition, the risk factors resulting from the vulnerability assessment must be relatively low and the need for MAARs must be considered prior to performing a desk review. Desk reviews are generally

DEFENSE CONTRACT AUDIT AGENCY
AUDIT LEADS

CONTRACTOR NAME _____   **AUDITOR** _____

Assignment Number _____   W/P Reference _____

AUDIT LEAD (Circle one or more):

1. Defective Pricing (Also Rate on FACS Form)   6. Overhead

2. Estimating System Deficiency   7. Other Direct Costs

3. Operations Audit   8. Cost Accounting Standards

4. Labor   9. Accounting System

5. Material   10. Internal Control

Other (*Explain*) _____

BRIEF EXPLANATION: _____

_____

_____

_____

_____

SUPERVISORY REVIEW: _____

_____

_____

_____

_____

_____

_____

_____

Distribution:
Original — Permanent File/Audit Lead File
    1 — Supervisor
    1— Working papers (*Assignment File*)

DISPOSITION (*Document permanent file copy*): _____

_____

_____

_____

DCAAForm 7640-22a   Supersedes DCAA Form 7640-22 October 1984
August 1987

Figure 13.8.

performed where auditors understand the contractors system and are confident that the government is at a minimum risk.

If the auditor feels that additional field work is required for any reason the scope of audit will be broader than a desk review. In some instances the scope of audit may be limited to evaluation of specific items or elements of cost. The reviews limited to specific items may be performed as the result of a request from the procuring agency or as the result of the auditor's evaluation of existing circumstances.

Comprehensive audits may occur where the audit values exceed the thresholds for a desk review or the audit planning process indicates a potential risk to the government, or MAARs must be performed.

Standardized preprinted audit programs are utilized to the maximum extent possible to promote consistency and efficiency in the performance of audits.

Summary

The auditors have a great deal of flexibility in planning audit activities and the scope or extent of the audit to be performed. Except for MAARs, the audit planning process depends heavily on the auditor's judgment. As a result, if the auditor perceives weaknesses or deficiencies, real or imagined, the extent of audit activity will be expanded significantly. Inversely, if the auditor has trust and confidence in the contractor's systems and controls, the extent of audit will be minimized.

TYPES OF AUDITS

Preaward Surveys

In a preaward survey, the procuring agency evaluates whether the prospective contractor is capable of performing the proposed contract. The survey can be utilized by the contracting officer to assist in determining if the offeror is responsible. The preaward evaluation may be accomplished by using data already in the agency files, data obtained from other government or commercial sources, on-site inspection of plants and facilities, or any combination of the above. A preaward survey is generally required when the information available to the contracting officer to make a determination regarding the responsibility of a prospective contractor is inadequate. This is normally the case when the agency has had no previous experience with the offeror or the anticipated level of activity with the company is to be significantly increased.

When a contracting officer determines that a preaward survey is desirable, his or her technical and financial advisors are directed to make the necessary reviews. The technical personnel will evaluate the prospective contractor's performance capability and productive capacity. The contract auditor will review the prospective contractor's financial capabilities, as well as the adequacy of the estimating and accounting systems.

The objective of the financial capability survey (see Fig. 13.9) is to determine whether the contractor's finances are adequate to perform the contract. In certain instances, a sound decision may be possible after a relatively simple review of a company's financial position and production commitments. In other circumstances, a more comprehensive review and analysis may be required. Where private financing is needed, in addition to any government financing

PREAWARD SURVEY OF PROSPECTIVE CONTRACTOR FINANCIAL CAPABILITY	If more space is needed, continue on page 3, back. Identify continued items.	SERIAL NO. (For surveying activity use)	FORM APPROVED OMB NO. 3090-0110
PROSPECTIVE CONTRACTOR		LOCATION	

SECTION I – BALANCE SHEET/PROFIT AND LOSS STATEMENT

PART A – LATEST BALANCE SHEET		PART B – LATEST PROFIT AND LOSS STATEMENT		
1. DATE	2. FILED WITH	1. CURRENT PERIOD		2. FILED WITH
		a. FROM	b. TO	

3. FINANCIAL POSITION					
a. Cash	$	3. NET SALES	a. CURRENT PERIOD	$
b. Other current assets			b. First prior fiscal year	
c. Working capital			c. Second prior fiscal year	
d. Current liabilities		4. NET PROFITS BEFORE TAXES	a. CURRENT PERIOD	$
e. Net worth			b. First prior fiscal year	
f. Total liabilities			c. Second prior fiscal year	

4. RATIOS			5. OTHER PERTINENT DATA
a. CURRENT ASSETS TO CURRENT LIABILITIES	b. ACID TEST (Cash, temporary investments held in lieu of cash and current receivables to current liabilities)	c. TOTAL LIABILITIES TO NET WORTH	
:	:	:	

6. FISCAL YEAR ENDS (Date)	7. BALANCE SHEETS AND PROFIT AND LOSS STATEMENTS HAVE BEEN CERTIFIED ➤	a. THROUGH (Date)	b. BY (Signature)

SECTION II – PROSPECTIVE CONTRACTOR'S FINANCIAL ARRANGEMENTS

Mark "X" in appropriate column.	YES	NO	4. INDEPENDENT ANALYSIS OF FINANCIAL POSITION SUPPORTS THE STATEMENTS SHOWN IN ITEMS 1, 2, AND 3
1. USE OF OWN RESOURCES			☐ YES ☐ NO (If "NO," explain)
2. USE OF BANK CREDITS			
3. OTHER (Specify)			

SECTION III – GOVERNMENT FINANCIAL AID

1. TO BE REQUESTED IN CONNECTION WITH PERFORMANCE OF PROPOSED CONTRACT			2. EXPLAIN ANY "YES" ANSWERS TO ITEMS 1a, b, AND c
Mark "X" in appropriate column.	YES	NO	
a. PROGRESS PAYMENT			
b. GUARANTEED LOAN			
c. ADVANCE PAYMENTS			

3. FINANCIAL AID CURRENTLY OBTAINED FROM THE GOVERNMENT

a. PROSPECTIVE CONTRACTOR RECEIVES GOVERNMENT FINANCING AT PRESENT	b. IS LIQUIDATION CURRENT?	c. AMOUNT OF UNLIQUIDATED PROGRESS PAYMENTS OUTSTANDING	Complete items below only if item a., is marked "YES."		
			DOLLAR AMOUNTS	(a) AUTHORIZED	(b) IN USE
			a. Guaranteed loans	$	$
☐ YES ☐ NO	☐ YES ☐ NO	$	b. Advance payments	$	$

4. LIST THE GOVERNMENT AGENCIES INVOLVED	5. SHOW THE APPLICABLE CONTRACT NOS

1407-101

STANDARD FORM 1407 (10-83)
Prescribed by GSA,
FAR (48 CFR) 53.209-1(e)

Figure 13.9. Preaward survey of prospective contractor financial capability, Standard Form 1407.

1. COMMENTS OF PROSPECTIVE CONTRACTOR'S BANK

2. COMMENTS OF TRADE CREDITORS

3. COMMENTS AND REPORTS OF COMMERCIAL FINANCIAL SERVICES AND CREDIT ORGANIZATIONS (Such as, Dun & Bradstreet, Standard and Poor, etc.)

4. MOST RECENT CREDIT RATING	a. DATE	b. BY

5. OTHER SOURCES (Business and financial reputation and integrity of the prospective contractor, or, if not established, of the principal executions, as determined by other sources.)

STANDARD FORM 1407 (10-83)
PAGE 2

Figure 13.9. (Continued)

6. DOES PRICE APPEAR UNREALISTICALLY LOW? ☐ YES ☐ NO

7. DESCRIBE ANY OUTSTANDING LIENS OR JUDGMENTS

SECTION V – SALES

CATEGORY	CURRENT DOLLAR BACKLOG OF SALES (a)	ANTICIPATED ADDITIONAL DOLLAR SALES FORECAST FOR NEXT 18 MONTHS (b)
1. Government *(Prime and subcontractor)*	$	$
2. Commercial	$	$
3. **TOTAL**	$	$

SECTION VI – RECOMMENDATION

1. RECOMMEND

☐ a. COMPLETE AWARD   ☐ b. PARTIAL AWARD *(Quantity:* _____ *)*   ☐ c. NO AWARD

2. REMARKS *(Cite those sections of the report which substantiate the recommendation. Give any other backup information in this space, on the back, or on additional sheet, if necessary.)*

If continuation sheets attached — mark here ☐

3. SURVEY MADE BY *(Signature and office)*	4. TELEPHONE NO. *(Include area code)*	5. DATE SUBMITTED

Figure 13.9. (Continued)

that may be provided, the auditor will normally verify the availability of such financing.

A preaward accounting system survey (see Fig. 13.10) is usually made for the purpose of determining the adequacy and suitability of the contractor's accounting practices to accumulate cost under the type of contract to be awarded. Accordingly, special emphasis may be given to the ability of the prospective contractor's cost accounting system to provide specific information the anticipated contract may require. The preaward accounting system survey should disclose the extent to which the proposed contract and the prospective contractor's cost accounting system are compatible. Additionally, if the contemplated contract is a cost-based contract, or a fixed-price contract with progress payment provisions, the auditor will normally review the accounting system to assure that it has the capability to accumulate cost by contract.

Because the preaward system survey is part of the overall determination of responsibility of the contractor, it is performed prior to contract award. The time available to complete the review is normally limited. Therefore, the review may not be extensive in scope or depth. Since a major deficiency in a cost accounting system could preclude the award of a contract, companies undergoing such a review should insist on knowing immediately any defects the government reviewers have noted. In anticipation of such a review by the government, it may be well for management to conduct its own survey and correct any deficiencies that are found.

Forward Pricing

Forward pricing entails price estimating for specific products or services to be provided in the future. Forward pricing may include price estimates for total contracts (proposals) or estimates for specific rates and factors (forward pricing rate agreements) to be used in all forward pricing efforts performed by a contractor for an established period of time. Regardless of the type of audit being performed, the underlying audit objective is to assist the procuring activity in determining a reasonable price for goods and services determined in accordance with applicable procurement regulations and cost accounting standards.

These objectives provide the auditors with significant latitude in determining the scope of a particular proposal audit. Virtually every aspect of a contractor's operations which impacts the price paid by the government is subject to audit scrutiny.

Proposal Audits

Proposal audits vary significantly from one contractor to another. These variations are principally due to the deviations in scope resulting from the audit planning process, discussed earlier in this chapter, and the unique characteristics of each procurement. The auditor will typically evaluate each element of cost proposed. Procedures performed in the course of a comprehensive audit of the proposed cost elements may include:

Review of the basis for proposed cost, i.e., historical data, quotation, engineering, estimates.

Verification and analysis of relevant historical data.

Review and analysis of kinds and quantities proposed, i.e., labor hours by category and material.

**PREAWARD SURVEY OF PROSPECTIVE CONTRACTOR
ACCOUNTING SYSTEM**

SERIAL NO. *(For surveying activity use)*

PROSPECTIVE CONTRACTOR

Mark "X" in the appropriate column	YES	NO	NOT APPLI- CABLE
1. Except as stated below, is the accounting system in accord with generally accepted accounting principles applicable in the circumstances?			
2. ACCOUNTING SYSTEM PROVIDES FOR:			
a. Proper segregation of costs applicable to proposed contract and to other work of the prospective contractor.			
b. Determination of costs at interim points to provide data required for contract repricing purposes or for negotiating revised targets.			
c. Exclusion from costs charged to proposed contract of amounts which are not allowable under terms of FAR 31, Contract Cost Principles and Procedures, or other contract provisions.			
d. Identification of costs by contract line item and by units if required by proposed contract.			
e. Segregation of preproduction costs from production costs.			
3. ACCOUNTING SYSTEM PROVIDES FINANCIAL INFORMATION:			
a. Required by contract clauses concerning limitation of cost (FAR 52.232-40 and 41) or limitation on payments (FAR 52.216-16).			
b. Required to support requests for progress payments.			
4. Is the accounting system designed, and are the records maintained in such a manner that adequate, reliable data are developed for use in pricing follow-on acquisitions?			

5. REMARKS *(Clarification of above deficiencies, and other pertinent comments. If additional space is required, continue on the back or on plain sheets of paper.)*

If continuation sheets attached — mark here ☐

6. SURVEY MADE BY *(Signature and office)*	7. TELEPHONE NO. *(Include area code)*	8. DATE SUBMITTED

Figure 13.10. Preaward survey of prospective contractor accounting system, Standard Form 1408.

Analysis of current cost data, i.e., last year end and year to date rates, factors and contract costs.

Analysis of proposed performance periods and economic adjustments proposed.

Analysis of forecasted business activities and their effects on rates and factors.

Comparison of proposed cost elements to same or similar activities.

Comparison of estimating techniques with accumulation and reporting techniques, i.e., CAS 401 and 402.

Forward Pricing Rates

The audits of forward pricing rates such as labor, indirect expense and scrap rates are accomplished via the same objectives and procedures discussed above. The principle difference is that the scope of audit is limited to the specific cost components of the proposed rates. In addition, procedures, internal controls and/or methods of developing the rates are more extensively examined.

Incurred Cost Audits

Incurred costs constitute monies spent both directly and indirectly in the performance of contracts. Incurred costs on flexibly priced contracts and subcontracts are subject to audit prior to contract settlement.

Indirect Expense Proposals

Indirect expense proposals are required and submitted for audit when a contractor is performing a flexibly priced contract (i.e., those contracts whose final remuneration is based on costs incurred during contract performance). The contractor's final indirect cost proposal is subsequently audited to some extent by the government. The objectives of the audit are to determine that 1) costs included in the indirect expense pools are allowable in accordance with applicable regulations and contract terms, 2) the indirect expenses have been homogeneously grouped for equitable allocation to contracts, 3) the bases used to distribute costs to contracts are appropriate given the types of expenses being distributed, and 4) the accumulation and distribution of indirect expenses have been consistently applied to all aspects of the contractor's operations, including government and nongovernment activities.

The audit procedures used by the auditor may vary significantly depending on the results of the vulnerability and risk results. However, as a minimum the auditor will:

Review accounts titles in each indirect expense pool to identify any obvious categories of unallowable expenses.

Review the allocation bases to ensure the propriety of the allocation.

Verify the mathematical accuracy of the proposed indirect expense pools, allocation bases, and indirect expense rates.

Verify that IR&D/B&P costs do not exceed established ceilings.

The minimum review will be a desk audit of the contractor's final indirect cost rate proposal without examination of any contractor records. More extensive indirect expense proposal audits, in addition to incorporating all of the steps summarized above, will include actual reviews of contractor accounting records and supporting documentation. Audit steps will include detailed testing to determine:

The adequacy of internal controls associated with the incurrence and recording of expenses.

The allowability of individual expenses within a variety of accounts.

The homogeneity of the indirect expense groupings (pools) to assure equitable distribution of expenses to cost objectives.

The propriety of the bases used to apportion expenses to cost objectives to insure cost allocations based on causal or beneficial relationships.

Material Cost Audits

The review of material costs is usually performed through several distinct audits encompassing determination of requirements, accounting for material costs, purchasing and subcontracting, receipt of materials, storing and issuing material.

Determination of Requirements

The audit steps will focus on assuring that:

Material requirements reflect timely buying practices at the most feasible economic order quantity.

Future requirements projections are based on proposal activity and major programs.

Material requirements are supported by a proper requisitioning system which reflects properly initiated and approved requisitions.

Information generated by stock level requirements established for standard items on bills of material are coordinated with production schedules.

Individual purchase requests from departments authorized to requisition material are used to determine the quantity and delivery date of material.

Controls are in effect to avoid repetitive requisitioning of small quantities of the same item and in excessive quantities.

Accounting (Payment) for Material Costs

The basic audit objectives in the accounting for material costs includes verification of proper payments and distribution of material charges to contracts, accounts and projects. Basic steps include verification that:

Invoices are supported by authorized purchase orders (P.O.).

Invoice terms agree with the P.O. on price, quantities, and other terms.

Paperwork is matched, that is, invoices are supported by receiving and inspection reports, debit and credit memos, etc.

The arithmetic accuracy of extension and discounts on invoices have been verified.

Documents are properly marked to show proper account distribution and cancellation to avoid duplicate payments.

Costs are paid before costs are claimed on public vouchers or progress payments (not applicable to small business concerns) .

Purchasing and Subcontracting

At large contractor locations, purchasing and subcontracting are usually reviewed every two years in a team effort by the procurement office and auditors. The Contractor Purchasing System Review (CPSR) team's objective is to determine if the purchasing system is effective and efficient in the expenditure of government funds and complies with public laws and contract requirements. The team reviews the internal controls over the organization and employees performing the functions, and procedures for obtaining quotes, negotiating purchase orders and subcontracts and issuance of purchase orders. The key areas for review are:

The existence and implementation of written policies and procedures.

The organizational independence of the purchasing department personnel from other departments and separation of the buying and receiving function.

Numerical control and accounting for purchase requisitions and orders to avoid unauthorized purchases.

Consistent trends reflect lower subcontract prices being negotiated after award of the prime contract.

Adequacy of the competitive bid process by the purchasing organization and adherence to the FAR and contractual terms.

Receipt

This review will focus on:

Independence of the receiving function from purchasing, accounting and shipping.

Adequacy of the receiving report to identify quantity and quality of materials and acceptability of the items received.

Central control, inspection and prompt distribution of incoming materials to storage or production.

Storage and Issue

Major areas for review include:

Separate control and accountability of contractor owned and government owned materials.

Documentation control over the distribution of materials to stores and production areas.

Controls to prevent theft and diversion of materials including special safeguards for high value materials which may be susceptible to personal use or sale.

Identification of stock levels and slow moving materials.

Controls over materials returned to stock noting appropriate credits and scrap material relative to disposition and credits.

Labor Costs

The review of labor costs is performed in several distinct audits for both direct and indirect costs:

Internal controls.
Personnel policies and procedures.
Recruitment costs and practices.
Payroll preparation and payment.
Overtime, extra pay shifts and multi-shift work policies and costing.
Verification of labor costs.

Three major audits cover most of the areas listed above: contractor's employee compensation system reviews (CECSR); labor distribution reviews and floor checks; and comprehensive labor audits.

CECSR

The CECSR is performed to determine the reasonableness of the total compensation paid to specific job classifications or categories for both direct and indirect employees. The review covers personnel policies and procedures, recruitment costs and practices, overtime and fringe benefit areas. When exceptions are found, such as excessive compensation, the contractor is afforded a reasonable compensation level that falls within the benchmark range. Adjustments are usually on a prospective basis.

Floor Checks

DCAA auditors will perform unannounced floor checks to determine the adequacy and accuracy of timekeeping systems for reimbursement of labor costs under cost reimbursable contracts. During these reviews the auditor will:

Determine whether the employees selected are at their assigned work sites.

Identify the projects currently being performed by selected employees.

Review the adequacy of written documentation to identify the project to be charged.

Determine employee adherence to established time reporting procedures (e.g., time report prepared daily in ink).

Determine whether the subsequent labor distribution properly reflects the charges observed on employee time reports.

Comprehensive Labor Audit

The Comprehensive labor audit focuses on reviewing and evaluating labor-related internal controls; testing labor transactions; and identifying and monetizing mischarged or misclassified labor and related costs.

Five basic points are key to the performance of this audit:

Current/comprehensive nature of the audit.

Risk/vulnerability assessment.

Preinterview analysis.

Detailed employee interviews.

Emphasis on internal controls - Employee "timecard preparation" awareness programs.

Current/Comprehensive Review

One of the underlying principles of an effective labor review is its performance on a current basis. Long lapses of time between when the labor effort is performed and when it is reviewed tend to diminish the effectivness and productivity of the review. Labor reviews are generally performed on a real time basis, with labor efforts being reviewed at the time of incurrence. Currency requires that the auditor monitor certain critical contracts and projects during the year to enable a comprehensive labor audit to begin when the area requires a detailed examination.

Another underlying principle is the comprehensive nature of the audit. Total conditions existing within a contractor's operations are considered before a review is performed. Verification of the incurrence of labor costs is only one facet of a comprehensive labor review. It also encompasses an evaluation of potential problem areas, such as:

Opportunity for, and impact of, mischarging labor costs (government participation and contract mix).

Adequacy of internal controls.

Significant overruns/underruns of Government contracts.

Probability of misclassified IR&D/B&P costs.

Consistency of indirect labor classifications.

Consistency in charging cost objectives for the same type of labor.

Unreasonable labor efforts (e.g., excessive nonproductive labor).

Labor incurred at offsite locations.

Risk/Vulnerability Analysis

Efforts are concentrated on those areas requiring immediate attention. The *risk analysis* is designed to identify those problem areas most likely to result in a *significant* adverse cost impact to the government.Vulnerability assessments are designed to determine the extent of government exposure to suspected irregular conduct.Factors that must be considered and reviewed are:

Internal controls.

Adequate policies and procedures and compliance.

Mix of contracts.

Overrun contracts.

Bid and proposal/IR&D costs.

Selling and marketing.

Prior experience audit lead sheets.

Significant increases in indirect labor accounts.

Reorganization/reclassification of employees.

Labor transfers through journal entries.

Budgetary system.

Contract definition contracts.

Contract provisions.

Related effort on multiple contracts.

Labor accounting by funding.

Preinterview/Inquiry Analysis

Once the high risk/vulnerability areas have been identified for review, a preinterview analysis is performed. The objective of this part of the review is to identify the population of employees associated with the high risk areas from which candidates will be selected for interviews. Sufficient data is gathered so that an informed decision can be made on the selection of employees for interview. Just as the risk analysis started with the contractor's entire labor system and narrowed the audit scope to selected areas of risk, preinterview analysis starts with all the employees charging the risk area and narrows the review to selected employees within that risk area.

To determine the high risk population, the following preinterview analysis steps are performed for each high risk area identified:

Labor distribution documents are reviewed to identify all employees charging labor effort to the risk area.

Other available documentation is reviewed, e.g., internal memos, status reports, organization charts, documentation logs, etc., to determine if employees who are *not* charging their time to the risk area, possibly should be.

Labor time charges are scheduled for an appropriate period of time e.g., 6 weeks to determine if any significant trends exist. Employees with irregular or inconsistent charging patterns are identified.

Timecards/Timesheets are physically inspected, starting with the most current time period for the following attributes:

Consistent splitting of time between two or more cost objectives.

Changes in time charging patterns.

Corrections, alterations, whiteouts.

Indications that someone other than the employee is completing the timecard.

Travel expense reports are reviewed to compare travel charges to labor distribution charges.

Detailed Employee Interviews

The principal criteria for selecting employees for interview are: (1) employees having the most questionable time charges and, (2) employees having charges that are useful in testing the contractor's system of internal controls. The actual employee interviews constitute a critical element in an effective comprehensive labor audit by providing sufficient information to form an opinion on (1) the adequacy of, and compliance with, internal controls and (2) the propriety of the recorded labor charges.

Emphasis on Internal Controls

If findings result from the comprehensive labor review, they can usually be traced to inadequate internal controls or a lack of compliance with written company policies and procedures. Adequate internal controls are essential if the labor system is to be relied upon for government contract costing purposes. Inadequate or ineffective internal controls may result in the suspension of labor costs and issuing a qualified opinion in pricing proposal audit reports.

Public Vouchers

Public vouchers submitted by a contractor under cost type contracts are not routinely audited. The frequency of these audits is directly affected by the extent of the auditor's reliance on the contractor's cost accumulation, reporting and billing systems and procedures.

The objective of a public voucher audit is to verify that the amounts billed on the contract are in accordance with the terms and conditions of the contract and are properly due the contractor. The voucher audit generally consists of procedures necessary to determine that the amounts billed have been determined based on applicable provisional, or actual indirect expense rates in effect, that fees claimed have been computed in accordance with contract terms and conditions, and that the request for payment has been properly prepared and includes only those costs authorized under the terms of the contract.

Progress Payments

Audit of progress payments on fixed-price contracts may be performed at the request of the contracting officer or when the auditor determines that the audit is necessary to protect the government's interest. Progress payments are in effect loans secured by materials charged to the contract and the government is interested in assurances that its investment is protected and that it is not overpaying the contractor for unliquidated progress payments.

The scope of the progress payment audit depends to a large extent on the auditor's understanding of the contractor's cost accounting and billing systems. When the auditor can rely on the contractor's systems and records, the audit scope may be limited to verification of reported costs to the contractor's books and records. However, when the auditor lacks confidence in the ability of thoe systems to produce accurate data in compliance with FAR requirements, the scope of audit may include more in-depth analysis to determine if the data generated by the systems for progress payments are reliable.

Cost Accounting Standards

The requirements imposed on contracts by cost accounting standards (CAS) have added to the auditor's audit responsibilities as well. The auditor is required to perform CAS reviews in order to render an opinion as to whether:

The disclosure statement adequately describes actual or proposed cost accounting practices.

Disclosed cost accounting practices are in compliance with CAS.

Failure to comply with applicable CAS or to follow consistently disclosed cost accounting practices has resulted, or may result in any increased cost paid by the government.

Proposed cost impact proposals submitted as a result of changes made to previously disclosed or established cost accounting practices, are fair and reasonable.

Disclosure Statement Audits

As previously discussed in Chapter 8, certain contractors must submit disclosure statements which describe the cost accounting practices applied to contracts containing the CAS clause. Upon submission of the disclosure statement government auditors will perform a review to ascertain whether it adequately describes the cost accounting practices to be used in estimating, accumulating and reporting costs. Either concurrent with or subsequent to the adequacy review, the auditor will perform a compliance review to ascertain whether disclosed practices comply with CAS and FAR requirements.

The determination of adequacy requires the auditor to validate the currency, accurateness and completeness of the practices described in the statement. For contractors subject to continuous audit surveillance, the adequacy review may be performed largely by reviewing data in existing files. For contractors audited on a more limited basis, the volume of CAS covered contracts will be a major consideration in establishing the scope of the adequacy review.

The auditor will compare the disclosed practices to the contractor's system, procedures and practices to ensure that current and/or planned practices have been described. To be current the statement must disclose current or planned practices which the contractor intends to follow in estimating, accumulating and reporting costs on CAS covered contracts.

The accuracy of the disclosure statement is determined by verifying that the practices have been clearly and distinctly disclosed. Vague, ambiguous and contradictory descriptions of the contractor's cost accounting practices may cause disputes and litigation; therefore, the auditor carefully reviews the described practices for specificity and clarity. Accuracy of the disclosure statement is also required, and the auditor's review will include verification that the appropriate boxes are checked, the applicable code letters have been inserted, and all applicable questions have been answered. This verification may incorporate review of policies, procedures and internal contracts as well as specific attribute testing to ensure the adequacy of the disclosure.

To be complete the statement must disclose all cost significant accounting practices the contractor intends to use in the process of estimating, accumulating and reporting costs and provide sufficient information to permit a full understanding of the accounting practices being described.

To determine compliance with CAS and applicable acquisition regulations, auditors will compare the disclosed practices to the requirements of the applicable standards. Noncompliances disclosed during the evaluation are reported to the administrative contracting officer. Initial compliance reviews are generally deferred until after completion of the adequacy review since an adequatcy statement is required prior to contract award.

Changes to established disclosure statements as a result of accounting practice changes are reviewed by the auditor concurrently for both adequacy and compliance.

Continuing CAS Compliance Reviews

When a contractor is subject to CAS, the auditor is responsible for reviewing the contractor's cost accounting practices used in estimating, accumulating and reporting costs under CAS covered contracts for compliance with the CAS Board's rules, regulations and standards.

Normally, audits of CAS compliance are integrated into the other normal audits performed by the auditor. For example, in a price proposal evaluation, the auditor will determine whether accounting practices used in pricing the proposal are consistent with the disclosure statement, if applicable, and/or established accounting practices for accumulating and reporting costs. In an incurred cost audit such as a final indirect expense rate submission, the auditor's review will include as a minimum an evaluation for compliance with applicable standards.

Separate reviews for CAS compliance may be performed when only infrequent audit requirements exist or when specific requirements of a standard cannot be integrated into normal audit reviews.

Cost Impact Proposal Reviews

Contractors and subcontractors subject to CAS are generally required to submit a cost impact proposal to the government when a disclosed or established accounting practice is changed, or when noncompliance with CAS or a disclosed or established accounting practice has been determined. The purpose of the proposal is to reflect the cost impact of the change or noncompliance on all applicable CAS covered contracts.

In a cost impact proposal review, the auditor is responsible for determining that:

All applicable CAS covered contracts are included in the proposal.

The proposal has been properly prepared and the method of presentation is adequate.

The proposed amounts (cost impact) are fair and reasonable.

The audit report must show the audit recommendations on a contract-by-contract basis. Finally, if the cost impact proposal is not submitted by the contractor, the auditor assists the contracting officer in estimating the cost impact.

Defective Pricing

In the past, DCAA has given postaward audits (reviews for compliance with Public Law 87-652) a priority exceeded only by that given to the reviews of contract pricing proposals. Because of this emphasis, the possibility that a particular contract will be selected for review is significant. The specific criteria for selection of specific contracts are established by DCAA headquarters. However, a substancial degree of flexibility to expand upon the number of contracts selected for review is given to each audit office.

In determining the number of contracts to review, the auditor rates major contractors by the quality of their proposal preparation policies and procedures. For those contractors that submit well-prepared and well-supported proposals, and prior experiance has disclosed little or no defective pricing, a limited number of contracts will be selected for review. At the other extreme, contractors that are known to be careless should expect to have a substantial number of contracts selected for postaward review.

Smaller contractors are generally not delt with individually but will have all of their contracts subject to defective pricing aggregated and be subject to selection based upon dollar size, chance, and lead sheets maintained for each contract and negotiation. The lead sheets are used to identify those specific pricing actions where the conditions that existed were such that the possibility of defective pricing was increased.

Notwithstanding the selection of specific pricing actions for review, DCAA will select actions which exceed a specified dollar amount by specific contract type and will sample contracts which do not meet the specific selection criteria. Generally all contracts over $50 million and firm fixed-price contracts over $10 million will be reviewed. Those between those costs will be sampled based upon criteria established by DCAA headquarters (anywhere from 5 to 50%). Cost type contracts below $50 million (other than incentive) will generally not be reviewed.

Guidance as to the specific items that should be considered by the auditor is contained in CAM[12] Section 14-104.4 which states:

> To most effectively achieve the basic objectives previously stated, the audit programs should be designed to identify and explore conditions indictive of defective pricing and to include specific information furnished by the contracting officer when applicable. Items normally examined for indications of defective pricing are historical unit cost records, vendors, quotes, purchase orders, voluntary refunds or credits from suppliers, cost trend records, sales and manufacturing volume projections, profit and loss statements, and product cost and profit analyses. The following should be considered in the development of the detailed audit program:
>
> (1) Significantly lower actual cost of the individual items and cost elements as compared with the amounts included in the contractor's proposal as certified. When the comparison does not disclose any significantly lower actual cost of the individual items and cost elements, the review of the contract for defective pricing may be considered complete unless unusual circumstances warrent further examination.
>
> (2) Operations not actually performed or items of cost not incurred, although included in the contractor's proposal (for example special testing program not performed, royalty expense not incurred, Goverment-owned equipment rental not paid, and changes in make-or-buy program).
>
> (3) Items of direct cost included in the contract pricing proposal at prices higher than were justified on the basis of information available to the contractor(and not disclosed to the Goverment) at the time the contract price was agreed upon or the date of contract, whichever is applicable. Examples are (i) subsequent to the submission of the original proposal but prior to the agreement on price, a firm quote was received from an established source at significantly less than the cost included in the original proposal or (ii) a previously used supplier who could be expected to submit a lower bid was not solicited, but the contractor subsequently purchased the material from this vendor. Where either of the forgoing situations is disclosed, the auditor should evaluate the circumstances involved to reach a conclusion as to whether defective pricing exists. A contract price is not defective soley because subsequent market price declines enabled the contractor to obtain lower material prices that the quotations obtained prior to award.
>
> (4) Less obvious instances of defective pricing that may include failure of the contractor to reflect in the proposal management decisions and information relating to budgets, production, autumation, time and motion studies on labor, etc. when the decisions were made and the information was available prior to agreement on the overall price and they would have been expected to result in lower costs under the prospective contract.
>
> (5) Closing or cut-off dates for recording transactions or for computing summary overhead rate or production cost data may not coincide with the date the contract price was negotiated. The contractor's proposal may be based upon overhead or other cost data as of a prior cut-off period. The contractor, is, however, responsible for the currency of its cost or pricing data. Even though a prior understanding is reached with the contracting officer on closing or cut-off dates, significant matters in the books or records as of the date of price agreement will be considered reasonably available to the contractor for purposes of defective pricing in spite of the fact that the data had not yet been summarized.

Other Audits and Review

The government may perform a variety of reviews in addition to those specifically discussed earlier in this chapter. These reviews may be performed by auditors, technical personnel, or contract administration personnel and may include such areas as 1) functional system reviews, 2) matters related to specific contract clauses, and 3) comprehensive system surveys. Most of these reviews address the contractor's ability to comply with applicable regulations and specific contract terms and conditions. One of the most significant reviews is the comprehensive operational review and evaluation (CORE) audit performed by the U.S. Air Force. These audits constitute a review of all functional areas involved in or associated with the performance of goverment contracts. They consist of reviews of written policies and procedures to determine that a contractor's operations are adequately documented and that the operations comply with applicable regulations. In addition, tests are conducted to determine that actual practices used in each functional area are as prescribed in the written policies and procedures.

The CORE selection process is performed on a periodic basis at major defense contractor locations or when conditions indicate that significant systems deficiencies may exist.

Fraud Detection

Contractor auditors are not generally assigned the responsibility to detect fraud; however, they are alert for indications of fraud which they may come across during the normal course of their audit activity.To assist auditors with the detection of fraud, the DODIG periodically issues indicators of fraud which identify transactions, events or conditions which may be associated with fraudulent activities.

Auditors may make a fraud referral when they believe they have detected irregularities or indicators of fraud. Under the referral process, auditors complete the "suspected irregularity referral form", Figure 13.11, and submit the form directly to the various investigative activities (e.g., local investigative offices, Defense Criminal Investigative Service, Department of Justice Defense Procurement Fraud Unit) and DCAA management. Prior approval of referrals by supervisory personnel within the audit agency is not required.

To avoid referrals of fraud, contractors should work as closely with the auditor as possible. Communication with the auditor may eliminate the possibility of a referral resulting from a misunderstanding and protect the company from extensive investigations and allegations of fraud.

MANAGING THE AUDIT PROCESS

Audit Liaison

Contract audit is an integral part of the process of pricing and costing negotiated procurements. Contractors who must undergo such reviews should endeavor to minimize both the time required to conduct the audit and the negative financial impact of thr review. To achieve this end, a company should make a concerted effort to demonstrate a spirit of cooperation and a genuine

SUSPECTED IRREGULARITY REFERRAL FORM

> Name of DCAA Employee
> Submitting Referral:
> _____
>
> FAO Location: _____
>
> Telephone Number: _____
>
> Cognizant FAO Managers'
> Name and Telephone Number:
>
> _____
> _____

Information which suggests a reasonable basis for suspicion of fraud, corruption or unlawful activity affecting Government contracts must be reported promptly. DCAA employees are encouraged to use this form. If there are any questions as to whether or not this referral should be made, please call your local DoD investigator.

You may not be able to supply all of the information. This form is designed to identify the type of information typically needed by an investigtor. Be as thorough as possible in order to assist the investigator in understanding the possible irregularity.

You are encouraged to discuss your suspicions and your written submission with your FAO manager to assure that adequate information has been developed.

Part I

a) - Name of contractor. _____

   Division, City and State. _____

   Location of Incident. _____

b) - Size, nature, and type of contracts in question. _____
_____
_____

c) - Name of affected major acquisition program, if any. _____
_____

d) - Contract number(s). _____

e) - Organization and location which administers the contract(s).
_____

f) - Organization and location which awarded the contract(s).
_____

Part II

a) - Is continued audit effort planned? _____

b) - If so, describe and expected start date. _____

(c - Is there pending a contract modification, adjustment, claim resolution or agreement that relates in any way to the suspected irregularity? Explain. _____
_____
_____

Figure 13.11. Suspected irregularity referral form, DCAA Form 2000.0

Part III

a) - To whom is distribution of this referral being made? _____

Part IV

Answer the following questions as fully as possible. Use as many pages as necessary.

a) - Thorough description of suspected irregularity. _____

_____
_____
_____
_____
_____
_____
_____
_____
_____
_____
_____
_____
_____
_____
_____
_____
_____
_____
_____
_____

-Type of audit performed when suspected irregularity was detected.

_____

- Identify indicators by which irregularity was accomplished (e.g., altered timecards, bogus invoices. _____

_____
_____
_____
_____

-Attach copies of any document(s) you believe are necessary to assist in an understanding of what irregular activity is suspected and why it is suspected.

b) - Full description of books and records pertinent to irregularity with contractor nomenclature for these books and records. _____

_____
_____
_____
_____
_____

c) - Name, job, city, and locaton of individuals who provided information or who may have relevant information. _____

_____
_____
_____
_____

Figure 13.11.   (Continued)

- Estimated loss or impact to Government contracts. _____
_____

d) - Extent of questioned practices, time span, isolated incident or a pattern. _____
_____

e) - Position or name of person(s) involved. _____
_____
_____

f) - Indicators of involvement of upper management. _____
_____
_____
_____
_____
_____
_____
_____

g) - Why do you think wrongdoing is intentional; i.e., that acts were done with fraudulent intent.
_____
_____
_____
_____
_____
_____

Figure 13.11. (Continued)

desire to facilitate the audit process. Such an effort should be effective in establishing a working relationship with the auditors that:

Minimizes conflicts.
Keeps the communication channels open.
Provides a basis for resolving differences of opinion.

However, in today's complex Federal procurement environment, it is also essential that a company act prudently to protect its own interest during the conduct of an audit. To facilitate the audit process, a company should concider designating a key staff representative for interface with contract auditors. This liaison person should:

Be knowledgeable of the contract audit process, federal acquisition regulations, cost accounting standards, and contractual terms.
Possess a high degree of interpersonal skills
Be knowledgeable of the accounting records and the system of internal control.
Be familiar with the work performed under the contracts.

In preparing for an audit, the designated liaison representative should try to anticipate the audit program and gather the books, records, and documents that, in the company's judgement, comprise all the support required to accomplish the audit objective.

DCAA policy requires the auditor to hold an entrance conference to advise the contractor of the purpose, scope of, and authority for the audit. Contractors should insist that this conference occurs. Contractors should be satisfied that the authority for the audit is solid and should have a good understanding of how the audit results will be used. Also, the conference should be used to identify what company can do to assist the auditor in the review.

The contractor should ask the auditor to request the information required for the audit from the designated liaison person. The liaison person should be responsible for making both requested data and personnel available to the auditor where management agrees that the request is appropriate. It is important that responses to the auditor, even when negative, be reasonably prompt. The liaison representative should accompany the auditor whenever the auditor is obtaining oral information from other company personnel.

Specific data requested by the auditor that is considered proprietary, is not normally produced by the accounting system and will require special effort to develope, or appears to be extraneous to the audit scope and objective, should be identified as early as possible. Conflicts occur because contractors tend to interpret the access to records requirements narrower than the goverment. If the right of goverment access is not reasonably clear, the auditor should be required to establish that the requested information is relevant to the audit objective.

Discuss with the auditor as the audit progresses should be encouraged. If issues are discussed as they arise, both the company's designated liaison person and the auditors will have greater assurance that there is an appropriate understanding of the facts involved before any decision is made concerning the audit recommendations.

Audit Conferences

Conferences regarding government audit activities should be conducted to protect both the contractor's and the government's interests. Contractors should always be aware of a government auditor's activities and the audit conference is a readily available means for monitoring such activities. Since the auditors are generally required to conduct conferences prior to and upon completion of the audit, contractors should make maximum use of the conferences for the reasons explained in the following paragraphs. The government auditor should also use such conferences to expedite the audit, enlist contractor support in obtaining the necessary records, and verify that the auditor's conclusions are based on a proper understanding of all important factual data.

Entrance Conference

The agency's general policy as outlined in the audit manual[13] (CAM Section 4-302) requires the auditor to conduct entrance conference with contractor personnel at the start of each audit assignment.The government's objective of this conference is to inform the contractor of the:

Purpose of audit.
Audit plan and scope of audit.
Authority for audit.
Types of contractor records required to perform the audit.
Duration of audit fieldwork.

Contractors should insist on such conferences and should be satisfied that the authority for the audit is valid. The conference should also be used to identify what the company can do to assist the auditor in the review.

Contractors should make every effort to understand the nature and extent of audit work to be performed, the types of records required to complete the audit, and how the audit results will be used. This understanding will generally enable the contractor to monitor the audit progress and assure that the auditor clearly understands the relevant data and systems associated with the audit issues. Ideally, the contractor should sufficiently understand the audit to assure that:

Pertinent data can be assembled for audit review.

Points of contact with company officials or employees can be arranged on a timely basis to provide pertinent information.

Contractor records and systems can be discussed or explained to avoid misunderstandings or incorrect conclusions by the auditor.

Exit Conferences

Auditors are required to conduct exit conferences (CAM Section 4-304[14]) at the completion of each audit assignment. The objectives of the exit conference vary depending on the type of audit performed. The principle differences in exit conference objectives are between contract price proposal and defective pricing audits versus incurred cost audits, systems reviews and other audits. Specific contract price proposal and defective pricing audit results are not generally discussed during the exit conference. However, auditors are required to disclose factual matters observed during the audit such as mistakes, system deficiencies, and failure to use specific historical data. Detailed discussions regarding these matters should provide insight areas as to basis for the auditor's findings. Nevertheless, the auditor is not allowed to disclose findings which are subject to contract negotiations.

Generally, results of incurred cost audits, system reviews and most other audits are fully discussed by the auditor. The audit findings are generally disclosed in an attempt to rectify any problems, misunderstandings, or deficiencies which the auditor has noted. In addition, audit findings related to cost allowability/ allocability issues which surface during incurred costs audits are discussed in an attempt to reach a final resolution of these costs prior to issuance of the report.

Contractors should document discussions at both entrance and exit conferences to establish an audit record which may assist in the resolution of any issues accruing subsequent to the audit report. For example, the record could be used to support a position as to whether certain cost or pricing data or other supporting data was provided to the auditor and in a timely basis. It could, as a result, be used in a defense against an allegation of defective pricing.

AUDIT REPORTS

Audit reports issued by government auditors may have a significant impact on a contractor's ability to obtain new government business or earn a reasonable profit on work performed or contemplated. Therefore, contractors should make every effort to minimize the potential negative effects of the audit report before it is released or determine to the extent practical, the basis for recommendations or findings contained in the report.

Auditors are not generally authorized to distribute copies of reports to the contractor. In most instances contractors must obtain copies of reports from the cognizant contracting officer. As a general rule contractors should not expect release of audit reports when the subject matter includes cost elements subject to future negotiation with the contracting officer or allegations of unlawful activity. However, working closely with the auditor may reveal vital information enabling the contractor to prepare for and deal with the issues contained in the report.

Contracting officers normally release reports relating to incurred cost, systems, compliance and functional/operations audits. Release of these reports is generally in the government's best interest since the release facilitates resolution of the issues.

The issuance of an adverse report by an audit agency will have various impacts on the contractor. An adverse proposal report may affect a contractor's ability to negotiate a reasonable price while a CAS noncompliance report or the withdrawal of a system approval may impact or complicate the process of negotiating new business.

Given the variety of subjects reported on by government auditors and contract administration personnel and the potential effects the report may have, it is not practical to address each possibility. However, contractors should determine the potential effects of each government report issued pertaining to their operations. Discussing the nature of the report to be issued and the potential impact associated with the report with the government representative should give contractors some idea as to what is in store for them in the future.

SUMMARY

Contract audits extend to virtually every stage of the procurement process. The scope of such audits is governed by specific provisions that are incorporated into solicitation documents, proposal forms, and resulting contracts.

Given the critical role of contract audit in the award, performance, and settlement of contracts, companies should carefully moniter the progress of such audits. The establishment of an audit liaison function and making full utilization of entrance and exit conferences are key elements in managing and facilitating that process.

NOTES

1. Superintendent of Documents, Government Printing Office, *Defense Contract Audit Manual*, Washington D.C. 20402 catalog no. D-1.461/2:7640.1/1283.
2. Grumman Aircraft Engineering Corporation, ASBCA no. 10309, September 15, 1966, 66-2 BCA 5,846.
3. SCM Corporation v. United States, (Ct. Cl. 1981) no. 6-76, March 11, 1981, 28 CCF 81,113.
4. Westinghouse Electric Corporation vs. U. S., Miscellaneous no. 11710, DC WD PA 1985, August 14, 1985, 33 CCF 73922; aff'd. CA-3 no. 85-3456, April 14, 1986, 33 CCF 74,342.
5. Newport News Shipbuilding and Dry Dock Company Reed, Misc. no 86-182 nn, EVA, March 20, 1987, 34 CCF 75,294.
6. Martin Marietta Corp. ASBCA nos. 31248, 31255, and 31271, May 7, 1987, 87-2 BCA 19,875.
7. Superintendent of Documents, Supra note 1.
8. Ibid.

9. Ibid.
10. Elmer B. Staats, Comptroller General of the United States, et al. v. Bristol Laboratories, Division of Bristol-Myers Company (S. Ct. 1981) no. 80-264, April 29, 1981, 28 CCF 81,339.
11. Charles A. Bowsher, Comptroller General of the United States, et al. v. Merck & Co., Inc; Merck & Co., Inc. v. Charles A. Bowsher, Comptroller General of the United States, and the United States (S. Ct. 1983) nos. 81-1273 and 81-1472, April 19, 1983, 30 CLF 70,944.
12. Superintendent of Documents, Supra note 1.
13. Ibid.
14. Ibid.

Chapter Fourteen
Disputes

BACKGROUND

Given the complexity and nature of the government contracting process, formal disputes are bound to arise. As in commercial contracting, no matter how clearly the intentions of each party are stated, no matter how carefully those intentions are included in a contractual document, and no matter how stable the environment, the diverse interests of the parties can easily create misunderstandings and disagreements. Disputes concerning government contract performance may arise in various ways. For example, the contracting parties may disagree on the amount of adjustment involved in a change order issued by the contracting officer. The allowability of costs resulting from contract terminations may likewise be grounds for a dispute as well as a contractor's claim for excess costs incurred because of government-caused delays.

Assuming that the intent of the parties is not always clearly stated, that contracts are not always carefully written, and that circumstances and personnel change, disagreements occur which must be resolved. These disagreements could be resolved solely through the judicial process; however, it would require considerable time and expense.

Often, such disagreements can be and are settled short of going to "court" or even avoided through advance planning. For example, as explained more completely in Chapter 7, FAR 31.109 provides for the use of advance agreements on particular cost items. Advance agreements can be used to avoid future disputes on the allowability of significant special or unusual costs, which are not specifically addressed in the cost principles.

Disputes can also be settled short of going to "court" through negotiation. This method of resolution should not be taken lightly. Many government contract disputes involve "gray" issues in which both parties have valid arguments. The better the case a contractor can make for its position, the better are the chances of achieving a favorable settlement. This is especially true in disagreements with the DCAA. It is important to present the best arguments before an audit report is issued. Once the report is issued, it is obviously more difficult to convince DCAA to change its position. When a significant disagreement with a DCAA auditor is involved, contractors should discuss the issue at progressively higher levels in the agency; however, once it is determined that the auditor is following DCAA policy, further discussion is probably not useful. Contractors may find it helpful to bring in an outside source with experience in the disputed area who can provide a fresh and perhaps more objective view of the issues in addition to providing potential arguments not yet considered.

The lines of communication with the contracting officer should be kept open as long as there is the possibility of a favorable settlement. Nevertheless, there may come a time when it is clear that further discussion is useless and the dispute must be resolved at another level.

As an alternative to the judicial process of resolving formal disputes, an administrative process was developed to provide a simpler means of resolution. Consequently, many government agencies have established administrative boards of contract appeals (BCAs). Until recently, the authority for using an administrative board to resolve government contract disputes was contained in the "disputes" clause included in a contract. This practice was approved by the Supreme Court in 1878.[1] Contractors should not avoid the judicial or administrative disputes process if the issue is significant and contractor representatives feel strongly about their position. Further, once the government is aware that a contractor will resort to the formal disputes process if necessary, it is less likely that the government would take an unreasonable position on future issues.

CONTRACT DISPUTES ACT OF 1978

Introduction

On November 1, 1978, the President signed Public Law 95-563, 92 Stat. 2383 (1978), the Contract Disputes Act of 1978. It was enacted based upon a report prepared six years earlier by the Commission on Government Procurement which called for sweeping reform in the system of legal and administrative remedies for resolving government contract disputes. The act implemented many of the commission's recommendations. As a result, there is now a uniform statutory basis for the settlement of contract disputes and claims. The Senate committee report on the proposed legislation provided a succinct description of its purpose:

> The Contract Disputes Act of 1978 provides a fair, balanced, and comprehensive statutory system of legal and administrative remedies in resolving Government contract claims. The Act's provisions help to induce resolution of more contract disputes by negotiation prior to litigation; equalize the bargaining power of the parties when a dispute exists; provide alternate forums suitable to handle the different types of disputes; and ensure fair and equitable treatment to contractors and Government agencies.[2]

The purpose of this chapter is to describe the disputes process under the act, while at the same time highlighting the changes to the prior disputes resolution process. The text also refers to applicable BCAs, Court of Claims, and other cases concerning interpretations of the act's provisions.

Applicability

The act became applicable to new contracts awarded by the federal executive agencies beginning on March 1, 1979 (120 days after it was signed by the President). In addition, the act contains a provision that states: "Notwithstanding any provision in a contract made before the effective date of this Act, the contractor may elect to proceed under this Act with respect to any claim pending then before the contracting officer or initiated thereafter."[3] Therefore, on contracts awarded prior to March 1, 1979, a contractor has the option of using the previous "disputes" clause procedures contained in the contract or the procedures available under the act. However, to have this option, the contractor's claim must have been "pending" before a contracting officer on March 1, 1979, or initiated thereafter. The Court of Claims in *Tapper and Associates*,[4] found that a claim is not "pending" once the contracting officer issues a final decision.

With few exceptions, the act (Section 3(a)) applies to any express or implied contract entered into by an executive agency for the:

Procurement of property, other than real property in being.

Procurement of services.

Procurement of construction, alteration, repair, or maintenance of real property.

Disposal of personal property.

Contracts of the Tennessee Valley Authority are accorded special treatment under the act (Section 3(b)). Further, the act (Section 3(c)) does not apply to contracts with foreign governments (or their agencies) or international organizations (or their subsidiary bodies) if the agency head determines that it would not be in the public interest.

Before getting too far into a discussion about the act, it is important to define the term *claim*, which will be used extensively throughout the chapter. The Office of Federal Procurement Policy (OFPP) provided the following definition in its Policy Letter 80-3, Subject:Regulatory Guidance on P.L 95-563, the Contract Disputes Act of 1978:

As used herein "claim" means a written demand by one of the contracting parties seeking, as a legal right, the payment of money, adjustment or interpretation of contract terms, or other relief, arising under or related to the contract.
A voucher, invoice, or request for payment that is not in dispute when submitted is not a claim for the purposes of the Act. However, where such submission is subsequently not acted upon in a reasonable time, or disputed either as to liability or amount, it may be converted to a claim under Section 6(a) of the Act. . . .[5]

The conversion to a claim is best made by submitting the payment request in writing to the contracting officer as part of a formal demand for a final decision. This is important because interest (discussed later in this chapter) accrues only on "claims".

Contracting Officer

The applicable contracting officer (CO) is the starting point for all claims "relating to a contract" whether initiated by the contractor or the government. The phrase "relating to a contract" includes breach of contract claims. Prior to the act, only disputes concerning a question of fact "arising under a contract" were subject to the administrative remedies process. Questions of law such as breach of contract claims were to be brought to a Federal district court (Tucker Act, 28 U.S.C. 1346(a)(2)) if the amount of the claim did not exceed $10,000 or to the Court of Claims for any amount. The Contract Disputes Act amended the Tucker Act to delete jurisdiction of the district courts over contract claims against the United States that are subject to jurisdiction of the Court of Claims. The distinction between questions of fact and questions of law will be discussed in more detail later in the chapter.

Contractor claims "relating to a contract" must be submitted to the CO for a decision. Government claims must also be formalized through a CO decision. However, claims assigned statutorily to another government agency are excluded. For example, in *Allied Painting & Decorating Co.*[6] the ASBCA found that disputes falling under the Davis-Bacon Act are subject to a review and decision by the Secretary of Labor.

Certification of Claims

Given the current government environment related to the concern of fraud, waste, and abuse, the act includes a requirement that contractors certify claims over $50,000. A review of the Senate committee report discloses that this requirement appears to have been added as a result of Admiral H. G. Rickover's testimony concerning "inflated" claims (i.e., unsupported claims inflated as a negotiation ploy with the objective of negotiating a more favorable settlement).

The act provides the following:

> For claims of more than $50,000, the contractor shall certify that the claim is made in good faith, that the supporting data are accurate and complete to the best of his knowledge and belief, and that the amount requested accurately reflects the contract adjustment for which the contractor believes the government is liable.[7]

FAR 33.001 states—in part—that a "claim" as "a written demand or written assertion . . . seeking the payment of money exceeding $50,000 is not a claim under the Act until certified. . . ." This issue has been heavily debated and will be covered in more detail later in the chapter under the section on interest. Also, the ASBCA in *Harnischfeger*[8] dismissed claims for lack of unqualified certification. It stated that the lack of a finite amount effectively precluded any meaningful consideration of the claim by the CO. In a related case, *Newell Clothing Co.,*[9] the contractor attempted to have the CO and ASBCA rule first on entitlement to a claim, reserving quantum (money damages) for disposition by negotiation or further appeal. As such, Newell did not submit a certified claim. While there was a dissenting opinion, the majority opinion was that the act required a certified claim because it exceeded $50,000 and, therefore, dismissed the appeal as premature. In *Paul E. Lehman, Inc.,*[10] the Court of Claims held that a claim over $50,000 is not a valid claim unless it has been certified, and dismissed a contractor's suit because of the lack of certification. The fact that a CO rendered a final decision on the claim was of no consequence as the court ruled that a CO has no authority to waive a requirement imposed by statute. This ruling has been affirmed in subsequent cases and should be considered firm. In Skelly and Loy,[11] the Court of Claims ruled that it did not have jurisdiction to hear an uncertified claim over $50,000. However, it stated that the contractor could correct the defect by resubmitting its claim with a proper certification. Further, in W. H. Moseley Co., Inc.,[12] the ASBCA decided that it is not barred from ordering a contracting officer to issue a new final decision when the contractor later submits a properly certified claim. It is important to keep these considerations in mind when submitting a claim. Disregarding them can cause delays in resolving a dispute and possibly lost interest if the contractor's claim is ultimately decided favorably.

The act has been interpreted to mean that when the government makes a claim against a contractor and withholds funds against a contract to obtain payment, the contractor does not have to certify its claim in order to get its money.[13]

Fraudulent Claims

Another requirement of the act provides for a potential penalty for unsupported claims. The provision states:

> If a contractor is unable to support any part of his claim and it is determined that such inability is attributable to misrepresentation of fact or fraud on the part of the contractor, he shall be liable to the Government for an amount equal to such unsupported part of the claim in addition to all costs to the Government attributable to the cost of reviewing said part of his claim. Liability under this subsection shall be determined within six years of the commission of such misrepresentation of fact or fraud.[14]

The phrase "misrepresentation of fact" is defined in the act. It should be noted that the penalty provided under the act does not relieve the contractor from liability under the False Claims Act (31 U.S.C. 231). Also, liability under this provision can exist regardless of the size of the claim and whether or not it was certified.

Required Notices

Government contractors should understand that some contract clauses require the contractor to notify the CO of circumstances that may entitle the contractor to submit a claim. For example, under the "changes-fixed-price" clause (FAR 52.243-1(c)) a contractor is required to assert a claim for an equitable adjustment within 30 days of receipt of the notification of change unless waived by the CO. Such notices or claims are usually required prerequisities to the issuance of a final decision by the CO. If they are required but not presented, the CO may not make a final decision and, therefore, there would be no basis for appeal. Further, time restraints imposed may preclude further consideration of a claim. Some other clauses which contain such notification requirements are the "differing site conditions" clause, "economic price adjustment—standard supplies" clause, and "government delay of work" clause.

Contracting Officer's Decision

As was the practice under the old "disputes" clause, the act specifically requires the CO's final decision to be in writing with a copy furnished to the contractor by mail or other means. FAR 33.211 states that the decision shall include a (i) description of the claim or dispute, (ii) reference to the pertinent contract terms, (iii) statement of the factual areas of agreement and disagreement, (iv) statement of the CO's decision, with supporting rationale, (v) comment that it is the final decision of the CO, and (vi) statement informing the contractor of its rights to appeal to the applicable BCA or Court of Claims.

As stated previously, a final decision is required before the appeals process can begin. Not every letter, order, instruction, or communication issued by a CO represents an appealable final decision. For example, the ASBCA in *R. G. Robbins Co., Inc.*,[15] ruled that a CO's letter, which suggested a no-cost settlement in response to the contractor's proposed settlement of a partial termination for convenience, did not constitute an appealable final decision. The Board stated that in determining if a communication from a CO represents a final decision, the standard to be applied is whether the "communication manifested objectively that the contractor's claim cannot be satisfied or settled by agreement or, alternatively, that there has been a failure of the parties to agree upon the amount. . . ." As was true prior to the act, it is important to make a valid attempt to resolve disagreements before entering the disputes process, which can be costly as well as time consuming. The ability to settle disputes in this manner depends on the government and contractor representatives' ability to maintain an open mind on the issues. OFPP regulatory coverage on the resolution of claims contains the following statement:

> In appropriate circumstances, before issuance of a contracting officer's decision on a claim, informal discussions between the parties, to the extent feasible by individuals who have not participated substantially in the matter in dispute, can aid in the resolution of differences by mutual agreement and should be considered.[16]

One of the problems experienced by contractors prior to the act was the tendency for some COs to hold claims for long periods of time before making a decision. As a result, the act provides (Section 6(c)(1)) that the CO's decision on any submitted claim of $50,000 or less shall be within 60 days of receipt of the claim if requested by the contractor. On certified claims of more than $50,000 the CO, within 60 days of receipt of the claim, is required to either issue a decision or notify the contractor when a decision is expected to be issued (Section 6(c)(2)). A key requirement is that the CO must issue a final decision within a reasonable time, considering the size of the claim, its complexity, and the adequacy of the contractor's support for the claim.

If the CO unreasonably delays issuing a final decision, a contractor may request the agency BCA to direct the CO to issue a decision within a specified time. Further, the failure by a CO to issue a decision on a contract claim within the required period will be considered a decision denying the claim. The contractor may then pursue the appeals process. In *SCM Corp.*,[17] the Court of Claims found that since the CO did not issue a decision within 60 days after receiving SCM's certified claim of over $50,000 and since he did not formally notify SCM within that period that a specified time beyond 60 days would be required, he was deemed to have denied the claim. In this case, the claim was pending before the CO for almost 2 years before SCM obtained relief in the Court of Claims, and the CO never advised the contractor that he would need additional time to reach a decision. In a related case, *Westclox Military Products*,[18] the ASBCA ruled that notwithstanding the inadequacy of a submitted certified claim for over $50,000, the CO is not relieved of the statutory duty to issue (within 60 days) a final decision or notify the contractor when a decision can be expected. In the event a contractor appeals or files suit without a CO's final decision, the tribunal reviewing the claim may suspend its proceedings to obtain such a decision.

The act states, in part:

> The contracting officer's decision on the claim shall be final and conclusive and not subject to review by any forum, tribunal, or Government agency, unless an appeal or suit is timely commenced as authorized by the Act. Nothing in this Act shall prohibit executive agencies from including a clause in government contracts requiring that pending final decision of an appeal, action, or final settlement, a contractor shall proceed diligently with performance of the contract in accordance with the contracting officer's decision.[19]

The "disputes" clauses in existence before the act generally required a contractor to continue diligent performance under a contract in accordance with the CO's decision while the dispute was being prosecuted. However, these clauses only related to questions of fact (i.e., claims arising under the contract). The legislative history of the act discloses that even breach of contract claims (questions of law) "relate to a contract." As a result, a question arose over the right of a contractor to stop work under a "breach of contract" issue. After much debate, this issue was resolved by the OFPP in its published standard "disputes" clause, effective June 1, 1980 (FAR 52.233-1). This clause, which applies to all solicitations and resulting contracts issued on or after that date, obligates a contractor to continue performance only if the dispute "arises under the contract." Nevertheless, procuring agencies are allowed to change the standard "disputes" clause included in contracts which may be vital to security or the public health and welfare to obligate a contractor to continue performance even if a breach of contract dispute arises (FAR 33.214). The ability of OFPP to publish such uniform rules of procedure was specifically granted by the act.

Appeals Process

Once the CO issues a final decision, a contractor has two options if it wants to contest the decision. It can appeal to the applicable agency BCA or it can file suit directly in the Claims Court (known as the Court of Claims Trial Division before enactment of the Federal Courts Improvement Act, Public Law 97-164, effective October 1, 1982). If it appeals to the BCA, it must do so within 90 days after receiving the decision. Prior to the act, an appeal had to be filed with the BCA within 30 days. The time allowed to submit a timely appeal may be extended if the CO's final decision does not adequately inform the contractor of its rights and options. Of course, on contracts awarded prior to March 1, 1979, a contractor has the option of using either the "disputes" clause in the contract or the Contract Disputes Act procedures. There are advantages and disadvantages of each. For example, under the old procedures, a contractor would not have to certify claims over $50,000 but also would have no option to bypass the BCA and go directly to court and could not receive interest on a claim unless some other provision is contained in the contract.

The burden of proof is on the contractor to show that an appeal is timely. The ASBCA in *Policy Research, Inc.*[20] reasserted that the 90-day provision in the act is jurisdictional and that it had no authority to waive or excuse a contractor's failure to file within that time period. This decision has been affirmed by the U.S. Court of Appeals for the Federal Circuit.[21]

The contractor must mail or otherwise furnish written notice of an appeal to the applicable BCA. A copy of the notice is to be provided to the CO. It is important that the notice (1) indicate that an appeal is being taken, (2) identify the department and agency or bureau involved, (3) reference the CO's final decision, and (4) identify the contract involved in the dispute by number and the amount in dispute, if known. The contractor must leave no doubt that an appeal is intended.

If the contractor decides to bypass the BCA process and proceed directly to the Claims Court, it must do so within 12 months after receiving the CO's decision. This option was not available to contractors prior to the act unless the action was for breach of contract. Actions brought directly to the Claims Court (and also actions brought to the BCAs) proceed de novo, which means that the CO's decision carries no presumption of correctness and the Court can either increase or decrease the award made in the contracting officer's decision.[22]

Agency Boards of Contract Appeals

The act contains a provision (Section 8(a)(1)) whereby, after consultation with the administrator of the OFPP and a determination that a workload study shows a need for at least three fulltime members, a BCA may be established within an executive agency. If the volume of claims is not enough to justify a board or if considered otherwise appropriate, the agency head can arrange for appeals to be decided by a BCA of another agency. Failing this, the agency head can submit the case to the administrator of OFPP for placement with an agency BCA.

Members selected for agency BCAs after the act's effective date must have at least five years' experience in public contract law. Members of agency BCAs as of the effective date of the act are considered "qualified" under a "grandfather" clause. The chairman and vice chairman of each BCA are selected from the members of the board by the agency head (or his/her designate). Board members are designated as administrative judges.

The act expanded the agency BCAs' jurisdiction to decide any appeal from a decision of a CO "relative to a contract." This jurisdiction now includes breach of contract claims, which previously had to be decided judicially, and claims arising under implied contracts. This supplants the pre-act requirement that jurisdiction was based on the existence of the "disputes" clause in the contract. Requests for relief under Public Law 85-804 (see FAR Part 50) are not considered to be claims under the act.

In exercising their additional jurisdiction, the BCAs are authorized to grant any relief that would be available to a litigant asserting a contract claim in the Claims Court. While money damages is the ordinary form of relief available in the Claims Court, the boards have also been granted contract rescission[23] and reformation authority.[24] However, specific performance cannot be ordered.[25]

In addition to the expansion of their jurisdiction, the boards now have the ability to administer oaths to witnesses, authorize depositions and discovery proceedings, and subpoena witnesses and production of books and papers. Subpoenas will be enforced in the federal district courts. The purpose of these increased powers is described in the Senate committee report accompanying the act. It states, in part:

> It is the intent of this increased authority to improve upon the quality of the board records, and to insure that the tools are available to make complete and accurate findings, thus minimizing the need for a court to supplement the board record on review.[26]

BCA Rules of Procedure

Introduction

The Contract Disputes Act of 1978 required the OFPP to issue guidelines for the procedures of the agency BCAs. OFPP published these guidelines on June 14, 1979.[27] To achieve maximum uniformity for government contract appeal practice, agency BCAs are expected to adopt these guidelines except when minor variances are justified due to a board's size or nature of its docket. The following discussion highlights some of the more significant provisions of the guidelines; however, those involved in a dispute should refer to the applicable board's rules of procedure. Further, it is not intended to be a legal analysis.

Docketing of Appeals

When a notice of appeal is received by a board, it will be docketed (placed on the board's docket). When docketed, the appellant should receive written notice from the board along with a copy of its rules of procedure.

Rule 4 File

Within 30 days after receiving notice that an appeal has been filed, the CO is to assemble and transmit to the board an appeal file (called the Rule 4 file) consisting of all documents pertinent to the appeal. The CO at the same time is to furnish the appellant copies of these documents. The appellant then has 30 days after receiving the file to transmit to the board any documents not contained in the file that are relevant to the appeal. Copies of such documents should be furnished to the government trial attorney. Since the Rule 4 file is considered part of the record upon which the board will make its decision, it is extremely important to assure that all relevant documents are included and that inappropriate documents are excluded. In some cases the board may not require a Rule 4 file if requested in the appeal or if stipulated thereafter.

Complaint

Within 30 days after receiving notice that the appeal has been docketed, the appellant is to file with the board a "complaint" setting forth simple, concise, and direct statements of each claim. The complaint should provide the basis for each claim, with references to the appropriate contract provisions, and the dollar amount claimed, if known. The rules allow for the complaint to be filed with the notice of appeal or, alternatively, the notice of appeal may serve as the complaint if it contains the required information.

Answer to Complaint

The government is required to prepare and submit to the board an "answer" to the complaint within 30 days after receiving the complaint. The government's answer is generally subject to the same requirements as the complaint. It should be simple, concise, and direct and, preferably, structured as a paragraph by paragraph admission or denial of corresponding paragraphs in the complaint. The appellant is provided a copy of the answer.

Amendments

Amendments to the complaint and answer are acceptable. This may be done by direction of the board to either party to make a more definitive statement of the complaint or answer, or to reply to an answer. In addition, the board, as its discretion may permit either party to amend its statements or "pleadings" under conditions fair to both parties.

Hearing Election

After the government's answer is filed, each party notifies the board whether it desires a hearing on the dispute or elects to have the case decided on the record without a hearing. Either party may elect to waive a hearing; however, this does not relieve the parties from the burden of proving the facts supporting their allegations or defenses. This may be accomplished through affidavits, depositions, answers to interrogatories (written questions), and stipulations to supplement other evidence in the record.

Prehearing Briefs

If a hearing is elected, the board may, at its discretion, require the parties to submit prehearing briefs to assure the issues are adequately addressed. Either party may voluntarily submit a prehearing brief to the board provided it notifies the other party. All briefs must be received by the board at least 15 days before the hearing date and a copy is to be furnished to the other party.

Conferences

Whether or not a hearing is elected, the board may, at its discretion or by application of either party, arrange a conference (by telephone if appropriate) to consider any matters that may aid in the disposition of the appeal. Such matters may include (1) simplification, clarification, or severing of the issues, (2) agreements that will avoid unnecessary proof, and (3) the possibility of a settlement of any or all issues in dispute. The results of any such conferences, including rulings and orders, will be in writing and will be added to the board's record.

Discovery

To further document the record on which the board's decision will be based, the parties to the dispute are encouraged to engage in voluntary discovery procedures, including (1) the taking of depositions, (2) requesting issuance of subpoenas, (3) serving written interrogatories, and (4) requesting admissions and the production, inspection, and copying of documents. The board will intervene when necessary to protect the parties from undue requests or to order compliance with discovery requests.

Discovery is an important part of litigation and in complex government contract cases, is critical to a successful prosecution or possible settlement of a case. Discovery can be used to identify weaknesses on the other side as well as its evidence. This information sometimes can be used as leverage for obtaining a favorable settlement.

The BCAs generally look to the federal rules of civil procedure for guidance regarding discovery disputes (i.e., what is available versus what can be protected). Generally, the boards use the criterion of "good cause" in deciding on what is or is not discoverable. In *Airco, Inc.,*[28] the Department of Interior BCA observed:

> the touchstones of discovery are:
> 1. probability that the discovery will lead to admissibile evidence (but it is not a ground for objection that a document or other material involved in discovery is not admissible per se), and
> 2. that the burden is commensurate with the need.
> The objections to discovery are (a) privilege—but privilege is not absolute, especially when a competing concern overweighs the reason for the privilege, and (b) burden, i.e., the benefit likely to be derived from the discovery is clearly much less than the burden of compliance.

If it can be shown that the requested information is relevant, needed, not subject to privilege from disclosure, and not relatively burdensome to obtain, discovery is likely. However, if the requested information is privileged or it is relatively burdensome to provide and is not relevant or needed, discovery will likely be denied. These are extremes, however, and disputes in between these extremes must be viewed on a case-by-case basis.

In 1966, the Freedom of Information Act (FOIA) was enacted which resulted in an additional discovery tool for government contractors. This Act provides for the right of access to information in the possession of most federal agencies. While this right to obtain information is available to virtually everyone, the discovery implications are extremely important to a government contractor when normal discovery procedures are unavailable. For example, it can be used to obtain information prior to initiating litigation. Such information may be used in deciding whether or not to litigate. Also, the FOIA can be used to obtain information which is so broad and general that it is outside the scope of normal discovery. Further, information can often be obtained faster through the FOIA than through discovery.

Of course, the FOIA provides for the exemption of certain records from disclosure such as classified material. Of the nine exemptions provided in the law, those more likely to be encountered by government contractors in requesting information for discovery purposes are no. 3, specific statutory exemptions of other statutes, no. 4, confidential business information such as trade secrets and commercial or financial information, and no. 5, agency communications which would be privileged and unavailable to a party in litigation with the agency.

While we have been discussing the use of the FOIA to obtain information, it is important for government contractors to understand their rights in preventing the disclosure of information they have submitted to the government. Normally, before information provided by a nongovernment source is released on an FOIA request, the source is notified of the intent to release. This gives the source an opportunity to object to the release and a chance to have its objections presented at a hearing.

Hearings and Representation

Hearings are held at places and at times determined appropriate by the board. The board may adjust the date of a hearing if requested and if for good reason. At least 15 days notice is to be given the parties of the time and place set for a hearing. In scheduling hearings, the board will consider the desires of the parties and the requirement for a just and inexpensive determination of appeals without unnecessary delay.

Hearings are conducted as informally as reasonable and appropriate in the circumstances. Evidence is offered in accordance with the federal rules of evidence and witnesses are examined orally under oath or affirmation unless the presiding administrative judge or examiner orders otherwise. Because of the complex nature of many government contracting issues, both contractors and the government rely on the testimony of expert witnesses to effectively present their case. If scientific, accounting, or other specialized technical knowledge will assist the hearing officer in understanding the evidence presented or a fact in issue, the federal rules of evidence applicable to board proceedings allow expert witnesses to present testimony in the form of an opinion. Expert witnesses can be used effectively not only to support a position but also to rebut the testimony of an expert witness used by the other side.

An appellant may be represented before the board by an appropriate member of the appellant's organization or by a duly-licensed attorney. In most cases, despite the relative informality of proceedings and especially if significant amounts are involved, the appellant should be represented by an attorney. At the conclusion of a hearing and if agreed upon by all parties, posthearing briefs will be submitted.

Decisions and Motions for Reconsideration

Board decisions on appeals will be made in writing with copies sent simultaneously to both parties. Generally, while hearings are conducted by a single administrative judge or examiner, decisions are made by a panel of administrative judges who decide the case by majority vote. The opinions of dissenting panel members are also provided.

A motion for reconsideration of the decision may be filed within 30 days after receiving the decision. Such motions are not looked upon favorably by a board unless (1) newly discovered evidence is presented, (2) there is a patent error in the decision such as a math error, or (3) the decision needs clarification to be implemented. Rehashing arguments already on the record is not accepted.

Optional Accelerated and Small Claims Procedures

One of the problems sought to be resolved by the Contracts Dispute act was the inflexible board system that had evolved as a result of Supreme Court decisions and the Wunderlich Act. The Senate committee report supporting the act's legislation stated, in part:

> The overriding problem with the present agency board system is that the boards attempt to adjudicate claims across the entire spectrum of size and complexity. Although the boards generally are doing an adequate job under the circumstances, this is not the most effective way to handle contract disputes.[29]

As a result, the act has provided for accelerated and small claims procedures on appeals. These procedures are used at the sole election of the contractor. The election should be made in writing within 60 days after receiving notice that the appeal has been docketed.

The act requires (Section 8(f)) that the rules of each agency board include a procedure for the *accelerated* disposition of claims for $50,000 or less. The objective is to resolve such appeals within 180 days from the date the contractor elects to use the procedure. Although the conduct of "accelerated" cases is similar to the normal disputes process, time periods may be shortened and pleadings, discovery, and other prehearing activities may be reduced or waived to enable the board to reach a decision within the 180 day period.

The act further requires (Section 9) that the rules of each agency board include a procedure for the *expedited* disposition of claims for $10,000 or less. The objective is to resolve such appeals within 120 days from the date the contractor elects to use the procedure. Once again, time periods of activities are shortened and rules are simplified to allow the board to reach a decision within the prescribed time. Decisions may be made by a single administrative judge and, unless fraudulent, are final and conclusive and may not be appealed or set aside. Further, such decisions have no precedential value for future cases (i.e., decisions in future cases cannot be based on the findings in expedited cases). The dollar threshold for "expedited" procedures is to be reviewed by the administrator of OFPP every 3 years and adjusted based upon selected economic indexes.

Board of Contract Appeals Workload

The ASBCA prepares an annual report of its activities after the end of each government fiscal year. The report provides such information as the number of appeals docketed and disposed of during the year, average dollar amount of claims, types and nature of contracts involved, principal contract clauses involved, and the average number of days from the date of docketing to the date of decision. For example, for government FYs 1984, 1985, and 1986 the ASBCA reported the following case workload:

	FY 1984	FY 1985	FY 1986
On hand at beginning of year	1,695	1,729	2,074
Docketed during year	1,369	1,638	1.960
Total requiring disposition	3,064	3,367	4,034
Disposed of during year	1,335	1,293	1,938
On hand at year end	1,729	2,074	2,096

As can be seen from a review of the workload data, there was a 20% increase in the number of cases docketed each year resulting in a relatively similar increase in the cases pending at year end except in 1986 when the increase was only 1%. Why has the Board's docket grown by only 22 appeals when a record number of new appeals (1960) were docketed in FY86? The answer is hard work, better use of the Board's resources, and a more active participation by the administrative judges in processing the appeals on their dockets. The Board members have used pre-trial methods to reduce records only to disputed facts resulting in the issuance of more summary judgment decisions, have limited hearing time and permissible discovery, and have played a more active role in the settlement process. The statistics reflect that in FY86, the Board disposed of approximately 50% more appeals than in FY85. The "changes" and "default" clauses were the two clauses most frequently identified as the principal issue in dispute. The number of disputes concerning allowable costs and contract specifications has been rising, however. An interesting statistic is that almost 50% of the cases disposed of are the result of a settlement prior to a decision,confirming the general desire to continue negotiations for a settlement even after a case is docketed. Of the cases disposed of in FY1986, about 15% of the appeals were denied and about 12% were sustained. One final statistic of interest involved the number of days from the date a case is docketed until the date of decision. For FY1985, the average time on docket for all cases was 484 days. In 1986 this figure was reduced to 440 days. For cases using the "accelerated" and "expedited" procedures, the average time on docket was 149 days. This figure has been steadily reducing from a high of 173 days in 1982 to the new low of 142 days in 1986.

Board Jurisdiction of Subcontractor Appeals

The Contracts Dispute Act act has apparently had little, if any, effect on the rights of subcontractors in board proceedings. Normally, a subcontractor has no right of direct access to the boards because there is no "privity of contract" between the subcontractor and the government (they are not parties to a contract). Nevertheless, there are exceptions to this general rule. Agency regulations or agreements may allow for direct access to the boards. Also, if the prime contractor is found as acting as a purchasing agent for the government, a subcontractor may be found to have "privity." Finally, subcontractors may have their appeals brought to the boards when the prime contractor agrees to sponsor an appeal on the subcontractor's behalf. In such cases, the prime files the appeal and may either conduct the appeal or agree to have the subcontractor conduct it. It has been held that when a prime contractor sponsors an appeal for a subcontractor in excess of $50,000, both the prime and subcontractor must certify the claim.[30] Because of potential problems concerning "privity of contract," it is important for the subcontractor to have provisions included in the subcontract for the prime to sponsor the subcontractor's appeal if the dispute is with the government. Furthermore, the subcontract should contain provisions for arbitration or other means for settling disputes between the prime and subcontractor.

Judicial Review of Board Decisions

The act provides (Section 8(g)(1)) that the decision of an agency BCA under regular or accelerated procedures is final unless (1) the contractor appeals the decision to the Court of Appeals for the Federal Circuit (CAFC) (known as the Court of Claims Appellate Division prior to enactment of the Federal Courts Improvement Act) within 120 days after receiving the decision or (2) the agency head, after approval by the Attorney General, transmits the decision to the Court of Appeals for judicial review, again within the 120 day period. (Appeals from BCA decisions under pre-Disputes Act procedures have gone to the Claims Court.) When there has been a motion for reconsideration of a BCA decision, the 120 day period runs from receipt of the decision on the motion, not the original decision.

Prior to the act, the ability of the government to appeal BCA decisions to the Court of Claims was virtually impossible, unless fraud or bad faith was found. In *S&E Contractors*,[31] the Supreme Court decided that the Wunderlich Act (41 U.S.C.) was not intended to confer the same rights to contractors and the government regarding judicial review of BCA decisions. This decision was nullified overturned by the Contract Disputes Act, which now provides the same standard for judicial review. According to the Senate committee report accompanying the act, the key reasons for allowing equal access to judicial review were that (1) the agency BCAs do not act as a representative of the agency and (2) BCA decisions may set important precedents in procurement law.

On appeals of agency BCA decisions by a contractor or the government, the act states, in part: ". . . the decision of the agency board on any question of law *shall not be* final or conclusive, but the decision on any question of fact *shall be* final and conclusive and shall not be set aside unless the decision is fraudulent, or arbitrary, or capricious, or so grossly erroneous as to necessarily imply bad faith, or if such decision is not supported by substantial evidence."[32] (Underscoring added.) This standard of review is essentially the same as set forth in the Wunderlich Act.

The differentiation of questions of law and questions of fact is not always easily determined. Some cases involve mixed questions of law and fact. For example, the elements that must be proven in order to establish a claim is a question of law. Whereas, whether a given cost is reasonable, allocable, and allowable in accordance with generally accepted accounting principles is a question of fact.

Prior to the act, the Supreme Court ruled that the Court of Claims was confined to a review of the administrative record under Wunderlich Act standards and could not receive new evidence.[33]

If further evidence was considered necessary, the Court was required to suspend its proceedings and remand the case to the BCA. This procedure was modified by the act (Section 10(c)) to allow the Court of Claims, at its option, to remand a case to the BCA for further action or to retain the case and take additional evidence or action necessary to conclude the case. The reason for this change was provided in the Senate committee report accompanying the bill for the act:

> The delays resulting from the requirement that cases be remanded to a busy agency board is too great a price to pay for maintaining the distinction between factfinding and reviewing findings of law, and is, furthermore, a waste of the readily accessible factfinding mechanisms available in the courts.[34]

Interest

The act states:

> Interest on amounts found due contractors on claims shall be paid to the contractor from the date the contracting officer receives the claim pursuant to Section 6(a) from the contractor until payment thereof. The interest provided for in this section shall be paid at the rate established by the Secretary of the Treasury pursuant to Public Law 92-41 (85 Stat. 97). . . .[35]

Therefore, a favorable disposition of a contractor's claim results in simple inter-est accruing from the CO's receipt of the claim until payment. A favorable disposition could involve a final judgment in a BCA or the Court of Claims, or a settlement between the government and contractor prior to a BCA or court decision.

There have been numerous controversies concerning the interest provision but the most prevalent issue has been the point at which interest begins to run. The House Judiciary Committee has stated that it was the intent of the act that the submission of a written claim to a CO under Section 6(a) of the act starts the "interest clock running," and that the "certification" requirement in Section 6(c) was intended only as a prerequisite to payment. However, some agencies, have concluded that they have not "received" a claim until certified. This argument received support from the *Lehman*[36] case discussed earlier. In that case, the Court of Claims held that without certification there is no claim for the Court to review. And since the Act allows interest only on "claims," if there is no claim there is nothing to which interest may be applied.

Another issue on interest was decided by the Court of Claims in *Brookfield Construction Co.*,[37] where the court held that on claims pending as of the act's effective date, interest is payable only from the effective date of the act (March 1, 1979) to the date of payment. In yet another case, *Fidelity Construction Company, Inc.*,[38] the Department of Transportation Contract Appeals Board decided, and the CAFC affirmed, that a contractor's submission of an uncertified and grossly overstated claim did not start the "interest clock running." Instead, interest was determined from the time a certified and reasonable claim was submitted.

Simple interest is calculated using all of the Treasury rates in effect for the periods during which a claim remains unpaid. This was the decision of the General Services BCA in *Honeywell Inc.*[39] Most of the BCAs reached this same conclusion, which was confirmed by the CAFC in J.F. Shea Co., Inc. in 1985.[40] The board had previously awarded interest under the act erroneously, using only the rate in effect at the time the claim was submitted to the CO.

Payments

The Act (Section 13) requires prompt payment of court judgments and BCA monetary awards to contractors on their claims. Payment is made from the U.S. Treasury and is backcharged to the procuring agency involved, to be paid out of available appropriated funds.

EQUAL ACCESS TO JUSTICE ACT

The Equal Access to Justice Act (EAJA), Public Law 99-80, has substantial implications for small business concerns doing business with the government. This act provides that agencies conducting an "adversary adjudication" will award to a "prevailing party" other than the United States, reasonable fees and other expenses (in-house as well as outside assistance) incurred by that party during the proceedings unless the position of the agency is found to be "substantially justified." In simple terms, this means that eligible "parties" who prevail over the government in certain civil actions brought by or against the government may be awarded reasonable attorney fees and other expenses, unless (1) the government acted reasonably during the conduct of a genuine dispute or (2) special circumstances make an award unjust. A "prevailing party" under the EAJA does not include (1) any individual whose net worth exceeds $1 million and (2) any sole owner of an unincorporated business, or any partnership, corporation, association, or organization with a net worth exceeding $5 million or with more than 500 employees. In determining the eligibility of applicants, the net worth and number of employees for affiliated entities may be aggregated. The act's purpose is to provide certain "parties" with limited resources the opportunity to seek review of, or defend against, unreasonable governmental action in situations when lack of financial capability would normally deter such action.

The act was originally enacted on a three-year trial basis. It has since been enacted permanently. However, the new legislation has several changes. First, the new legislation expressly provides BCAs with authority to award attorneys fees and other expenses. Since the earlier EAJA did not expressly provide the BCAs with this authority, the court had held in Fidelity Construction Company[41] that the EAJA did not permit the boards to award such fees. In addition, the new legislation makes this section retroactive, thus allowing recovery by contractors who previously sought but were unable to obtain relief from a board.

Second, the new legislation attempts to clarify the standard for awarding attorneys fees. The original act provided that fees would not be awarded if the government's position was "substantially justified." The new act replaces this language and now provides the following:

> Whether or not the position of the agency was substantially justified shall be determined on the basis of the administrative record as a whole, which was made in the adversary adjudication for which fees and other expenses are sought.

Although the change does not obviate all of the problems associated with the recovery of fees, it creates a less subjective criterion.

The Department of Justice has taken the position that attorney fees generated prior to the EAJA's effective date are not recoverable. Its position is based on the decision in Brookfield Construction Co., Inc.,[42] in which the court held that the contractor was not entitled to interest on claims prior to the Contract Dispute Act's effective date, and absence of specific statutory language retroactively waiving the government's sovereign immunity. Nevertheless, several court decisions have allowed recovery of attorney fees incurred prior to the Act's effective date. These decisions were confirmed in Kay Manufacturing Co.[43] where the court ruled that the EAJA allows recovery of fees and expenses incurred both before and after its effective date if the action was pending on the effective date or initiated thereafter.

DEBARMENT AND SUSPENSION

While we are on the subject of disputes in government contracting, it is important to discuss the subject of debarment and suspension. Debarment and suspension are remedies available to the government to prohibit the award of contracts to a contractor who has committed (debarment), or where there is probable cause to believe that it has committed (suspension), an act indicating a serious lack of business integrity or honesty which would affect its present "responsibility" as a government contractor.

There are two types of debarment: statutory and administrative. Statutory, as the name implies, relates to willful violations of certain statutes such as the Davis-Bacon and Walsh-Healey Acts.

The grounds for administrative debarment or suspension are set out in FAR 9.406-2 and in agency regulations. However, the decision to debar is discretionary. Normally, administrative debarment prevents a contractor from receiving a government contract or subcontract for a period of up to three years. If a contractor is suspended before being debarred, the suspension period should be considered in determining the debarment period. The period of a statutory debarment depends on the requirements of the applicable statute. Normally, contractors are to be accorded due process rights before debarment actions are taken. The grounds for administrative suspension are set out in FAR 9.407-2. A suspension is a temporary prohibition against the awarding of contracts to a contractor when there is probable cause that the contractor has committed an act which would justify debarment. The time of suspension varies, depending on the length of the investigations and any ensuring legal proceedings. Suspensions may be imposed without prior notice to the contractor. An opportunity to be heard is normally given after receiving notice unless it is based on an indictment or other compelling reason.

On June 24, 1982 the OFPP issued Policy Letter No. 82-1 to provide uniform *administrative* debarment and suspension policies and procedures for the executive branch.[44] The letter, provided several changes to the administrative suspension and debarment rules including:

Debarments and suspensions are normally imposed government-wide rather than just agency-wide.

Company-wide debarment and suspension is possible rather than just the division or other organizational element involved.

The agency head or an authorized desumate is the "debarring official" and "suspending official".

A consolidated list of all debarred, suspended, and ineligible contractors is to be maintained by the GSA.

More detailed criteria is established on the effect of the imputed actions of others in debarment proceedings. For example, the fraudulent, criminal, or other seriously improper conduct of any officer, director, shareholder, partner, employee, or other individual associated with a contractor may be imputed to the contractor when it occurred in connection with the performance of the individual's duties for or on behalf of the contractor or with the contractor's knowledge, approval, or acquiescence. Acceptance of the benefits derived from the conduct is evidence of knowledge, approval, or acquiescence.

This policy represents just another step in the current attack on perceived fraud, waste, and abuse in government and government procurement. The changes represent important new considerations that government contractors should be aware of, especially the extension of the imputed actions of others. It also represents a current trend in the statutory and regulatory framework in government contracting which emphasizes even more the need for a complete understanding of the rules involved and the need for adequate accounting and internal control systems to assure compliance with those rules.

The requirements of Policy Letter No. 82-1 are incorporated into FAR Subpart 9.4.

SUMMARY

During the performance of government contracts, disagreements arise and a means must be available to resolve them if they cannot be settled through negotiation. Although settlement is the preferred approach and is used to resolve most disagreements, sometimes an outside party must be used to help reach a decision. Such disagreements could be resolved solely by the courts but this would be expensive and time-consuming. Therefore, many government agencies have established administrative boards of contract appeals as an administrative alternative to the courts.

Until the Contract Disputes Act of 1978, this process was authorized through a "disputes" clause contained in the contract. The contract Disputes Act provided a statutory basis for the administrative process and made several changes to the prior disputes-resolving system, including: certification of claims over $50,000, penalties for fraudulent claims, time restraints on contracting officer decisions, accelerated and expedited handling of appeals cases, and interest on claims ultimately decided in the contractor's favor. The major problem with the Contract Disputes Act has been the overwhelming number of board and court cases involved in interpreting the act's provisions. The controversies are continuing in cases regarding the jurisdiction of federal courts provided by the Federal Courts Improvement Act of 1982.

Small businesses have been encouraged to challenge unreasonable government actions through the Equal Access to Justice Act. This act allows small businesses, as defined by the act, to recover reasonable attorney fees and other expenses when the position of the government is not found to be "substantially justified." While courts have the authority to make awards in appropriate cases, contractors have not been very successful in recovering costs because of the difficulty in showing that the government's position was not substantially justified even if it was wrong.

Finally, the government policy on debarment and suspension actions has been added to the list of "iron hand" government statutory and regulatory pronouncements aimed at stamping our perceived fraud, waste, and abuse. Contractors should be aware of the policy's provisions which provide heavy penalties for actions that seriously affect a contractor's "responsibility" to perform as a government contractor.

NOTES

1. Kihlberg v. United States, 97 U.S. 398 (1878).
2. *Report of the Committee on Government Affairs and the Committee on the Judiciary,* United States Senate, to accompany S.3178, Senate Report 95-1118, August 15, 1978, p. 1.
3. Contract Disputes Act of 1978, Public Law 95-563, 92 Stat. 2383 (1978), sec. 16.
4. Monroe M. Tapper and Associates v. United States, (Ct. Cl. 1979), December 12, 1979, 26 CCF 83,903.
5. OFPP Policy Letter 80-3, "Regulatory Guidance on P.L. 95-563, the Contract Disputes Act of 1978," para. I.1.(b), April 29, 1980.
6. Allied Painting & Decorating Co., ASBCA no. 25099, September 17, 1980, 80-2 BCA 14,710.
7. Contract Disputes Act of 1978, sec. 6(c) (1).
8. Harnischfeger Corp., ASBCA nos. 23918 and 24733, June 11, 1980, 80-2 BCA 14,541.
9. Newell Clothing Co., ASBCA no. 24482, October 15, 1980, 80-2 BCA 14,774.
10. Paul E. Lehman, Inc. v. United States, (Ct. Cl. 1982), February 24, 1982, 29 CCF 82,266.
11. Skelly and Loy v. United States, (Ct. Cl. 1982) August 11, 1982, 30 CCF 70,214.
12. W. H. Moseley Co., Inc., ASBCA no. 27370-18, January 13, 1983, 83-1 BCA 16,272.
13. Teton Construction Co., ASBCA nos. 27700, 28968, April 11, 1986, 86-2 BCA 18971.
14. Contract Disputes Act of 1978, sec. 5.
15. R. G. Robbins Co., Inc. ASBCA no. 26521, January 7, 1982, 82-1 BCA 15,643.
16. OFPP Policy Letter 80-3, para. I.1.(c).
17. SCM Corp. v. United States, (Ct. Cl. 1980), October 10, 1980, 28 CCF 80,789.
18. Westclox Military Products, ASBCA no. 25592, August 4, 1981, 81-2 BCA 15,270.
19. Contract Disputes Act of 1978, sec. 6(b).
20. Policy Research, Inc., ASBCA no. 26144, January 26, 1982, 82-1 BCA 15,618.
21. Cosmic Construction Co. v. United States (CAFC 23-82, 1982), December 10, 1982, 30 CCF 70,732.
22. The Assurance Company v. United States, CAFC 86-1350, 1987, March 10, 1987.
23. PAVCO, Inc., ASBCA no. 23783, April 8, 1980, 80-1 BCA 14,407.
24. Paragon Energy Corp. v. United States (Ct. Cl. 1981), April 8, 1981, 28 CCF 81,290.

25. Arcon/Pacific Contractors, ASBCA no. 25057, September 18, 1980, 80-2 BCA 14,709.
26. *Report of the Committee on Government Affairs and the Committee on the Judiciary,* supra note 2, p. 31.
27. OFPP "Final Rules of Procedure for Boards of Contract Appeals under the Contract Disputes Act of 1978," June 14, 1979, Government Contracts Reports, Commerce Clearing House, para. 79,604.
28. Airco, Inc., IBCA no. 1074-8-75, October 17, 1977, 77-2 BCA 12,809.
29. *Report of the Committee on Government Affairs and the Committee on the Judiciary,* supra note 2, p. 13.
30. Harrington Associates, Inc., GSBCA no. 6795, October 15, 1982, 82-2 BCA 16,103.
31. S&E Contractors, Inc. v. United States, (S. Ct. 1972), April 24, 1972, 17 CCF 81,265.
32. Contract Disputes Act of 1978, sec. 10(b).
33. United States v. Carlo Bianchi & Company, Inc. (S. Ct. 1963), June 3, 1963, 9 CCF 72,126.
34. *Report of the Committee on Government Affairs and the Committee on the Judiciary,* supra note 2, p. 30.
35. Contract Disputes Act of 1978, sec. 12.
36. Paul E. Lehman, Inc. v. United States, supra note 11.
37. Brookfield Construction Co., Inc. and Baylor Construction Corp. (a joint venture) v. United States, (Ct. Cl. 1981), September 23, 1981, 29 CCF 81,878.
38. Fidelity Construction Company, Inc., DOTCAB nos. 1113 and 1219, February 11, 1982, 82-1 BCA 15,633, aff'd. CAFC see footnote number 42.
39. Honeywell, Inc., GSBCA no. 5458, September 30, 1981, 81-2 BCA 15,383.
40. J.F. Shea Co., Inc. v. United States, CAFC no. 84-1166, February 1, 1985, 32 CCF 73224.
41. Fidelity Construction Company, Inc. v. United States (CAFC 27-82, 1983), February 18, 1983, 30 CCF 70,827.
42. Brookfield Construction Co., Inc. and Baylor Construction Corp. (a joint venture) v. United States, supra note 36.
43. Kay Manufacturing Co. v. United States (CAFC 478-73, 1983), February 18, 1983, 30 CCF 70,828.
44. OFPP Policy Letter No. 82-1, "Government-wide Debarment, Suspension and Ineligibility," June 24, 1982.

List of Acronyms

ACO	Administrative Contracting Officer
ADP	Automatic Data Processing
AFPR	Air Force Plant Representative
AFPRO	Air Force Plant Representative Office
AGBCA	Department of Agriculture Board of Contract Appeals
AICPA	American Institute of Certified Public Accountants
AID	Agency For International Development
APA	Administrative Procedures Act
ASBCA	Armed Services Board of Contract Appeals
ASPA	Armed Services Procurement Act
ASPM	Armed Services Procurement Manual for Contract Pricing
ASPR	Armed Services Procurement Regulation (subsequently changed to DAR)
BAFO	Best and Final Offer
BA	Basic Agreement
BCA	Board of Contract Appeals
BOA	Basic Ordering Agreement
B&P	Bid and Proposal
CA	Court of Appeals
CACO	Corporate Administrative Contracting Officer
CAFC	Court of Appeals for the Federal Circuit
CAO	Contract Administration Office
CAS	Cost Accounting Standards
CASB	Cost Accounting Standards Board
CBD	Commerce Business Daily
CCF	Contract Cases Federal
CFC	Cost of Facilities Capital
CFR	Code of Federal Regulations
CICA	Competition in Contracting Act
Cl Ct	Claims Court
CMC	Contract Monitoring Coordinator
CO	Contracting Officer

COC	Certificate of Competency
CODSIA	Council of Defense and Space Industry Associations
COM	Cost of Money
COR	Contracting Officer's Representative
COTR	Contracting Officer's Technical Representative
CPAF	Cost Plus Award-Fee Contract
CPFF	Cost Plus Fixed-Fee Contract
CPIF	Cost Plus Incentive-Fee Contract
CPM	Critical Path Method
CR	Cost Reimbursable Contract
C/SCS	Cost/Schedule Control Systems
C/SCSC	Cost/Schedule Control Systems Criteria
CtCl	Court of Claims (now Claims Court)
CWAS	Contractor's Weighted Average Share in Cost Risk
DAC	Defense Acquisition Circular
DAR	Defense Acquisition Regulation (formerly ASPR)
DARC	Defense Acquisition Regulatory Council
DCAA	Defense Contract Audit Agency
DCAAM	Defense Contract Audit Agency Manual
DCAS	Defense Contract Administration Services
DCASMA	Defense Contract Administration Services Management Area
DCASR	Defense Contract Administrative Services Region
DC D of C	District Court of the District of Columbia
DCIS	Defense Criminal Investigative Service
DISAO	Designated Independent Senior Acquisition Official
DLA	Defense Logistics Agency
DOD	Department of Defense
DOE	Department of Energy
DOI	Department of Interior
DOL	Department of Labor
DOT	Department of Transportation
DOT CAB	Department of Transportation Contract Appeals Board
EAJA	Equal Access to Justice Act
ECP	Engineering Change Proposal
ENG BCA	Corps of Engineers Board of Contract Appeals
ERISA	Employee Retirement Income Security Act
FAA	Federal Aviation Administration
FAR	Federal Acquisition Regulation
FAS	Financial Accounting Standards
FASB	Financial Accounting Standards Board
FBI	Federal Bureau of Investigation
FCOM	Facilities Cost of Money
FCPA	Foreign Corrupt Practices Act
FFP	Firm Fixed-Price Contract
FFRDC	Federally Funded Research and Development Center
FHWA	Federal Highway Administration
FIFO	First-In-First-Out
FMS	Foreign Militray Sales
FOIA	Freedom of Information Act
FP	Fixed-Price Contract
FPI	Fixed-Price Incentive Contract
FPR	Federal Procurement Regulations

FRA	Federal Railroad Administration
FTC	Federal Trade Commission
FY	Fiscal Year
G&A	General and Administrative
GAAP	Generally Accepted Accounting Principles
GAO	General Accounting Office
GATT	General Agreement on Tariffs and Trade
GSA	General Services Administration
GSBCA	General Services Board of Contract Appeals
HHS	Department of Health and Human Services
HUD	Department of Housing and Urban Development
HUDBCA	Department of Housing and Urban Development Board of Contract Appeals
IBCA	Department of Interior Board of Contract Appeals
ICA	International Communications Agency
ICMO	Indirect Cost Monitoring Office
IFB	Invitation for Bids
IG	Inspector General
IQC	Indefinite Quantity Contract
IR&D	Independent Research and Development
IRC	Internal Revenue Code
IRS	Internal Revenue Service
LBCA	Department of Labor Board of Contract Appeals
LIFO	Last-In-First-Out
LSA	Labor Surplus Area
MOU	Memorandum of Understanding
MPR	Material Planning Requirements
NASA	National Aeronautics & Space Administration
NASA BCA	National Aeronautics & Space Administration Board of Contract Appeals
NASA PR	National Aeronautics & Space Administration Procurement Regulation
NATO	North Atlantic Treaty Organization
NIH	National Institute of Health
NSIA	National Security Industrial Association
OFPP	Office of Federal Procurement Policy
OMB	Office of Management and Budget
OSHA	Occupational Safety and Health Act
PCM	Postal Contracting Manual
PCO	Procuring Contracting Officer
PERT	Program Evaluation and Review Technique
P.L.	Public Law
PNM	Price Negotiation Memorandum
PR	Purchase Request; Procurement Requisition
PSBCA	Postal Service Board of Contract Appeals
QA	Quality Assurance
R&D	Research and Development
RFP	Request for Proposals
RFQ	Request for Quotations
RFTP	Request for Technical Proposals
ROI	Return on Investment
SBA	Small Business Administration

SCA	Service Contract Act
S.Ct.	Supreme Court
SEC	Securities & Exchange Commission
SF	Standard Form
TCO	Termination Contracting Officer
T&M	Time and Materials Contract
TRA 86	Tax Reform Act of 1986
TSCO	Tri-Service Contracting Officer
UMTA	Urban Mass Transportation Administration
U.S.C.	United States Code
USDA	United States Department of Agriculture
VA	Veteran's Administration
VE	Value Engineering
VECP	Value Engineering Change Proposal
WBS	Work Breakdown Structure

Glossary

ACTUAL COST: An amount determined on the basis of cost incurred as distinguished from forecasted cost. Includes standard cost properly adjusted for applicable variance.

ADVANCE AGREEMENT: An agreement between the contractor and the government regarding the treatment of specified costs negotiated either before or during contract performance but preferably before the cost covered by the agreement is incurred.

ADVANCE PAYMENT: Remittance by the government to a contractor prior to, in anticipation of, and for the purpose of performance under a contract or contracts.

ALLOCABLE COST: A cost that is assignable or chargeable to one or more cost objectives in accordance with the relative benefits received or other equitable relationship.

ALLOCATION: Assignment of an item of cost, or a group of items of cost, to one or more cost objectives. Includes both direct assignment of cost and the reassignment of a share from an indirect cost pool.

ALLOWABLE COST: A cost which meets the tests of reasonableness; allocability; compliance with standards promulgated by the Cost Accounting Standards Board, if applicable, otherwise generally accepted accounting principles and practices appropriate in the circumstances; contractual terms; and limitations set forth the acquisition regulations.

BID AND PROPOSAL COST: Costs incurred in preparing, submitting and supporting bids and proposal (solicited or unsolicited) on potential government and non-government contracts.

BUSINESS UNIT: Any segment of an organization, or an entire business organization which is not divided into segments.

BUYING IN: The practice of bidding, particularly in connection with government contracts, whereby a price or cost estimate submitted is known to be less than the anticipated actual cost to perform the contractually required effort.

COMMERCIAL ITEM: An item, including both supplies and services, of a class or kind which is used regularly for other than government purposes, and is sold or traded in the course of conducting normal business operations.

COMPENSATED PERSONAL ABSENCE: Any absence from work for reasons such as illness, vacation, holidays, jury duty or military training, or personal activities, for which an employer pays compensation directly to an employee in accordance with a plan or custom of the employer.

COMPETITIVE NEGOTIATION: A negotiated procurement that (1) is initiated by a request for proposals, which sets out the government's requirements and the criteria for evaluation of offers, (2) contemplates the submission of timely proposals by the maximum number of possible offerors, (3) usually provides discussion with those offerors found to be within the competitive range, and 94) concludes with the award of a contract to the one offeror whose offer, price and other factors considered, is most advantageous to the government.

CONSTRUCTIVE CHANGE: A contract change directed by an authorized representative of the government, other than a formal change order, or a change resulting from government action or inaction.

CONTINGENCY: A possible future event or condition arising from presently known or unknown causes, the cost outcome of which is indeterminable.

CONTRACT: A term used to describe a variety of agreements or orders for the procurement of supplies or services. An agreement, enforceable by law, between two or more competent parties, to do or not do something not prohibited by law, for a legal consideration.

CONTRACT AUDIT: The examination of books, records, documents and other evidence and accounting procedures and practices pertaining to costs incurred or estimated to be incurred in the performance of one or more contracts. Includes providing advice on accounting and financial matters to assist in the negotiation, award, administration, repricing, and settlement of contracts.

CONTRACTING OFFICER: Any person who, either by virtue of his/her position or by appointment in accordance with prescribed regulations, is vested with the authority to enter into and administer contracts on behalf of the government and make determinations and findings with respect thereto, or with any part of such authority.

CONTRACT FINANCING: Methods utilized by the government to provide financial assistance to contractors in advance of or during contract performance but prior to delivery and acceptance. In order of government preference, these methods are: progress payments (customary), guaranteed loans, progress payments (unusual), and advance payments.

CONTRACT MODIFICATION: Any unilateral or bilateral written alteration in the specifications, delivery point, rates of delivery, contract period, price, quantity, or other provision of an existing contract resulting from a change order.

CONTRACT PRICING PROPOSAL: The submission required of an offeror which identifies appropriate cost or pricing data. The Standard Form 1411 provides a standard format for submitting to the government a summary of estimated (or in some instances incurred) costs suitable for detailed review and analysis.

CONTRACT TYPE: Refers to specific pricing arrangements employed for the performance of work under contract. Specific pricing or remunerative arrangements, expressed as contract types, include firm fixed-price, fixed price incentive, cost plus fixed-free, cost plus incentive fee, and several others. Among special arrangements that use fixed-price or cost reimbusement pricing provisions are contract types called indefinite delivery contracts, basic ordering agreements, letter contracts, and others.

COST ACCOUNTING: A system of accounting and reporting the costs of producing goods or services, or of operating programs, activities, functions or organizational units. The system may also embrace cost estimating and determining actual and standard costs for the purpose of aiding cost control.

COST ACCOUNTING STANDARDS: Standards promulgated by the Cost Accounting Standards Board under the authority of Public Law 91-379 and with the objective of achieving uniformity and consistency in the cost accounting practices followed by defense contractors.

COST ANALYSIS: The review and evaluation of cost or pricing data and of the judgmental factors applied in projecting from the data to estimated costs. Includes appropriate verification of cost data, evaluation of specific elements of costs, and projection of these data to determine the effects on price factors like cost necessity, allowances for contingencies, and the basis used for allocation of overhead costs.

COST ESTIMATING: The process of forecasting a future result in terms of cost, based upon information available at the time.

COST INCURRED: A cost identified through the use of the accrual method of accounting and reporting, or otherwise actually paid. Cost of direct labor, direct materials, and direct services identified with and necessary for the performance of a contract, and all properly allocated and allowable indirect costs.

COST INPUT: The cost, except G&A expenses, which for contract costing purposes is allocable to the production of goods and services during a cost accounting period.

COST OBJECTIVE: A function, organizational subdivision, contract, or other work unit for which cost data are desired and for which provision is made to accumulate and measure the cost of processes, products, jobs, capitalized projects, etc.

COST OR PRICING DATA: Facts existing up to the time of agreement on price which prudent buyers and sellers would reasonably expect to have a significant effect on price negotiations.

COST REIMBURSEMENT: A family of pricing arrangements that provide for payment of allowable costs incurred in performing the contract. Under a cost-plus fixed fee arrangement, the dollar amount of fee is not subject to adjustment by reason of cost experience during contract performance.

DEFECTIVE COST OR PRICING DATA: Certified cost or pricing data, subsequently found to have been inaccurate, incomplete, or noncurrent as of the effective date of the certificate.

DEFENSE ACQUISITION REGULATION: The uniform policies and procedures which, prior to implementation of the Federal Acquisition Regulation, governed the procurement of supplies and services by the Department of Defnse components. (Until July 1978, the DAR was known as the Armed Services Procurement Regulation (ASPR).

DEFERRED COMPENSATION: An award made by an employer to compensate an employee in a future cost accounting period or periods for services rendered in one or more cost accounting periods prior to the date of the receipt of compensation by the employee. Does not include year-end accruals for salaries, wages, or bonuses that are to be paid within a reasonable period of time after the end of a cost accounting period.

DIRECT COST: Any cost which is identified specifically with a particular final cost objective, but not limited to items which are incorporated in the end product as material or labor. Costs identified specifically with a contract are direct costs of that contract.

DISCLOSURE STATEMENT: The document (Form CASB-DS-1) designed to meet the requirements of Public Law 91-379 for describing contract cost accounting practices.

EQUITABLE ADJUSTMENT: An adjustment in the contract price and/or delivery schedule to compensate the contractor for changes in the contract.

ESTABLISHED CATALOG PRICE: A price included in a catalog, price list, schedule, or other form that is regularly maintained, published, or made available to customers and states prices at which sales are made to a significant number of buyers constituting the general public.

ESTABLISHED MARKET PRICE: A current price, established in the ordinary course of trade between buyers and sellers free to bargain, which can be independently substantiated.

EXPRESSLY UNALLOWABLE COST: A particular item or type of cost which, under the provisions of an applicable law, regulation, contract, or mutual agreement of the contracting parties, is specifically named and stated to be unallowable.

FACILITIES CAPITAL: The net book value of tangible capital assets and of those intangible capital assets that are subject to amortization.

FEDERAL ACQUISITION REGULATIONS: The policies and procedures which, effective April 1984, govern the procurement of supplies and services by federal agencies.

FEDERAL PROCUREMENT REGULATIONS: The policies and procedures issued by the General Services Administation (under authority of the federal property & Administration Services Act) which, prior to implementation of the Federal Acquisition Regulation, governed the procurement of supplies and services by federal agencies other than the Department of Defense and the National Aeronautics and Space Administration.

FINAL COST OBJECTIVE: A cost objective which has allocated to it both direct and indirect costs, and, in the contractor's accumulation system, is one of the final accumulation points.

FIXED PRICE: A family of pricing arrangements whose common discipline is a ceiling beyond which the government bears no responsibility for payment in connection with performance under a contract. Under a firm fixed-price arrangement, the negotiated price is not subject to any adjustment by reason of the contractor's cost experience in the performance of the contract.

FORMAL CHANGE ORDER: A written order signed by the contracting officer, or an authorized representative, directing the contractor to make changes in accordance with the Changes clause of the contract.

FORWARD PRICING RATE AGREEMENT: A written understanding negotiated between a contractor and the government to make certain rates (e.g., labor, indirect) available for use during a specified period in preparing contract cost estimates or contract modifications.

GENERAL AND ADMINISTRATIVE (G&A) EXPENSE: Any management, financial, and other expense which is incurred by or allocated to a business unit and which is for the general management and administration of the business unit as a whole.

GUARANTEED LOAN: A loan by a lending institution in which the government agrees to purchase a guaranteed portion or to share in a loss if requested by the lending institution.

HOME OFFICE: An office responsible for directing or managing two or more, but not necessarily all, segments of an organization. It typically establishes policy for, and provides guidance to the segments in their operations; performs management, supervisory, or administrative functions; and may also perform service functions in support of the operations of the various segments. An organization which has intermediate levels, such as groups, may have several home offices which report to a common home office.

INCENTIVE ARRANGEMENT: A negotiated pricing arrangement which rewards a contractor for performance in accordance with contract-specified criteria.

INDIRECT COST: Any cost not directly identified with (and to be allocated to) two or more cost objectives but not identified specifically with any final cost objective.

INDIRECT COST POOL: A grouping of incurred costs identified with (and to be allocated to) two or more cost objectives but not identified specifically with any final cost objective.

INTANGIBLE CAPITAL ASSET: An asset that has no physical substance, has more than minimal value, and is expected to be held by an enterprise for continued use or possession beyond the current accounting period for the benefits it yields.

INTERNAL CONTROLS: The organizational plan and all the methods and measures coordinated within a business to safeguard its assets, check the accuracy and reliability of accounting data, promote operational efficiency, and encourage adherence to prescribed management policies. Internal controls are subdivided into administrative controls and accounting controls.

INVITATION FOR BIDS: The solicitation document used in formal advertising.

JOB ORDER COSTING: A method of cost accounting whereby costs are accumulated for a specific quantity of products, equipment, repairs, or other services that move through the production process as a continuously identifiable unit; applicable material, direct labor, direct expense, and usually a calculated portion of overhead being charged to a job order; distinguished from process costing.

LETTER CONTRACT: A contractual instrument that authorizes the immediate commencement of activity under its terms and conditions, pending definitization of a fixed-price or cost-reimbursement pricing arrangement for the work to be done. Must specify the maximum liability of the government and be superseded by a definite contract within a specified time.

MOVING AVERAGE COST: An inventory costing method under which an average unit cost is computed after each acquisition by adding the cost of the newly acquired units to the cost of the units of inventory on hand and dividing this figure by the new total number of units.

NASA PROCUREMENT REGULATION: The policies and procedures which, prior to implementation of the Federal Acquisition Regulation, governed the procurement of supplies and services by the NASA buying activities.

NEGOTIATING: One of the major methods of procurement which is employed under certain permissive circumstances prescribed by statute when formal advertising is determined to be infeasible and impracticable. In its more general context, a bargaining process between two or more parties, each with its own viewpoints and objectives, seeking to reach a mutually satisfactory agreement on, or settlement, of, a matter of common concern.

OPERATING REVENUE: Amounts accrued or charged to customers, clients, and tenants, for the sale of products manufactured or purchased for resale, for services, and for rentals or perperty held primarily for leasing to others. Includes reimbursable costs and fees under cost-type contracts and percentage-of-completion sales accruals except that it includes only the fee for management contracts under which the contractor acts essentially as an agent of the government in the erection or operation of government-owned facilities. Excludes incidental interest, dividents, royalty and rental income, and proceeds from the sale of assets used in the business.

PENSION PLAN: A deferred compensation plan established and maintained by one or more employers to provide systematically for the payment of benefits to plan participants after their retirement.: Provided, that the benefits are paid for life or are payable for life at the option of the employees.

PREPRODUCTION COSTS: Costs required to initiate production on particular orders.

PRICE ANALYSIS: The process of examining and evaluating a prospective price without evaluation of the separate cost elements and proposed profit.

PRICING: The process of establishing the amount or amounts to be paid in return for goods or services.

PROCESS COSTING: A method of cost accounting in which the costs incurred for a process are assigned to the units (both complete and incomplete) that have been produced or are in process during the cost acounting period.

PRODUCTION UNIT: A grouping of activities which either uses homogeneous inputs of direct material and direct labor or yields homogeneous outputs such that costs or statistics related to these homogeneous inputs or outputs are appropriate as bases for allocating variances.

PROFIT CENTER: A discrete, organizationally independent segment of a company, which has been charged by management with profit and loss reponsibilities.

PROGRESS PAYMENT: A payment made as work progresses under a contract on the basis of percentage of completion accomplished or costs incurred, or for work performed at a particular stage of completion.

PROPOSAL: Any offer or other submission used as a basis for pricing a contract, contract modification, or termination settlement or for securing payments thereunder.

PROSPECTIVE PRICING: A pricing decision made in advance of performance, based on analysis of comparative prices, cost estimates, past costs, or combinations of such considerations.

REASONABLE COST: A cost which, in its nature or amount, does not exceed what would be incurred by an ordinarily prudent person in the conduct of competitive business.

REPORTING COSTS: Selection of relevant cost data and its presentation in an intelligible manner for use by the recipient.

REQUEST FOR PROPOSALS:A solicitation document used in negotiated procurements in which the government reserves the right to award a contract based on initial offers received without any written or oral discussion with offerors.

REQUEST FOR QUOTATIONS: A solicitation document used in negotiated procurements which is a request for information. Since the document is not an offer, the government cannot initially accept it without confirmation or discussion with the offerors.

RESIDUAL VALUE: The net proceeds realized upon disposition of a tangible capital asset or the asset's fair value if it is traded in on another asset.

SEALED BIDDING: One of the major methods of procurement which employs competitive bids, public opening of bids, and award to the responsible bidder whose bid is most advantageous to the government, price and other factors considered.

SEGMENT: One of two or more divisions, product departments, plants, or other subdivisions of an organization reporting directly to a home office, usually identified with responsibility for profit and/or producing a product or service. The term includes government-owned contractor-operated (GOCO) facilities, and joint ventures and subsidiaries (domestic and foreign) in which the organization has a majority ownership or has less than a majority of ownership but over which it exercises control.

SERVICE LIFE: The period of usefulness of a tangible capital asset (or group of assets) to its current owner, as expressed in units of time or output. The estimated service life of a tangible capital asset (or group of assets) is a forecast of its service life and is the period over which depreciation cost is to be assigned.

STANDARD COST: Any cost computed with the use of pre-established measures.

SUPPLEMENTAL AGREEMENT: A modification to an existing contract that is accomplished by the mutual action of the parties.

TANGIBLE CAPITAL ASSET: An asset that has physical substance, more than minimal vlaue, and is expected to be held by an enterprise for continued use or possession beyond the current accounting period for the services it yields.

UNALLOWABLE COST: Any cost which, under the provisions of any pertinent law, regulation, or contract, cannot be included in prices, cost reimbursements, or settlements under a government contract.

WEIGHTED AVERAGE COST: An inventory costing method under which an average unit cost is computed periodically by dividing the sum of the cost of beginning inventory plus the cost of acquisitions, by the total number of units included in these two categories.

Table of Cases

Selected Costs

Advertising
Aerojet-General
ASBCA no. 13372, 73-2 BCA 10,164; 73-2 BCA 10,307

Blue Cross Association and Blue Shield Association ASBCA no. 25944,
83-1 BCA 16,524

Bid and Proposal costs
Dynatrend
ASBCA no. 23463, 80-2 BCA 14,617

Compensation
Boeing
ASBCA no. 24089, 81-1 BCA 14,864, 81-1 BCA 15,121
Boeing
ASBCA no. 28342, 85-3 BCA 18,435
Burt Associates
ASBCA no. 25884, 82-1 BCA 15,764
Data-Design Laboratories
ASBCA no. 24534, 83-2 BCA 16,665
Honeywell
ASBCA no. 28814, 29140, 84-3 BCA 17,690
Lulejean and Associates
ASBCA no. 20094, 76-1 BCA 11,880
Singer, Kearfott Division
ASBCA no. 18857, 75-1 BCA 11,185; 81-2 BCA 15,167; 82-1
BCA 15,684 Ct. Cl. no. 381-79C, 28 CCF 80,741
Space Services of Georgia
ASBCA no. 26021, 82-2 BCA 15,952

Depreciation
Marquardt
ASBCA no. 29888, 85-3 BCA 18,245
Gould Defense Systems
ASBCA no. 24881, 83-2 BCA 16,676

Goodwill
Gould Defense Systems
ASBCA no. 24881, 83-2 BCA 16,676

Patents
Rocket Research
ASBCA no. 24972, 81-2 BCA 15,307

Professional and Consulting Services/
Defense of Fraud Proceedings
Celesco Industries
ASBCA no. 20569, 77-1 BCA 12,445

Montag-Halvorson-Cascade-Austin
CCA 1121 (1958)
Pacific Architects and Engineers
203 Ct. Cl. 449, 9 CCF 82,415

Acceleration

Ashton
IBCA no. 1070-6-75, 76-2 BCA 11,934
Dynamics of America, Fermont Division
ASBCA no. 15806, 75-1 BCA 11,139

Deductive Change

Nager Electric and Keystone Engineering
194 Ct. Cl. 835, 14 CCF 83,571; 16 CCF 80,367

Defective Specification

Hol-Gar Mfg.
175 Ct. Cl. 518, 11 CCF 80,438

Delay Claims

Idle Labor
Hardemann-Monier-Hutcherson
ASBCA no. 11785, 67-1 BCA 6,210

Performance in a Later Period
Keco Industries
ASBCA nos. 15184 and 15547, 2-2 BCA 9,576

Unabsorbed Overhead
Allegheny Sportswear
ASBCA no. 4163, 58-1 BCA 1,684
Capital Electric
GSBCA nos. 5316 and 5317, 83-2 BCA 16,548
CAFC no. 83-965-31 CCF 72,119
Carteret Work Uniforms
ASBCA no. 1647, 6 CCF 61,561
Dawson Construction
GSBCA no. 4956, 79-2 BCA 13,989
Eichleay
ASBCA no. 5183, 60-2 BCA 2,688
McMullan & Son, Robert
ASBCA no. 19023, 76-1 BCA 11,728
Propserv
ASBCA no. 20768, 78-1 BCA 13,066
Savoy Construction
Ct. Cl. no. 579-81C, 31 CCF 71,109
ASBCA nos. 21218, 21925, 22300, 22336, 22691, 22763,
22915, 85-2 BCA 18,073

Index